Flea Market Trader

Thirteenth Edition

**THOUSANDS OF
ITEMS WITH
CURRENT
VALUES**

COLLECTOR BOOKS

A Division of Schroeder Publishing Co., Inc.

Editorial Staff

Editors

Sharon and Bob Huxford

Research and Editorial Assistants

Michael Drollinger, Donna Newnum, Loretta Suiters

Cover Design: Beth Summers
Book Design: Holly C. Long

The current values in this book should be used only as a guide. They are not intended to set prices, which vary from one section of the country to another. Auction prices as well as dealer prices vary greatly and are affected by condition as well as demand. Neither the editors nor the publisher assumes responsibility for any losses that might be incurred as a result of consulting this guide.

Searching For A Publisher?

We are always looking for people knowledgeable within their fields. If you feel that there is a real need for a book on your collectible subject and have a large comprehensive collection, contact Collector Books.

COLLECTOR BOOKS
P. O. Box 3009
Paducah, Kentucky 42002-3009

www.collectorbooks.com

INTRODUCTION

The *Flea Market Trader* is a unique price guide, geared specifically for the convenience of the flea market shopper. Several categories have been included that are not often found in general price guides, while others on antiques not usually seen at flea markets have been omitted. The new categories will serve to introduce you to collectibles that are currently coming on, the best and often the only source for which is the market place. As all of us who religiously pursue the circuits are aware, flea markets are the most exciting places in the world to shop; but unless you're well informed on current values those 'really great' buys remain on the table. Like most pursuits in life, preparation has its own rewards; and it is our intention to provide you with the basic tool of education and awareness toward that end. But please bear in mind that the prices in this guide are meant to indicate only general values. Many factors determine actual selling prices; values vary from one region to another, dealers pay various wholesale prices for their wares, and your bargaining skill is important too.

We have organized our listings into general categories for easy use; if you have trouble locating an item, refer to the index. The values we have suggested reflect prices of items in mint condition. NM stands for minimal damage, VG indicates that the items will bring 40% to 60% of its mint price, and EX should be somewhere between the two. Glassware is assumed clear unless a color is noted. Only generally accepted abbreviations have been used.

The Editors,
Sharon and Bob Huxford

ABBREVIATIONS

dia — diameter	NRFB — never removed from box
ea — each	pc — piece
EX — excellent	pr — pair
gal — gallon	pt — pint
lb — pound	qt — quart
lg — large	sm — small
med — medium	sq — square
M — mint	VG — very good
MIB — mint in box	(+) — has been reproduced

Action Figures

The first line of action figures Hasbro developed in 1964 was GI Joe. It met with such huge success that Mego, Kenner, Mattel, and a host of other manufacturers soon began producing their own lines. Though GI Joe, Marx's Best of the West series, and several of Mego's figures were 12", others were 8" or 9" tall, and the most popular size in the last few years has been 3¾". Many lines came with accessory items such as vehicles, clothing, guns, etc. Original packaging (most now come on cards) is critical when it comes to evaluating your action figures, especially the more recent issues — they're seldom worth more than a few dollars if they've been played with. Values given MIB or MOC can be reduced by 40% to 60% when appraising a 'loose' figure in even the best condition. For more information, you'll want to read *Collectible Action Figures* by Paris and Susan Manos, *Mego Toys* by Wallace M. Crouch, and *Schroeder's Toys, Antique to Modern,* all published by Collector Books.

See also GI Joe; Star Wars.

Action Jackson, accessory, baseball or football outfit, Mego, MIB, ea.............................**12.00**

Action Jackson, figure, Action Jackson, blue jumpsuit, Mego, 8", NMIB **35.00**

Aliens, accessory, Queen Hive playset, Kenner, MIB **50.00**

Aliens, figure, King, Queen, Swarm, or Arachnid, Kenner, MOC, ea..............................**25.00**

Batman (animated), accessory, Batcycle, Kenner, MOC.**15.00**

Batman (animated), accessory, Batmobile, Kenner, MIB.......**45.00**

Batman (animated), accessory, Joker Mobile, Kenner, MIB, from $35 to **45.00**

Batman (animated), accessory, Triple Attack Jet, Kenner, MOC.**20.00**

Batman (animated), figure, any, Kenner, MOC, ea from $25 to.**30.00**

Batman Forever, accessory, Batboat, Kenner, MIB **25.00**

Batman Returns, accessory, Laser Blade, Kenner, MIB.......**30.00**

Batman Returns, accessory, Wayne's Custom Coupe, w/figure, Kenner, MIB...**40.00**

Batman Returns, figure, Bola Strike Batman, Kenner/Toys R Us, MIB.......................**25.00**

Batman Returns, figure, Firebolt Batman, Kenner, MIB...**55.00**

Battlestar Galactica, accessory, Cylon Raider, Mattel, MIB............**60.00**

Battlestar Galactica, figure, any, Mattel, 3¾", MOC, ea from $20 to.............................**25.00**

Best of the West, accessory, Circle X Ranch, Marx, complete, MIB.............................**175.00**

Best of the West, accessory, Jeep & Trailer, Marx, MIB, from $150 to..........................**175.00**

Best of the West, figure, Chief Cherokee, Marx, complete, NMIB..........................**175.00**

Best of the West, figure, General Custer, Marx, complete, NM (VG box)........................**75.00**

Best of the West, figure, Jamie West, Marx, complete, NMIB 75.00

Best of the West, figure, Jane West, Marx, NMIB, $70.00.

Best of the West, figure, Johnny West, Marx, complete, EX .50.00

Best of the West, figure, Princess Wildflower, Marx, complete, MIB 150.00

Best of the West, figure, Sheriff Garret, Marx, complete, NMIB............................185.00

Best of the West, horse, Pancho, cream-colored, Marx, complete, VG.........................30.00

Big Jim, accessory, Kung Fu Studio, Mattel, MIB.............85.00

Big Jim, accessory, Sports Camper w/Boat, Mattel, MIB 50.00

Big Jim, figure, any, Mattel, complete, EX, ea from $25 to ..30.00

Bionic Woman, accessory, Carriage House, Kenner, MIB, from $200 to 250.00

Black Hole, figure, Alex Durant, 12", MIB, from $65 to 85.00

Buck Rogers, figure, any, Mego, 3¾", MOC, ea 25.00

Buck Rogers, figure, any, Mego, 12", MIB, ea....................75.00

Capt Action, accessory, Inter-Galactic Jet Mortar, Ideal, MIB...............................150.00

Capt Action, carrying case, opens to headquarters, Ideal, EX...85.00

Capt Action, figure, Batman, Ideal, 12" complete, EX............200.00

Capt Action, figure, Capt America, Ideal, 12", complete, EX .175.00

Capt Action, figure, Steve Canyon, Ideal, 12", MIB.............200.00

Capt Planet & the Planeteers, accessory, Skumm Copter, Kenner, MIB 25.00

Capt Planet & the Planeteers, figure, any, Tiger/Kenner, MOC, ea 12.00

CHiPs, figure, any, Mego, 3¾", MOC, ea..........................15.00

Dark Knight, figure, Batman Blast Shield, Kenner, MIB 35.00

Dr Who, figure, any, 4", MOC, ea from $30 to 35.00

Dukes of Hazzard, figure, any, Mego, 8", MOC, ea from $35 to 40.00

Flash Gordon, figure set, Beastman, Lizard Woman & Ming, Mattel, MIB...................40.00

Flash Gordon, figure set, Flash, Dr Zarkov & Thun, Mattel, MIB..............................40.00

Generation X, figure, any, Toy Biz, MOC, ea from $15 to......20.00

He-Man, figure, any, Mattel, MOC, ea..........................15.00

Land of the Lost, figure, any, MOC, ea from $10 to......**15.00**

Last Action Hero, figure, any except Evil Eye Bandit, Mattel, MOC, ea **5.00**

Last Action Hero, figure, Evil Eye Bandit, Mattel, MOC.....**10.00**

Lone Ranger Rides Again, figure, any, Gabriel, 9", MIB, ea..**50.00**

Major Matt Mason, accessory, Astro Trac, Mattel, 1966, MIB **125.00**

Major Matt Mason, accessory, Space Station, Mattel, MIB ...**200.00**

Major Matt Mason, accessory, Talking Back Pack, Mattel, EX....................................**30.00**

Major Matt Mason, figure, Callisto, Mattel, 6", MOC............**200.00**

Major Matt Mason, figure, Capt. Laser, Mattel, 12", complete, EX, $60.00.

Marvel Super Heroes, figure, Capt America, Mego, complete, NMIB.............................**175.00**

Marvel Super Heroes, figure, Catwoman, Mego, complete, NM.............................**125.00**

Marvel Super Heroes, figure, Falcon, Mego, complete, NMIB **150.00**

Marvel Super Heroes, figure, Green Arrow, Mego, complete, EX....................................**95.00**

Marvel Super Heroes, figure, Joker, Mego, complete, NMIB **165.00**

Marvel Super Heroes, figure, Mr Fantastic, Mego, complete, NMIB............................**100.00**

Masters of the Universe, accessory, Flight Zone playset, Mattel, MIB **85.00**

Masters of the Universe, accessory, Road Ripper, Mattel, MOC **20.00**

Masters of the Universe, figure, any, Mattel, MOC, ea from $15 to...............................**25.00**

Micronauts, accessory, Cosmic Warp Chamber, Hourtoy, MOC (sealed)...................**50.00**

Micronauts, figure, Acroyear or Hydra, Mego, NMIB, ea ..**50.00**

Micronauts, figure, Giant Acroyear, Mego, NMIB ..**75.00**

Mortal Combat, accessory, Dragon Wing w/figure, Hasbro, MIP **25.00**

Mortal Combat, figure set & arena, Goro Vs Johnny Cage, Hasbro, MIP...................**25.00**

Official Scout High Adventure, accessory, Avalanche..., Kenner, MIB **35.00**

Official Scout High Adventure, accessory, Jeep & Trailer, Kenner, MIB **35.00**

Official Scout High Adventure, figure, Craig Cub, Kenner, MIB **30.00**

Official Scout High Adventure, figure, Steve Scout, Kenner, M 25.00

Official WG Super Heroes, accessory, Amazing Spider Car, Mego, MIB 100.00

Official WG Super Heroes, accessory, Batcopter, Mego, NMIB 175.00

Official WG Super Heroes, figure, Aquaman, Mego, 8", MIB.175.00

Official WG Super Heroes, figure, Batman, Bend 'n Flex, Mego, 5", NMOC 50.00

Official WG Super Heroes, figure, Penguin, Mego, 8", MOC (sealed) 125.00

Official WG Super Heroes, figure, Riddler Fist Fighting, Mego, 8", MOC 175.00

Official WG Super Heroes, figure, Spider-Man, Bend 'n Flex, Mego, MOC 75.00

Official WG Super Heroes, figure, Spider-Man, Mego, 8", EX 35.00

Official World's Greatest Super-Gals, figure, Catwoman, Mego, 8", EX 95.00

Official World's Greatest Super-Gals, figure, Wonder Woman, Mego, 8", NM 150.00

Planet of the Apes, accessory, Throne, Mego, MIB........75.00

Planet of the Apes, figure, Astronaut, Mego, 8", complete, M.......65.00

Planet of the Apes, figure, Cornelius, Mego, 8", complete, M........50.00

Planet of the Apes, figure, Gen Ursus, Mego, 8", MOC .200.00

Planet of the Apes, figure, Soldier Ape, Bend 'n Flex, Mego, 5", MOC 50.00

Predator, figure, any, Kenner, MOC, ea..........................20.00

Princess of Power, accessory, Crystal Castle, Mattel, complete, MIB 125.00

Princess of Power, figure, any, Mattel, MOC, ea from $20 to 25.00

Rambo, figure, any except Rambo, Coleco, 6", MOC, ea 20.00

Rambo, figure, Rambo, Coleco, 6", MOC 25.00

Real Ghostbusters, figure, any except Stay Puft or Slimer, Kenner, MOC 12.00

Real Ghostbusters, figure, Stay Puft or Slimer, Kenner, MOC, ea 20.00

RoboCop, figure, any, Kenner, rare, MOC, ea.................25.00

Shogun Warriors, figure, Poseidon, Mazinga, or Dragun, Mattel, MOC, ea..............40.00

Shogun Warriors, figure, Raider or Dragun, Mattel, MOC, ea..60.00

Six Million Dollar Man, accessory, Bionic Mission Vehicle, Kenner, MIB 65.00

Six Million Dollar Man, accessory, Mission Control, Kenner, MIB 65.00

Six Million Dollar Man, accessory, OSI Headquarters, Kenner, MIB...............................85.00

Six Million Dollar Man, figure, Oscar Goldman, Kenner, 12", MIB...............................85.00

Space: 1999, accessory, Moon Base Alpha Deluxe Set, Mattel, MIB 300.00

Space: 1999, figure, Com Koenig or Prof Bergman, Mattel, 9", MOC, ea........................75.00

Spawn, figure, any from 1st or 2nd series, Todd Toys, MOC, ea....................................**30.00**

Spawn, figure, any from 3rd or 4th series, Todd Toys, MOC, ea....................................**15.00**

Spawn, figure, Violator, Todd Toys, 13", MOB..............**50.00**

Super Naturals (Ghostlings), accessory, Tomb of Doom, Tonka, MIB....................**25.00**

Super Naturals (Ghostlings), figure, any, Tonka, 1986, MOC, ea..**8.00**

Super Naturals (Warriors), figure, any, Tonka, 1986, MOC, ea.......**10.00**

Super Powers, accessory, Batcopter, Kenner, MIB........**95.00**

Super Powers, accessory, Lex-Soar 7, Kenner, MIB......**25.00**

Super Powers, figure, Batman, Kenner, MOC..................**50.00**

Super Powers, figure, DeSaad, Kenner, MOC..................**25.00**

Super Powers, figure, Flash, Kenner, MOC........................**15.00**

Super Powers, figure, Joker, Kenner, complete w/ID card & comic, NM........................**35.00**

Super Powers, figure, Martian Manhunter, MOC..........**50.00**

Super Powers, figure, Robin, Kenner, MOC........................**50.00**

Super Powers, figure, Wonder Woman, Kenner, MOC ..**35.00**

Superman Man of Steel, accessory, Superboy VTOL Cycle, Kenner, MOC..................**15.00**

Superman Man of Steel, figure, Power Flight Superman, Kenner, MOC........................**10.00**

Superman Man of Steel, figure, Ultimate Superman, Kenner, MOC **25.00**

Swamp Thing, figure, Bayou Jack or Tomahawk, Kenner, MOC, ea **22.00**

Swamp Thing, figure, Dr Deemo or Weed Killer, Kenner, MOC, ea **15.00**

Swamp Thing, figure, Skinman or Snare Arm, Kenner, MOC.**15.00**

Team America, accessory, Scramble Rig, Ideal, MOC................**20.00**

Team America, figure, any, Ideal, MOC, ea from $8 to........**12.00**

Terminator 2, figure, any except John Conner, Kenner, MOC, ea **20.00**

Terminator 2, figure, John Conner, Kenner, MOC.........**25.00**

Thunderbirds, figure, any, Tyco, MOC, ea...........................**5.00**

Thundercats, accessory, Mutant Skycutter, LJN, MIB.....**25.00**

Thundercats, accessory, Stilt Runner, LJN, MIB................**20.00**

Thundercats, accessory, Thundertank, LJN, MIB.............................**40.00**

Thundercats, figure, any, LJN, MOC, ea from $25 to......**35.00**

Toxic Crusaders, figure, any, Playmates, MOC..........**100.00**

Venom, figure, any from 1st or 2nd series, Toy Biz, MOC, ea..**15.00**

Waltons, accessory, Country Store, Mego, 1974, MIB..........**100.00**

Waltons, accessory, Farmhouse, Mego, 1974, MIB..........**150.00**

Waltons, figure set, any, Mego, 1974, MIB, ea from $30 to...........**40.00**

WWF, figure, Adam Bomb, Hasbro, MOC (green)...........**30.00**

WWF, figure, Doink the Clown, Hasbro, MOC (purple)...**16.00**

WWF, figure, Mr Perfect, Hasbro, MOC (red).....................**20.00**

Wizard of Oz, figure, Scarecrow, Mego, 8", MIB, $65.00.

WWF, figure, Razor Ramone, Hasbro, MOC (blue)..............**25.00**
WWF, figure, Texas Tornado, Hasbro, MOC **50.00**
WWF, figure, Ultimate Warrior, Hasbro, purple trunks, MOC **50.00**
X-Men (animated), figure, any, Toy Biz, MOC, ea...........**15.00**
X-Men (Mutant Armor Series), figure, any, Toy Biz, MOC, ea from $15 to **20.00**

Advertising Collectibles

As far back as the turn of the century, manufacturers used characters that identified with their products. They were always personable, endearing, amusing, and usually succeeded in achieving just the effect the producer had in mind, making their product line more visual, more familiar, and therefore one the customer would more often than not choose over the competition. Magazine ads, display signs, product cartons, and TV provided just the right exposure for these ad characters. Elsie the Cow became so well known that at one point during a random survey, more people recognized her photo than one of the President!

There are scores of advertising characters, and many have been promoted on a grand scale. Today's collectors search for the dolls, banks, cookie jars, mugs, plates, and scores of other items modeled after or bearing the likenesses of their favorites, several of which are featured below.

Condition plays a vital role in evaluating vintage advertising pieces. Our estimates are for items in at least near-mint condition, unless another condition code is present in the description. Try to be very objective when you assess wear and damage.

For more information we recommend *Advertising Character Collectibles* by Warren Dotz; and *Huxford's Collectible Advertising*. Both are published by Collector Books.

See also Breweriana; Bubble Bath Containers; Cereal Boxes and Premiums; Character and Promotional Glassware; Novelty Telephones; Pin-Back Buttons; Radios. See Clubs and Newsletters for information concerning *The Prize Insider* newsletter for

Cracker Jack collectors; Peanut Pals, a club for collectors of Planters Peanuts; and The Soup Collector Club (Campbell's Soups).

Actigall Guy doll, squeeze vinyl, Summit, 1989, 8", M, from $55 to 65.00

Admiral bank, vinyl figure, 1970s, 7", M 25.00

Alka-Seltzer's Speedy bank, vinyl, 5½", EX, minimum value 200.00

Alka-Seltzer's Speedy doll, vinyl, 1960, 8", EX, from $500 to 700.00

Allied Van Lines doll, stuffed cloth, 1970s, 17", NM, minimum value......................25.00

Aunt Jemima Breakfast Bear, blue plush, 13", M........175.00

Aunt Jemima canister, products on nostalgic background, 1983, EX..........................42.00

Aunt Jemima Perfect Cornbread magazine ad, color, 1958, 13x10", EX......................18.00

Aunt Jemima Restaurant plate, Wellsville China, 1950s, 10", EX..............................225.00

Aunt Jemima Restaurants brochure, lists 28 locations, 1950s, EX 45.00

Baby Ruth doll, beanbag body w/vinyl head & hands, EX................35.00

Bazooka Joe doll, stuffed cloth, 1973, EX 20.00

Betty Crocker doll, stuffed cloth, Kenner, 1974, 13", VG...20.00

Big Boy Christmas ornament, Happy Holidays, M........20.00

Big Boy doll, stuffed cloth w/name printed on chest, 1978, 14", MIP..............................30.00

Big Boy Dolly doll, stuffed, w/dress, hands on hips, 1978, 14", MIP........................30.00

Big Boy game, complete, NMIB......................225.00

Big Boy kite, image on paper, M............................500.00

Big Boy lunch/pencil box, red plastic, M..............................25.00

Big Boy pen, Parker, MIB 20.00

Big Boy trading cards, Famous Americans, set of 30.......80.00

Blue Bonnet Sue doll, stuffed cloth w/yarn hair, 1980s, NM, minimum......................20.00

Borden's Beauregard bank, red plastic figure, Irwin, 1950s, 5", EX..............................65.00

Borden's Elsie doll, plush w/vinyl head, 16", M 135.00

Borden's Elsie figure, PVC, 1993, 3½", M, from $10 to 20.00

Borden's Elsie push-button puppet, wood, EX 125.00

Borden's Elsie the Cow place mat, ...Over 125 Years..., M ...25.00

Borden's Elsie the Cow tie clasp, gold-tone bar w/Elsie on chain, EX......................55.00

Bosco the Clown doll, vinyl, NM 45.00

Brach's Candy Scarecrow doll, stuffed cloth, minimum value......35.00

Brach's Peppermint watch, 1980s, MIB..............................15.00

Breck's Bonnie Breck doll, original outfit, Hasbro, 1972, 9", VG 40.00

Brown's Chicken Farmer Brown doll, stuffed cloth, 1970s, 16", NM..............................65.00

Buster Brown doll, stuffed cloth, 1974, 14", NM **40.00**

Buster Brown Shoes kite, 1940s, NM **40.00**

Buster Brown watch, red costume, 1970s, VG **75.00**

Camel Cigarettes' Joe Camel backpack, M **30.00**

Camel Cigarettes' Joe Camel coaster set, square, MIB..........**10.00**

Camel Cigarettes' Joe Camel drink holder, figural, M.**20.00**

Camel Cigarettes' Joe Camel thermometer, diecut, 18½", EX..**50.00**

Campbell Kids Cheering Soup Kids phone card, 1996, unused, M.....................**10.00**

Campbell Kids dancing chefs salt & pepper shakers, 1991, MIB, pr....................................**10.00**

Campbell Kids doll, baseball player, Animal Fair, 1985, 14", VG.........................**55.00**

Campbell Kids doll, cheerleader, vinyl, 1967, 8", EX **75.00**

Campbell Kids doll, chef, vinyl, 8", EX...................................**50.00**

Campbell Kids doll, girl, cloth outfit, Ideal, 1955, 8", EX, minimum............................**125.00**

Campbell Kids dolls, boy & girl rag-type, 1970s, MIB, pr......**125.00**

Campbell Kids jigsaw puzzle, All Aboard, 28-pc, 1986, VG..**25.00**

The Campbell Kids Shopping Game, Parker Bros., 1955, complete, NM (EX box), $150.00 at auction.

Campbell Kids sign, diecut cardboard baseball player, 1980, 18", EX............................**8.00**

Campbell Kids tea set, 4 cups, plates, tray, dish & utensils, 1982, M........................**50.00**

Campbell Kids tool caddy w/tools, Westwood, 1992, M.........**8.00**

Campbell Kids Vegetable Soup watch, 1994, M...............**50.00**

Cap'n Crunch bank, painted plastic figure, 1973, VG.......**65.00**

Cap'n Crunch doll, stuffed plush, 14", EX, from $30 to.......**50.00**

Cap'n Crunch wallet & money, thin cardboard, 1982, EX **10.00**

Ceresota Boy doll, stuffed cloth, 1972, EX, minimum value **30.00**

Charlie the Tuna watch, faces right, 1973, VG...............**50.00**

Cheer's Cheeroo Kangaroo doll, stuffed plush, Proctor & Gamble, NM **20.00**

Cheetos' Chester Cheeta doll, plush, w/sunglasses, 1980, 20", EX............................**70.00**

Chicken of the Sea Mermaid doll, stuffed cloth, 1974, 15", NM.....................**20.00**

Chiquita Banana Girl doll, stuffed cloth, premium, 1974, minimum........................**20.00**

Chocks Vitamins Charlie Chocks doll, cloth, 1970s, 20", NM, minimum......................**35.00**

Cracker Jack Boy doll, vinyl w/cloth clothes, Vogue, 1980, MIP.**65.00**

Curad Band Aids Taped Crusader doll, vinyl, 1975, 7½", NM, $25 to **30.00**

Curity's Miss Curity Nurse figure, plastic, w/stand, 21", VG..**10.00**

Del Monte Big Top Bonanza Clown bank, plastic, 1985, 7", $10 to **15.00**

Del Monte Country Yumkin Fruits doll, plush, 1980, 8", M, $10 to **15.00**

Del Monte Shoo Shoo Scarecrow doll, plush, 1983, NM **15.00**

Del Monte Veggies doll, plush, 1980, 11", M, $10 to **15.00**

Diaparene Baby doll, vinyl w/original diaper, vinyl, 1980s, M, $50 to **75.00**

Dole Bananimal Banabear, plush, Trudy Toys, 1989, 10", M .**15.00**

Dole Piney Pals doll, plush, Sundara, 1992, 12", M, $10 to **15.00**

Domino's The Noid dolls, vinyl, 1980s, 2½"-4½", NM, ea $4 to...............................**6.00**

X Dow Scrubbing Bubble figure, vinyl, 1989, EX...............**20.00**

Dunkin' Donuts watch, 1999, M **10.00**

Eggo Waffles Eggosaurus watch, 1990, M..........................**15.00**

Eskimo Pie Man doll, rag-type, EX **20.00**

Frito Bandito eraser, figural, 1960s, 1½", NM, from $30 to **40.00**

Fruit Stripe Gum Yipes doll, plush, 15", M **50.00**

General Mills Sippin' Sam doll, vinyl w/cloth clothes, 1972, NM...............................**40.00**

Gerber Baby duffel bag, rayon canvas, Windjammer, 1983, M **18.00**

Gerber Baby mug, insulated, 1988, M..........................**6.00**

Gerber Kid dolls, stuffed w/cloth clothes, Atlanta, 1981, 12", EX, ea **25.00**

Gerber squeaker dolls, Atlanta Novelty, girl and boy, vinyl, 1985, 8", EX, $20.00 each. (Photo courtesy Joan Stryker Grubaugh)

Gerber's Tender Loving Care Bear, Atlanta Novelty, 1978, 20", EX...........................**25.00**

Green Giant doll, stuffed cloth, 1960s, 12", NM, from $15 to...............................**20.00**

Green Giant Farm Factory, complete, MIB......................**20.00**

Green Giant kite, thin plastic, 1960s, 48", from $20 to ..**30.00**

Green Giant's Little Sprout bank, composition, musical, NM...............................**45.00**

Green Giant's Little Sprout doll, stuffed cloth, 1974, 10½", NM...............................**15.00**

Green Giant's Little Sprout doll, vinyl, 1970-90, 6½", EX, $10 to **20.00**

Green Giant's Little Sprout flashlight, MIB......................**45.00**

Green Giant's Little Sprout jump rope, MIB......................**20.00**

Hamburger Helper Helping Hand doll, plush, EX...............**20.00**

Harley-Davidson's Harley Hog doll, w/leather jacket, 9", M............................**25.00**

Hawaiian Punch Punchy doll, stuffed cloth, 20", NM....**65.00**

Icee Bear bank, w/drink in front of him, rubber, 7", EX........**30.00**

Icee Bear ring, EX.................**15.00**

IGA Tablerite Kid doll, stuffed cloth, 12", EX..................**25.00**

Jack Frost Sugar doll, stuffed cloth, 17", M **50.00**

Jell-O's Sweet Tooth Sam hand puppet, 1960s, EX+........**85.00**

Keebler Elf bank, ceramic figure, lg, NM..............................**60.00**

Keebler Elf doll, stuffed cloth, 1981, NM.........................**35.00**

KFC's Colonel Sanders finger puppet, vinyl w/black trim, EX **15.00**

KFC's Colonel Sanders nodder, painted composition, 1960s, 7", EX...............................**75.00**

KFC's Colonel Sanders poker chip, plastic, w/portrait, 1960s, M.........................**18.00**

KFC's Colonel Sanders windup walker figure, 3¼", NM.**15.00**

Kleenex Bears figures, mail-in premium, set of 3, NM...**50.00**

Kool-Aid Kid doll, w/pigtails & freckles, 1989, MIB, from $25 to **35.00**

Kool-Aid Man bank, pitcher on yellow base, plastic, 7", 1970, NM **60.00**

Little Debbie doll, vinyl w/cloth outfit & straw hat, 1984, 11", M....................................**85.00**

M&M doll, red, plush, 12", M..**15.00**

M&M magnet, plain or peanut, plush, 2", M, ea **8.00**

M&M Plain cookie cutter, standing w/arms up, plastic, 3"....................................**4.00**

Mack Trucks' Mack Bulldog doll, plush, NM......................**40.00**

Mars Snickers' Anniversary watch, 1990, M...............**35.00**

Maypo's Marky Maypo bank, vinyl, 1960s, 9", NM **50.00**

Michelin Man ashtray, ceramic, seated on rim, 1-rest, M .**55.00**

Michelin Man bank, PVC figure, made for 100-year birthday, 14"...**30.00**

Michelin Man coffee cup, plastic, figure on side, EX.............**5.00**

Morton Salt Girl doll, Mattel, 1974, 10", MIB **40.00**

Mott's Apple of My Eye Bear, plush, 1988, M...............**15.00**

Mr Bubble Tub Pal doll, vinyl, 1990, 8", NM, from $35 to **40.00**

Mr Clean doll, painted vinyl, 1961, 8", EX...................**80.00**

Mr Peanut wristwatch, yellow face, 1966, VG **50.00**

Nabisco Pretzels Mr Salty doll, stuffed cloth, 1983, NM, minimum..............................**25.00**

Nestlé Chocolate Man doll, plastic w/cloth clothes, 1969, 12½", NM **50.00**

Nestlé Chocolate Man doll, stuffed cloth, Chase Bag Co, 1970, 15", EX.................**20.00**

Nestlé Morsels dolls, plush, 5 various, 1984, 15"-20", NM, ea from $15 to **20.00**

Nestlé Quik Bunny doll, plush, 1980s mail-in, M............**35.00**

Old Crow key chain, M **15.00**

Old Crow playing cards, Two Crows You See..., 2 decks, 1967, EX......................**40.00**

Oreo Cookie watch, 1998, M ..**50.00**

Oscar Mayer, bank, Weinermobile, plastic, 1988, 10", M, $25.00. (Photo courtesy June Moon)

Oscar Mayer's Little Oscar ring, plastic, 1970s, EX **25.00**

Pillsbury Doughboy address book, spiral-bound, EX **6.00**

Pillsbury Doughboy bank, ceramic, 1980s mail-in premium, M **35.00**

Pillsbury Doughboy beanie, 2 different styles, M, ea from $10 to **20.00**

Pillsbury Doughboy coffee mug, 1988, M........................**100.00**

Pillsbury Doughboy doll, plush, 1982, scarce, EX.............**30.00**

Pillsbury Doughboy Jelly Bean Machine, Carousel, Taiwan, 13", $125.00. (Photo courtesy Charlie Reynolds)

Pillsbury Doughboy doll, stuffed cloth, 1972, 11", EX........**20.00**

Pillsbury Doughboy doll, stuffed cloth talker, Mattel, 16", NM **100.00**

Planters Mr Peanut doll, jointed wood, blue hat version, 9", EX...............................**200.00**

Planters Mr Peanut doll, stuffed cloth, Chase Bag Co, 1967, 21", EX...........................**30.00**

Planters Mr Peanut doll, stuffed cloth, Chase Bag Co, 1970, 18", NM **25.00**

Planters Peanuts, Mr Peanut nodder, Lego, papier-mache, NM, $150.00. (Photo courtesy Joleen Ashman Robinson and Kay Sellers)

Planters Mr Peanut pillow doll, 1967, EX **25.00**

Planters Mr Peanut tray, Fresh Roasted Since 1906, 1982, 14" oval, M..........................**20.00**

Planters Mr Peanut umbrella, blue & yellow w/single image, 1982, M..........................**40.00**

Pops-Rite Popcorn doll, stuffed cloth, NM......................**30.00**

14

Raid Bug doll, plush, 5 various, 1980s, M, ea from $50 to 125.00

Raid Bug wind-up figure, 5", EX............................50.00

Ralston Purina Scarecrow doll, stuffed w/vinyl head, 1965, NM, $35 to......................40.00

Red Barn Restaurant Hamburger Hungry doll, plush & felt, 1970, EX........................30.00

Reddy Kilowatt, penknife, 2-blade, Zippo, EX.............50.00

Reddy Kilowatt, stick pin, figural, gold-tone w/red enamel, 1", M............................30.00

Reddy Kilowatt doll, plush & vinyl w/suction cups on hands, 1980s, EX 35.00

Reddy Kilowatt figure, glow-in-the-dark, 1960s, MOC (EX mail-in box)..................225.00

Reddy Kilowatt night light, Panelescent, Sylvania, 3" dia, from $35 to 40.00

Reddy Kilowatt note paper holder, 1" Reddy on 3x5" holder, EX................................25.00

Ritz Cracker watch, 1971, MIB..200.00

Royal Gelatin's King Royal bank, vinyl, 1970, scarce, NM 225.00

Sarah Lee Bagels doll, stuffed plush, M..........................30.00

Smokey Bear ashtray, Snuffit, magnetized to stay on dashboard, M 25.00

Smokey Bear badge, Junior Forest Ranger, tin w/embossed lettering, M...........................8.00

Smokey Bear bank, plastic, stands on stump holding shovel, 8".....................25.00

Smokey Bear belt buckle, cast metal, 2½x1¾", M.........18.00

Smokey Bear belt buckle, heavy metal, 40th anniversary, #414, M......................125.00

Smokey Bear handkerchief, picnic scenes, 8", EX.................25.00

Smokey Bear ruler, Smokey's Friends Don't Play w/Matches, M 8.00

Smokey Bear trading cards, 1987, set of 15, M.....................12.00

Snuggle Fabric Softener bear, Lever Bros, 1983, 6", EX..20.00

Snuggle Fabric Softener bear, Lever Bros, 1986, 15", EX..........35.00

Star-Kist's Charlie Tuna bank, 1988, 9½", M 75.00

Star-Kist's Charlie Tuna belt buckle, brass oval w/embossed Charlie.......35.00

Star-Kist's Charlie Tuna camera, ca 1970, 10", VG...........100.00

Star-Kist's Charlie Tuna doll, stuffed talker, Mattel, 1969, 14", NM 85.00

Star-Kist's Charlie Tuna lamp base, composition, 1970, 13", EX 85.00

Star-Kist's Charlie Tuna patch, w/Sorry Charlie sign, 1975, 3", NM 12.00

Sunbeam's Little Miss Sunbeam doll, stuffed cloth, 17", NM........35.00

Swiss Miss doll, stuffed cloth w/vinyl face, EX, minimum value 25.00

Swiss Miss watch, mechanical windup, 1981, EX...........50.00

Swiss Miss wristwatch, 1981, EX 50.00

Tastee Freeze doll, hard plastic, 1950s, 7", NM.................20.00

Texaco, tanker truck, Buddy L, 1950s, 25", NMIB, from $350.00 to $450.00. (Photo courtesy Dunbar Gallery)

Toppie Elephant, 1950s, G.**100.00**
Tropicana Orange Juice Tropic-Ana doll, stuffed cloth, 1977, 17", NM **35.00**
Tyson Chicken Quick doll, stuffed cloth, 13", VG **15.00**
Vlasic's Stork doll, fluffy white fur, Trudy Toys, 1989, 22", NM **40.00**
Wrangler's Cody or Missy doll, Ertl, 1982, 11½", MIB, ea**55.00**

Advertising Tins

Attractive packaging has always been a powerful marketing tool; today, those colorful tin containers that once held products ranging from cookies and dog food to motor oil and tobacco are popular collectibles. There are several interesting books on this topic you may want to refer to: for the older tins, *Antique Tins, Books I, II,* and *III,* by Fred Dodge; *Encyclopedia of Advertising Tins, Volume II,* by David Zimmerman; and *Modern Collectible Tins* by Linda McPherson. All are published by Collector Books.

Ad Rem, G&S Majoie, Holland, tobacco tin, from $50 to.**75.00**

Amaco Home Oil, American Oil Co, 5½x2¼x¾", from $25 to **50.00**
Barnum's Animal Crackers, pail, plastic handle, 1991, 6", $12 to **16.00**
Bazooka Bubble Gum, pail, red/white/blue, bail handle, 1991, 7", $8 to................**10.00**
BDV Cigarettes, vertical, 3x3½x1", from $300 to.**350.00**
Big Mac, hamburger shape & graphics, 1996, 4¼", $8 to.**10.00**
Blue Boar Rough Cut, American Tobacco Co, 4¼x4¼" dia, from $25 to **50.00**
Bob White Mixture, Marburg Bros, 3½x4x2½", from $250 to................................**300.00**
Campbell's Tomato Soup, soup can bank, 125th Anniversary, $5 to **8.00**
Chicago Cubs Chewing Tobacco, Rock City Tobacco, Quebec, 3¼x6" dia......................**85.00**

Cinnamon Rose Tea, Celestial Seasonings, 1983, 3¾x4¾x2¾", from $5.00 to $8.00. (Photo courtesy Linda McPherson)

Coca-Cola, bottle shape, 1996, 7¼", $6 to........................**8.00**

Cocoa Puffs, vertical box, cereal graphics on brown, 5¼", $4 to **7.00**

✕Cracker Jack, vertical round, white, 1990, 8", $10 to ...**14.00**

✕Crayola, square box, Christmas scene, 1992, 6", $10 to....**12.00**

Grape-Nuts, rectangular, breakfast graphics on yellow, 6x8", $14 to **18.00**

Havana Sticks, embossed cigar box, 5¾x3½x3½", from $25 to..................................**50.00**

Keebler Animal Crackers, pail, Ernie in tree, 1992, 6", $14 to..................................**18.00**

La Resta Cigars, flat box, 1½x 5¼x3¾", from $25 to....**50.00**

Land O' Lakes, recipe box, Indian maiden scouting river, $20 to..........................**25.00**

✕Log Cabin Syrup, cabin shape, 100th Anniversary, 1987, 4¾", $15 to.....................**20.00**

✕M&M Cookies, round, graphics on brown, 4¼x10", $12 to....................................**16.00**

✕Maxwell House Coffee, vertical box, 1892 graphics, 1992, from $10 to **14.00**

Mick McQuaid Cut Plug, PJ Carroll Co, 1½x7½x3¼", from $50 to **75.00**

No 3 Toaster Navy Cut, 1¼x3¼" dia, from $50 to..............**75.00**

No 10 Cut Plug, 1¼x3¼" dia, from $25 to **50.00**

Ogden's Fine Cut, Imperial Tobacco, Canada, 4x4½" dia, from $1 to **25.00**

Oily Bird Household Lubricant, Ronson, 6x2x1", from $25 to **50.00**

Oreo Cookies, rectangular, Unlock the Magic!, 1991-1992, 8", ea from $6 to **10.00**

Oreo Cookies, rectangular, Unlock the Magic!, 1993-1996, 8", ea $5 to..................................**8.00**

Osmundo Cigars, 1¾x5x3¼", from $25 to..............................**50.00**

Pioneer Smoking Tobacco, Eagle Tobacco, 1¾x5x3½", from $100 to..........................**150.00**

Player's Navy Cut, HD & HO Wills, 1x3½" dia, from $25 to **50.00**

Pride of Virginia Cut Plug, J Wright Co, ¾x4½x2¾", from $1 to...............................**25.00**

Pride of Virginia Cut Plug, J Wright Co, ¾x4½x2¾", from $1 to...............................**25.00**

✕Quaker Old Fashioned Oats, vertical round, blue/red, 7¼", $10 to.....................................**15.00**

✕Quaker Rolled Oats, cylinder, 1886 label on yellow, 1984, 8", $12 to.............................**16.00**

✕Ritz Crackers, vertical box, Limited Edition, 1986, 8¾", $12 to .**16.00**

Singer Sewing Machine Oil, Singer Manufacturing Co., Left: 5¼x2½x1", Right: 3¼x2¼x1", from $1.00 to $25.00 each. (Courtesy Fred Dodge/Lawson and Lin Veasey)

Snickers Fun Size, radio, hinged lid, 1990, 7¼", $8 to **12.00**

Starbucks Coffee Company, box, truck graphics, 6¾x10¼", $18 to **23.00**

Sun-Maid Oatmeal Raisin Cookies, rectangular, red, 8¼", $10 to **14.00**

Whitman's Candies, egg shape, lace & floral design, 4¼", $3 to **4.00**

Whitman's Sampler, rectangular, hinged lid, 1996, 8¼x10½", $8 to **10.00**

York Peppermint Pattie, resembles foil-wrapped pattie, 6¼", $5 to **8.00**

3 Kings, Plain Tobacco Co, England, 2½x5x3½", from $1 to **25.00**

Aluminum

From the late 1930s until early in the 1950s, kitchenwares and household items were often crafted of aluminum, usually with relief-molded fruit or flowers on a hammered background. Today many find that these diversified items make an attractive collection. Especially desirable are those examples marked with the manufacturer's backstamp or the designer's signature.

You've probably also seen the anodized (colored) aluminum pitchers, tumblers, sherbet holders, etc., that were popular in the late '50s – early '60s. Interest in these items has exploded, as prices on eBay attest. Be sure to check condition, though, as scratching and wear reduce values drastically. The more uncommon forms are especially collectible.

For more information refer to *Collectible Aluminum, An Identification and Value Guide* (Collector Books), by Everett Grist.

Ashtray, Arthur Armour, water lilies & pads (lotus), 6" sq............**30.00**

Ashtray, Everlast, bamboo, bowl shape w/single rest, 5" ...**15.00**

Basket, Cromwell, fruit & flowers, hexagonal, 2-loop handle, 6" **5.00**

Basket, Everlast, flower & leaf band, fluted bowl, handled, 9" **10.00**

Basket, Everlast, tomato band, plate w/sq-knot handle, 11"........**10.00**

Basket, Federal, ship sailing, bowl w/ruffled rim, sq-knot handle, 9"....................................**25.00**

Basket, Forman, mums, scalloped bowl w/sq handle twisted in middle, 8" **10.00**

Basket, Hand Forged, angelfish/hammered, shallow, sq-knot handle, 12"........**26.00**

Beverage server, Kromex, plain bottle w/ring design, ball stopper, 11" **25.00**

Bowl, Bascal, anodized, 6", set of 8.....................................**35.00**

Bowl, Buenilum, daisy ring, resembles 8-petal flower, serrated, 6½" **5.00**

Bowl, Continental, wild rose, well w/wide flat rim, scalloped, 11" **25.00**

Bowl, DePonceau, bittersweet, notched rim, 11"............**20.00**

Bowl, dessert; w/glass inserts, anodized, 3½", set of 8 ...**50.00**

Bowl, W August Forge, dogwood, fluted & crimped rim, 7"..**20.00**

Buffet server, R Kent, tulip finial, ribbon/flower handles & feet............**35.00**

Buffet server/bun warmer, II Faberware, S-shaped feet w/tulip design.............**20.00**

Cake salver, hot pink w/black handles on cover, Regal, 13" plate, EX..........**30.00**

Candelabrum, unmarked, 3-sockets on half-circle base, hammered, 21"..........**25.00**

Candlesticks, II Farberware, S-shaped w/tulip design, beaded, 8", pr..........**45.00**

Candy dish, Cromwell, fruit & flowers, 2 bowls w/center handle, 13"............**10.00**

Candy dish, Manning Bowman, open grape & leaf pattern on 1 end, 13".............**15.00**

Casserole, Everlast, bamboo pattern w/bamboo finial, no handles, 7"............**10.00**

Casserole, Everlast, pea vine pattern w/pea pod finial, 7"..**10.00**

Chocolate pot, Continental, mums, petal finial, 10"..**85.00**

Cigarette box, Laid Argental, applied duck figure, 1½x3x5"............**75.00**

Coaster, DePonceau, bird on branch, fluted rim, 5".....**20.00**

Coaster, Everlast, angelfish, serrated, 5"............**5.00**

Coaster set, anodized, set of 8..**25.00**

Coaster set, Everlast, concentric spiral, serrated, dish-rack tray..............**10.00**

Coaster set, Everlast, 5-petal flowers, serrated, w/display box.......**25.00**

Compote, Continental, wild rose, serrated, 5"...............**20.00**

Creamer & sugar bowl w/tray, Buenilum, polished, looped handles............**15.00**

Cups, anodized, 5½", set of 6..**30.00**

Dresser set, R Kent #403, tulip lids on 2 glass dishes, w/tray............**45.00**

Folding server, Everlast, pine cone, fluted, hammered handle, 13½".............**25.00**

Fruit bowl & knives, unmarked, fruit & flowers, handled, footed.**15.00**

Gravy boat & tray, Buenilum, polished, beaded rim, loop handle, 6x3"............**20.00**

Hurricane lamps, Everlast, grape & leaf, loop handle, 8x3⅜", pr **40.00**

Ice bucket, Buenilum, hammered interior, beaded, twisted handle, 6"..............**10.00**

Ice bucket, Continental, mums, mushroom & leaf finial, ribbon handles.............**40.00**

Ice bucket, Kromax, hammered, black handles & knob finial, 12"..**10.00**

Ice bucket, red apple shape, anodized, 7"..............**25.00**

Key chains, DeMarsh Forge, various patterns, ea.............**12.00**

Lazy Susan, Cromwell, 2-tier, fruit & flowers, fluted, serrated, 13"............**10.00**

Lazy Susan, unmarked, 2-tier, tulip spray, serrated, 10".........**15.00**

Lobster tray, Bruce Fox, lobster form w/enlarged pinchers, 11x15"...........**35.00**

Match box covers, W August Forge, pine cone or bittersweet, ea...............**65.00**

Measuring scoops, ½-cup, ⅓-cup & ¼-cup, anodized, set of 3 ....**20.00**

Measuring spoon set, Tallscoops, MIB, from $25 to............**30.00**

Mint dish, unmarked, single mum on fluted pansy shape, flower finial **20.00**

Money clips, DeMarsh Forge, various patterns, ea..............**12.00**

Napkin holder, unmarked, flower & ribbon, 4 leaf-shaped legs, 6"..**15.00**

Napkin rings, anodized, narrow, set of 8, MIB...................**28.00**

Paperweight, W August Forge, 2 flying ducks, 5x3"............**75.00**

Pitcher, Buenilum, hammered, looped & twisted handle, 8"................**25.00**

Pitcher, Continental, lg mum on stem, applied leaf on handle, 9"...**35.00**

Pitcher, gold w/ice lip, anodized, no mark **28.00**

Plate, Arthur Armour, dogwood branch & butterfly, fluted, 10" **45.00**

Plate, W August Forge, scenic river w/jumping fish, crimped, 9"..**50.00**

Popcorn popper, W August Forge, ducks on lid, black handle, 9" **75.00**

Popcorn set, anodized, 11" bowl & four 5" individuals **30.00**

Salad fork & spoon set, unmarked, hammered, riveted handles, 12"..............**45.00**

Salad set, Bascal, lg bowl & 8 footed individuals, anodized.**65.00**

Sauce pan, unmarked, floral band on lid, twisted handle w/end loop **10.00**

Sherbet dishes, unmarked, glass inserts in anodized bases, set of 6 ....**15.00**

Shot glasses on tray, anodized, late 1950s – 60s, NM, $30.00.

Silent butler, Continental, wild rose, 6" dia......................**20.00**

Silent butler, Everlast, tomatoes in center, fluted, 6" dia..**10.00**

Syrup pitcher, Stratford-on-Avon, hammered tankard w/black handle, 6" **15.00**

Tidbit, Continental, 2-tier, mums, sq, fluted, coiled handle, 10" tall...................................**35.00**

Tidbit, Everlast, 2-tier, bamboo, bamboo finial, 9" **10.00**

Tidbit, unmarked, 3-tier, dogwood & pine cone, marble finial, 12".........................**5.00**

Tray, Arthur Armour, 4-part, flying geese, self-handled, 5x16"............................**75.00**

Tray, Continental, roses & geometrics, leaf handles, 17" dia **10.00**

Tray, Everlast, pine cone, well w/flat rim, no handles, 8x20".............................**10.00**

Tray, Everlast, 2 horse heads in bridles, bar handles, 12x16" **25.00**

Tray, Kensington, polished, fox hunt scene on handles, 14x23" **10.00**

Tray, Keystone, flower & vine, cradle style, applied handles, 10x14".............................**10.00**

Tray, Lehman, 2 bird dogs in oval scene, fluted rim, 12" sq..**20.00**

Tray, Stewart, deer landscape in well, flat hammered rim, 7x13"..............................**35.00**

Tray, unmarked, 2 flying ducks & cattail, self-handles, 9x16".**30.00**

Tray, W August Forge, Amish scene, hammered ground & rim, 5x10"......................**65.00**

Tray, W August Forge, bittersweet, upturned rim, 8x11"......................**25.00**

Tray, W August Forge, grapes, acorns & flowers oval, 7x11"...............**45.00**

Tray, W August Forge, sailboat, hammered ground & rim, 5x8"............................**45.00**

Tray, W. August Forge, vegetable pattern, 9x14", $65.00. (Photo courtesy Dannie Woodard)

Tumblers, anodized, 5", set of 6..**25.00**
Vase, Continental, single mum on stem, incurvate serrated rim, 10"..................................**65.00**

Anchor Hocking

From the 1930s until the 1970s Anchor Hocking (Lancaster, Ohio) produced a wide and varied assortment of glassware including kitchen items such as reamers, mixing bowls, measuring cups, etc., in many lovely colors. Many patterns of dinnerware were made as well. Their Fire-King line was formulated to produce heat-proof glassware so durable that it was guaranteed for two years against breakage caused by heat. Colors included Jade-ite, Azur-ite, Turquoise and Sapphire Blue, Ivory, Milk White (often decorated with fired-on patterns), Royal Ruby, and Forest Green. Collectors are beginning to reassemble sets, and for the most part, prices are relatively low, except for some of the rarer items. For more information, we recommend *Anchor Hocking's Fire-King & More, Second Edition,* by Gene Florence (Collector Books).

Bubble, pitcher, ruby, with ice lip, 64-ounce, $60.00. (Photo courtesy Gene Florence).

Bubble, bowl, cereal; crystal, 5¼"..............................**8.00**

Bubble, platter, light blue, oval, 12"....................................**16.00**

Bubble, tumbler, juice; crystal, 5-oz..**3.50**

Charm, bowl, salad; azur-ite or white, 7⅜" **17.50**

Charm, creamer or sugar bowl, jade-ite or ivory, ea **20.00**

Charm, platter, forest green, 8x11"..............................**22.00**

Classic, bowl, deep; white, 11"..**22.50**

Classic, cup, snack; crystal, 5-oz...................................**3.00**

Classic, plate, ruby, 14½" **35.00**

Early American Prescut, bowl, crystal, smooth rim, #726, 4¼" **22.00**

Early American Prescut, cake plate, crystal, footed, #706, 13½"................................**35.00**

Early American Prescut, coaster, crystal, #700/702..............**2.00**

Early American Prescut, plate, snack; crystal, #780, 10".**10.00**

Early American Prescut, relish, crystal, 5-part, 13½" **40.00**

Early American Prescut, tray, hostess; crystal, #750, 6½x12" **12.50**

Early American Prescut, vase, crystal, #742, 10" **12.50**

Forest Green, pitcher, 86-ounce, $40.00. (Photo courtesy Gene Florence)

Forest Green, ashtray, 3½" sq..**5.00**

Forest Green, pitcher, 36-oz...**25.00**

Forest Green, stem, cocktail; 4½-oz....................................**12.50**

Forest Green, tumbler, footed, 10-oz, 4½" **6.50**

Forest Green, tumbler, iced tea; 15-oz **14.00**

Forget Me Not, custard, white w/decals **8.00**

Forget Me Not, loaf pan, white w/decals, w/lid **25.00**

Forget Me Not, mug, white w/decals, 8-oz **15.00**

Game Birds, ashtray, white w/decals, 5¼"..................**18.00**

Game Birds, tumblers: iced tea, 11-ounce, $12.00; water, 9½-ounce, rare, $100.00; juice, 5-ounce, $35.00. (Photo courtesy Gene Florence)

Game Birds, platter, white w/decals, 9x12"...............**50.00**

Gay Fad, cake pan, Poppy, 8" dia **65.00**

Gay Fad, casserole, French; Peach Blossom, 12-oz...............**20.00**

Gay Fad, loaf pan, Fruits, 5x9"..**30.00**

Gay Fad, mixing bowl, Ivy, 1½-qt...................................**50.00**

Gay Fad, pie plate, Apple, 9"..**45.00**

Gay Fad, refrigerator container, Distlefink, 4x4" **55.00**

Gray Laurel, bowl, dessert; 4⅞" **7.00**

Gray Laurel, creamer, footed .**5.00**

Gray Laurel, plate, dinner; 9⅛".**10.00**

Harvest, bowl, dessert; white w/decals, 4⅝" **5.00**

Harvest, cup, white w/decals, 7½-oz **4.00**

Harvest, saucer, white w/decals, 5¾" **2.00**

Homestead, bowl, vegetable; white w/decals, 8¼" **18.00**

Homestead, platter, white w/decals, 9x12"...............**18.00**

Honeysuckle, creamer, white w/decals **5.00**

Honeysuckle, relish, white w/decals, 3-part, 9¾" ...**100.00**

Honeysuckle, sugar bowl, white w/decals, w/lid................**10.00**

Jade-ite Ovenware, custard, individual; 6-oz **70.00**

Jade-ite Ovenware, loaf pan, 5x9" **50.00**

Jade-ite Ovenware, skillet, 1-spout, 7"..........................**75.00**

Jane Ray, bowl, dessert; jade-ite, 4⅞"...................................**12.00**

Jane Ray, bowl, vegetable; Vitrock (white), 8¼" **25.00**

Jane Ray, cup, ivory..............**20.00**

Meadow Green, cake dish, white w/decals, 8" sq **6.00**

Meadow Green, casserole, white w/decals, crystal lid, 2-qt..**9.00**

Meadow Green, loaf pan, white w/decals, 5x9"...................**6.50**

Moonstone, bowl, opalescent hobnail, crimped, 9½".........**25.00**

Moonstone, candle holders, opalescent hobnail, pr....**18.00**

Moonstone, creamer or sugar bowl, opalescent hobnail, ea **9.00**

Moonstone, goblet, opalescent hobnail, 10-oz.................**18.00**

Peach Lustre (Laurel), bowl, vegetable; 8¼"......................**10.00**

Peach Lustre (Laurel), creamer or sugar bowl, footed, ea **4.00**

Peach Lustre (Laurel), cup, 8-oz..**3.50**

Peach Lustre (Laurel), plate, dinner; 9⅛" **5.00**

Peach Lustre (Laurel), soup plate, 7⅝" **10.00**

Philbe, bowl, vegetable; crystal, oval, 10" **60.00**

Philbe, plate, grill; green or pink, 10½" **75.00**

Philbe, tumbler, iced tea; blue, 15-oz, 6½" **90.00**

Prescut (Oatmeal), bowl, berry; crystal, 4¼"......................**2.00**

Prescut (Oatmeal), sherbet, crystal, 5-oz **1.50**

Prescut (Oatmeal), tumbler, water; crystal, 9-oz...........**2.00**

Prescut (Pineapple), box, crystal w/ruby lid, 4¾"...............**25.00**

Prescut (Pineapple), pitcher, crystal, 12-oz **8.00**

Prescut (Pineapple), sugar bowl, crystal, handles, w/lid....**12.00**

Primrose, casserole, white w/decals, knob lid, 1½-qt.................**12.00**

Primrose, sauce boat, white with fired-on design, rare, $250.00. (Photo courtesy Gene Florence)

Primrose, plate, dinner; white w/decals, 9⅛"....................**7.00**

Primrose, tumbler, white w/decals, 11-oz **25.00**

Restaurant Ware, cup, jade-ite, extra heavy, 7-oz............**10.00**

Restaurant Ware, flat soup, jade-ite, 9½" **110.00**

Restaurant Ware, plate, luncheon; crystal or white, 8".........**20.00**

Restaurant Ware, plate, pie or salad; crystal or white, 6¾".............**6.00**

Restaurant Ware, plate, 5-part; jade-ite, 9⅝" **38.00**

Restaurant Ware, platter, jade-ite, oval, 11½"................**50.00**

Royal Lustre & White, bowl, dessert; lustre, 4¾" **6.00**

Royal Lustre & White, flat soup, Anchorwhite or lustre, 9"..**20.00**

Royal Lustre & White, plate, dinner; Anchorwhite or lustre, 10"....................................**12.00**

Royal Ruby, bowl, vegetable; oval, 8"......................................**32.00**

Royal Ruby, creamer, footed...**9.00**

Royal Ruby, ice bucket..........**35.00**

Royal Ruby, plate, 13¾" **25.00**

Royal Ruby, punch bowl **40.00**

Royal Ruby, sugar bowl, footed..**7.50**

Sandwich, bowl, cereal; crystal, 6¾"....................................**45.00**

Sandwich, bowl, gold, scalloped, 5¼"......................................**6.00**

Sandwich, bowl, pink, smooth, 5¼"......................................**7.00**

Sandwich, custard cup, green.**3.50**

Sandwich, pitcher, juice; crystal, 6"......................................**65.00**

Sandwich, plate, dinner; crystal, 9"......................................**20.00**

Sandwich, tumbler, crystal, footed, 9-oz.............................**33.00**

Sapphire Blue, baker, 1-pt, 4½x5" **8.00**

Sapphire Blue, bowl, utility; 1½-qt, 8⅜" **20.00**

Sapphire Blue, casserole, w/pie plate lid, 1-qt.................**18.00**

Sapphire Blue, measuring cup, 1-spout, 8-oz **22.00**

Sapphire Blue, pie plate, 1½x9" dia..................................**10.00**

Sapphire Blue, refrigerator jar, w/lid, 5⅛x9⅛".................**32.50**

Sheaves of Wheat, bowl, dessert; jade-ite, 4½" **85.00**

Sheaves of Wheat, plate, dinner; crystal, 9" **20.00**

Sheaves of Wheat, tumbler, water; crystal, 9-oz **15.00**

Shell, bowl, cereal; peach lustre, 6⅜"....................................**10.00**

Shell, creamer or sugar bowl (open), peach lustre, ea..**10.00**

Shell, flat soup, Aurora (mother-of-pearl), 7⅝"..................**25.00**

Shell, plate, dinner; milk white or peach lustre, 10" **7.00**

Shell, plate, salad; Golden Shell (white w/gold trim), 7¼" **4.00**

Shell, platter, jade-ite, oval, 9½x13"............................**85.00**

Swirl, bowl, dessert/fruit; azur-ite, 4⅞"....................................**12.00**

Swirl, bowl, vegetable; pink, 8¼" **30.00**

Swirl, creamer, azur-ite, ivory or white, flat **10.00**

Swirl, cup, lustre w/pastel trim, 8-oz **12.00**

Swirl, plate, dinner; azur-ite, ivory or white, 9⅛".........**10.00**

Swirl, plate, dinner; jade-ite, 9⅛"....................................**80.00**

Swirl, plate, salad; Sunrise (ivory w/red trim), 7⅜"...............**8.00**

Swirl, sugar bowl, azur-ite, ivory or white, flat, tab handles ...**10.00**

Thousand Line 'Stars & Bars,' bowl, vegetable; crystal, 8".........**12.00**

Thousand Line 'Stars & Bars,' candy jar, crystal, w/lid .**17.00**

Thousand Line 'Stars & Bars,' plate, luncheon; crystal, 8".........**10.00**

Three Bands, bowl, dessert/fruit; ivory, 4⅞"........................**10.00**

Three Bands, cup, peach lustre..**3.00**

Three Bands, plate, dinner; ivory, 9⅛"...................................**25.00**

Three Bands, saucer, peach lustre, 5¾".............................**1.00**

Turquoise Blue, bowl, cereal/chili; 2⅜" H...............................**15.00**

Turquoise Blue, creamer or sugar bowl (open), ea.................**8.00**

Turquoise Blue, cup.................**5.00**

Turquoise Blue, plate, 9"......**12.00**

Wheat, baking dish, white w/decals, w/lid, 5x9".......**16.00**

Wheat, bowl, vegetable; white w/decals, 8¼"..................**12.00**

Wheat, cake pan, white w/decals, round, 8".........................**11.00**

Wheat, platter, white w/decals, 9x12"...............................**14.00**

1700 Line, bowl, vegetable; ivory, 8½".....................................**35.00**

1700 Line, cup, jade-ite, Ransom, 9-oz **22.00**

1700 Line, platter, milk white, oval, 9x12"........................**15.00**

Ashtrays

Even though the general public seems to be down on smoking, ashtrays themselves are beginning to be noticed favorably by collec-tors, who perhaps view them as an 'endangered species'! Some of the more desirable examples are those with embossed or intaglio designs, applied decorations, added figures of animals or people, Art Deco styling, an interesting advertising message, and an easily recogniz-able manufacturer's mark.

For further information we recommend *Collector's Guide to Ashtrays, Identification and Values,* by our advisor, Nancy Wanvig (published by Collector Books). She is listed in the Directory under Wisconsin.

Advertising, Camel, cobalt glass w/yellow name, green palm trees, 8" L.......................**35.00**

Advertising, Dairy Queen, clear glass w/white name on red, 3½" L **12.00**

Advertising, Hershey's Chocolate World, glass, 6" L...........**12.00**

Advertising, Holiday Inn/Nations Innkeeper, clear glass, 4" sq..**13.00**

Advertising, Olympia Premium Lager Beer, white ceramic, 4⅛" dia............................**15.00**

Advertising, Pizza Hut, clear glass, impressed stylized logo, 5" dia................................**7.00**

Advertising, Stork Club, ceramic, blue on beige, 7" dia.......**30.00**

Advertising, Wise Potato Chips, painted metal, saleman's sample, 7" L....................**16.00**

Card table, clown set, ceramic, lustre suit card shapes, 4-pc, 1⅞".**45.00**

Casino, Harrah's/Reno & Lake Tahoe, glass w/red center, 3½" sq **8.00**

Casino, Landmark Hotel Las Vegas, green glass w/gold lettering, 4⅛".....................**10.00**

Decorative, Wurlitzer baby grand piano, registered name, wood and metal, 3⅝", with box, $83.00. (Photo courtesy Nancy Wanvig)

Decorative, Art Deco nude smoking, brass dish shape, 6½" L..........................**80.00**

Decorative, brass, dragonfly in relief, 6 rests, Victorian, 7" dia **135.00**

Decorative, bronzed pot-metal ship w/mermaid, 4¼".....**23.00**

Decorative, cloisonne, bowl w/brass cells & sm flower rests, 3¼".........................**16.00**

Decorative, copper, hammered, octagonal w/1 rest, Roycroft, 4¾"...............................**100.00**

Decorative, copper, sq w/round bowl, 4 rests on flat rim, hammered, 5" **18.00**

Decorative, glass fish shape, clear w/stainless steel cover, 4½"..**15.00**

Decorative, pottery leaf shape, cream w/yellow & blue, Winfield, 4".............................**5.00**

Fraternal, Boy Scouts National Jamboree 1910-60, glass, 8" dia **18.00**

Fraternal, Masonic, ceramic, round w/3 rests, white w/gold, 5" dia................................**8.00**

Fraternal, Rotary International, ceramic cogwheel form, 5¾" dia..................................**15.00**

Novelty, cat w/umbrella in center of ashtray, solid brass, 4".....**21.00**

Novelty, clown-head smoker on book, bee between eyes, Japan, 4x4"....................**58.00**

Novelty, Confederate hat, ceramic, blue & black w/flag, 6½".**12.00**

Novelty, lady on bed w/nodding legs, multicolor porcelain, 5⅜" **55.00**

Novelty, man nodder, ceramic, Yes Dear, Yes Dear, Japan, 4" L **48.00**

Novelty, smoker-fisherman, Holt Howard, vents in mouth and ears, 1960, 5¼", $135.00. (Photo courtesy Nancy Wanvig)

Novelty, skull smoker, Poor Old Fred — He Smoked in Bed, Japan, 6" L **35.00**

Souvenir, California, ceramic, embossed cable-car form, 9½" **10.00**

Sports, Indianapolis 500, cranberry-color glass, winners to 1969 ....**38.00**

Tire Ashtrays

Tire ashtrays were introduced in the 'teens as advertising items. The very early all-glass or glass-and-metal types were replaced in the early 1920s by the more familiar rubber-tired varieties. Hundereds of different ones have been produced over the years. They are still distributed (by the larger tire companies only), but no longer contain the detail or color of the pre-World War II tire ashtrays. Although the common ones bring modest prices, rare examples demand retail prices of up to several hundred dollars.

Our tire ashtray advisor is Jeff McVey; he is listed in the Directory under Idaho. You'll also find information on how to order his book, *Tire Ashtray Collector's Guide,* which we recommend for further study.

Armstrong Miracle SD Rhino Flex, clear glass insert w/6 rests **20.00**

Atlas Plycron, clear insert, 8"..**70.00**

BF Goodrich Comp T/A, imprinted insert, 6" **30.00**

Continental Titan, truck tire, clear embossed insert, 6¾" **50.00**

Diamond Balloon 33x6.00 to fit 5" rim 21" wheel, blue embossed insert **80.00**

Dunlop Guardian 6.95L 14, clear imprinted insert, 6" **30.00**

Firestone Steel Radial 500, clear imprinted insert, 6" **25.00**

General Steelex Radial, truck tire, clear imprinted insert, 6½" **30.00**

Firestone, Century of Progress, 1934, amber embossed insert, $85.00.

General Streamline Jumbo, green embossed insert, 5" **65.00**

Goodrich Silvertown Super 6-Ply, green embossed insert, 7" .**60.00**

Goodyear Wrangler Radial, clear imprinted insert, 6½" **40.00**

Hercules Tires, red & black plastic insert, 6" **20.00**

Hood Deep Cleat HB, tractor tire w/clear imprinted insert, 6⅛" **50.00**

Kelly-Springfield Tom Cat, solid truck tire, clear embossed insert **100.00**

Laramie Tires, plastic w/metal insert, 6" **20.00**

Mohawk Ultissimo, clear imprinted insert, 6" **100.00**

Orban TX-9, clear insert w/manufacturer imprint, 6"........**40.00**

Seiberling RT/78 Steel Radial, clear imprinted insert, 6⅛"......**50.00**

Toyo Radial Z-2, red, green or black w/clear imprinted insert, 5⅜"......**40.00**

Western Auto, plastic w/red & black plastic insert, 6"...**40.00**

Winston Cup/25th Anniversary, plastic w/glass insert, 2"......**28.00**

Automobilia

Many are fascinated with vintage automobiles, but to own one of those 'classy chassis' is a luxury not all can afford! So instead they enjoy collecting related memorabilia such as advertising, owners' manuals, horns, emblems, and hood ornaments. The decade of the 1930s produced the items that are most in demand today, but the 1950s models have their own band of devoted fans as well.

Badge, Studebaker Employee, brass w/celluloid insert, EX **35.00**

Bank, Chevrolet the Symbol of Savings..., tin globe, Chein, 5", EX+......**60.00**

Bank, Ford, dog figure, marked Florence Ceramics, 1960s **35.00**

Booklet, Studebaker, A Trip Through the...Factory, ca 1950, VG......**10.00**

Brochure, Indian Motorcycles, 40th Anniversary, 1941, EX **90.00**

Brochure, Oldsmobile Six & Eight, color, 1930s, 9x10", VG+.**40.00**

Calendar, Chevrolet Motor Cars, 1920, paper, framed, 33½", EX......**80.00**

Cigar box, Ford, wood, 2½x9", VG......**160.00**

Cigarette case, Ford V-8, blue w/silver trim & V-8 emblem, 3", EX......**275.00**

Clock, Cadillac, sq desk-type lightup w/center emblem, 1960, 9x10", NM **200.00**

Clock, Ford Cars/Trucks/Parts/Accessories, octagonal lightup, 18", VG......**750.00**

Coin, 1954 Corvette, Motorama commemorative, gold-tone, EX......**15.00**

Compass, Union 76, suction-cup mount, EX **15.00**

Desk accessory, GMC truck in bronze on base, 3x4x7", EX......**100.00**

Display rack, Ford Color Patch, 3 stepped shelves w/marquee, 19", G......**100.00**

Display rack, Greyhound Bus literature, 4-tiered, wood, 7x15x4", EX......**200.00**

Foldout, Harley-Davidson/Running & Adjusting Instructions, 1940, EX **50.00**

Hood ornament, Ford Mustang, chrome horse logo, 5¾", NMIB **175.00**

Hood ornament, Packard's Goddess of Speed mascot, chrome, 1930s, EX **170.00**

Hubcaps, Hudson Super Six, aluminum, screw-on, 1925, NM, pr......**90.00**

Jar, Volkswagen, amber glass figural VW Bug w/cork stopper, 6", EX......**40.00**

Jigsaw puzzle, Dodge Bros New Eight Sedan/Six Sedan, 2-sided, 16", EX...............**125.00**

Key chain, '66 Olds Super Salesman, M **15.00**

License plate attachment, Chrysler, tin, hat/gloves/cane, 6x9", VG+ **275.00**

Lighter, Downtown Ford Sales, 1950s-60s emblem, Zippo type, EX..........................**20.00**

Magazine, Automobile Quarterly, Vol 7 #2, M **15.00**

Magazine, Motor Magazine's Annual, Oct 1939, cover by Radchaugh, VG.............**30.00**

Map, Greyhound route, dated Nov 1 1934, 20x31", EX.........**30.00**

Mechanical pencil, Pontiac, Safety Shift, late 1940s, EX......**15.00**

Mug, Chevrolet Truck Sales Award, shows 1947 stake-bed truck, 1961, NM.............**15.00**

Necklace, Buick Rivera, silver car-shaped pendant, Anson, 1963, EXIB...............................**45.00**

Owner's guide, '66 Chevrolet Truck, Series 10-30, EX..**10.00**

Paperweight, GM Golden Milestones 1908-1958, token in Lucite cube, EX..............**45.00**

Picnic set, Ford, complete w/case, VG...............................**275.00**

Pin, Cadillac Craftsman, gold w/logo, 1947, NM **35.00**

Pin, Chevrolet Corvette Owner, round w/crossed flag logo, 1955-56, NM.................**260.00**

Playing cards, Cadillac emblem, double deck in plastic box, EX...............................**10.00**

Pocketknife, Ford, blue logo on red plastic casing, 3½", EX...**60.00**

Postcard, Nash Ambassador 600, pictures auto, NM..........**20.00**

Postcard, 1972 Mustang, black & white photo, 5x7", unused..**2.00**

Promotional vehicle, 1950 Ford Sedan, maroon w/mirrored windows, EX................**125.00**

Promotional vehicle, 1959 Thunderbird convertible, 8", EX, $150.00.

Promotional vehicle, 1965 Pontiac GTO, metallic green, NM (w/case).........................**200.00**

Promotional vehicle, 1974 Chevy Corvette, metallic burnt orange, NM **165.00**

Salt & pepper shakers, Greyhound Bus, metal bus shapes, EX, pr **100.00**

Shop manual, Packard, 1937 Series, black & white, 71 pages, EX.........................**55.00**

Sign, DeSoto/Authorized Dealer/Top Value, diecut emblem, 16x36", VG **235.00**

Sign, FoMoCO Genuine Ford Auto Parts, metal, 2-sided, 14x18", EX **60.00**

Sign, Fordor Sedan, cardboard, 1940s vehicle, framed, 25x37", EX+...................**75.00**

Sign, Harley-Davidson logo/Insist on Genuine..., tin, 29x16", EX..................**200.00**

Sign, Plymouth, neon, flag shape w/block lettering, 22x25", NM **325.00**

Tape measure, DeSoto Six, Product of Chrysler, 1½", EX+ **50.00**

Windshield scraper, Packard logo, plastic, M in envelope **18.00**

Thermometer, Buick Motor Cars, porcelain, 27x7", VG, from $250.00 to $300.00. (Photo courtesy Dunbar Gallery)

Thermometer, Buick Motor Cars, porcelain, white on dark blue, 27", NM **350.00**

Thermometer, Chevrolet Corvair/OK, tin, white ground, vertical, EX **225.00**

Thermometer, Mack Trucks, dial type w/glass front, VG+...**200.00**

Tie pin, Cadillac crest w/V underneath, sterling................**20.00**

Tip tray, Aero, cars/airplane, 4" dia, EX+........................**150.00**

Token, Chrysler Industrial Association, aluminum, octagonal, M....................................**10.00**

Watch fob, Cadillac, silver emblem on black fabric strap, NM **200.00**

Autumn Leaf

Autumn Leaf dinnerware was a product of the Hall China Company, who produced this extensive line from 1933 until 1978 for exclusive distribution by the Jewel Tea Company. The Libbey Glass Company made co-ordinating pitchers, tumblers, and stemware. Metal, cloth, plastic, and paper items were also available. Today, though very rare pieces are expensive and a challenge to acquire, new collectors may easily reassemble an attractive, usable set at a reasonable price. Hall has produced special club pieces (for the NALCC) as well as some limited editions for an Ohio company, but these are well marked and easily identified as such. Refer to *The Collector's Encyclopedia of Hall China, Third Edition,* by Margaret and Kenn Whitmyer (Collector Books) for more information.

Our advisor for this category is Gwynne Harrison; she is listed in the Directory under California. See Clubs and Newsletters for information concerning *Autumn Leaf.*

Baker, cake; Mary Dunbar, Heatflow clear glass, 1½-qt................**85.00**

Baker, French; 3-pint...........**20.00**

Baker, souffle; 4⅛" **80.00**

Blanket, vellux, Autumn Leaf color, full sz **175.00**

Book, Autumn Leaf Story.....**60.00**

Bottle, Jim Beam, broken seal..**110.00**

Bowl, salad; 9".....................**20.00**
Bowl, vegetable; Melmac, oval..**50.00**
Bowl, vegetable; Royal Glasbake,
milk glass, divided.......**150.00**
Butter dish, regular ruffled lid, 1-
lb..................................**500.00**
Cake safe, motif on top.........**50.00**
Candlestick, Douglas, metal, pr..**100.00**
Cards, playing; 75th Anniversary
deck, 1974.......................**50.00**
Casserole, w/lid, round, 2-qt..**45.00**
Catalog, Jewel, paper...........**20.00**
Coffee dispenser..................**400.00**
Coffeepot, all china, 4-pc....**350.00**
Cookbook, National Autumn Leaf
Collector's Club..............**45.00**
Cooker, pressure; metal, Mary
Dunbar.........................**225.00**
Creamer & sugar bowl, Rayed,
1930s style.....................**80.00**
Cup, coffee; Jewel's Best.......**30.00**
Cup, custard; Radiance.........**10.00**
Flatware, stainless steel, serving
pcs, ea...........................**130.00**

Gravy boat, $30.00.

Gravy boat, w/underplate.....**55.00**
Mug, Irish coffee.................**150.00**
Pan, loaf; Mary Dunbar......**125.00**
Pan, sauce; w/lid, 2-qt.........**100.00**
Plate, salad; Melmac, 7".......**20.00**
Plate, 10"..............................**18.00**
Platter, oval, 11½"................**28.00**
Saucer, St Denis.....................**8.00**
Scales, Jewel Family...........**200.00**
Table cloth, plastic, 54x54"..**150.00**

Teapot, Newport, dated 1978, from $200.00 to $250.00.

Teapot, Aladdin.....................**70.00**
Teapot, New York, Club pc...**700.00**
Tidbit, 2-tier.......................**100.00**
Tin, fruitcake; tan.................**10.00**
Toy, Jewel truck, semi trailer,
white.............................**400.00**
Tumbler, Brockway, 13-oz....**45.00**
Tumbler, iced tea; Libbey, frosted,
5½"..................................**20.00**
Tumbler, Libbey, gold & frost on
clear, 10-oz.....................**65.00**
Warmer, oval.....................**200.00**

Avon

Originally founded in 1886 under the title California Perfume Company, the firm became officially known as Avon Products Inc. in 1939. Among collectors they are best known not for their cosmetics and colognes but for their imaginative packaging and figural bottles. Avon offers something for almost everyone as such cross-collectibles including Fostoria, Wedgwood, commerative plates, Ceramarte steins, and hundreds of other quality items. Also sought are product samples, awards, magazine ads, jewelry, and catalogs. Their Cape Cod glassware has been sold in vast quantities since the '70s and is becoming a common sight at flea markets and antique malls. For more information we recommend *Hastin's Avon Collector's Price Guide* by Bud Hastin. See also Cape Cod. For information concerning the National Association of Avon Collectors and the newsletter *Avon Times*, see Clubs and Newsletters.

Asparagus (Garden Fresh) Decanter, glass, 1979-80, 10-oz, MIB **5.00**

Bird of Paradise Decanter, glass w/gold head, 1970-72, 8", MIB **12.00**

Bon Bon Poodle Decanter, black or white milk glass, 1972-73, MIB, ea **7.00**

Calculator Decanter (It All Adds Up), black glass, 1979-80, 4-oz, MIB **8.00**

Candle, Ho Ho Glow Santa, ceramic, 1982-83, 5", MIB........**16.00**

Candle, Sea Shell Trinket Box, pearlized ceramic, 1987, 3½", MIB...................................**7.00**

Candle, Sparkling Turtle Candlette, glass, 1976-79, 4½" L, MIB...................................**9.00**

Candle, Year-to-Year Birthday (clown on block), ceramic, 1983-84, MIB..................**10.00**

Christmas Sparkler Bubble Bath Bottle, colors, 1968-69, 4-oz, MIB, ea...........................**13.00**

Cornucopia Decanter, milk glass w/gold cap, 1971-76, 5½", MIB **9.00**

Doll, Howdy Partner, 5th in Childhood Dreams series, 1993, 10", MIB **40.00**

Doll, Nigerian Adama, 4th in series, 1990, 8½", MIB...**35.00**

Doll, Southern Belle, porcelain, 1988, 8¼", MIB **30.00**

Doll, Spring Petals Barbie, 1997, 11½", MIB **40.00**

Egg, crystal, Majestic, w/pewter base, 1993, 4½", MIB.....**30.00**

Egg, porcelain, Winter's Treasure, w/wood base, 1987, 3", MIB **10.00**

Egg, tin, Spring Flowers design, held butter mints, 1995, 6" L, MIB...................................**5.00**

Eiffel Tower Decanter, glass w/gold cap, 1970, 3-oz, MIB.........................**10.00**

Elizabeth Fashion Figurine, glass w/plastic top, 1972, 4-oz, MIB **20.00**

Forget-Me-Not Heart Box, porcelain, w/matching pin, 1989, MIB...................................**8.00**

French Telephone Decanter, milk glass w/gold cap, 1971, 6-oz, MIB...................................**30.00**

Golden Harvest Corn Cob Pump Decanter, glass, 1977-80, 10-oz, MIB **6.00**

Heavenlight Face Powder, pink feather decor, 1944, MIB, $12.50.

Holiday Hostess Candlesticks, glass w/holly decal, 1981, 3", MIB, pr.............................**12.00**

Holiday Hostess Platter, glass w/holly decal, 1981, 11" dia, MIB...............................**15.00**

Hummingbird Bell, glass, etched frosted design, 1983, MIB.**12.00**

Hummingbird Cup & Saucer Set, crystal, 1994, MIB.........**25.00**

Hurricane Lamp Decanter, milk glass w/glass shade, 1973-74, 6-oz, MIB........................**13.00**

Icicle Perfume Bottle, glass w/gold cap, 1967-68, 1 dram, MIB.......................................**8.00**

Key Note Perfume, glass key shape w/gold plastic cap, 1967, MIB......................**20.00**

Little Bo Peep Decanter, painted milk glass & plastic, 1976-78, MIB....................................**8.00**

Love Bird Perfume Bottle, frosted w/gold cap, 1973-74, ¼-oz, MIB...............................**10.00**

Mad Hatter Bubble Bath Decanter, plastic, 1970, 6-oz, MIB.....................................**6.00**

Mrs Quackles Decanter, painted glass w/plastic top, 1979-80, 2-oz, MIB..........................**7.00**

No Tears Shampoo Six Shooter, plastic, 1962-63, 6-oz, MIB..........................**24.00**

Ornament, Baby's First...1986, porcelain, Joan W Anglund, 4", MIB.........................**10.00**

Ornament, Hummingbird 1986, lead crystal w/etched design, 3½", MIB.........................**12.00**

Ornament, Melvin P Merrymouse, plastic, 2nd series, 1983, 2¾", MIB.................................**8.00**

Ornament, Sparkling Angel, silver plate w/gold 1990 star, 3¼", MIB................................**10.00**

Partridge Decanter, milk glass w/white plastic cap, 1973-75, 5-oz, MIB.........................**6.00**

Peacock Decanter, glass w/gold cap, 1973-74, 4-oz, MIB.**11.00**

Picture Frame Cologne, painted glass, w/stand, 1970-71, 4-oz, MIB................................**17.00**

1933 Pierce Arrow Deep Woods After Shave, cobalt glass bottle with plastic top, 7¾", MIB, $77.00 at auction. (Photo courtesy Monsen and Baer)

Precious Turtle Sachet Jar, gold w/plastic lid, 1975-76, MIB.............................**6.00**

Sea Treasure Sea Shell Decanter, glass w/gold cap, 1971-72, 7", MIB...............................**10.00**

Snail Perfume Bottle, glass w/gold cap, 1968-69, ¼-oz, MIB..**14.00**

Snoopy Come Home Soap Dish & Soap, raft w/Snoopy on sail, 1973-74, MIB...................**6.00**

Stylish Lady Pig Pump Decanter, milk glass, 1982-83, 8-oz, MIB.................................**9.00**

Tic Toc Tiger Bubble Bath Decanter, plastic, 1967-69, MIB.................................**9.00**

Tot 'N Tyke Shampoo Good Habit Rabbit Decanter, plastic, 1967, MIB......................**12.00**

Banks

After the Depression, everyone was aware that saving 'for a rainy day' would help during bad times. Children of the '40s, '50s, and '60s were given piggy banks in forms of favorite characters to reinforce the idea of saving. They were made to realize that by saving money they could buy that expensive bicycle or a toy they were particularly longing for.

Glass

Interest in glass banks has recently grown by leaps and bounds, and you'll be amazed at the prices some of the harder-to-find examples are bringing. Charlie Reynolds has written the glass bank 'bible,' called *Collector's Guide to Glass Banks*, which you'll want to read if you think you'd like to collect them. It's published by Collector Books. In our listings, we've included only those banks with punched factory slots or those with molded, raised slots. There are other types as well. Because of limited space, values listed below are mid range. Expect to pay as much as 50% more or less than our suggested prices.

Baby Bottle, various pyro labels, Samuel Callet Co, 6½"...**55.00**

Barbasol, black lid, letters in panels, 3"............................**55.00**
Baseball, St Louis Cardinals, white paint inside, red letters, 3½".................................**110.00**
Baseball, State Bank of Long Beach, white paint inside, black lid base.................**55.00**
Block, diamond pattern on inside, slot molded in seam, 5¾"..**55.00**
Block, distorted panels, slot molded in seam on top, 5¾"...**25.00**
Bud Light, bottle w/slot cut in back shoulder, 9", up to .**15.00**
Coca-Cola, green glass bottle, 20"...............................**110.00**
Domino Sugar Bear, Bear's a Bank Too on lid, 4½"......**25.00**
Feed the Kitty Bucket, Spanish Olives info on lid, 4¾"..**225.00**
For Your Lincoln Pennies (Lincoln bust), twist-off lid, 9"......................**115.00**
Fred Fear Pig, lg lid, fur detail, 8"......................................**55.00**
Galaxy Asteroid Commander, pyro identification, 8½", up to..**15.00**
Garfield, clear, Anchor Hocking, 7½", up to **15.00**
Gattuso Rabbit, 16-oz (embossed), Bambino Olives info on lid, 6½"...............................**450.00**
Grapette Elephant, product info on lid, 7¼" **55.00**
Kiddy Bank Tic Tic Relish (clock), info on label, Pat 95888, 4½"...................**55.00**
Kinsey Silver Display Bottle, amber w/whiskey label, 13½"............................**25.00**
Liberty Bell, amber glass, Anchor Hocking, raised long slot, 3¾" **225.00**

34

Louisiana Vinegar Clown, Grapette Family Beverage information on lid, 7", from $35.00 to $75.00. (Photo courtesy Charlie Reynolds)

Lucky Barrel, carnival glass, raised slot, 4⅜"...............**55.00**
Lucky Joe (head), Nash's Prepared Mustard on lid, paper lips, 4½".........................**25.00**
Milk Bottle, Whitestone Farms (red pyro), steel lid w/lock, ½-pt...................................**110.00**
Old Fashioned Stove (burning fire label), Fresh Pak Candy, 5¼" **25.00**
Pig, carnival glass, Anchor Hocking, raised slot, 4⅞", up to **15.00**
Pig, carnival glass, Save w/Marathon, raised slot, 3"........................**55.00**
Pillsbury Little Sprout Jelly Bean Machine, plastic/zinc base, Taiwan...........................**125.00**
Snow Crest Penguin, Patent Pend Mfrd by Snow Crest Beverages, 7½" **450.00**
Stewert's Root Beer, amber with pyro message, 5" **25.00**
Wise Old Owl (marked on bottom, amber glass, 6", up to **15.00**

World Globe, raised continents in glass, Pat Applied For, 5¼"..............................**55.00**
1929 Car, grill marked FP 1929, 4¾" L **25.00**

Character Related

Today, on the flea market circut, figural ceramic banks are popular collectibles, especially those that are character-related — advertising characters and Disney in particular. For more information on banks of this type, we recommend *Ceramic Coin Banks* by Tom and Loretta Stoddard, and *Collector's Guide to Banks* by Beverly and Jim Mangus, both published by Collector Books. See also Advertising.

Andy Panda, litho tin book shape, EX.................................**125.00**
Barney Rubble & Bamm-Bamm, hard plastic, Homecraft, 13", M.....................................**75.00**
Batman, vinyl, Transogram, 1966, 20", VG **45.00**
Big Bird on toy box, ceramic, NM **20.00**
Big Bird w/egg, composition, NM **20.00**
Bozo the Clown, plastic, 1972, lg, NM.................................**35.00**
Bugs Bunny holding present, ceramic, Warner Bros, 1981, EX.................................**50.00**
Casper the Friendly Ghost, ceramic, NM.................**200.00**
Dino & Pebbles, Hamilton/ Made in Japan, from $60 to.................................**75.00**

35

Donald Duck, Ucago, 1960s, MIB **55.00**

Dr. Dolittle with monkey and dog at feet, pink and blue plastic, NM, $50.00. (Photo courtesy Matt and Lisa Adams)

Dr Zaius (Planet of the Apes), plastic, Play Pal, 1967, 10", NM.................................**30.00**

Elmer Fudd standing beside tree stump, metal, Metal Moss, 6", NMIB...........................**250.00**

Elmo in train, ceramic, Enesco, 1993, M.........................**50.00**

Ernie in train, ceramic, Applause, NM.................................**40.00**

ET standing on round green base, 6", M **30.00**

Felix the Cat sitting, Applause, 1989, 5¾".........................**50.00**

Flipper, plastic, 1960s, 17½", NM.................................**45.00**

Fred Flintstone, Pebbles & Bamm-Bamm on can shape, Kanley, 1988, NM..........**30.00**

Fred Flintstone standing by rock, plastic, 1973, EX.............**30.00**

Garfield in rabbit suit sitting on egg, ceramic, Enesco, 1978, NM.................................**40.00**

Garfield w/knife & fork, ceramic, Enesco, NM **35.00**

General Urus (Planet of the Apes), plastic, Apac, 1967, 18", NM........................**30.00**

Huckleberry Hound, plastic, 1960, 10", EX....................**35.00**

Incredible Hulk bust, plastic, Renzi, 1979, 15", NM.....**25.00**

King Kong, painted plaster, Universal Statuary, 1952, 11", M..................................**100.00**

King Kong, plastic, 17", NM ..**35.00**

Lambchop, plastic, Sheri Lewis Enterprises/China, 1993..**12.00**

Li'l Abner, composition, Capp Enterprises, 1975, 7", M............**100.00**

Linus the Lion-Hearted, plastic, Transogram, 1965, 10", EX.............**55.00**

Little Lulu, plastic, Play Pal Plastics, 7½", NM..................**50.00**

Little Red Riding Hood, ceramic, NAPCO, NM **125.00**

London Tour Bus w/Warner Bros characters, ceramic, China, 1995 ....**55.00**

Lucy at desk (Peanuts), ceramic, NM.................................**30.00**

Marilyn Monroe (Funtime Savings), vinyl, China, 1960s, 12", MIB **175.00**

Marvin the Martian (Happiness Is a Vacation), China, 1994, M **25.00**

Miss Piggy, ceramic, Sigma, NM **50.00**

Mufusa & Simba (Lion King), Sigma #650, from $75 to..**95.00**

Pebbles Flintstone, plastic, Transogram, 1960s, EX...............**45.00**

Popeye sitting w/spinach can, vinyl, Alan Jay, 1958, 8", EX...**75.00**

Raggedy Ann & Andy, papiermache, Determined, 1971, 6", M..................................**25.00**

Raggedy Ann seated w/puppy, ceramic w/yarn hair, 1981, 6", M.....................................**25.00**

Rainbow Brite, vinyl, M........**15.00**

She-Ra Princess of Power, painted vinyl, HG Toys/Hong Kong, MIB.................................**10.00**

Sketetor, plastic, HG Toys, 1984, 6", MOC.........................**30.00**

Snoopy, chalkware, Lego, 1950s, 8", VG.............................**45.00**

Snoopy on hot dog, United Features Syndicate, from $20 to.....................................**25.00**

Snoopy on rainbow, composition, NM.................................**25.00**

Spider-Man bust, plastic, Renzi, 1979, 15", EX.................**25.00**

Superman, ceramic, Enesco, 1987, MIB.................................**85.00**

Superman, plastic, NPPI, 1974, NM.................................**55.00**

Sylvester lying on treasure chest, ceramic, WB, 1981, from $25 to.....................................**35.00**

WC Fields as policeman, Sigma, M.....................................**70.00**

Wilma Flintstone & Pebbles, plastic, NM..........................**30.00**

Woodstock (Peanuts), yellow plastic, 1972, 6", NM............**35.00**

Barbie Dolls

Barbie doll was first introduced in 1959, and soon Mattel found themselves producing not only dolls but tiny garments, fashion accessories, houses, cars, horses, books, and games as well. Today's Barbie doll collectors want them all. Though the early Barbie dolls are very hard to find, there are many of her successors still around. The trend today is toward Barbie doll exclusives — Holiday Barbie dolls and Bob Mackies are all very 'hot' items. So are special-event Barbie dolls.

When buying the older dolls, you'll need to do a lot of studying and comparisons to learn to distinguish one Barbie doll from another, but this is the key to making sound buys and good investments. Remember, though, collectors are sticklers concerning condition; compared to a doll mint in box, they'll often give an additional 20% if that box has never been opened! If you want a good source for study, refer to one of these fine books: *A Decade of Barbie Dolls and Collectibles, 1981 – 1991,* by Beth Summers; *The Wonder of Barbie* and *The World of Barbie Dolls* by Paris and Susan Manos; *Barbie Fashions, Volume I* and *II,* by Sarah Sink Eames; *Barbie Exclusives, Books I* and *II,* by Margo Rana; *Thirty Years of Mattel Fashion Dolls, The Barbie Doll Boom,* and *Collector's Encyclopedia of Barbie Doll Exclusives and More* by J. Michael Augustyniak; *The Story of Barbie, Second Edition,* by Kitturah Westenhouser; *The Barbie Doll Years* by Patrick C. and Joyce L. Olds; *Skipper — Barbie Doll's Little Sister,* by Scott Arend, Karla Holzerland, and Trina Kent; *Collector's Guide to Barbie Doll Vinyl Cases*; and *Schroeder's Collectibles Toys, Antique to Modern* (Collector Books).

Dolls

Allan, 1964-67, painted red hair, straight legs, MIB........**145.00**

Barbie, #3, 1960, blond hair, original swimsuit, NM **950.00**

Barbie, #6, 1962, Ponytail, MIB .**600.00**

Barbie, American Girl, 1964, platinum hair, original swimsuit, NM **650.00**

Barbie, American Girl wearing Fashion Editor outfit, brunette hair, 1964, NM, from $600.00 to $650.00. (Photo courtesy Cindy Sabulis)

Barbie, Angel Face, 1982, NRFB **40.00**

Barbie, Beach Blast, 1989, NRFB ..**25.00**

Barbie, Beautiful Bride, 1976, NRFB...........................**25.00**

Barbie, Blockbuster, 1998, NRFB..........................**50.00**

Barbie, Dance & Twirl, 1994, NRFB............................**50.00**

Barbie, Day-to-Night, 1985, NRFB **75.00**

Barbie, Deluxe Tropical, 1985, NRFB...........................**40.00**

Barbie, Dolls of the World, 1985, Peruvian, NRFB **85.00**

Barbie, Dolls of the World, 1996, Arctic, NRFB.................**20.00**

Barbie, Frills & Fantasy, 1988, Wal-Mart, NRFB **65.00**

Barbie, Gold Medal Swimmer, 1975, NRFB.................**100.00**

Barbie, Great Shape, 1983, NRFB...........................**25.00**

Barbie, Harley-Davidson, 1997, 1st edition, NRFB........**600.00**

Barbie, Holiday, 1988, red gown, NRFB, minimum value **1,000.00**

Barbie, Holiday, 1989, NRFB **250.00**

Barbie, Holiday, 1990, NRFB ..**250.00**

Barbie, Holiday, 1991, NRFB ..**250.00**

Barbie, Holiday, 1992, NRFB ..**150.00**

Barbie, Holiday, 1993, NRFB ..**200.00**

Barbie, Holiday, 1994, NRFB ..**175.00**

Barbie, Holiday, 1995, NRFB **75.00**

Barbie, Holiday, 1996, NRFB **50.00**

Barbie, Holiday, 1997, NRFB **35.00**

Barbie, Jewel Jubilee, 1991, MIB...............................**85.00**

Barbie, Lilac & Lovely, 1988, Sears Exclusive, NRFB .**60.00**

Barbie, Live Action on Stage, 1971, NRFB..................**165.00**

Barbie, Magic Curl (Black), 1982, NRFB...........................**35.00**

Barbie, Moonlight Rose, 1991, Hills, NRFB...................**50.00**

Barbie, Oreo Fun, 1997, NRFB ..**35.00**

Barbie, Pretty Changes, 1980, NRFB...........................**50.00**

Barbie, Rappin' Rockin', 1991, NRFB...........................**40.00**

Barbie, Sun Valley, 1973, NRFB .**100.00**

Barbie, Twist 'N Turn, 1968, blond hair, MIB...........**700.00**

Barbie, Wedding Fantasy (Black), 1989, NRFB...................**35.00**

Barbie, Western Stampin' (Black), 1993, NRFB....................**30.00**

Brad, Talking, 1997, MIB...**250.00**

Brad, 1969, bendable legs, NRFB........................**200.00**

Chris, 1967, blond hair, original outfit, NM.....................**125.00**

Chris, 1974, auburn hair, original outfit & shoes, EX..........**75.00**

Christie, Rappin' Rockin', 1991, NRFB............................**45.00**

Fluff, Living, 1971, NRFB, minimum value **175.00**

Francie, Growin' Pretty Hair, 1970, original outfit, NM.........**150.00**

Francie, Twist 'N Turn, 1966, blond hair, original outfit, NM..............................**350.00**

Jamie, New & Wonderful Walking, blond hair, original outfit, EX.........................**225.00**

Ken, painted hair, straight legs, 1962, MIB, $150.00.

Ken, Busy Talking, 1972, original outfit, VG........................**85.00**

Ken, Doctor, 1987, MIB........**35.00**

Ken, Hawaiian Fun, 1983, MIB **50.00**

Ken, Jewel Secrets, 1986, NRFB **65.00**

Ken, Prince Charming, 1991, NRFB............................**35.00**

Ken, Professor Higgins, 1996, NRFB............................**75.00**

Ken, Sun Valley, 1973, NRFB..**125.00**

Ken, Walking Lively, 1972, MIB **150.00**

Ken, 30th Anniversary, 1991, NRFB...........................**225.00**

Midge, All Stars, 1990, MIB ..**40.00**

Midge, California Dream, 1988, MIB.................................**50.00**

Midge, 1963, blond hair, bendable legs, MIB **500.00**

PJ, Dream Date, 1983, MIB .**50.00**

PJ, Sweet Roses, 1983, NRFB..**65.00**

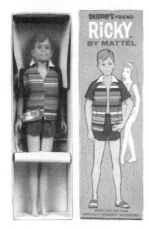

Ricky, 1965, MIB, $175.00. (Photo courtesy McMasters Auctions)

Ricky, 1965, original outfit & shoes, NM......................**75.00**

Skipper, Deluxe Quick Curl, 1976-77, NRFB......................**125.00**

Skipper, Dramatic New Living, 1970. original swimsuit, NM........**50.00**

Skipper, Horse Lovin', 1982, NRFB.............................**40.00**

Skipper, Sunset Malibu, 1971-74, NRFB...............75.00

Skipper, Twist 'N Turn, 1970-71, NRFB............300.00

Skooter, Funtime, 1976, NRFB, minimum value............200.00

Skooter, 1965, blond hair, bendable legs, MIB..............225.00

Stacey, Twist 'N Turn, 1968, blond hair, NRFB........900.00

Stacey, Twist 'N Turn, 1969, blond hair, replica swimsuit, NM.............225.00

Steffie, Walk Lively, 1968, original outfit & scarf, NM................175.00

Teresa, Baywatch, 1994, NRFB..35.00

Teresa, Island Fun, 1988, MIB...40.00

Tutti, 1966, brunette hair, original outfit, NM..............85.00

Whitney, Perfume Party, 1987, NRFB..............85.00

Whitney, Style Magic, 1988, NRFB..............35.00

Cases

Golden Dream Barbie, 1980, $10.00. (Photo courtesy Beth Summers)

Barbie, Francie & Casey Doll Trunk, NM, from $75 to.100.00

Barbie & Her Friends Travel Trunk, rare, EX, minimum value...........................125.00

Barbie & Ken Costume Trunk, rare, EX, from $125 to.175.00

Barbie & Midge Travel Pals, 1963, round w/zipper closure, black, NM.................50.00

Fashion Queen Barbie, 1963, w/mirror & wig stand, EX........100.00

Midge, Barbie's Best Friend, 1963, NM, from $25 to.............35.00

Slipper & Skooter, 1965, oval portraits, vinyl, NM, from $25 to...........................35.00

Tuttie & Todd House, vinyl, NM...........................50.00

World of Barbie, 1968, vinyl, NM...........................25.00

Clothing and Accessories

Barbie, Add-Ons Fashion Pak, 1968, MOC..................300.00

Barbie, Backyard Barbecue, #5719, 1983, MIB...........25.00

Barbie, Dancing Lights, #3437, 1971, MIB....................350.00

Barbie, Dreamy Pink, #1857, 1968, MIB....................150.00

Barbie, Fancy Trimmin's Fashion Pak, 1967, MIP............300.00

Barbie, Flower Wower, #1453, 1970, MIB.....................75.00

Barbie, Friday Night Date, #979, complete, NM..............100.00

Barbie, Garden Wedding, #1658, complete, M.................300.00

Barbie, Gaucho Gear, #3436, 1971, MIB....................275.00

Barbie, Glowin' Out, #3404, 1971, MIB...........................125.00

Barbie, Model of the Year (Superstar), 1988, NRFB.............25.00

Barbie, Overall Denim, #3488, 1972, MIB....................150.00

Barbie, Pedal Pushers Fashion Pak, 1968, MIP............100.00

Barbie, Rainbow Wraps, #1796,
complete, NM **135.00**

Barbie, Registered Nurse, #991,
complete, NM **90.00**

Barbie, Sport Star, #3353, complete, NM **25.00**

Barbie, Student Teacher, #1622,
1965, complete, M **250.00**

Barbie, Victorian Velvet, #3431,
1971, MIB **175.00**

Francie, Concert in the Park,
#1256, complete, NM+ ... **85.00**

Francie, Dance Party, #1257, complete, M **150.00**

Francie, Little Knits, #3275, 1971,
MIB **100.00**

Francie, Twilight Twinkle, #3459,
1971, MIB **225.00**

Francie, Zig-Zag Zoom, #3445,
1971, MIB **100.00**

Ken in Mexico, MIB, $150.00; Time for
Tennis, #790, MIB, $125.00. (Photo cour-
tesy June Moon)

Ken, Campus Corduroys, #1410,
1964, MIB **125.00**

Ken, College Student, #1416,
1965, MIB **550.00**

Ken, In Training, #780, 1961,
MIB **125.00**

Ken, Midnight Blues, #1719,
1972, NRFB **175.00**

Ken, Pet Show Fashions, several variations, 1986, NRFB, ea **20.00**

Ken, Special Date, #1401, complete, NM+ **85.00**

Ken, TV Sports Reporter, #9086,
1984, NRFB **20.00**

Ken, Wide Awake Stripes, #3378,
1972, MIB **60.00**

Skipper, Chill Chasers, #1926,
complete, NM+ **55.00**

Skipper, Young Ideas Fashion Pak, Sears Exclusive,
MIP **150.00**

Tutti, Pinky PJ's, #3616, 1968,
NRFB **150.00**

Tutti, Plantin' Posies, #3609,
1967, complete, M **65.00**

Houses, Furnishings, and Vehicles

**Barbie and Ken Dune Buggy, Irwin,
scarce, MIB, $200.00.**

Barbie & Skipper's Speedboat, Sears
Exclusive, 1964, MIB **300.00**

Barbie Country Living House,
1973-77, complete, EX ... **75.00**

Barbie Dream Cottage, 1983, complete, M **65.00**

Barbie Fashion Plaza, 1975, complete, NMIB **100.00**

Barbie Glamour Home, 1985,
MIB **125.00**

Barbie Loves McDonald's, 1983,
NRFB **50.00**

Barbie's Buggy, 1971-72, MIB .. **75.00**

Barbie's Room-Fulls Studio Bedroom, 1974, NRFB **60.00**

Barbie Starlight Bed, 1990, complete, MIB......................30.00
California Dream Barbie Hot Dog Stand, 1988, NRFB........50.00
Camp Barbie Sun Cruiser, 1994, M......................................20.00
Go-Together Lawn Swing & Planter, 1964, complete, MIB 150.00
Olympic Ski Village, 1975, MIB............................60.00
Skipper's Travelin' Trailer Deluxe Set, 1983, MIB 50.00
Star Traveler Motorhome, 1980, MIB..............................65.00

Gift Sets

Barbie & Friends, 1983, NRFB..55.00
Barbie & Ken Wedding Fantasy, 1993, NRFB..................100.00
Birthday Beauties, Tutti, #3617, 1968, NRFB..................175.00
Dance Magic Barbie & Ken, 1990, NRFB..............................50.00
Loving You Barbie, 1984, NRFB..........................75.00
Night Night Sleep Tight Tutti, NRFB............................300.00
Pretty Pairs Angie 'n Tangie, 1970, MIB.....................250.00
Skipper's Holiday Party, #1021, 1965, MIB....................900.00

Skipper on Wheels, 1965, complete, MIB, $600.00. (Photo courtesy Paris and Susan Manos)

Sun Sensation Barbie Spray & Play Fun, 1992, MIB 60.00
Western Stampin' Barbie, 1993, complete, MIB................50.00

Bauer

The Bauer Company moved from Kentucky to California in 1909, producing crocks, gardenware, and vases until after the Depression when they introduced their first line of dinnerware. From 1932 until the early 1960s, they successfully marketed several lines of solid-color wares that are very collectible today. Some of their most popular lines are Ring, Plain Ware, and Monterey Modern. Refer to *The Collector's Encyclopedia of Bauer Pottery* by Jack Chipman (Collector Books) for more information.

Brusche Al Fresco, plate, dinner; lime, 11½"......................12.00
Cal-Art, bowl, matt green, swirl, 8" 40.00
Cal-Art, vase, matt pink, 10" ..85.00
Gloss Pastel Kithenware, pitcher, ivory, 1-qt 35.00
La Linda, plate, dinner; green, 9" 15.00
La Linda, saucer, matt yellow ..6.00
Monterey Moderne, cup & saucer, black, minimum value ...45.00
Monterey Moderne, plate, dinner; turquoise/olive green, 9½"..............................20.00
Plain ware, bowl, salad; blue, 10½", from $85 to.........125.00
Plain ware, butter plate, black, 4½", minimum value ...135.00

Plainware, open coffee server, wood handle, from $50.00 to $65.00.

Plain ware, coffee server, wood handle, w/lid, from $65 to **95.00**

Plain ware, creamer, midget, red, from $45 to **65.00**

Plain ware, lamp base, green, 4½", from $300 to.........**450.00**

Plain ware, pitcher, 12", from $350 to...........................**525.00**

Plain ware, pudding dish, orange, #6, 10¼", from $80 to...**120.00**

Ring, bowl, batter; 2-qt, from $85 to....................................**125.00**

Ring, bowl, berry; 4", from $20 to................................**30.00**

Ring, bowl, fruit; 5", from $25 to **35.00**

Ring, bowl, mixing; #18, from $45 to.....................................**65.00**

Ring, bowl, punch; 14", from $350 to....................................**525.00**

Ring, bowl, salad; low, 9", from $60 to.............................**90.00**

Ring, bowl, vegetable; oval, 8", from $85 to **125.00**

Ring, candle holder, 2½", from $45 to.....................................**65.00**

Ring, cigarette jar, w/lid, from $300 to minimum value **450.00**

Ring, coffeepot, drip; from $300 to................................**400.00**

Ring, cookie jar, from $400 to..**600.00**

Ring, creamer, from $20 to...**30.00**

Ring, gravy bowl, from $100 to...........................**150.00**

Ring, mustard jar, w/notched lid, from $250 to **375.00**

Ring, nappy, #9, from $65 to..**95.00**

Ring, pitcher, 3-qt, from $125 to...........................**175.00**

Ring, plate, bread & butter; 5", from $30 to **45.00**

Ring, plate, dinner; 10½", from $65 to..............................**95.00**

Ring, plate, salad; 7½", from $30 to **45.00**

Ring, platter, oval, 9", from $30 to **45.00**

Ring, relish plate, divided, from $85 to............................**125.00**

Ring, saucer, AD; from $60 to .**90.00**

Ring, tumbler, w/handle, 3-oz, from $75 to **100.00**

Ring, spice jar, #1, from $100.00 to $150.00. (Photo courtesy Jack Chipman)

Beanie Babies

Though everyone agrees Beanie Babies are on the downside of their highest peak, they're still a force to deal with, and you'll still find Beanie Baby tables by the score in any large flea market field. New ones are still being cranked out, thanks to collector demand — these are valued at $7.00 to $10.00 each. (See *Schroeder's Collectible Toys, Antique to Modern,* or *Garage Sale and Flea Market Annual* for a comprehensive listing of both current and retired Beanies as well as information on hang tags. Both are published by Collector Books.) All of those we've listed here have been retired; values reflect examples in mint condition. Style numbers are the last four digits of the UPC code on the back of Beanie Babies' swing tags.

Ally the Alligator, #4032 ......**50.00**
Amber the Cat, #4243, gold tabby, ...**10.00**
Baldy the Eagle, #4074........**20.00**
Batty the Bat, #4035, tie-dyed.**15.00**
Beak the Kiwi Bird, #4211 ...**10.00**
Bessie the Cow, #4009, brown.**45.00**
Blizzard the Tiger, #4163, white...........................**20.00**
Bones the Dog, #4001 ....**15.00**
Bongo the Monkey, #4067 ....**10.00**
Britannia the British Bear, #4601, Ty UK exclusive..............**60.00**
Brownie the Bear, #4010, w/swing tag, minimum value .**1,900.00**
Bubbles the Fish, #4078 ....**50.00**
Bucky the Beaver, #4016......**15.00**
Butch the Bull Terrier, #4227..**10.00**
Caw the Crow, #4071..........**325.00**
Chilly the Polar Bear, #4012..**1,100.00**
Chipper the Chipmunk, #4259 .**10.00**
Chops the Lamb, #4019 ....**80.00**
Clubby the Bear, BBOC exclusive, blue **30.00**
Coral the Fish, #4079, tie-dyed .**75.00**

Cubbie the Bear, #4010, brown .**25.00**
Daisy the Cow, #4006 ....**15.00**
Derby the Horse, #4008, 1st issue, fine yarn mane & tail .**1,600.00**
Derby the Horse, #4008, 3rd issue, brown w/white star **10.00**
Digger the Crab, #4027, orange...........................**475.00**
Doby the Doberman, #4110 ..**15.00**
Dotty the Dalmatian, #4100.**10.00**
Ears the Rabbit, #4018.........**20.00**
Eggbert the Baby Chick, #4232.**10.00**
Eucalyptus the Koala, #4240 .**10.00**

Fetch the Golden Retriever, #418, 10.00.

Fleece the Lamb, #4125...........**10.00**
Flitter the Butterfly, #4255..**10.00**
Flutter the Butterfly, #4043, tie-dyed **475.00**
Freckles the Leopard, #4066..**15.00**
Garcia the Bear, #4051, tie-dyed .**110.00**
Gigi the Poodle, #4191........**10.00**
Glory the Bear, #4188 ....**25.00**
Gobbles the Turkey, #4034...**10.00**
Goochy the Jellyfish, #4230..**10.00**
Groovy the Bear, #4256 ....**15.00**
Halo the Angel Bear, #4208 .**15.00**
Happy the Hippo, #4061, 2nd issue, lavender **20.00**
Hippity the Bunny, #4119 ....**20.00**
Honks the Goose, #4258 ....**10.00**
Hope the Praying Bear **10.00**

Humphrey the Camel, #4060 .**1,000.00**

Inch the Worm, #4044, felt antenna **80.00**

Inky the Octopus, #4028, 1st issue, tan, no mouth **500.00**

Jabber the Parrot, #4197 ......**10.00**

Jolly the Walrus, #4082 ....**15.00**

Kiwi the Toucan, #4070, 85.00.

Kuku the Cockatoo, #4192 ....**10.00**

Legs the Frog, #4020 ....**20.00**

Lips the Fish, #4254 ....**10.00**

Lizzy the Lizard, #4033, 2nd issue, blue **20.00**

Lucky the Ladybug, #4040, 1st issue, w/7 spots **165.00**

Lucky the Ladybug, #4040, 3rd issue, 11 spots **20.00**

Mac the Cardinal, #4225 ......**10.00**

Manny the Manatee, #4081 ..**90.00**

Maple the Bear, #4600, Ty Canada exclusive **50.00**

Mel the Koala Bear, #4162 ...**10.00**

Millennium the Bear, #4226 ..**15.00**

Mystic the Unicorn, #4007, 1st issue, soft fine mane & tail **240.00**

Mystic the Unicorn, #4007, 3rd issue, iridescent horn **10.00**

Nana the Monkey, #4067, 1st issue of Bongo **2,500.00**

Neon the Seahorse, #4239 ....**10.00**

Nibbly the Rabbit, #4217 ......**10.00**

Nip the Cat, #4003, 2nd issue, all gold **425.00**

Nuts the Squirrel, #4114 ......**15.00**

Osito the Mexican Bear, #4244 .**15.00**

Patti the Platypus, #4025, 2nd issue, purple **20.00**

Peace the Bear, #4053, 15.00.

Pecan the Bear, #4251 ....**10.00**

Pinchers the Lobster, #4026 .**20.00**

Pouch the Kangaroo, #4161 ..**10.00**

Prance the Cat, #4123 ....**10.00**

Puffer the Puffin, #4181 ....**10.00**

Pugsly the Pug Dog, #4106 ...**10.00**

Quackers the Duck, #4024, 1st issue, no wings **1,000.00**

Radar the Bat, #4091 ....**85.00**

Rex the Tyrannosaurus, #4086 .**450.00**

Ringo the Raccoon, #4014 .....**20.00**

Roary the Lion, #4069 ....**15.00**

Rocket the Bluejay, #4202 ....**10.00**

Rover the Dog, #4101 ....**20.00**

Sammy the Bear, #4215 ....**15.00**

Scaly the Lizard, #4263 ....**10.00**

Schweetheart the Orangutan, #4252 ....**10.00**

Scorch the Dragon, #4210 .....**10.00**

Seamore the Seal, #4029 ......**75.00**

Sheets the Ghost, #4620 ....**10.00**

Signature Bear (2000), #4266 .**20.00**

Slippery the Seal, #4222.......**10.00**

Slowpoke the Sloth, #4261 ...**10.00**

Sly the Fox, #4115, 2nd issue, white belly.................................**15.00**

Snip the Siamese Cat, #4120.**15.00**

Snowball the Snowman, #4201.**25.00**

Spangle the American Bear, #4245, white face.........**15.00**

Speedy the Turtle, #4030......**25.00**

Spinner the Spider, #4036....**10.00**

Spooky the Ghost, #4090......**35.00**

Spot the Dog, #4000, 2nd issue, black spot on back..........**40.00**

Squealer the Pig, #4005........**15.00**

Stilts the Stork, #4221 ....**10.00**

Stinger the Scorpion, #4193.**10.00**

Stretch the Ostrich, #4182 ...**10.00**

Strut the Rooster, #4171 ......**15.00**

Swirly the Snail, #4249 ....**10.00**

Tank the Armadillo, #4031, 1st issue, 7 lines & no shell .**180.00**

Tank the Armadillo, #4031, 3rd issue, w/shell.................**90.00**

Teddy Bear, #4050, brown, new face.................................**65.00**

Teddy Bear, #4051, teal, old face.............................**1,000.00**

Teddy Bear, #4055, violet, new face, minimum value.**1,075.00**

The Beginning Bear, #4267..**20.00**

Tiny the Chihuahua, #4234..**10.00**

Tracker the Basset Hound, #4198.**10.00**

Tuffy the Terrier, #4108 ....**15.00**

Tusk the Walrus, #4076 ....**85.00**

Ty 2K the Bear, #4262.........**20.00**

Valentino the Bear, #4058, white w/red heart.....................**20.00**

Waddle the Penguin, #4075..**15.00**

Waves the Whale, #4084 ......**15.00**

Weenie the Dachshund, #4013.**15.00**

Wise the 1998 Graduation Owl, #4187 ....**15.00**

Wrinkles the Bulldog, #4103..**10.00**

Ziggy the Zebra, #4063......**20.00**

Zip the Cat, #4004, 2nd issue, all black **685.00**

1997 Holiday Teddy, #4200 ..**30.00**

1998 Holiday Teddy, #4204 ..**30.00**

2000 Holiday Teddy, #4332 ..**10.00**

Beatles

Beatles memorabilia is becoming increasingly popular with those who grew up in the '60s. Almost any item that could be produced with their pictures or logos was manufactured and sold by the thousands in department stores. Some have such a high collector value that they have been reproduced, beware!

Our advisor for this category is Bojo (Bob Gottuso), who is listed in the Directory under Pennsylvania. Refer to *The Beatles: A Reference and Value Guide* by Michael Stern, Barbara Crawford, and Hollis Lamon (Collector Books) for more information.

Ashtray, white china w/black head images & names, EX+ .**250.00**

Autograph book, vinyl w/photo image, 1964, unused, rare, NM, $500 to.................**700.00**

Balloon, various colors, United Industries, 1964, MIP, ea...........................**150.00**

Book, Out of the Mouths of Beatles, softcover, 1964, VG **15.00**

Book, Yellow Submarine, softcover, Signet, EX, form $15 to.......................**20.00**

Brooch, gold-tone banjo w/figures, movable beaded eyes, EX..**65.00**

Bubble bath container, Paul McCartney likeness, Colgate's, MIB, $150.00. (Photo courtesy Greg Moore and Joe Pizzo)

Cake decorations, The Swingers, MIP................................**175.00**

Calendar cards, plastic coated w/various images, 1964-65, NM, ea **25.00**

Charm bracelet, photos of ea member, Nicky Byrne/Nems Ent Ltd, NMOC **175.00**

Coin holder, rubber squeeze type, 2x3", VG+ **75.00**

Concert booklet, black & white photos w/3-color cover, 1964, 12", EX.............................**45.00**

Dis-Go-Case, plastic with group photo, blue, NM, from $175.00 to $225.00. (Photo courtesy Bob Gottuso)

Doll, Mascot, cloth & felt, w/guitar & tag, Remco, 22", VG **275.00**

Figures, Hey Jude, complete w/cardboard backdrop, set of 4, M..............................**100.00**

Figures, Magical Mystery Tour, lead, set of 4, M...........**100.00**

Guitar, New Beat, 4-string w/faces & autographs, Selcol, 32", EX **500.00**

Hairbrush, blue or red, Genco, MIP (EX header card)..**100.00**

Harmonica, Hohner, 1964, MOC.........................**450.00**

Hat, beach type w/faces & autographs, NM **175.00**

Hummer, cardboard w/head shots, Louis F Dow, 1960s, NM.**150.00**

Key chain, Love Songs promo, record shape w/logo, EX..**15.00**

Megaphone, head shots on white, orange, or yellow NEMS, 1964, EX, ea **600.00**

Mobile, cardboard popouts, Sunshine Art Studios, unused, MIP..............................**140.00**

Mug, plastic w/paper portrait insert, 4", EX (reproduction).............................**20.00**

Necklace, oval pendant w/black & white photo under dome, EX...............................**100.00**

Nodders, plastic, set of 4, 4" .**40.00**

Notebook, doorway photo, spiral or regular, 11x8½", unused, M, ea **90.00**

Pennant, felt, We Luv You Beatles w/heart-shaped images, EX...............................**200.00**

Picture cube, fan club, cardboard w/apple logo, 1970, M (EX mailer) **75.00**

Pin-back button, flasher, I Like the Beatles surrounded by names, NM **30.00**

Playing cards, group photo w/2 sitting, orange, complete, EX (G box) **280.00**

Purse, silk-like w/gold clasp, color image of John, Canada, 1970s, EX **35.00**

Rings, flashes from phrase to picture, chrome, set of 4, EX..**75.00**

Rub-ons, Wheat Honeys or Rice Honeys cereal premium, unused, ea sheet **50.00**

Scarf, triangular w/tie strings, white w/red graphics & trim, M.....................................**90.00**

Stick-ons, Yellow Submarine, Dal Mfg Corp, 1968, set of 4, MIP **75.00**

Official Tie Tack Pin, silver color, 1964, set of four, M on card, $150.00. (Photo courtesy Gene Klompus)

Tote bag, vinyl, cartoon bodies w/photo heads, Wako/Japan, 14x13", EX....................**180.00**

Tumbler, plastic w/paper insert, original issue (beware of repros), VG **85.00**

Wallet, plastic w/group photo on front, NJ map on back, gold trim, M **250.00**

Watercolor set, Yellow Submarine, Craft Master, complete, MIB **145.00**

Beer Cans

Beer has been sold in cans since 1935, when the Continental Can Company developed a method of coating the inside of the can with plastic. The first style was the flat top that came with instructions on how to open it. Because most breweries were not equipped to fill a flat can, most went to the 'cone top,' but by the 1950s, even that was obsolete. Can openers were the order of the day until the 1960s, when tab-top cans came along. The heyday of beer can collecting was during the 1970s, but the number of collectors has since receded, leaving a huge supply of beer cans, most of which are worth no more than a few dollars each. The basic rule of thumb is to concentrate your collecting on cans made prior to 1970. Beware, condition is critical.

Cone top, American Beer, American Brewing/Baltimore, 1940s, VG **70.00**

Cone top, Berghoff 1887 Beer, Berghoff Brewing/Fort Wayne, 1940s, VG.........**35.00**

Cone top, Cardinal Premium Beer, Standard Brewing/Scranton, 12-oz, NM 90.00

Cone top, Carling's Ale, Brewing Corp of America/Cleveland, 1940s, EX 85.00

Cone top, Copper Club Beer, A Hass Brewing/Hancock, 12-oz, EX+ 80.00

Cone top, E&B Special Beer, E&B Brewing/Detroit, 1940s, EX+ 40.00

Cone top, Edelweiss, S Edelweiss Brewing/Chicago, IRTP, 12-oz, EX..............................30.00

Cone top, Falstaff Beer, Falstaff Brewing/Omaha, 1950s, G+ 15.00

Cone top, Gibbons Beer, Lion Inc/ Wilkes-Barre, 12-oz, EX.45.00

Cone top, Goetz Country Club Beer, Goetz Brewing/St Joseph, 1950s, EX+ 40.00

Cone top, Gold Star Beer, Hoff-Brau Brewing/Ft Wayne, IRTP, 12-oz, EX 55.00

Cone top, Kuebler Pilsner Beer, Kuebler Brewing/Easton, 1930s, G+......................100.00

Cone top, Maier Select Beer, Maier Brewing/Los Angeles, 1940s, VG 50.00

Cone top, Peerless Beer, Lacrosse Brewing/Lacrosse, 1950s, EX+ 120.00

Cone top, Schlitz, Schlitz Brewing/ Milwaukee, 1940s, EX ...50.00

Crowntainer, Altes Lager Beer, Tivoli Brewing/Detroit, 1940s, VG.................................40.00

Crowntainer, Ebling Premium Beer, Ebling Brewing/New York, 1940s, EX 45.00

Crowntainer, Fehr's X/L, Fehr Brewing/Louisville, 1940s, G+ 15.00

Crowntainer, Gluek's Beer, Gluek Brewing/Minneapolis, 1940s, EX+ 35.00

Crowntainer, Grossvater Beer, Renner Brewing/Youngstown, 1940s, EX 50.00

Crowntainer, Old Shay Beer, Fort Pitt Brewing/Jeannette, 1940s, G+......................70.00

Ebling Premium Beer, crowntainer, 1940s, New York NY, G, $50.00; National Bohemian Pale Beer, cone top, 1940s, Baltimore MD, EX, $55.00; Falstaff Beer, cone top, 1940s, St. Louis MO, NM, $65.00.

Flat top, Balboa Export Beer, Southern Brewing/Los Angeles, 1940s, VG.................65.00

Flat top, Ballantine XXX Ale, Ballantine Brewing/Newark, 12-oz, NM 25.00

Flat top, Budweiser Lager Beer, Anheuser-Busch/St Louis, 1950s, EX 20.00

Flat top, Bull Dog Ale, Grace Bros/Santa Rosa, 1950s, EX+ 20.00

Flat top, Fox Head Malt Liquor, Fox Head Brewing/Waukesha, 12-oz, EX 40.00

Flat top, Keglet Beer, Esslinger Inc/Philadelphia, 12-oz, EX+ **45.00**

Flat top, Krueger Cream Ale, Krueger Brewing/Newark, 1950s, VG **50.00**

Flat top, Old German Brand Beer, Lebanon Valley/Lebanon, 1950s, NM+ **40.00**

Flat top, Senate 250 Beer, Heurichs Brewing/Washington, 1950s, EX+ **70.00**

Hull's Cream Ale, Hull Brewing/New Haven, 12-oz, EX+ **40.00**

Pull tab, Fauerbach Beer, Fauerbach Brewing/Madison, 1960s, VG+ **20.00**

Pull tab, Gibbons Season's Best, Lion Inc, Wilkes-Barre, 1960s, EX+ **100.00**

Pull tab, Hudson House Beer, Maier Brewing/Los Angeles, 1960s, NM+ **15.00**

Pull tab, Jax Draft Beer, Jackson Brewing/New Orleans, 1960s, EX+ **15.00**

Pull tab, Orbit Premium Beer, Orbit Brewing/Miami, 1960s, NM+................................**10.00**

Scheidt's Rams Head Ale, Adam Scheidt Brewery, Norristown PA, 12-ounce, EX, $130.00; Trommer's Malt Beer, 12-ounce NM, $110.00.

Pull tab, Ox-Bow Beer, Walter Brewing/Pueblo, 1970s, EX+ **25.00**

Pull tab, Schmidt's Ale, Schmidt's Brewing/Philadelphia, 1960s, NM................................**15.00**

Birthday Angels

Here's a collection that's a lot of fun, inexpensive, and takes relatively little space to display. They're not at all hard to find, but there are several series, so completing 12-month sets of them all can provide a bit of a challenge. Generally speaking, angels are priced by the following factors: 1) company — look for Lefton, Napco, Norcrest, and Enesco marks or labels (unmarked or unknown sets are of less value); 2) application of flowers, bows, gold trim, etc., (the more detail, the more valuable; 3) use of rhinestones, which will also increase price; 4) age; and 5) quality of the workmanship involved, detail, and accuracy of painting.

#1194, angel of the month series, white hair, 5", ea, from $14 to...................**16.00**

#1300, boy angel, wearing suit, white hair, 6", from $18 to **20.00**

#1600, Pal Angel, month series of both boy & girl, 4", from $10 to **12.00**

Arnart, Kewpies, in choir robes w/rhinestones, 4½", ea, from $10 to **12.00**

**Josef, angel holding numeral, 4½",
$15.00; 5½", $20.00.**

Enesco, angels on round base
w/flower of the month, gold
trim, ea **15.00**
Kelvin, #250, holding flower of the
month, 4½" **16.00**
Kelvin, C-230, holding flower of
the month, 4½", ea **16.00**
Lefton, #1323, angel of the month,
bisque, ea **18.00**
Lefton, #2600, birthstone on skirt,
3¼", ea **24.00**
Lefton, #556, boy w/blue wings,
5", ea **26.00**

**Lefton, #6224, applied flower, birth-
stone on skirt, 4½", $15.00.** (Photo cour-
tesy Loretta DeLozier)

Lefton, #574, day of the week
series, like #8281 but not as
ornate, ea **28.00**
Lefton, #627, day of the week
series, 3½", ea **26.00**
Lefton, #6949, day of the week
series in wooden frame, 5",
ea **26.00**
Lefton, #8281, day of the week
series, applied roses, ea ..**28.00**
Lefton, #985, flower of the month,
5", ea **24.00**
Lefton, AR-1987, w/ponytail, 4",
ea **18.00**
Napco, A1360-1372, angel of the
month, ea **20.00**
Napco, A1917-1929, boy angel of
the month, ea **20.00**
Napco, A4307, angel of the month,
sm, ea **20.00**
Napco, C1361-1373, angel of the
month, ea **20.00**
Napco, S1291, day of the week
'Belle', ea **20.00**
Napco, S1307, bell of the month,
ea **20.00**
Napco, S1361-1372, angel of the
month, ea **20.00**
Napco, S1392, oval frame angel of
the month, ea **24.00**
Napco, S429, day of the week
angel (also available as
planters), ea **24.00**
Norcrest, F-120, angel of the
month, 4½", ea **18.00**
Norcrest, F-167, bell of the month,
2¾", ea **10.00**
Norcrest, F-210, day of the week
angel, 4½", ea **18.00**
Norcrest, F-340, angel of the
month, 5", ea **20.00**
Norcrest, F-535, angel of the
month, 4½", ea **20.00**

Relco, 4¼", ea **15.00**
Relco, 6", ea **18.00**
TMJ, angel of the month, w/flower, ea **20.00**
UCAGCO, white hair, 5¾" ...**12.00**
Wales, wearing long white gloves, white hair, Made in Japan, 6⅜" **22.00**

Black Americana

This is a wide and varied field of collector interest. Advertising, toys, banks, sheet music, kitchenware items, movie items, and even the fine arts are areas that offer Black Americana buffs many opportunities to add to their collections. Caution! Because some pieces have become so valuable, reproductions abound. Watch for a lot of new ceramic items, less detailed in both the modeling and the painting.

Our advisor for this category is Judy Posner, who is listed in the Directory under Pennsylvania. Refer to these books for more information: *Black Collectibles Sold in America* by P.J. Gibbs, and *Black Dolls, An Identification and Value Guide, 1820 – 1991*, by Myla Perkins. (Both are published by Collector Books.)

Activity book, Sambo's Circus, by Bill Wooden, premium, 1960s, M **50.00**
Ashtray, Dinah's Pancake & Chicken House, glass, 1940s, 4½" dia, EX **70.00**
Bank, baby nodder w/alligator, painted bisque, Kenmar, 1950s, 7", EX................**125.00**

Birthday card, Say! What's Cookin'?, black skin tone, bright colors, M...............**25.00**
Book, Little Alexander, Besse Schiff, Wartburg Press, 1955, EX...................................**90.00**

Book, Little Black Sambo, Helen Bannerman, Saalfield, 1942, soft cover, folio size, 16 pages including covers, Ethel Hays illustrations, VG, $125.00. (Photo courtesy Marvelous Books)

Book, Little Black Sambo Magic Drawing Book, Platt & Munk #937A, EX **100.00**
Book, Meg & Moe, Lothrop, Lee & Shepard, 1938, EX.......**125.00**
Book, Music Is My Mistress, Duke Ellington, 1973, 1st edition, EX **50.00**
Book, Polly & Her Dollys, by Ajo, Blackie & Son LTD, 1933, EX....................**125.00**
Candy box, Amos 'N Andy, black/white/orange on cardboard, 1930, VG **350.00**
Clicker, Minstrel Sam, litho tin, 1920s, 1¾", EX.............**100.00**
Coloring book, Little Black Sambo & Peter Rabbit, 1941, unused, EX **65.00**

Cookbook, Rebecca's Cookbook, by Rebecca West, 1942, 9x6", M.................................**135.00**

Crate, wood & cardboard, Mammy eating orange on label, 1940s, 18", EX.........................**135.00**

Dolls, cloth with curly yarn hair, applied eyes, stitched mouths, original clothes, 1940s – 1950s, 12", from $200.00 to $225.00 for the pair. (Photo courtesy P.J. Gibbs)

Doll, golliwogg, stuffed plush, googly eyes, clothed, 1970s, 20", EX...................................**75.00**

Doll, My Lovely Topsee, side-glance eyes, pigtails, 1940s, 5", MIP............................**60.00**

Doll, Raggedy Ann's Mammy friend, stocking knit, 1950s, 14", EX............................**75.00**

Doll, Tod-L-Tot, glass-type eyes, w/squeaker, Sun Rubber, 10", EX...................................**65.00**

Doll Kit, Mammy, 1930s, 18", scarce, MIB **125.00**

Figure, cast-iron man on fence eating watermelon, Manoil, 3", EX...........................**150.00**

Figure, ceramic boy holding up basket, 1930-40, 5½", EX, $60 to.....................................**70.00**

Figure, ceramic Mammy upper torso w/cloth skirt, 1930-40, 5½", EX.........................**55.00**

Figures, chalkware, Amos 'N Andy, multicolor, 1930s, EX, pr **275.00**

Figures, wood, carved minstrels standing on log-type bases, 2", pr...................................**95.00**

Flower holder, girl next to ear of corn, ceramic, 1950, 5", EX...............................**75.00**

Game, Amos 'N Andy Card Party, AM Davis, 1930, NMIB .**165.00**

Game, Skillets & Cakes, Milton Bradley, 1946, complete, EXIB, $150 to..............**200.00**

Handkerchiefs, embroidered w/Sambo, multicolor, set of 3, 1930s, MIB..................**135.00**

Hose caddy, diecut wood Sambo, 33", EX..........................**275.00**

Lobby card, Little Rascals, Fishy Tales, Monogram Pictures, 1951, EX.........................**50.00**

Magazine, Jet, any 1963 issue, EX.................................**15.00**

Magazine, Life, Martin Luther King 1929-1968, April 12, 1968, EX.......................**80.00**

Menu, Sambo's Restaurants souvenir, 4-panel, glossy, 1967, EX.................................**85.00**

Movie Poster, Amos & Andy Check & Double Check, framed, 18x14", EX......**175.00**

Mug, Golliwogg's Joy Ride, gold rim, unmarked, 1930s, EX......**125.00**

Noisemaker, litho tin, man in dancing pose, 1940s, EX.........**50.00**

Noisemaker, painted tin, unmarked, 1920 – 1940, 4", EX, $65.00. (Photo courtesy P.J. Gibbs)

Notepad holder, Mammy w/plastic torso, skirt forms pad, 1940s, EX **100.00**

Paper dolls, Betty & Billy, Whitman, 1955, NM **125.00**

Paper hat, Sambo's Restaurant, colorful logo, Cellucap, 1960s, EX **85.00**

Phonograph jigger, Dancing Dandy, wood, EX..........**225.00**

Pin, Art Deco style lady w/leather hat & celluloid fruit, 3".**100.00**

Pin-back button, Black Students Union, black on white, 1½", $30 to **40.00**

Plaque, chalkware figure of man wearing straw hat, 1950, 6", EX **65.00**

Plate, Sambo's Restaurant, Jackson China, 1950s, 8" dia, VG **70.00**

Pocket mirror, round image of 2 Black women, swing handle, 3½", EX.............................**55.00**

Pot holder caddy, chalkware chef w/red lips, wall hanger, 6¼", MIB.................................**50.00**

Pull toy, Snowflakes & Swipes, boy walking dog w/toothache, tin, EX **350.00**

Puppet, Jambo the Jiver Marionette, Talent Products, 1948, 14", VG **225.00**

Puzzle, frame-tray, Jumbo & Mumbo, 1945, M............**75.00**

Ramp Walker, Mammy, wood w/cloth print dress, 1920s, 4½", scarce, M................**75.00**

Record, Little Brave Sambo, Peter Pan, 1950, EX (EX sleeve)................................**65.00**

Record set, Uncle Remus Stories, RCA, 78 rpm, 1940s, EX (w/cover).........................**110.00**

Salt & pepper shakers, maid & chef, Japan, 1950s, 2", EX, pr **60.00**

Sheet music, Blue Boogie, by John W Schaum, 1946, EX.....**65.00**

Shopping pegboard, wood, Mammy saying 'Reckin' Ah Needs...,' 1940s, EX **90.00**

Stacking blocks, features Sambo & Tiger, set of 5, 1940s, EX........................**125.00**

Tea Set, matt porcelain w/graphics by Florence Upton, 1904, 5-piece, M **250.00**

Teapot, figural Mammy chef w/goggly eyes, Japan, 1930s, 4½", EX.........................**200.00**

Top, litho tin w/natives atop various animals in comical poses, 6", EX............................**175.00**

Towel, handmade applique of Mammy w/watermelon, embroidered fruit, EX....**60.00**

Toy figure, Dancing Dan, plastic, moves to sound, Bell Products, NMIB...................**225.00**

Toy figure, Dancing Sambo, jointed cardboard, 1940s-50s, 12", MIP...............................**75.00**

Toy figure, Mammy Tinker, wood w/decal, Toy Tinkers, 1920, 7½", NM **125.00**

Tumbler, Showboat, Old Plantations, banjo player, frosted, 1940s, M **30.00**

Wind-up toy, Mammy, litho tin, Lindstrom, ca 1939, 8", $400 to **500.00**

Black Cats

This line of fancy felines was marketed mainly by the Shafford (importing) Company, although black cat lovers accept similarly modeled, shiny glazed kitties of other importing firms into their collections as well. Some of the more plentiful items may be purchased for $15.00 to $35.00, while the Shafford six-piece spice set in a wooden rack usually sells for around $175.00. These values and the ones that follow are for items in mint paint, a very important consideration in determining a fair market price. Shafford items are often minus their white whiskers and eyebrows, and this type of loss should be reflected in your evaluation. An item in poor paint may be worth even less than half of given estimates. Note: Unless 'Shafford' is included in the descriptions, values are for cats that were imported by other companies.

Ashtray, flat face, Shafford, 4¾"..........................**18.00**

Bank, upright, Shafford-like features, marked Tommy, 2-part, $150 to **175.00**

Cigarette lighter, sm cat stands on book by table lamp....**65.00**

Condiment set, 2 joined heads, yellow eyes **65.00**

Creamer & sugar bowl, Shafford ..**45.00**

Cruet, upright, open mouth, paw spout, yellow eyes **30.00**

Decanter, long cat w/red fish in mouth as stopper **60.00**

Demitasse pot, tail handle, bow finial, Shafford, 7½".....**165.00**

Pincushion, cushion on back, tongue measure..............**25.00**

Pitcher, squatting, pour through mouth, Shafford, scarce, 4½"..................**75.00**

Pitcher, Shafford, squatting cat, mouth pour, very rare size: 5", $90.00.

Planter, cat sitting on knitted boot w/gold string, Elvin, 4½"..**30.00**

Salt & pepper shakers, seated, blue eyes, Enesco label, 5¾", pr.....................................**15.00**

Salt & pepper shakers, upright range size, Shafford, scarce, 5"....................................**65.00**

Spice set, 6 sq shakers in wooden frame, yellow eyes........**125.00**

Stacking tea set, 3 w/red collar, gold ball, yellow eyes, 3-pc.......**80.00**

Sugar bowl/planter, sitting, red bow w/gold bell, Elvin, 4" **25.00**

Teapot, upright w/paw spout, red bow, yellow eyes, Wales, 8¼" **60.00**

Teapot, 1-cup, yellow eyes **30.00**

Thermometer, stands w/paw on round thermometer face, yellow eyes **30.00**

Wall pocket, flat-backed 'teapot' cat, Shafford, $125 to...**150.00**

Blade Banks

In 1903 the safety razor was invented, making it easier for men to shave at home. But the old, used razor blades were troublesome, because for the next twenty-two years, nobody knew what to do with them. In 1925 the first patent was filed for a razor blade bank, a container designed to hold old blades until it became full, in which event it was to be thrown away. Most razor blade banks are 3" or 4" tall, similar to a coin bank with a slot in the top but no outlet in the bottom to remove the old blades. These banks were produced from 1925 to 1950. Some were issued by men's toiletry companies and were often filled with shaving soap or cream. Many were made of tin and printed with an advertising message. An assortment of blade banks made from a variety of materials — ceramic, wood, plastic, or metal — could also be purchased at five-and-dime stores.

For information on blade banks as well as many other types of interesting figural items from the same era, we recommend *Collectibles for the Kitchen, Bath & Beyond* (featuring napkin dolls, egg timers, string holders, children's whistle cups, baby feeder dishes, pie birds, and laundry sprinkler bottles) by Ellen Bercovici, Bobbie Zucker Bryson, and Deborah Gillham (available through Antique Trader Books).

Barber, wood w/Gay Blade bottom, Woodcroft, 1950, 6", from $65 to **75.00**

Barber, wood w/key & metal holders for razor & brush, 9", from $85 to **95.00**

Barber bust w/handlebar mustache, in coat & tie, from $55 to **65.00**

Barber bust w/handlebar mustache (no tie), Lipper & Mann, from $75 to **95.00**

Barber chair, lg, from $100 to....**125.00**

Barber chair, sm, from $100 to..**125.00**

Barber head, different colors on collar, Cleminson, from $30 to **40.00**

Barber holding pole, Occupied Japan, 4", from $50 to....**60.00**

Barber head, Gay Blade, Cleminson, 4", $40.00. (Photo courtesy Jack Chipman)

Barber pole, red & white w/ or w/out attachments, from $20 to 25.00

Barber pole w/barber head & derby hat, white, from $35 to 40.00

Barber pole w/face, red & white, from $30 to 35.00

Barber standing in blue coat & stroking chin, from $75 to 80.00

Barber w/buggy eyes, full-figure, Gleason look-alike, from $65 to 75.00

Barbershop quartet, 4 singing barber heads, from $95 to .125.00

Box w/policeman, metal, marked Used Blades, from $95 to..125.00

Dandy Dans, plastic w/brush holder, from $30 to...............40.00

Frog, green, marked For Used Blades, from $65 to........75.00

Half barber pole, hangs on wall, may be personalized, from $60 to...............70.00

Half shaving cup, hangs on wall, marked Gay Blades, from $65 to 75.00

Half shaving cup, hangs on wall, marked Old Gay Blade, from $65 to 75.00

Listerine donkey, from $20 to 30.00

Listerine elephant, from $25 to..35.00

Listerine frog, from $15 to....20.00

Looie, right- or left-hand version, from $85 to 100.00

Man shaving, mushroom shape, Cleminson, from $25 to .30.00

Razor Bum, from $95 to......125.00

Safe, green, marked Razor, from $55 to 65.00

Tony the barber, Ceramic Arts Studio, from $85 to 95.00

Shaving brush, APCO, marked USA, 6¼", from $50.00 to $60.00. (Photo courtesy Mary Jane Giacomini)

Blue Garland

Bell, from $50 to...............60.00

Bowl, fruit; 5⅛", from $4.50 to..6.00

Bowl, oval, 10¾" L 65.00

Beverage server (teapot/coffeepot), with lid, 11", from $60.00 to $70.00.

Bowl, soup; 7⅝", from $9 to..12.00

Bowl, vegetable; 8½" dia, from $25 to 35.00

Butter dish, ¼-lb, from $45 to ..55.00

Butter pat 10.00

57

Candlesticks, 3½x4", pr, from $75 to **85.00**
Casserole, w/lid, 12" W, from $55 to **65.00**
Chamberstick, metal candle cup w/handle, 6" dia **75.00**
Coaster/butter pat, 3¾" dia, from $9 to **12.00**
Creamer, from $15 to.............**18.00**
Cup & saucer, flat, from $5 to..**8.00**
Cup & saucer, footed, from $9 to **12.00**
Gravy boat, w/attached under-plate, from $35 to...........**45.00**
Plate, bread & butter; 6¼", from $3 to **4.00**
Plate, dinner; 10", from $8 to..**10.00**
Plate, salad; 7¾" dia, from $7 to **9.00**
Platter, 13", from $22 to **28.00**
Platter, 14½", from $30 to **40.00**
Platter, 15½", from $45 to **50.00**
Salt & pepper shakers, 4¼", pr, from $35 to **40.00**
Sugar bowl, w/lid, from $18 to ..**22.00**
Teakettle, porcelain w/stainless steel lid **25.00**
Teapot, 7", from $60 to.........**65.00**
Tidbit tray, 1-tier **45.00**
Tidbit tray, 3-tier **90.00**

Blue Ridge

Some of the most attractive American dinnerware made in the twentieth century is Blue Ridge, produced by Southern Potteries of Erwin, Tennessee, from the late 1930s until 1956. More than four hundred patterns were hand painted on eight basic shapes. Elaborate or appealing designs sell for 25% more than the prices we suggest for simple, plain patterns. The Quimper-like peasant-decorated line is one of the most treasured and should be priced at double the amounts recommended for the higher-end patterns. Refer to *Blue Ridge Dinnerware, Revised Third Edition,* by Betty and Bill Newbound (Collector Books) for more information.

Ashtray, Mallard box shape .**40.00**
Bowl, hot cereal....................**12.00**
Bowl, mixing; sm...................**20.00**
Bowl, soup/cereal; Premium, 6"............................**25.00**
Bowl, vegetable; oval, 9".......**25.00**
Box, Sherman Lily **800.00**
Butter pat/coaster **35.00**
Celery, Skyline **35.00**
Chocolate tray **450.00**
Creamer, Fifties shape **15.00**
Cup & saucer, Premium **60.00**

Dinner plates, Floral Spray and Apple Tart, $22.00 each.

Egg cup, Premium.................**55.00**
Lamp, china.........................**250.00**
Leftover, w/lid, lg **35.00**
Pitcher, Betsy, china...........**195.00**
Pitcher, Rebecca..................**195.00**
Plate, advertising, lg...........**450.00**
Plate, dinner; 10½" **22.00**
Plate, sq, 7"...........................**15.00**

Pitcher, Sculptured Fruit, black handle, 7½", $95.00.

Plate, turkey w/acorns **90.00**
Ramekin, w/lid, 7½" **40.00**
Relish, deep shell, china **85.00**
Salad fork, Earthenware **40.00**
Shakers, range style, pr **45.00**
Sugar bowl, Waffle, w/lid......**20.00**
Teapot, Chevron handle **165.00**
Teapot, Colonial **125.00**
Teapot, Piecrust **100.00**
Tidbit, 3-tier **35.00**
Toast, Premium, w/lid **200.00**
Tray, snack; Martha **160.00**
Vase, boot shape, 8" **95.00**

Blue Willow

Inspired by the lovely blue and white Chinese exports, the Willow pattern has been made by many English, American, and Japanese firms from 1950 until the present. Many variations of the pattern have been noted — mauve, black, green, and multicolor Willow ware can be found in limited amounts. The design has been applied to tin-ware, linens, glassware, and paper goods, all of which are treasured by today's collectors. Refer to *Blue Willow* by Mary Frank Gaston (Collector Books) for more information. See also Royal China. See Clubs and Newsletters for information concerning *The Willow Word* newsletter.

Ashtray, oval, various phrases in center, Japan, 6", ea from $45 to **55.00**
Baking dish, tapered, Japan, 2½x6" dia........................**40.00**
Bank, 3 stacked pigs, 1-pc, Japan, from $65 to **75.00**
Batter pitcher, w/lid, Moriyama/ Japan, 9½" **300.00**

Biscuit jar, unmarked English, silver-plated lid and bail handle, 7", from $225.00 to $250.00. (Photo courtesy Mary Frank Gaston)

Biscuit jar, w/lid, cane handle, Moriyama (Japan) **175.00**
Bowl, flat soup; Homer Laughlin, 8"....................................**15.00**

Bowl, Homer Laughlin, 5"......**6.00**

Bowl, salad; England, 4x9" sq, from $80 to **90.00**

Bowl, serving; oval or round, Homer Laughlin.............**30.00**

Bowl, vegetable; divided oval, Allerton/England, 7¼".**130.00**

Bowl, vegetable; sq w/scalloped edge, bow-knot border, England, 8" **30.00**

Butter dish, round w/dome lid, open loop finial, England, 3x8" dia.........................**175.00**

Cake plate, Traditional, open handles, dome lid, Moriyama (Japan), 11" **275.00**

Casserole w/lid, Homer Laughlin **45.00**

Coffeepot, swan-neck spout w/ear-shaped handle, footed, Japan, 7"....................................**120.00**

Condiment set, 3-pc on 6" cloverleaf tray, Old Willow, 6" **225.00**

Cookie jar, pitcher form, pictorial medallion, McCoy, 9" **80.00**

Creamer, Homer Laughlin ...**18.00**

Creamer & sugar bowl (w/lid), sq w/Canton design, GL Ashworth, 5", set **100.00**

Cruets, necked ball form w/handles & lids, marked O & V, Japan, 6", pr.................**120.00**

Cup, cream soup; 2-handled, John Maddock (England), 2½x4" dia.............................**30.00**

Cup, Homer Laughlin **10.00**

Cup & saucer, handleless; Mandarin, Aynsley (England), 2" & 4"...............................**130.00**

Cup & saucer, Washington Pottery (England), 3" cup, from $5 to **10.00**

Egg cup, Homer Laughlin.....**25.00**

Egg cup, pedestal foot, Japan, 1½"................................**40.00**

Ginger jar, ball form w/medallions on side & lid, Arthur Wood, 5"........................**45.00**

Gravy or sauce boat, Homer Laughlin...........................**30.00**

Gravy or sauce boat, Wood & Sons (England), 7", from $55 to.**65.00**

Instant Coffee jar, w/lid, Japan, 6", from $60 to................**75.00**

Jam dish, individual; restaurant ware, Wood & Sons (England)...**15.00**

Lamp, kerosene; w/reflector plate, Japan, 8" **140.00**

Mug, thick handle, USA, 3¾"...**12.00**

Pie plate, unglazed base, Moriyama (Japan), 10" dia, from $70 to **80.00**

Pie/pastery server, Moriyama (Japan), 10", from $35 to..**45.00**

Pitcher, scalloped top & bottom, Allerton (England), 6"..**165.00**

Plate, grill; 3-part, Booth's pattern, bow-knot border, England, 11" **40.00**

Plate, Homer Laughlin, 6¼"...**8.00**

Plate, Homer Laughlin, 9¼".**15.00**

Plate, Traditional, sq, scalloped corners, gold trim, England, 6½"..................................**25.00**

Platter, Homer Laughlin, 11"..**20.00**

Platter, Homer Laughlin, 13"..**30.00**

Platter, Traditional, oval, Made in Occupied Japan, 9½ x 12¾"..............................**75.00**

Relish dish, round w/lug-style handle, divided, Adderley (England), 8" **140.00**

Teacup, Homer Laughlin......**10.00**

Teapot, Homer Laughlin **60.00**

Teapot, 6-cup, Royal China Co (unmarked), from $50 to .**60.00**

Teapot, marked North Staffordshire Pottery Co., Ltd, 1940s, four-cup, from $60.00 to $75.00. (Photo courtesy Mary Frank Gaston)

Tumbler, juice; ceramic, Japan, 3½", from $30 to..............**35.00**
Tureen, sq w/tab handles, scalloped foot, Japan (unmarked), 6x10"............................**175.00**

Bookends

Bookends have come into their own as a separate category of collectibles. They are so diversified in styling, it's easy to find those that appeal to you, no matter what your personal tastes and preferences. Metal examples seem to be most popular, especially those with the mark of their manufacturer, and can still be had at reasonable prices. Glass and ceramic bookends by noted makers, however, may be more costly — for example, those made by Roseville or Cambridge, which have a cross-over collector appeal.

Because our space is limited, assume all bookends in our listings to be made of cast iron, unless another material is noted. Our advisor for this category is Louis Kuritzky, author of *Collector's Guide to Bookends* (Collector Books); he is listed in the Directory under Florida. See Clubs and Newsletters for information concerning the Bookend Collectors Club.

Angelus Call to Prayer, gray metal, K&O, ca 1925, pr...........**125.00**
Appeal to the Great Spirit, Indian on horseback, ca 1926, 7¼", pr........................**195.00**
As w/Wings, female figures hold skirt wide, ca 1925, 9", pr........**275.00**
Cameo Girls, female figures, 1926, 4¼", pr **75.00**
Cocker Spaniel, Frankart, ca 1934, 6¼", pr **150.00**

Discus Thrower, Littco, ca 1928, 7", $110.00 for the pair. (Photo courtesy Louis Kuritzky)

Galahad in Archway, ca 1925, 6", pr.....................................**50.00**
Head Up Horse, glass, New Martinsville, ca 1940, 8", pr............................**190.00**
Leaping Horse, Nuart, ca 1934, 5¾", pr **85.00**

Lincoln's Cabin, Judd, ca 1925, 3¾", pr **50.00**

Lion, glass, Cambridge, ca 1940, 6", pr **200.00**

Minute Man, gray metal, Jennings Brothers, mk JB 1755, ca 1930, 9", pr **175.00**

Nude on Sphinx, att Armor Bronze, bronze clad, ca 1925, 6", pr **175.00**

Owl in Archway, #506, ca 1925, 4¼", pr **125.00**

Parrot on Book, K&O, ca 1928, 6", pr **125.00**

Pirate w/Chest, Littco, ca 1928, 5¼", pr **80.00**

Polo Player on white horse, Littco, ca 1928, 5½", pr..............**85.00**

Ram, gray metal, SCC, 1974, 7", $35.00 for the pair. (Photo courtesy Louis Kuritzky)

Retro Scottie, Frankart, ca 1930, 4½", pr **125.00**

Sailfish & Wave, Jennings Brothers, #1258, ca 1928, 5", pr **110.00**

Sailor Boy & Dog, Frankart, ca 1934, 6¾", pr **185.00**

Sea Horse Family, adult between 2 babies, ca 1925, 5¾", pr ..**75.00**

Seated Lincoln, Nuart, gray metal, 1924, 6½", pr.....**110.00**

Setters (dogs), Littco, ca 1925, 5", pr **115.00**

Tryst, Hubley #301, ca 1924, 5½", pr......................................**75.00**

Working for Peanuts, elephant, ca 1925, 4¼", pr **85.00**

Bottles

Bottles have been used as containers for commercial products since the late 1800s. Specimens from as early as 1845 may still be occasionally found today (watch for a rough pontil to indicate this early production date). Some of the most collectible are bitters bottles, used for 'medicine' that was mostly alcohol, a ploy to avoid paying the stiff tax levied on liquor sales. Spirit flasks from the 1800s were blown in the mold and were often designed to convey a historic, political, or symbolic message. Even bottles from the 1900s are collectible, especially beer or pop bottles and commercial containers from defunct bottlers. Refer to *Bottle Pricing Guide, Third Revised Edition,* by Hugh Cleveland (Collector Books) for more information.

Dairy Bottles

The storage and distribution of fluid milk in glass bottles became commonplace around the turn of the century. They were replaced by paper and plastic containers in the mid-1950s. Perhaps 5% of all US dairies are still using some glass, and glass bottles are still widely used in Mexico and some Canadian provinces.

Milk-packaging and distribution plants hauled trailer loads of glass bottles to dumping grounds during the conversion to the throwaway cartons now in general use. Because of this practice, milk bottles and jars are scarce today. Most collectors search for bottles from hometown dairies; some have completed a fifty-state collection in the three popular sizes.

Bottles from 1900 to 1920 had the name of the dairy, town, and state embossed in the glass. Nearly all of the bottles produced after this period had the copy painted and then pyro-glazed onto the surface of the bottle. This enabled the dairyman to use colors and pictures of his dairy farm or cows on the bottles. Collectors have been fortunate that there have been no serious attempts at this point to reproduce a particularly rare bottle!

AJ Dorr Dairy, Watertown NY, pyro, tall, 1-pt...................**8.00**
Asgard Dairy, green pyro cow w/child, sq, ½-pt...............**8.00**
Barlow Dairy, Sugar Grove PA, pyro, sq, 1-qt.....................**4.00**
Buy Burn Boost, Anthracite Coal, pryo, 1945, ½-pt.............**15.00**
Cloverdale Dairy, Chippewa Falls WI, cloverleaves, orange pyro, ½-pt...................................**3.00**
Cloverleaf, Stockton CA, ribbed cream top, pyro, ½-pt.....**18.00**

Cloyed's Dairy Farm, pyro letters, ½-gal..............................**25.00**
Danville Producers Dairy, Buy War Bonds & Stamps, pyro, 1-qt...............................**90.00**
Deerfoot Farm, embossed, pear form w/screw lid, ca 1900, 1-pt...................................**30.00**
Diamond Farms, Salem NH, pyro, 10-oz................................**7.00**
Eastside Creamery Saratoga Springs NY, embossed name, 1-qt....................................**8.00**
Estey's Farm Dairy, orange pyro, 1-qt....................................**9.00**
Fischer's Dairy Farm, green pryo & embossed, 1-qt............**14.00**
Frates Dairy Inc, embossed name, ½-pt....................................**5.00**
Gibb's Farm Dairy, Rochester MA, embossed name, 1-pt.......**6.00**
Helfand Dairy Products, red pyro, w/cap, 2x1¼" dia, NM....**16.00**
Hood & Sons Boston, embossed name, 1-qt.........................**6.50**
Howell & Demarest Farm Dairies, embossed, wire bail, ca 1900, ½-pt...................................**30.00**
Indian Hill, Greenville ME, pyro, 1-qt...................................**12.50**
It's Hoods, orange pyro, sq, 1-qt................................**5.00**
Johns Hopkins Hospital, embossed, ca 1940, 1-qt.....................**17.50**
Jordan's Dairy, Hobbs NM, pyro, ca 1945, 1-qt..................**17.50**
Lake View Dairy, Ithaca NY, pyro, cream top, ca 1940, 1-pt..**12.50**
Land-O-Sun, Phoenix AZ, pyro, 1950s, ½-gal...................**20.00**
Lone Oak Dairy, coffee creamer, embossed, ca 1930, 2-oz..**10.00**
Lueck Dairy, pyro, 1-pt...........**8.00**

Maple City Dairy, Monmouth IL, A Nourishing Treat, red pyro, cream top, one-quart, $32.00.

Maple City Dairy, Monmouth IL, war slogan, red pryo, 1-qt..**65.00**

Meadow Brook, Clarksville NY, pyro, sq, 1-qt......................**7.50**

Morlen, baby's face on front, embossed, sq, 1-qt..........**45.00**

Newsom's Pride Dairy, Milk the Champion of Drinks, black pyro, 1-qt.........................**30.00**

Producers, embossed, sq, 1-qt..**5.00**

Protect the Children, Golden Jersy Milk, pyro colors, ca 1937, 1-qt......................**15.00**

Quality Dairy The Best..., Gloversville NY, pyro lettering, sq, 1-qt.....................**28.00**

Reehl's Dairy, Grand Ledge MI, amber, pyro, sq, 1-qt......**10.00**

Reynold's Dairy, pyro, w/cow, sq, 1-qt.....................................**7.50**

Rojeck's Delicious Sour Cream, pyro, wide mouth...........**10.00**

Roosevelt Dairy, pryo, ½-gal ..**38.00**

Rosebud Creamery, pyro, sq, 1940s-50s, ¾-oz................**7.50**

Shade's Dairy, Sante Fe NM, pyro, ca 1940, 1-qt..........**17.50**

Silver State Dairy, Denver CO, pyro, 1950s, 1-qt.............**28.00**

Sun Glo, embossed, amber, sq, ca 1950, 2-qt.........................**6.00**

Sunnymede Farm, Missouri Pacific Lines, red pryo, squat, ½-pt.....................**22.00**

Sunshine Dairy, orange pyro, baby top, 1-qt, VG..........**45.00**

Thatcher Farms, Milton MA, cream top, pyro, sq, 1-qt .**17.50**

University of Georgia, pyro, ca 1950, ½-pt.......................**12.50**

University of Tennessee, Knoxville TN, embossed, ca 1945, 1-qt.........**12.50**

Wallas Dairy, New Castle PA, pyro, 1-gal......................**30.00**

Walnut Crest Farm, Westbrook ME, pyro, 1-qt................**14.00**

Wauregan Dairy, It Whips, rhyme on back, 2-color, cream top, 1-pt......................................**35.00**

Wilson Goat Farm, San Bernadino CA, pyro, ca 1950, 1-qt ..**30.00**

Soda Bottles with Applied Color Labels

This is a specialized area of advertising collectibles that holds the interest of bottle collectors as well as those who search for soda pop items; both fields attract a good number of followers, so the market for these bottles is fairly strong right now. See also Coca-Cola; Soda Pop.

Acme Club Beverage Co, green, 1-qt.....................................**20.00**

Badger State, clear, 7-oz.......**15.00**

Bell's, clear, 7-oz **20.00**

Bingo, clear, 10-oz................**15.00**

Buckeye Sparkling Beverages, green, 7-oz **10.00**

Buffalo Rock, clear, 7-oz **15.00**

Cherie Cola, clear, 12-oz.......**10.00**

Choc-ola, clear, 9-oz **10.00**

Chocolate Soldier, clear, 10-oz..**15.00**

Clicquot Club, clear, 7-oz......**10.00**

Cotton Club Beverages, clear, 12-oz.....................................**15.00**

Cow Boy, clear, Chicago, 6-oz..**15.00**

Dillon Beverages, orange label on clear, 16-ounce, $10.00.

Dodge City, amber, throw-away, 10-oz **25.00**

Down East, clear, 6-oz **20.00**

Dr Swetts, clear, 12-oz..........**10.00**

English Club, clear, 7½-oz....**25.00**

Fizz, Low in Calories, green, 12-oz.....................................**8.00**

Flores Bros, clear, 10-oz........**25.00**

Frostie Root Beer, clear, 10-oz or 12-oz, ea...........................**10.00**

Garden Island, clear, 7-oz.....**15.00**

Good Guy, clear, 12-oz **25.00**

Grilli's Club Soda, clear, 1-qt .**8.00**

Hage-n-Hage, green, 12-oz ...**20.00**

Hamakua, clear, 7-oz **10.00**

Independence, clear, 7-oz......**15.00**

Isaly's Mountain Air, clear, 12-oz...**20.00**

Keep Kool, clear, 10-oz..........**20.00**

Kenton's, clear, 10-oz............**15.00**

Leary's, clear, 12-oz **15.00**

Liberty Beverage, green, 7-oz .**20.00**

MacFuddy, clear, 10-oz.........**35.00**

Mountaineer, clear, 9-oz.......**20.00**

Nugget, clear, 12-oz **15.00**

Old Scotch, clear, 7-oz...........**20.00**

Padgett Beverage, clear, 10-oz .**6.00**

Pal Cola, amber, 12-oz..........**15.00**

Quench, green, 8-oz...............**15.00**

Roxo, clear, 12-oz **25.00**

Scot, Dog Gone Good Drink, clear, 7-oz **15.00**

Solo, clear, 12-oz...................**25.00**

Sparkle, clear, 7-oz...............**10.00**

Sun Crest, blue and white label on clear, King Size, 1964, $5.00.

Sunny Kid Beverages, Buffalo NY, clear, 7-oz **8.00**

Turners Club Soda, 7-oz **6.00**

US Beverages, clear, 7-oz **15.00**

Veep, green, 12-oz **10.00**

Vess, clear, 10-oz..................**10.00**

White Rock Quinine Water, clear, 7-oz **10.00**

Yacht Club, clear, 7½-oz.......**15.00**

Zee, clear, 7-oz......................**25.00**

Miscellaneous

AC Grant German Magnetic Linament, aqua, beveled, 5", from $10 to..............**25.00**

Alkavis Sure Cure for Malaria, amber w/label, ring top, 8¼"............................**25.00**

Baker's Blood & Liver Cure, amber, lg crown w/a flag, 9½"...........................**100.00**

Bonney Barrel Ink, aqua, 2½", from $10 to....................**20.00**

Bromo-Seltzer Emerson Drug, Baltimore MD, cobalt, machine made, 8"..........**20.00**

Brown & Lyons Blood Bitters, amber, 8"........................**90.00**

Brown's Blood Cure, green, 6½", from $80 to..................**100.00**

Caracas Bitters, dark green, 8¼", from $25 to....................**50.00**

Caroni Bitters, amber, 1-pt..**50.00**

Carson's Ague Cure, aqua, ring top, 7¼", from $10 to......**20.00**

Carter's Rubber Stamp Ink, cobalt, 6½"......................**8.00**

Chesebrough Mfg Co (horseshoe lettering) Vaseline, clear, 3"..**25.00**

Chicago Fancy Bottler Brandy, ruby, ribbed shoulder & bottom, 11¾"........................**25.00**

Clarkes Sherry Wine Bitters, blue-green, 8", from $40 to.....**60.00**

Coopers Well Water, aqua, BCOO on back base, 9¾", from $20 to...................**30.00**

David's Turtle Ink, green, from $100 to..........................**120.00**

Don Lorenzo, dark olive, tapered sq w/beveled corners, 10"......**15.00**

Dr Belding's Wild Cherry Sarsaparilla, aqua, 10"............**15.00**

Dr Bullock's Nephreticurn, aqua, 7", from $30 to...............**40.00**

Dr Daniel's Veterinary Colic Cure No 1, clear, sq, 3½"........**75.00**

Duffy Malt Whiskey Company/ Patd Aug 1886, amber, 10½", from $25 to.....................**60.00**

Eiffel Tower Lemonade, clear, 2¾", from $30 to..............**40.00**

Fletcher's Vege-Tonic, amber, sq w/beveled corners, 8½"..**12.00**

Frog Pond Chill & Fever Tonic, cobalt, 7", from $8 to......**12.00**

Garnet Dry Gin, clear, 8¾", from $6 to................................**10.00**

GO Blake's Kentucky Whiskey, aqua, 12½"......................**10.00**

Guilford Mineral Spring Water, blue-green, 9¾", from $20 to................................**35.00**

GW House Clemens Indian Tonic, aqua, ring top, 5", from $40 to...................**80.00**

Hathorn Water Saratoga NY, amber, paper label, 9½"..**10.00**

Hilleman's American Chicken Cholera Cure, cobalt, flared top, 6½"...............................**75.00**

Hires Cough Cure, Phila PA, aqua, 4½", from $20 to...**30.00**

JH Cutter Old Bourbon, Louisville KY, amber, 1-qt, from $20 to...................**50.00**

JH Henkes, green, tapered top, 10⅜", from $25 to...........**35.00**

JM Clark Pickle Co, Louisville KY, clear, round, 5", from $15 to.............................**30.00**

Kennedy's East India Bitters, clear, 6½", from $20 to...**40.00**

Kobole Tonic Med Co, Chicago IL, amber or aqua, 8½", from $150 to.........................**200.00**

Kobole Tonic Med Co, Chicago IL, milk glass, 8½", from $200 to......................**250.00**

Lincoln Foods Inc, Abe Lincoln figural bank, clear, Pat 1959, 8½".................................**35.00**

Nyal's Emulsion of Cod Liver Oil, amber, 9".........................**18.00**

Paines Celery Compound, amber, 10", from $4 to...................**8.00**

Paines Celery Compound, aqua, 10", from $8 to.................**10.00**

Phillips' Emulsion (N backwards), amber, 9½", from $20 to **30.00**

Poison/Not To Be Taken, cobalt, 6-sided, 7¾", from $45 to ..**60.00**

Sea Horse Hollands Gin, green, tapered top, 3 dots on bottom, 9½"..................................**50.00**

Teaberry for the Teeth & Breath, clear, 3½", from $6 to.......**8.00**

Tonex patent medicine, paper label, Pantine Michigan, 8¾", $25.00.

Wait's Wild Cherry Tonic, amber, sq w/beveled corners, 8½", $30 to.............................**45.00**

Warners Imported B Gin, sky blue, 9", from $20 to.......**30.00**

Boyd Crystal Art Glass

Since it was established in 1978, this small glasshouse located in Cambridge, Ohio, has bought molds from other companies as they went out of business, and they have designed many of their own as well. They may produce several limited runs of a particular shape in a number of the lovely colors of glass they themselves formulate, none of which are ever reissued. Of course, all of the glass is handmade, and each piece is marked with their 'B-in-diamond' logo. Most of the pieces we've listed are those you're more apt to find at flea markets, but some of the rarer items may be worth a great deal more.

Our advisor for this category is Joyce Pringle who is listed in the Directory under Texas. See Clubs and Newsletters for information concerning a Boyd's Crystal Art Glass newsletter.

Airplane, Mirage...................**11.00**

Airplane, Cobalt Blue Carnival, 3½x4", $25.00. (Photo courtesy Joyce Pringle)

Angel, Vaseline Carnival **22.00**

Artie the Penguin, Banana Cream (R) **10.25**

Artie the Penguin, Classic Black **15.00**

Aunt Sheila's Pin Tray, Candyland **5.00**

Bingo the Deer, Potpourri (R)..**25.00**

Bow Slipper, Aqua Diamond ..**8.75**

Bunny Salt, Kumquat...........**16.50**

Bunny Salt, Mountain Haze...**17.50**

Candy the Carousel Horse, Bernard Boyd Black.......**15.00**

Candy the Carousel Horse, Purple Frost **8.00**

Cat Slipper, Rosie Pink...........**9.50**

Chick Salt, Nutmeg Carnival..**9.50**

Chick Salt, Orange Spice **18.00**

Debbie & 3 Ducklings, Old Lyme **8.00**

Eli & Sarah, Chocolate **12.00**

Elizabeth, Alpine Blue (R)......**8.50**

Fuzzy Bear, Capri Blue (R) **9.00**

JB Scotty, Buckeye (R) **40.00**

JB Scotty, Daffodil (R) **35.00**

JB Scotty, Heatherbloom (R).**35.00**

JB Scotty, Mountain Haze (R)..**32.00**

JB Scotty, Spring Suprise (R) ...**85.00**

Jeremy Frog, Pacifica (R) **9.25**

Joey the Horse, Delphinium (R)..**18.00**

Joey the Horse, Touch of Pink (R) ...**27.50**

Lil Joe the Horse, Country Red (R)................................**18.00**

Lil Luck the Unicorn, Classic Black Carnival (R) **15.00**

Lil Luck the Unicorn, Summer Haze (R)...........................**8.50**

Louise Doll, Alpine Blue, hand painted............................**26.00**

Louise Doll, Persimmon........**25.00**

Louise Doll, Violet Slate **12.00**

Nancy Doll, Cobalt **10.50**

Nancy Doll, Pacifica Green.....**9.25**

Owl, Light Rose....................**31.00**

Owl, Pecan............................**10.00**

Owl Bell, Vacation Swirl **10.00**

Patrick Bear, Shasta White (R) ..**16.00**

Rooster Holder, Sunflower Yellow **20.00**

Sammy Squirrel, Alexandrite (R) **15.00**

Skate Boot, Snow **28.50**

Skippy Dog, Cornsilk **6.00**

Susie the Pig, Chasmine Pink..**11.50**

Taffy the Carousel Horse, Spring Suprise **18.00**

Teddy the Tugboat, Mint Green ..**21.50**

Tractor, Cardinal Red (R).....**15.00**

Tucker Car, Cobalt Carnival...**18.00**

Turkey Salt, Lemon Custard ..**10.00**

Willie the Mouse, Buckeye **9.50**

Willie the Mouse, Peach **8.00**

Woodsie Owl (sm), Lemon Custard..**8.50**

Zack the Elephant, Bermuda Slag **45.00**

Zack the Elephant, Flame, $60.00.

Zack the Elephant, Sandpiper .**15.00**

Breweriana

Beer can collectors and antique advertising buffs as well

enjoy looking for beer-related memorabilia such as tap knobs, beer trays, coasters, signs, and the like. While the smaller items of a more recent vintage are quite affordable, signs and trays from defunct breweries often bring three-digit prices. Condition is important in evaluating early advertising items of any type.

Ashtray, Anheuser-Busch, brass emblem w/red enamel A-&-eagle logo, VG+ 60.00

Ashtray, Cambden Beer, red-painted logo on clear glass, EX...................................8.00

Bank, Lone Star Beer/Certified Quality, plaster keg form, VG 35.00

Blimp, Genessee Beer/Good Beer, inflatable vinyl, 1970s, 14x30", NM.....................25.00

Book, Schlitz Brewing Co, Quality Control Story, 1940s, 20 pages, EX........................10.00

Bottle, Schlitz, ruby glass w/paper label, 7-oz, 12-oz, or 32-oz, ea 10.00

Bottle opener, Barbarossa Beer, wood bottle w/foil label, 1950s, EX 20.00

Calendar, Budweiser, wall hanging, bottle & glass on tray, 1940s, EX 60.00

Calendar, Pabst, plastic wallet size, 1940s, EX..............10.00

Clock, Budweiser King of Beers, plastic light-up pocket watch, 17", NM 100.00

Clock, Gibbons/Is Good Anytime, plastic, 1950s, 3x14", EX...................................45.00

Coaster, Busch, pressed paper, red & green logo, 3x3½", NM .10.00

Corkscrew, Anheuser-Busch, wooden handle, preprohibition, EX...........................50.00

Display, California Gold Label covered wagon, light-up, 1950s, NM 100.00

Display figure, Acme singing trio, chalkware, EX.............200.00

Display figure, Bud Man, hard foam w/2 capes & string, 19", NM................................165.00

Display figure, Goebel rooster by bottle of beer, chalkware, EX....................65.00

Display figure, Spuds MacKenzie, vinyl light-up, NM.......150.00

Display sign, Hamm's Bear leaning on beer can, molded plastic, 13", NM 30.00

Door push, Pabst Blue Ribbon Beer, painted metal, 4x9", VG..55.00

Figural display, Anteek Beer, composition, 22½", $300.00. (Photo courtesy B.J. Summers)

Foam scraper, Piels 'light beer' w/Burt & Harry characters, 1950s, EX 35.00

Foam scraper, Yuengling, red w/white logo, 1950s, EX ..35.00

Glass, Acme, bucking horse in black & red enamel, 1950s, EX..................................**25.00**

Glass, Falstaff, shield logo in red & white enamel, 1960s, EX ...**5.00**

Globe, Schlitz Beer, plastic, revolving wall mount, light-up, 16", EX......................**15.00**

Knife/corkscrew, Anheuser-Busch, embossed, EX..................**75.00**

Light fixtures, Schlitz Draft, plastic, hanging, 1970s, 12", pr......**65.00**

Lighter, Schlitz can shape, 1960s, 5", EX..............................**15.00**

Measuring stick/ruler, Eilert's Supreme Lager, 6x1", EX .**18.00**

Miniature bottle, Eastside, gold foil label, 1950s, EX.........**5.00**

Miniature bottle, Fort Pitt, stubby, decal label, 1950s, EX....**10.00**

Miniature mug, Coors, ceramic w/red logo, 1960s, EX.......**6.00**

Miniature mug, glass w/red logo, 1970s, EX **3.00**

Mirror, Marathon, brown-painted logo, 1940s, 3x10"..........**10.00**

Mug, Hamm's, Octoberfest, ceramic, 1973, 8", EX.....**15.00**

Necktie, Schlitz Beer, 1950s, NM..............................**20.00**

Neon sign, Bud Dry/Cold Filtered Draft, red & blue, 23", EX **40.00**

Neon sign, Miller/Made the American Way, 1980s, NM..........................**75.00**

Paperweight, Schlitz, glass w/encased brewery scene, VG..............................**100.00**

Plaque, Budweiser King of Beers, lighted, early 1960s, 14x19", NM+...............................**55.00**

Plaque, Schlitz/No Bitterness/Just the Kiss of Hops, composition, VG+................................**50.00**

Playing cards, Ballantine Beer, 3-ring design, 1960s, complete, MIB................................**25.00**

Seltzer bottle, Balboa, clear glass w/red logo, metal top, 1940s **25.00**

Sign, Ballantine Draught Beer, pressed wood, dated 1951, 10x14", EX.....................**25.00**

Sign, Brew 102, cardboard, blond woman holding beer, 1950s, EX.................................**20.00**

Mug, Miller High Life, red painted label on clear, 5½", $12.00.

Sign, Heinekin Beer, one-sided porcelain pillow style, seven colors, 23¹/₂x16", EX, $250.00.

Sign, Wiedemann Fine Beer, 3-D plastic light-up, 1960s, 15x10", NM......................**25.00**

Tap handle, Falstaff, chrome ball style w/red logo, 1940s, EX.**30.00**

Tip tray, Budweiser King of Beers, w/logo, red & white, 1950s, EX **15.00**

Toy tractor-trailer, Budweiser, metal, logo on side, 1960s, 24", EX.............................**80.00**

Tray, Grand Prize, blue shield on yellow, 1950s, EX...........**45.00**

Anheuser-Busch Steins by Ceramarte

A&E Eagle logo, CSL2, w/lid, 1975, 9¾", EX...............**100.00**

American Homestead, Holiday Series, retired 1996, 7", EX..............**50.00**

Bavarian house, ½-litre......**200.00**

Bud man, hollow head, ½-litre..**250.00**

Busch, CS-44, 1980, EX......**100.00**

Busch Gardens, blue & gray, 6½", EX...................................**75.00**

Christmas, Holiday Series, signed by artist, w/lid, 1997, 8¼", EX **70.00**

Declaration of Independence, 1976, 7⅝", EX...............**100.00**

JFK, American Heritage Collection, pewter lid, 1993, 12", EX...............................**120.00**

LA Olympic Committee, 1980, 10", EX...........................**90.00**

Breyer Horses

Breyer collecting has grown in popularity throughout the past several years. Though horses dom-inate the market, cattle and other farm animals, dogs, cats, and wildlife have also been produced, all with exacting details and life-like coloration. They've been made since the early 1950s in both glossy and matt finishes. (Earlier models were glossy, but from 1968 until the 1990s when both glossy and semigloss colors were revived for special runs, matt colors were preferred.) Breyer also manufactures dolls, tack, and accessories such as barns for their animals.

For more information we recommend *Schroeder's Collectible Toys, Antique to Modern*, and *Breyer Animal Collector's Guide* by Felicia Browell. (Both are by Collector Books.)

Adios Standing Quarter Horse Stallion, 1988-89............**30.00**

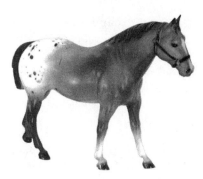

Appaloosa Gelding, #97, 1971 – 1980, $35.00.

Arabian Foal, alabaster, 1973-82...............................**30.00**

Black Beauty, 1980-93..........**15.00**

Bucking Bronco, matt gray, 1961-67 ....**150.00**

Cantering Welsh Pony, seal brown
w/blue ribbons, 1971-74.**125.00**

Clydesdale Stallion, woodgrain,
1960-65 ....**250.00**

Family Arabian Stallion, glossy
palomino, 1961-66..........**30.00**

Grazing Mare Buttons, black,
1965-70 ....**100.00**

Kelso, dark matt bay, 1975-90..**20.00**

Lady Phase (Sears Spirit of the
West), bay pinto **50.00**

**Old Timer, #20, 1966 – 1976, alabaster,
missing hat, $40.00.**

Old Timer, dapple gray, 1966-
87 ....**75.00**

Old Timer, red roan, 1991-93 ..**40.00**

Proud Arabian Mare, red chest-
nut, 1991-92 ....**40.00**

Quarter Horse Foal, matt black,
1975-82 ....**20.00**

Racehorse, glossy chestnut, 1956-
67 ....**150.00**

Rearing Stallion, palomino, 1965-
85 ....**25.00**

Running Foal Spice, glossy dapple
gray, 1963-73..................**45.00**

Scratching Foal, liver chestnut,
1970-71 ....**125.00**

Sham (Marguerite Henry), 1984-
88 ....**45.00**

Silky Sullivan, matt brown, 1975-
90 ....**35.00**

Stud Spider, chestnut blanket
appaloosa, 1990-91 ....**35.00**

Swaps, chestnut, 1975-90 .....**25.00**

Western Horse, glossy chestnut
pinto, 1956-67 ....**50.00**

Western Prancer, matt bay, 1961-
71 ....**75.00**

Bubble Bath Containers

Figural bubble bath containers were popular in the 1960s and
have become highly collectible
today. The Colgate-Palmolive Company produced the widest variety
called Soakies. Purex's Bubble
Club characters were also popular.
Most Soaky bottles came with
detachable heads made of brittle
plastic which cracked easily. Purex
bottles were made of a softer plastic but lost their paint easier. Condition affects price considerably.

The interest collectors displayed in the old bottles prompted
many to notice foreign-made products. Some of the same characters
have been licensed by companies
in Canada, Italy, the UK, Germany, and Japan, and the bottles
they've designed have excellent
detail. They're usually a little
larger than domestic bottles, and
though fairly recent, are often
reminiscent of those made in the
US during the 1960s.

For more information, we recommend *Collector's Guide to Bubble Bath Containers* and
*Schroeder's Collectible Toys,
Antique to Modern.* Both are published by Collector Books. The fol-

lowing prices are for containers in excellent to near-mint condition, unless noted otherwise.

Augie Doggie, Purex, original tag, EX.....................45.00
Baloo Bear, Colgate-Palmolive, 1966, NM.......................40.00
Bambi, Colgate-Palmolive, sitting & smiling, NM................25.00
Bamm-Bamm, Purex, NM....35.00
Batman, Colgate-Palmolive, 1966, NM................................75.00

Batman, DC Comics Inc., Tsumura International Inc., plastic, 1991, 10", $10.00. (Photo courtesy Mary Jane Lamphier)

Batman, Kid Care, M............10.00
Beauty & the Beast, Cosrich, original tag, M, from $5 to.....8.00
Bozo the Clown, Colgate-Palmolive, 1960s, NM..............30.00
Bugs Bunny, Colgate-Palmolive, NM................................25.00
Bullwinkle, Colgate-Palmolive, NM................................45.00
Casper the Ghost, Colgate-Palmolive, EX..........................30.00
Cement Truck, Colgate-Palmolive, EX+...............................35.00

Charlie Brown, Avon, red baseball outfit, NM.....................20.00
Dick Tracy, Colgate-Palmolive, 1965, NM.......................50.00
Dum Dum, Purex, 1964, rare, EX.............................100.00

Felix the Cat, Colgate-Palmolive, 1960s, M, $50.00. (Photo courtesy Greg Moore and Joe Pizzo)

Felix the Cat, Colgate-Palmolive, EX...............................30.00
Garfield, Kid Care, lying in tub, NM................................10.00
Harriett Hippo, Merle Norman, NM................................10.00
Incredible Hulk, Benjamin Ansehl, standing on rock, M 25.00
Jiminy Cricket, Colgate-Palmolive, 1960s, EX+ 30.00
Kermit the Frog, Calgon, Treasure Island outfit, w/tag, M......8.00
Little Orphan Annie, Lander, 1977, NM, from $25 to...30.00
Mighty Mouse, Colgate-Palmolive, lg head, EX.....................25.00
Mr Jinks w/Pixie & Dixie, Purex, w/contents, MIB.............40.00
Mummy, Colgate-Palmolive, 1960s, NM 100.00

Pinocchio, Colgate-Palmolive, 1960s, M **25.00**

Pluto, Colgate-Palmolive, 1960s, NM **25.00**

Popeye, Colgate-Palmolive, 1977, NM **35.00**

Porky Pig, Colgate-Palmolive, 1960s, EX+ **25.00**

Power Rangers, Kid Care, 1994, any, M, ea **8.00**

Ricochet Rabbit, Purex, movable arms, VG **35.00**

Robin, Colgate Palmolive, 1966, EX **75.00**

Secret Squirrel, Purex, 1966, rare, VG..................................**45.00**

Smokey Bear, Colgate-Palmolive, 1960s, NM **25.00**

Snaggle Puss, Purex, 1960s, NM **50.00**

Snoopy, Avon, 1971, in tub of bubbles, MIB **20.00**

Speedy Gonzales, Colgate-Palmolive, 1960s, EX **30.00**

Splash Down (Space Capsule), Avon, 1970, MIB **20.00**

Spouty Whale, Roclar (Purex), originial card, M.............**25.00**

Superman, Avon, 1978, MIB..**40.00**

Sylvester the Cat, Colgate-Palmolive, 1960s, w/microphone, EX **30.00**

Teenage Mutant Ninja Turtle, Kid Care, 1990, any, M, ea **8.00**

Tennessee Tuxedo, Colgate-Palmolive, 1965, w/ice-cream cone, NM **30.00**

Thumper, Colgate-Palmolive, 1960s, EX **25.00**

Tic Toc Turtle, Avon, 1968, MIB............................**20.00**

Touche Turtle, Purex, standing, NM **40.00**

Wally Gator, Purex, 1963, rare, VGs **35.00**

Wendy the Witch, Colgate-Palmolive, 1960s, NM **30.00**

Winsome Witch, Purex, 1965, rare, NM........................**30.00**

Yogi Bear, Purex, NM, $30.00.

Cake Toppers

The first cake toppers appeared on wedding cakes in the 1880s and were made almost entirely of sugar. The early 1900s saw toppers carved from wood and affixed to ornate plaster pedestal bases and backgrounds. A few single-mold toppers were even made from poured lead. From the 1920s to the 1950s bisque, porcelain, and chalkware figures reigned supreme. The faces and features on many of these were very realistic and lifelike. The beautiful Art Deco era was also in evidence.

Celluloid kewpie types made a brief appearance from the late 1930s to the 1940s. These were quite fragile because the celluloid they were made of could be easily dented and cracked. The true Rose O'Neill kewpie look-alike also appeared for awhile during this period. During and after World War II and into the Korean Conflict of the 1950s, groom figures in military dress appeared. Only a limited amount was ever produced; they are quite rare. From the 1950s into the 1970s, plastics were used almost exclusively. Toppers took on a vacant, assembly-line appearance with no specific attention to detail or fashion.

In the 1970s, bisque returned and plastic disappeared. Toppers were again more lifelike. For the most part, they remain that way today. Wedding cakes now often display elegant and elaborate toppers such as those made by Royal Doulton and Lladro.

Toppers should not be confused with the bride and groom doll sets of the same earlier periods. While some smaller dolls could and did serve as toppers, they were usually too unbalanced to stay upright on a cake. The true topper consisted of a small bride and groom anchored to (or a part of) a round flat base which made it extremely stable for resting on a soft, frosted cake surface. Cake toppers never did double-duty as play items.

Our advisor for this category is Jeannie Greenfield, who is listed in the Directory under Pennsylvania.

Kissing couple, bisque, newer..**20.00**

Sailor uniform on groom, all plaster, 4½" **35.00**
1900s couple, carved wood figures on plaster stand **50.00**
1920s couple, all bisque, bride in dropped-waist gown, 4" .**30.00**
1920s couple, single mold, poured lead **45.00**

1920s couple, single mold, poured lead, cloth flowers, 5", from $50.00 to $60.00. (Photo courtesy Jeannie Greenfield)

1940s, basalt carved figures, single-pc **20.00**
1940s couple, plaster/chalkware combination....................**25.00**
1940s couple, standing in front of 3 lg bells, all plastic **30.00**
1950s (early) couple, chalkware.**20.00**

California Potteries

In recent years, pottery designed by many of the artists who worked in their own small studios in California during the 1940s through the 1960s has become highly sought after, and prices on the secondary market have soared. As more research is completed and collectors are introduced to the work of previously unknown artists, the field continues to expand. Items made by Kay Finch, Florence Ceramics, Brayton, Howard Pierce, and Sascha Brastoff often bring high prices and have been considered very collectible for several years. Now such names as Matthew Adams, Marc Bellair, and deLee are attracting their share of attention as well.

It's a fascinating field, one covered very well in Jack Chipman's *Collector's Encyclopedia of California Pottery, Second Edition.* Specific companies/designers are featured in these books: *Collector's Encyclopedia of Howard Pierce Porcelain* by Darlene Hurst Dommel; *Collector's Encyclopedia of Sascha Brastoff* by Steve Conti, A. Dewayne Bethany, and Bill Seay; and *Collector's Guide to Don Winton Designs* by Mike Ellis. All are published by Collector Books. Mike Nickel and Cynthia Horvath have written *Kay Finch Ceramics, Her Enchanted World* (Schiffer), a must for collectors interested in Kay Finch ceramics. See also Bauer; Cookie Jars; Franciscan; Metlox.

Adams, Matthew

Ashtray, husky, #061, 13x10"..**40.00**
Bowl, iceberg on lid, #158,
 4x6½" **75.00**
Creamer & sugar bowl, walrus,
 5" **125.00**
Tray, seal on ice flow, sq,
 15x11" **85.00**
Vase, seals & brown splashes,
 cylindrical, #127, 18" ...**150.00**

Bellaire, Marc

Bowl, Jamaican theme, boat
 shape, 12" L...................**95.00**
Bowl, Jamaican theme, free-form,
 16" L, from $120 to **145.00**
Box, Luau, 2x4½x3¾" **50.00**
Figurine, island man, seated on
 keg, bent over bongo drums,
 8½"...............................**400.00**

Plate, stylized leaves, teal, maroon, and gold, 12", $100.00; Matching 5" vase, $75.00.

Platter, island fisherman w/nets,
 16" dia..........................**150.00**

Platter, reclining woman with blue bird in hand on gray background, 14" long, $175.00.

Vase, leafy spray, white outlines on charcoal, pedestal
 base, 9" **68.00**

Brayton Laguna

Candy jar, chicken shape, sm .**225.00**
Chess piece, Castle, 1946, 10½"..**200.00**
Cookie jar, Christina, Swedish
    maid, ca 1941, 11".......**550.00**
Figurine, bear seated, front legs
    apart, 1950s, 3½" **75.00**
Figurine, Dutch boy & girl, pr..**250.00**
Figurine, Eric & Inga, Swedish
    boy & girl, pr **300.00**
Figurine, Gepetto, Walt Disney
    series, 8" **800.00**
Figurine, Little Red Riding
    Hood..........................**275.00**
Figurine, Mexican man, yellow
    pancho, w/sombrero, 9" .**250.00**
Figurine, mule, w/yoke,
    7¼x10" **250.00**
Figurine, Pluto, howling, Walt
    Disney series, 6"...........**180.00**
Figurine, Rosita, Mexican girl
    w/flower basket, 5½"....**100.00**
Figurine, toucan, polychrome high
    glaze, 9" **200.00**
Flower holder, Swedish woman,
    ca 1939, 11½" **350.00**
Plate, eggplant glaze, handmade,
    early, 9" **125.00**
Vase, bud; blue w/entwined snake,
    8"..................................**400.00**
Vase, waisted neck, bulbous body,
    yellow, 5½" **250.00**
Wall hanging, man standing,
    arms over head, Webton Ware
    mark, 13" **275.00**

Cleminson Pottery

Ashtray, fruit, footed, 10" **35.00**
Bread tray, Distlefink, 12½"..**35.00**
Butter dish, Distlefink, w/lid ..**50.00**
Egg cup, from $30 to **35.00**

Gravy bowl, Distlefink, w/ladle,
    5½"...............................**50.00**
Jar, Chinese man, white w/black
    hat, w/lid **60.00**
Plate, crowing rooster decoration,
    9½".................................**30.00**
Razor blade bank, Gay Blade,
    4"...................................**40.00**
Salt & pepper shakers, artist
    w/palette, 6¼", pr...........**75.00**
Spoon rest, floral dec, 8½"..**25.00**
Toothpick holder, butler, 4½" ..**50.00**
Tray, Galagray; 12"..............**25.00**
Wall pocket, fireplace bellows
    shape, 10½" **40.00**
Wall pocket, kettle shape, w/verse,
    7¼"................................**30.00**
Wall pocket, key shape, 7¼" ..**35.00**
Wall pocket, little house on top of
    world, 8" **50.00**

DeForest of California

Condiment, Horace Radish...**50.00**
Garlic holder, comical man's head,
    lid is hat, 5" **25.00**
Tray, pig head shape, Go Ahead...,
    13x13", from $30 to........**45.00**

deLee

Bank, Stinkie, skunk, unmarked,
    7"...................................**20.00**

**Figurines,
Danny and
Daisy, from
$35.00 to
$50.00 each.**
(Photo courtesy Joanne
and Ralph
Schafer)

77

Figurine, June, girl seated w/open book, 4", from $65 to **85.00**

Figurine, Mickey, kitten playing w/ball, 4", from $45 to....**60.00**

Figurine, Whitey, white lamb, standing, 4", from $30 to..............**40.00**

Head vase, Bobby Pin Up, lady w/locket, 3½", from $60 to ..**90.00**

Finch, Kay

Bank, Sissy, looking up, #166, 3¾x4"............................**175.00**

Figurine, bear, Tubby, sitting, #4847, 4¼"....................**250.00**

Figurine, Chinese boy, #4629, 6¾" **125.00**

Figurine, dog, Beggar, #5262, 8" **600.00**

Figurine, Dog Show Boxer, #5025, 5x5"...............................**400.00**

Figurine, elephant, Peanuts, #191, 8½".......................**350.00**

Figurine, Littlest Angel, #4803, 2½"................................**175.00**

Figurine, Pajama Girl, #5002, 5½"..............................**225.00**

Figurine, Quail, Mama, blue, #5984, 7"......................**450.00**

Fountain, Bird Bath w/Bird, #5388, 6".......................**150.00**

Planter, Baby Block w/Bear, 6½"............................**100.00**

Vase, South Sea Girl, #4912, 8¾"............................**200.00**

Florence Ceramics

Note: The amount of applied decoration — lace, flowers, etc. — has a great deal of influence on values. Our ranges reflect this factor.

Diana, powder box, 6¼"......**400.00**

Gibson Girl, painted mark, 11", from $350 to **375.00**

Grandmother & I, from $2,500 to **3,000.00**

Irene, white dress w/gold, Godey **70.00**

John Alden, gray, white & black, 9¼", from $250 to.........**275.00**

Karlo, Oriental lady, w/fan, 14", from $400 to **450.00**

Kay, fur trim w/gold, 6" **100.00**

Linda Lou, red or teal, 7¾", from $160 to **400.00**

Figurines, rooster and hen, Mr. and Mrs. Banty Jr., #4843 and #4844, $175.00 for the pair.

Marie Antoinette and Louis XVI, $750.00 for the pair. (Photo courtesy Doug Foland)

Martin, red coat w/cane, 10½",
from $375 to **400.00**
Mikado, Oriental man, 14", from
$400 to **450.00**
Priscilla & John Alden, pr..**600.00**
Suzanna, lace, gold, 8¾", from
$375 to **400.00**

Keeler, Brad

Bowl, lettuce, #959, 4¾x11¼"..**55.00**
Figurine, bird of paradise, 11",
from $140 to **165.00**

Figurine, Blue Jay, #735, 9", $85.00.
(Photo courtesy Jack Chipman)

Figurine, crested heron, #43, 16",
minimum value............**225.00**
Figurine, Siamese cat, 12", from
$75 to **85.00**
Plate, lobster & leaf, 3-section,
11x9½"...........................**55.00**
Platter, turkey, #197, 10x12" .**145.00**
Server, lobster & leaf, 3-section,
#868, 8¾x9" **35.00**

Schoop, Hedi

Candle holder, mermaid holding
shells in ea hand, 13½"..**450.00**

Figurine, boy angel, waist up,
8" **85.00**
Figurine, Chinese musicians, 11",
pr **275.00**
Figurine, Conchita, w/2 baskets,
12½"............................**165.00**
Figurine, Debutante, handmade
flowers, 12½"................**165.00**
Figurine, hula dancer, 11", from
$225 to **250.00**
Figurine, Josephine, holding sm
black bowl, 13" **250.00**
Figurine, Love Boat, 1939,
6x10½" **280.00**
Figurine, Vienna, w/baskets,
13½" **175.00**
Flower frog, dancing girls, 8"..**250.00**
Flower holder, Marguerita, 12½",
from $125 to **145.00**
Jardiniere, Chinese style, blue
w/gold trim, 7½"..........**100.00**

**Tray, lady figural, flowing skirt
forms tray, 10x13", $185.00. (Photo
courtesy Pat and Kris Secor)**

Twin Winton

Ashtray, Bambi, 6x8"..........**100.00**
Ashtray, Hillbilly Line (Ladies
of the Mountain), sm,
4½x4¼" **20.00**
Bank, lamb, 8"......................**40.00**
Bank, Ranger Bear, 8".........**50.00**

Candle holder, Aladdin, 9½x6½" **45.00**

Candle holder, Verdi, 9½x4" ...**15.00**

Candy jar, shoe, 10x10" **75.00**

Canister, Canisterville, house, coffee, 4x8" **75.00**

Creamer & sugar bowl, hen & rooster, 5x6" **200.00**

Figurine, cocker spaniel, 7" ..**50.00**

Lamp, squirrel, 12" **175.00**

Napkin holder, cocktail; horse, 4x6" **150.00**

Napkin holder, Dutch girl, 8½x5½" **75.00**

Napkin holder, Ranger Bear, 4x9" **75.00**

Salt & pepper shakers, sheriff, pr **50.00**

Stein, Bamboo Line, 8" **35.00**

Weil Ware

Baker, Mango, 9x6½" **15.00**

Butter dish, Blossom, ¼-lb ...**22.00**

Flower holder, Dutch girl, #3041, 7¼" **45.00**

Flower holder, sailor boy, stamped mark, 10¾" **50.00**

Gravy boat, blossom **22.00**

Snack tray & cup, Birchwood, rare **15.00**

Tray, Bambu, 6x12" **25.00**

Tumbler, Blossom, 4¼" **16.00**

Pitcher, Hillbilly Line (Men of the Mountain, #H-101, 7½", $85.00. (Photo courtesy Michael L. Ellis)

Planter, squirrel, 4x8" **50.00**

Punch cup, Hillbilly Line (Men of the Mountain), #H-111, 3" **15.00**

Salt & pepper shakers, apple, pr **75.00**

Salt & pepper shakers, cart, pr **50.00**

Salt & pepper shakers, donkey, pr................................ **40.00**

Salt & pepper shakers, house, pr................................ **75.00**

Vases, lady in rose dress with flower decoration and lady in green with black lace fan, from $50.00 to $60.00 each.

Yona

Decanter, clown figural, cold-painted, 13" **65.00**

Figure vase, girl in blue bonnet w/rose trim, #47, 7" **30.00**

Figurine, medieval ladies, in gold-trimmed attire, facing pr, 10" **135.00**

Figurines, Siamese dancers, overglaze gold embellishment, 1950s, 13½", 12½", $200.00 for the pair. (Photo courtesy Jack Chipman)

Figurine, Oriental man & woman, #15/#16, 9", pr **50.00**
Pill jar, plump lady, hair is lid, Shafford label, ca 1960 ..**45.00**
Pretzel jar, red & white striped, Country Club #8741 ....**150.00**
Salt & pepper shakers, clowns (Salty & Peppy), 1957, MIB, pr.....................................**40.00**

California Raisins

In the fall of 1986, the California Raisins made their first commercials for television. In 1987 the PVC figurines were introduced. Initially there were four: a singer, two conga dancers, and a saxophone player. At this time, Hardee's issued similar but smaller figures. Later that year Blue Surfboard (horizontal), and three Bendees (which are about 5½" tall with flat pancake-style bodies) were issued for retail sale.

In 1988 twenty-one Raisins were made for sale in retail stores and in some cases used for promotional efforts in grocery stores: Blue Surfboard (vertical), Red Guitar, Lady Dancer, Blue/Green Sunglasses, Guy Winking, Candy Cane, Santa Raisin, Bass Player, Drummer, Tambourine Lady (there were two styles), Lady Valentine, Male Valentine, Boy Singer, Girl Singer, Hip Guitar Player, Sax Player with Beret, and four Graduates. The Graduates are identical in design to the original four characters released in 1987 but stand on yellow pedestals and are attired in blue graduation caps and yellow tassels. Bass Player and Drummer were initially distributed in grocery stores along with an application to join the California Raisin Fan Club located in Fresno, California. Later that year Hardee's issued six more: Blue Guitar, Trumpet Player, Roller Skater, Skateboard, Boom Box, and Yellow Surfboard. As was true with the 1987 line, the Hardee's characters were generally smaller than those produced for retail sales.

Eight more made their debut in 1989: Male in Beach Chair, Green Trunks with Surfboard, Hula Skirt, Girl Sitting on Sand, Piano Player, 'AC,' Mom, and Michael Raisin. During that year the Raisins starred in two movies: *Meet the Raisins* and *The California Raisins — Sold Out*, and were joined in figurine production by five movie characters (their fruit and vegetable friends): Rudy Bagaman, Lick Broccoli, Banana White, Leonard Limabean, and Cecil Thyme.

The latest release of Raisins came in 1991 when Hardee's issued four more — Anita Break, Alotta Stile, Buster, and Benny. All Raisins issued for retail sales and promotions in 1987 and 1988, including Hardee's issues for those years, are dated with the year of production (usually on the bottom of one foot). Of those Raisins released for retail sale in 1989, only the Beach Scene characters are dated, and they are actually dated 1988. Hardee's Raisins, issued in 1991, are also undated.

In the last two years, California Raisins have become extremely popular collectible items and are quickly sold at flea markets and toy shows. On Friday, November 22, 1991, the California Raisins were enshrined in the Smithsonian Institution to the tune of *I Heard It Through the Grapevine*. We recommend *Schroeder's Collectible Toys, Antique to Modern*, for further information about the many miscellaneous items relating to California Raisins that are available. Listings are for loose items in mint condition unless noted otherwise.

Beach Theme Issue, girl sitting in sand w/boom box, green shoes, '88 ....**20.00**
Beach Theme Issue, girl w/grass hula skirt, white gloves, 1988..............................**20.00**

Beach Theme Issue, male in beach chair, orange sandals & glasses, 1988..........................**20.00**
Beach Theme Issue, male in green trunks, surfboard, white gloves, 1988....................**20.00**

California Raisin boy in beach chair, Beach Theme Edition, 1988, M, $15.00.

Christmas Issue, Santa Hat, red cap & green sneakers, 1988............................**12.00**
First Commercial Issue, Singer, w/microphone, 1988........**6.00**
First Key Chains, Hands, hands up, thumbs at head, 1987 ....**5.00**
First Key Chains, Saxophone, gold sax, no hat, 1987 ....**5.00**
Graduate Key Chains, Sunglasses, fingers touch face, Applause, 1988...............**85.00**
Hardee's 1st Promotion, Hands, thumbs touch head, 1987, sm **3.00**
Hardee's 1st Promotion, Microphone, right hand points up, 1987, sm **3.00**
Hardee's 2nd promotion, FF Strings, blue guitar, Applause, 1988, $1 to.......**3.00**

Hardee's 2nd Promotion, Waves Weaver, yellow surfboard, Applause, 1988.................**3.00**

Hardee's 4th Promotion, Benny, bowling ball & bag, Applause, 1992 ....**15.00**

Meet the Raisins 1st Edition, Banana White, yellow dress, 1989 ....**20.00**

Meet the Raisins 1st Edition, Piano, red hair, blue piano, 1989 ....**20.00**

Meet the Raisins 2nd Edition, Cecil Thyme, orange, carrot-like, 1989.....................**225.00**

Meet the Raisins 2nd Edition, Lenny Limabean, purple coat, 1989 ....**200.00**

Post Raisin Bran Issue, Hands, hands point opposite ways, 1987 ....**2.00**

Post Raisin Bran Issue, Sunglasses, orange sunglasses, 1987....**2.00**

Second Commercial Issue, Bass Player, gray slippers, 1988, M......................**8.00**

Second Key Chains, Hip Band Hip Guitarist (Hendrix), w/headband, 1988......................**65.00**

Special Raisin Club Issue, Tambourine Female, Applause, 1988 ....**15.00**

Unknown Issue, Blue Surfboard (vertical), connected to right foot, '88 ....**35.00**

Cameras

Whether buying a camera for personal use, adding to a collection, or for resale, use caution. Complex usable late-model cameras are difficult to check out at sales, and you should be familiar with the camera model or have confidence in the seller's claims before purchasing one for your personal use. If you are just beginning a camera collection, there are a multitude of different types and models and special features to select from in building your collection; you should have on hand some of the available guide books listing various models and types. Camera collecting can be a very enjoyable hobby and can be done within your particular funding ability.

Buying for resale can be a very profitable experience if you are careful in your selection and have made arrangements with buyers who have made their requirements known to you. Generally, buying low-cost, mass-produced cameras is not advisable; you may have a difficult time finding a buyer for such cameras. Of these low-cost types, only those that are mint or new in the original box have any appreciable appeal to collectors.

Very old cameras are not necessarily valuable — it all depends on availability. The major criterion is quality; prices offered for mint-condition cameras may be double or triple those of average-wear items. You can expect to find that foreign-made cameras are preferred by most buyers because of the general perception that their lenses and shutters are superior. The German- and Japanese-made cameras dominate the 'classic' camera market. Polaroid cameras and movie cameras have yet to gain a significant collectors' market.

The cameras listed here represent only a very small cross section of thousands of cameras available. Values are given for examples with average wear and in good working order; they represent average retail prices with limited guarantees. It is very important to note that purchase prices at flea markets, garage sales, or estate sales would have to be far less for them to be profitable to a resaler who has the significant expense of servicing the camera, testing it, and guaranteeing it to a user or collector.

Our advisor, C.E. Cataldo, is listed in the Directory under Alabama.

Agfa, Billy, early 1930s.........**15.00**
Agfa, Karat 3.5, 1940............**35.00**
Ansco, Memar, 1954-58 ....**20.00**
Ansco, Super Speedex, 75/3.5 lens, 1953-58.........................**175.00**
Argus A2F, 1939-41 ....**20.00**
Argus C4, 50/2.8 lens w/flash ..**30.00**
Asahiflex 1, first Japanese SLR.**500.00**
Bolsey, B2.............................**30.00**
Canon III **275.00**
Canon J, Seiki Kogaku, 1939-44, from $4,500 to **6,000.00**
Canon 7, 1961-64 ....**450.00**
Compass Camera, 1938, from $1,000 to...................**1,300.00**
Contessa 35, 1950-55, from $100 to................................**150.00**
Eastman Folding Brownie Six-20 ....**12.00**

Edinex, by Wirgin **30.00**
Exakta VX, 1951 ....**80.00**
Graflex Pacemaker Crown Graphic, various sizes, ea, from $80 to **150.00**
Hasselbland 1000F, 1952-57 ....**700.00**
Kodak Baby Brownie, Bakelite ..**12.00**
Kodak Box Brownie 2A...........**7.00**
Kodak Gignet 35 ....**30.00**
Kodak Hawkeye, plastic **10.00**
Kodak No 3A Folding Pocket ..**40.00**
Kodak Retina I **50.00**
Kodak Retina IIa...................**90.00**
Kodak Retina IIIc **180.00**
Kodak 35 w/range finder, 1940-51............................**30.00**
Konica Autoreflex T4.........**125.00**
Konica III, Rangefinder, 1956-59 ....**80.00**
Leica I, several models, from $400 to.....................................**450.00**
Leica IID, 1932-38, from $250 to...............................**400.00**
Leica M3, 1954-66, from $600 to...............................**1,400.00**
Mamiyaflex 1, TLR, 1951, from $125 to **150.00**
Mercury, Model II, CX, 1945 .**35.00**
Minolta HiMatic Series, various models, from $15 to........**30.00**
Minolta SRT 101 ....**75.00**
Minolta XG-1........................**60.00**
Minolta 35, early models, Rangefinder, 1947-50, ea, from $300 to **500.00**
Minox B (Spy Camera) **125.00**
Nikon F, various finders & meters, ea, from $150 to............**275.00**
Nikon 2, 1954-58, from $300 to ..**500.00**
Olympus CM-2 ....**150.00**
Olympus Pen F, compact half-frame SLR, from $150 to **200.00**
Pax-M3, 1957 ....**40.00**

Nikon S Rangefinder, 1951 – 1954, from $450.00 to $950.00. (Photo courtesy C.E. Cataldo)

Pentax ME...........................**100.00**
Pentax Super Program **160.00**
Petri 7, 1961.........................**20.00**
Polaroid, most models, from $5 to................................**10.00**
Praktica Super TL, 1968-74 .**60.00**
Regula, King, various models, fixed lens **40.00**
Ricoh Diacord L, TLR, built-in meter, 1958 ....**75.00**
Rolleicord II, 1936-50, from $70 to **90.00**
Rolleiflex 3.5, 1960-81 ....**300.00**
Samoca 35, 1950s.................**25.00**
Tessina, miniature, chrome, from $400 to..........................**700.00**
Topcon Super D, 1963-74....**125.00**
Topcon Uni **50.00**
Tower 50 (Sears), w/Cassar lens **20.00**
Voigtlander Bessa, various folding models, 1931-49, ea, from $15 to.....................................**35.00**
Voigtlander Vitessa L, 1954 ..**175.00**
Yashica A, TLR **45.00**
Yashica FX-1, 1975 ....**50.00**
Zeiss-Ikon Box Tengor 43/2, 1934-38 ....**40.00**
Zeiss-Ikon Nettar, folding, various sizes, ea, from $20 to **35.00**
Zenit E, Russian...................**35.00**

Candlewick

Candlewick was one of the all-time bestselling lines of The Imperial Glass Company of Bellaire, Ohio. It was produced from 1936 until the company closed in 1982. More than 741 items were made over the years; and though many are still easy to find today, some (such as the desk calendar, the chip and dip set, and the dresser set) are a challenge to collect. Candlewick is easily identified by its beaded stems, handles, and rims characteristic of the tufted needlework of our pioneer women for which it was named. For a complete listing of the Candlewick line, we recommend *Elegant Glassware of the Depression Era* by Gene Florence (Collector Books).

Ashtray, #1776/1, eagle, 6½" .**55.00**

Basket, 6½", $275.00. (Photo courtesy Gene Florence)

Bell, #400/108, 5" **75.00**
Bowl, #400/10F, round, 9" **50.00**

Bowl, #400/232, sq, 6".........**135.00**
Bowl, #400/63B, belled, 10½"..**60.00**
Bowl, celery boat; #400/46, oval, 11"..................**65.00**
Bowl, fruit; #400/3F, 6".........**12.00**
Calender, desk; 1947 ....**235.00**
Candle holder, #400/207, 3-toed, 4½"....................**85.00**
Candy box, #400/59, 5½" dia..**45.00**
Compote, #400/63B, 4½".......**40.00**
Cup, coffee; #400/37 ....**7.50**
Knife, butter; #4000...........**350.00**
Mirror, standing, 4½" dia ...**135.00**
Oil, #400/274, bulbous bottom, 4-oz.....................**45.00**
Pitcher, #400/19, low footed, 16-oz...............**225.00**
Plate, #4001/24, oval, 12½" ..**85.00**
Plate, bread & butter; #400/1D, 6"......................**8.00**
Plate, luncheon; #400/7D, 9"...**13.50**
Plate, salad; #400/3D, 7".........**8.00**
Plate, torte; #400/17D, 14" ...**45.00**
Punch ladle, #400/91.............**30.00**
Salt & pepper shakers, #400/109, individual, pr...................**11.00**
Salt dip, #400/61, 2".............**10.00**
Stem, brandy; #3800.............**35.00**
Stem, cordial; #40/190, 1-oz..**70.00**
Stem, oyster cocktail; #3400, 4-oz.....................**15.00**
Stem, wine; #4000, 5-oz........**28.00**
Sugar bowl, #400/33, plain foot...**6.50**
Tray, #400/113E, handled, 14"..**45.00**
Tray, #400/29, 6½"...............**15.00**
Tumbler, juice; #400/18, 5-oz..**45.00**
Tumbler, tea; #400/19, 14-oz..**25.00**
Tumbler, water; #400/18, 9-oz..**45.00**
Tumbler, wine; #400/19, footed, 3-oz.....................**22.00**
Vase, #400/193, footed, 10"..**185.00**
Vase, #400/198, 6" dia.........**300.00**
Vase, bud; #400/187, footed, 7"..**215.00**

Candy Containers

If you're old enough to be the parents of a baby boomer, you'll remember the glass candy containers we used to buy at the 5-&-10¢ store filled with tiny, multicolored candies. Dogs, guns, lanterns, cars, ships, rabbits, horns, busses, trains, and lamps were common. But as each new design hit the store counters, we'd scurry to buy it up, and add the container to the rows and rows we already had at home. Today's collectors have a little more serious approach to their shopping — some of the rarer examples can carry four-figure price tags. For instance, Felix on the Pedestal with original black paint intact carries a value of $4,000.00! A Flossie Fisher Bed realized an auction price of over $5,000.00! But there are many that can still be bought for under $100.00, so don't let those extremely high prices discourage you.

For more information, we recommend *The Collector's Guide to Candy Containers* by Doug Dezso and Leon and Rose Poirier (Collector Books). References to plate numbers in the descriptions that follow correspond with this book. Our values are given for candy containers that are undamaged, in good original paint, and complete (with all parts and closure). See Clubs and Newsletters for information concerning *The Candy Gram*.

Airplane (P-38 Lightning), plate #82, from $200 to.........**250.00**

Apothecary jar, plate #113, 1940s, 5¼", from $120 to.........**125.00**

Baby Nurser, plate #121, 1939, 2½", from $35 to.............**50.00**

Bulldog, plate #17, oblong base, ca 1945, 3¾", from $40 to...**50.00**

Bus (New York/San Francisco), plate #154, 1938, 4⅛" L, from $500 to..........................**600.00**

Camel, plate #4, seated on sq base, clear or amber, 1970s, from $75 to....................**100.00**

Chicken on nest, plate #10, 4¼x2½", from $25 to......**35.00**

Fire ladder truck, plate #254, front/rear figures, 1930s, 5", $200 to.........................**275.00**

Flapper girl, plate #203, ca 1931, 10½", from $80 to.........**120.00**

Gun (Kolt), plate #393, 1923-30, from $100 to.................**200.00**

Helicopter, plate #91, 2-blade rotor, from $250 to.......**300.00**

Iron, plate #305, w/string cord & paper plug, 1940s, 4½".................................**60.00**

Lamp, plate #329, hobnail, cardboard shade, 1940s, 2¼", $250 to...................................**350.00**

Lamp, plate #335, metal shade/screw cap, 1970s, 3½", from $40 to.....................**60.00**

Lantern, plate #364, all glass w/screw cap, bail handle, 1950s, 3½".......................**25.00**

Liberty Bell, plate #96, ribbed, marked 2, 1940s, 2¼", from $33 to.............................**70.00**

Locomotive, plate #525, all glass w/rear screw cap, 5¼", $400 to.............**500.00**

Pencil (Baby Jumbo), plate #218, w/label, 5½" L, from $100 to.....................**135.00**

Santa's boot, plate #273, paper insert, 1940s-50s, 3¼", from $20 to.............................**40.00**

Sign (Don't Park Here), plate 423, 1920s, 4½", from $250 to.**300.00**

Snowman, plate #289, styrofoam head, 1960s, 4½", from $15 to..........................**20.00**

Tank, plate #412, man in turret, 1940s, 4½", from $50 to ..**60.00**

Telephone (Tot), plate #234, 1940s, 2½", from $30 to.............**40.00**

Turkey Gobbler, plate #75, stippled feathers, ca 1924, 3½", from $175.00 to $225.00. (Photo courtesy Doug Dezso and Leon and Rose Poirier)

Windmill (Dutch), plate #534, 1940s, 4¾", w/blade from $90 to..................................**100.00**

Cape Cod by Avon

Though now discontinued, the Avon company sold this dark ruby red glassware through their catalogs since the 1970s, and there seems to be a good supply of it around today. In addition to the place settings (there are plates in three sizes, soup and dessert bowls, a cup and saucer, tumblers in two sizes, three different goblets, a mug, and a wine glass), there are many lovely accessory items as well. Among them you'll find a cake plate, a pitcher, a platter, a hurricane-type candle lamp, a butter dish, napkin rings, and a pie plate server. Note: Mint-in-box items are worth about 20% more than the same piece with no box.

Our advisors for this category, Debbie and Randy Coe, are listed in the Directory under Oregon.

Bell, hostess; marked Christmas, 1979, 6½"........................**22.50**
Bell, hostess; unmarked, 1979-80, 6½"...............................**17.50**
Bowl, dessert; 1978-90, 5" **14.50**
Bowl, rim soup; 1991, 7½"....**20.00**
Bowl, vegetable; marked Centennial Edition, 1886-1986, 8¾" **38.00**
Bowl, vegetable; unmarked, 1986-90, 8¾"...........................**24.50**
Box, heart form, w/lid, 1989-90, 4" wide **18.00**
Butter dish w/lid, 1983-84, ¼-lb, 7" long............................**22.50**
Cake knife, red plastic handle, Regent Sheffield, 1981-84, 8"....................................**18.00**
Candle holder, hurricane-type w/clear chimney, 1985, 13".**38.00**
Candlestick, 1975-80, 8¾", ea.**12.50**
Candlestick, 1983-84, 2½", ea ..**9.75**
Candy dish, 1987-90, 3½x6" dia..**19.50**

Christmas ornament, 6-sided, marked Christmas, 1990, 3¼" **10.00**
Creamer, footed, 1981-84, 4"..**12.50**
Cruet, oil; w/stopper, 1975-80, 5-oz.................................**12.50**
Cup & saucer, 15th anniversary, marked 1975-1990 on cup, 7-oz.................................**24.50**
Cup & saucer, 1990-93, 7-oz..**19.50**
Decanter, w/stopper, 1977-80, 16-oz, 10½" **20.00**
Goblet, champagne; 1991, 8-oz, 5¼" **12.50**
Goblet, claret; 1992, 5-oz, 5¼" .**9.50**

Goblet, water; 1976 – 1990, from $9.00 to $12.00.

Goblet, wine; 1977-80, 3-oz, 4½" **2.50**
Mug, pedestal foot, 1982-84, 6-oz, 5"....................................**12.50**
Napkin ring, 1989-90, 1¾" dia..**9.50**
Pie plate, 1992-93, 10¾" dia ..**24.50**
Pitcher, water; footed, 1984-85, 60-oz **50.00**
Plate, bread & butter; 1992-93, 5½" **7.50**
Plate, cake; pedestal foot, 1991, 3½x10¾" dia..................**50.00**
Plate, dessert; 1980-90, 7½" ...**9.50**

Plate, dinner; 1982-90, 11"...**22.50**
Platter, oval, 1986, 13".........**38.00**
Relish, rectangular, 2-part, 1985-
86, 9½"............................**19.50**

Salt and pepper shakers, marked May 1978, MIB, from $18.00 to $22.00 for the pair.

Salt & pepper shakers, 1978-80,
unmarked, pr.................**10.00**
Sauce boat, footed, 1988, 8"
long...........................**25.00**
Sugar bowl, footed, 1980-83.**12.50**
Tidbit tray, 2-tiered, (7x10" dia),
1987, 9¾"......................**49.50**
Tumbler, straight-sided, footed,
1988, 8-oz, 3⅗"................**9.50**
Tumbler, straight-sided, 1990, 12-
oz, 5½"........................**12.50**
Vase, footed, 1985, 8"...........**20.00**

Carnival Chalkware

Chalkware statues of Kewpies, glamour girls, assorted dogs, horses, etc., were given to winners of carnival games from about 1910 until the 1950s. Today's collectors especially value those representing well-known personalities such as Disney characters and comic book heroes. Refer to *The Carnival Chalk Prize* by Tom Morris for more information. Mr. Morris is in the Directory under Oregon.

Air Raid Warden, holding US flag,
1940s, 14"......................**95.00**
Bathing Beauty, ca 1940, 9x7".**65.00**
Boy & Dog, marked Pals, ca 1935-
45, 10x9"......................**45.00**
Cowgirl, marked Rainwater, ca
1936, 10¾"....................**80.00**
Devil Kewpie, ca 1925-40, 6½"..**80.00**
Donald Duck, head bank, Disney,
ca 1940-50, 10½"............**80.00**
Fan Dancer, ashtray, ca 1940,
10½"............................**95.00**
Girl w/Sombrero, ca 1930, 14"..**85.00**
Indian w/Drum, marked KC Art
Statuary, ca 1940-50, 13"..**60.00**
Little Mail Boy, ca 1935-45, 7"..**30.00**
Nude Child, kneeling w/arms
crossed, ca 1920-30, 6"...**40.00**
Nude w/Feather, ca 1930-40,
12"............................**125.00**
Penguin w/Top Hat, glass eyes, ca
1935-45, 7¼"..................**50.00**
Pirate Girl, marked Rainwater, ca
1936, 10¾"....................**95.00**
Pluto sitting, ca 1930-40, 6".**65.00**

Sailor Boy, Remember Pearl Harbor, JY Jenkins, 1942, $175.00. (Photo courtesy Tom Morris)

Scottish Lass, ca 1940-50, 15"....**70.00**

Sweater Girl, ca 1930-40, 11½"..**40.00**

Uncle Scrooge, standing w/money
bag, ca 1940-50, 8".........**50.00**

US Air Force Pilot, picture frame,
1940s, 7¼x5½"..............**55.00**

US Sailor, w/arms folded, ca 1935-
45, 13".............................**95.00**

Cat Collectibles

Cat lovers are often quite fervent in their attachment to their pets, and for many their passion extends into the collecting field. There is no shortage of items to entice them to buy, be they figural pieces, advertising signs, postcards, textiles, books, candy containers, or what have you. Marbena Fyke has written two amusing and informative books called *Collectible Cats, Identification and Value Guide, Volume I* and *Volume II.* If you're a cat lover yourself, you're sure to enjoy them.

See also Black Cats; Character Collectibles; Garfield; Kliban; Clubs and Newsletters.

Ashtray, lustreware, black & white kitten on dish, 6 rests, Japan.............................**25.00**

Bank, chalkware, cat standing w/pipe in mouth, 10"......**95.00**

Bottle, perfume; blue metal w/embossed white kitten, China.............................**60.00**

Box, porcelain, kitten on pillow, metal hinge, Limoges, 3" L.........................**185.00**

Dish, pottery, gold w/brown flowers, CA USA, 7¼x6¼"....**15.00**

Doorstop, pink metal w/red hearts & blue bow, American Folk Art, 11".............................**8.00**

Figurine, brass cat on 7" sq marble base, 11"..................**150.00**

Figurine, ceramic, orange striped tabby w/closed eyes, 16"..**80.00**

Figurine, ceramic, turquoise long-haired cats, China, 6½", pr......................................**38.00**

Figurine, pewter cat playing fiddle, 1½".........................**25.00**

Figurine, Red Persian Tabby, Shafford (Japan), 1967, 10" long, $45.00. (Photo courtesy Marilyn Dipboye)

Matchbox holder, metal w/cat on top, 2¼x1½x3"................**50.00**

Mirror, Smoke Black Cat Cigarettes, 9x15", NM........**175.00**

Paperweight, aluminum, 2 cats curled together, Arthur Court, 1992, 3"..............**35.00**

Plaque, black cats w/colorful row of houses, pink ground, 12x5½"...........................**6.00**

Ring holder, brass stylized cat, 6" tail...............................**5.00**

Salt & pepper shakers, Sad Eye Cat, hugs trash can, 1960s, 4¾", pr...........................**35.00**

Sugar bowl & creamer, yellow tabby cats, Norcrest, 1980s, 4½", pr..........................**12.00**

Suncatcher, Cheshire Cat, Wonderland Miniature Series, Glassmasters...................**35.00**

Thermometer, white hammered aluminum cat on base, 5¼"....**40.00**

Tray, long-haired white cat w/blue eyes on black w/gold outlines, 18"...................................**45.00**

Cat-Tail Dinnerware

Cat-Tail was a dinnerware pattern popular during the late 1920s until sometime in the 1940s. So popular, in fact, that ovenware, glassware, tinware, and even a kitchen table was made to coordinate with it. The dinnerware was made primarily by Universal Potteries of Cambridge, Ohio, though a catalog from Hall China Co. circa 1927 shows a three-piece coffee service, and there may have been other pieces made by Hall as well. Cat-Tail was sold for years by Sears Roebuck and Company, and some items bear a mark with their name.

The pattern is unmistakable — a cluster of red cattails (usually six but sometimes only one or two) with black stems on creamy white. Shapes certainly vary; Universal used a minimum of three of their standard mold designs — Camwood, Old Holland, Laurella — and there were possibly others. Some Cattails say 'Wheelock' on the bottom. Wheelock was a department store in Peoria, Illinois.

If you are trying to decorate a '40s vintage kitchen, no other design could afford you more to work with. To see many of the pieces that are available and to learn more about the line, read *The Collector's Encyclopedia of American Dinnerware* by Jo Cunningham (Collector Books).

Our advisors for Cattail Dinnerware are Ken and Barbara Brooks, who are listed in the Directory under North Carolina.

Batter jug, w/metal lid, from $80 to...................................**100.00**

Bowl, mixing; 9", from $28 to ..**30.00**

Bowl, Old Holland shape, marked Wheelock, 6"......................**7.00**

Butter dish, w/lid, 1-lb..........**50.00**

Cake cover & tray, tinware ..**35.00**

Canister set, tinware, 4-pc, from $45 to **60.00**

Casserole, w/lid **30.00**

Coffeepot, 3-pc......................**70.00**

Cookie jar, from $85 to **100.00**

Cracker jar, barrel shape, from $75 to **85.00**

Creamer, from $20 to............**25.00**

Cup and saucer, $10.00.

Custard cup **8.00**

Gravy boat, w/liner, from $35 to...............................**45.00**

Jug, refrigerator; w/handle...**35.00**

Jug, side handle, cork stopper..**35.00**
Kitchen scales, tinware.........**40.00**
Match holder, tinware **35.00**
Pie plate.................................**30.00**
Pie server, hole in handle for hanging, marked Universal Potteries **25.00**
Pitcher, glass, w/ice lip, from $100 to....................................**125.00**
Pitcher, utility or milk..........**30.00**
Pitcher, w/ice lip, from $75 to..**80.00**
Plate, dinner; Laurella shape, from $15 to **20.00**
Plate, dinner; 3-compartment..**30.00**
Plate, salad or dessert; round...**6.50**
Plate, serving; early, marked Universal Potteries-Oven Proof...**40.00**
Platter, oval...........................**30.00**
Salad set (fork, spoon & bowl), from $50 to **60.00**
Salt & pepper shakers, different styles, ea, pr, from $15 to..**20.00**
Saucer, Old Holland shape, marked Wheelock **6.00**
Shaker set (salt/pepper/flour/ sugar), glass, on red metal tray, $40 to **45.00**
Stack set, 3-pc, w/lids, from $35 to **40.00**
Sugar bowl, w/lid, from $20 to ..**25.00**
Tablecloth..............................**90.00**
Teapot, w/lid, from $40 to.....**50.00**
Tumbler, iced tea; glass, from $35 to.................................**40.00**
Tumbler, marked Universal Potteries, scarce, from $65 to ...**70.00**
Tumbler, water; glass **35.00**
Waste can, step-on, tinware .**35.00**

Ceramic Arts Studio

Whether you're a collector of American pottery or not, chances are you'll like the distinctive styling of the figurines, salt and pepper shakers, and other novelty items made by the Ceramic Arts Studio of Madison, Wisconsin, from about 1938 until approximately 1952. They're not especially hard to find — a trip to any good flea market will usually produce at least one good buy from among their vast array of products. They're easily spotted, once you've seen a few examples; but if you're not sure, check for the trademark — most are marked.

Our advisors for this category are BA Wellman and John Canfield; they are listed in the Directory under Massachusetts. The CAS Collector's Association is listed under Clubs and Newsletters in the back of this book. They not only publish a quarterly newsletter but a comprehensive value guide as well.

Accessory, garden shelf, metal, for Mary Contrary, 4x12"....**95.00**
Accessory, sofa, metal, for Maurice & Michelle, from $60 to..**80.00**
Accessory, spider web, corner; metal, for Miss Muffet, 4"............**95.00**
Ashtray, hippo, 3½" **165.00**

Figurine, Archibald the Dragon, 8", minimum value $275.00.

Figurine, Adonis, 9" **275.00**
Figurine, angel w/star, standing, 5½" **80.00**
Figurine, Autumn Andy, 5", from $85 to **95.00**
Figurine, Bashful Girl, 4½" ..**90.00**
Figurine, Billie, boxer (dog), sprawling, 2" L...............**95.00**
Figurine, bunny, 1¾" **50.00**
Figurine, cellist man, 6½" ..**295.00**
Figurine, collie pup sleeping, 2¼" **45.00**
Figurine, cow, snuggle, 5½".**120.00**
Figurine, Egyptian woman, 9½" **325.00**
Figurine, fawn, 4¼" **50.00**
Figurine, Frisky the Colt, 3¾" ..**125.00**
Figurine, horse, mother, 4¼" **125.00**
Figurine, Katrinka, chubby, 6¼" **95.00**
Figurine, kitten washing, 2" ..**45.00**
Figurine, lion & lioness, 5" L, pr **450.00**

Figurines, Lucindy and Colonel Jackson, $125.00 for the pair.

Figurine, Lu-Tang (man), 6" ..**60.00**
Figurine, Mr Monkey, scratching, 4" **95.00**
Figurine, Palomino colt, 5¾" ..**150.00**

Figurine, Pepita, Pan-American, 4½" **45.00**
Figurine, Pied Piper, early & rare, 6¼" **195.00**
Figurine, Polish boy & girl, 6½", 6½", pr **120.00**
Figurine, Rebekah, 10" **165.00**
Figurine, Rhumba woman, 7" ..**85.00**
Figurine, saxophone boy, 5" .**75.00**
Figurine, shepherd & sherpherdess, 8½", pr **275.00**
Figurine, Spaniel pup, 2"......**50.00**
Figurine, Tembino the baby elephant, 2½" **150.00**
Figurine, tortoise w/cane, standing, 2¼"...........................**95.00**
Figurine, Wendy, 5¼" **95.00**
Head vase, Becky, 5¼"........**165.00**

Head vase, Bonnie, 7", $175.00.

Jug, rose; 3" **45.00**
Lamp, Bali-Lao **400.00**
Mug, Barber Shop Quartet, 3½" **150.00**
Plaque, Arabesque, 9¼".......**70.00**
Plaque, cockatoos, A & B, 7½", pr **165.00**
Plaque, Comedy & Tragedy masks, 5", pr **165.00**
Plaque, Lotus lantern woman, 8" **95.00**

Salt & pepper shakers, bear &
cub, brown, snuggle type, pr,
$65 to **90.00**
Salt & pepper shakers, cocks
fighting, pr, from $70 to **80.00**
Salt & pepper shakers, fish on
tail, pr **75.00**
Salt & pepper shakers, frog & toad-
stool, pr, from $75 to..........**95.00**
Salt & pepper shakers, mouse &
cheese, snuggle, 2", 3", pr..**65.00**
Salt & pepper shakers, Peek &
Boo, Siamese cats, snuggle,
pr **185.00**
Salt & pepper shakers, sea horse &
seaweed, snuggle, 3½", pr.**185.00**
Salt & pepper shakers, Wee Chinese
girl & boy, 3", pr....................**35.00**
Salt & pepper shakers, Wee Scot-
tish boy & girl, pr...........**80.00**
Shelf sitter, Balinese boy & girl,
5½", pr **295.00**
Shelf sitter, canary, 5" **65.00**
Shelf sitter, Dutch boy & girl,
4½", pr **65.00**
Shelf sitter, farm girl & boy fish-
ing w/pole & fish, pr.....**195.00**
Shelf sitter, Mexican girl & boy,
pr **195.00**
Shelf sitter, Pete & Polly parrot,
7½", pr **195.00**
Teapot, grapes, 2" **75.00**

Cereal Boxes and Premiums

When buying real estate, they
say 'location, location, location.'
When cereal box collecting its
'character, character, character.'
Look for Batman, Quisp, Superman, or Ninja Turtles — the so-
called 'Grain Gods' emblazoned
across the box. Dull adult and
health cereals such as Special K or
Shredded Wheat, unless they have
an exciting offer, aren't worth picking up (too boring). Stick to the
cavity-blasting presweets aimed at
kids, like The Jetsons, Froot Loops,
or Trix. You can hunt down the
moldy FrostyOs and Quake from
childhood in old stores and
pantries or collect the new stuff at
your supermarket. Your local cereal aisle — the grain ghetto — is
chock full of future blue chips, so
squeeze the moment! The big ques-
tion is: once you've gotten your
flaky treasures home, how do you
save the box? If you live where
pests (bugs or mice) aren't a prob-
lem, display or store the box
unopened. Otherwise, eat its con-
tents, then pull out the bottom
flaps and flatten the package along
the fold lines. If you don't want to
flatten the box, empty it by gently
pulling out the bottom flaps and
removing the bag. Be sure to save
the prize inside, called an inpack,
if it has one; they're valuable too —
often more so than the box! For
further information we recommend
*Cerealizing America, The Unsweet-
ened Story of American Breakfast
Cereal,* by Scott Bruce and Bill
Crawford; and *Cereal Box Bonanza*
and *Cereal Boxes & Prizes: 1960s,*
also by Bruce.

Boxes

All Stars, Huckleberry Hound cartoon cutouts, 1960, EX..**125.00**

Apple Jacks, glow-in-the-dark
  stickers, 1971, NM........**85.00**

Cheerios, General Mills, 1958, Annette
doll and outfits on back, EX, $300.00.
(Photo courtesy Scott Bruce)

Post Alpha-Bits, 1963, features
Jack E. Leonard Postman, Cowboys and Indians set for two box-
tops, NM, $175.00. (Photo courtesy
Scott Bruce)

Cheerios, Wyatt Earp initial ring
  offer, 1958, EX **125.00**
Cocoa Krispies, Jose the Monkey
  on front, 1958, EX........**150.00**
Cocoa Puffs, Train Station offer,
  1961, 9½", EX...............**250.00**
Corn Flakes, Yogi Bear Birthday
  Dell Comic, 1962, EX...**300.00**
Cornfetti, Captain Jolly comic
  book, 1954, EX **150.00**
Frosted Flakes, Superman Stero-
  Pix, 1954, EX................**300.00**
Fruity Pebbles, Flintmobile, 1972,
  NM...............................**100.00**
Grape-Nut Flakes, Bugs Bunny
  mask, 1961, NM...........**150.00**
Kix, New Ideas from Ding Dong
  School, 1953, EX **50.00**
OKs, Play the Big Otis Catapult
  Game, 1959, EX **100.00**
Post Alpha Bits, monkey & camel
  cutouts, 1958, EX...........**35.00**

Post Toasties, Li'l Abner cutout,
  1958, VG......................**100.00**
Quaker Puffed Rice, Gabby Hayes
  Shooting Cannon Ring offer,
  1951, EX **350.00**
Quaker Puffed Wheat, Gabby
  Hayes Western Wagons offer,
  1952, EX **200.00**
Raisin Bran, California Raisin fig-
  ure offer, 1988, EX.........**15.00**
Raisin Bran, Disney Joinies, 1950,
  EX **150.00**
Rice Honeys, Rin-Tin-Tin & Rusty
  w/Barrels of Fun Free!, 1956,
  EX **100.00**
Rice Krispies, Howdy Doody doll
  offer, 1953, EX **300.00**
Rice Krispies, Woody Woodpecker
  Swimmer, 1967, NM....**127.00**
Shredded   Wheat   Juniors,
  Spoonman premium inside,
  EX................................**150.00**

Sugar Pops, Wild Bill Hickok's Famous Gun Series, 1952, EX................................**150.00**

Sugar Rice Krinkles, Ford Thunderbird inside, EX.................**100.00**

Sugar Smacks, Smaxey the Seal cutouts, 1959, EX.........**100.00**

Trix, Tonto belt offer, 1955, EX **350.00**

Wheat Honeys, Bert the Chimney Sweep pop-up toy, 1964, EX................................**150.00**

Wheaties, Disneyland Park Light-Ups, 1956, EX, $100 to **200.00**

Wheaties, Paul Bunyon mask, 1940s, EX **35.00**

Quake, friendship ring, 1966, blue plastic, EX, $300.00. (Photo courtesy Scott Bruce)

Premiums

Buffalo Bee or Jolly Clown bowl riders, plastic, 1961, 2", NM, ea **10.00**

Cap'n Crunch hand puppets, Cap'n, Dave, or Sea Dog, vinyl, 9", M, ea **35.00**

Cap'n Crunch wiggle figures, 3 different, 1969, EX, ea...**50.00**

Cocoa Puffs train, 1959-61, 12", NM................................**100.00**

Count Chocula or Frankenberry mask, plastic, 1970s, NM, ea...................................**35.00**

Frankenberry secret compartment ring, NM.......................**275.00**

Kellogg's Prize Catalog, 1951, EX **50.00**

Magic Pup w/ring, Wheat Chex, 1951, NM......................**100.00**

Post Junior Detective Corps Manual, NM...........................**50.00**

Post's Ford 2-door hardtop, metallic blue, F&F Mold, M..**125.00**

Quangaroo free-wheeler, 1964, EX.................................**50.00**

Quisp bank, ceramic figure on base, 1960s, NM...........**100.00**

Sherman & Peabody wiggly picture, 1960, 1", EX...........**10.00**

Smaxey the Seal pin-back button, 1957, 1" dia, EX **10.00**

Snap! Crackle! & Pop hand puppets, cloth & vinyl, 1950, EX, ea **75.00**

Sweetheart of the Corn doll, vinyl w/cloth outfit, Kellogg's, 1953, NM.................................**10.00**

Tony the Tiger glow-in-the-dark iron-on patch, 1974, MIP.**12.00**

Toucan Sam bicycle license plate, blue plastic, 1973, 3x6", EX......................**10.00**

Toucan Sam doll, stuffed cloth, 1964, 8", EX....................**30.00**

Twinkles the Elephant bank, red, 1960, 9", EX.................**375.00**

Woody the Woodpecker swimmer, 1967, 7", NM **100.00**

Character and Promotional Glassware

Once routinely given away by fast-food restaurants and soft-drink companies, these glasses have become very collectible; and though they're being snapped up by avid collectors everywhere, you'll still find there are bargains to be had. The more expensive are those with Disney or Walter Lantz cartoon characters, super-heroes, sports greats, or personalities from Star Trek or the old movies. For more information refer to *Collectible Drinking Glasses* by Mark E. Chase and Michael J. Kelley (Collector Books) and *The Collector's Guide to Cartoon and Promotional Drinking Glasses* by John Hervey (L-W Book Sales). See Clubs and Newsletters for information on *Collector Glass News*.

Al Capp's Dog Patch, 1975, flat, 6 different, ea from $50 to..**80.00**

Al Capp's Dog Patch, 1975, footed, 6 different, ea from $40 to **90.00**

Apollo Series, Marathon Oil, Apollo 11-14, ea from $2 to............**4.00**

Apollo Series, Marathon Oil, carafe, from $6 to **10.00**

Arby's Actor Series, 1979, 6 different, smoked glass, ea from $5 to **7.00**

Arby's Bicentennial Cartoon, 1976, 10 different, 5", ea from $18 to..............................**25.00**

Arby's Bicentennial Cartoon, 1976, 10 different, 6", ea from $20 to..............................**30.00**

Armour Peanut Butter, Transportation Series, 1950s, 8 different, ea **4.00**

Battlestar Galactica, Universal, 1979, 4 different, ea from $7 to ...**10.00**

BC Ice Age, Arby's, 1981, 6 different, ea from $3 to **5.00**

Burger Chef, Friendly Monsters, 1977, 6 different, ea from $20 to **35.00**

Burger King, Dallas Cowboys, Dr Pepper, 6 different, ea from $7 to **15.00**

Burger King, Have It Your Way 1776-1976 Series, 4 different, ea from $4 to **6.00**

Cinderella, Disney/Libby, 1950s-60s, set of 8...................**120.00**

Currier & Ives, Arby's 1975-76, 4 different, ea from $3 to **5.00**

Disney, 1990, 6 different face images on frosted glass, ea from $5 to **8.00**

Domino's Pizza, Avoid the Noid, 1988, 4 different, ea **7.00**

Elsie the Cow, Borden, 1960, yellow daisy image, from $10 to **12.00**

ET, Pizza Hut, 1982, footed, 4 different, ea from $2 to.........**4.00**

Flintstone Kids, Pizza Hut, 1986, Betty, from $2.00 to $4.00.

Flintstones, Pizza Hut, 1986, 4 different, ea from $2 to **4.00**

Flintstones, Welch's, 1962, 1963, 1964, 14 different, ea from $8 to **12.00**

Goonies, Godfather's Pizza/ Warner Bros, 1985, 4 different, ea from $4 to **8.00**

Great Muppet Caper, McDonald's, 1981, 4 different, 6", ea....**2.00**

Happy Days, Dr Pepper, 1977, 5 different, ea from $8 to ..**12.00**

Happy Days, Dr Pepper/Pizza Hut, 1977, Fonz or Richie, ea from $10 to **15.00**

Happy Days, Dr Pepper/Pizza Hut, 1977, Joanie, Potsie, Ralph, ea from $8 to **12.00**

Harvey Cartoons, Pepsi, 1970s, action pose, 4 different, ea from $8 to **15.00**

Harvey Cartoons, Pepsi, 1970s, static pose, 5 different, ea from $12 to **25.00**

James Bond 007, 1985, 4 different, ea from $10 to **15.00**

Jungle Book, Disney/Pepsi, 1970s, Bagheera or Shere Kahn, ea from $60 to **90.00**

Jungle Book, Disney/Pepsi, 1970s, Mowgli, from $40 to **50.00**

Jungle Book, Disney/Pepsi, 1970s, Rama, from $50 to **60.00**

Keebler Soft Batch Cookies, 1984, 4 different, ea from $7 to....**10.00**

King Kong, Coca-Cola/Dino De Laurentis Corp, 1976, from $5 to.**8.00**

Mark Twain Country Series, Burger King, 1985, 4 different, ea from $8 to **10.00**

Masters of the Universe, Mattel, 1986, 7 different, ea from $3 to **10.00**

McDonald's, McDonaldland Action Series, 1977, 6 different, ea.**5.00**

McDonald's, McDonaldland Collector Series, 1970s, 6 different, ea.**4.00**

McDonald's, McVote, 1986, 3 different, ea from $4 to........**6.00**

Mickey's Christmas Carol, Coca-Cola, 1983, 3 different, ea..**10.00**

Night Before Christmas, Pepsi, 1982-83, 4 different, ea from $4 to **6.00**

Norman Rockwell, Summer Series, Arby's, 1987, 4 different, tall, ea **4.00**

Norman Rockwell, Winter Series, Arby's/Pepsi, 1979, 4 different, ea **4.00**

PAT Ward, Pepsi, Rocky & Bullwinkle Series, 1970s, any from $8 to **30.00**

Peanuts, Camp Snoopy, McDonald's, 1983, white plastic, any, from ea $5 to **8.00**

Peanuts, Kraft, 1988, 4 different, ea **2.00**

Popeye's Pals, Popeye's Chicken, 1979, 4 different, ea from $10 to **20.00**

Return of the Jedi, Burger King/Coca-Cola, 1983, 4 different, ea from $6 to........**8.00**

Rufus, Brockway/Pepsi, 1977, NM, $25.00.

Ringling Bros Circus Clowns, Pepsi, 1980s, 8 different, ea **12.00**

Smurf's, Hardee's, 1982 (8 different), 1983 (6 different), ea from $1 to **3.00**

Star Trek, Dr Pepper, 1976, 4 different, ea from $20 to **25.00**

Star Wars Trilogy: Empire Strikes Back, Burger King/Coca-Cola, 1980, Luke Skywalker, from $7.00 to $10.00.

Super Heroes, Moon Series, Pepsi/DC Comics, 1976, any, from $10 to **50.00**

Superman, NPP/M Polanar & Son, 1964, 6 different, ea from $20 to **35.00**

Universal Monsters, Universal, 1980, footed, 6 different, ea from $100 to **160.00**

Walter Lantz, Pepsi, 1970s, Chilly Willy or Wally Walrus, ea from $35 to **55.00**

Walter Lantz, Pepsi, 1970s, Cuddles, from $60 to.............**80.00**

Walter Lantz, Pepsi, 1970s, Space Mouse, from $150 to **250.00**

Walter Lantz, Pepsi, 1970s, Woody Woodpecker, from $10 to..**20.00**

Warner Bros, Arby's Adventure Series, 1988, 4 different, ea from $35 to **45.00**

Warner Bros, Collector's Series, 1979, 6 different, ea from $7 to **10.00**

Warner Bros, Pepsi, 1973, 12-oz, 6 different, ea from $10 to..**15.00**

Warner Bros, Welch's, 1974, 8 different w/phrases, ea from $2 to **4.00**

Warner Bros, Welch's, 1976-77, 8 different w/names, ea from $5 to **7.00**

Wild West Series, Coca-Cola, Buffalo Bill or Calamity Jane, ea from $10 to **15.00**

Ziggy, 7-Up Collector Series, 4 different, ea from $4 to.........**7.00**

Character Collectibles

One of the most active areas of collecting today is the field of character collectibles. Flea markets usually yield some of the more common items — toys, books, lunch boxes, children's dishes, and sheet music are for the most part quite readily found. Trade papers are also an excellent source. Often you will find even the rare and hard-to-find listed for sale. Disney characters, television personalities, and comic book heroes are among the most sought after.

For more information, refer to *Schroeder's Collectible Toys, Antique to Modern*; *Cartoon Toys & Collectibles* by David Longest; *Collector's Guide to TV Toys & Memorabilia, 2nd Edition,* by Greg Davis and Bill Morgan; *G-Men and FBI Toys and Col-*

lectibles by Harry and Jody Whitworth; *Howdy Doody, Collector's Reference and Trivia Guide,* by Jack Koch; and *Cartoon Friends of the Baby Boom Era* by Bill Bruegman (see the Directory under Ohio). Books on Disney include *Character Toys and Collectibles, First* and *Second Series,* and *Antique and Collectible Toys, 1869 – 1950,* by David Longest; *Stern's Guide to Disney Collectibles* by Michael Stern (there are three in the series); and *The Collector's Encyclopedia of Disneyana* by Michael Stern and David Longest. With the exception of the Bruegman book, all are published by Collector Books.

See also Advertising; Banks; Bubble Bath Containers; California Raisins; Cereal Boxes and Premiums; Character and Promotional Glassware; Children's Books; Cookie Jars; Fast Food Collectibles; Games; Garfield; Kliban; Lunch Boxes; Novelty Telephones; Peanuts; Puzzles; Radios; Star Wars; Western Heroes.

Addams Family, hand puppet, Gomez, cloth & vinyl, Ideal, 1964, EX.........................**75.00**

Aladdin, doll, Jasmine or Prince Ali, Mattel, 1992, 8", MIB, ea..................................**25.00**

Aladdin, pin, Genie holding lamp, cloisonne, 1993, M.........**10.00**

Alice in Wonderland, figurine, ceramic, Japan, 1970s, 6", M................................**30.00**

Alice in Wonderland, paint set, Hasbro, 1969, M (sealed).........**50.00**

Alvin & the Chipmunks, dolls, any, Knickerbocker, 1964, 14", NM, ea.......................**5.00**

Alvin & the Chipmunks, harmonica, Plastic Inject Corp, 1959, 4", MOC..........................**85.00**

Astro Boy, slide-tile puzzle, Roalex, 1960s, MIB, $100 to..............................**125.00**

Atom Ant, magic slate, Watkins/Strathmore, 1967, NM................................**45.00**

Babes in Toyland, doll, Soldier, Gundkins, 1961, 9½", scarce, NM................................**40.00**

Baby Huey, bop bag, inflatable vinyl, Doughboy, 1966, 54", EX...............................**65.00**

Bambi, pencil sharpener, Bakelite, Plastic Novelties, 1¾", EX.......................................**85.00**

Banana Splits, figures, painted soft rubber, Hasbro, 1969, 4", MOC, ea.........................**25.00**

Banana Splits, Stich-A-Story set, Hasbro, 1969, unused, MIB............................**50.00**

Batman, banner, Batman Vs the Riddler, cloth, 1966, 27", EX.....................**100.00**

Batman, bowl, Joker image on white, Melmac, 1966, 5", EX...............................**15.00**

Batman, charm bracelet, w/6 brass charms, 1966, EX (EX card)............................**75.00**

Batman, Colorforms, 1966, complete, NMIB...................**55.00**

Batman, figure, Batman, rubber, Fun Things/NPPI, 1966, 5", NMOC.......................**125.00**

Batman, figure, Robin, rubber, Fun Things/NPPI, 1966, 5", NMOC 85.00

Batman, flashlight, plastic figure, Nasta, 1981, 4", MOC 15.00

Batman, Joker make-up kit, 1989, MIP 15.00

Batman, lamp, plastic, Vanity Fair Industries, 7½" wide with expandable arm for light, EX, $135.00.

Batman, marker pens, Batman or Robin, 1980, MIP, ea 15.00

Batman, pencil case, Batman & Robin, vinyl w/zippered pouch, 1977, EX 15.00

Batman, push-button puppet, Kohner, 1960s, NM......100.00

Batman, slide-tile puzzle, American Publishing, 1977, MOC ...25.00

Batman, wristwatch, swinging from rope, leather band, Dabbs, 1977, MIB 200.00

Batman, yo-yo, flasher seal, Duncan, early 1980s, MIP................30.00

Battlestar Galactica, ring, Lieutenant Starbuck photo, MIB 75.00

Beany & Cecil, Beany Copter hat, plastic, Mattel, 1962, EX..65.00

Beany & Cecil, carrying case, red vinyl, 1961, 9" dia, VG...50.00

Beany & Cecil, doll, Cecil, talker, Mattel, 1961, 18", EX.....80.00

Beany & Cecil, Soap on a Rope, Roclar, 1961, unused, MIB............50.00

Beauty & the Beast, doll, Beast, plush w/clothes, Mattel, 1993, NMIB.............................30.00

Beetle Bailey, magic slate, Lowe, 1963, M...........................35.00

Beetle Bailey, magic slate, Lowe, 1963, EX........................27.50

Ben Casey, doctor kit, Transogram, 1960s, EX.............35.00

Betty Boop, Colorforms Big Dress-Up Set, 1970s, MIB, $35 to...........................45.00

Beverly Hillbillies, Colorforms Cartoon Kit, 1963, MIB.75.00

Bionic Woman, Action Club Kit, Kenner, 1975, M 65.00

Bionic Woman, tattoos & stickers, Kenner, 1976, MIP.........20.00

Bionic Woman, wristwatch, vinyl band, MZ Berger, 1970s, NM, $60 to 80.00

Blondie & Dagwood, crayons, 1952, EXIB 30.00

Bozo the Clown, bank, plastic, 1972, NM........................35.00

Bozo the Clown, decal Decorator Kit, Meyercord, 1950s, unused, EXIB 40.00

Bozo the Clown, figure, bendable, Jesco, 1988, 6", MIP.........6.00

Bozo the Clown, Stitch-a-Story, Hasbro, 1967, MIB.........50.00

Brady Bunch, Brain Twisters, Larami, 1973, MOC 25.00

Brady Bunch, Fan Club Kit, Tiger Beat, 1972, MIB, $150 to..200.00

Brady Bunch, magic slate, Whitman, 1973, unused, NM, $50 to 75.00

Buck Rogers, Colorforms Adventure Set, 1979, MIB.........30.00

Buck Rogers, Official Utility Belt, plastic, Remco, 1979, NMIB 55.00

Bugs Bunny, doll, stuffed, Mighty Star, 18", NM 15.00

Bugs Bunny, jack-in-the-box, Mattel, 1970s, VG.................15.00

Bugs Bunny, lamp, in chair, name on base, Holiday Fair, 1970, 11", M 55.00

Bugs Bunny, sleeping bag, image of Bugs & friends, 1977, EX.....................25.00

Bugs Bunny, vase, ceramic, Bugs leaning against tree, 1940s, 7", NM+ 60.00

Bugs Bunny, wall clock, black, electric, Seth Thomas, 1970, 10", NM 85.00

Buster Brown, pocketwatch, 1960s, VG 75.00

California Raisins, baseball cap, 1988, EX 5.00

California Raisins, beach towel, CALRAB, M 50.00

California Raisins, picture album, 1988, EX 25.00

California Raisins, puzzle, American Publishing, 1988, 500 pcs, MIB...............................20.00

Capt America, bicycle license plate, litho tin, Marx, 1967, NM 50.00

Capt America, flashlight, plastic, Gordy Int, 1980, 3½", MIP......................................30.00

Capt Kangaroo, fingerpaint set, Hasbro, 1956, EXIB 55.00

Capt Kangaroo, TV Eras-O-Board Set, Hasbro, 1956, M (VG box)................................30.00

Capt Marvel, key chain, Capt Marvel Club, plastic, 1940s, EX 75.00

Care Bears, bank, Wish Bear on a Star, composition, NM 20.00

Casper the Ghost, jewelry set, 10-pc, AAI Inc, 1995, MOC ..15.00

Casper the Ghost, Rub-A-Pencil Set, Saalfield, 1960, EXIB 50.00

Casper the Ghost, toss-up balloon, Pioneer Rubber, 1950s, 36", MOC 70.00

Cat in the Hat, bookends, cast iron, Midwest of Cannon Falls, MIB 55.00

Cat in the Hat, doll, plush, Mattel & Arcotoys, 1997, 39", NM 45.00

Cat in the Hat, jack-in-th-box, He's a Jolly Good Fellow, Mattel, EX....................105.00

Cat in the Hat, store banner, vinyl, 1995, 16x36", NM...........80.00

Cat in the Hat, wristwatch, 1972, NM...............................250.00

Charlie's Angels, backpack, vinyl w/group photo, Travel Toys, 1977, M...........................75.00

CHiPs, bullhorn, plastic, Placo Toys, 1977, M................35.00

CHiPs, poster, Ponch & John, Dargis Associates, 1977, 35x23", EX.....................25.00

CHiPs, sunglasses, Fleetwood, 1977, MOC 15.00

CHiPs, wallet, various colors, Larami, 1979, MOC 30.00

Cinderella, apron pattern, JC Penney, 1950s, uncut, EX+ 35.00

Cinderella, purse, green slipper w/zipper closure, 1970s, 5", MIP 25.00

Cinderella, wastebasket, metal, tells story w/graphics, 1950s, 19", EX............................50.00

Cinderella, wristwatch, w/plastic figure, Timex, 1958, EXIB ..150.00

Cool Cat, poster, 1968, M 10.00

Daffy Duck, bank, Daffy leaning on tree trunk, painted metal, 6", EX............................135.00

Daffy Duck, candle holder, painted bisque, 1980, M 35.00

Daisy Duck, figurine, croquet player, bisque, WDP, 1960s, 4" 40.00

Dennis the Menace, mug, plastic head form, Kellogg's, 1960, 3½", EX............................18.00

Dennis the Menace & Ruff, lamp, vinyl figures, Hall, 1960, 7", EX 75.00

Deputy Dawg, doll, stuffed w/vinyl head, Ideal, 1960s, 14", EX 100.00

Dick Tracy, Candid Camera, Seymour/New York News, 1950s, complete with instructions, EX (EX box), $100.00. (Photo courtesy Larry Doucet)

Dick Tracy, Crimestoppers Set, Larami, 1967, NMIP......40.00

Dick Tracy, magnifying glass, Larami, 1979, MOC 20.00

Donald Duck, bank, Ucago, 1960s, MIB................................55.00

Donald Duck, bread wrapper, Debus, 1950s, 16x17", EX.10.00

Donald Duck, doll, Dancing Donald, Hasbro, 1977, 18", EX......35.00

Donald Duck, nodder figure, plastic, Marx, 1960s, 2", EX+.......45.00

Donald Duck, Rolykin, Marx, 1960s, 1½", NM..............22.00

Donald Duck, squirt gun, plastic head figure, 1974, EX....25.00

Donald Duck, sweeper, Ohio Art/WDE, lithographed wood, EX, $125.00.

Donald Duck, Whirl-A-Tune Music Maker, Ideal, 1965, NMIB..80.00

Dondi, pencil box, cardboard, w/drawer, Hasbro, 1961, EX 25.00

Dr Dolittle, medical playset, Hasbro, NM 75.00

Dr Dolittle, Stitch-A-Story, Hasbro, NMIP......................25.00

Dukes of Hazzard, Colorforms, 1981, NMIB..................30.00

Dukes of Hazzard, TV tray, 1981, 13x17", EX.....................**25.00**

Dumbo, wall pocket/shelf planter, in tree, ceramic, 1940s, 4", EX **40.00**

Dumbo & Timothy, wall plaques, diecut cardboard, WDP, 1951, pr.....................................**40.00**

Elmer Fudd, pistol/flashlight, EX **15.00**

ET, bank, ET standing on round green base, 6", EX..........**30.00**

ET, figure, talker, 1982, 7", MIB **60.00**

ET, photo album, M (sealed).**12.00**

Family Affair, Colorforms Cartoon Kit, 1970, MIB **35.00**

Fat Albert & the Cosby Kids, figures, Tedro Enterprises, 1982, MOC, ea................**30.00**

Felix the Cat, apron, Determined Products, 1990, adult size, EX **30.00**

Felix the Cat, ashtray, on pedestal, metal, 1990, 20" H, EX ...**60.00**

Felix the Cat, color & wipe-off book, 1958, EX **32.00**

Felix the Cat, watch, antique style w/leather band, Fossil, 1993, EXIB **50.00**

Figaro, doll, plush, Disney Classics, 1980s, 5", MIB **16.00**

Flash Gordon, slide-tile puzzle, Defenders of Earth, Ja-Ru, 1985, MOC **18.00**

Flintstones, alarm clock, Fred, 'Yabba Dabba Doo,' 1973, M **65.00**

Flintstones, bank, Barney & Bamm-Bamm, hard plastic, 13", M **75.00**

Flintstones, bank, Fred, hard plastic, Homecraft, 14", M **75.00**

Flintstones, bubble pipe, Bamm-Bamm, 1960s, 8", EX **20.00**

Flintstones, doll, Baby Pebbles, vinyl, Ideal, 1960s, 14", EXIB............................**55.00**

Flintstones, doll, Fred, plush & vinyl, Knickerbocker, 1960s, 12", NM **100.00**

Flintstones, Fred figure, vinyl, 1960, 12", NM, $70.00. (Photo courtesy Martin and Carolyn Berens)

Flintstones, Fuzzy Felt, characters & accessories, Toykraft, 1961, MIB.......................**50.00**

Flintstones, night light, Barney, Snapit, 1964, 4", MIC **20.00**

Flintstones, pillow, Fred, 1970s, M.....................................**15.00**

Flintstones, squeak toy, Barney, vinyl, 1960, M **15.00**

Flipper, Activity Box, Whitman, 1966, complete, MIB......**40.00**

Flipper, bank, plastic, 1960s, 17½", NM **45.00**

Flipper, wristwatch, glow-in-the-dark image, ITF/MGM, M.............................**125.00**

Flying Nun, chalkboard, Hasbro, 1967, 16x24", MIP..........**75.00**

Foghorn Leghorn, doll, plush, w/tag, Warner Bros, recent, $15 to **20.00**

Fonz, belt buckle, brass finish, 2 embossed styles, 1976, M, ea **22.00**

Fonz, book covers, 4 different in package, SPCE, 1976, MIP **20.00**

Fonz, Bubb-A-Loons, Imperial, 1981, MIP **15.00**

Fonz, bumper sticker, Fonzie for President, Pinning, 1976, 4x12", M **10.00**

Fonz, wristwatch, photo image, vinyl band, Time Trends, 1976, MIB.......................**75.00**

Fonz & the Happy Days Gang, puffy stickers, Imperial, 1981, MIP **10.00**

Gilligan's Island, baseball cap, American Needle, 1994, EX..............**10.00**

Gilligan's Island, doll set, 3-pc, soft rubber, Playskool, 1977, M **35.00**

Gilligan's Island, 10¢ tablet, pictures Skipper & Gilligan, 1960s, NM **35.00**

Good Times, socks, Dyn-O-Mite/JJ, Expression Wear, 1975, unused, pr **22.00**

Goofy, bank, head figure, Play Pal Plastics, 1971, 12", NM .**30.00**

Goofy, Weebles figure, 1973, EX..**15.00**

Green Hornet, balloon, Black Beauty, 1966, MIP.......**100.00**

Green Hornet, kite, Roalex, 1967, MIP..............................**200.00**

Gumby & Pokey, Modeling Dough, Chemtoy, 1967, unused, MIB.................**50.00**

Gumby & Pokey, Super-Flex Figure, Lakeside, 1965, 6", MOC, either, ea **50.00**

Hardy Boys, Pocket Flix Cassette, Ideal, 1978, MIP **15.00**

Hardy Boys, wristwatch, 1970s, NM, $50 to.....................**75.00**

He-Man, Superblobo, inflatable, Unique, 1984, expands to 7 ft, MIP...............................**20.00**

Heckle & Jeckle, magic slate, Lowe, 1952, NM.............**25.00**

Herman & Katnip, kite, Saalfield, 1960, MIP.......................**25.00**

Howdy Doody, alarm clock, Howdy on Bronco, Leadworks, 1988, 10", EX......**65.00**

Howdy Doody, Circus Kee 'N Lite, semi-truck shape, pocket-size, MIB..............................**150.00**

Howdy Doody, doll, stuffed cloth, Applause, 1988, 18", EX .**30.00**

Howdy Doody, football, 1950s, 8", EX.................................**85.00**

Howdy Doody, night light, ceramic, Howdy on bull, 1988, unused, M....................**185.00**

Howdy Doody, Phono Doodle, Shuratone, 1950s, EX, from $250.00 to $300.00.

Howdy Doody, swim ring, inflatable vinyl, 1950s, 24" dia, EX...............................**65.00**

Howdy Doody, wash mitt, Clarabell, terry, Bernard Ulmann, 1950s, EX+ **45.00**

HR Pufnstuf, pennants, plastic, Kellogg's premium, 1970, 8½", M, pr **75.00**

HR Pufnstuf, tote bag, canvas, Sid & Marty Kroft Productions, 1965, M **125.00**

Huckleberry Hound, bank, plastic, 1960, 10", EX **35.00**

Huckleberry Hound, gumball machine, Candy Factory, 1960, 11", EX **40.00**

Huckleberry Hound, ring, plastic, EX **50.00**

Huckleberry Hound, utility belt, Remco, 1978, complete, NMIB **25.00**

Hunchback of Notre Dame, doll, Applause, 1996, 9", MIB, ea **12.00**

I Dream of Jeannie, Magic Locket, Harmony, 1975, MOC....**45.00**

I Dream of Jeannie, party plates, cartoon, paper, 1973, 9", MIP **25.00**

Incredible Hulk, paint-by-number set, Hasbro, 1982, unused, MIB **30.00**

Incredible Hulk, wastebasket, litho metal, EX **45.00**

Incredible Hulk, yo-yo, w/flasher seal, Duncan, early 1980s, NM **18.00**

James Bond, hand puppet, full figure, Gilbert, 1965, 14", EX **150.00**

James Bond, pencil case, vinyl, 1960s, 4x8", EX............. **100.00**

Jetsons, magic slate, Watkins/Strathmore, 1963, NM **50.00**

Jetsons, puffy magnets, George & Jane, 1970s, 4", EX, pr ..**10.00**

Jonny Quest, Annual, Authorized TV Edition, hardcover, 1965, EX **30.00**

Jonny Quest, Paint-by-Number Coloring Set, Transogram, 1965, MIB **125.00**

Josie & the Pussycats, Crossword Puzzles book, Tempo, 1976, unused **25.00**

Josie & the Pussycats, Marvy Markers, Uchida of America, 1974, MIB **40.00**

Kermit the Frog, figure, Bend 'Ems, MOC **10.00**

King Kong, Colorforms Panoramic Playset, 1976, complete, EXIB............................ **25.00**

Knight Rider, Self-Inking Stamp Kit, Larami, 1982, MOC.**30.00**

Lady & the Tramp, wallet, vinyl, WDP, 1950s, $30 to........**40.00**

Lambchop, bank, plastic, Shari Lewis Enterprises/China 1993, M........................... **12.00**

Lariat Sam, Colorforms Cartoon Kit, 1962, complete, EXIB........**35.00**

Laurel & Hardy, Stuff & Lace Dolls, Transogram, 1962, MIB, ea.......................... **30.00**

Laverne & Shirley, paint-by-number set, Hasbro, 1981, MIB **35.00**

Li'l Abner, mug, ceramic, profile image, 1968, NM...........**12.00**

Lion King, Colorforms, 1994, EXIB.............................**6.00**

Lion King, spoon rest, Timon, Treasure Craft, M.........**20.00**

Little Audrey, doll, vinyl, 13", EX................................**50.00**

Little Lulu, bank, Play Pal Plastics, 7½", NM.................**50.00**

Little Lulu, crossword puzzle book, Whitman, 1974, unused, M **45.00**

Little Red Riding Hood, tea set, tin, 11-pc, Ohio Art, 1960s, NM **100.00**

Ludwig Von Drake, Pencil Crayons Set, Empire Pencil, 1961, unused, NM **85.00**

Magilla Gorilla, change purse, vinyl w/zipper, Estelle, 1960s, NMOC **35.00**

Magilla Gorilla, doll, plush w/vinyl head, Ideal, 1960s, 18½", NM **125.00**

Man From UNCLE, bop bag, vinyl, Dean/MGM, 1966, NMIP............................... **175.00**

Man From UNCLE, Secret Print Putty, Colorforms, 1965, NMOC **80.00**

Marvel Super Heroes, checkers set, 1976, MIP (sealed) ..**45.00**

Marvel Super Heroes, finger puppets, any, Imperial Toy, 1978, NM, ea **15.00**

Marvel Super Heroes, light-up drawing desk, Lakeside, 1977, EXIB **40.00**

Mary Poppins, plate, Sun Valley Melmac, 9½", unused, M .**30.00**

Mary Poppins, spoon, silver-plated, figure at end of handle, 1964, M **20.00**

Mary Poppins, Talking Telephone, battery-op, w/records, Hasbro, MIB.............................. **200.00**

Max Headroom, Fingertronic Puppet, Bendy Toys, 1987, 6", MIB.............................. **20.00**

Max Headroom, wall clock, shaped like wristwatch, NMIB............................ **65.00**

Mickey Mouse, alarm clock, Bayard, 1964, NM........**300.00**

Mickey Mouse, belt buckle, brass w/colorful Mickey, 1970s, 2" sq, EX+ **25.00**

Mickey Mouse, bookends/banks, cast iron, WDP, 1960s, 5x4", pr **275.00**

Mickey Mouse, CB radio, 1977, MIB, $16.00. (Photo courtesy June Moon)

Mickey Mouse, doll, Chatterchum, Mattel, 1976, 7", VG **30.00**

Mickey Mouse, doll, Posie, Ideal, 1950s, EXIB **45.00**

Mickey Mouse, figurine, ceramic, Dan Brechner, 1960s, 8", NM+ **45.00**

Mickey Mouse, gumball machine, head on red base, Hasbro, 1968, NM........................ **50.00**

Mickey Mouse, lamp base, dancing figure, ceramic, 8", EX+ ..**40.00**

Mickey Mouse, music box, ceramic, 50th birthday cake, Schmid, MIB **75.00**

Mickey Mouse, nodder figure, plastic, Marx, 1960s, 2", EX+ **45.00**

Mickey Mouse, planter, ceramic, Mickey w/cart, Brechner, 1960s, 5", EX **65.00**

Mickey Mouse, Rub 'N Play Magic Transfer Set, Colorforms, 1978, unused **30.00**

Mickey Mouse, scarf, red, white & blue printed cotton, 1960s, MIB **30.00**

Mickey Mouse, toy wristwatch, Marx, 1971, MOC **55.00**

Mickey Mouse, wastebasket, litho tin, Chein, 1974, 13", EX..**25.00**

Mighty Mouse, Candy Factory, Remco, 1973, NMIB.......**75.00**

Mighty Mouse, doll, rubber w/cloth cape, 1955, 10", EX........**75.00**

Mighty Mouse, Presto-Paints, Kenner, 1963, complete, EXIB..............................**65.00**

Minnie Mouse, bank, Minnie in house, composition, WDP/Japan **50.00**

Minnie Mouse, Disneykin, 1st series, Marx, 1960s, NM .**10.00**

Minnie Mouse, doll, cloth w/leather-type shoes, Gund, 1940s, 18", VG..............**280.00**

Minnie Mouse, doll, plush & vinyl, Applause, 1981, 16", VG....................................**15.00**

Minnie Mouse, figurine, bisque, Minnie w/golf clubs, 1970s, 4", NM **20.00**

Miss Piggy, bank, ceramic, Sigma, NM..................................**50.00**

Miss Piggy, doll, stuffed w/vinyl head, Fisher-Price, 1980, 14", NM..................................**20.00**

Mork, gumball machine, figure on top, Hasbro, 1980, EX....**25.00**

Mork & Mindy, Colorforms Rub 'N Play, 1979, MIB **35.00**

Mork from Ork, alarm clock, talking, Concept 2000, 1980, NM, $40 to **50.00**

Mortimer Snerd, teeth, Pilo Novelty, 1940s, unused, NMIP.**65.00**

Mother Goose, magic slate set, Strathmore, 1945, complete, EXIB **35.00**

Mr Ed, hand puppet, talker, Mattel, 1962, MIB **200.00**

Mr Magoo, doll, Ideal, stuffed cloth with vinyl head, felt jacket, knitted scarf, Ideal, 1964, 15", EX, minimum value $75.00.

Mr Magoo, playing cards, double deck in plastic casing, 1960s, NM..................................**15.00**

Munsters, doll, baby Herman, vinyl w/cloth clothes, Ideal, 1965, NM......................**65.00**

Munsters, flasher ring, Lily w/name, 1965, EX..........**18.00**

Mushmouse, pull toy, vinyl figure on wagon, Ideal, 1964, 6", EX **30.00**

Olive Oyl, push-button puppet, Kohner, NM **75.00**

Oswald Rabbit, magic slate, Saalfield, 1962, EX................**20.00**

Partridge Family, bulletin board, 1970s, 18x24", EX..........**75.00**

Partridge Family, wristwatch, family photo, 1970s, NM, $150 to **200.00**

Pee Wee's Playhouse, doll, Vance the Talking Pig, Matchbox, 1988, MIB, $55.00. (Photo courtesy Martin and Carolyn Berens)

Peter Pan, bell, Tinkerbell figure atop bell, gold-tone, 1950s, 3", EX **60.00**

Peter Pan, key chain, Tinkerbell, fluorescent, 1970s, 3", NM **15.00**

Peter Pan, pin, Peter Pan or Capt Hook, gold-tone, 1950s, EX, ea **35.00**

Peter Pan, place mat, Tinkerbell & the magic castle, vinyl, 1960s, EX **25.00**

Peter Potamus, playing cards, Whitman, 1965, EX **25.00**

Phantom, poster, advertising DC Comic Books, 1984, 22x14", NM..................................**25.00**

Pink Panther, Cartoonarama, 1970, complete, EXIB **60.00**

Pink Panther, picture frame, Royal Orleans, about 4x3" w/oval opening **60.00**

Pink Panther, shakers, Royal Orleans, 1982, 3½", pr, minimum..............................**225.00**

Pinky Lee, doll, Lose Your Head, squeeze rubber, 9", NM.................................**95.00**

Pinocchio, clicker, Jiminy Cricket, plastic head figure, 1950s, NM **45.00**

Pinocchio, cup, Jiminy Cricket, plastic head w/flicker eyes, 1950s, NM **30.00**

Pinocchio, figurine, Geppetto or Pinocchio, bisque, Multi, 2", NM, ea..........................**100.00**

Pinocchio, figurine, Gideon or Honest John, bisque, Multi, 2", ea...............................**75.00**

Pinocchio, figurine, Jiminy Cricket, bisque, Multi, 1940s, 5", NM..............................**100.00**

Pixie & Dixie, Punch-O Punching Bag, vinyl, Kestral, 1959, 18", NMIB...............................**25.00**

Planet of the Apes, bank, Dr Zaius, Play Pal Plastics, 1967, 10", NM **30.00**

Planet of the Apes, bank, Gen Urus, Play Pal Plastics, 1967, 18", M **40.00**

Planet of the Apes, squirt gun, Cornelius, plastic, AHI, 1970s, M **75.00**

Pluto, alarm clock, on doghouse watching chicks, Bayard, 1964, NM.....................**250.00**

Pluto, figurine, ceramic, Brayton Laguna, 1940s, 6", M...**135.00**

Pluto, nodder figure, plastic, Marx, 1960s, 1¾", EX+..**45.00**

Pluto, rocking chair, stuffed vinyl w/wood rockers, 1950s, 32", EX **200.00**

Pluto, Rolykin, Marx, 1960s, 1½",
NM **22.00**

Popeye, bank, sitting w/spinach
can, vinyl, Alan Jay, 1958, 8",
EX **75.00**

Popeye, boxing gloves, red, Everlast, 1950s, MIP **75.00**

Popeye, flasher ring, silver-tone
plastic, Vari-Vue, 1960s,
NM **30.00**

Popeye, Paint 'N Foil Kit, Crafco,
1978, MIP (sealed) **25.00**

**Popeye,
sparkler, litho-
graphed tin,
lever action,
Chein, NMIB,
$385.00.**

Porky Pig, bank, standing beside
tree trunk, pot metal, 1940s,
EX **100.00**

Porky Pig, gum machine, plastic
figure, Banko Matic, 1970s,
EXIB **25.00**

Quick Draw McGraw, gloves,
western-style cloth w/image,
EX **25.00**

Raggedy Ann, coin purse, vinyl
figure, Hallmark/Bobbs-Mer-
rill, NM **15.00**

Raggedy Ann & Andy, bank,
musical, 4½", NM **20.00**

Raggedy Ann & Andy, beach ball,
Ideal, 1974, 20" dia, MIP ..**30.00**

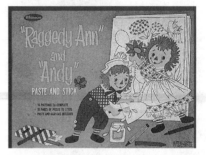

**Raggedy Ann and Andy, Paste and
Stick, Whitman, 1968, MIB, $30.00.**

Rambo, walkie-talkies, w/head-
band, 1985, MOC **30.00**

Rat Fink, decal, 1990, NM **5.00**

Rat Fink, ring, plastic w/detach-
able figure, Macman Ent,
1963, MIP **30.00**

Ricochet Rabbit, pull toy, Ideal,
1964, EX **100.00**

Road Runner, doll, plush w/wire
frame, Mighty Star, 1971,
17", EX **35.00**

Road Runner, figure, PVC, Shell
gas premium, MIP **3.00**

Road Runner, yo-yo, John Hart
Toys Inc, 1974, MIP **40.00**

RoboCop, pencil sharpener,
MIP **5.00**

Rocketeer, doll, vinyl, Applause,
9", EX **20.00**

Rocketeer, Poster Pen Set, Rose
Art #1921, 1991, MOC, $20
to **30.00**

Rocketeer, sleeping bag, NM ..**45.00**

Rocketeer, wallet, Pyramid Hand-
bag Co, M **40.00**

Rocky & Bullwinkle, bank, Bullwinkle, vinyl, Play Pal, 1973, 12", M **75.00**

Rocky & Bullwinkle, bank, Mr Sherman, ceramic, PAT Ward, 1960, 6", VG **300.00**

Rocky & Bullwinkle, blackboard, diecut figure atop, Frolic, 1970s, VG **50.00**

Rocky & Bullwinkle, sewing cards, Rocky & Friends, Whitman, 1961, NMIB **100.00**

Roger Rabbit, doll, talker, Playskool, 1988, NRFB..**95.00**

Rootie Kazootie, magic set, 1950s, NMIB............................**125.00**

Scooby Doo, doll, plush, Sutton, 1970s, EX **40.00**

Scooby Doo, gumball machine, plastic head, Hasbro, 1968, EX....................................**25.00**

Scooby Doo, rubber stamp, 1982, MOC **10.00**

Sesame Street, doll, Big Bird, talker, Playskool, 1970s, 22", VG **25.00**

Sesame Street, doll, Ernie, stuffed cloth, 18", EX..................**20.00**

Sesame Street, figure set, PVC, set of 8, Applause, 1993, M..**20.00**

Sesame Street, key chain, any character, Fisher-Price, rare, MIB, ea............................**25.00**

Simpsons, alarm clock, Maggie, MIB, from $100 to........**125.00**

Simpsons, doll, Bart, stuffed cloth & vinyl, Dandee, 16", MIB **15.00**

Simpsons, figure, any w/5 balloons, PVC, Mattel, MOC, ea, from $20 to **25.00**

Simpsons, frisbee, Radical Dude, Betras Plastics, M............**5.00**

Simpsons, poster book, Button-Up, 8 posters, NM............**8.00**

Six Million Dollar Man, CB Headset Radio Receiver, Kenner, 1977, MIB......................**45.00**

Six Million Dollar Man, tattoos & stickers, Kenner, 1976, MOC............................**12.00**

Sleeping Beauty, Disneykin, second series, Marx, 1960s, NM **45.00**

Sleeping Beauty, paint-by-number set, Transogram, 1959, unused, EX **65.00**

Sleeping Beauty, sewing kit, Transogram, 1959, unused, scarce, EX......................**65.00**

Sleeping Wand, Magic Bubble Wand, 1950s, MIP **40.00**

Smurfs, barrettes, set of 2, 1983, MIP **3.00**

Smurfs, figurine, Papa Smurf, ceramic, VG....................**30.00**

Smurfs, greeting card, Hallmark, M, from $5 to....................**8.00**

Smurfs, Smurf Village, ceramic, VG....................................**35.00**

Smurfs, toothbrush & cup set, MIB..............................**25.00**

Snow White, night light, plastic, 1950s, EX **125.00**

Snow White, planter, ceramic, Leeds, 1940s, 6½", NM..**50.00**

Snow White, Talking Telephone, Hasbro, 1967, MIB......**225.00**

Speedy Gonzales, hand puppet, vinyl, 1970s, EX.............**15.00**

Spider-Man, Code Breaker, Gordy, 1980, MOC **35.00**

Spider-Man, doll, talker, Mego, 1974, 28", M **45.00**

Spider-Man, finger puppet, 1970, NM................................**12.00**

Spider-Man, squirt gun, plastic head figure, 1974, EX **25.00**

Spider-Man, wallet, brown plastic w/image on yellow circle, 1978, NM.........................**18.00**

Spider-Man, wristwatch, blue plastic band, Dabs, 1981, MIB..............................**200.00**

Spider-Man, wristwatch, flip-top head, vinyl strap, Hope, 1990, MOC **25.00**

Starsky & Hutch, Poster Put-Ons, Bi-Rite, 1876, MIP.........**12.00**

Steve Canyon, school bag, canvas, 1959, EX **75.00**

Super Powers, poster, Super Powers Collection, 1984, 24", M (w/mailer).......................**65.00**

Superman, doll, Applause, 1988, 18", NM **25.00**

Superman, gym bag, vinyl w/image & logo, DC Comics, 1971, NM........................**50.00**

Superman, kite, Hi-Flier, 1984, MIP.................................**30.00**

Superman, Kryptonite Rock, glow-in-the-dark, DC Comics, 1978, MIB...............................**25.00**

Sylvester the Cat, roly-poly, EX..............................**25.00**

Tarzan, Weebles Jungle Hut, Romper Room/Hasbro, 1976, MIB, $85.00. (Photo courtesy June Moon)

Tarzan, Jungle Animal Set, Salco/Banner, 1966, unused, NMIB............................**200.00**

Tarzan, Rub-Off Picture Set, Whitman, 1966, VG (VG box).**25.00**

Tasmanian Devil, yo-yo, plastic, Magic Mountain souvenir, 1990s, NM **4.00**

Teenage Mutant Ninja Turtles, cereal bowl, ceramic, Mirage, 1990, NM.........................**8.00**

Teenage Mutant Ninja Turtles, mug, mask changes color, Mirage, 1991, M...............**8.00**

Teenage Mutant Ninja Turtles, tote bag, Mirage Studios, 1989, NM.........................**20.00**

Tennessee Tuxedo, pencil-by-number set, Transogram, 1963, NMIB............................**100.00**

Terminator, doll, Classic Plastic, 1992, 11½", EX+.............**10.00**

That Girl, wig case, 1960s, NM, from $75 to **100.00**

Three Little Pigs, birthday card, White & Wyckoff Co, 1938, unused, NM...................**60.00**

Three Little Pigs, switch plate, plastic, 1950s, MIP **35.00**

Three Stooges, figure set, original tags & stands, 1988, 14", M........................**140.00**

Three Stooges, flasher rings, any 3, EX, ea **25.00**

Three Stooges, wristwatch, photo image, Columbia Pictures, 1980, VG......................**125.00**

Tom & Jerry, cups, ceramic, 3 different, Staffordshire/MGM, 1970, ea **45.00**

Tom & Jerry, guitar, plastic, Mattel, 1960s, NM, from $100 to **125.00**

Top Cat, doll, vinyl, yellow w/red jacket & hat, 1960s, 8", VG **15.00**

Top Cat, viewer, plastic house shape, 8 action scenes, 3x2½", NMIB **95.00**

Topo Gigio, hand puppet, American Character, 1960s, 12", MIB **125.00**

Toy Story, doll, Woody, talker, Think Way, NRFB **50.00**

Toy Story, pocketwatch, Buzz or Woody, Fossil, 1996, MIB (tin), ea **125.00**

Tweety Bird, alarm clock, talking, battery-op, Janex, 1978, EX................................**75.00**

Tweety Bird, charm, plastic figure, 1950s, ¾", NM **15.00**

Underdog, iron-on transfers, set of 3, Vortex, 1960s, 8x10", unused **55.00**

Universal Monsters, Stick 'N Lift Monsters Kit, American, 1980s, MIB **65.00**

Universal Monsters, sticker sheet, set of 8, 1960s, EX..........**50.00**

Welcome Back Kotter, bulletin board, Board King, 1976, M **50.00**

Welcome Back Kotter, mug, plastic, The Sweathogs, Dawn, 1976, EX **12.00**

Welcome Back Kotter, Poster Art Kit, Board King, 1976, MIB **45.00**

Welcome Back Kotter, towel set, Sweathogs, Cannon, 1976, 3-pc, unused **75.00**

Winky Dink, paint set, Pressman, 1950s, unused, NMIB **75.00**

Winnie the Pooh, doll, Piglet, stuffed cloth, Sears, 1960s, 7", NM **75.00**

Winnie the Pooh, figurine, Eeyore seated, ceramic, 1960s, EX................................**55.00**

Winnie the Pooh, lamp base, Pooh in wagon pulled by Eeyore, plastic **55.00**

Winnie the Pooh, squeak toy, Tigger, vinyl, Hollandhall, 1966, 7", NM **125.00**

Wizard of Oz, sunglasses, Scarecrow, Multi-Kids/Lowes, 1989, MOC **20.00**

Wolfman, flashlight key chain, Basic Fun, 1995, MOC...**12.00**

Wonder Woman, poster, Lynda Carter, Thought Factory, 1977, 35x23", EX............**75.00**

Wonder Woman, wristwatch, Dabbs, 1977, EXIB **200.00**

Wonder Woman, yo-yo, paper insert seal, Duncan, 1970s, NM **15.00**

Woody Woodpecker, mug, brown plastic w/painted face, 1965-73, NM............................**15.00**

Woody Woodpecker, Picture Dominoes, Saalfield, 1963, MIB (sealed) **50.00**

Woody Woodpecker, TV Coloring Pencil Set, 1958, EXIB ..**35.00**

Yogi Bear, bubble pipe, red plastic figure, Transogram, 1963, MIP................................**35.00**

Yogi Bear, camera, 1960s, MIB, $65.00.

Yogi Bear, doll, stuffed cloth, Playtime, 1960s, 17", NM.........**50.00**

Yogi Bear, push-button puppet, Kohner, 1960s, M..........**65.00**

Yogi Bear & Friends, wastebasket, tin litho, 1960s, 13", VG.**65.00**

Yosemite Sam, hand puppet, toothpaste premium, M.**12.00**

Cherished Teddies

First appearing on dealers' shelves in the spring of 1992, Cherished Teddies found instant collector appeal. They were designed by artist Priscilla Hillman and produced in the Orient for the Enesco company. Besides the figurines, the line includes waterballs, frames, plaques, and bells.

#617253, Baby in Basket, ornament, Christmas 1994 ...**38.00**

#914894, Jointed Bear in Santa Cap, ornament, Christmas 1993 ....**20.00**

L/R 900362, Abigail, Inside We're All the Same, Easter 1993 ......**65.00**

L/R 910708, Heidi & David, Special Friends, 1993 ....**75.00**

L/R 910724, Priscilla, Love Surrounds Our Friendship, 1993...............................**45.00**

L/R 950424, Camille, I'd Be Lost Without You, 1992.........**75.00**

L/R 950513, Nathaniel & Nellie, It's Twice As Nice..., 1992 .....**85.00**

L/R 950548, Benji, Life Is Sweet Enjoy, 1992/retired 1995 .**80.00**

L/R 950564, Beth & Blossom, Friends Are Never Far Apart, 1992 ....**135.00**

L/R 950734, Jacob, Wishing For Love, Christmas 1992....**50.00**

L/R 951196, Theodore, Samantha, Tyler, Friends Come..., 1992, 9".....................................**160.00**

3/R 624888, Father, A Father Is the Bearer of Strength, 1994 ....**22.00**

3/R 910694, Chelsea, Good Friends Are a Blessing, 1993/retired 1995.........**135.00**

3/R 911313, Through the Years Age 3, Three Cheers For You, 1993 ....**22.00**

3/R 911402, Robbie & Rachel, Love Bears All Things, 1993...**60.00**

3/R 911739, Thomas, Chuggin' Along, 1993....................**40.00**

3/R 912921, Carolyn, Wishing You All Good Times, Christmas 1993 ....**45.00**

3/R 916315, Nancy, Your Friendship Makes..., Valentines 1994 ....**55.00**

3/R 916390, Courtney, Springtime Is a Blessing From Above, Easter 1994 ....**65.00**

3/R 916447, Kathleen, Luck Found Me a Friend in You, St Pats 1994........................**35.00**

3/R 916641, Oliver & Olivia, Will You Be Mine, Valentines 1994 ....**50.00**

4/R 103551, Boy Bear Cupid, Sent With Love, 1995.............**20.00**

4/R 103594, Boy & Girl Cupid, Aiming For Your Heart, 1995 ....**38.00**

4/R 617148, Stacie, You Lift My Spirit, Halloween 1994..**30.00**

4/R 624810, Tom Tom The Piper's Son, Wherever You Go..., 1994...............................**45.00**

5/R 103829, Melissa, Every Bunny Needs a Friend, 1995.....**20.00**

Children's Books

Books were popular gifts for children in the latter 1800s; many were beautifully illustrated, some by notable artists such as Frances Brundage and Maxfield Parrish. From this century tales of Tarzan by Burroughs are very collectible, as are those familiar childhood series books — for example, The Bobbsey Twins and Nancy Drew. For more information we recommend *Collector's Guide to Children's Books, Volumes I* and *II*, by Diane McClure Jones and Rosemary Jones (Collector Books).

Big Little Books

Probably everyone who is now fifty to sixty-five years of age owned a few Big Little Books as a child. Today these thick hand-sized adventures bring prices from $10.00 to $75.00 and upwards. The first was published in 1933 by Whitman Publishing Company. Dick Tracy was the featured character. Kids of the early '50s preferred the format of the comic book, and the Big Little Books were gradually phased out. Stories about super heroes and Disney characters bring the highest prices, especially those with an early copyright. For more information see *Big Little Books, a Collector's Reference and Value Guide,* by Larry Jacobs (Collector Books).

Andy Panda in the City of Ice, Whitman #1441, NM **40.00**

Buck Jones in the Roaring West, Whitman #1174, VG **25.00**

Chester Gump at Silver Creek Ranch, Whitman #734, EX..............**35.00**

Dick Tracy in Chains of Crime, Whitman #1185, NM **75.00**

Flame Boy & the Indians' Secret, Whitman #1464, VG **25.00**

Gene Autry & the Hawk of the Hills, Whitman #1493, NM.........**50.00**

Hairbreath Harry in Dept QT, Whitman #1101, EX **35.00**

In the Name of the Law, Whitman #1124, VG......................**25.00**

Jungle Jim & the Vampire Woman, Whitman #1139, NM **75.00**

Junior Nebb on the Diamond Bar Ranch, Whitman #1422, 1938, VG, $20.00.

Little Annie Roonie & the Orphan House, Whitman #1117, VG..**30.00**

Little Woman, Whitman #757, EX................................**45.00**

Mickey Mouse & the Magic Lamp, Whitman #1429, NM **70.00**

Mutt & Jeff, Whitman #1113, NM..............................**75.00**

Once Upon a Time, Whitman #718, EX **50.00**

Phantom & the Sky Pirates, Whitman #1468, NM **65.00**

Roy Rogers & the Deadly Treasure, Whitman #1437, VG.......**40.00**

Sombrero Pete, Whitman #1136, VG.................................**25.00**

Tarzan & the Golden Lion, Whitman #1448, NM **75.00**

Uncle Don's Strange Adventures, Whitman #1114, VG **30.00**

Zip Sauder's King of the Speedway, Whitman #1465, EX **25.00**

Little Golden Books

Little Golden Books (a registered trademark of Western Publishing Company Inc.), introduced in October of 1942, were an overnight success. First published with a blue paper spine, the later spines were of gold foil. Parents and grandparents born in the '40s, '50s, and '60s are now trying to find the titles they had as children. From 1942 to the early 1970s, the books were numbered from 1 to 600, while books published later had no numerical order. Depending on where you find the book, prices can vary from 25¢ to $30.00 plus. The most expensive are those with dust jackets from the early '40s or books with paper dolls and activities. The three primary series of books are the Regular (1 – 600), Disney (1 – 140), and Activity (1 – 52).

Television's influence became apparent in the '50s with stories like the Lone Ranger, Howdy Doody, Hopalong Cassidy, Gene Autry, and Rootie Kazootie. The '60s brought us Yogi Bear, Huckleberry Hound, Magilla Gorilla, and Quick Draw McGraw, to name a few. Condition is very important when purchasing a book. You normally don't want to purchase a book with large tears, crayon or ink marks, or missing pages.

As with any collectible book, a first edition is always going to bring the higher price. To determine what edition you have on the 25¢ and 29¢ cover price books, look on the title page or the last page of the book. If it is not on the title page, there will be a code of 1/(a letter of the alphabet) on the bottom right corner of the last page. A is for first edition, Z would refer to the twenty-sixth printing.

There isn't an easy way of determining the condition of a book. What is 'good' to one might be 'fair' to another. A played-with book in average condition is generally worth only half as much as one in mint, like-new condition. To find out more about Little Golden Books, we recommend *Collecting Little Golden Books* (published by Books Americana) by Steve Santi.

Animals of Farmer Jones, #11, H edition, EX......................**14.00**

Beany Goes to the Sea, #537, A edition, VG **30.00**

Bozo the Clown, #446, C edition, EX **8.00**

Bugs Bunny at the Easter Party, #183, D edition, EX......**100.00**

Captain Kangaroo, #421, D edition, EX..............................**6.00**

Darby O'Gill, #D81, A edition, EX.................................**15.00**

Donald Duck Toy Sailboat, #D40, E edition, EX..................**10.00**

Howdy Doody & His Magic Hat, #184, A edition, EX........**28.00**

I Have a Secret, #495, A edition, EX..................................**14.00**

Little Tip-Yip & His Bark, #73, A edition, EX......................**20.00**

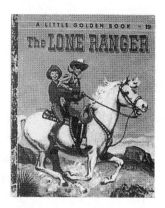

Lone Ranger, #263, A edition, EX, $25.00.

Maverick, #354, A edition, EX ..**25.00**

My Snuggly Bunny, #250, A edition, EX............................**20.00**

Pussycat Tiger, #362, B edition, EX...................................**16.00**

Road to Oz, #144, A edition, EX **30.00**

Smokey the Bear, #224, A edition, EX..................................**20.00**

Tin Woodsman of Oz, #159, A edition, EX..........................**22.00**

Ugly Duckling, #D22, C edition, EX...................................**15.00**

Woody Woodpecker Joins the Circus, #330, E edition, VG............**12.00**

Zorro & the Secret Plan, #D77, B edition, EX.....................**12.00**

Series

Everyone remembers a special series of books they grew up with: The Hardy Boys, Nancy Drew Mysteries, Tarzan — there were countless others. And though these are becoming very collectible today, there were many editions of each, and most are very easy to find. As a result, common titles are sometimes worth very little. Generally the last few in any series will be the most difficult to locate, since fewer were printed than the earlier stories which were likely to have been reprinted many times. As is true of any type of book, first editions or the earliest printing will have more collector value. For further reading see *Collector's Guide to Children's Books, 1850 to 1950,* by Diane McClure Jones and Rosemary Jones (Collector Books).

Augustus & the Mountains, Henderson Le Grand, Bobbs Merril, 1941, EX..................**25.00**

Betty Gordon at Boarding School, Alice B Emerson, 1930s, sm, EX....................................**10.00**

Blondie & Dagwood's Snapshot Clue, Authorized Editions, 1940s, EX.......................**15.00**

Boy's King Arthur, Sidney Lanier, Scribner Classics, 1947 edition, EX............................**50.00**

Clue of the Leaning Chimney (Nancy Drew), Carolyn Keen, 1949, EX.......................**20.00**

Gene Autry & the Ghost Riders, Lewis B Patton, Whitman, 1955, EX.........................**20.00**

Girl Scouts' Canoe Trip, Edith Lavell, 1930s, EX...........**10.00**

Mike Mars Around the Moon, Donald Wolheim, Doubleday, 1964, EX.........................**15.00**

Mystery of the Brass Bound Box (Rick & Ruddy), H Garis, 1930s, EX **30.00**

Mystery of the Mississippi (Trixie Beldon), K Kenny, Whitman, 1970, EX..........................**10.00**

Outdoor Girls in the Air, Laura Lee Hope, Whitman, 1933, EX.**10.00**

Paddington Takes to TV, Michael Bond, 1st American edition, 1974, EX.........................**45.00**

Radio Boys at the Sending Station, Allen Chapman, 1910s, EX..**10.00**

Robinson Crusoe, Whitman Classics, 1930s, EX **10.00**

Rushton Boys at Treasure Cove, Spencer Davenport, 1916, EX **10.00**

Secret Sky Express (Slim Tyler Air Stories), Richard Stone, 1920s, EX **15.00**

Story of Dr Dolittle, Hugh Lofting, Lippincott, 1948 edition, EX................................**15.00**

Walt Disney's Annette, Sierra Summer; Doris Schroeder, 1960, EX........................**10.00**

Whitman Tell-A-Tale Books

Though the Whitman Company produced a wide variety of children's books, the ones most popular with today's collectors (besides the Big Little Books which are dealt with earlier in this category) are the Tell-A-Tales. They were published in a variety of series, several of which centered around radio, TV, and comic strips. For more information, photos, and current values, we recommend *Whitman Juvenile Books, Reference & Value Guide*, by David and Virginia Brown (Collector Books).

Pan Am Jet Flight Story Book, 1960s, $35.00 (1980s, $10.00). (Photo courtesy Diane McClure Jones and Rosemary Jones)

Tarzan and the City of Gold, Whitman, hardcover, 1954, VG, $15.00. (Photo courtesy David and Virginia Brown)

Alphabet Rhymes, #24002-2, 1956, VG..........................**6.00**

Casey the Clumsy Colt, #2403, 1965, EX.........................**10.00**

Daffy Duck, #2453-36, 1977, EX..**5.00**

Flintstones at the Circus, #2552, 1963, VG......................**12.00**

Gingerbread Man, Top Top Tale, #2444, 1967, EX..............**6.00**

Hello Joe, #2526-15, 1961, VG..**6.00**

Katy's First Day, #2403, 1972, EX................................**8.00**

Magilla Gorilla Takes a Banana Holiday, #2552, 1965, VG........**14.00**

Night Before Christmas, #2517, 1969, VG..........................**5.00**

Polka Dot Tots, #864, 1946, VG..**10.00**

Puffy, #2546, 1952, VG.........**12.00**

Raggedy Andy's Treasure Hunt, #2420, 1973, VG...............**8.00**

Snoozy, #2564, 1944, w/dust jacket, EX.............................**20.00**

Two Stories About Lollipop, #2470, 1969, VG.............**10.00**

Woody Woodpecker's Peck of Trouble, #2562, 1951, VG.........**12.00**

Wonder Books

Though the first were a little larger, the Wonder Books printed since 1948 have all measured 6½" x 8". They've been distributed by Random House, Grosset Dunlap, and Wonder Books Inc. They're becoming very collectible, especially those based on favorite TV and cartoon characters. Steve Santi's book *Collecting Little Golden Books* includes a section on Wonder Books as well.

Baby Huey, #787, 1975, VG...**25.00**

Casper & Wendy, #805, 1963, EX...............................**10.00**

Doll Family, #802, 1962, VG..**20.00**

Flash Gordon & the Baby Animals, 1956, EX..............**30.00**

Freddy & the Indians, #816, 1963, VG................................**12.00**

Hungry Baby Bunny, #847, 1951, EX, $10.00.

Little Cowboy's Christmas, #570, 1951, EX.........................**12.00**

Luno the Soaring Stallion, #831, 1964, EX.........................**15.00**

Pelle's New Suits, #803, 1962, EX...............................**12.00**

Playtime for Nancy, #560, 1951, G.....................................**5.00**

Runaway Baby Bird, #748, 1960, EX.....................................**6.00**

Snow White & the Seven Dwarfs, #659, 1955, VG.................**8.00**

This Magic World, #723, 1959, VG **8.00**

Who Has My Shoes?, #801, 1963, EX.....................................**8.00**

Wonder Book of Fun, #576, 1951, VG..................................**10.00**

Miscellaneous

Ali & the Ghost Tiger, Elaine Masters, 1st edition, 1970, EX.................................**15.00**

Alice in Wonderland, Elf/Rand McNally, 1951, EX.........**25.00**

Bumble, Magdalen Eldon, Collins, 1950, EX........................**20.00**

Captain's Daughter, Elizabeth Coatsworth, MacMillan, 1950, EX...................................**25.00**

Country School, Jerrold Beim, 1st edition, Morrow, 1955, EX...............................**10.00**

Elephant's Child, Rudyard Kipling, 1st hardcover, Folett, 1969, EX.......................**20.00**

Freaky Friday, Mary Rogers, 1st edition, Harper & Row, 1972, EX....................................**10.00**

Giant John, Arnold Lobel, 1st edition, Harper, 1964, EX ..**15.00**

Good Morning Miss Dove, Frances Gray Paton, Dodd Mead, 1954, EX........................**10.00**

Grandpa, Barbara Borack, Harper, 1967............................**10.00**

Grin & Giggle Book, Robert Pierce, 1st edition, Golden Press, 1972, EX..............**35.00**

Hong Kong Phooey & the Fortune Cookie Caper, Jean Lewis, 1975, EX........................**10.00**

Hopalong Cassidy Lends a Helping Hand, Bonnie Books, pop-ups, 1950, EX.................**75.00**

Ken Follows the Chuck Wagon, Basil Miller, Zondervan, 1950, EX.........................**10.00**

Koko's Circus, Hank Hart, Animated Book Co, 1942, VG....**55.00**

Lighthouse Keeper's Son, Nan Chauncy, 1st edition, Oxford, 1969, EX.......................**15.00**

Look Through My Window, Jean Little, 1st edition, Harper & Row, EX.........................**45.00**

Peppermint Pig, Nina Bawden, 1st edition, Victor Gollancz, 1975, EX.........................**20.00**

Rainbow Round-A-Bout, 2 pop-ups & revolving pictures, 1992, EX........................**15.00**

Resident Witch, Marian Place, Washburn, 1970, EX......**15.00**

Santa Mouse, Michael Brown, DeWitt color illustrations, NY, 1968, VG, $15.00. (Photo courtesy Marvelous Books)

Secret Gold, Madeleine Raillon, 1st American edition, 1965, EX...................................**10.00**

Treasure in the Sun, Adeline Atwood, 1st edition, 1954, EX...................................**15.00**

Unfriendly Book, Charlotte Zolotow, 1st edition, 1975, EX **15.00**

Wonderful Ice Cream Cart, Alice Rogers Hager, 1st edition, 1955, EX........................**20.00**

Christmas

No other holiday season is celebrated to such an extravagant extent as Christmas, and vintage decorations provide a warmth and charm that none from today can match. Ornaments from before 1870 were imported from Dresden, Germany — usually made of cardboard and sparkled with tinsel trim. Later, blown glass ornaments were made there in literally thousands of shapes such as fruits and vegetables, clowns, Santas, angels, and animals. Kugles, heavy glass balls (though you'll sometimes find fruit and vegetable forms as well), were made from about 1820 to late in the century in sizes up to 14". Early Santa figures are treasured, especially those in robes other than red. Figural bulbs from the '20s and '30s are popular, those that are character related in particular. Refer to *Christmas Collectibles*, by Margaret and Kenn Whitmyer, and *Christmas Ornaments, Lights & Decorations, Volumes I, II* and *III*, by George Johnson (all by Collector Books) for more information.

Bank, Father Christmas, cast iron, US, early 1900s, 6", $185 to **225.00**
Bank, Santa & Mrs Claus, Norcrest, NM.......................**45.00**
Bubble light, C-7 base, old, ea, $2 to **7.00**
Bubble light mantle set, 9 lights on plastic base, complete **50.00**
Bubble light w/Santa figure, plastic, 1950s, 8"....................**28.00**
Candy container, bell, paper w/scrap trim, US, 1930s, 5½", $25 to **35.00**

Candy container, boot, red plastic, Merry Christmas, Rosbro, 1955, 4".............................**6.00**

Candy container, paper, commercially made cornucopia with applied lithograph, large, from $60.00 to $75.00. (Photo courtesy George Johnson)

Candy container, Santa in Chimney, plastic, 1950s, NM..............................**35.00**
Candy container, Santa in sled w/running deer, plastic, US, 1950s, 4".........................**24.00**
Candy container, Santa on skis, plastic, US, 1955, 3½"....**10.00**
Candy container, snowball, crushed glass over cardboard, 1980-90s, 3"......................**4.00**
Candy container, snowman, plastic, Rosbro Plastics, 1955, 5", $12 to..............................**15.00**
Decoration, Santa head wall display, papier-mache, 17", EX............................**135.00**
Doll, Santa, Steiff, all ID, 1985, 12", NM **250.00**
Figure, reindeer, plastic, stamped Rudolph, 3¾", $5 to..........**6.00**
Figure, Santa w/toy bag, bisque, 4", VG **50.00**
Lantern, Santa face on red base, glass, battery-op, 5", MIB.**100.00**

Light bulb, apple, painted milk glass, embossed leaves, Japan, 2½"......................**12.00**

Light bulb, bear sitting, milk glass, Japan, 1950s, 2¾", $75 to.....................**85.00**

Light bulb, cat sitting on bow, painted clear glass, Japan, $30 to..............................**35.00**

Light bulb, clown head (Joey), painted clear glass, Japan, 2", $25 to..............................**35.00**

Light bulb, clown w/mask, milk glass, Japan, 1950s, 3", $25 to **35.00**

Light bulb, Dutch boy, milk glass, Japan, 1950s, 3", $75 to..**85.00**

Light bulb, ear of corn, milk glass, lg leaves, Japan, 4", $20 to............................**30.00**

Light bulb, horn player, painted clear glass, 2¾", $50 to..**60.00**

Light bulb, large hump-backed Santa, from $15.00 to $25.00; Snowman with stick, 4", from $20.00 to $25.00. (Photo courtesy George Johnson)

Light bulb, morning glory, muted colors, Mazda, 1940, 2½", $60 to....................................**75.00**

Light bulb, Mother Goose, milk glass, Paramount, Japan, 1955, $15 to...................**25.00**

Light bulb, ocean liner, milk glass, Japan, 1950, 2¾", $75 to..**100.00**

Light bulb, rabbit sitting, milk glass, Japan, 1950, 2", $25 to................................**35.00**

Light bulb, raspberry, painted clear glass, embossed, 1½", $20 to.............................**30.00**

Light bulb, squirrel eating nut, painted clear glass, US, mini, $70 to..............................**80.00**

Light bulb, St Nicholas, milk glass, Japan, 1925-50, 2¾", $25 to..............................**35.00**

Light bulb set, 8 Disney characters, C-7 base, Paramount, 1960s, MIB...................**100.00**

Light reflector, snowflake, hard plastic, 2-sided, 1940s, 5"..**8.00**

Light shade set, 8 Mickey Mouse shades on a strand, Noma, 1930s, MIB....................**35.00**

Light-up Santa figure, painted molded figure, 1950s, 10", NM...............................**50.00**

Mask, Santa, papier-mache w/crepe hat & cloth beard, Germany, 12", NM.......**175.00**

Nativity scene, 1-pc diecut cardboard foldout, 14x22"...**110.00**

Ornament, acorn, mold-blown, Corning Glass, ca 1939, 2", $5 to.....................................**10.00**

Ornament, angel, scrap w/crepe gown, wing collar, no arms, 6", $14 to.........................**16.00**

Ornament, angel on harp, mold-blown, Germany, 1970, 3½", $10 to..............................**15.00**

Ornament, apple, free-blown, covered in crushed glass, 2".**30.00**

Ornament, baby buggy, coated cardboard, 2¼"..............**12.00**

Ornament, basket, wooden w/glass fruit, 3", $40 to ..**50.00**

Ornament, bear in cone hat w/paw to ear, mold-blown, 1950s, 4", $35 to **45.00**

Ornament, bell, chenille, 4½", $12 to **15.00**

Ornament, berries on heart, mold-blown, 1¾", $2 to **5.00**

Ornament, bird, cardboard, flat, sm, $20 to **35.00**

Ornament, bird, glitter on cardboard, Japan, ca 1960, 3½", $4 to ...**5.00**

Ornament, bird, mold-blown w/spun-glass crest, clip-on, 1991, 3½" **18.00**

Ornament, butterfly, filigree wings, Dresden, 1980s-90s, 4½", $5 to **10.00**

Ornament, candy cane, chenille, 5" **25.00**

Ornament, carrot, mold-blown, Germany, 3½-4", $25 to .**45.00**

Ornament, cross, cardboard, flat, $20 to **35.00**

Ornament, duck, mold-blown, Germany, 1950s-70s, 2¾-3", $25 to **30.00**

Ornament, dwarf w/pick, mold-blown, Germany, 1980s, 2½", $50 to **75.00**

Ornament, Father Christmas, scrap w/spun-glass skirt, 7½", $50 to **60.00**

Ornament, ice cream cone, free-blown, 4", $5 to **10.00**

Ornament, lighthouse, mold-blown, 1950s-60s, 3", from $35 to **45.00**

Ornament, pear, pressed cotton, 3½", $18 to......................**20.00**

Ornament, Santa, vinyl w/flocking, Japan, 1970s-80s, 4½" **4.00**

Ornament, Santa w/bag & toys, mold-blown, 3-3¾", $30 to .**35.00**

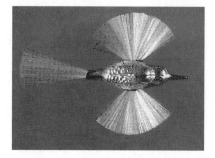

Ornament, songbird with spun-glass wings (also referred to as hummingbird), from $30.00 to $40.00. (Photo courtesy George Johnson)

Ornament, teapot, silvered embossed plastic, ca 1960, 3"................**9.00**

Rattle, Santa figure holding box of fruit, celluloid, NM **150.00**

Roly Poly, celluloid, Irwin, 1930s, 3½", NM **65.00**

Store display, Santa w/letter, velvet-covered diecut cardboard, 21"................................**25.00**

Toy, Santa, latex rubber squeaker, 1950s, 10½", MIB, $30.00. (Photo courtesy Linda Baker)

Tree, aluminum w/'star-burst' tips, 1960s, 18"...............**18.00**

Tree, shredded green or white Visca, 1950s, 42" to 60", ea $30 to **45.00**

Tree stand, Eight Light Automatic, Noma, ca 1948, 19" dia, $20 to **25.00**

Tree topper, Santa w/tree, Inge Glass, late 1980s, 11", $20 to **25.00**

Village pieces, coated cardboard, Japan, 4" to 5", ea, $12 to..**15.00**

Village pieces, coated cardboard, Japan, 5" to 6", ea, $15 to..**20.00**

Wind-up Santa figure, litho tin, Chein, 1920s-30s, 5½".**100.00**

Wreath, choir boy w/candle at center, plastic, 1955-60, 6¾", $20 to **25.00**

Wreath w/light-up candle, Noma Electric Candle Auto Wreath, EXIB **50.00**

Cigarette Lighters

Pocket lighters were invented sometime after 1908 and were at their peak from about 1925 to the 1930s. Dunhill, Zippo, Colibri, Ronson, Dupont, and Evans are some of the major manufacturers. An early Dunhill Unique model if found in its original box would be valued at hundreds of dollars. Quality metal and metal-plated lighters were made from the 1950s to about 1960. Around that time disposable lighters never needing a flint were introduced, causing a decline in sales of figurals, novelties, and high-quality lighters.

What makes a lighter collectible? — novelty of design, type of mechanism (flint and fuel, flint and gas, battery, etc.), and manufacturer (and whether or not the company is still in business). For further information, we recommend *Collector's Guide to Cigarette Lighters, Books I* and *II,* by James Flanagan.

Advertising, Canadian Ale, bottle form, 1950s, 5", $15 to ...**25.00**

Advertising, Mack, chrome w/brass logo, Zippo, 1976, 2¼", $25 to **35.00**

Advertising, Marlboro, brass, Zippo, 1991, 2½", $25 to..**35.00**

Advertising, Phillip Morris Commander, Japan, 1960s, 2", $15 to **20.00**

Advertising, Santa Fe, musical, Crown, 1940s, 2⅝x1⅜", $75 to **90.00**

Advertising, Winston, Japan, 1960s, 1¾x2⅛", $10 to ...**20.00**

ASR, dagger-shaped letter opener/lighter, metal/plastic, 1950s, 10" **35.00**

ASR, plastic marble-like bowl body w/brass pedestal & top, 1950s, 3" **30.00**

Colibri, metal pouch style, 1954, 2⅛x2", $20 to **30.00**

Continental, Pigeon, ivory-look carved roses on brass, 1960s, 1½" **25.00**

Evans, brass egg shape w/hinged lid, footed, 1950s, 2½x3" **50.00**

Evans, chromium, vertical ribbing, 1950s, 5¾x3¼", $70 to....**90.00**

Evans, fur-covered brass cylinder w/brass top, 1934, 3", $35 to **50.00**

Evans, hammered chromium lift-arm sq case, 1930s, 3⅛", $75 to **90.00**

124

Evans, hammered chromium w/black enamel design, 1930s, 4¼", $60 to.....................**80.00**

Evans, silver-plated gondola form on pedestal, 1950s, 2½x3", $15 to.............................**45.00**

Evans, stitched leather bucket shape w/brass emblem, 1930s, 4¼"....................................**60.00**

Figural, barrel, silver-plated, Occupied Japan, 1948, 3", $60 to......................................**80.00**

Figural, brass and leather bellows, squeeze to light, 1960s, 2x7¼", from $20.00 to $30.00. (Photo courtesy James Flanagan)

Figural, camera lighter/flashlight, chrome & leather, Aurora, 1960, 2"........................**35.00**

Figural, candle in chamber stick holder, Giv-A-Gift, 1960s, 6¼"...................................**30.00**

Figural, horse, ceramic, saddled, chain reins, Japan, 1955, 5½"...................................**25.00**

Figural, knight's helmet, push down on visor to light, 1950s, 5"....................................**20.00**

Figural, lighthouse, silver-plated, Occupied Japan, 1948, 4¼"...................................**75.00**

Figural, nude w/basket lighter on head, chrome, 1950, 6", $15 to **30.00**

Figural, owl, silver-plated w/glass eyes, Occupied Japan, 1948, 3"....................................**100.00**

Figural, penguin, gold & silver-plated, 1960, 2", $40 to ..**70.00**

Figural, Stature of Liberty, batteries & butane, 1950s, 7½", $90 to............................**115.00**

Figural, tankard w/embossed knight & castle, chromium, 1980s, 4¼".....................**25.00**

Figural, Thompson machine gun, chromium, butane, 1988, 11¼", $35 to....................**60.00**

Parker, chromium, vertical ribbing, 1930s, 3", $35 to...............**50.00**

Prince, Rotary, chromium w/medallion design, 1950s, 1⅞" dia, $20 to **30.00**

Rex Mfg Co, brass lift-arm, 1930s, 2x1⅜", $30 to..................**50.00**

Ronson, ball-shaped white-on-green Wedgwood style, 1962, 2¾x2⅛"..........................**60.00**

Ronson, reproduction of 'Banjo' lighter in gold plate and black enamel, 1960s, 3⅜x1⅞", from $60.00 to $80.00. (Photo courtesy James Flanagan)

Ronson, Decanter, silver-plated, 1936, 4½", $40 to...........**60.00**

Ronson, Decor, saucer shape w/legs, 1954, 2¾x4¼" dia, $25 to 40.00

Ronson, Essex, leather & chromium, 1954, 2⅛", $20 to 30.00

Ronson, Nordic, glass & chromium, ca 1955, 3½x3⅜" dia, $25 to 40.00

Ronson, Pal, chromium, 1941, 4⅛x2", $40 to 60.00

Zippo, Corinthian, chromium, 1960, 3⅞x2" dia, $35 to .50.00

Zippo, Moderne, chromium, 1966, 4⅛x2¼" dia at base, $35 to 50.00

Clothes Sprinkler Bottles

From the time we first had irons, clothes were sprinkled with water before ironing for the best results. During the 1930s until the 1950s when the steam iron became a home staple, some of us merely took sprinkler tops and stuck them into bottles to accomplish this task, while the more imaginative enjoyed the bottles made in figural shapes and bought the ones they particularly liked. The most popular, of course, were the Chinese men marked 'Sprinkle Plenty.' Some bottles were made by American Bisque, Cleminson of California, and other famous figural pottery makers. Many were made in Japan for the export market.

Cat, various designs & colors, handmade, $75 to 150.00

Chinese man, Sprinkle Plenty, hands over belly, handmade, $50 to 100.00

Chinese man, towel over arm, $300 to 400.00

Clothespin, red, yellow & green plastic, $20 to.................40.00

Dutch girl, white w/green & pink trim, wetter-downer, $175 to......................250.00

Elephant, pink & gray, $60 to..85.00

Emperor, various designs & colors, handmade, $150 to.......200.00

Iron, green ivy, $50 to...........75.00

Iron, man & woman farmer, $200 to.................................275.00

Iron, souvenir of Wonder Cave, $250 to.........................300.00

Mary Poppins, Cleminson, $250 to 350.00

Myrtle, ceramic, Pfaltzgraff, from $250.00 to $350.00. (Photo courtesy Ellen Bercovici)

Poodle, gray & pink or white, $200 to.........................300.00

Coca-Cola

Introduced in 1886, Coca-Cola advertising has literally saturated our lives with a never-ending variety of items. Some of the earlier calendars and trays have been known to bring prices well into the four figures. Because of these heady prices and extreme collector demand for good Coke items, reproductions are everywhere so beware! In addition to reproductions, 'fantasy' items have also been made, the difference being that a 'fantasy' never existed as an original. Don't be deceived. Belt buckles are 'fantasies.' So are glass doorknobs with an etched trademark, bottle-shaped knives, pocketknives, and others.

When the company celebrated its 100th anniversary in 1986, many 'centennial' items were issued. They all carry the '100th Anniversary' logo. Many of them are collectible in their own right, and some are already high priced.

If you'd really like to study this subject, we recommend these books: *Coca-Cola Commemorative Bottles, 2nd Edition,* by Bob & Debra Henrich; *Collector's Guide to Coca-Cola Items, Vols I* and *II,* by Al Wilson; *Petretti's Coca-Cola Collectibles Price Guide* by Allan Petretti; *B.J. Summers' Guide to Coca-Cola;* and *B.J. Summers' Pocket Guide to Coca-Cola, Third Edition.*

Blotter, Friendliest Drink on Earth, 1955, NM+..........15.00
Blotter, How About a Coke?, 3 girls w/bottles, 1944, M .15.00
Bookends, brass bottle shapes, 1963, 8", NM, pr...........325.00
Bottle caddy for shopping cart, wire w/tin sign, 2-bottle, EX...............65.00
Bottle carrier, aluminum, Delicious/Refreshing, 6-bottle, 1950s, VG+..................230.00

Bottle opener, metal flat bottle shape, 1950s, EX+..........22.00
Calendar, 1941, complete, VG.........................200.00
Calendar, 1945, complete, EX+......................320.00
Calendar, 1957, complete, NM+.....................175.00

Calendar, 1960, Be Really Refreshed, couple with skis and bottle, full pad, M, $80.00. (Photo courtesy B.J. Summers)

Calendar holder, Drink...Refreshes You Best!, fishtail logo, 19", NM 325.00
Carton display, cardboard, 2-tier, Shop Here, 1950s, 38", EX+ 200.00
Clock, clear plastic dome over brass case, w/4 bottles, 1950s, 6", EX............................550.00
Clock, Sessions, 1980 reproduction w/oak case, pendulum, NM 325.00
Clock, Things Go Better w/Coke, plastic, sq, 1960s, EX 100.00

Decal, King/Size/Ice Cold, bottle on yellow, 1950s, 17x8", NM..............**35.00**

Dispenser, wood barrel, red w/chrome bands, 2 spigots, 1950s, 28", NM............**750.00**

Display bottle, green glass, 1980s, 20", NM........................**50.00**

Doll, Buddy Lee in Coca-Cola uniform w/hat, composition, 1950s, EX+...................**750.00**

Doll, Frozen Coca-Cola mascot, stuffed stripes cloth, 1960s, NM+..............................**145.00**

Door plate, ½-litre bottle, white on red, Canada, 1970s, 10", NM+..............................**70.00**

Door pull, plastic figural bottle on metal bracket, 1950s, 8", NMIB...........................**425.00**

Door push bar, Coke Is It!, contour logos flank phrase, 1970s-80s, NM+.............**65.00**

Festoon piece, Shop Refreshed, couple/silhouette, 1950s-60s, VG+..............................**200.00**

Game, Down the Mississippi Race Game, salesman's incentive, 1956, EX+......................**50.00**

Game, NFL Football Game, ca 1964, NM........................**15.00**

Glass, bell shape, 50th Anniversary, gold-dipped, w/stand, 1950s, lg **250.00**

Handkerchief, cloth, Kit Carson, early TV & C-C premium, 21x21", EX...................**120.00**

Ice bucket, waxed cardboard, striped swag around top, EX+.....**50.00**

Lighter, bottle shape, Bakelite, 1950s, 2½", NM.............**30.00**

Matchbook cover, Season's Greetings..., Santa w/bottle, NM.**35.00**

Menu board, cardboard, Coca-Cola/Sign of Good Taste, 1959, 29x19 ", EX.........**200.00**

Menu board, menu slots flank fishtail logo, 1960s, 16x57", NM **575.00**

Patch, Drink Coca-Cola in bottles, red disk logo, 1950s, 7" dia, VG+................................**20.00**

Patch, Drink...In Bottles red disk logo, 1950s, 7" dia, VG+...**20.00**

Pencil holder, ceramic 1896 dispenser, 1960s, 7", EX...**150.00**

Pillow, race-car shape, stuffed cloth w/other ads, 1970s, 15", NM..............................**100.00**

Pin-back button, Member Hi-Fi Club, multicolored, 1950s, EX................................**20.00**

Playing cards, Coca-Cola Adds Life to...Everything Nice, 1976, MIB......................**30.00**

Playing cards, Coke Refreshes You Best, bowling girl, 1961, EX+................................**60.00**

Radio, red plastic cooler form, Drink Coca-Cola Ice Cold, 1950s, VG+...................**450.00**

Radio, vending machine, Drink...logo on white top panel, 1963, VG...**65.00**

Record, Bobby Curtola Sings for C-C, 45-rpm, scarce, EX.....**20.00**

Record holder, Hi-Fi Club, holds 45 rpm records, NM.......**55.00**

Sign, cardboard, Have a Coke, bottle on iceberg, 1944, 20x36", NM **300.00**

Sign, cardboard, Have a Coke, cheerleader, 1946, 20x36", EX+..............................**300.00**

Sign, cardboard, Things Go Better..., girl on phone, 1960s, 27x16", EX....................**200.00**

Sign, cardboard, Coke Belongs, boy and girl with bottle, horizontal, 1944, EX, $700.00. (Photo courtesy Gary Metz/B.J. Summers)

Sign, cardboard diecut stand-up, Santa by lamppost, 1958, 28x15", M 325.00

Sign, celluloid, C-C over bottle on red, gold border, 1950s, 9", NM+.............................325.00

Sign, light-up disk on rotating base, Shop Refreshed, 1950s, NM...............................950.00

Sign, plastic w/wrought-iron frame, Drink...In Bottles, 1950s, NM+..................150.00

Sign, porcelain, Delicious/ Refreshing flank bottle, 24x24", EX....................250.00

Sign, porcelain bottle shape, 1950s, 12", VG+............150.00

Sign, tin, Drink/C-C/Trademark Reg, curved corners, 1970s, 12x24", NM+ 25.00

Sign, tin, Enjoy That Refreshing...Ice Cold, w/bottle, 1963, 20x28", M 300.00

Sign, tin, Pick Up 6..., shows 6-pack, raised rim, 1964, 50x16", EX....................450.00

Sign, tin button w/silver arrow, Drink...on red, 1950s, 16", NM+.............................700.00

Sign, tin diecut ribbon, Sign of Good Taste, red on yellow, 10x42", EX.................75.00

Sign, wood diecut girl on metal base, 2-sided, 1950s-60s, EX+ 425.00

Stadium vendor, wood, red, w/strap, 1950s, NM (new old stock)...........................325.00

Syrup jug, paper label, shows paper cup & Coke glass, 1960s, EX 20.00

Thermometer, dial, Things Go Better w/Coke, white, 1964, 12", dia, EX+...............250.00

Thermometer, plastic, Drink..., orange & white, 1960s, 18", EX..................................30.00

Thermometer, tin bottle shape, gold, 1956, 8", EX...........40.00

Thermometer, tin cigar shape, ...Sign of Good Taste, 1950s, 30", VG 200.00

Tie, men's, silk-screened Sprite Boy w/bottle, 5" wide at bottom, NM 225.00

Tie clip, gold & enameled bar, 5-Year, NM......................75.00

Toy airplane, 1973-74 Albatros, red & white w/black markings, EX+.....................100.00

Toy truck, Buddy L#5270J, tractor-trailer, 1980s, 14", NM+.40.00

Toy truck, Linemar, squash cab, litho tin, friction, 1950s, 3", EX+...............................140.00

Tray, 1938, Girl in Afternoon, 10½x13¼", EX, $275.00. (Photo courtesy Mitchell Collection/B.J. Summers)

Toy truck, Matchbox #37, diecast, yellow/red, 1950s-60s, 2¼", NMIB............................**115.00**

Tray, 1940, fishing girl, 10½x13¼", EX..............**250.00**

Tray, 1942, Roadster, 10½x13¼", NM+.............................**425.00**

Tray, 1950, Girl w/Wind in Hair, screened ground, 10½x13¼".**85.00**

Tray, 1957, Umbrella Girl, 10½x13¼", M...**375.00**

the gold is worn or faded, value is minimal.) Numbers included in our descriptions were company-assigned stock numbers that collectors use as a means to distinguish variations in stems and shapes. For further information we recommend *Collectible Glassware from the 40s, 50s & 60s,* by Gene Florence (Collector Books).

Coin Glass

Coin glass was originally produced in crystal, ruby, blue, emerald green, olive green, and amber. Lancaster Colony bought the Fostoria Company in the mid-1980s and reproduced this line in crystal, green, blue, amber, and red. Except for the red and crystal, the colors are 'off' enough to be pretty obvious, but the red is so close it's impossible to determine old from new. Here are some (probably not all) of the items currently in production: bowl, 8" diameter; bowl, 9" oval; candlesticks, 4½"; candy jar with lid, 6¼"; cigarette box with lid, 5¾" x 4½"; creamer and sugar bowl; footed comport; decanter, 10¼"; jelly; nappy with handle, 5¼"; footed salver, 6½"; footed urn with lid, 12¾"; and wedding bowl, 8¼". Know your dealer!

Emerald green is most desired by collectors. You may also find some crystal pieces with gold-decorated coins. These will be valued at about double the price of plain crystal if the gold is not worn. (When

Cruet, #1372/531, green, with stopper, 7-ounce, $225.00; Wedding bowl, #1372/162, green, with lid, $200.00. (Photo courtesy Milbra Long and Emily Seate)

Ashtray, #1372/123, amber, 5"..**17.50**

Ashtray, #1372/124, blue, 10" ...**50.00**

Ashtray/cover, #1372/110, crystal, 3".....................................**25.00**

Bowl, #1372/189, olive, oval, 9"..**30.00**

Bowl, #1372/199, green, footed, 8½"...............................**125.00**

Bowl, wedding; #1372/162, amber, w/lid...............................**70.00**

Candle holder, #1372/326, ruby, 8", pr............................**125.00**

Candy box, #1372/354, blue, 4⅛"..............................**60.00**

Cigarette box, #1372/374, crystal, 5¾x4½".......................**40.00**

Cigarette urn, #1372/381, green, footed, 3⅜"......................**50.00**

Condiment set, #1372/737, tray, cruet & 2 shakers, olive, 4-pc **225.00**

Condiment tray, #1372/738, olive, 9⅝"................................**75.00**

Creamer, #1372/680, ruby **16.00**

Decanter, #1372/400, crystal, w/stopper, 1-pt, 10¼".....**95.00**

Lamp, coach; #1372/320, amber, oil, 13½"......................**135.00**

Lamp, courting; #1372/311, blue, electric, handled, 10⅛"..**200.00**

Lamp, patio; #1372/459, amber, oil, 16½"......................**275.00**

Lamp, patio; #1372/466, amber, electric, 16½"................**160.00**

Lamp chimney, coach or patio; #1372/461, blue.............**60.00**

Lamp chimney, courting; #1372/292, amber, handled................**45.00**

Nappy, #1372/499, crystal, w/handle, 5⅜"..........................**15.00**

Pitcher, #1372/453, green, 32-oz, 6¼"................................**175.00**

Plate, #1372/550, olive, 8" **20.00**

Punch bowl base, #1372/602, crystal **165.00**

Shakers, #1372/652, crystal, w/chrome top, 3¼", pr....**25.00**

Stem, goblet; #1372/2, crystal, 10½-oz **38.00**

Stem, sherbet; #1372/7, olive, 9-oz, 5¼" **45.00**

Stem, wine; #1372/26, ruby, 5-oz, 4"....................................**95.00**

Sugar bowl, #1372/673, blue or ruby, w/lid **45.00**

Tumbler, iced tea; #1372/58, ruby, 14-oz, 5¼" **75.00**

Tumbler, iced tea/highball; #1372/64, crystal, 12-oz, 5⅛"..........**37.50**

Tumbler, juice/old fashioned; #1372/81, crystal, 9-oz, 3⅝"............................**30.00**

Tumbler, scotch & soda; #1372/73, crystal, 9-oz, 4¼"...........**30.00**

Urn, #1372/829, olive, ftd, w/lid, 12¾"................................**80.00**

Vase, #1372/818, crystal, footed, 10"..................................**45.00**

Vase, bud; #1372/799, amber, 8" **22.00**

Coloring Books

This is a branch of toy collecting that has become so popular that it now stands on its own merit. Throughout the '50s and even into the '70s, coloring and activity books were produced by the thousands. Whitman, Saalfield, and Watkins-Strathmore were some of the largest publishers. The most popular were those that pictured well-known TV, movie, and comic book characters, and these are the ones that are bringing top dollar today. The better the character, the higher the price, but condition is important as well. Compared to a coloring book that was never used, one that's only partially colored is worth from 50% to 70% less.

Alley Oop, Treasure Books, 1962, unused, EX.....................**25.00**

Archies, Whitman, 1969, unused, M...................................**40.00**

Baby Alive, Whitman, 1976, unused, VG....................**12.00**

Beany & Cecil, Whitman, 1953, unused, EX....................**45.00**

Beverly Hillbillies, Whitman, 1963, unused, EX, from $25 to **35.00**

Bob Hope, Saalfield, 1954, unused, EX.....................**20.00**

Bonnie Braids, Saalfield, 1951, unused, NM....................**40.00**

Brady Bunch, Whitman, 1973, unused, EX, from $25.00 to $35.00. (Photo courtesy Greg Davis and Bill Morgan)

Bugs Bunny, Whitman, 1970, unused, M.......................**15.00**

Car 54 Where Are You?, Whitman, 1962, rare, NM **50.00**

Casper & Nightmare, Saalfield, 1964, unused, EX...........**30.00**

Chilly Willy, Saalfield, 1962, unused, NM....................**35.00**

Cinderella, Playmore, 1975, unused, M.......................**15.00**

Daffy Duck, Watkins-Strathmore, 1963, unused, M..............**35.00**

Daniel Boone, Whitman, 1961, unused, EX.....................**25.00**

Dennis the Menace, Watkins-Strathmore, 1960, unused, EX **25.00**

Dick Van Dyke, Saalfield, 1963, unused, EX.....................**40.00**

Donny & Marie, Whitman, 1977, unused, NM....................**15.00**

Felix the Cat, Saalfield, 1965, unused, M......................**30.00**

Flash Gordon & His Adventures in Space, Artcraft, 1965, unused, EX....................**25.00**

Flying Nun, Saalfield, 1968, unused, NM....................**35.00**

Frankenstein Jr, Whitman, 1967, few pages colored, NM...**30.00**

Fun w/Elmer Fudd, Watkins-Strathmore, 1963, few pages colored, EX **15.00**

George of the Jungle, Whitman, 1968, unused, EX...........**30.00**

Gilligan's Island, Whitman, 1965, unused, NM....................**50.00**

Green Acres, Whitman, 1967, unused, EX.....................**35.00**

Heart Family, Golden, 1985, unused, NM....................**10.00**

Huey, Dewey & Louie, Whitman, 1961, unused, M.............**20.00**

Humpty Dumpty, Lowe, 1950s, unused, NM....................**15.00**

I Love Lucy, Whitman, 1954, unused, NM, $75.00.

Jackie Gleason's TV Show, Abbott, 1956, unused, VG...........**40.00**

Jolly Santa, Whitman, 1965, unused, EX......................**12.00**

King Leonardo, Whitman, 1961, unused, EX......................**15.00**

Lady & the Tramp, Whitman, 1955, unused, EX...........**25.00**

Laurel & Hardy, Whitman, 1968, unused, M.......................**25.00**

Lone Ranger, Whitman, 1959, unused, M.......................**45.00**

Mille the Lovable Monster, Saalfield, 1963, unused, EX................**30.00**

Million Dollar Duck, Whitman, 1971, unused, EX............**15.00**

New Kids on the Block, Golden, 1990, unused, NM.............**8.00**

Pebbles & Bamm-Bamm, Whitman, 1964, unused, NM.............**25.00**

Pink Panther, Whitman, 1975, unused, EX......................**12.00**

Popeye, Lowe, 1959, unused, VG...............................**35.00**

Porky Pig, Whitman, 1969, unused, M.......................**20.00**

Raggedy Ann, Saalfield, 1951, unused, EX, $20.00. (Photo courtesy Kim Avery)

Roger Ramjet, Whitman, 1966, unused, NM...................**50.00**

Shari Lewis & Her Puppets, Saalfield, 1962, oversized, unused, NM.................................**40.00**

Skippy, Whitman, 1970, unused, EX.................................**12.00**

Superman, Saalfield, 1947, oversized, unused, NM.......**200.00**

That Girl, Saalfield, 1967, unused, NM.................................**30.00**

Tom & Jerry, Whitman, 1960s, unused, M.......................**20.00**

Tom Terrific, Treasure Books, 1957, unused, EX...........**25.00**

Underdog, Whitman, 1965, unused, VG....................**20.00**

Yogi Bear, Charlton, 1971, unused, NM...................**25.00**

Comic Books

Factors that make a comic book valuable are condition, content, and rarity, not necessarily age. In fact, comics printed between 1950 and the late 1970s are most in demand by collectors who prefer those they had as children to the earlier comics. Issues where the hero is first introduced are treasured. While some may go for hundreds, even thousands of dollars, many are worth very little; so if you plan to collect, you'll need a good comic book price guide such as Overstreet's to assess your holdings. Condition is extremely important. Compared to a book in excellent condition, a mint issue might be worth six to eight times as much, while one in only good condition should be priced at less than half the price of the excellent example. For more information see

Schroeder's Collectible Toys, Antique to Modern (Collector Books).

Alvin & His Pals Merry Christmas, Dell, 1963, NM....................**20.00**

Andy Griffith, Dell, #1252, EX..**75.00**

Annie Oakley & Tagg, Dell #575, EX....................................**30.00**

Bat Masterson, Dell Four-Color #1013, 1959, VG.............**15.00**

Beatles, Dell Giant #1, 1964, EX, from $75 to **125.00**

Best of Donald Duck & Scrooge, Dell #2, 1967, EX...........**30.00**

Bewitched, Dell #2, 1965, NM, from $40 to **50.00**

Bionic Woman, Charlton #1, 1977, NM.................................**15.00**

Brady Bunch, Dell #2, 1970, NM **50.00**

Capt Marvel Jr, Master Comics #73, 1946, G **30.00**

Christmas & Archie, Archie Comics #1, 1974, EX......**10.00**

Cisco Kid, Dell #17, VG **20.00**

Dale Evans Queen of the West, Dell #479, EX...............**100.00**

Daniel Boone, Gold Key #10, 1967, EX..........................**10.00**

Dark Shadows, Gold Key #5, 1970, NM.......................**50.00**

Dark Shadows, Gold Key #15, 1972, EX, $10.00.

Donald Duck Beach Party, Dell Giant #1, EX...................**35.00**

F-Troop, Dell #4, 1967, VG...**20.00**

Family Affair, Gold Key #1, 1970, NM.................................**40.00**

Flintstones, Gold Key Giant #1, EX....................................**50.00**

Garrison's Gorillas, Dell #5, 1967, VG....................................**20.00**

Gene Autry, Dell #51, VG.....**20.00**

Get Smart, Dell #1, 1965, NM..**35.00**

Gunsmoke, Dell Four-Color #844, EX....................................**45.00**

Happy Days, Gold Key #1, 1979, M **15.00**

Hardy Boys, Gold Key #2, 1970, photo cover, NM.............**10.00**

Hawkman, DC Comics #1, 1964, NM...............................**500.00**

Hogan's Heroes, Dell #4, 1966, NM.................................**10.00**

Howdy Doody, Dell #4, 1950, EX **40.00**

HR Pufnstuff, Gold Key #2, 1971, EX....................................**40.00**

Huckleberry Hound, Dell #10, 1961, VG.........................**10.00**

Human Torch, 1954, EX, $125.00.

I Dream of Jeannie, Dell #1, 1966, NM, from $50 to.............**75.00**

I Love Lucy, Dell #35, 1959, NM..............................**35.00**

Josie & the Pussycats, Archie Comics #6, 1964, NM.....**20.00**

Krofft Supershow, Gold Key #1, 1976, NM........................**15.00**

Lady & the Tramp, Dell #1, 1955, VG....................................**30.00**

Mary Poppins, Gold Key, 1964, EX.................................**20.00**

Moby Dick, Dell #717, 1956, EX..**25.00**

Mod Squad, Dell #1, 1969, NM....**40.00**

Monkees, Dell #1, 1967, NM..**40.00**

Partridge Family, Charlton #19, 1973, EX.........................**15.00**

Phantom, Gold Key, 1964, EX..**25.00**

Popeye, Dell #8, 1959, EX.....**15.00**

Raggedy Ann & Andy, Dell #1, 1964, NM........................**35.00**

Raggedy Ann & Andy, Gold Key #2, 1972, NM..................**25.00**

Red Ryder, Dell #69, 1949, NM..**35.00**

Richie Rich, Dell #23, EX.....**20.00**

Rifleman, Dell #5, 1960, photo cover, EX........................**35.00**

Robin Hood, Dell #413, 1952, EX **30.00**

Sheena Queen of the Jungle, Jumbo Comics #140, 1950, VG.................................**30.00**

Simpsons, Bongo Comic Group #8, NM....................................**4.00**

Six Million Dollar Man, Charlton #1, 1976, NM..................**15.00**

Snagglepuss, Gold Key #2, 1964, VG...................................**10.00**

Steve Canyon, Dell Four-Color #641, 1955, NM.............**35.00**

Tarzan's Jungle Annual, Dell #2, 1953, EX.......................**40.00**

Tex Ritter, Fawcett #17, 1953, photo cover, EX..............**30.00**

Three Stooges, Dell #1170, 1961, VG...................................**30.00**

Tom Corbett Space Cadet, Dell #9, EX...................................**50.00**

Top Cat, Charlton #3, 1971, EX **15.00**

Tweety & Sylvester, Dell #11, NM **20.00**

Two-Gun Kid, Marvel Comics, 1964, NM.......................**18.00**

Voyage to the Bottom of the Sea, Gold Key #6, 1966, EX...**15.00**

Wacky Witch, Gold Key #7, 1972, NM...................................**5.00**

Wild Wild West, Dell #2, 1966, EX...............................**15.00**

Yogi Bear Jellystone Jollies, Gold Key #11, 1963, EX..........**15.00**

101 Dalmatians, Dell Four-Color #1183, 1961, EX.............**25.00**

Shadow, DC #1, 1973, EX, $15.00.

Compacts

Prior to World War I, the use of cosmetics was frowned upon. It was not until after the war when women became liberated and entered the work force that their use became acceptable. A compact became a necessity as a portable container for cosmetics and usually contained a puff and mirror. They were made in many different styles, shapes, and motifs and from every type of natural and man-made material. The fine jewelry houses made compacts in all of the precious metals — some studded with precious stones. The most sought-after compacts today are those made of plastic, Art Deco styles, figurals, and any that incorporate gadgets. Compacts that are combined with other accessories are also very desirable.

Our advisor for this category is Roselyn Gerson; she is listed in the Directory under New York. For further information we recommend these books: *Collector's Encyclopedia of Compacts, Carryalls & Face Powder Boxes, Volumes I* and *II,* by Laura M. Muller; and *Vintage Ladies' Compacts* by Ms. Gerson. All are published by Collector Books. See Clubs and Newsletters for information concerning the *Compact Collector Chronicles.*

Columbia Fifth Avenue, brushed gold-tone with door knocker motif in high relief, puff with logo, mirror, ca 1946, 3¼" diameter, from $25.00 to $35.00. (Photo courtesy Laura M. Mueller)

Daniel, satin gold-tone square w/courting scene under dome, $80 to **125.00**

Delettrez, Wildflower, round pale blue paper w/floral spray, $50 to **60.00**

DF Briggs, engine-turned silvered carryall w/figure on black oval **175.00**

Dorothy Gray, engine-turned gold-tone resembling lady's hat, $125 to **175.00**

Eisenberg, brushed gold-tone square w/applied rhinestones, 3", $125 to **200.00**

Evans, antique gold-tone oval encrusted w/faux cabochon jade & pearls **60.00**

Evans, gold-tone tap shift w/gold-tone floral branch on red enamel **60.00**

Evening in Paris, wood square w/stylized decorated lid, $40 to **60.00**

France, square w/beaded flowers on beaded sunburst design, $75 to **100.00**

Fuller, round plastic w/comb in pocket on lid, $40 to **60.00**

Alwyn, blue enamel suitcase form, $80 to **120.00**

Coty, Buckle, gold-tone rectangular vanity w/white enamel belt buckle **125.00**

Coty, plastic hand mirror design w/lipstick in handle, $50 to **75.00**

Gucci, round black enamel lid w/gold-tone thumb opening & hinge..............**100.00**

Gwenda, octagonal w/sailing ship painted on foil, $40 to....**80.00**

Halston/Elsa Peretti, gold-tone stylized heart shape, 2x½"......................**175.00**

Houbigant, 6-sided w/basket of flowers, gold-tone trim, sm version............................**60.00**

K&K, satin-finished bracelet/compact, hinged top, $200 to..**250.00**

Kigu, brass-type basket w/pearl in center of filigree floral wreath **175.00**

La Mode, flapjack w/cloisonne floral decor, $50 to **70.00**

Melba, engraved gold-tone rectangular vanity w/tassel & chain, $40 to.............................**60.00**

Melba, gold-tone oblong w/enameled tropical scene, $40 to.........**60.00**

Melissa, fan shape w/enamel gondola on cracked eggshell, 4½x2½"........................**125.00**

Plate, Trio-ette, plastic vanity case designed as hand mirror, $125 to.........................**250.00**

Rex Fifth Avenue, gold-tone flapjack case with embossed ribboned spray inset with faux emeralds, mirror, 4" diameter, from $65.00 to $75.00. (Photo courtesy Laura M. Mueller)

Rex, half-moon shape w/decorated gold-tone band on blue enamel, 5½"..........................**100.00**

Rex, red enamel oval w/mirror inset, gold-tone trim, $80 to.............................**100.00**

Richard Hudnut, vanity clutch in white & gold Tree of Life fabric................................**100.00**

Richelieu, yellow egg-shaped vanity w/monogrammed lid, $40 to............................**60.00**

Roger & Gallet, Lucite square w/applied gold medallion, $125 to..........................**225.00**

Terri, blue plastic diagonal square w/silver dancers on round lid **40.00**

Tiffany & Co, sterling oval, case signed, 1¼x2¾".............**125.00**

Volupte, gold-tone mesh square w/buckle closure, $80 to.**100.00**

Volupte, Lucky Purse, satin-finish, 1940s, $80 to.........**100.00**

Volupte, mink-covered square w/gold-tone braid trim, 3", $75 to............................**100.00**

Wadsworth, bolster shape in black enamel & gold-tone, $100 to........................**150.00**

Wadsworth, clear plastic square w/crossbar design, gold-tone back **125.00**

Wadsworth, polished & satin-finish scalloped fan w/embossed design **80.00**

Yardley, gold-tone oblong vanity w/sliding mirror, $60 to.**80.00**

Yardley, gold-tone rectangular vanity w/3-color embossed design **75.00**

Zell, engraved gold-tone flower basket shape, $100 to..**150.00**

Zell, vanity clutch in black suede w/metal trim, snap closure, $60 to **80.00**

Cookbooks

Cookbook collecting can be traced back to the turn of the century. Good food and recipes on how to prepare it are timeless. Cookbooks fall into many subclassifications with emphasis on various aspects of cooking. Some specialize in regional or ethnic food; during the World Wars, conservation and cost-cutting measures were popular themes. Because this field is so varied, you may want to decide what field is most interesting and specialize. Hardcover or softcover, Betty Crocker or Julia Childs, Pillsbury or Gold Medal — the choice is yours!

Our advisor for this category is Colonel Bob Allen, author of *A Guide to Cookbook Collecting*. Other suggested reading: *The Price Guide to Cookbook and Recipe Leaflets* by Linda Dickinson. (Both are published by Collector Books.)

Advertising

Cookbooks featuring specific food items are plentiful. Some are diecut to represent the product — for instance, a pickle or a slice of bread. Some featured a famous personality, perhaps from a radio show sponsored by the food company.

Anheuser-Busch's How To Cook w/Budweiser, 1952, paperback, 34 pages **30.00**

Arm & Hammer Baking Soda, New Fashioned Old Fashioned Recipes, 1953..........**6.00**

Baker's Best Chocolate Recipes, Walter Baker & Co, 1932, 60 pages..............................**12.00**

Ball Blue Book, 1932, 56 pages .**15.00**

Betty Crocker, Holiday Heritage, 1966, 14 pages..................**6.00**

Betty Crocker, Pie & Pastry Cook Book, 1968, 1st edition, 160 pages..............................**10.00**

Big Boy Barbecue Book, Tested Recipe Institute, 1956, 1957 ....**10.00**

Campbell's Soup, Canape Book, 1935 ....**35.00**

Clabber Girl Baking Book, 1934, 19 pages..........................**12.00**

Del Monte Peaches, 11 Food Experts Tell Us How To Serve Them, 1927....................**20.00**

Dromedary Cocoanut, Foods From Sunny Lands, 1925, 18 pages **16.00**

Duncan Hines Adventures in Good Cooking & the Art of Carving..., 1960................**8.00**

Hershey's Bitter-Sweet Chocolate Recipes, 1940, 16 pages .**10.00**

Hip-O-Lite Marshmallow Creme, Home Desserts & Confections..., 1930s **12.00**

Jewel Tea Co, Mary Dunbar's New Cook Book, 1933 ....**14.00**

Kerr Home Canning Book, 1953, 56 pages............................**8.00**

Knox Gelatine Desserts, Salads, Candies, Frozen Dishes, 1933, 71 pages....................**12.00**

Kraft Cheese Treasury of Good Food Ideas, 3-ring hardcover, 1955 ....**12.00**

Kroger, Ways To Save Sugar, 1940s, flyer.....................**12.50**

Libby's Fancy Red Alaska Salmon, 1935, die-cut can shape, 31 pages...............**15.00**

LL Bean Game & Fish Cookbook, A Cameron, 1959, hardcover.....................**15.00**

Minute Tapioca, Cook's Tour, 1931, 46 pages................**12.00**

Nestlé Semi-Sweet Chocolate Kitchen Recipes, 1959, 64 pages...................................**8.00**

Pet Milk, Tempting Dishes the Easy Way for 2..., 1930s, 16 pages................................**14.00**

Planters, Mr Peanut's Guide to Entertaining, 1960s.........**8.00**

Robin Hood Flour, Let's Bake the ...'No-Sift' Way, 1964, 64 pages................................**4.00**

Star-Kist Tuna, Food and Fun, endorsed by Arthur Godfrey, 1953, $45.00. (Photo courtesy Colonel Bob Allen)

Swans Down, How To Bake by the Ration Book, Wartime Recipes, 1943..................**10.00**

Towle's Log Cabin Syrup, set of 24 recipe cards **35.00**

Watkins Products, Spices in Fine Foods..., 1962, 23 pages...**6.00**

Welch's, Wonder World of..., 1968, spiral-bound, 97 pages.....**5.00**

Appliances

Appliance companies often published their own cookbooks, and these appeal to advertising buffs and cookbook collectors alike, especially if they illustrate pre-1970s kitchen appliances.

Amana recipes, 1948.............**11.00**

Blender Cookbook, Seranne, 1961, 288 pages.........................**6.50**

Blender Way to Better Cooking, B Sullivan, 1965, hardcover, 208 pages.........................**8.00**

Edison Electric, Manual of Miracle Cookery, 1935, paperback, 64 pages...........................**5.00**

Frigidaire, Carefree Cooking w/...Electric Range, 1940, 48 pages.................................**6.00**

Kelvinator Book of Delicacies, 1926, paperback, 23 pages **2.00**

Majestic Cookstove, 1900 .....**12.00**

Malleable Iron Range, Monarch, 1906 ....**25.00**

New Art Refrigerator Recipe Book, General Electric Kitchen Institute, 1940, $12.50. (Photo courtesy Colonel Bob Allen)

Mirro Cook Book, 1954 ....**6.00**

Sears Food Processor, ca 1970, 73 pages **2.00**

Waring Cookbook for 8 Push Button Blender, 1967, 128 pages...**6.00**

Westinghouse Sugar & Spice Book, 1951, leaflet **3.00**

Jell-O

The Jell-O® Story: Peter Cooper dabbled with and patented a product which was 'set' with gelatin, a product that had been known in France since 1682. His patent for an orange-flavored gelatin was granted in 1845 and was marketed from the 1890s through the early 1900s. Suffice it to say, it never did 'jell' with the American public.

In 1897 Pearl B. Wait, a carpenter in Le Roy, New York, was formulating a cough remedy and laxative tea in his home. He experimented with gelatin and came up with a fruit-flavored dessert. His wife coined the name Jell-O®, and production began with four flavors: lemon, orange, raspberry, and strawberry.

Jell-O® is 'America's Most Famous Dessert.' In the infancy of advertising campaigns, this was the campaign slogan of a simple gelatin dessert that would one day become known around the world. The success story is the result of advertising and merchandising methods, new and different, having never before been employed. Well-groomed, well-trained, and well-versed salesmen went out in 'spanking' rigs drawn by beautiful horses into the roads, byroads, fairs, country gatherings, church socials, and parties to advertise their product. Pictures, posters, and billboards covered the American landscape, and full-page ads in magazines carried Jell-O® with her delicious flavored product into American homes.

A Calendar of Desserts, 365 New Ideas & Recipes, 1940, 48 pages **10.00**

Jack & Mary's Jell-O Recipe Book, 1937 ....**35.00**

Jell-O Girl Entertains, Rose O'Neill illustrated **32.00**

Jell-O Today — What Salad, What Dessert..., 1926, 32 pages..**12.50**

New Jell-O Book of Surprises, 1930, 23 pages **6.00**

Polly Put the Kettle On, 1923, Maxfield Parrish illustrated **65.00**

Thrifty Jell-O Recipes, 1931, 23 pages................................**5.50**

Thru the Menu w/Jell-O, 1927..**4.00**

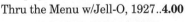

What Mrs. Dewey Did with the New Jell-O!, 1933, 23 pages, $15.00.

48 Recipes — Want Something Different, 23 pages...........**3.00**

Pillsbury

Perhaps no single event in the 1950s attracted more favorable attention for the Pillsbury Flour Company than the one first staged in 1949. Early in the year, company officials took the proposal to its advertising agency. Together they came up with a plan that would become an American institution — the Pillsbury Bake-Off contest. On December 12, 1949, in the grand ballroom of the Waldorf Astoria Hotel in New York City, ninety-seven women and three men were standing nervously over one hundred ranges ready to compete for $100,000.00 in cash prizes. Phillip Pillsbury, Eleanor Roosevelt, and Art Linkletter presented the awards to the winners. The Duke and Duchess of Windsor were in attendance as guests. The bake-offs have been held each year since that time.

A Book for a Cook, 1905, 128 pages, $25.00.

Best Loved Foods of Christmas, 1958, 65 pages.................**8.00**
Best of the Bake Off Collection, 1959 ....**38.00**
Butter Cookie Booklet, 1961, 22 pages...............................**4.00**
Diamond Anniversary Recipes, 1944, paperback...............**8.00**
Grand National Recipe & Baking Contest, 1950s, #3 through #10, $15 to......................**18.00**
Let's Have a Barbecue, paperback...............................**3.50**
Silver Anniversary Bake-Off, 1974, paperback, 92 pages..........**5.00**
Treasury of Bake-Off Favorites, 1969, 96 pages.................**3.00**
100 New Bundt Ideas, 1977, softcover, 90 pages.................**4.00**
100 Prize Winning Recipes, 3rd Grand National, 1953, $15 to...............................**18.00**

Miscellaneous

American Home All Purpose Cookbook, 1966, hardcover, 563 pages........................**15.00**
Best in Cookery in the Middle West, Clark, 1956, hardcover...............................**20.00**
Better Homes & Gardens, Hot & Spicy Cooking, 1984, hardcover, 96 pages **8.00**
Boston Cooking-School Cookbook, Fanny Farmer, 1924, 808 pages..............................**25.00**
Complete American Cook Book, Stella Standard, revised, 1957, 512 pages..............**20.00**
Dinners That Wait: A Cook Book, 1954, hardcover, 216 pages........................**25.00**

Eat Italian Once a Week, Jarratt, 1967, hardcover..............15.00

Fannie Farmer Junior Cook Book, Perkins, 1942, hardcover, 208 pages..............................35.00

Farmer's Almanac Cookbook, 1964, hardcover, 390 pages 12.00

Fifty Ways To Cook Most Everything, 1992, hardcover, 477 pages...............................20.00

French Pastry Book, Crippen, 1932, hardcover..............30.00

Good Housekeeping Cook Book, 1933, 1st edition, hardcover, 254 pages........................25.00

Grandma's Cooking, Keller, 1956, hardcover........................20.00

Holiday Party Casseroles, Beileyson, 1956, hardcover, 60 pages...............................15.00

Hungarian Cookery Book, Grudel, 1958, 114 pages..............48.00

Jack Bailey's What's Cookin', 1949, hardcover, 187 pages........................15.00

James Beard's Treasury of Outdoor Cooking, 1960, hardcover, 282 pages 15.00

Joy of Cooking, Irma Rombaur, 1976, hardcover, 915 pages........................25.00

Low-Fat Cookery, Stead & Warren, 1959, hardcover 15.00

McCall's Basic Cake Book, 12 Perfect recipes, 1953..............8.00

Modern French Culinary Art, Pelaprat, 1st edition, 1966........................25.00

Murder on the Menu, Larmoth & Turgeon, 1972, hardcover, 268 pages........................10.00

Practical Candy Making, Porter, 1930, hardcover..............30.00

Stillmeadow Cookbook, Taber, 1965, hardcover, 335 pages.................42.00

Tested Tasties, Naylor, 1967, hardcover........................15.00

The 5 Minute Dessert, 1961, hardcover 10.00

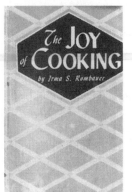

The Joy of Cooking, 1946, $20.00. (Photo courtesy Colonel Bob Allen)

Thoughts for Buffets, Barass, 1954, hardcover..............20.00

Woman's Home Companion Cook Book, 1946, hardcover ...25.00

Working Girls Must Eat, Young, 1938, hardcover..............35.00

Cookie Cutters and Shapers

Cookie cutters have come into their own in recent years as worthy kitchen collectibles. Prices on many have risen astronomically, but a practiced eye can still sort out a good bargain. Advertising cutters and product premiums, especially in plastic, can still be found without too much effort. Aluminum cutters with painted wooden handles are usually worth several dollars each if in good condition. Red and green are the usual handle colors, but other colors are more highly prized by many. Hallmark plastic cookie cutters, especially those with painted backs, are always worth considering, if in good condition.

Be wary of modern tin cutters being sold for antique. Many present-day tinsmiths chemically antique their cutters, especially those done in a primitive style. These are often sold by others as 'very old.' Look closely, because most tinsmiths today sign and date these cutters.

To learn more, check *The Cookie Shaper's Bible* by Phyllis Wetherill and Rosemary Henry. Ms. Henry also publishes *Cookies*, a newsletter for collectors. She is listed in the Directory under Virginia. See Clubs and Newsletters for information concerning *Cookies*.

Angel, terra cotta, Brown Bag Cookie Art, 1983, M.......**25.00**

Betty Crocker Gingerbread Boy, red or blue plastic, marked Betty Crocker Gingerbread Mix, Made in USA, $3.00 each. (Photo courtesy Rosemary Henry)

Borden's Elsie & Beulah, plastic, 2½" dia, pr......................**25.00**
Cat, ceramic, Brown Bag Cookie Art, 1988, M..................**20.00**
Cat, Hartstone Pottery, 1983, 6½x4½", NM..................**12.50**
Duck, flat back, w/handle, 5x5"............................**9.00**
Easter Basket, Brown Bag Cookie Art, 1984, w/ribbon & recipe book, NM......................**110.00**
Father Christmas, Longaberger, 1990, NM........................**25.00**
Flower/fruit/cornucopia/fish/bird/castle/ship, wooden, Springerle, VG+................................**70.00**
Graduation, plastic, Congrats/Great Grad/cap/diploma, Wilson, 4 for........................**11.50**
Heart, tin flat-back, w/handle, 9x10½"............................**40.00**
Kermit the Frog, plastic, Henson Associates, 1956/1978, 4¼", MIP................................**10.00**
Little John & Crusader, plastic, Robin Hood Flour, 4½", pr.**15.00**
Mr Peanut, hard plastic, w/Planters premium ad, 1989-90, NMIP...............**18.00**
Penguin, copper, mk Martha Stewart, in original box, 4", EX.................................**12.50**

Rabbit, machine-formed metal with self handle, marked Forma, ca 1930, 6", G, $10.00. (Photo courtesy Rosemary Henry)

Pink Panther, plastic, Hallmark, 1978, M..........................8.00

Rabbit, metal, green wood handle, mk A&J in a diamond, 2¼", EX..................................50.00

Rabbit, plastic, mk HRM, VG+ ..12.50

Scooby-Doo, plastic, Hallmark, 1978, M..........................12.00

Snowman/Gingerbread Boy, metal, 2-in-1, 1940s, 5¾x7¾", EXIB...............................12.00

Swan, pottery, Brown Bag Cookie Art, 1983, 4¼x5¼", NM .55.00

Teddy Bear, ceramic, Pampered Chef, 1991, M..................27.50

Tigger, clay, Wilton, 6x4½", MIP.............................25.00

Cookie Jars

McCoy, Metlox, Twin Winton, Robinson Ransbottom, and American Bisque were among the largest producers of cookie jars in the country. Many firms made them to a lesser extent. Today cookie jars are one of the most popular of modern collectibles. Figural jars are the most common (and the most valuable), made in an endless variety of subjects. Early jars from the 1920s and 1930s were often decorated in 'cold paint' over the glaze. This type of color is easily removed — take care that you use very gentle cleaning methods. A damp cloth and a light touch is the safest approach.

For further information we recommend *Collector's Encyclopedia of Metlox Potteries* by Carl Gibbs, *Collector's Guide to Don Winton Designs* by Mike Ellis, *Collector's Encyclopedia of McCoy Pottery* by Sharon and Bob Huxford, *Collector's Encyclopedia of Cookie Jars* by Joyce and Fred Roerig (there are three in the series), and *An Illustrated Value Guide to Cookie Jars* by Ermagene Westfall (all published by Collector Books). Values are for jars in mint condition unless otherwise noted. Beware of modern reproductions! See Clubs and Newsletters for information concerning *Cookie Jarrin' With Joyce: The Cookie Jar Newsletter.*

Abingdon, clock, #653.........100.00

Abingdon, hippo w/yellow daisy, marked Abingdon USA #549.................250.00

Abingdon, Little Ol' Lady (Black face), #471, 1942, 7½", from $375.00 to $400.00. (Photo courtesy Ermagene Westfall)

Abingdon, Miss Muffet, #622 ..200.00

American Bisque, Acorn & Leaves, corner jar, from $275 to ...350.00

American Bisque, Cheerleaders, w/flasher, from $350 to ..425.00

American Bisque, Cookie Time Clock, gold trim, from $115 to 135.00

American Bisque, Grandma, #CJ-752, from $125 to.........150.00

American Bisque, Schoolhouse (After School Cookies), marked USA #741..........**70.00**

Brush, Clown Bust, #W49, minimum value **325.00**

Brush, Donkey w/Cart, ears up, #W33, minimum value ..**800.00**

Brush, Granny, pink apron, blue dots on skirt **325.00**

Brush, Little Boy Blue, gold trim, #K25, sm **700.00**

Brush, Night Owl................**125.00**

Brush, Raggedy Ann, #W16, from $475 to **525.00**

Brush, Teddy Bear, feet apart ..**250.00**

California Originals, Airplane with Pilot, marked 2629 USA, from $100.00 to $125.00. (Photo courtesy Fred and Joyce Roerig)

California Originals, Coffee Grinder, from $40 to **50.00**

California Originals, Lion w/Cub, open mouth, from $200 to **225.00**

California Originals, Santa Claus, #871 ....**275.00**

California Originals, Teakettle, from $25 to **35.00**

California Originals, Disney, Mickey Mouse Leaning on Drum, $350 to **425.00**

Cardinal China, Castle, #307 ..**175.00**

Cardinal China, Soldier, from $250 to **285.00**

Certified International, Happy Hatters Dapper Cow, from $20 to **25.00**

Clay Art, Baby Cat, from $30 to................................**35.00**

Clay Art, Fishbowl Cafe, from $30 to **35.00**

Cleminson, King, 10½" **550.00**

DeForest of California, Beans Pig, 1959 ....**125.00**

DeForest of California, Monk, from $75 to **100.00**

Department 56, Cowboy in Silhouette, 10½" **110.00**

Doranne of California, Camel, from $100 to **125.00**

Doranne of California, Duck w/Ears of Corn, from $35 to......**55.00**

Doranne of California, Mother Goose, white, from $135 to **165.00**

Doranne of California, Pig w/Pork Barrel, from $50 to **60.00**

Doranne of California, Volkswagen, from $225 to **255.00**

Fitz & Floyd, Bacon & Eggs Hog **95.00**

Fitz & Floyd, Dog w/Bone, from $75 to.............................**100.00**

Fitz & Floyd, Hippo Limpix, from $50 to **85.00**

Fitz & Floyd, Night Before Christmas **225.00**

Fitz & Floyd, Rain Forest Elephant, from $75 to **100.00**

Fitz & Floyd, Sheriff, from $250 to **300.00**

Goebel, Eagle Head, from $140 to...............................**165.00**

Happy Memories, Marilyn Monroe, from $300 to **325.00**

Hearth & Home (H&HD), Elephant, from $45 to **55.00**

Hirsch, Buddha, from $85 to ..**100.00**

Hirsch, Potbelly Stove, from $40 to **50.00**

Japan, Cookies Can w/Raccoon & Ladybugs **20.00**

Japan, Rag Doll (Raggedy Ann type), pink w/white pinafore, orange hair **30.00**

Lefton, Miss Priss, blue cat head...........................**135.00**

Maddux of California, Humpty Dumpty, #2113.............**300.00**

McCoy, Appollo Age, minimum value **1,000.00**

McCoy, Basket of Eggs **40.00**

McCoy, Bugs Bunny, cylinder, from $165 to **200.00**

McCoy, Chef, bust...............**110.00**

McCoy, Clown in Barrel, blue, yellow or green....................**85.00**

McCoy, Cook Stove, white w/gold trim, marked McCoy USA, 1961-69...........................**35.00**

McCoy, Cookie Jug, double loop..**35.00**

McCoy, Covered Wagon **95.00**

McCoy, Davy Crockett........**600.00**

McCoy, Dutch Boy.................**45.00**

McCoy, Flowerpot, plastic flower on top............................**500.00**

McCoy, Globe, from $300 to .**375.00**

McCoy, Hobby Horse, from $125 to **150.00**

McCoy, Indian, brown.........**350.00**

McCoy, Kittens in Low Basket, minimum value, $600.00.

McCoy, Kangaroo, McCoy USA, 1965, original **425.00**

McCoy, Lollipops....................**80.00**

McCoy, Mother Goose.........**175.00**

McCoy, Pepper, yellow or green **40.00**

McCoy, Rabbit Shopper, from $135 to **165.00**

McCoy, Strawberry, 1955-57 .**65.00**

McCoy, Tepee, straight top..**300.00**

McCoy, Turkey, green & brown, marked McCoy, 1945 ...**325.00**

Metlox, Acorn w/Woodpecker Finial, stained finish ...**375.00**

Metlox, Bear on Roller Skates ..**150.00**

Metlox, Cow (Yellow) w/Floral Collar & Butterfly on Back, blue **375.00**

Metlox, Gingham Dog, blue ..**225.00**

Metlox, Lamb, says Baa **125.00**

Metlox, Pine Cone w/Baby Bluebird Finial, brown stain **75.00**

Metlox, Rose Bud, light pink w/green leaves..............**425.00**

Metlox, Slenderella Pig, $150.00. (Photo courtesy Carl Gibbs)

North American Ceramics, Corvette, #ACC J9, 1986.....................**150.00**

North American Ceramics, Thunderbird, from $200 to.................**225.00**

Omnibus, Bear Scout, from $60 to **85.00**

Omnibus, Devonshire Rabbit, from $55 to **60.00**

Omnibus, Homestead House, from $40 to **50.00**

Omnibus, Seals on Iceberg, from $40 to **50.00**

Red Wing, Grapes, green, marked, from $250 to **275.00**

Red Wing, Pineapple, yellow.....**200.00**

Regal, Davy Crockett, marked..**550.00**

Regal, Quaker Oats, marked....**125.00**

Robinson-Ransbottom, Chef, from $125 to **165.00**

Shawnee, Corn King, marked Shawnee #66 .... **300.00**

Shawnee, Puss 'n Boots, gold trim, minimum value, $375.00. (Photo courtesy Marilyn Dipboye)

Sierra Vista, Circus Wagon, from $125 to **135.00**

Sierra Vista, Pig, from $125 to...**150.00**

Sigma, Circus Ringmaster....**75.00**

Sigma, Rag Doll **225.00**

Treasure Craft, Bowling Ball..**45.00**

Treasure Craft, King Kong...**275.00**

Treasure Craft/Henson, Kermit the Frog, serenading w/banjo..**75.00**

Twin Winton, Cookie Elf, green, 8½x12" **65.00**

Twin Winton, Mother Goose, from $100 to **150.00**

USA Pottery By JO, Nancy (head) **150.00**

Vandor, Greatful Dead Bus, from $100 to **130.00**

Vandor, Real Monsters Garbage Can **36.00**

Warner Bros, Bugs Bunny Bust w/Carrot **45.00**

Warner Bros, Road Runner (Acme TNT) **650.00**

Copper Craft

Sold during the 1960s and 1970s through the home party plan, these decorative items are once again finding favor with the buying public. The Coppercraft Guide of Taunton, Massachusetts, made a wonderful variety of wall plaques, bowls, pitchers, trays, etc. Not all were made of copper, some were of molded plastic. Glass, cloth, mirror, and brass accents added to the texture. When uncompromised, by chemical damage or abuse, the finish they used on their copper items has proven remarkably enduring. Collectors are beginning to take notice, but prices are still remarkably low. If you enjoy the look, now is the time to begin your collection.

Bowl, footed, plain, 4⅛x8¾" .**12.50**

Candle holders, copper & gold-colored metal, 10" w/chimney, pr **30.00**

Carafe, glass w/copper collar, w/copper stand, 13"........**20.00**

Coffee server, 7½" **15.00**

Console set, footed bowl, 4½x7" & 2 4x3¾" candle holders, 3-pc **38.00**

Creamer & sugar bowl, brass handles, w/9½x6" tray **25.00**

Demitasse pot, 7½", $15.00.

Dish, embossed floral rim, 1½x11".............................**15.00**
Flower bowl, 4-footed, 3⅞x9⅞"..**25.00**
Gravy boat, w/strand & candle warmer, 8½" L **22.00**
Lazy susan, w/6 glass serving pcs, 13" dia..............................**15.00**
Mirror w/eagle finial, molded w/copper-tone finish, 21x14½"..**35.00**
Mug, brass handle, sterling interior, 4 for **12.50**
Planter, gold-tinted spinning wheel on front, 4 brass ball feet, 4x10"........................**15.00**
Plaque, Last Supper, in wooden frame, 9¾x20¾" **20.00**
Plate, floral shape, 10" dia ...**15.00**
Punch bowl, pedestal-type base, 7-qts, 6x12", w/12 cups, 8-oz **60.00**
Serving tray, raised rim, 13" dia **20.00**
Tidbit tray, ornate etchings, 2-tiered, 8" & 11" plates, 8" H **15.00**
Tray, ornate etchings in bottom, oval, 9½x6½" **15.00**
Tray, scalloped rim, 12" L **10.00**

Cracker Jack

The name Cracker Jack was first used in 1896. The trademark as well as the slogan 'The more you eat, the more you want,' were registered at that time. Prizes first appeared in Cracker Jack boxes in 1912. Prior to then, prizes or gifts could be ordered through catalogs. In 1910 coupons that could be redeemed for many gifts were inserted in the boxes.

The Cracker Jack boy and his dog Bingo came on the scene in 1916 and have remained one of the world's most well-known trademarks. Prizes themselves came in a variety of materials, from paper and tin to pot metal and plastic. The beauty of Cracker Jack prizes is that they depict what was happening in the world at the time they were made.

To learn more about the subject, you'll want to read *Cracker Jack Toys, The Complete Unofficial Guide for Collectors*, and *Cracker Jack Advertising Collectibles*, both by our advisor, Larry White; he is listed in the Directory under Massachusetts.

Alphabet animals, plastic, marked Nosco, various colors, ea..**4.00**
Badge, Smitty, plastic...........**42.00**
Bike stickers, Z-1380, various colors, set of 10, ea................**4.50**
Book, Liddle Riddles, paper, several different, ea...............**7.50**
Bubble pipe, ceramic w/dog face bowl, red, blue & pink **9.50**

Charm, eagle, bird, owl, Indian, etc, white metal, flat, ea ..**5.75**

Clicker, Dutch Boy, litho tin.**45.00**

Coin, plastic, red **5.00**

Finger Faces, clown, elephant or jester, paper, ea..............**36.00**

Fortune-Telling wheel, two-piece paper litho, turn for fortune, marked Cracker Jack, 1¾", $70.00 (same made of tin, $55.00).

Kaleidoscope cards, #46, set of 15, ea **3.75**

Magic slate, #1388, ea..............**3.75**

Magic square, hidden pictures, paper, several different, ea ..**4.00**

Magnifying glass, plastic, various edge designs, unmarked, ea .**3.00**

Nits, plastic, marked R&L Australia, set of 20, ea **4.50**

Pin, Pied Piper, metal...........**65.00**

Pin-back button, movie star, baseball player or western heroes, ea **10.00**

Sled, metal w/silver finish **18.00**

Spoon rider, astronaut, cowboy, monkey, etc, plastic, ea....**7.50**

Stickers, Creatures of the Deep, set of 8, ea.............................**50**

Tattoos, Z-1366, set of 9, ea **1.25**

Tools, hammer, saw, pipe wrench, etc, plastic, unmarked, ea..**4.00**

Top, embossed metal, marked Cracker Jack **20.00**

Train, w/engine, coal tender, boxcar, tanker & caboose, plastic, EX **10.00**

Wheel walker, elephant, police dog, pig, etc, unmarked, ea **28.00**

Whistle, gun shape, metal....**20.00**

Crackle Glass

Most of the crackle glass you see on the market today was made from about 1930 until the 1970s. At the height of its popularity, almost five hundred glasshouses produced it; today it is still being made by Blenko, and a few pieces are coming in from Taiwan and China. It's hard to date, since many pieces were made for years. Some colors, such as red, amberina, cobalt, and cranberry, were more expensive to produce; so today these are scarce and therefore more expensive. Smoke gray was made for only a short time, and you can expect to pay a premium for that color as well. For more information we recommend *Crackle Glass, Books I* and *II,* by Stan and Arlene Weitman (Collector Books).

Apple, cobalt, Blenko, 1950s-60s, 4½", $50 to.....................**75.00**

Ashtray, dark blue bowl form w/3 rests, unknown, 7¼" **30.00**

Basket, blue, thick handle, Kanawha, 1957-87, 3¾", $40 to **55.00**

Basket, topaz w/crystal handle, Pilgrim, 1960s, 4¾"........**65.00**

Beaker, crystal w/applied green leaves, Blenko, 1940s-50s, 13".....................**150.00**

Bottle, amber fish form w/green eyes, sits on fins, unknown, 15"..........................**75.00**

Bowl, crystal w/sea-green stem & foot, Blenko, 1940s-50s, 8", $75 to.........................**100.00**

Bowl, light blue, scalloped, Blenko, 1960s, 5½x2½"..**50.00**

Candle holder, sea green, bulbous w/narrow neck, Blenko, 1960s, 5¼"....................**50.00**

Case, amethyst, stick neck, Hamon, 1940s-66, 9½", $100 to...............................**125.00**

Creamer, blue, drop-over handle, Rainbow, 1957-87, 3".....**40.00**

Creamer & sugar bowl, amber, drop-over handles, Bonita, 1931-53, pr.....................**85.00**

Cruet, blue, pulled-back handle, Pilgrim, 1949-69, 6¾"....**75.00**

Decanter, blue, ruffled rim, Blenko, 1940s-50s, 10¾"..............**110.00**

Decanter, captain's; ruby, Pilgrim, 1949-69, 10x8"..............**165.00**

Decanter, crystal, bulbous, ball stopper, Blenko, 1950s, 11½".........................**125.00**

Decanter, crystal, bulbous, ball stopper, Bonita, 1931-53, 6¼".**90.00**

Decanter, topaz, slim w/ball stopper, Rainbow, 1953, 11".**125.00**

Hat, turquoise, Blenko, 1950s-60s, 3".....................................**65.00**

Jug, blue w/clear drop-over handle, Pilgrim, 1949-69, 4".......**30.00**

Patio light, topaz, Viking, 1944-60, 3x5"...........................**45.00**

Perfume bottle, olive ball base, metal top, Rice, 3"..........**25.00**

Perfume bottle, rose crystal, ball form, ball stopper, unknown, 6¾"................................**100.00**

Pitcher, amberina, pulled-back handle, flared rim, unknown, 5"....................................**60.00**

Pitcher, blue, drop-over handle, Rainbow, 1957-87, 3".....**40.00**

Pitcher, blue w/crystal handle, Rainbow, 1940s-60s, 6"..**65.00**

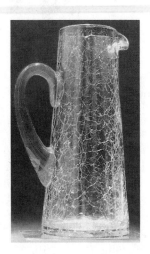

Pitcher, crystal with green drop-over handle, Blenko, 1940s, 10", from $75.00 to $100.00. (Photo courtesy Stan and Arlene Weitman)

Pitcher, crystal, amber drop-over handle, Hamon, 1960s, 5¼".......**50.00**

Pitcher, topaz, very slim, drop-over handle, Kanawha, 1957-87, 8"...............................**80.00**

Tumbler, ruby, pinched, Bischoff, 1950s, 3½"......................**55.00**

Vase, blue-gray penguin shape, polished pontil, 6½".....**115.00**

Vase, crystal w/sea-green foot, flared rim, Blenko, 1940s-50s, 9"....................................**100.00**

Vase, green ruffled rim, Jamestown, 1959-68, 5".**45.00**

Vase, orange, waisted, ruffled top, Rainbow, 1940s-50s, 5"..**50.00**

Vase, tangerine, waisted w/smooth rim, Blenko, 1960s, 12¼"..**125.00**

Vase, teal, flared cylinder w/ruffled rim, Rainbow, 1940s-60s, 9"....................................**125.00**

Czechoslovakian Glass

Czechoslovakia was established as a country in 1918. It was an area rich in the natural resources needed to produce pottery and glassware. Wonderful cut and pressed scent bottles were made in a variety of colors with unbelievably well detailed intaglio stoppers. Vases in vivid hues were decorated with contrasting applications of enamel work. Refer to *Czechoslovakian Glass and Collectibles* by Dale and Diane Barta and Helen M. Rose (Collector Books) for more information. See Clubs and Newsletters for information concerning the *Czechoslovakian Collectors Guild International.*

Atomizer, cased, bright orange w/gold trim, 3"................**70.00**

Atomizer, frosted satin w/painted flowers, amber stem & foot, 5½".................................**95.00**

Basket, red, cased, applied black rim & handle, 6½"..........**80.00**

Bottle, scent; clear, ribbed, rectangular, w/stopper, 5¼".....**50.00**

Bowl, cased, black w/red interior, 5"....................................**85.00**

Bowl, cobalt, silver design & rim, 3¼"..................................**65.00**

Bowl, cased, cream w/multicolor wavy design, inverted rim, 4½"..................................**85.00**

Candlestick, black w/orange interior, wide flared rim, 3", pr......**190.00**

Candlestick, cased, varicolored, 8½"..................................**80.00**

Candy dish, cased, cream w/mottled colors, w/lid, 7½".....**85.00**

Candy dish, cased, red w/black design & knob, 7"...........**95.00**

Champagne glass, cranberry w/crystal stem, 6"...........**45.00**

Decanter, clear w/hand-painted flowers, 10½"..................**60.00**

Decanter, clear w/painted floral design, w/stopper, 10½".**70.00**

Honey pot, dark blue iridescent w/enameled decor, w/lid, 5"..**95.00**

Lamp, electric, rust color satin glass base and shade with hand-painted and enameled windmills and trees, 9", $250.00. (Photo courtesy Jackson's Auctions)

Mustard pot, cased knob, orange w/black design, 4½".......**85.00**

Paperweight, clear w/multicolor base, 3 pink & white flowers, 3"....................................**45.00**

Perfume bottle, crystal w/clear cut base & stopper, 5½".......**85.00**

Perfume bottle, patterned white band on green-painted glass, 6"......................................**90.00**

Pitcher, cased, mottled colors, applied cobalt handle, 9".**125.00**

Pitcher, clear w/painted scene, bulbous, clear handle, 6¾"..**175.00**

Puff box, cased, red w/black & white enameling, 3½"....**95.00**

Salt & pepper shakers, crystal w/red porcelain duck head tops, 2", pr......................**45.00**

Shot glass, clear enameled design, 1¾"..................................**25.00**

Toothpick holder, cased, orange w/black & green design, 2¼"................**35.00**

Tumbler, clear w/green base overlay, cobalt threading, 5".**65.00**

Tumbler, hunt scene enameled on bubbly green, 5¾"..........**65.00**

Vase, cased, light blue w/pink interior, ruffled top, 6¾".......**95.00**

Vase, cased, orange w/black applied serpentine design, 8"........**90.00**

Vase, cased, red & orange mottle, 4¼"....................................**60.00**

Vase, cased, red & orange mottle, w/metal flower arranger, 4"..**75.00**

Vase, cased, variegated pattern, 5½"....................................**65.00**

Vase, cased, white w/green aventurine, applied black rim, 8⅞"....................**110.00**

Vase, crystal, floral intaglio, ball form, 5"..........................**90.00**

Vase, crystal w/blue variegated design, 8½"...................**185.00**

Vase, crystal w/intaglio-cut design, ball form, 5".......**80.00**

Dakin

From about 1968 through the late 1970s, the R. Dakin Company produced a line of hollow vinyl advertising and comic characters licensed by such companies as Warner Brothers, Hanna-Barbera, and the Disney corporation as well as others. Some figures had molded-on clothing; others had felt clothes and accessory items. Inspiration for characters came from TV cartoon shows, comic strips, or special advertising promotions. Dakins were offered in different types of packaging. Those in colorful 'Cartoon Theatre' boxes command higher prices than those that came in clear plastic bags. Plush figures were also produced, but the vinyl examples we've listed below are the most collectible. Assume all to be complete with clothes, accessories, and original tags unless otherwise noted. For further information and more listings we recommend *Schroeder's Collectible Toys, Antique to Modern* (Collector Books).

Banana Splits, Fleegle, 1970, 7", NM, $75.00.

Bambi, Disney, 1960s, MIP..**35.00**

Bozo the Clown, Larry Harmon, 1974, EX..........................**35.00**

Bugs Bunny, Warner Bros, 1978, MIP (Fun Farm Bag).....**20.00**

Deputy Dawg, Terrytoons, 1977, EX....................................**50.00**

Donald Duck, Disney, 1960s, straight or bent legs, EX..**20.00**

Dream Pets, Midnight Mouse, cloth, w/original tag, EX.**15.00**

Fred Flintstone, Hanna-Barbera, 1970, EX..........................**40.00**

Goofy Gram, Frog, Happy Birthday, EX..........................**25.00**

Hokey Wolf, Hanna-Barbera, 1971, MIP....................**100.00**

Hoppy Hopperroo, Hanna-Barbera, 1971, EX+.............**75.00**

Louie Duck, Disney, straight or bent legs, EX.................**30.00**

Merlin the Magic Mouse, Warner Bros., 1970, EX+, $25.00.

Mickey Mouse, Disney, cloth clothes, EX.....................**20.00**

Olive Oyl, King Features, 1976, MIB (TV Cartoon Theater box)..................................**40.00**

Pebbles Flintstone, Hanna-Barbera, 1970, EX...............**35.00**

Pink Panther, Mirisch-Freleng, 1971, EX+......................**50.00**

Ren & Stimpy, water squirters, Nickelodeon, 1993, EX.**100.00**

Road Runner, Warner Bros, 1968, EX....................................**30.00**

Scooby Doo, Hanna-Barbera, 1980, EX..........................**75.00**

Second Banana, Warner Bros, 1970, EX..........................**35.00**

Snagglepuss, 1971, EX.......**100.00**

Stan Laurel, Larry Harmon, 1974, EX+..................................**30.00**

Sylvester, Warner Bros, 1968, EX....................................**20.00**

Top Banana, Warner Bros, NM..**25.00**

Wile E Coyote, Warner Bros, 1968, MIB......................**30.00**

Yogi Bear, Hanna-Barbera, 1970, EX....................................**60.00**

Yosemite Sam, Warner Bros, 1968, MIB......................**40.00**

Decanters

The James Beam Distilling Company produced its first ceramic whiskey decanter in 1953 and remained the only major producer of these decanters throughout the decade. By the late 1960s, other companies such as Ezra Brooks, Lionstone, and Cyrus Noble were also becoming involved in their production. Today these fancy liquor containers are attracting many collectors.

Our advisors for decanters are Judy and Art Turner of Homestead Collectibles, who are listed in the Directory under Pennsylvania.

Beam, Anniversary Series, University of Toledo Centennial.**40.00**

Beam, Automative Series, 1968 Corvette, blue................**60.00**

Beam, Automotive Series, Mississippi Valley Pumper...................**125.00**

Beam, Automotive Series, Police Paddy Wagon...............**170.00**

Beam, Automotive Series, Thomas Flyer, ivory......................**60.00**

Beam, Automotive Series, 18 Wheeler, Dump Truck...**45.00**

Beam, Automotive Series, 1913 Model T, green...............**55.00**

Beam, Automotive Series, 1968 Corvette, white............**100.00**

Beam, Bobby Unser Gurney Eagle Racing Car, white with multicolor decals, ca 1975, MIB, $75.00.

Beam, Casino Series, Harold's Club Covered Wagon, 1969.............**6.00**

Beam, Centennial Series, Cheyenne.......................**10.00**

Beam, Centennial Series, Lombard IL.............................**7.00**

Beam, Club Series, California Missions..........................**12.00**

Beam, Club Series, Hawaii Aloha w/Medallion....................**15.00**

Beam, Club Series, Twin Bridges........................**25.00**

Beam, Convention Series, #1, Denver............................**9.00**

Beam, Convention Series, #10, Norfolk Waterman, pewter.................**30.00**

Beam, Convention Series, #16, Boston Minuteman, pewter.............**55.00**

Beam, Convention Series, #19, Kansas City...................**40.00**

Beam, Convention Series, #3, Detroit.........,...............**15.00**

Beam, Convention Series, #7, Louisville........................**9.00**

Beam, Customer Series, Armanetti, Bacchus.......................**9.00**

Beam, Customer Series, Broadmoor Hotel.......................**8.00**

Beam, Customer Series, Ponderosa Ranch...................**6.00**

Beam, Customer Series, Travelodge Bear.....................**20.00**

Beam, Customer Series, Zimmerman, Blue Daisy...............**7.00**

Beam, Executive Series, 1967 Prestige..........................**18.00**

Beam, Executive Series, 1969 Sovereign.............................**12.00**

Beam, Executive Series, 1973 Phoenician......................**12.00**

Beam, Executive Series, 1982 American Pitcher, District 5, brown........**40.00**

Beam, Executive Series, 1990 Nutcracker, Drummer Boy.........**30.00**

Beam, Foreign Series, Australia, Galah Bird......................**25.00**

Beam, Foreign Series, Boys Town of Italy.............................**8.00**

Beam, Foreign Series, Germany, Wiesbaden.......................**9.00**

Beam, Foreign Series, Germany, 1970.................................**8.00**

Beam, Foreign Series, Seoul Korea.............................**20.00**

Beam, Organization Series, Chili Society..........................**12.00**

Beam, Organization Series, Ducks Unlimited, #1, 1974, Mallard..........................**36.00**

Beam, Organization Series, Ducks Unlimited, #3, 1977, 40th..**41.00**

Beam, Organization Series, Ducks Unlimited, #12, 1986, Red Head **45.00**

Beam, Organization Series, Elks National Foundation **10.00**

Beam, Organization Series, Fleet Reserve **7.00**

Beam, Organization Series, Pearl Harbor Survivors, 1976 .**11.00**

Beam, Organization Series, Tall Cedars of Lebanon **8.00**

Beam, Organization Series, Telephone, #2, 1897 Desk Set **36.00**

Beam, Organization Series, Telephone, #6, Battery **44.00**

Beam, People Series, General Stark **14.00**

Beam, People Series, John Henry **30.00**

Beam, People Series, Martha Washington **14.00**

Beam, Political Series, 1976 Donkey & Elephant, On Drum, pr **24.00**

Beam, Regal China Series, Antique Clock.................**40.00**

Beam, Regal China Series, Bell Ringer, plaid...................**10.00**

Beam, Regal China Series, Franklin Mint **10.00**

Beam, Regal China Series, Portland Rose Festival **10.00**

Beam, Regal China Series, Submarine Redfin **8.00**

Beam, Regal China Series, Truth or Consequences...............**7.00**

Beam, Sports Series, Kentucky Derby, 98th Running **26.00**

Beam, Sports Series, Preakness, 1975 ....**40.00**

Beam, States Series, Illinois..**10.00**

Beam, States Series, Ohio **15.00**

Beam, Train Series, Box Car, brown..............................**70.00**

Beam, Train Series, Caboose, red...............................**75.00**

Beam, Train Series, Casey Jones Locomotive & Tender.....**50.00**

Beam, Train Series, Casey Jones Tank Car **35.00**

Beam, Train Series, Combination Car...................................**50.00**

Beam, Train Series, Locomotive, General.........................**130.00**

Beam, Train Series, Locomotive, JB Turner.....................**150.00**

Beam, Train Series, Lumber Car **45.00**

Beam, Train Series, Tank Car **45.00**

Beam, Train Series, Wood Tender, for JB Turner **75.00**

Beam, Trophy Series, Birds, Cardinal, male....................**35.00**

Beam, Trophy Series, Fish, Sailfish **22.00**

Brooks, Animal Series, Ram..**17.00**

Brooks, Cars, 1937 Cord.......**31.00**

Brooks, Clydesdale...............**30.00**

Brooks, Fordson Tractor, 1971, $20.00.

Brooks, Owl Series, #2, Eagle Owl...............................**65.00**

Early Times, Bicentennial Series, USA **60.00**

Famous Grouse, very rare bisque finish..........................**150.00**

Fraternal Order of Eagles, Louisville, 1990 ....**32.00**

Garnier, Bouquet **20.00**

Hoffman, Dalmatian, miniature..............................**30.00**

Hoffman, Queen's Ranger, Drummer.................................**25.00**

Jack Daniels, Maxwell House ..**60.00**

Kessler, Football Player **30.00**

Lionstone, Firefighter #2, Carrying Child.........................**95.00**

Lionstone, Squawman **20.00**

Lord Calvert, #1, Canadian Goose............................**46.00**

McCormick, Bicentennial Series, Betsy Ross **27.00**

McCormick, Elvis Series, #1, white, 1977 ....**75.00**

McCormick, Gunfighter Series, Black Bart, $35.00.

McCormick, Silver Tribute w/out Presentation Box **150.00**

Old Crow, Pawns, yellow or green...........................**21.00**

Old Bardstown, Coal Miner #2, w/pick **45.00**

Old Bardstown, Surface Miner..**25.00**

Old Mr Boston, West Virginia National Guard.............**28.00**

Pacesetter, Tractor Series, Steiger 4 Wheel Drive **195.00**

Paramount, Ohio Governor James Rhodes **25.00**

Seagram, Tiffany Bicentennial, 1976 ....**20.00**

Ski Country, Animal Series, Mountain Cat Family **60.00**

Ski Country, Banded Waterfowl Series, 1982, Wood Duck .**90.00**

Ski Country, Bird Series, Peacock...........................**100.00**

Ski Country, Circus Series, Clown Bust **65.00**

Ski Country, Falcon Series, Peregrine, gallon, 450 made.................**295.00**

Ski Country, Hawk Series, Redtail, miniature...............**45.00**

Ski Country, Inidan Series, Ceremonial Dancers, Eagle.................**150.00**

Ski Country, Owl Series, Screech Owl Family...................**110.00**

Wild Turkey, Series II, Lore, #2...**35.00**

Wild Turkey, Series III, #10, Turkey & Coyote............**95.00**

Wild Turkey, Series III, #2, Turkey & Bobcat..........**140.00**

Degenhart

Elizabeth Degenhart and her husband John produced glassware in their studio at Cambridge, Ohio, from 1947 until John died in 1964. Elizabeth restructured the company and hired Zack Boyd who had previously worked for the Cambridge Glass Company, to help her formulate almost 150 unique and original colors which they used to press small-scale bird and animal figures, boxes, wines, covered dishes, and toothpick holders. Degenhart glass is marked with a 'D in heart' trademark. After her death and at her request, this mark was removed from the molds, some of which were bequeathed to the Degenhart museum. The remaining molds were acquired by Boyd, who added his own logo to them and continued to press glassware very similar to Mrs. Degenhart's. (See Boyd Crystal Art Glass.)

Baby Shoe (Hobo Boot) Toothpick Holder, Dark Caramel ...**20.00**
Baby Shoe (Hobo Boot) Toothpick Holder, Toffee.................**15.00**
Basket Toothpick Holder, Taffeta................................**25.00**
Beaded Oval Toothpick Holder, Emerald Green..............**20.00**
Beaded Oval Toothpick Holder, Tomato..........................**45.00**
Bell, Sea Foam **12.00**
Bicentennial Bell, Custard ...**25.00**
Bicentennial Bell, Lavender Blue **12.00**
Bird Salt & Pepper, Crystal .**25.00**
Bird Salt w/Cherry, Crown Tuscan.................................**25.00**
Bird Salt w/Cherry, Milk Blue..**20.00**
Bow Slipper, Custard Slag ...**35.00**
Buzz Saw Wine, Bittersweet .**30.00**
Buzz Saw Wine, Bloody Mary..**65.00**
Buzz Saw Wine, Lemon Custard **40.00**
Chick Covered Dish, 2", Mint or Lime Custard **20.00**
Coaster, Crystal **8.00**
Coaster, Pearl Gray **15.00**
Colonial Drape Toothpick Holder, Sunset...........................**20.00**
Daisy & Button Creamer & Sugar Bowl, Milk White...........**90.00**

Daisy & Button Salt, Elizabeth's Blue **30.00**
Daisy & Button Toothpick Holder, Mint Green.....................**20.00**
Daisy & Button Wine, Vaseline **25.00**
Elephant Head Toothpick Holder, Heliotrope.......................**30.00**
Forget-Me-Not Toothpick Holder, Blue Green **20.00**
Forget-Me-Not Toothpick Holder, Champagne **15.00**
Forget-Me-Not Toothpick Holder, White w/Gold Trim, rare .**35.00**
Gypsy Pot Toothpick Holder, Blue Fire **20.00**
Gypsy Pot Toothpick Holder, Tomato...........................**50.00**
Hand, Fog.............................**20.00**
Heart & Lyre Cup Plate, Brown **8.00**
Heart Jewel Box, Brown.......**20.00**
Heart Jewel Box, Teal **20.00**

Heart Toothpick Holder, Cobalt, $20.00.

Heart Toothpick Holder, Crystal Slag..................................**40.00**
Heart Toothpick Holder, Ruby ..**35.00**
Hen Covered Dish, Cambridge Pink, 3" **30.00**

Hen Covered Dish, Holly Green, 3".................................25.00
Hen Covered Dish, Nile Green, 3" 25.00
Hen Covered Dish, Vaseline, 5"..50.00
Kat Slipper (Puss & Boots), Baby Green Slag......................35.00
Kat Slipper (Puss & Boots), Tiger 40.00
Lamb Covered Dish, Forest Green, 5"........................50.00
Lamb Covered Dish, Rose Marie, 5"....................................45.00
Mini Slipper w/o Sole, Amethyst..15.00
Mini Slipper w/Sole, Persimmon..35.00
Owl, Baby Green Slag...........75.00
Owl, Concord Grape..............50.00
Owl, Dark Amber..................35.00
Owl, Honey...........................35.00
Owl, Lime, Sherbet...............35.00
Owl, Unique Blue................150.00
Pooch, Bluebell......................15.00
Pooch, Brownie......................15.00
Pooch, Fantastic....................50.00
Pooch, Lavender Gray...........25.00
Pooch, Peach (clear)..............15.00
Priscilla, Periwinkle 95.00
Robin Covered Dish, Amethyst Slag, 5" 75.00
Robin Covered Dish, Opalescent, 5"....................................60.00
Robin Covered Dish, Tangerine, 5"..................................175.00
Seal of Ohio Cup Plate, Custard Slag................................30.00
Star & Dew Drop Salt, Custard...20.00
Stork & Peacock Child's Mug, Blue Green 25.00
Stork & Peacock Child's Mug, Chocolate........................20.00
Texas Boot, Willow Blue.......20.00
Texas Creamer & Sugar, Amberina..................................100.00

Tomahawk (Hatchet), Bluebell...25.00
Turkey Covered Dish, Amethyst, 5"....................................50.00
Turkey Covered Dish, Peach Blo, 5"....................................50.00
Turkey Covered Dish, Sapphire, 5"....................................40.00
Wildflower Candle Holder, Bluebell 25.00
Wildflower Candy Dish, Crown Tuscan 30.00
Wildflower Candy Dish, Custard 35.00

Depression Glass

Depression glass, named for the era when it sold through dime stores or was given away as premiums, can be found in such varied colors as amber, green, pink, blue, red, yellow, white, and crystal. Mass produced by many different companies in hundreds of patterns, Depression glass is one of the most sought-after collectibles in the United States today. For more information, refer to *The Pocket Guide to Depression Glass, 12th Edition; Collector's Encyclopedia of Depression Glass, 15th Edition;* and *Collectible Glassware of the 40s, 50s, & 60s, 6th Edition;* all are by Gene Florence (Collector Books). See also Anchor Hocking/Fire-King. See Clubs and Newsletters for information concerning the National Depression Glass Association and the *Depression Glass Daze.*

Adam, bowl, green, handle, 9".27.50

Adam, cup, green 25.00
Adam, plate, grill; green, 9" .25.00
American Pioneer, candlesticks, green, 6½", pr 125.00
American Pioneer, coaster, crystal, green or pink, 3½" ...35.00
American Pioneer, cup, crystal green or pink 15.00
American Sweetheart, bowl, flat berry; pink, 3¾" 85.00
American Sweetheart, plate, salver; monax, 12" 22.00
American Sweetheart, tidbit, 2-tier, monax or pink, 8" & 12" 60.00
Aunt Polly, creamer, blue 55.00
Aunt Polly, plate, luncheon; 8" 20.00
Aunt Polly, vase, footed, blue, 6½" 55.00
Aurora, bowl, cobalt or pink, deep, 4½" 60.00
Aurora, creamer, cobalt or pink, 4½" 25.00
Avocado, bowl, handles, crystal, 5¼" 10.00
Avocado, plate, luncheon; pink, 8¼" 17.00
Avocado, tumbler, crystal 35.00
Beaded Block, bowl, red, handle, 5½" 32.00
Beaded Block, candy jar, pear shaped, amber, crystal, green or pink 295.00
Beaded Block, plate, milk white, 7¾" 30.00
Block Optic, butter dish, green, w/lid 50.00
Block Optic, plate, green or yellow, 12¾" 30.00
Block Optic, tumbler, green, 3" ..55.00
Cameo, cake plate, pink, flat, 10½" 175.00

Cameo, plate, grill; yellow, 6".2.50
Cameo, salt & pepper shakers, green, footed, pr 70.00
Cameo, vase, green, 8" 40.00
Cherry Blossom, bowl, berry; pink, 4¾" 20.00
Cherry Blossom, bowl, green, handles, 9" 75.00
Cherry Blossom, pitcher, green or pink, pattern at top, flat, 8" 60.00
Cherry Blossom, tumbler, pink, pattern at top, flat, 3½" .22.00
Cherryberry, comport, crystal or iridescent, 5¾" 18.00
Cherryberry, plate, sherbet; crystal or iridescent, 6"...........6.00

**Cherryberry, salad plate, blue, 7½",
$20.00. (Photo courtesy Gene Florence)**

Chinex Classic, bowl, vegetable; decal decorated, 7" 25.00
Chinex Classic, plate, dinner; decal decorated, 9¾" 8.50
Chinex Classic, saucer, brown-stone or plain ivory 2.00
Circle, bowl, green, 4½" 8.00
Circle, saucer, pink, w/cup ring 3.00
Circle, tumbler, tea; green, 5"...18.00

Cloverleaf, bowl, salad; green, deep, 7".............55.00

Cloverleaf, cup, black...........20.00

Cloverleaf, sherbet, yellow, footed, 3"...................14.00

Colonial, bowl, berry; crystal, 9".............................25.00

Colonial, cup, white...............8.00

Colonial, stem, cocktail; green, 4".............................25.00

Colonial Block, bowl, crystal, 4".4.00

Colonial Block, butter dish, green or pink, w/lid.................45.00

Colonial Block, sugar bowl, white, w/lid..............................10.00

Colonial Fluted, bowl, berry; green, 7½".....................22.00

Colonial Fluted, sherbet, green..........................7.00

Columbia, bowl, crystal, ruffled edge, 10½".......................20.00

Columbia, plate, bread & butter; pink, 6"...........................15.00

Columbia, tumbler, water; crystal, 9-oz.................................30.00

Coronation, bowl, berry; pink or ruby, handles, 4¼"...........7.00

Coronation, sherbet, green...75.00

Cremax, plate, dinner; 9¾".....4.50

Cremax, saucer, demitasse, blue or decorated...................10.00

Cube, butter dish, pink, w/lid..70.00

Cube, plate, luncheon; green, 8"............................11.00

Diamond Quilted, cake salver, green, tall, 10" dia..........60.00

Diamond Quilted, creamer, blue..17.50

Diamond Quilted, plate, sandwich; green, 14"..............15.00

Diana, bowl, salad; pink, 9"..22.00

Diana, plate, amber, 9½"........9.00

Diana, salt & pepper shakers, crystal, pr......................30.00

Dogwood, cup, green, thin....40.00

Dogwood, plate, bread & butter; cremax or monax, 6"......21.00

Dogwood, tumbler, pink, molded band...............................25.00

Doric, bowl, vegetable; green, oval, 9"..........................45.00

Doric, candy dish, 3-part......10.00

Doric, cup, pink....................10.00

Doric, plate, grill; green, 9"..25.00

Doric & Pansy, cup, crystal or pink...............................12.00

Doric & Pansy, plate, dinner; green or teal, 9"..............38.00

Doric & Pansy, tray, green or teal, handles, 10"...................33.00

English Hobnail, ashtray, pink, 4½" sq............................25.00

English Hobnail, candy dish, green, 3-footed................55.00

English Hobnail, vase (straw jar), pink, 10"..........................95.00

Floral, bowl, berry; pink, 4"..20.00

Floral, butter dish, green, w/lid.90.00

Floral, plate, salad; green, 8".....16.00

Floral & Diamond Band, creamer, pink, 4¾".......................18.00

Floral & Diamond Band, tumbler, iced tea; pink, 5".............40.00

Florentine No 1, bowl, cereal; pink or yellow, 6"....................30.00

Florentine No 1, plate, dinner; crystal, 10".....................18.00

Florentine No 1, sugar bowl, cobalt, ruffled.................60.00

Florentine No 2, candy dish, pink, w/lid..............................145.00

Florentine No 2, comport, cobalt, ruffled, 3½".....................65.00

Florentine No 2, platter, yellow, oval, 11"..........................22.50

Flower Garden w/Butterflies, comport, amber or crystal, 7¼x8¼"...60.00

Flower Garden w/Butterflies, plate, blue or yellow, 2 styles, 8", ea............25.00

Flower Garden w/Butterflies, tumbler, amber or crystal, 7½-oz............175.00

Fortune, bowl, crystal or pink, rolled edge, 5¼"............18.00

Fortune, tumbler, juice; crystal or pink, 3½"............10.00

Fruits, bowl, berry; pink, 8".45.00

Fruits, plate, luncheon; green or pink, 8"............10.00

Georgian, creamer, green, footed, 3"............12.00

Georgian, plate, dinner; green, 9¼"............25.00

Georgian, tumbler, green, flat, 4"............65.00

Hex Optic, bowl, mixing; green or pink, 9"............22.00

Hex Optic, bucket reamer, green or pink............55.00

Hex Optic, plate, luncheon; green or pink, 8"............5.50

Hobnail, cup, pink............6.00

Hobnail, decanter, crystal, w/stopper, 32-oz............30.00

Hobnail, pitcher, crystal, 67-oz..25.00

Homespun, bowl, berry; crystal or pink, 8¼"............24.00

Homespun, cup, crystal or pink..11.00

Indiana Custard, creamer....16.00

Indiana Custard, plate, dinner; 9¾"............30.00

Iris, bowl, soup; iridescent, 7½"............60.00

Iris, goblet, crystal, 5½"........26.00

Iris, vase, iridescent, 9"........25.00

Jubilee, bowl, pink, 3-footed, 5⅛x8"............250.00

Jubilee, plate, sandwich; yellow, handles, 13½"............50.00

Jubilee, tumbler, juice; yellow, footed, 5"............95.00

Laced Edge, bowl, opalescent, oval, 11"............150.00

Laced Edge, plate, salad; opalescent, 8"............35.00

Laced Edge, saucer, opalescent.15.00

Lake Cameo, bowl, vegetable; white w/blue scene, 9¾"..55.00

Lake Cameo, platter, white w/blue scene, 11"............75.00

Laurel, plate, grill; ivory, round or scalloped, 9⅛"............15.00

Laurel, sherbet/champagne, ivory, 5"............50.00

Laurel, tumbler, green or white opalescent, flat, 4½"......60.00

Lincoln Inn, creamer, blue or red............22.50

Lincoln Inn, plate, 8"............10.00

Lincoln Inn, tumbler, blue or red, footed, 9-oz............30.00

Little Jewel, bowl, colors, 6½"..15.00

Little Jewel, bowl, honey; crystal, 5½" sq............10.00

Little Jewel, pickle dish, crystal, 6½"............12.50

Lorain, bowl, vegetable; yellow, oval, 9¾"............65.00

Lorain, relish, crystal or green, 4-part, 8"............20.00

Lorain, tumbler, yellow, footed, 4¾"............35.00

Madrid, bowl, sauce; pink, 5".8.00

Madrid, platter, blue, oval, 11½"............24.00

Madrid, trivet, amber or green, w/indent............55.00

Manhattan, bowl, fruit; crystal, open handles, 9½"............35.00

Manhattan, comport, pink, 5¾".38.00

Manhattan, relish tray, crystal, 4-part, 14"............30.00

Mayfair (Federal), plate, dinner; amber or green, 9½"......**14.00**

Mayfair (Federal), plate, salad; crystal, 6¾"......**4.50**

Mayfair (Federal), platter, amber or green, oval, 12"......**4.00**

Mayfair (Open Rose), bowl, cereal; pink, 5½"......**30.00**

Mayfair (Open Rose), pitcher, blue, 6"......**165.00**

Mayfair (Open Rose), platter, crystal, oval, divided, open handles, 12"......**12.50**

Mayfair (Open Rose), vase, blue, ruffled rim, 5½", $125.00. (Photo courtesy Gene Florence)

Miss America, cake plate, pink, footed, 12"......**60.00**

Miss America, cup, green......**14.00**

Miss America, goblet, juice; crystal, 4¾"......**27.00**

Miss America, salt & pepper shakers, crystal, pr......**33.00**

Moderntone, butter dish, cobalt, w/metal lid......**100.00**

Moderntone, custard, amethyst..**15.00**

Moderntone, plate, dinner; cobalt, 8⅞"......**21.00**

Moondrops, celery dish, blue or red, boat shape, 11"......**32.00**

Moondrops, creamer, colors other than blue or red, miniature, 2¾"......**11.00**

Moondrops, decanter, blue or red, 11¼"......**100.00**

Mt Pleasant, candlesticks, green or pink, single, pr......**20.00**

Mt Pleasant, cup, amethyst, black or cobalt......**14.00**

Mt Pleasant, mayonnaise, green or pink, 3-footed, 5½"......**18.00**

New Century, ashtray/coaster, crystal or green, 5⅜"......**28.00**

New Century, cup, amethyst, cobalt or pink......**20.00**

New Century, saucer, amethyst, cobalt or pink......**7.50**

Newport, bowl, berry; cobalt, 4¾"......**22.00**

Newport, saucer, amethyst or cobalt......**5.00**

Newport, tumbler, cobalt, 4½"......**42.00**

No 610 Pyramid, pitcher, green..**225.00**

No 610 Pyramid, tray for creamer & sugar bowl, yellow......**55.00**

No 612 Horseshoe, bowl, vegetable; yellow, oval, 10½"......**33.00**

No 612 Horseshoe, relish, green, 3-part, footed, 9-oz......**30.00**

No 616 Vernon, plate, luncheon; crystal, 8"......**6.00**

No 616 Vernon, saucer, green or yellow......**4.00**

No 616 Vernon, tumbler, crystal, footed, 5"......**15.00**

No 618 Pineapple & Floral, ashtray, crystal, 4½"......**17.50**

No 618 Pineapple & Floral, comport, amber or red, diamond shape......**8.00**

No 618 Pineapple & Floral, plate, salad; amber, crystal or red, 8⅜"......**8.50**

Normandie, creamer, pink, footed......**14.00**

Normandie, salt & pepper shakers, amber, pr.................**50.00**

Normandie, tumbler, juice; pink, 4"................................**90.00**

Old Cafe, bowl, cereal; crystal or pink, 5½".......................**20.00**

Old Cafe, pitcher, crystal or pink, 80-oz............................**125.00**

Old Cafe, tumbler, water; crystal or pink, 4"........................**20.00**

Old Colony, bowl, pink, plain, 9½"...................................**28.00**

Old Colony, butter dish, pink, w/lid, 7¾"..........................**67.50**

Old Colony, plate, pink, solid lace, 13"...............................**85.00**

Old English, bowl, amber, green or pink, flat, 4"................**20.00**

Old English, creamer, amber, green or pink..................**17.50**

Old English, sugar bowl, amber, green or pink, w/lid........**52.50**

Orchid, bowl, yellow, square, 4⅞"...................................**25.00**

Orchid, cake stand, black, blue or red, sq, 2" high.............**150.00**

Ovide, candy dish, black, w/lid..**45.00**

Ovide, plate, dinner; decorated white, 9"........................**20.00**

Parrot, plate, dinner; green, 9"..............................**55.00**

Parrot, platter, amber, oblong, 11¼"...............................**75.00**

Parrot, saucer, amber or green.........................**15.00**

Patrician, bowl, cream soup; amber or crystal, 4¾".....**18.00**

Patrician, plate, salad; amber, crystal or pink, 7½"........**15.00**

Patrick, bowl, fruit; pink, handles, 9"...................................**175.00**

Patrick, goblet, juice; pink, 4¾"..**80.00**

Patrick, saucer, yellow..........**12.00**

Peacock & Wild Rose, plate, any color, 8".........................**25.00**

Peacock & Wild Rose, vase, bowl, any color, flat, 8½".......**125.00**

Peacock Reverse, bowl, any color, sq, 4⅞"............................**42.00**

Peacock Reverse, plate, luncheon; any color, 8½"..............**60.00**

Petalware, creamer, pink, ftd.**8.00**

Petalware, tumbler, red trim floral, 4⅝"...........................**37.50**

Pillar Optic, mug, crystal, 12-oz...**10.00**

Pillar Optic, tumbler, water; crystal, 9-oz............................**2.50**

Primo, coaster/ashtray, green or yellow................................**8.00**

Primo, saucer, green or yellow...**3.00**

Princess, ashtray, green, 4½"..**75.00**

Princess, plate, sherbet; green or pink, 5½".........................**10.00**

Princess, tumbler, iced tea; apricot or topaz, 5¼".............**33.00**

Queen Mary, bowl, cereal; crystal, 6"...................................**6.00**

Queen Mary, candy dish, pink, w/lid, #490, 7¼".............**40.00**

Queen Mary, relish tray, pink, 3-part, 12"...........................**18.00**

Radiance, bowl, nut; ice blue or red, handles, 5"..............**20.00**

Radiance, bowl, punch; amber, 9"...................................**100.00**

Radiance, salt & pepper shakers, amber, pr......................**20.00**

Ribbon, bowl, berry; green, 4".**30.00**

Ribbon, tumbler, green, 6"....**33.00**

Ring, decanter, decorated, w/stopper................................**40.00**

Ring, pitcher, crystal, 8½"....**22.00**

Ring, vase, crystal, 8"..........**17.50**

Rock Crystal, cup, red, 7-oz..**70.00**

Rock Crystal, ice dish, crystal, 3 styles, ea........................**40.00**

Rock Crystal, plate, crystal, scalloped edge, 9".................**18.00**

Rose Cameo, plate, salad; green, 7"................................**14.00**

Rose Cameo, tumbler, green, footed, 2 styles, ea, 5"...........**25.00**

Rosemary, cup, green...............**9.50**

Rosemary, platter, pink, oval, 12".............................**32.00**

Roulette, bowl, fruit; crystal, 9"................................**9.50**

Roulette, sugar bowl, green, footed....................................**12.50**

Round Robin, bowl, berry; green, 4".......................................**10.00**

Round Robin, plate, sherbet; green or iridescent, 6"......**2.50**

Roxana, bowl, yellow or white, 4½x2⅜"..........................**15.00**

Roxana, plate, yellow, 5½"...**10.00**

Royal Lace, butter dish, green, $265.00.
(Photo courtesy Gene Florence)

Royal Lace, candlesticks, green, straight edge, pr.............**85.00**

Royal Lace, salt & pepper shakers, green, pr...................**85.00**

Royal Lace, tumbler, blue, 4⅛"..**50.00**

S Pattern, cup, amber, crystal or yellow, thick or thin.........**4.50**

S Pattern, tumbler, amber, crystal or yellow, 3½"..................**8.00**

Sandwich, basket, amber or crystal, 10"...........................**35.00**

Sandwich, butter dish, teal, w/domed lid..................**155.00**

Sandwich, salt & pepper shakers, red, pr.............................**45.00**

Sharon, bowl, berry; amber, 5".....**8.50**

Sharon, bowl, fruit; pink, 10½"...**45.00**

Sharon, candy jar, green, w/lid.**160.00**

Ships, cocktail shaker, blue/white.............................**38.00**

Ships, saucer, blue/white......**17.00**

Sierra, bowl, cereal; pink, 5½"..**16.00**

Sierra, cup, green..................**16.00**

Sierra, platter, green, oval, 11"..**60.00**

Spiral, bowl, berry; green, 4¾"..**5.00**

Spiral, creamer, green, flat or footed...............................**7.50**

Spiral, platter, green, 12".....**30.00**

Starlight, bowl, cereal; pink, closed handles, 5½"........**12.00**

Starlight, creamer, crystal or white, oval.......................**8.00**

Starlight, plate, sandwich; pink, 13"...................................**18.00**

Strawberry, bowl, crystal or iridescent, 2x6¼".............**55.00**

Strawberry, plate, salad; green or pink, 7½".......................**18.00**

Strawberry, tumbler, green or pink, 3⅝".........................**38.00**

Sunburst, bowl, berry; crystal, 8½"...............................**18.00**

Sunburst, relish, crystal, 2-part.**12.00**

Sunflower, ashtray, pink, center design only, 5"..................**9.00**

Sunflower, saucer, green......**10.00**

Sunflower, tumbler, green or pink, footed, 4¾".....................**35.00**

Swirl, bowl, salad; pink, 8"...**10.00**

Swirl, salt & pepper shakers, ultramarine, pr.............**45.00**

Swirl, tumbler, pink, 4"........**22.00**

Tea Room, bowl, finger; green or pink................................**60.00**

Tea Room, creamer, amber, foot-
ed, 4½"............................**75.00**
Tea Room, plate, luncheon; pink,
8¼".................................**30.00**
Thistle, plate, luncheon; green,
8" **22.00**
Thistle, saucer, green or pink..**10.00**
Tulip, bowl, amethyst or blue,
oval, 13¼"......................**110.00**
Tulip, creamer, crystal or
green..........................**20.00**
Twisted Optic, creamer, blue or
canary yellow **12.50**
Twisted Optic, plate, salad; blue
or canary yellow, 7"..........**6.00**
Twisted Optic, sandwich server,
amber, green or pink, center
handle............................**20.00**
US Swirl, butter dish, green or
pink, w/lid **120.00**
US Swirl, comport, pink **20.00**
US Swirl, plate, sherbet; green or
pink, 6⅛" **2.50**
Victory, bowl, cereal; amber,
green or pink, 6½"..........**14.00**
Victory, plate, luncheon; black or
blue, 8"...........................**30.00**
Vitrock, plate, salad; white,
7¼" **2.50**
Vitrock, platter, white, 11½"..**33.00**

**Windsor Diamond, pink tumblers: 3",
$25.00; 5", $33.00.**

Waterford, ashtray, crystal, 4"..**7.50**
Waterford, plate, dinner; crystal,
9⅝"..................................**11.00**
Waterford, tumbler, pink, footed,
4⅞"..................................**25.00**
Windsor, bowl, vegetable; green,
oval, 9½".........................**30.00**
Windsor, candle holder, crystal, 1-
handle............................**15.00**
Windsor, plate, chop; crystal,
13"................................**14.00**

Desert Storm

On August 2, 1990, Saddam
Hussien invaded Kuwait, taking
control of that small nation in less
than four hours and capturing
nearly a fourth of the world's oil
supply. Saudi Arabia seemed to be
his next goal. After a plea for pro-
tection by the Saudis, President
Bush set a January 15, 1991,
deadline for the removal of Iraqui
soldiers from Kuwait. January 16
saw the bombing of Baghdad and
other military targets, followed by
SCUD missile attacks. The brief
but bloody war ended in March
1991, with Iraqi soldiers leaving
Kuwait and US combat forces
returning home.

Many Desert-Storm related
items were created as remembrances for this brief time in history. Topps Desert Storm trading
cards are popular among collectors, along with Barbie and Ken in
Desert Storm uniforms. Patches,
goggles, and key chains were also
made. Actual battle-related items
are extremely scarce, but highly
coveted by collectors.

Air War Playset, Marx, limited
edition, 100+ pcs, MIB...**65.00**

Bosson head, USAF Fighter
Pilot, orig tag, sm nicks,
7x6", VG......................**90.00**

Combat boots, military issue, sz
11½, new **45.00**

Flyers coveralls, many pockets
w/velcro straps, sz 42 reg,
new **45.00**

Gas mask, MCU-2P 864-55, w/can-
vas carrying case, EX.....**35.00**

Helmet, camouflage, Iraqi,
w/burlap sandbag & rubber
band, VG+ **45.00**

Helmet, US Army Kevlar Ballis-
tic; w/booklet/sweatband, SM,
unissued **55.00**

Knife, bayonet; Russian, w/scab-
bard, 11", NM.................**45.00**

Knife, National Guardsman, bead-
blasted blade, w/scabbard,
6¾", NM **65.00**

Lithograph, Yosemite Sam in uniform w/US flag, Freleng,
16x20, M..........................**35.00**

Medal, Saudi Arabian Service;
w/ribbon, in presentation box,
M.....................................**40.00**

Parka, night; US military issue,
sz med, unissued, new ...**35.00**

Patch, Carrier Air II Wing; shield
shape, 5x4", NM.............**85.00**

Patch, CV67-CVW3, USS JFK D/S
in center, 4½" dia, M......**45.00**

Patch, USS Midway/Carrier
Wing 5, plastic coating,
4x3¼", M......................**40.00**

Sleeping bag, Iraqi; roll-up type,
NM.................................**65.00**

Trading card, Gen Schwarzkopf,
gold border, plexiglass case,
1991, NM......................**35.00**

Dollhouse Furnishings

Collecting antique dollhouses
and building new ones is a popular hobby with many today, and
all who collect houses delight in
furnishing them right down to the
vase on the table and the scarf on
the piano! Flea markets are a
good source of dollhouse furnish-
ings, especially those from the
1940s through the 1960s made by
Strombecker, Tootsietoy, Renwal,
or the Petite Princess line by
Ideal. For an expanded listing, see
*Schroeder's Collectible Toys,
Antique to Modern.*

Patch, U.S.S. Midway CVW5, embroidered cloth, 5x4¾", $110.00.

**Boudoir chaise lounge, Petite
Princess Fantasy Furniture, MIB,
$25.00.**

Armoire, Tomy Smaller Homes..**10.00**

Bathroom set, dark ivory, hard plastic, 8-pc, Marx **20.00**

Bathroom set, Fisher-Price #253 ....**6.00**

Bed, bright yellow, Superior...**5.00**

Buffet, brown, opening drawer, Renwal..............................**8.00**

Buffet, Ideal Petite Princess, complete **25.00**

Chair, club; blue w/brown base, Renwal..............................**8.00**

Chair, dining room; brown or ivory, Tootsietoy, ea **7.00**

Chair, living room; aqua, Strombecker....................**10.00**

Chair, living room; Mattel Littles................................**4.00**

Chaise lounge, ivory w/pink, Marx Little Hostess.................**10.00**

Chest of drawers, various colors, Superior, ea......................**5.00**

Clock, mantel; ivory or red, Renwal, ea **10.00**

Dinette Set, Fisher-Price #251, MIB....................................**4.00**

Hamper, ivory, Renwal...........**3.00**

Hutch, brown, soft plastic, Marx **3.00**

Hutch, dining room; marbleized maroon, Ideal Young Decorator **25.00**

Ideal, radio, floor...................**10.00**

Ironing board, pink or blue, w/iron, Renwal, ea **22.00**

Kitchen set, Tootsietoy, MIB, $325.00.

Lamp, table; Ideal.................**20.00**

Lounge chair & grill, Fisher-Price #272, MOC **4.00**

Nightstand, ivory, stenciled, Plasco.....................................**5.00**

Piano, baby grand; walnut, Strombecker..................**20.00**

Piano, red or yellow, hard plastic, Marx **15.00**

Potty chair, Ideal, blue **15.00**

Refrigerator, pink or white, no-base style, Plasco, ea **3.00**

Refrigerator, white w/blue base, Plasco................................**5.00**

Rocking chair, bentwood; Fisher-Price #273, MOC..............**4.00**

Sink, kitchen; wht, Donna Lee...**6.00**

Sink & dishwasher w/2 racks, Tomy Smaller Homes **15.00**

Sofa, brocade, Ideal Petite Princess **25.00**

Sofa, Mattel Littles.................**8.00**

Stove, ivory or white, hard plastic, Marx, ea...........................**5.00**

Table, cocktail; brown, Renwal..**10.00**

Table, coffee; Tomy Smaller Homes...........................**10.00**

Table, dining; brown, stenciled, Renwal..........................**20.00**

Table, kitchen; Donna Lee, wht..............................**6.00**

Telephone, yellow w/red, Renwal **22.00**

Tub, bathroom; yellow or red, Superior, ea.....................**5.00**

Vanity, ivory w/blue, Ideal ...**18.00**

Vanity bench, pink w/speckled seat, Tootsietoy **15.00**

Dolls

Doll collecting is no doubt one of the most popular fields today.

Antique as well as modern dolls are treasured, and limited edition or artists' dolls often bring prices in excess of several hundred dollars. Investment potential is considered excellent in all areas. Dolls have been made from many materials — early to middle nineteenth-century dolls were carved of wood, poured in wax, and molded in bisque or china. Primitive cloth dolls were sewn at home for the enjoyment of little girls when fancier dolls were unavailable. In this century from 1925 to about 1945, composition was used. Made of a mixture of sawdust, clay, fiber, and a binding agent, it was tough and durable. Modern dolls are usually made of vinyl or molded plastic.

Learn to check your intended purchases for damage which could jeopardize your investment. In the listings, values are for dolls in excellent condition unless another condition is noted in the line. They are priced 'mint in box' only when so indicated. Played-with, soiled dolls are worth from 50% to 75% less, depending on condition.

Patsy Moyer's books, *Modern Collector's Dolls, Volume 1 through Volume 5,* are filled with wonderful color photos and a wealth of valuable information; we recommend them highly. Also recommended is *Dolls of the 1960s and 1970s* by Cindy Sabulis. All of these books are published by Collector Books. See also Action Figures; Advertising Collectibles; Character Collectibles; Holly Hobbie and Friends; Strawberry Shortcake Collectibles; Trolls. See Clubs and Newsletters for information on *Doll Castle News* Magazine.

American Character

In business by 1918, this company made both composition and plastic dolls, all of excellent quality. Many collectors count them among the most desirable American dolls ever made. The company closed in 1968, and all of their molds were sold to other companies. The hard plastic dolls of the 1950s are much in demand today. See also Betsy McCall.

Eloise, cloth w/painted features, yarn hair, 15", EX........**260.00**

Little Miss Echo, 1964, 28", MIB, $225.00. (Photo courtesy Marcia Fanta)

Magic Make-up, grow hair, 1965-66, 11½", EX...................**75.00**

Sweet Sue, walker, 15", VG..**75.00**

Talking Marie, record player in body, battery-operated, 1963, 18", EX............................**90.00**

Toodle-Loo, plastic, 1961, 18", VG **50.00**

Toodles, complete w/wardrobe & accessories, 11", EXIB .**285.00**

Annalee

Annalee Davis Thorndike made her first commercially sold dolls in the late 1950s. They're characterized by their painted felt faces and the meticulous workmanship involved in their manufacture. Most are made entirely of felt, though Santas and rabbits may have flannel bodies. All are constructed around a wire framework that allows them to be positioned in imaginative poses. Depending on rarity, appeal, and condition, some of the older dolls have increased in value more than ten times their original price. Dolls from the 1950s carried a long white red-embroidered tag with no date. The same tag was in use from 1959 until 1964, but there was a copyright date in the upper right-hand corner. In 1970 a transition period began. The company changed its tag to a white satiny tag with a date preceded by a copyright symbol in the upper right-hand corner. In 1975 they made another change to a long white cotton strip with a copyright date. In 1982 the white tag was folded over, making it shorter. Many people mistake the copyright date as the date the doll was made — not so! It wasn't until 1986 that they finally began to date the tags with the year of manufacture, making it much easier for collectors to identify their dolls. Besides the red-lettered white Annalee tags, numerous others were used in the 1990s, but all reflect the year the doll was actually made.

Our advisor for this category is Jane Holt; she is listed in the Directory under New Hampshire. For more information, refer to *Teddy Bears, Annalee's, and Steiff Animals,* by Margaret Fox Mandel, and *Garage Sale and Flea Market Annual.* Both are published by Collector Books. Values are given for dolls in clean, near-mint condition.

Baby in pajamas, 1989, 8" **40.00**
Bunny girl, red hair, 1978, 21" ..**95.00**
Caroller girl, 1974, 8"...........**50.00**
Clown, yellow hat & clothes, 1990, 30"...................................**75.00**
Cupid Kid in hanging heart, 1984, 7"......................................**95.00**
Leprechaun w/sack, 1974, 10" **75.00**
Monk in black robe, 1963, 10" ..**150.00**
Mouse bride & groom, 1995, 3", pr **35.00**
Skeleton Kid w/trick-or-treat bag, 1988, 7"...........................**35.00**
Snowy Owl, green earmuffs, 1990, 10"....................................**35.00**
Thorny the Ghost, 1989, 18"..**125.00**
Unicorn, 1986, 10"................**50.00**

Yum Yum bunny, 12", $550.00; 7", $300.00. (Photo courtesy Jane Holt)

Betsy McCall

Tiny 8" Betsy McCall was manufactured by the American Character Doll Company from 1957 until 1963. She was made from fine quality hard plastic with a bisque-like finish and had hand-painted features. Betsy came with four hair colors — tosca, blond, red, and brown. She has blue sleep eyes, molded lashes, a winsome smile, and a fully jointed body with bendable knees. On her back is an identification circle which reads ©McCall Corp. The basic doll could be purchased for $2.25 and wore a sheer chemise, white taffeta panties, nylon socks, and Maryjane-style shoes.

There were two different materials used for tiny Betsy's hair. The first was soft mohair sewn onto mesh. Later the rubber skullcap was rooted with saran which was more suitable for washing and combing.

Betsy McCall had an extensive wardrobe with nearly one hundred outfits, each of which could be purchased separately. They were made from wonderful fabrics such as velvet, felt, taffeta, and even real mink fur. Each ensemble came with the appropriate footware and was priced under $3.00. Since none of Betsy's clothing is tagged, it is often difficult to identify other than by its square snap closures (although these were used by other companies as well).

Betsy McCall is a highly collectible doll today but is still fairly easy to find at doll shows. The prices remain reasonable for this beautiful clothes horse and her many accessories, some of which we've included below.

Our advisor for this category is Marci Van Ausdall; she is listed in the Directory under California. For further information we recommend her book, *Betsy McCall, A Collector's Guide.* See Clubs and Newsletters for information concerning the *Betsy McCall's Fan Club.*

Doll, American Character, original outfit, jointed, 29", MIB..250.00
Doll, American Character, Playtime outfit, 14", EX................**250.00**
Doll, American Character, Town & Country outfit, 8", M**175.00**
Doll, Horsman, 1974, 12½", EX.**75.00**
Doll, Ideal, all original, MIB **225.00**
Doll, Rothchild, 35th Anniversary, 1986, 12", EX.................**45.00**
Doll, Uneeda, all original, 11½", EX...............................**45.00**
Outfit, Bar-B-Q, MOC **125.00**
Outfit, Prom Time Formal, blue, EX..................................**50.00**

Outfit, #8204, Birthday Party, MOC, $95.00 (also shown, 8" doll). (Photo courtesy Marci Van Ausdall)

Pattern, McCall's #2247, uncut......................**25.00**

TV Time, #9153, all original, complete w/TV, M..............**150.00**

Celebrities

Dolls that represent movie or TV personalities, fictional characters, or famous sports figures are very popular collectibles and can usually be found for well under $100.00. Mego, Horsman, Ideal, and Mattel are among the largest producers. Condition is vital. To price a doll in mint condition but without the box, deduct about 65% from the value of one mint in the box. Dolls in only good or poorer condition drop at a very rapid pace.

Our advisor for this category is Henri Yunes; he is listed in the Directory under New Jersey. For an expanded listing, see *Schroeder's Collectible Toys, Antique to Modern*.

Angie Dickinson (Police Woman), Horsman, 1976, 9", MIB..**60.00**

Beverly Hills 90210, 5 different, Mattel, 1991, 11½", MIB, ea **65.00**

Captain & Tenille, Mego, 1970s, 12", MIB, ea....................**60.00**

Dennis Rodman (Bad As I Wanna Be), Street Players, 1995, 11½", MIB **55.00**

Diana Ross, Mego, 1977, white & silver dress, 12", NRFB .**125.00**

Donnie & Marie Osmond, gift set, Mattel, 1976, 11½", NRFB **125.00**

Laverne & Shirley, Mego, 1977, 12", NRFB, pr...............**125.00**

MC Hammer, purple outfit, Mattel, 1991, 11½", MIB **70.00**

Mr. T, 1st edition, bib overalls, 12", MIB **60.00**

Pam Dawber (Mork & Mindy), Mattel, 1979, 8½", MIB ..**50.00**

Rosie O'Donell, Mattel, 1998, 11½", NRFB **50.00**

Vanna White, 20 different, Pacific Media/HSN, 1990, 11½", NRFB, ea **50.00**

Eegee

The Goldberger company made these dolls, Eegee (E.G.) being the initials of the company's founder. Dolls marked 'Made in China' were made in 1986.

Annette, vinyl, teen fashion, rooted hair, 1963, 11½", EX.**55.00**

Brooke Shields, Prom Party, LJN, 1983, 3rd issue, rare, 11½", NRFB, $200.00. (Photo courtesy Henry Yunes)

Baby Bunting, vinyl with molded hair, sleep eyes, two upper teeth, clothes by Mollye Goldman, 1956, 25½", $40.00. (Photo courtesy Pat Smith)

Baby Carrie, w/carriage or carry seat, 1970, 24", EX.........**60.00**

Baby Susan, 1958, 8½", EX..**20.00**

Ballerina, hard plastic w/vinyl head, 1964, 31", EX......**100.00**

Shelly, Tammy-type, grow hair, 1964, 12", EX..................**18.00**

Sniffles, marked 13/14 AA-EEGEE, 1963, 12", EX ..**20.00**

Susan Stroller, walker, ca 1955, 26", EX............................**80.00**

WC Fields, ventriloquist, vinyl, 1980, 30", EX................**210.00**

Effanbee

This company has been in business since 1910, continually producing high quality dolls, some of all composition, some composition and cloth, and a few in plastic and vinyl. In excellent condition, some of the older dolls often bring $300.00 and up. For more information we recommend *Effanbee Dolls* by Pat Smith, published by Collector Books.

Patsy Ann, composition head and five-piece body, blue tin sleep eyes, original clothes, 19", $465.00.

Alyssa, walker, 1960-61, 23", EX **225.00**

Andy, vinyl, teen-type w/molded hair, painted features, 1963, 12", EX............................**35.00**

Bud, molded hair, jointed, 1960-61, 22", EX......................**75.00**

Button Nose, cloth body w/vinyl head, 1968-71, 18", EX ..**35.00**

Miss Chips (Black), 15", EX..**45.00**

Patsy Ann, limited edition, marked, 1959, 15", EX..**285.00**

Patsy Ann, marked Official Girl Scout, 1959, 15", EX **250.00**

Precious Baby, Limited Edition Club, 1975, EX.............**350.00**

Pun'kin, toddler, 1966-83, 11", EX..**30.00**

Scarecrow, designed by Faith Wick, 1983, 18", MIB...**100.00**

Sweetie Pie, hard plastic, 1952, 27", VG **65.00**

Wee Patsy, #V571, painted features, 1997, 5½", MIB....**35.00**

Fisher-Price

Since the mid-1970s, this well-known American toy company has been making a variety of dolls. Many have vinyl heads, rooted hair, and cloth bodies. Most are marked and dated. You'll find more information on these dolls in *Fisher-Price Toys* by Brad Cassity (Collector Books).

Billie, #242, 1979-80, M........**10.00**

Elizabeth (Black), #205, 1974 – 1976, cloth and vinyl with removable skirt, M, $25.00. (Photo courtesy Brad Cassity)

Bundle-Up Baby, #244, w/bassinet & quilt, 1980-82, MIB....**20.00**

Honey, #208, 1977-80, M......**20.00**

Muffy, #241, 1979-80, M.......**10.00**

Musical Baby Ann, #204, 1975-76, MIB................................**25.00**

My Friend Becky, #218, 1982-84, MIB................................**20.00**

My Friend Christie, #8120, 1990, M......................................**75.00**

My Friend Nicky (Black), #206, 1985, MIB........................**30.00**

My Sleepy Baby, #207, 1978-80, M......................................**20.00**

Natalie, #202, 1974-76, M **25.00**

Gerber Babies

The first Gerber Baby dolls were manufactured of cloth by an unknown maker in 1936. Since that time six different doll companies have attempted to capture the charm of the charcoal drawing done by Dorothy Hop Smith of her friend's baby, Ann Turner (Cook).

Gerber began to issue premium items in the 1930s but discontinued them during World War II (1941 – 1945) and began again in 1946. In the 1970s Gerber began to expand their interest beyond food items into merchandising their related baby-care line and insurance. Then in the 1980s Gerber initiated a sales program of promotional items that were available to those who were in any way connected with the company. The 1990s saw emphasis shift toward mass merchandising, and the company developed a line of toys designed to grow with the child.

However, the sale of high quality food items for infants and toddlers remains their first priority.

Besides premiums and sale items, Gerber made many 'freebie' souvenirs available through its company tours, the Tourist Center, and special events which they sponsored.

Joan Stryker Grubaugh is the author of an excellent book, *Gerber Baby Dolls and Advertising Collectibles*. She is listed in the Directory under Ohio.

Amsco, baby & feeding set, vinyl, 1972-73, complete, 14", NMIB **85.00**

Amsco, pink & white rosebud sleeper, vinyl, 10", NM ..**55.00**

Amsco, pink & white rosebud sleeper (Black), vinyl, 10", NM, $60 to....................**100.00**

Arrow Rubber & Plastic Corp, bib & diaper, 1965-67, 14", MIB, $45 to..............................**60.00**

Atlanta Novelty, 'mama' voice (White or Black), 17", NRFB, ea **85.00**

Atlanta Novelty, Baby Drink & Wet, 1979-81, 17", complete, M,.....................................**85.00**

Atlanta Novelty, Baby Drink & Wet (Black), 1979-81, 12", complete, M..................**100.00**

Atlanta Novelty, Bathtub Baby, 1985, 12", complete, MIB .**85.00**

Atlanta Novelty, christening gown, porcelain head, 1981, 14", NRFB **350.00**

Atlanta Novelty, christening gown, vinyl, 1981, 12", NRFB **85.00**

Atlanta Novelty, jacket, pillow & coverlet, 1979, 17", NRFB.......**95.00**

Atlanta Novelty, rag doll, pink or blue, 1984, 11½", EX, ea..**20.00**

Atlanta Novelty, snowsuit w/hood (White or Black), 17", NRFB, $75 to..............................**95.00**

Atlanta Novelty, velour dress w/white blouse (Black), 17", M, $75 to........................**85.00**

Atlanta Novelty, 50th Anniversary, 17", NRFB, from $75 to....................................**95.00**

Lucky LTD, Birthday Party Twins, 1989, 6", NRFB..**40.00**

Lucky LTD, christening gown, cloth & vinyl, 1989, 16", EX.............................**40.00**

Sun Rubber, nightgown, 1955-58, M....................................**175.00**

Toy Biz, Baby Care Set, 1996, MIB **25.00**

Toy Biz, Food & Playtime Baby, 1995, MIB, from $25.00 to $35.00.
(Photo courtesy Joan S. Grubaugh)

Toy Biz, Lullaby Baby, 1995, 11", NRFB..............................**25.00**

Toy Biz, Potty Time Baby, 1994-95, 15", NRFB **25.00**

Horsman

During the 1930s, this company produced composition dolls of the highest quality. Today many of their dolls are vinyl. Hard plastic dolls marked '170' are also Horsmans.

Answer Doll, back button moves head, 1966, 10", EX........**15.00**

Baby First Tooth, 1966, 16", EX.............................**40.00**

Betty, 1951, 14", EX..............**60.00**

Cindy, 1950s, 17", VG..........**65.00**

Lullabye Baby, #2580//B144 8, Sears, 1967-68, 12", EX.**15.00**

Poor Pitiful Pearl, 1964, 11", VG..............................**35.00**

Tynie Baby, 1950s, 15", EXIB..**110.00**

Ideal

For more than eighty years, this company produced quality dolls that were easily affordable by the average American family. Their Shirley Temple and Toni dolls were highly successful. They're also the company who made Miss Revlon, Betsy Wetsy, and Tiny Tears. For more information see *Collector's Guide to Ideal Dolls* by Judith Izen. See also Dolls, Shirley Temple and Tammy.

Baby Dreams, cloth body w/flocked vinyl arms & legs, 1975-76, 17", NM **20.00**

Baby Kissy, 1962, 23", NRFB..**325.00**

Betsy Wetsy, vinyl, rooted hair, sleep eyes, w/suitcase, 1956, 12", EX.............................**50.00**

Cinnamon, painted eyes, growing hair, 1972-74, 13½"........**40.00**

Crissy (Country Fashion), 1982-83, EX **20.00**

Crissy (Movin' Groovin'), vinyl, swivel waist, grow hair, 1971, MIB **75.00**

Dina, purple playsuit, 1972-73, EX **50.00**

Kerry, green romper, EX **55.00**

Mary Hartline, hard plastic, fully j o i n t e d , blond nylon wig, 16", M I B , **$ 7 0 0 . 0 0 .** (Photo courtesy McMasters Auctions)

Miss Revlon, #IT-18, complete w/stand & hang tag, 1956-59, 18", NM **350.00**

Miss Revlon, #VT/V-22, complete w/ribbon tag, 1956-59, 21", EX **100.00**

Patty Play Pal, #G-35, 1960-61, rare, 35", NM **500.00**

Pepper, rooted hair, painted eyes, rigid torso, 1960s, 9", EX...**25.00**

Plassie, composition, painted eyes, molded hair, 1942, 24", NM **150.00**

Princess Mary, wig, sleep eyes, 1954, 19", NM **175.00**

Saucy Walker, marked T28X-60, 1960-61, 28"..................**175.00**

Snoozie, cloth & vinyl body, she squirms, 1964, 20", MIB.**55.00**

Swirla Curla Crissy, 1973, EX..**35.00**

Swirla Curla Crissy (Black), 1973, EX **100.00**

Tara (Black), 1976, MIB **85.00**

Thumbelina, cloth body, w/original hang tag, 1983-85, 18", NM **45.00**

Tiny Thumbelina, 1962-68, 14", MIB...............................**185.00**

Whoopsie, Black, #H298, rooted hair, painted eyes, 13", NM **55.00**

Jem

The glamorous life of Jem mesmerized little girls who watched her Saturday morning cartoons, and she was a natural as a fashion doll. In 1985 Hasbro introduced the Jem line of 12" dolls representing her, the rock stars from Jem's musical group, the Holograms, and other members of the cast, including Rio, the only boy, who was Jem's road manager and Jerrica's boyfriend. Production was discontinued in 1987. Each doll was poseable, jointed at the waist, heads, and wrists, so that they could be positioned at will with their musical instruments and other accessory items. Their clothing, their makeup, and their hairdos were wonderfully exotic, and their faces were beautifully molded. More information on Jem dolls may be found in *Modern Collectible Dolls* by Patsy Moyer (Collector Books).

Accessory, Glitter 'n Gold Roadster, M **150.00**

Accessory, Jem Roadster, AM/FM radio in trunk, scarce, EX..**150.00**

Accessory, Jem Soundstage, Starlight House #14, EX, from $40 to **50.00**

Accessory, New Wave Waterbed, M....................................**35.00**

Accessory, Star Stage, M **30.00**

Doll, Aja (Holograms), 1st issue, M **45.00**

Doll, Aja (Holograms), 2nd issue, M....................................**90.00**

Doll, Ashley (Starlight Girl), 11", M **40.00**

Doll, Banee (Starlight Girl), 11", M **25.00**

Doll, Clash, MIB **40.00**

Doll, Danse, pink & blond hair, complete, 11", MIB.........**40.00**

Doll, Danse (Holograms), NRFB **60.00**

Doll, Jem (Flash 'n Sizzle), NRFB...........................**40.00**

Doll, Jem (Rock 'n Curl), M ..**20.00**

Doll, Jem/Jerrica, 1st issue, M ..**30.00**

Doll, Jem/Jerrica (Glitter 'n Gold), 11", MIB **50.00**

Doll, Jetta, silver-streaked black hair, complete, 11", MIB..**40.00**

Doll, Kimber (Holograms), 1st issue, M **40.00**

Doll, Kimber (Holograms), 2nd issue, M **75.00**

Doll, Krissie (Starlight Girl), 11", M....................................**35.00**

Doll, Pizzaz (Misfits), chartreuse hair, 11", MIB **40.00**

Doll, Raya, 11", MIB **40.00**

Doll, Rio, 1st issue, M **25.00**

Doll, Rio (Glitter 'n Gold), M ..**25.00**

Doll, Rio (Glitter 'n Gold), pale vinyl, M **125.00**

Doll, Roxy (Misfits), 1st or 2nd issue, M, ea....................**50.00**

Doll, Shana (Holograms), 1st issue, M **40.00**

Doll, Shana (Holograms), 2nd issue, M **225.00**

Doll, Stormer (Misfits), 2nd issue, M.....................................**60.00**

Doll, Video, complete, 11", MIB ..**40.00**

Outfit, City Lights, MIP **15.00**

Kenner

This company's dolls range from the 12" jointed teenage glamour dolls to the tiny 3" Mini-Kins with the snap-on changeable clothing and synthetic 'hair' ponytails. (Value for the latter: doll only, $8.00; doll with one outfit, $15.00; complete set, $70.00.)

Baby Bundles (Black), 16", M .**25.00**

Baby Yawnie, 1975, 15", M...**20.00**

Butch Cassidy or Sundance Kid, 4", M, ea..........................**15.00**

Dusty, teen doll, 1974, 11", M....**20.00**

Rose Petal, scented, 1984, 7", M...**20.00**

Skye (Black), teen friend of Dusty, 11", M **25.00**

Steve Scout, 1974, 9", M **20.00**

Liddle Kiddles

Produced by Mattel between 1966 and 1971, Liddle Kiddle dolls and accessories were designed to suggest the typical 'little kid' in the typical neighborhood. These

Doll, Rio (Glitter 'n Gold), MIB, (not shown), $50.00. (Photo courtesy Lee Garmon)

dolls can be found in sizes ranging from ¾" to 4", all with poseable bodies and rooted hair that can be restyled. Later, two more series were designed that represented storybook and nursery rhyme characters. The animal kingdom was represented by the Animiddles and Zoolery Jewelry Kiddles. There was even a set of extraterrestrials. And lastly, in 1979 Sweet Treets dolls were marketed.

Items mint on card or mint in box are worth about 25% more than one in mint condition but with none of the original packaging. Based on mint value, deduct 50% for dolls that are dressed but lack accessories. For further information we recommend *Dolls of the 1960s and 1970s* by Cindy Sabulis, and *Schroeder's Collectible Toys, Antique to Modern*; both are published by Collector Books.

Our advisor is Cindy Sabulis; she is listed in the Directory under Connecticut.

Electric Drawing Set, Lakeside, 1969, MIB, $25.00. (Photo courtesy Tamela Storm and Debra Van Dyke)

Alice in Wonderliddle, complete, NM...............................**175.00**

Baby Din-Din, #3820, complete, M...............................**75.00**
ChocoLottie's House, #2501, MIP............................**40.00**
Florence Niddle, #3507, complete, M...............................**75.00**
Frosty Mint Kone, #3653, complete, M...........................**75.00**
Greta Griddle, #3508, complete, M...............................**85.00**
Heart Pin Kiddle, #3741, MIP..**50.00**
Howard Buff Biddle, #3502, complete, M...........................**75.00**
Kiddle Komedy Theatre, #3592, EX...............................**50.00**
Liddle Kiddles Pop-Up Boutique, #5170, M........................**30.00**
Lola Locket, #3536, MIP.......**75.00**
Luscious Lime, #3733, complete, M...............................**55.00**
Olivia Orange Kola Kiddle, #3730, MIP..............................**80.00**
Pretty Priddle, #3549, complete, M...............................**75.00**
Slipsy Sliddle, #3754, complete, M..............................**125.00**
Swingy Skediddle, #3789, MIP..**200.00**
Vanilla Lilly, #2819, MIP.....**25.00**

Madame Alexander

Founded in 1923, Beatrice Alexander began her company by producing an Alice in Wonderland doll which was all cloth with an oil-painted face. By the 1950s there were more than 600 employees making dolls of various materials. The company is still producing lovely dolls today. For further information, we recommend *Madame Alexander Dolls* by Pat Smith and *Madame Alexander*

Collector's Doll Price Guide by Linda Crowsey; both are published by Collector Books.

Aladdin, Storybook Series, hard plastic, #482, 1993, 8"...............**60.00**

Alice in Wonderland, hard plastic, synthetic wig, sleep eyes, closed mouth, 1949 – 1952, 17", $425.00.

Allison, cloth/vinyl, 1990-91, 18".**110.00**

Butch, cloth/vinyl, 1965-66 only, 12" **125.00**

Classic Ballerina, white tulle & satin, #22700, 1999, 16"...**170.00**

Dorothy, hard plastic, blue check dress, basket & Toto, 1998-99, 8" **60.00**

Friar Tuck, hard plastic, Storybook Series, #493, 1998-91, 8"....**85.00**

Heidi, hard plastic, green dress, straw hat, goat, #15100, 1998-99, 8"....................................**80.00**

Janie, toddler, #1146, 1964-66 only, 12" **275.00**

Kathy Tears, vinyl, new face, 1960-61, 12" **75.00**

Little Bitsy, all vinyl nurser, Sweet Tears, 1967-68, 9'..............**150.00**

Madonna & Child, Christmas Series, #10600, 1995, 10" **105.00**

Mr. and Mrs. Frankenstein set, 1996, 8"..............................**155.00**

Panama, #555, 1985-87, 8".......**85.00**

Queen Esther, Bible Series, #14584, 1995 only, 8"....................**100.00**

Rusty, cloth/vinyl, 1967-68 only, 20"..................................**300.00**

Scout, Americana Series, #367, 1991-92 only, 8"...........................**95.00**

Spanish Matador, Wendy, #530, 1992-93 only, 8"..................**65.00**

Mattel

Though most famous, of course, for Barbie and her friends, the Mattel company also made celebrity dolls, Liddle Kiddles, Chatty Cathy, talking dolls, a lot of action figures (the Major Matt Mason line and She-Ra, Princess of Power, for example), and in more recent years, Baby Tenderlove and P.J. Sparkles. See also Barbie; Dolls, Liddle Kiddles.

To learn more about Mattel dolls, consult *Talking Toys of the 20th Century* and *Chatty Cathy Dolls, An Identification and Value Guide*, both by Kathy and Don Lewis. They are listed in the Directory under California.

Baby First Step, 1964, M, $50.00. (Photo courtesy Cindy Sabulis)

Baby Beans, bean bag body w/terry or tricot, 12", EX..............**25.00**

Baby Beans, talker, bean bag body w/terry or tricot, 1971-75, 12", EX......................35.00

Baby Cheryl, talker, 1965, MIB 200.00

Baby Drowsy (Black), talker, 1968, 15", MIB 175.00

Baby Love Light, battery-operated, 16", EX.......................18.00

Baby Love Notes, plays tunes when hands & feet are pressed, 1974, 10"..........15.00

Beddie Bye Talk, Patter Pal, 1970, MIB.......................80.00

Chatty Baby, talker, brunette hair, brown eyes, early, M 160.00

Chatty Cathy, talker, reissue, blond hair, blue eyes, MIB.........80.00

Cheerful Tearful, face changes from smile to pout, 1966-67, 7", EX............................100.00

Crawling Baby, keywind, 1984, 15", M 18.00

Dancerina, battery-operated, 1968, 24", NM 125.00

Drowsy Sleeper-Keeper, talker, 1966, MIB.....................125.00

Gramma Doll, talker, Sears only, 1970-73, 11", EX 20.00

My Child, stuffed flannel, stitched fingers, 1985, 15"..........25.00

Rainbow Brite, 1983, 18"......30.00

Shrinkin' Violet, talker, cloth w/yarn hair, 1964-65, 16", VG 25.00

Singin' Chatty, talker, blond hair, M....................................250.00

Teachy Talk, talker, 1970, MIB...50.00

Tearful Baby Tender Love, 1972, 17", EXIB.......................25.00

Raggedy Ann and Andy
Designed by Johnny Gruelle

in 1915, Raggedy Ann was named by combining two James Whitcomb Riley poem titles, *The Raggedy Man* and *Orphan Annie*. The early cloth dolls he made were dated and had painted-on features. Though these dolls are practically nonexistent, they're easily identified by the mark, 'Patented Sept. 7, 1915.' P.F. Volland made these dolls from 1920 to 1934; theirs were very similar in appearance to the originals.

The Mollye Doll Outfitters were the first to print the now-familiar red heart on her chest, and they added a black outline around her nose. These dolls carry the handwritten inscription 'Raggedy Ann and Andy Doll/Manufactured by Mollye Doll Outfitters.' Georgene Averill made them ca 1938 to 1950, sewing their label into the seam of the dolls. Knickerbocker dolls (1963 to 1982) also carry a company label. The Applause Toy Company made these dolls for two years in the early 1980s, and they were finally taken over by Hasbro, the current producer, in 1983.

Besides the dolls, scores of other Raggedy Ann and Andy items have been marketed, including books, radios, games, clocks, bedspreads, and clothing. Over the past several years, collector interest has really taken off, and just about any antique mall you visit today will have an eye-catching display. For more information see *The World of Raggedy Ann Collectibles* by Kim Avery.

Applause, sleeping bag dolls, original tags, NM, ea, from $15 to.............................**20.00**

Applause, Sleepytime, 17", EX, ea, from $30 to **35.00**

Georgene Novelties, 15½", 1930s – 1960s, 15½", 15", $375.00 for the pair, (Photo courtesy Debbie Crume and Patsy Moyer)

Georgene Novelties, Awake/ Asleep, 1940-45, 12½", EX, from $275 to **375.00**

Georgene Novelties, 1946-63, 19", EX, ea, from $95 to **125.00**

Georgene Novelties, 1960-63, 15", EX, ea **110.00**

Ideal/Bobbs-Merrill, inflatable vinyl, 1973, 21" & 22", MIP, ea....................................**40.00**

Knickerbocker, NY, mid-1960s, 15", EX, ea, from $35 to ..**40.00**

Knickerbocker, sewn in China, 35", MIB, ea, from $145 to....**165.00**

Knickerbocker, Taiwan, 1970s-80s, 19", EX, ea, from $30 to **35.00**

Knickerbocker, talker, 1974, 12", EX....................................**100.00**

Knickerbocker, Teach & Dress, Hong Kong, 20", EX, ea, from $50 to **55.00**

Playskool, Christmas edition, 1990, 12", MIB **40.00**

Remco

The plastic and vinyl dolls made by Remco during the 1960s and 1970s are gaining popularity with collectors today. Many have mechanical features that were activated either by a button on their back or batteries. The Littlechap Family of dolls (1964), Dr. John, his wife Lisa, and their two children, Judy and Libby, came with clothing and fashion accessories of the highest quality. Children found the family less interesting than the more glamorous fashion dolls on the market at that time, and as a result, production was limited. These dolls in excellent condition are valued at about $15.00 to $20.00 each, while their outfits range from about $30.00 (loose and complete) to a minimum of $50.00 (MIB).

Littlechap Family: Libby (front), Judy (left), John (back), and Lisa (right), EX, from $15.00 to $20.00 each. (Photo courtesy Cindy Sabulis)

Baby Crawl-Along, 1967, 20",
MIB **25.00**
Baby Grow-a-Tooth, 1968, 15",
MIB **25.00**
Baby Know-It-All, 1969, 17",
MIB **20.00**
Growing Sally, 6¼", MIB......**45.00**
Jumpsy, 1970, 14", MIB **20.00**
Jumpsy (Black), 1970, 14",
MIB **25.00**
Mimi, singer, battery-operated,
1973, 19", MIB **50.00**
Mimi (Black), singer, battery-
operated, 19", MIB.........**60.00**

Shirley Temple

The public's fascination with Shirley was more than enough reason for toy companies to literally deluge the market with merchandise of all types decorated with her likeness. Dolls were a big part of that market, and the earlier composition dolls in excellent condition are often priced at a minimum of $600.00 on today's market. Many were made by the Ideal Company, who in the 1950s also issued a line made of vinyl.

Bisque, painted, molded hair,
Japan, 6" **250.00**
Composition, Bright Eyes, all orig-
inal, 1934, 18", EX **750.00**
Vinyl, Captain January, 1958,
12" **200.00**
Vinyl, Cinderella, 1961, 15",
NM **325.00**
Vinyl, Ideal, 1961, 12", MIB..**200.00**
Vinyl, Little Red Riding Hood,
1950s, 15", NM.............**265.00**
Vinyl, Little Stowaway, Ideal,
1982, 8"......................**45.00**

Vinyl, Ideal, hazel sleep eyes, open/closed mouth with six upper teeth, five-piece body, original clothes, 1950s, 12", M, $225.00. (Photo courtesy McMasters Auctions)

Tammy

In 1962 the Ideal Novelty & Toy Company introduced their teenage Tammy doll. Slightly pudgy and not quite as sophisticated as some of the teen fashion dolls on the market at the time, Tammy's innocent charm captivated consumers. Her extensive wardrobe and numerous accessories added to her popularity with children. Tammy had everything including a car, a house, and a catamaran. In addition, a large number of companies obtained licenses to issue products using the 'Tammy' name. Everything from paper dolls to nurses' kits were made with Tammy's image on them. Tammy's success was not confined to the United States. She was also successful in Canada and in several European countries. Doll values listed here are for mint-in-box examples. (Loose dolls are generally about half mint-in-box value as they are relatively common.) Other values are for mint-condition items without their original packaging. (Such items with their original packaging or in less-than-mint condition would then vary up or down accordingly.

Our advisor for this category is Cindy Sabulis; she has co-authored a book with Susan Weglewski entitled *Collector's Guide to Tammy, The Ideal Teen* (Collector Books), which we highly recommend. Cindy is listed in the Directory under Connecticut.

Accessory Pak, #9244-5, w/sweater scarf & hanger, NRFP..............................25.00
Accessory Pak, #9345-2, w/afternoon dress & shoes, NRFP.........................25.00
Case, Dodi, green, EX...........30.00
Case, Tammy Model Miss, EX..25.00
Case, Tammy Traveler, EX..45.00
Doll, Misty, MIB..................100.00
Doll, Patti, MIB...................200.00
Doll, Pepper, MIB.................65.00

Doll, Pepper, 'carrot'-colored hair, MIB, $75.00. (Photo courtesy Cindy Sabulis)

Doll, Pos'n Pete, MIB..........125.00
Doll, Pos'n Tammy, MIB 100.00
Doll, Tammy, MIB 75.00

Outfit, Pepper, Flower Girl, #9332-8, complete, M.....45.00
Outfit, Tammy, Private Secretary, #9939-0, MIP.................75.00
Pepper's Jukebox, M.............65.00
Pepper's Treehouse, MIB....150.00
Tammy's Bubble Bath Set, NRFB 75.00
Tammy's Car, MIB................75.00

Vogue

This is the company that made the Ginny doll famous. She was first made in composition during the late 1940s, and if you could find her in mint condition, she'd bring about $450.00 on today's market. (Played with and in relatively sad condition, she's still worth about $90.00.) Ginnys from the 1950s were made of rigid vinyl. The last Ginny came out in 1969. Tonka bought the rights in 1973, but the dolls they produced sold poorly. After a series of other owners, Dakin purchased the rights in 1986 and began producing a vinyl doll that resembled the 1950-style Ginny very closely. For more information, we recommend *Collector's Guide to Vogue Dolls* by Judith Izen and Carol Stover (Collector Books).

Baby Dear, original, 1960s, 16", EX..................................165.00
Brikette, ball-jointed twist & turn body, 1960, 16", EX........15.00
Cheryl (Tiny Miss), 8", EX..400.00
Ginnette, open mouth, 1964, 8", MIB..............................200.00
Ginny (Gym Kids), walker, ca 1956-57, 8"....................150.00

Ginny (Kinder Crowd), walker, 1956, 8"......................**200.00**

Ginny (Nurse), walker, 1956, 8", EX................................**325.00**

Ginny (Sasson), slimmer body, 1981-82, 8", EX..............**35.00**

Jan, rigid body w/swivel waist, 1958-60, 10½", EX.......**150.00**

Jill, blond ponytail, pink tulle formal, original accessories, replaced hair wreath, 1959, 10½", EX, $200.00. (Photo courtesy Bonnie Groves)

Jeff (Bridegroom), 1957-59, 11"..**75.00**

Jimmy (Ginny's baby brother), open mouth, 8", EX........**60.00**

Kay (Kindergarten Series), 1952, 8", EX............................**450.00**

Toddles Dutch Boy & Girl, original, 7", pr.....................**300.00**

Doorstops

Doorstops, once called door porters, were popular from the Civil War period until after 1930. They were used to prop the doors open during the hot summer months so that the cooler air could circulate. Though some were made of brass, wood, and chalk, cast iron was by far the most preferred material, usually molded in amusing figurals — dogs, flower baskets, frogs, etc. Hubley was one of the largest producers. Refer to *Doorstops, Identification and Values,* by Jeanne Bertoia (Collector Books) for more information. Beware of reproductions! Assume all the examples in the listing that follows to be made of cast iron and with original paint; ranges reflect conditions from VG to M. See Clubs and Newsletters for information concerning the Doorstop Collectors of America.

Amish Man, standing w/hand in pocket, 8½x3¾", from $225 to **275.00**

Apple Blossom Basket, Hubley, #329, 7½x5½", from $100 to **150.00**

Armored Knight, standing, 13¼x6", from $250 to...**300.00**

Cat, cleaning paw, Sculptured Metal Studios, 11x7½", from $400 to **475.00**

Cockatoo, on branch, multicolored, 14", from $200 to..........**275.00**

Cocker Spaniel, Hubley, 6¾x11", from $225 to **275.00**

Covered Wagon, horse-drawn, Hubley, #375, 9½x5", from $150 to **225.00**

Doberman Pinscher, full figure, Hubley, 8x8½", from $325 to..............................**400.00**

Dog, yawning, full figure, 7x5", from $250 to **325.00**

Dutch Girl, w/flower baskets, Hubley, #10, 9¼x5½", from $175 to **250.00**

El Capitan, 7¾x5¼", from $175 to **250.00**

Elephant, S117, 6½x8¼", from $150 to **225.00**

Fruit & Flower Basket, 13x7¼", from $200 to **275.00**

Geisha Girl, seated on pillow w/instrument, Hubley, 7x6", from $200 to **275.00**

Grape Bowl, #20, 4⅛x7", from $100 to **150.00**

Lantern, 13x5", from $150 to ..**225.00**

Malamute, 7¾x6¼", from $175 to **200.00**

Organ Grinder & Monkey, flat-cast, 10x5¾", from $375 to **450.00**

Owl, on stump, 10x6", from $200 to **275.00**

Overhead Swinging Golfer, #238, EX, $425.00; Putting Golfer, #34, VG+, $220.00.

Pansy Bowl, Hubley, #256, 7x6½", from $125 to **175.00**

Parrot, on perch, 7x3½", from $100 to **150.00**

Policeman, standing w/billy club, no base, 8x4", from $275 to **350.00**

Poppies & Cornflowers, Hubley, #3265, 7¼x6½", from $100 to **150.00**

Rooster, full figure, 15½x6", from $275 to **350.00**

Rose Vase, Hubley, #441, 10½x8", from $100 to **175.00**

Sailor, standing, 8½x3½", from $250 to **325.00**

Spanish Girl, Hubley, #192, 9x5", from $175 to **250.00**

Totem Pole, 12", from $100 to ..**150.00**

Windmill, AA Richardson, 8x5½", from $125 to **175.00**

Woman w/Muff, 9¼", from $225 to **275.00**

Egg Timers

The origin of the figural egg timer appears to be Germany, circa 1920s or 1930s, with Japan following their lead in the 1940s. Some American companies may have begun producing figural timers at about the same time, but evidence is scarce in terms of pottery marks or company logos.

Figural timers can be found in a wide range of storybook characters (Oliver Twist), animals (pigs, ducks, rabbits), career and vocational uniformed people (chef, London Bobby, housemaid), or people in native costume.

All types of timers were a fairly uniform height of 3" to 4". If a figural timer no longer has its sand tube, it can be recognized by the hole which usually goes through the back of the figure or the stub of a hand. Most timers were made of ceramic (china or bisque), but a few are of cast iron and carved wood. They can be detailed or quite plain. Listings below are for timers with their sand tubes completely intact.

Bellhop on phone, ceramic, Japan, 3".....................................**40.00**

Black chef standing w/frying pan, chalkware, Japan.........**125.00**

Boy w/lg red bow, ceramic, Germany, from $85 to........**100.00**

Cat standing by base of grandfather clock, ceramic, Germany, 4¾"..................................**65.00**

Chef holding platter of food, ceramic, Japan, 3½".......**50.00**

Chicken on nest, green plastic, England, 2½"..................**30.00**

Dutch boy standing, ceramic, German, 3½" **65.00**

Golliwog, bisque, English, 4½", $200.00.
(Photo courtesy Ellen Bercovici)

Mexican boy playing guitar, ceramic, Germany, 3½".**65.00**

Mouse, chalkware, Josef Originals/ Japan, 1970s, 3¼"..........**35.00**

Parlor maid w/cat, ceramic, Japan, 4".........................**65.00**

Pixie, ceramic, Enesco/Japan, 5½"...............................**40.00**

Sailor w/sailboat, ceramic, Germany, 4" **85.00**

Santa Claus and present, ceramic, Sonsco, Japan, 5½", $75.00.
(Photo courtesy Ellen Bercovici)

Telephone, black glaze on clay, Japan, 2".........................**35.00**

Welsh woman, ceramic, German, 4½"................................**85.00**

Elegant Glass

To quote Gene Florence, Elegant glassware 'refers mostly to hand-worked, acid-etched glassware that was sold by better departmant and jewelry stores during the Depression era through the 1950s, differentiating it from dime store and give-away glass that has become known as Depression glass. Cambridge, Duncan & Miller, Fostoria, Heisey, Imperial, Morgantown, New Martinsville, Paden City, Tiffin, U.S. Glass, and Westmoreland were major producers. For further information we recommend *Elegant Glassware of the Depression Era, 9th Edition,* by Mr. Florence (Collector Books).

Cambridge

Apple Blossom, bowl, cream soup; yellow or amber, w/underplate **55.00**

Apple Blossom, plate, dinner; green or pink, 9½".........**85.00**

Apple Blossom, tumbler, yellow or amber, footed, #3400, 12-oz...................................**40.00**

Candlelight, bowl, crystal, 2-handled, footed, #3900/28, 11½".............................**85.00**

Candlelight, creamer or sugar bowl, crystal, #3900/41, ea **25.00**

Candlelight, plate, dinner; crystal, #3900/24, 10½"...............**85.00**

Caprice, bonbon, crystal, 2-handled, #154, 6" sq.............**15.00**

Caprice, cake plate, crystal, footed, #36, 13"....................**150.00**

Caprice, tumbler, blue or pink, footed, #11, 5-oz **50.00**

Chantilly, bowl, celery/relish; crystal, 3-part, 9" **35.00**

Chantilly, plate, salad; crystal, 8" **12.50**

Chantilly, tumbler, tea; crystal, footed, #3779, 12-oz **25.00**

Cleo, bowl, vegetable; blue, Decagon oval, 9½"........**145.00**

Cleo, candlestick, 3-light; blue ..**150.00**

Cleo, plate, grill; amber, green, pink or yellow, 9½" **100.00**

Daffodil, bonbon, crystal, #1181...**30.00**

Daffodil, comport, crystal, footed, #533, 5½"........................**45.00**

Daffodil, tumbler, crystal, footed, #1937, 5-oz **22.00**

Decagon, bowl, cereal; pastel colors, flat rim, 6" **22.00**

Decagon, ice tub, blue...........**65.00**

Decagon, tray, pickle; pastel colors, 9"..............................**25.00**

Diane, bowl, berry; crystal, 5" .**30.00**

Diane, creamer or sugar bowl, crystal.............................**20.00**

Diane, vase, bud; crystal, 10"..**60.00**

Elaine, basket, crystal, upturned sides, 2-handled, 6"........**22.00**

Elaine, comport, crystal, 5½"..**35.00**

Elaine, salt & pepper shakers, crystal, footed, pr...........**40.00**

Gloria, bowl, cereal; crystal, 6" sq **35.00**

Gloria, creamer, pink, tall, footed, $25.00. (Photo courtesy Gene Florence)

Gloria, platter, crystal, 11½".**75.00**

Gloria, tumbler, juice; crystal, #3135, 5-oz **18.00**

Marjorie, jug, crystal, #93, 3-pt...**155.00**

Marjorie, nappy, crystal, #4111, 4"....................................**20.00**

Mt Vernon, bowl, cereal; amber or crystal, #32, 6" **12.50**

Mt Vernon, plate, dinner; amber or crystal, #40, 10½"......**35.00**

Mt Vernon, salt & pepper shakers, amber or crystal, #28, pr .**22.50**

Number 520, candy box, green or peach blo, #300...............**95.00**

Number 520, gravy/sauce boat, green or peach blo..........**75.00**

Number 704, cheese plate, all colors, #468 ....**35.00**

Number 704, pickle tray, all colors, #907, 9"....................**30.00**

Number 704, sugar bowl, all colors, flat, #944 ....**20.00**

Portia, bonbon, crystal, tab handles, footed, 7"................**35.00**

Portia, celery tray, crystal, 11"...........................**40.00**

Portia, creamer, crystal, footed............................**20.00**

Rosalie, bowl, cream soup; amber......................**20.00**

Rosalie, cup, blue, green or pink.........................**35.00**

Rosalie, platter, amber, 15".**100.00**

Rose Point, bowl, fruit; crystal, #3500/10, 5"....................**85.00**

Rose Point, pitcher, crystal, w/ice lip, #3400/100, 76-oz....**215.00**

Rose Point, plate, luncheon; crystal, #3400/63, 9½"..........**42.00**

Tally Ho, ashtray, amber or crystal, 4"..............................**12.50**

Tally Ho, bowl, pan; green, 10"..**75.00**

Tally Ho, candlestick, blue, 6"..**45.00**

Tally Ho, mug, ruby, $40.00.

Valencia, mayonnaise, crystal, #3500/59, 3-pc................**45.00**

Valencia, plate, sandwich; crystal, handled, #1402, 11½"....**35.00**

Valencia, salt & pepper shakers, crystal, #3400/18............**65.00**

Wildflower, butter dish, crystal, #3400/52, 5"..................**135.00**

Wildflower, plate, salad; crystal, #3900/22, 8"...................**17.50**

Wildflower, tumbler, water; crystal, #3121, 10-oz.............**22.00**

Duncan and Miller

Canterbury No 115, ashtray, crystal, 5"...............................12.00

Canterbury No 115, basket, crystal, oval, handled, 3½"...**25.00**

Canterbury No 115, mayonnaise, crystal, 3¼x6"................**17.50**

Canterbury No 115, stem, claret or wine; crystal, 4-oz, 5".....**20.00**

Caribbean, plate, dinner; crystal, 10½"................................**65.00**

Caribbean, relish, blue, oblong, 4-part, 9½".........................**60.00**

Caribbean, tumbler, iced tea; crystal, footed, 11-oz, 6½"....**27.50**

First Love, bowl, crystal, #115, 4¾x10¾"........................**42.50**

First Love, cake plate, crystal, #115, 14".........................**50.00**

First Love, cheese stand, crystal, #111, 3x5¼"...................**25.00**

Lily of the Valley, candy dish, crystal, w/lid...................**85.00**

Lily of the Valley, plate, crystal, 9", **$45.00.** (Photo courtesy Gene Florence)

Lily of the Valley, sugar bowl, crystal............................**25.00**

Nautical, ashtray, crystal, 6"..**12.50**

Nautical, cake plate, transparent blue, 2-handled, 6½"......**25.00**

Nautical, sugar bowl, crystal ..**15.00**

Sandwich, oil bottle, crystal, 5¾" **35.00**

Sandwich, plate, salad; crystal, 8" **10.00**

Sandwich, tray, crystal, oval, 8" **18.00**

Spiral Flutes, bowl, grapefruit; amber, green or pink, 6¾"..**7.50**

Spiral Flutes, platter, amber, green or pink, 13' **50.00**

Spiral Flutes, sugar bowl, amber, green or pink, oval **8.00**

Tear Drop, nappy, dessert; crystal, 6" **6.00**

Tear Drop, plate, dinner; crystal, 10½" **40.00**

Tear Drop, stem, wine; crystal, 3-oz, 4¾" **18.00**

Terrace, cup, amber or crystal..**15.00**

Terrace, plate, amber or crystal, 11"....................................**47.50**

Terrace, stem, cordial; amber or crystal...............................**17.50**

American, butter dish, crystal, w/lid, ¼-lb.......................**25.00**

American, pitcher, crystal, flat, 1-qt......................................**30.00**

Baroque, bowl, vegetable; crystal, oval, 9½".......................**25.00**

Baroque, cake plate, blue, 10"..**35.00**

Baroque, comport, blue, 4¾"..**38.00**

Brocade (Grape #287), whipped cream pail, green, #2375..**40.00**

Brocade (Oakleaf #290), mint dish, crystal, #2394, 4½".........**35.00**

Brocade (Oakwood #72), candy dish, blue or orchid, w/lid, #2395 ....**200.00**

Brocade (Palm Leaf #73), plate, green or rose, #2419, 8" sq...........**35.00**

Brocade (Paradise #289), tumbler, green or orchid, footed, #877, 9-oz **60.00**

Colony, bowl, salad; crystal, 9¾"..............................**37.50**

Colony, candlestick, crystal, 9"..**30.00**

Colony, salt & pepper shakers, crystal, 3⅝", pr..............**28.00**

Fostoria

American, creamer, crystal, rare, $400.00. (Photo courtesy Gene Florence)

American, bonbon, crystal, 3-footed, 7" **12.50**

Fairfax, butter dish, amber, $115.00; Salad dressing bottle, amber, $125.00. (Photo courtesy Milbra Long and Emily Seate)

Fairfax No 2375, baker, green or topaz, oval, 9"................**30.00**

Fairfax No 2375, pickle dish, blue, orchid or rose, 8½" **25.00**

Fairfax No 2375, platter, blue, orchid or rose, oval, 12" .**42.00**

Fuchsia, bowl, crystal, #2479, 12".............................**90.00**

Fuchsia, plate, salad; crystal, #2440, 7".........................**15.00**

Fuchsia, tumbler, crystal, #833, 8-oz...................................**22.00**

Hermitage, bowl, cereal; azure, #2449½, 6".......................**20.00**

Hermitage, mug, crystal, #2449, footed, 9-oz......................**12.50**

Hermitage, plate, sandwich; amber, green or topaz, #2449, 12"...................................**12.50**

June, bowl, baker; crystal, oval, 10"...................................**40.00**

June, candlestick, blue or rose, 2"....................................**33.00**

June, compote, topaz, #2375, 7"..............................**70.00**

Kashmir, candlestick, green or yellow, 9½".......................**40.00**

Kashmir, plate, dinner; blue, 10"...............................**70.00**

Kashmir, tumbler, iced tea; green or yellow, 13-oz **25.00**

Lafayette, bowl, sweetmeat; burgundy or Regal Blue, 4½".............................**35.00**

Lafayette, cup, demitasse; amber or crystal........................**17.50**

Lafayette, sugar bowl, green, rose or topaz, footed, 3⅝" **25.00**

Navarre, bowl, crystal, handled, footed, #2496, 5".............**20.00**

Navarre, cup, crystal, #2440 ..**20.00**

Navarre, plate, cracker; crystal, #2496, 11"......................**50.00**

New Garland, celery dish, amber or topaz, 11" **22.00**

New Garland, creamer or sugar bowl, rose, ea...................**15.00**

New Garland, tumbler, amber or topaz, #4120, 10-oz **14.00**

Pioneer, baker, amber, crystal or green, oval, 9"................**35.00**

Pioneer, egg cup, rose or topaz ..**25.00**

Pioneer, platter, amber, crystal or green, 15" **27.50**

Rogene, marmalade, crystal, w/lid, #1968.............................**30.00**

Rogene, plate, salad; crystal, #2283, 7".........................**10.00**

Rogene, vase, crystal, rolled edge, 8½"..................................**95.00**

Royal, bowl, salad; amber or green, #2350, 10" **35.00**

Royal, celery, amber or green, #2350, 11".......................**25.00**

Royal, platter, amber or green, #2350, 10½"....................**30.00**

Royal, vase, amber or green, flared, #2292 ....**125.00**

Seville, plate, dinner; amber, #2350, 10½"....................**35.00**

Seville, stem, parfait; green, #870 ....**35.00**

Sun Ray, bowl, fruit; crystal, 5"................................**8.00**

Sun Ray, pitcher, crystal, 64-oz **65.00**

Sun Ray, plate, sandwich; crystal, 12"...................................**35.00**

Trojan, candlestick, rose, #2394, 2"....................................**25.00**

Trojan, goblet, wine; topaz, #5099, 3-oz, 5½".........................**45.00**

Trojan, plate, chop; topaz, #2375, 13"...................................**65.00**

Versailles, bowl, soup; green or pink, #2375, 7"...............**80.00**

Versailles, platter, green, pink or yellow, #2375, 12".........**85.00**

Versailles, relish dish, green or
pink, #2375, 8½"............**33.00**
Vesper, bowl, green, 8⅞".......**32.00**
Vesper, cheese dish, amber, foot-
ed, #2368........................**25.00**
Vesper, plate, luncheon; blue,
#2350, 8½".......................**25.00**

Heisey

Charter Oak (Acorn & Leaves),
bowl, finger; pink, #3362..**17.50**
Charter Oak (Acorn & Leaves),
plate, luncheon; pink, #1246,
8"....................................**15.00**
Chintz, bowl, pickle & olive; crys-
tal, 2-part, 13"................**15.00**
Chintz, cup, yellow................**25.00**
Chintz, platter, crystal, oval, 14"..**35.00**
Crystolite, candle block, crystal,
swirl, 1-light...................**20.00**
Crystolite, mustard, crystal,
w/lid..............................**55.00**
Crystolite, relish tray, crystal, 3-
part, 12"..........................**35.00**
Empress, bonbon, yellow, 6".**25.00**
Empress, comport, pink, 6"
sq **70.00**
Empress, platter, yellow, 14"..**45.00**
Greek Key, creamer, crystal..**50.00**
Greek Key, sherbet, crystal, foot-
ed, straight rim, 4½-oz ..**30.00**
Greek Key, tumbler, crystal,
flared rim, 5-oz...............**50.00**

**Ipswich,
candy dish,
Sahara,
half-pound,
$300.00.**

Ipswich, creamer, crystal......**35.00**
Ipswich, pitcher, crystal, ½-
gal..................................**350.00**
Lariat, bowl, cream soup; crystal,
handles...........................**50.00**
Lariat, plate, dinner; crystal,
10½"...............................**125.00**
Lariat, tumbler, iced tea; crystal,
footed, 12-oz **28.00**
Minuet, bowl, shallow salad; crys-
tal, 13½"..........................**75.00**
Minuet, plate, luncheon; crystal,
8"....................................**30.00**
Minuet, tumbler, juice; crystal,
#5010, 5-oz **34.00**
New Era, bowl, crystal, 11"..**60.00**
New Era, saucer, after dinner;
crystal.............................**10.00**
New Era, stem, claret; crystal, 4-
oz....................................**20.00**
Octagon, basket, crystal, #500,
5"....................................**100.00**
Octagon, mayonnaise, pink, foot-
ed, #1229, 5½"................**25.00**
Octagon, platter, orchid, oval,
12¾"...............................**50.00**
Old Colony, celery tray, yellow,
13" **40.00**
Old Colony, grapefruit, yellow,
#3380, footed **20.00**
Old Colony, pitcher, yellow,
#3390, 3-pt **230.00**
Old Sandwich, comport, crystal,
6"....................................**40.00**
Old Sandwich, plate, green, 8"
sq....................................**32.00**
Old Sandwich, tumbler, iced
tea; green or pink, footed,
12-oz **45.00**
Orchid, bell, dinner; crystal,
#5022 or #5025...............**35.00**
Orchid, marmalade, crystal,
w/lid **235.00**

Orchid, plate, torte; crystal, rolled edge, 14".........................**65.00**

Plantation, butter dish, crystal, oblong, w/lid, ¼-lb........**115.00**

Plantation, oil bottle, crystal, w/#125 stopper, 3-oz....**130.00**

Plantation, sugar bowl, crystal, footed..............................**40.00**

Pleat & Panel, cup, pink.......**15.00**

Pleat & Panel, plate, dinner; crystal, 10¾".........................**15.00**

Pleat & Panel, tumbler, green, ground bottom, 8-oz.......**22.50**

Provincial, nappy, crystal, 4½"..**15.00**

Provincial, plate, luncheon; crystal, 8".............................**15.00**

Provincial, salt & pepper shakers, crystal, pr........................**40.00**

Queen Ann, bowl, cream soup; crystal.............................**18.00**

Queen Ann, cup, after dinner; crystal.............................**20.00**

Queen Ann, stem, sherbet; crystal, 4-oz...........................**15.00**

Ridgeleigh, bowl, salad; crystal, 9"....................................**40.00**

Ridgeleigh, plate, torte; crystal, footed, 13½"....................**45.00**

Ridgeleigh, tumbler, old-fashioned; crystal, pressed, 8-oz.......**40.00**

Rose, water pitcher, crystal, Waverly blank, 73-ounces, $575.00. (Photo courtesy Gene Florence)

Rose, bowl, crystal, crimped, Waverly, 13"................**110.00**

Rose, candlestick, crystal, 3-light, Cascade, #142................**85.00**

Rose, plate, salad; crystal, Waverly, 8"................................**30.00**

Saturn, bowl, baked apple; crystal................................**25.00**

Saturn, marmalade, crystal, w/lid..............................**45.00**

Saturn, plate, luncheon; crystal, 8"....................................**10.00**

Stanhope, bowl, salad; crystal, 11"....................................**90.00**

Stanhope, saucer, crystal......**10.00**

Stanhope, tumbler, soda; crystal, #4083, 5-oz....................**20.00**

Twist, bonbon, Marigold, handles, 6"....................................**30.00**

Twist, celery tray, green or pink, 10"....................................**50.00**

Twist, ice tub, crystal...........**50.00**

Victorian, cigarette box, crystal, 4"....................................**80.00**

Victorian, cup, punch; crystal, 5-oz....................................**10.00**

Victorian, stem, wine; crystal, 2½-oz....................................**30.00**

Waverly, bowl, vegetable; crystal, 9"....................................**35.00**

Waverly, cruet, crystal, w/#122 stopper, 3-oz..................**75.00**

Waverly, plate, crystal, dinner; 10½"..................................**50.00**

Yeoman, bowl, banana split; green, footed..................**35.00**

Yeoman, cup, after dinner; pink or yellow.............................**40.00**

Yeoman, platter, crystal, 12"..**10.00**

Imperial

Cape Cod, ashtray, crystal, #160/134/1, 4"................**14.00**

Cape Cod, bowl, dessert; crystal, tab handles, #160/197, 4½"....**23.00**

Cape Cod, bowl, punch; crystal, #160/20B, 12".............**65.00**

Cape Cod, comport, crystal, #160/45, 6"...................**25.00**

Cape Cod, gravy bowl, crystal, #160/202, 18-oz.............**85.00**

Cape Cod, pitcher, crystal, #160/240, 1-pt.................**45.00**

Cape Cod, plate, dinner; crystal, #160/10D, 10".............**37.50**

Cape Cod, salt & pepper shakers, crystal, footed, #160/116, pr...............**20.00**

Cape Cod, tumbler, crystal, 12-ounce, $12.50.

Cape Cod, tumbler, juice; crystal, #1600, 6-oz.......................**8.00**

Cape Cod, vase, crystal, footed, #160/21, 11½".................**70.00**

Morgantown

Golf Ball, bell, colors other than cobalt, green or red........**60.00**

Golf Ball, creamer or sugar bowl, green or red, ea............**175.00**

Golf Ball, stem, cocktail; green or red, 3½-oz, 4⅛"..............**25.00**

Queen Louise, bowl, finger; crystal w/pink, footed........**200.00**

Queen Louise, plate, salad; crystal w/pink..........................**150.00**

Queen Louise, stem, water; crystal w/pink, 9-oz.............**385.00**

Sunrise Medallion, cup, crystal.**40.00**

Sunrise Medallion, stem, wine; blue, 2½-oz.....................**85.00**

Sunrise Medallion, tumbler, green or pink, footed, 9-oz, 4¾".**40.00**

Tinkerbell, bowl, finger; azure, footed...........................**75.00**

Tinkerbell, stem, cocktail; azure, 3½-oz.............................**95.00**

Tinkerbell, vase, azure, ruffled top, footed, Uranus #36, 10".**350.00**

Tinkerbell, vase, green, ruffled top, footed, Uranus #36, 10", $350.00. (Photo courtesy Gene Florence)

New Martinsville

Janice, basket, crystal, 11"...**75.00**

Janice, bowl, fruit; blue or red, ruffled top, 12".............**100.00**

Janice, plate, cheese; crystal, 11"..............................**22.50**

Meadow Wreath, bowl, crystal, crimped, #4220/26, 10"..**40.00**

Meadow Wreath, candy box, crystal, w/lid, #42/26.............**65.00**

Meadow Wreath, plate, crystal, 11".....................................**35.00**

Paden City

Black Forest, bowl, green or pink, center handle, 9¼".........**85.00**
Black Forest, cake plate, amber, 2" pedestal foot...............**75.00**
Black Forest, candy dish, amber, w/lid, several styles, ea.**135.00**
Black Forest, plate, bread & butter; green or pink, 6½"...**25.00**
Black Forest, stem, wine; crystal, 2-oz, 4¼".......................**17.50**
Black Forest, tumbler, old-fashioned; green or pink, 8-oz, 3⅞"................................**65.00**
Gazebo, candlestick, crystal, 5¼" **45.00**
Gazebo, plate, crystal, bead handles, 12½".......................**55.00**

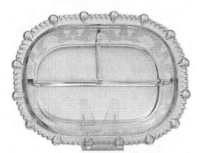

Gazebo, relish, crystal, three-part, 9¾", $60.00. (Photo courtesy Gene Florence)

Gazebo, relish, blue, 3-part, 9¾"..............................**60.00**
Gazebo, tumbler, juice; crystal, footed **22.00**

Tiffin

Cadena, bowl, finger; crystal ..**25.00**

Cadena, creamer or sugar bowl, crystal, ea.......................**20.00**
Cadena, plate, pink or yellow, 6"..**12.00**
Cherokee Rose, bowl, salad; 7".....**45.00**
Cherokee Rose, plate, luncheon; crystal, 8" **15.00**
Cherokee Rose, stem, sherry; crystal, 2-oz **35.00**
Classic, cup, crystal **60.00**
Classic, plate, pink, 8" **20.00**
Classic, sherbet, crystal, 6½-oz, 3⅛"................................**17.50**
Flanders, ashtray, crystal, 2¼x3¾".......................**55.00**
Flanders, crystal, 2 styles.....**50.00**
Flanders, mayonnaise, pink, w/liner **100.00**
Flanders, relish dish, pink, 3-part..............................**90.00**
Fontaine, candlestick, amber, green or pink, #9758, low...........**35.00**
Fontaine, creamer or sugar bowl, Twilight, footed, #4, ea ..**65.00**
Fontaine, plate, amber, green or pink, #8818, 10" **65.00**
Fuchsia, bowl, salad; crystal, 10" **65.00**
Fuchsia, cup, crystal, #5831.**80.00**
Fuchsia, saucer, crystal, #5831.**15.00**
Julia, candy jar, amber trim, footed, w/lid **125.00**

Julia, creamer, amber trim, $30.00. (Photo courtesy Gene Florence)

Julia, plate, dessert; amber trim **12.00**

Julia, stem, water; amber trim..........................**30.00**
June Night, bowl, crystal, crimped, 12"..................**65.00**
June Night, plate, sherbet; crystal, 6"..............................**6.00**
June Night, relish dish, crystal, 3-part, 6½"..........................**35.00**
Jungle Assortment, basket, #151, 6"....................................**85.00**
Jungle Assortment, candy jar, footed, #15179...............**55.00**
Jungle Assortment, vase, sweet pea; #151, 7"...................**65.00**

Elvis Presley

The King of rock 'n roll, the greatest entertainer of all time (and not many would disagree with that), Elvis remains just as popular today as he was at the height of his career. Over the past few years, values for Elvis collectibles have skyrocketed. The early items marked 'Elvis Presley Enterprises' bearing a 1956 or 1957 date are the most valuable. Paper goods such as magazines, menus from Las Vegas hotels, ticket stubs, etc., make up a large part of any Elvis collection and are much less expensive. His 45s were sold in abundance, so unless you find an original Sun label (one sold at auction for $2,800.00), a colored vinyl or a promotional cut, or EPs in wonderful condition, don't pay much! The picture sleeves are usually worth much more than the record itself! Albums are very collectible, and even though you see some stiff prices on them at antique malls, there's not many you can't buy for well under $25.00 at any Elvis convention.

Remember, the early mark is 'Elvis Presley Enterprises'; the 'Boxcar' mark was used from 1974 to 1977, and the 'Boxcar/Factors' mark from then until 1981. In 1982, the trademark reverted back to Graceland.

Our advisor is Rosalind Cranor, author of *Elvis Collectibles* and *Best of Elvis Collectibles* (Overmountain Press); see the Directory under Virginia for ordering information.

Ballpoint pen, From Elvis & the Colonel, Las Vegas.........**25.00**
Beach hat, w/original photo hang tag, 1956, EX...............**125.00**
Board game, Elvis, guitar-shaped board w/record game cards, 1987, EXIB.....................**75.00**
Booklet, Legendary Performer, early 1970s.......................**8.50**
Bracelet, diecut ELVIS on gold-tone metal, 1970s, EX......**8.00**
Bracelet, dog tag, EP Enterprises, 1950s, EX.....................**150.00**
Calendar, pocket size, Strictly Elvis Generation, 1977, M........**15.00**
Charm, RCA record, 1956, M..**28.00**
Christmas ornament, Hallmark, 1992, MIB......................**20.00**
Concert ticket, Terre Haute IN, September 26, 1977, unused, M.......................................**35.00**
Decanter, McCormick, 1979, Elvis '77 Mini, Love Me Tender..**55.00**
Decanter, McCormick, 1980, Elvis '55 Mini, Loving You......**65.00**

Decanter, McCormick, 1984, Elvis Karate Mini, Don't Be Cruel **125.00**

Decanter, McCormick, 1986, Elvis & Gates, Welcome to My World **150.00**

Decanter, McCormick, 1986, Elvis Season's Greetings, White Christmas......................**195.00**

Doll, World Doll, 1984, available in 3 different outfits, 21", MIB, ea..........................**110.00**

Fan club kit, w/button, membership card & letter, 1956, EX..................**400.00**

Guitar, Lapin, 1984, MOC....**75.00**

Gum cards, Boxcar Enterprises, 1978, set of 66 (some multicolored), M, $65.00.

Key chain, flasher, full figure w/yellow background, EX.........**20.00**

Lighter, Zippo Slim Line, Aloha Elvis, from $75 to.........**100.00**

Locket, gold-plated, Elvis picture on front............................**15.00**

Menu, from Sahara Tahoe show, folding record form, mid-1970s..............................**55.00**

Necklace, dog tag w/blue letters on silver, M.....................**45.00**

Paper dolls, 1982, uncut, M..**15.00**

Pen, 1956 Tickle Me promotion, feathers at top................**18.00**

Pencil, Sincerely Yours Elvis Presley '56 on side, unused, M **18.00**

Pennant, I Love Elvis, red w/white letters, stars & hearts, 1960s, MIP........**45.00**

Photo, Elvis Special Concert edition, 14x7" **15.00**

Photo, 1970s tour, color, in caped swimsuit, 11x14", VG+.............................**12.00**

Photo album, came w/Golden Hits Album, color photos & giant pinup, EX **20.00**

Pin-back, Don't Be Cruel, white w/red broken heart, 1950s, 1", EX **25.00**

Pin-back, Jailhouse Rock, gold album w/portrait in center, 3x3", EX.........................**15.00**

Plate, Elvis Goes Country, by Susie Morton, 8½", M **50.00**

Pitcher and four mugs, multicolored decals of Elvis, from $100.00 to $125.00 for the set.

Poster, Easy Come Easy Go, 1-sheet, EX **90.00**

Poster book, Vol 1, all color, 8x16" **15.00**

Recipe book, Are You Hungry Tonight..., hardcover, 64 pages, 1992, VG **12.00**

Ring, flasher, 1957, EX.........**50.00**

Rubber stamp, Takin' Care of Business **20.00**

Scarf, blue or purple w/silkscreen signature, M...................**15.00**

Sheet Music, All Shook Up, EX ..**25.00**

Socks, Dog Tag anklet, 1956, MOC.............................**45.00**

Standee, Elvis Lives!, MIB (sealed) **60.00**

Statue, bisque, Royal Orleans..**50.00**

Thermometer, Some Like It Cool, shows Elvis in white, 36" .**80.00**

Wallet, blue vinyl w/glittery graphics, EP Enterprises, 1956, EX.......................**300.00**

Enesco

Enesco is an importing company based in Elk Grove, Illinois. They're distributors of ceramic novelties made for them in Japan. There are several lines styled around a particular character or group, and with the emphasis collectors currently place on figurals, they're finding these especially fascinating. During the 1960s, they sold a line of novelties originally called 'Mother-in-the Kitchen.' Today's collectors refer to them as 'Kitchen Prayer Ladies.' Ranging from large items such as canisters and cookie jars to toothpick holders and small picture frames, the line was fairly extensive. Some of the pieces are very hard to find, and those with blue dresses are much scarcer than those in pink. Where we've given ranges, pink is represented by the lower end, blue by the high side. If you find a white piece with blue trim, add another 10% to 20% to the high end.

Another Enesco line that has become very collectible is called 'Kitchen Independence.' It features George Washington with the Declaration of Independence scroll held at his side, and Betsy Ross wearing a blue dress and holding a large flag.

Both lines are pictured in *The Collector's Encyclopedia of Cookie Jars, Volumes 1, 2,* and *3,* by Joyce and Fred Roerig. See also Cookie Jars.

Air freshener, Kitchen Prayer Lady..............................**150.00**

Bank, Human Bean series, This Is A Retired Human Bean, from $20.00 to $25.00.

Bank, Kitchen Prayer Lady, from $175 to.........................**250.00**

Bell, Human Bean, 7 pictured on bell, 6"............................**16.00**

Candle holders, Kitchen Prayer Lady, pr **200.00**

Clock, mantle; Pinocchio, plays 'I've Got No Strings,' MIB **135.00**

Cookie jar, Kitchen Prayer Lady, blue **495.00**

Cookie jar, Kitchen Prayer Lady, pink **395.00**

Crumb tray or brush, Kitchen Prayer Lady, from $125 to **200.00**

Egg timer, Kitchen Prayer Lady, from $100 to **135.00**

Egg timer, windmill w/2 Dutch kids kissing, 4⅜", NMIB.**68.00**

Figurine, Basil the Basset Hound, standing & begging........**65.00**

Figurine, Dear God Kids, nurse, Let's Do Rounds..., 1983, 4¾".................................**40.00**

Figurine, Echo, Coral Kingdom Collection, 1994, M **95.00**

Figurine, Eggbert, Dentist, 2x3", MIB **20.00**

Figurine, Jeffery, Bein' a Fireman Sure Is Hot & Thirsty Work, MIB **95.00**

Figurine, Mayor Mistletoe, North Pole Village Collection, 3⅜", MIB **85.00**

Figurines, Saints Marching Band, 9-pc, from 6" to 8½", MIB **95.00**

Head vase, nurse w/white hat w/red cross, 3½", NM...**165.00**

Head vase, teenager, pink outfit, flowers & ribbons in hair, 5½", M **95.00**

Jack-in-the-box, Cowardly Lion, Wizard of Oz, 1988, MIB........**165.00**

Mug, Human Bean Loves Jelly Beans **10.00**

Mug, Kitchen Prayer Lady.**125.00**

Music box, Dear God Kids, couple getting married, 1984, 4¾", M **60.00**

Music box, roller coaster, plays 6 tunes, MIB **100.00**

Music box, sewing machine w/mice, 6", MIB.............**90.00**

Music box, typewriter w/mice, 1991, EX........................**90.00**

Music box, Wee Wedding Wishes, 1989, MIB....................**160.00**

Napkin holder, Kitchen Prayer Lady, pink, from $25 to .**30.00**

Night light, Eggbert, coming out of soccer ball, 1989, MIB ...**364.00**

North Pole Station, 1987 ......**80.00**

Ornament, Partners in Crime, dog & cat in shopping bag, 1994, 2½" **30.00**

Ornament, Partners in Crime, dog & cat in wreath, 1994 ....**30.00**

Ornament, Santa knitting scarf, 1994, 2¼" **25.00**

Picture frame, Wilfred, Brambly Hedge series, 5", M **65.00**

Planter, Kitchen Prayer Lady..**75.00**

Plaque, Kitchen Prayer Lady, full-figure **100.00**

Ring holder, Kitchen Prayer Lady **50.00**

Salt and pepper shakers, Kitchen Independence, Betsy Ross and George Washington, 4¼", $20.00 for the pair.

Salt & pepper shakers, Kitchen Prayer Lady, pr, from $12 to **20.00**

Snow dome, Eggbert in snow dome on top of golf ball..........**435.00**

String holder, Kitchen Prayer Lady, wall mount, from $135 to....................................**145.00**

Sugar bowl, Kitchen Prayer Lady, w/spoon..........................**60.00**

Toothpick holder, Kitchen Prayer Lady, 4½", from $20 to ..**24.00**

Tumbler, Dearie the Wearie, 3¾"............................**165.00**

Vase, bud; Kitchen Prayer Lady, from $100 to.................**125.00**

Ertl Banks

The Ertl company was founded in the mid-'40s by Fred Ertl, Sr., and until the early 1980s, they produced mainly farm tractors. In 1981 they made their first bank, the 1913 Model T Parcel Post Mail Service #9647; since then they've produced thousands of models with the logos of countless companies. The size of each run is dictated by the client and can vary from a few hundred up to several thousand. Some clients will later add a serial number to the vehicle; this is not done by Ertl. Other numbers that appear on the base of each bank are a four-number dating code (the first three indicate the day of the year up to 365, and the fourth number is the last digit of the year, '5' for 1995, for instance). The stock number is shown only on the box, never on the bank, so be sure to keep them in their original boxes. Our values are for banks that are mint and in their original boxes.

For more information, see *Schroeder's Collectible Toys, Antique to Modern* (Collector Books).

A&W Root Beer, 1918 Ford, #2972............................**40.00**

Ace Hardware, 1925 Kenworth, #F397............................**20.00**

Atlanta Falcons, 1913 Ford, #1248............................**35.00**

Baby Ruth, 1926 Mack Bulldog, #9096, M..........................**45.00**

Bell Telephone, 1932 Ford, #9803............................**35.00**

Brach's Candy, 1923 Chevy, #7675............................**35.00**

Bumper to Bumper, 1923 Chevrolet Van, 1992, $35.00.

Canada Dry, 1913 Ford, #2133..**125.00**

Caterpiller, 1931 Hawkeye, #2353............................**25.00**

Cheetos, Step Van, #9023.....**30.00**

Coca-Cola, Trolley Car, #B902..**30.00**

Coors Beer, Stearman Plane, #F583............................**25.00**

Dairy Queen, 1950 Chevy, #9178..........................**135.00**

DuPont, 1923 Chevy, #1353 .**75.00**

Elmer's Glue, 1918 Ford, #F608......................**20.00**

Eskimo Pie, 1931 Hawkeye, #H120............................**22.00**

Fina Oil, 1932 Ford, #9285...**25.00**

Global Van Lines, 1913 Ford, #1655 ....**45.00**

Grapette Soda, 1932 Ford, #9885 ....**65.00**

Hamm's Beer, 1913 Ford, #2145 ....**75.00**

Hershey Chocolate, 1931 Hawkeye, #9349 ....**30.00**

Hostess Cupcakes, 1913 Ford, #9422 ....**30.00**

IGA, 1917 Ford Pickup, #F951..**20.00**

JI Case, 1923 Chevy, #0255 .**25.00**

John Deere, 1926 Mack, #5534......................**115.00**

Kodak, 1905 Ford, gold spokes, #9985 ....**225.00**

Lake of the Ozarks, 1923 Chevy, B380...............................**30.00**

Lipton Tea Co, 1932 Ford, #9087..........................**35.00**

Maurices, 1932 Ford, #9476.**35.00**

Mountain Dew, Vega Plane, #35040 ....**30.00**

Nestle's Crunch, 1931 Hawkeye, #1316 ....**32.00**

Oliver Tractors, Orion Plane, #42501 ....**32.00**

Pabst Beer, 1938 Chevy, #F587 ....**20.00**

Pepsi-Cola, 1931 International, JLE, #5025 ....**75.00**

Quaker State Oil, 1913 Ford, #9195 ....**95.00**

Red Crown Gasoline, 1918 Ford, #1367 ....**25.00**

Reese's Pieces, 1950 Chevy, #9809...........................**28.00**

Safeguard Soap, 1950 Chevy, #7508 ....**35.00**

Schwan's Ice Cream, 1950 Chevy, #9210 ....**95.00**

Smokey Bear, 1913 Ford, #9124 ....**85.00**

Sunmaid Raisins, 1905 Ford, #9575 ....**35.00**

Tabasco Sauce, 1905 Ford, #9878 ....**25.00**

Texaco Petroleum Products, Ford Model A Tanker, Liberty Classics, $60.00. (Photo courtesy June Moon)

Thomas English Muffins, 1932 Ford, #9129 ....**50.00**

Tonka, 1913 Ford, #9739 ......**35.00**

Toys R Us, 1918 Ford, #4587..**28.00**

United Parcel Service, 1912 Ford, #9704 ....**35.00**

US Mail, 1918 Ford, #9843...**45.00**

V&S Variety Store, 1905 Ford, #9622 ....**45.00**

Very Fine Juice, 1923 Chevy, #B109..............................**25.00**

Wix Filters, 1932 Ford, #9810..**125.00**

Wolfgang Candy, 1913 Ford, #9440 ....**35.00**

Fast-Food Collectibles

Everyone is familiar with the kiddie meals offered by fast-food restaurants, but who knew that the toys tucked inside would become so collectible! Played-with items are plentiful at garage sales for nearly nothing, but it's best if they're still in the packages they originally came in. The ones to concentrate on are Barbie dolls, the old familiar Disney characters, and those that tie in with the big blockbuster kids' movies. Collectors look for the boxes the meals came in, too, and even the display signs that the restaurants promote each series with are valuable. The toys don't have to be old to be collectible.

Our values are for toys that are still in the original packaging. A loose example is worth about 35% to 50% less than one still sealed.

Our advisors for McDonald's® are Joyce and Terry Losonsky, authors of *Illustrated Collector's Guide to McDonald's® Happy Meal® Boxes, Premiums and Promotions; McDonald's® Happy Meal® Toys in the USA; McDonald's® Happy Meal® Toys Around the World;* and *Illustrated Collector's Guide to McDonald's® McCAPS®.* Terry and Joyce are listed in the Directory under Maryland. Another reference is *McDonald's Collectibles, 2nd Edition* by Gary Henriques and Audre DuVall (Collector Books). Our advisors for restaurants other than McDonald's are Bill and Pat Poe (see Florida). See also Character and Promotional Glassware. For information concerning a McDonald's club and newsletter see Clubs and Newsletters.

Arby's, Babar's World Tour, finger puppets, 1990, ea **3.00**
Arby's, Looney Tunes Car Tunes, 1989, ea **3.00**
Arby's, Winter Wonderland Crazy Cruisers, 1995, ea **4.00**

Arby's, Yogi Bear Fun Squirters, 1994, ea **4.00**
Burger King, Aladdin, 1992, ea..**3.00**
Burger King, Beauty & the Beast, 1991, 4 different, ea **4.00**
Burger King, Bone Age, 1989, 4 different, ea **5.00**

Burger King, Burger King doll, stuffed cloth, 1973, 16", NM, $20.00.

Burger King, Glo Force, 1996, 5 different, ea **3.00**
Burger King, Gobots, 1986, Odd Ball/Monster....................**8.00**
Burger King, Good Gobblin', 1989, 3 different, ea **3.00**
Burger King, Good Gobblin', 1989, 3 different, ea **3.00**
Burger King, Minnie Mouse, 1992..............................**2.00**
Burger King, Nerfuls, 1989, 3 different, ea **5.00**
Burger King, Pocahontas, 1995, 8 different, ea **3.00**
Burger King, Pranksters, 1994, 5 different, ea **3.00**
Burger King, Toy Story, 1995, Action Wing Buzz............**2.00**
Burger King, Z-Bots w/Pogs, 1994, 5 different, ea **2.00**
Dairy Queen, Baby's Day Out Books, 1994, 4 different, ea **5.00**

Dairy Queen, Dennis the Menace, 1994, 4 different, ea........**2.00**

Dairy Queen, Space Shuttle, 6 different, ea **2.00**

Denny's, Dino-Makers, 5 different, ea **2.00**

Denny's, Jetson's Go Back to School, 1992, 4 different, ea.............**2.00**

Denny's, Jetson's Space-Age Puzzle Ornaments, 1992, ea **2.00**

Dominos Pizza, Avoid the Noid, 1988, 3 different, ea.........**2.00**

Dominos Pizza, Keep the Noid Out, 1987, 3 different, ea **3.00**

Hardee's, Apollo Spaceship, 1995, 3-pc set **12.00**

Hardee's, Breakman's World, 1995, 4 different, ea.........**2.00**

Hardee's, Camp California, 1994, 4 different, ea...................**2.00**

Hardee's, Pound Puppies, 1986, plush, 4 different, ea **2.00**

Hardee's, Swan Princess, 1994, 5 different, ea......................**2.00**

Jack-in-the-Box, Garden Fun Seed Packages, 1994, 3 different, ea..........................**3.00**

Jack-in-the-Box, Jack Pack Make-A-Scene, 1990, 3 different, ea..........................**3.00**

Jack-in-the-Box, Star Trek the Next Generation, 1994, 6 different, ea **3.00**

Long John Silver's, Berenstain Bears Books, 1995, 4 different, ea **2.00**

Long John Silver's, Free Willy II, 1995, 5 different, ea.........**2.00**

Long John Silver's, Map Activites, 1991, 3 different, ea.........**2.00**

McDonald's, Amazing Wildlife, 1995, ea **2.00**

McDonald's, Barbie/Hot Wheels, 1997, Barbie, 5 different, ea......................**2.00**

McDonald's, Batman, 1992, 6 different, ea **2.00**

McDonald's, Bedtime, 1989, Ronald, set of 4................**3.00**

McDonald's, Changeables, 1987, 6 different, ea......................**2.00**

McDonald's, Crazy Creatures w/Popoids, 1985, 4 different, ea **3.00**

McDonald's, Ducktails II, 1988, Webby on tricycle.............**4.00**

McDonald's, Feeling Good, 1985, Fry Guy on duck **2.00**

McDonald's, Flintstone Kids, 1988, under age 3, Dino...**8.00**

McDonald's, Friendly Skies, 1991, Ronald or Grimace, ea **3.00**

McDonald's, Fun w/Food, 1989, ea **6.00**

McDonald's, Hamburgler doll, stuffed cloth, Chase Bag Co., 1972, 12", M, minimum value $20.00. (Photo courtesy Mary Jane Lamphier)

McDonald's, Happy Pail, 1986, 5 different, ea **3.00**

McDonald's, Little Golden Book, 1982, 5 different, ea.........**2.00**

McDonald's, Little Mermaid, 1989, 4 different, ea.........**2.00**

McDonald's, Mac Tonight, 1988, any except under age 3, ea........**3.00**

McDonald's, McDonald's Star Trek, 1979, from $5 to **6.00**

McDonald's, McDonaldland Dough, 1990, ea.................**3.00**

McDonald's, Moveables, 1988, any, ea **5.00**

McDonald's, Oliver & Co, 1988, 4 different, ea.....................**2.00**

McDonald's, Ronald McDonald bank, ceramic, 7½", M, from $20.00 to $25.00.

McDonald's, School Days, 1984, eraser, pencil or ruler, ea.**2.00**

McDonald's, Sea World of Texas, 1988, 4 different, M, ea....**8.00**

McDonald's, Sports Balls, 1990, ea.......................................**2.00**

McDonald's, VR Troopers, 1996, under age 3......................**2.00**

McDonald's, 101 Dalmatians, 1991, 4 different, ea.........**2.00**

Pizza Hut, Beauty & the Beast, 1992, hand puppets, 4 different, ea..............................**2.00**

Pizza Hut, Eureeka's Castle, 1990, hand puppets, 3 different, ea **2.00**

Pizza Hut, Marvel Comics, 4 different, 1994, ea **2.00**

Pizza Hut, Mascot Misfits, 4 different, 1995, ea **2.00**

Pizza Hut, Pagemaster, 4 different, 1994, ea.....................**2.00**

Sonic, All-Star Mini Baseballs, 1995, 5 different, ea.........**2.00**

Sonic, Animal Straws, 1995, 4 different, ea **2.00**

Sonic, Brown Bag Bowlers, 1994, 4 different, ea....................**3.00**

Sonic, Flippin' Food, 1995, 3 different, ea **2.00**

Sonic, Holiday Kids, 1994, 4 different, ea **2.00**

Subway, Bobby's World, 1995, 4 different, ea......................**2.00**

Subway, Cone Heads, 1993, 4 different, ea **2.00**

Subway, Hackeysack Balls, 1991, 4 different, ea...................**2.00**

Subway, Monkey Trouble, 1994, 5 different, ea......................**2.00**

Subway, Save the Wildlife, 1995, 4 different, ea...................**2.00**

Taco Bell, Hugga Bunch, Fluffer, Gigglet or Tuggins, 1984, plush, ea **3.00**

Taco Bell, Mask, 1995, It's Party Time switchplate or Milo w/mask, ea.......................**3.00**

Taco Bell, The Tick, 1996, Arthur w/wings or Sewer Urchin, ea......................**2.00**

Target Markets, Muppet Twisters, 1994, 3 different, ea.........**2.00**

Target Markets, Roll-O-Fun Coloring Kit, 1995, 3 different, ea **2.00**

Wendy's, Alf Tales, 1990, 6 different, ea.............................**2.00**

Wendy's, Ballsasaurus, 1992, 4 different, ea......................**4.00**

Wendy's, Fast-Food Racers, 1990, 6 different, ea **2.00**

Wendy's, Glofriends, 1989, 9 different, ea **2.00**

Wendy's, George Jetson in spaceship, 1st series, 1989, M, $2.50.

Kenn Whitmyer; two of their later lines, Hobnail and Silver Crest, are shown in Gene Florence's book called *Collectible Glassware of the '40s, '50s, and '60s.* All are published by Collector Books. See also Glass Animals; Glass Shoes; Slag Glass. For information on Fenton Art Glass Collectors of America, see Clubs and Newsletters.

Wendy's, Potato Head II, 1988, 5 different, ea......................**3.00**

Wendy's, Weird Writers, 1991, 3 different, ea......................**2.00**

Wendy's, World of Teddy Ruxpin, 1987, 5 different, ea.........**2.00**

White Castle, Bow Biters, 1989, Blue Meany......................**1.00**

White Castle, Castleburger Friends, 1989, 6 different, ea............**3.00**

White Castle, Fat Albert & the Cosby Kids, 1990, ea........**5.00**

Fenton

The Fenton glass company, organized in 1906 in Martin's Ferry, Ohio, is noted for their fine art glass. Over one hundred thirty patterns of carnival glass were made in their earlier years, but even their new glass is considered collectible. Only since 1970 have some of the pieces carried a molded-in logo; before then paper labels were used. For information on Fenton, we recommend *Fenton Art Glass, 1907 to 1939,* and *Fenton Art Glass, 1939 – 1980,* by Margaret and

Ashtray, Apple Blossom, #7377, 1960-61, from $35 to......**45.00**

Ashtray, leaf; Daisy & Button, Colonial Green, #1976, 1968-70......................................**8.00**

Ashtray, Silver Crest, #7377, 1970-71, from $35 to......**45.00**

Banana bowl, Hobnail, milk glass, #3720, 1959-80, from $25 to...........................**35.00**

Basket, Aqua Crest, #36, 1942-43, 6¼", from $85 to.............**95.00**

Basket, Black Rose, #7237, 1953-55, from $145 to...........**185.00**

Basket, Coin Dot, blue opalescent, #1522/1430, 1947-51, 10"................................**165.00**

Basket, Coin Dot, cranberry opalescent, #203/1427, 1947-65, 7"............................**115.00**

Basket, Diamond Optic, Mulberry, #203, 1942, 7", from $100 to **150.00**

Basket, Emerald Crest, #680/7236, 1949-54, 5", from $100 to..........................**125.00**

Basket, Rose Crest, #36, 1946-47, 4½", from $75 to.............**85.00**

Basket, Silver Crest, Apple Blossom decor, #7436, 1969-71, sm, from $45 to **65.00**

Basket, Silver Crest, cone shape, #36, 1943-47, 8", from $60 to 75.00

Basket, Spanish Lace, Violets in Snow decor, #3538, 1974-80+, 8½" 125.00

Basket, Spiral Optic, Cameo (amber) opalescent, #3137, 1979-1980 ....45.00

Bell, Daisy & Button, carnival, #1966, 1971-76, from $27 to 35.00

Bell, Daisy & Button, Lime Sherbet, #1966, 1973-80, from $20 to 25.00

Bell, Hobnail, Blue Bell decor on milk glass, #3667, 1971-73, 6" 35.00

Bell, Hobnail, Cameo (amber) opalescent, #3667, 1979-81 ....28.00

Bell, Hobnail, Colonial Amber, #3667, 1967-80+, 6", from $10 to 14.00

Bell, Spanish Lace, Silver Crest trim, #3567, 1973-80+....40.00

Berry dish, Hobnail, Blue Pastel, #3928, 1954-55, from $15 to 18.00

Bonbon, Blue Crest, #7428, 1963, 8", from $45 to...............55.00

Bonbon, Gold Crest, #7428, 1963-65, from $12 to 14.00

Bowl, Coin Dot, blue opalescent, #203/1427, 1947-53, 7", from $35 to 45.00

Bowl, Crystal Crest, flared, #203, 1942, 8½", from $30 to.....................................40.00

Bowl, Peach Crest, double-crimped, #1522/#7224, 1940-70, 10"............................80.00

Bowl, Silver Crest, #205, 1943-48, 8½"..................................45.00

Bowl, Silver Crest, Yellow Rose decor, #7423, 1969-71, 9½", from $45 to 55.00

Butter dish, Cactus, milk glass, #3477, 1959-61, from $20 to 30.00

Butter dish, Hobnail, milk glass, oval, #3777, 1963-80+, ¼-lb 28.00

Cake plate, Blue Crest, #7213, 1963, 13", from $125 to..150.00

Cake plate, Diamond Lace, blue opalescent, #1948-A, 1949-51, 11"...................................65.00

Cake plate, Emerald Crest, low foot, #5813, 1954-56, from $90 to..................................125.00

Cake plate, Hobnail, milk glass, footed, 12½", from $35.00 to $45.00.

Candle holder, Apple Blossom, #7271, 1960-61, from $35 to 42.50

Candle holder, Crystal Crest, #1523, 1942, from $40 to..45.00

Candle holder, Peach Crest, #7272, 1956-62, from $35 to.....45.00

Candy box, Hobnail, Blue Marble, w/lid, #3886, 1970-74, from $40 to............................55.00

Candy jar, Hobnail, Blue Pastel, #3883, 1954-55, from $60 to 70.00

Chip 'n Dip, Hobnail, milk glass, #3703, 1958-80, from $55 to **65.00**

Cigarette lighter, Hobnail, Colonial Blue, #3692, 1965-69........**20.00**

Comport, Black Crest, footed, flared, #7429, from $75 to **85.00**

Creamer, #1924, 1947-48, from $50 to **60.00**

Creamer, Coin Dot, blue opalescent, #33, 1948-49, from $35 to **45.00**

Cruet, Hobnail, blue opalescent, #3863, 1941-55, from $100 to **125.00**

Cruet, Polka Dot, cranberry, #2273, 1955-56, from $175 to **200.00**

Cup, child's; Burred Hobnail, milk glass, #489, 1950-52.......**28.00**

Epergne & block, Silver Crest, #1522, 1946-51 ....**45.00**

Epergne set, Silver Turquoise, #7200, 1956-59, 3-pc, from $150 to **175.00**

Fairy light, Hobnail, blue satin, #3608, 1974-81, from $30 to **35.00**

Finger bowl, Aqua Crest, #202, 1941-43, from $25 to **30.00**

Frog, Silver Crest/Violets in Snow decor, #5166, 1979-80+, $35 to **45.00**

Goblet, water; Priscilla, blue, #1890, 1950-52 ....**30.00**

Hurricane lamp, Hobnail, green pastel, #3998, 1954-56, 11", from $90 to **110.00**

Jug, Gold Crest, handled, #192, 1943-44, 5½", from $30 to.............**40.00**

Jug, Peach Crest, handled, #711/#7166, 1949-70, 6"..**45.00**

Jug, syrup; Hobnail, coral, #3762, 1961-62, 12-oz, from $35 to **45.00**

Lavabo, Hobnail, Honey Amber, #3867, 1962-67, from $100 to **150.00**

Pitcher, Ring Optic, French opalescent, #201, 7", from $150 to **185.00**

Pitcher, Spiral Optic, blue opalescent, #3166, 1979-80, 10-oz, $35 to **45.00**

Plate, Crystal Crest, #682, 1942, 10", from $65 to.............**85.00**

Plate, Silver Crest, #7211, 1956-72, 12½", from $25 to.....**35.00**

Powder jar, Coin Dot, cranberry opalescent, #92/1485, 1948-56, from $125 to **150.00**

Puff box, Peach Crest, #192-A, 1943-48 ....**48.00**

Punch bowl, Hobnail, blue opalescent, flared, #3827, 1950-55, from $225 to **250.00**

Punch cup, Hobnail, blue opalescent, #3837, 1950-55 .....**20.00**

Relish, Silver Rose, heart shaped, handled, #7333, 1956-58, from $50 to **60.00**

Salt and pepper shakers, Rib Optic, cranberry opal, mold blown, #1605, 5", 4", scarce, $110.00 for the pair.

Shaker, kitchen; Hobnail, black, #3602, 1962-66, from $12 to **15.00**

Tidbit, Black Crest, 2-tier, #7294, from $75 to **85.00**

Toothpick holder, Hobnail, Colonial Amber, #3795, 1966-76, from $6 to **8.00**

Top hat, Peach Crest, #1923, 1940-43, 6", from $45 to.**55.00**

Top hat, Snowcrest, amber, #1921, 1951-52, 7", from $100 to..**125.00**

Tumbler, Diamond Optic, ruby overlay, #1353, 1942-49, 10-oz.**27.00**

Tumbler, Hobnail, cranberry opalescent, #3947, 1941-68..........**38.00**

Vanity set, Gold Crest, #192-A, 1943-44, 3-pc, from $150 to **175.00**

Vase, Aqua Crest, double-crimped, #187, 1941-43, 6", from $50 to **60.00**

Vase, Block & Star, milk glass, #5659, 1955-56, 9", from $30 to **45.00**

Vase, Bubble Optic, coral, pinched, #1358, 1961-62, 8", from $60 to **85.00**

Vase, Coin Dot, topaz opalescent, #1456, 1959-60, 6"..........**95.00**

Vase, Hobnail, Colonial Blue, #3752, 1977-78, 11"........**25.00**

Vase, Ivory Crest, tulip, #894, 1940-41, 10"....................**90.00**

Vase, Silver Jamestown, #7350, 1957-59, 5", from $45 to..**55.00**

Vase, Snowcrest, blue, #4516, 1950-51, 8½", from $45 to.........**55.00**

Vase, Spiral Optic, topaz opalescent, #1925, 1940, 6", from $65 to **80.00**

Vase, Wild Rose w/Bow Knot, blue overlay, #2855, 1961, 5" ..**35.00**

Fiesta

Since it was discontinued by Homer Laughlin in 1973, Fiesta has become one of the most popular collectibles on the market. Values have continued to climb until some of the more hard-to-find items now sell for several hundred dollars each. In 1986 HLC reintroduced a line of new Fiesta that buyers should be aware of. To date these colors have been used: cobalt (darker than the original), rose (a strong pink), black, white, apricot (very pale), yellow (a light creamy tone), turquoise, sea mist (a light mint green), lilac, persimmon, periwinkle (country blue), sapphire blue (very close to the original cobalt), chartreuse (brighter), gray, juniper (teal), cinnabar (maroon), and sunshine yellow. When old molds were used, the mark will be the same, if it is a molded-in mark such as on pitchers, sugar bowls, etc. The ink stamp differs from the old — now all the letters are upper case.

'Original colors' in the listings indicates values for three of the original six colors — light green, turquoise, and yellow. The listing that follows is incomplete due to space restrictions; refer to *The Collector's Encyclopedia of Fiesta, Ninth Edition*, by Sharon and Bob Huxford (Collector Books) for more information. See also Clubs and Newsletters for information on *Fiesta Collector's Quarterly*.

Ashtray, '50s colors **88.00**
Ashtray, cobalt, ivory or red ...**65.00**
Bowl, covered onion soup; red ..**750.00**
Bowl, cream soup; light green, turquoise or yellow **45.00**
Bowl, dessert; 6", cobalt, ivory or red **52.00**
Bowl, footed salad; light green or yellow **340.00**
Bowl, fruit; 4¾", '50s colors ..**40.00**
Bowl, fruit; 4¾", light green, turquoise or yellow **28.00**
Bowl, fruit; 5½", cobalt, ivory or red **35.00**
Bowl, individual salad; med green, 7½" **120.00**
Bowl, nappy; 8½", '50s colors ..**65.00**
Bowl, nappy; 8½", light green or yellow **42.00**
Cake plate, light green or yellow, minimum value **900.00**
Candle holders, bulb; light green or yellow, pr **110.00**
Candle holders, tripod; light green or yellow, pr **485.00**
Carafe, cobalt, ivory, red or turquoise **340.00**
Casserole, French; yellow ...**300.00**
Casserole, light green, turquoise or yellow **165.00**
Coffeepot, cobalt, ivory or red ..**255.00**
Coffeepot, light green, turquoise or yellow **195.00**
Compote, sweets; light green or yellow...........................**80.00**
Compote, 12", light green or yellow...........................**150.00**
Creamer, regular; med green ..**90.00**
Creamer, stick handle; light green or yellow **48.00**
Cup, demitasse; cobalt, ivory or red..............................**80.00**
Egg cup, '50s colors **160.00**

Covered onion soup bowl, light green, $600.00; Dessert bowl, cobalt, 6", $52.00; Individual salad bowl, red, 7½", $105.00; Fruit bowl, yellow, 5½", $28.00; Fruit bowl, rose, 4¾", $40.00.

Marmalade, light green or yellow **245.00**
Mixing bowl #1, cobalt, ivory, red or turquoise **245.00**
Mixing bowl #2, light green or yellow **115.00**
Mixing bowl #3, cobalt, ivory, red or turquoise **135.00**
Mixing bowl #4, light green or yellow **130.00**
Mixing bowl #5, light green or yellow **160.00**
Mixing bowl #6, cobalt, ivory, red or turquoise **275.00**
Mixing bowl #7, light green or yellow **350.00**
Mug, Tom & Jerry; '50s colors ..**100.00**
Mustard, light green or yellow ..**210.00**
Pitcher, disk juice; Harlequin yellow **60.00**
Pitcher, disk water; cobalt, ivory or red **170.00**
Pitcher, ice; light green or yellow **140.00**

Pitcher, jug; 2-pt, light green, turquoise or yellow **88.00**
Plate, calendar; 1955, 9"......**50.00**
Plate, chop; 13", light green, turquoise or yellow **42.00**
Plate, chop; 15", '50s colors..**145.00**
Plate, compartment, 12", cobalt, ivory or red......................**60.00**
Plate, compartment; 10½", '50s colors..............................**75.00**
Plate, deep; light green, turquoise or yellow **38.00**
Plate, deep; med green **140.00**
Plate, 6", cobalt, ivory or red ..**7.00**
Plate, 7", '50s colors **13.00**
Plate, 9", med green...............**45.00**
Plate, 10", '50s colors **52.00**
Platter, '50s colors.................**58.00**
Platter, cobalt, ivory or red...**45.00**
Relish tray base, light green or yellow................................**75.00**
Relish tray center insert, cobalt, ivory, red or turquoise ...**60.00**
Salt & pepper shakers, cobalt, ivory or red, pr **30.00**
Salt & pepper shakers,'50s colors, pr.....................................**45.00**
Sauce boat, cobalt, ivory or red ..**85.00**
Saucer, '50s colors **6.00**
Saucer, demitasse; cobalt, ivory or red...................................**22.00**
Saucer, original colors.............**4.00**
Sugar bowl, w/lid, '50s colors, 3¼x3½"............................**75.00**
Sugar bowl, w/lid, cobalt, ivory or red, 3¼x3½" **58.00**
Syrup, cobalt, red or turquoise..**425.00**
Teacup, '50s colors **38.00**
Teacup, cobalt, ivory or red ..**35.00**
Teapot, lg; light green or yellow **210.00**
Teapot, med; light green, turquoise or yellow **165.00**

Tray, utility; light green or yellow **38.00**
Tumbler, juice; cobalt or ivory..**45.00**
Tumbler, juice; red................**60.00**
Tumbler, water; light green or yellow **65.00**
Vase, bud; light green or yellow...**85.00**
Vase, 8", light green or yellow, minimum value............**600.00**

Kitchen Kraft

Bowl, mixing; 6", light green or yellow..............................**72.00**
Bowl, mixing; 8", cobalt or red ..**95.00**
Cake plate, cobalt or red.......**65.00**
Casserole, individual; cobalt or red **160.00**
Covered jar, lg; light green or yellow **320.00**
Covered jar, sm; cobalt or red..**300.00**
Fork, cobalt or red...............**135.00**
Pie plate, 9", cobalt or red **48.00**
Platter, spruce green **350.00**
Spoon, light green or yellow..**135.00**
Stacking refrigerator lid, ivory...**225.00**
Stacking refrigerator unit; cobalt or red **58.00**

Post 86 Fiesta Colors

Bowl, chili; 18-oz, lilac **50.00**
Bowl, vegetable; lg, 39-oz, apricot **20.00**

Individual creamer and sugar bowl on tray, lilac, from $80.00 to $95.00.

Candlestick, round (bulb), sapphire, ea...........................**45.00**
Creamer, individual; lilac.....**35.00**
Lamp, apricot.......................**100.00**
Pitcher, disk; lg, w/anniversary logo, sapphire.................**75.00**
Plate, chop; 11¾", lilac..........**65.00**
Salt & pepper shakers, apricot, pr.................................**22.00**
Saucer, jumbo; 6¾", sapphire...**12.00**
Tumbler, apricot **15.00**
Tumbler, lilac.......................**40.00**
Tumbler, sapphire.................**20.00**

Castles, 2½", from $10.00 to $15.00; 3½", from $18.00 to $22.00. (Photo courtesy of Carole Bess White)

Fishbowl Ornaments

Mermaids, divers, and all sorts of castles have been devised to add interest to fishbowls and aquariums, and today they're starting to attract the interest of collectors. Many were made in Japan and imported decades ago to be sold in 5-&-10¢ stores along with the millions of other figural novelties that flooded the market after the war. The condition of the glaze is very important; for more information we recommend *Collector's Guide to Made in Japan Ceramics* by Carole Bess White (Collector Books). Unless noted otherwise, the examples in the listing that follows were produced in Japan.

Bathing beauty on turtle, tan & green on white, 2½", $20 to.................................**30.00**
Boy riding dolphin on wave, multicolored matt glazes, 3¾", $20 to...........................**30.00**

Castle towers w/3 arches, tan lustre w/red, green & white, 5¼"..............................**22.00**
Colonade w/palm tree, green, blue & white, 3¾x4"...............**20.00**
Coral deep sea diver, glossy orange w/black image of diver, 3½"..**20.00**
Diver holding dagger, white suit & helmet, blue gloves, 4¾"......................................**22.00**
Doorway, stone entry w/open aqua wood-look door, 2".........**15.00**
Fish riding waves, 2 white fish on cobalt waves, 3½x3".......**22.00**
Lighthouse, tan, black, brown & green, 6½x4"..................**26.00**
Mermaid on sea horse, glossy white, green & orange, 3¼", $20 to.............................**30.00**
Mermaid on snail, 4", $35 to..**45.00**
Nude on starfish, bisque, 4½", $40 to.....................................**50.00**
Pagoda, triple roof, blue, green & maroon, 5½x3¼"...........**20.00**
Sign on tree trunk, No Fishing, brown, black & white, 2½x4"...........................**12.00**
Torii gate, glossy multicolored glazes, 3¾"....................**22.00**

Fisher-Price

Since about 1930 the Fisher-Price Company has produced distinctive wooden toys covered with brightly colored lithographed paper. Plastic parts were first added in 1949. The most valuable Fisher-Price toys are those modeled after well-known Disney characters and having the Disney logo. A little edge wear and some paint dulling are normal to these well-loved toys and to be expected; pricing information reflects items that are in very good played-with condition. Mint-in-box examples are extremely scarce.

Our advisor for this category is Brad Cassity. For further information we recommend *Fisher-Price Toys* by Brad Cassity (Collector Books); *A Pictorial Guide to the More Popular Toys, Fisher-Price Toys, 1931 – 1990*, by Gary Combs and Brad Cassity; *Fisher-Price, A Historical Rarity Value Guide*, by John J. Murray and Bruce R. Fox (Books Americana); and *Schroeder's Collectible Toys, Antique to Modern* (Collector Books). See also Dolls, Fisher-Price; and Clubs and Newsletters for information on the Fisher-Price Collectors Club.

Adventure People Alpha Recon, #360, 1982-84 ....**15.00**
Adventure People Dune Buster, #322, 1979-82 ....**15.00**
Big Bill Pelican, #794, 1961-63, w/cardboard fish.............**85.00**

Bizzy Bunny Cart, #306, 1957-59 ....**40.00**
Bucky Burro, #166, 1955-57 ..**250.00**
Bulldozer, #311, 1976-77 ......**25.00**
Bunny Basket Cart, #301, 1957-59 ....**40.00**
Bunny Egg Cart, #28, 1950 ..**75.00**
Chick Basket Cart, #304, 1960-64................................**40.00**
Chubby Cub, #164, 1969-72 .**20.00**
Chuggy Pop-Up, #616, 1955-56.............................**100.00**

Doggy Racer, #7, 1942, $200.00. (Photo courtesy Brad Cassity)

Dr Doodle, #132, 1957-60 .....**85.00**
Happy Hauler, #732, 1968-70 ..**35.00**
Happy Hippo, #151, 1962-63...**85.00**
Happy Hopper, #121, 1969-76...**20.00**
Husky Cement Mixer, #315, 1978-82 ....**30.00**
Husky Dump Truck, #302, 1978-84 ....**20.00**
Jack & Jill TV Radio, #155, 1968-70, wood & plastic.........**40.00**
Jeep CJ-7 Renegade, #4552, 1985 ....**25.00**
Jiffy Dump Truck, #156, 1971-73 ....**25.00**
Katie Kangaroo, #158, 1976-77 ....**25.00**
Lift & Load Road Builders, #789, 1978-82 ....**20.00**
Little People Construction Set, #2352, 1985, MIB...........**20.00**

Little People Floating Marina, #2582, 1988-90, MIB......**15.00**

Little People Indy Racer, #347, 1983-90 ....**8.00**

Magnetic Chug-Chug, #168, 1964-69 ....**50.00**

McDonald's Happy Meal, #2155, 1989-90, MIB.................**15.00**

Milk Carrier, #637, 1966-85 .**15.00**

Mini Snowmobile, #705, 1971-71 ....**45.00**

Oscar the Grouch, #177, 1977-84 ....**20.00**

Pick-Up & Peek Puzzle, #500, 1972-86.........................**100.00**

Piggy Bank, #166, 1981-82, pink plastic **15.00**

Play Family Animal Circus, #135, 1974-76...........................**60.00**

Play Family Children's Hospital, #931, 1976-78...............**115.00**

Play Family Farm Barnyard, #117, 1972-74.................**25.00**

Play Family Fun Jet, #183, 1970, 1st version......................**25.00**

Pontiac Firebird, #4551, 1985 ..**24.00**

Pop-Up-Pal Chime Phone, #150, 1968-78...........................**40.00**

Power Dump Truck, #4581, 1985-86 ....**20.00**

Pull-A-Long Lacing Shoe, #146, 1970-73, w/6 figures.......**60.00**

Puppy Playhouse, #110, 1978-80 ....**10.00**

Push Pullet, #194, 1971-72...**25.00**

Queen Buzzy Bee, #314, 1956-58................................**40.00**

Roller Grader, #313, 1977 ....**25.00**

Roly Poly Boats Chime Ball, #162, 1967-69...........................**10.00**

Roly Raccoon, #172, 1980-82 .**10.00**

Running Bunny Cart, #312, 1960-64 ....**45.00**

Shovel Digger, #301, 1975-77...**25.00**

Squeaky the Clown, #777, 1958-59 ....**250.00**

Three Men in a Tub, #142, 1974-75, w/flag......................**10.00**

Wobbles, #130, 1964 – 1967, $40.00.
(Photo courtesy Brad Cassity)

Fishing Collectibles

Very much in evidence at flea markets these days, old fishing gear is becoming popular with collectors. Because the hobby is newly established, there are some very good buys to be found. Early twentieth-century plugs were almost entirely carved from wood, sprayed with several layers of enamel, and finished off with glass eyes. Molded plastics were of a later origin. Some of the more collectible manufacturers are James Heddon, Shakespeare, Rhodes, and Pflueger. Rods, reels, old advertising calendars, and company catalogs are also worth your attention, in fact, any type of vintage sporting goods is now collectible. For more information we recommend *19th-Century Fishing Lures* by Arlan Carter; *The Fishing Lure Collector's Bible* by R. L. Streater with Dudley Murphy and

Rick Edmisten; *Fishing Lure Collectibles* by Dudley Murphy and Rick Edmisten; and *Collector's Guide to Creek Chub Lures and Collectibles* by Harold E. Smith, MD. All are published by Collector Books.

Our advisor for this category is Dave Hoover; he is listed in the Directory under Indiana.

Lures

Arbogast, Sunfish Tin Liz, glass eyes, 1⅝", VG+ **190.00**
Creek Chub, Baby Beetle #6000, mother-of-pearl rear spinner, 2", EX................................**75.00**
Creek Chub, Baby Dingbat #5200, silver flash, 1⅝", EX **50.00**

Creek Club, Baby Pikie in Chrome, wooden with chrome finish, #940-P, from $10.00 to $15.00. (Photo courtesy Harold E. Smith, M.D.)

Creek Chub, Big Bomber, Golden Shiner, 3¾", EX **300.00**
Creek Chub, Dive Bomber (Kreeker), 3 dots & dash finish, EX............................**50.00**
Creek Chub, Fly Rod Hum-Bird F305, green & yellow, EX............**200.00**
Creek Chub, Fly Rod Mouse #F200, gray, EX **250.00**
Creek Chub, Husky Pikie #2300, tiger-striped, 6", EX.......**80.00**
Creek Chub, Husky Surfster #7300, silver flash, 6", EX...........**90.00**

Creek Chub, Snook Plunker #7100, blue flash, 5", EX...........**100.00**
Creek Chub, The Champ #S50, 3¼", EX...........................**40.00**
Creek Chub, Wiggler #100, Chub scale finish, VG..............**40.00**
Heddon, Crazy Crawler, movable wings, 2½", EX...............**40.00**
Heddon, Fly Rod Flapfish, yellow finish, 1⅛", EX..............**15.00**
Heddon, Lung Frog #3500, VG ..**85.00**
Heddon, Sea Runt #160, yellow perch finish w/glass eyes, 2⅝", EX...........................**30.00**
Heddon, SOS Minnow #160, yellow perch w/glass eyes, 3½", EX **100.00**
Heddon, Torpedo, rainbow finish w/glass eyes, 3½", VG **40.00**
Jamison, Fly Rod Wiggler, striped w/painted eyes, 2⅛", EX..**50.00**
Jamison, Musky Wig-Wag (Gep Bait), 2-part head & body, 6", EX **125.00**
Jennings, Torpedo, silver-plated hollow metal w/trim, 2⅞", VG **350.00**
JK Rush, Deluxe Tango, metal head plate, 4¼", EX+ .**100.00**
Keeling, Bass Crawfish, black & yellow, 2½", EX **75.00**
Keeling, Crab, black & yellow, EX................................**55.00**
Martin, Redhead, white, glass eyes, lg, MIB **50.00**
Moonlight/Paw Paw, Moonlight Crawfish, rubber legs, tack eyes, NM......................**125.00**
Moonlight/Paw Paw, Paw Paw Bullhead, spotted, tack eyes, 4¼", NM **100.00**
Pflueger, Flocked Mouse, 2¾", NM **200.00**

Pflueger, Razum Minnow, rubber w/perch finish, attached keel, 2", VG **30.00**

Pflueger, Soft Rubber Frog, loop-end weed guards over hooks, EX **40.00**

Shakespeare, Barnacle Bill, wire runs from nose to tail, glass eyes, two trebles, 1921, 2⅞", from $75.00 to $125.00. (Photo courtesy Dudley Murphy and Rick Edmisten)

Shakespeare, No-Grip Minnow, red & white w/pressed eyes, 4", VG **110.00**

Shakespeare, Pad-Ler, red & white, Musky size, 3¾", VG **80.00**

South Bend, Lunge-Oreno #966, glass eyes, steel prop, 5¾", NM **150.00**

South Bend, Perch-Oreno, nickel finish, deep front hook cup, EX **55.00**

South Bend, Spin-Oreno, glass eyes (uncommon), 2", EX **20.00**

Winchester, Spinner #9783, feathered treble, EX **100.00**

Woods, Expert Minnow, traces of silver w/yellow glass eyes, 3", G **200.00**

Reels

AH Fox, marked Bait Casting..., w/8-sided metal plates, VG.......**55.00**

Brookline #16, EX **8.00**

Coronet #25, JA Coxe, aluminum, EX **40.00**

Dam Quick 550, spinning, rare right-handed model, EX..**55.00**

Hardy, Longstone 'Center Pin,' 4", VG...............................**110.00**

Hardy, Silex, 1950s, 4", EX..**165.00**

Heddon #3-15, silver, EX......**75.00**

HH Kiffe, marked Non Level Wind 100-yd Bait Casting, VG..**115.00**

Langley Whitecap #410, star drag, free spool, EX **20.00**

Meek, BF & Son #3, EX......**100.00**

Meissekbach, sm fresh-water Neptune Take-Apart, VG **60.00**

Shakespeare Precision, jeweled, EX **15.00**

South Bend #666, free cast, level winding, EX....................**10.00**

Westly Richards & Co, Rolo, Pat #20113, 4½", VG **250.00**

Rods

Foster Bros Ashbourne Manifold, 2-pc trout, w/case, 108", VG....................................**85.00**

Gene Edwards, spinning, w/original bag & tube, 78" **140.00**

Goodwin Granger 9-Ft Champion Trout, w/tube, G...........**110.00**

Hardy Palakona, 2-pc fly rod, 1 tip, w/canvas case, 105", VG..**330.00**

Heddon #105, 2-pc bait casting, 5½", VG **75.00**

LL Bean's Atlantic Salmon, w/extra tip & cork handle, w/case, EX.**100.00**

Orvis Midge Nymph Combination Trout, 2 tips, w/tube, M.**470.00**

South Bend #59, fly, bamboo, EX **85.00**

Stubby, w/reel, hand brake, 23" L, EX **45.00**

Miscellaneous

Bobber, Kingfish, multicolored, w/instructions, EX+ on card **15.00**

Catalog, Heddon, 1964, tackle, color, 63-pgs, VG+ **70.00**

Catalog, Makinen, 1947, tackle, color, 16 pgs, NM **30.00**

Catalog, Shakespeare, 1925, 39-pgs, VG **275.00**

Catalog, South Bend, 1939, multicolored charts, EX+ **75.00**

Creel, willow w/leather binding, hinges & strap, lg offset hole, VG **130.00**

Decoy, Northern Pike, Carl Christenson, glass eyes, 9¾", EX+ ..**75.00**

Decoy, Trout, Dennis Wolf, glass eyes, 12", EX+ **200.00**

Fly holder, leather, King Sport, 6x4½", EX **35.00**

Hook, Stanley's Perfection Weedless, MOC **25.00**

Minnow trap, CF Orvis Manchester VT, all original, EX ..**85.00**

Sign, Pflueger, cardboard pop-out, 2 in boat w/lg fish, 22x17", EX **330.00**

Split-shot container, Pflueger, tin, EX **10.00**

Split-shot container, Selby BB, celluloid, round, EX **70.00**

Tackle box, leather, 10 cantilevered trays, Knickerbocker, 16x9", EX **85.00**

Flashlights

The flashlight was invented in 1898 and has been produced by the Eveready Company for these past ninety-six years. Eveready dominated the flashlight market for most of this period, but more than 125 other U.S. flashlight companies have come and gone, providing competition along the way. Add to that number more than 35 known foreign flashlight manufacturers, and you end up with over one thousand different models of flashlights to collect. They come in a wide variety of styles, shapes, and sizes. The flashlight field includes tubular, lanterns, figural, novelty, litho, etc. At present, over 45 different categories of flashlights have been identified as collectible. For further information we recommend consulting the *Flashlight Collectors of America*, see Clubs and Newsletters.

Our advisor for this category is Bill Utley; he is listed in the Directory under California.

Bantam Lite, Roy Rogers, 1940s-50s, EX **50.00**

Crown Royal, bottle shape, VG+ **105.00**

Daco Lite, WWII, mk tropical use, hand energized, 1944, EX+ ..**55.00**

Daimon, WWII German Army, sheet steel, 3 colored lens, EX **50.00**

Dyna-lite, ivory Bakelite w/streamline design, EXIB **95.00**

Eveready, Vest Pocket, silver-plated Victorian design, 1912, 3x2", VG **95.00**

Franco, 2 C cells, EX..........**115.00**

GE, Automotive Lamp, w/17" L 'snake' neck, EX **25.00**

Flasher Is Your Friend, plastic dog with tail switch, made in various colors, NM, $28.00 each. (Photo courtesy Bill Utley)

Kwik-Lite, mk Pat 12/29/1914 & 5/16/1916, 5¾", VG+ **30.00**

Niagara Searchlight Co, chrome-plated brass, dated 4/28/1914, VG+ **25.00**

Ray-O-Vac, red plastic screw-on top, 1950s, NMIB **65.00**

Ray-O-Vac, Sportsman Premium Grade, 5" dia lens, 19" L, EX .**55.00**

Ray-O-Vac, Theater Usher's Flashlight, bull-shaped end, EX **30.00**

Saja, hand-generated, Bakelite, 4", EX **45.00**

Winchester, #A3200, EX (w/Winchester paper band & box) **55.00**

Winchester, chrome-plated brass, dated 1920, 5¾", EX **85.00**

Flower Frogs

Nearly every pottery company and glasshouse in America produced their share of figural flower frogs, and many were imported from Japan as well. They were probably most popular from about 1910 through the 1940s, coinciding not only with the heyday of American glass and ceramics, but with the gracious, much less hectic style of living the times allowed. Way before a silk flower or styrofoam block was ever dreamed of, there were fresh cut flowers on many a dining room sideboard or table, arranged in shallow console bowls with matching frogs such as we've described in the following listings. For further information see *Collector's Guide to Made in Japan Ceramics, Identification and Values*, by Carole Bess White (Collector Books). See also specific pottery and glass companies.

Bird on grassy base, ceramic, orange w/yellow & black wings, 4x3" **22.50**

Bird on stump, ceramic, shiny multicolors, 3 holes, Japan, 4½" **36.00**

Butterfly on flower, majolica-like pottery, multicolor, 2x2½" **30.00**

Cherub w/cornucopia & basket, ceramic, multicolor, Japan, 6⅝" **20.00**

Fish, Jamieson's, Capistrano, Calif. (with maple leaf), 6½", in matching bowl, from $45.00 to $55.00. (Photo courtesy Nada Sue Knauss)

215

Fish lying flat, pottery, glossy blue, 5 holes in back, 1½x3¾" **22.50**

Frog on lily pad, ceramic, Dept 56 B St John, 3x6½" **30.00**

Hedgehog, ceramic, blue & white, marked Delfts, 2¼" **48.00**

Loop holder, cast iron, marked JPO Patd 1930s, 4½", VG.........**43.00**

Nude on rock, ceramic, glossy white, Japan, 7x5x4" **28.00**

Owl, ceramic, brown w/white, Japan, 3¾" **18.00**

Parrot, ceramic, multicolor lustre, 6 holes, Japan, 2¾x1¾" .**20.00**

Rooster, ceramic, multicolor, 14 holes, 10½" **30.00**

Snowflake, cast iron, 12 sm holes, Japan, EX.......................**35.00**

Turtle, cast iron, removable insert, 3x6" **60.00**

Woodpecker at side of stump, ceramic, multicolor, Czech, 4¾", NM **45.00**

40s, 50s, and 60s Glassware

Remember the lovely dishes mother used back when you were a child? Many collectors do. With the scarcity of the older Depression glassware items that used to be found in every garage sale or flea market, glass collectors have refocused their interests and altered buying habits to include equally interesting glassware from more recent years, often choosing patterns that bring back warm childhood memories. For an expanded listing and more information, see *Collectible Glassware from the 40s, 50s, and 60s, 6th Edition,* by Gene Florence (Collector Books). See also Anchor Hocking.

Cambridge

Cascade, candlestick, green or yellow, 5" **35.00**

Cascade, celery dish, crystal, 3-part, 10".........................**20.00**

Cascade, creamer or sugar bowl, green or yellow, ea **20.00**

Cascade, plate, bread & butter; crystal, 6½".......................**5.50**

Cascade, plate, torte; crystal, 4-footed, 14".......................**22.50**

Cascade, punch bowl, crystal, 15" **125.00**

Cascade, punch cup, crystal ...**7.50**

Cascade, tumbler, crystal, footed, 5-oz **10.00**

Cascade, two-part relish, crystal, 6½" long, $13.00. (Photo courtesy Gene Florence)

Square, bowl, salad; crystal, #3797/49, 9"....................**22.50**

Square, comport, crystal, #3797/54, 6"....................**25.00**

Square, plate, crystal, #3797/26, 11½"..............................**25.00**

Square, stem, cocktail; crystal, #3798 ....**17.50**

Square, vase, crystal, footed, #3797/79, 11"..................**40.00**

Federal

Golden Glory, bowl, soup; white w/gold decor, 6⅜".............8.00

Golden Glory, plate, dinner; white w/gold decor, 9⅛".............5.00

Golden Glory, platter, white w/gold decor, oval, 12" ...11.00

Golden Glory, tumbler, white w/gold decor, 10-oz, 5"....10.00

Heritage, bowl, berry; crystal, 5".................8.00

Heritage, cup, crystal............7.00

Heritage, saucer, crystal.........4.00

Park Avenue, ashtray, crystal, 3½" sq..............5.00

Park Avenue, bowl, dessert; crystal, 5", $2.00. (Photo courtesy Gene Florence)

Park Avenue, bowl, vegetable; amber, 8½".................15.00

Park Avenue, tumbler, amber, 10-oz, 4¾"..............7.00

Park Avenue, tumbler, juice; crystal, 4½-oz, 3½".................3.00

Star, bowl, dessert; amber, 4⅝"...........7.00

Star, pitcher, crystal, 60-oz, 7"..............12.00

Star, platter, amber, round, 11"............15.00

Star, tumbler, water; crystal, 9-oz, 3⅞".................5.50

Yorktown, bowl, fruit; amber or crystal, footed, #2902, 10"........17.50

Yorktown, plate, amber or crystal, #2904, 11½".....................8.50

Yorktown, vase, amber or crystal, 8"...................16.00

Fostoria

Buttercup, bowl, salad; crystal, #2364, 9".......................50.00

Buttercup, comport, crystal, #2364, 8".......................40.00

Buttercup, creamer, crystal, footed, #2350½, 3¼"............16.00

Buttercup, plate, crystal, #2337, 7½"..................12.00

Buttercup, relish, crystal, 3-part, #2364, 10x7¼"...............33.00

Buttercup, sugar bowl, crystal, footed, #2350½, 3⅛".......15.00

Buttercup, tumbler, iced tea; crystal, #6030, 12-oz, 6"........30.00

Camellia, bowl, cereal; crystal, 6"..................25.00

Camellia, bowl, serving; crystal, oval, 9½"........................45.00

Camellia, candy dish, crystal, w/lid, 7"..........................55.00

Camellia, ice bucket, crystal..75.00

Camellia, plate, salad; crystal, 7½"..............................10.00

Camellia, relish, crystal, 2-part, 7⅜".................18.00

Camellia, salt & pepper shakers, crystal, 3⅛", pr..............45.00

Camellia, tray, crystal, center handle, 11½".................38.00

Century, bowl, fruit; crystal, 5"..14.00

Century, bowl, salad; crystal, 8½"..............................25.00

Century, candlestick, crystal, 4½"............................17.50

Century, ice bucket, crystal..**65.00**

Century, mayonnaise, crystal, 3-pc **30.00**

Century, pitcher, crystal, 16-oz, 6⅛" **60.00**

Century, plate, dinner; crystal, 10½" **32.00**

Century, salt & pepper shakers, crystal, 3⅛", pr..............**20.00**

Century, tidbit, crystal, 3-footed, upturned edge, 8⅛"........**18.00**

Century, tray, crystal, center handle, 11½" **30.00**

Chintz, bowl, fruit; crystal, #2496, 5" **30.00**

Chintz, candlestick, crystal, #2496, 5½" **35.00**

Chintz, plate, luncheon; crystal, #2496, 8½" **21.00**

Chintz, relish, crystal, 5-part, #2419 ....**40.00**

Chintz, sauce boat, crystal, oval, #2496 ....**65.00**

Chintz, tumbler, juice; crystal, #6026, 5-oz **27.50**

Corsage, bowl, crystal, flared, #2496, 12" **55.00**

Corsage, crystal, #2535, 5½"..**35.00**

Corsage, mayonnaise, crystal, 2-part, #2440 ....**25.00**

Corsage, plate, crystal, 16" ...**85.00**

Corsage, tidbit, crystal, 3-footed, #2496 ....**15.00**

Heather, bowl, fruit; crystal, 5" **16.00**

Heather, candlestick, crystal, 4½" **22.00**

Heather, mayonnaise, crystal, 3-pc..................................**37.50**

Heather, plate, luncheon; crystal, 8½" **15.00**

Heather, relish, crystal, 3-part, 11⅛" **32.50**

Heather, salt & pepper shakers, crystal, 3⅛", pr..............**47.50**

Heather, tray, crystal, center handle, 11½" **37.50**

Heather, vase, crystal, footed, #2470, 10", $115.00. (Photo courtesy Gene Florence)

Holly, bowl, fruit; crystal, #2364, 13" **40.00**

Holly, celery, crystal, #2364, 11"..**25.00**

Holly, goblet, water; crystal, #6030, 10-oz, 7⅞" **20.00**

Holly, plate, salad; crystal, #2337, 7½" **10.00**

Holly, plate, sandwich; crystal, #2364, 11" **30.00**

Horizon, bowl, salad; brown, crystal or green, 8½"..............**18.00**

Horizon, coaster, brown, crystal or green **10.00**

Horizon, plate, dinner; brown, crystal or green, 10".......**15.00**

Horizon, platter, brown, crystal or green, oval, 12"..............**22.00**

Jamestown, bowl, salad; amber or brown, #2719/211, 10" ...**21.00**

Jamestown, cake plate, blue, pink or ruby, handled, #2719/306, 9½" **40.00**

Jamestown, plate, amethyst, crystal or green, #2719/550, 8" **16.00**

Jamestown, sauce dish, amber or brown, w/lid, #2719/635, 4½".............18.00

Jamestown, tumbler, blue, pink or ruby, #2719/64, 12-oz, 5⅛".............26.00

Lido, bowl, blue or crystal, handles, 8½".............40.00

Lido, candlestick, blue or crystal, 4'.............20.00

Lido, cup, blue or crystal, footed.............15.00

Lido, plate, torte; blue or crystal, 14".............40.00

Lido, sugar, individual; blue or crystal.............10.00

Lido, vase, blue or crystal, 5"..75.00

Mayflower, comport, crystal, 5½".............30.00

Mayflower, plate, crystal, #2560, 9½".............37.50

Mayflower, salt & pepper shakers, crystal, pr.............65.00

Mayflower, vase, crystal, #2430..110.00

Meadow Rose, bonbon, blue or crystal, 3-footed, 7⅜".....27.50

Meadow Rose, candlestick, blue or crystal, 4".............25.00

Meadow Rose, plate, dinner; blue or crystal, 9½".............45.00

Meadow Rose, stem, water; blue or crystal, #6016, 10-oz, 7⅝".............30.00

Romance, bowl, baked apple; crystal, #2364.............20.00

Romance, comport, crystal, #6030, 5".............25.00

Romance, plate, sandwich; crystal, #2364, 11".............37.50

Romance, vase, crystal, #2614, 10".............85.00

Seascape, bowl, opalescent, shallow, 8".............50.00

Seascape, creamer or sugar bowl, opalescent, ea.............25.00

Seascape, mayonnaise, opalescent, 3-pc set.............50.00

Hazel Atlas

Capri, ashtray, blue, triangular, 3¼".............6.00

Capri, candy jar, blue, footed, w/lid.............32.00

Capri, cup, blue, octagonal.....6.00

Capri (Colony Swirl), bowl, blue, 5⅝".............9.00

Capri (Colony Swirl), plate, salad; blue, 7".............7.00

Capri (Colony Swirl), tumbler, blue, 12-oz, 5".............10.00

Capri (Colony), bowl, blue, rectangular, 7¾".............14.00

Capri (Colony), bowl, blue, round w/sq bottom, 6".............8.00

Capri (Dots), bowl, blue, round, 4⅞".............7.00

Capri (Dots), vase, blue, 8"...20.00

Capri (Hobnails), cup, blue, round.............5.00

Capri (Hobnails), plate, salad; 7¼".............6.50

Capri (Hobnails), saucer, blue, round, 6".............1.00

Colony Swirl, bowl, blue, 5⅝", $9.00.
(Photo courtesy Gene Florence)

219

Moderntone Platonite, bowl, cream soup; pastel colors, 4¾"....**6.50**

Moderntone Platonite, creamer or sugar bowl, pastel colors, ea......**5.00**

Moderntone Platonite, cup, white or white w/stripes **2.50**

Moderntone Platonite, tumbler, pastel colors, 9-oz.............**9.00**

Modertone Platonite, saucer, Blue Willow, Deco or red.........**5.00**

Moroccan Amethyst, ashtray, amethyst, triangular, 3¼" .**5.50**

Moroccan Amethyst, bowl, amethyst, 10¾".............**30.00**

Moroccan Amethyst, goblet, water; amethyst, 9-oz, 5½".......**10.00**

Moroccan Amethyst, plate, salad; amethyst, 7¼"..................**7.00**

Newport, bowl, berry; white, 4¾"..............................**3.50**

Newport, creamer or sugar bowl, fired-on colors, ea.............**7.50**

Newport, plate, sandwich; white, 11½"................................**10.00**

Newport, sherbet, fired-on colors...................................**6.00**

Ovide, bowl, berry; fired-on colors, 4¾"....................................**5.50**

Ovide, cup, decorated white .**12.50**

Ovide, saucer, Art Deco **20.00**

Ovide, sherbet, white w/trims ..**5.50**

Ripple, bowl, cereal; all colors, deep, 5⅝" **8.00**

Ripple, plate, sandwich; all colors, 10½"..............................**15.00**

Ripple, tidbit, any color, 3-tier..**30.00**

Heisey

Cabochon, bonbon, crystal, sloped sides w/sq handle, #1951, 6¼" **24.00**

Cabochon, butter dish, crystal, #1951, ¼-lb.....................**25.00**

Cabochon, cup, crystal, #1951 ..**6.00**

Cabochon, plate, sandwich; crystal, #1951........................**18.00**

Cabochon, sherbet, crystal, #1951, 6-oz....................................**4.00**

Cabochon, stem, cordial; crystal, #6091, 1-oz **22.50**

Cabochon, tumbler, juice; crystal, footed, #6091, 5-oz **7.00**

Lodestar, candy dish, Dawn, w/lid, 5"....................................**135.00**

**Lodestar, divided relish, Dawn, 7½",
$70.00. (Photo courtesy Gene Florence)**

Lodestar, plate, Dawn, 8½" ..**65.00**

Lodestar, sauce dish, Dawn, #1626, 4½".....................**40.00**

Lodestar, tumbler, juice; Dawn, 6-oz.....................................**40.00**

New Era, cup, crystal............**10.00**

New Era, goblet, crystal, 10-oz..**16.00**

New Era, saucer, crystal.........**5.00**

Rose, candlestick, crystal, #112 ....**45.00**

Rose, mint dish, crystal, footed, 5½"....................................**37.50**

Rose, plate, service; crystal, Waverly, 10½"................**75.00**

Rose, tumbler, iced tea; crystal, footed, #5072, 12-oz **65.00**

Imperial

Crocheted Crystal, basket, 6" .**30.00**

Crocheted Crystal, basket, 12", $70.00.
(Photo courtesy Gene Florence)

Crocheted Crystal, cake stand, crystal, footed, 12"........**40.00**

Crocheted Crystal, hurricane lamp, 11"........................**50.00**

Crocheted Crystal, plate, 14"..**25.00**

Crocheted Crystal, vase, 8"..**35.00**

Indiana

Christmas Candy, bowl, crystal, 5¾"....................................**4.50**

Christmas Candy, creamer or sugar bowl, teal, ea........**32.50**

Christmas Candy, cup, crystal..**22.00**

Christmas Candy, plate, dinner; crystal, 9⅝"....................**11.00**

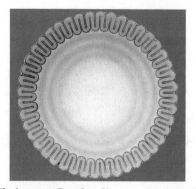

Christmas Candy, dinner plate, teal, 9⅝", $47.50. (Photo courtesy Gene Florence)

Daisy, bowl, berry; green, 4½"..**6.00**

Daisy, bowl, cereal; crystal, 6"..**10.00**

Daisy, creamer or sugar bowl, amber or red, footed, ea...**8.00**

Daisy, plate, dinner; crystal, 9⅜".................................**5.50**

Daisy, platter, green, 10¾".....**8.50**

Daisy, tumbler, crystal, footed, 12-oz...................................**20.00**

Pretzel, bowl, soup; crystal, 7½"..............................**10.00**

Pretzel, pickle dish, crystal, handles, 8½"........................**5.50**

Pretzel, plate, salad; crystal, 8⅜"..**6.00**

Pretzel, tumbler, crystal, 12-oz, 5½"..................................**65.00**

Sandwich, bowl, teal blue, hexagonal, 6"............................**14.00**

Sandwich, plate, teal blue, 13"..**25.00**

Sandwich, sherbet, teal blue, 3¼"..................................**12.00**

Wild Rose, plate, sherbet; multicolored **10.00**

Wild Rose, relish, crystal, crystal sanitized or milk glass, handles................................**7.00**

Wild Rose, tray, iridescent, handles................................**18.00**

Jeannette

Anniversary, bowl, soup; crystal, 4⅞"...................................**3.50**

Anniversary, candlestick, iridescent, 4⅞", pr...................**25.00**

Anniversary, creamer, crystal, footed **5.00**

Anniversary, pickle dish, pink, 9"..................................**15.00**

Anniversary, plate, dinner; iridescent, 9"............................**6.00**

Anniversary, sugar bowl, crystal................................**4.50**

Camellia, bowl, vegetable; crystal, 8⅞".................10.00

Camellia, candle holder, crystal.........................10.00

Camellia, creamer or sugar bowl, crystal, footed, ea.............5.00

Camellia, tray, crystal, handles..15.00

Dewdrop, bowl, crystal, 8½".12.00

Dewdrop, butter dish, crystal, w/lid................................27.50

Dewdrop, lazy susan, crystal, complete, 13".........................45.00

Dewdrop, plate, crystal, 11½"..17.50

Dewdrop, tumbler, iced tea; crystal, 12-oz, 6".....................20.00

Floragold, bowl, iridescent, ruffled, 9½"...........................8.00

Floragold, butter dish, iridescent, round w/sq base, w/lid, 6¼"...............................45.00

**Floragold, fruit bowl, iridescent, 12",
$7.00. (Photo courtesy Gene Florence)**

Floragold, plate, dinner; iridescent, 8½".........................40.00

Floragold, platter, iridescent, 11¼"...............................25.00

Floragold, tumbler, iridescent, footed, 10-oz or 11-oz, ea........20.00

Harp, ashtray/coaster, crystal ..5.00

Harp, plate, crystal, 7"..........15.00

Harp, vase, crystal, 7½".........25.00

Holiday, bowl, vegetable; pink, oval, 9½".........................27.50

Holiday, butter dish, pink, w/lid.............................40.00

Holiday, pitcher, milk; crystal, 16-oz, 4¾"...........................15.00

Holiday, tray, sandwich; iridescent, 10½"......................15.00

Holiday, tumbler, pink, flat, 10-oz, 4"....................................22.50

Iris, bowl, sauce; iridescent, ruffled, 5"..........................28.00

Iris, butter dish, crystal, w/lid .47.50

Iris, goblet, crystal, 4-oz, 4¼"..27.50

Iris, pitcher, iridescent, footed, 9½"................................42.50

Iris, plate, dinner; crystal, 9".55.00

Iris, tumbler, crystal, footed, 6"....................................18.00

National, bowl, blue, crystal, pink or Shell Pink, flat, 12" ...14.00

National, lazy susan, blue, crystal, pink or Shell Pink ...35.00

National, punch bowl, blue, crystal, pink or Shell Pink, 12"....................................25.00

National, vase, blue, crystal, pink or Shell Pink, 9".............18.00

Shell Pink Milk Glass, bowl, Pheasant, footed, 8".......37.50

Shell Pink Milk Glass, cake stand, Harp, 10".......................45.00

Shell Pink Milk Glass, candy dish, Floragold, 4-footed, 5¼"....................................20.00

Shell Pink Milk Glass, honey jar, beehive shape, w/notched lid................40.00

Shell Pink Milk Glass, tray, five-part, two-handled, 15¾"...............................85.00

Shell Pink Milk Glass, vase, 7"..30.00

Paden City

Emerald Glo, bowl, salad; green, 10"...................................30.00

Emerald Glo, candle holders, green, ball form w/metal cups, pr.................................**35.00**

Emerald Glo, creamer or sugar bowl, green, ea **20.00**

Emerald Glo, relish, green, heart shape **25.00**

U. S. Glass

King's Crown/Thumbprint, ashtray, ruby-flashed, 5¼" sq.........**25.00**

King's Crown/Thumbprint, cheese stand, ruby-flashed........**25.00**

King's Crown/Thumbprint, cup, ruby-flashed **8.00**

King's Crown/Thumbprint, plate, bread & butter; ruby-flashed, 5".......................................**8.00**

King's Crown/Thumbprint, relish, ruby-flashed, 5-part, 14"..............................**110.00**

King's Crown/Thumbprint, tumbler, juice; ruby-flashed, footed, 4-oz...........................**12.00**

King's Crown/Thumbprint, water pitcher, ruby-flashed, $185.00. (Photo courtesy Gene Florence)

Viking

Prelude, bonbon, crystal, handled, 6".....................................**18.00**

Prelude, bowl, crystal, shallow, 13".................................**45.00**

Prelude, cake salver, crystal, 11", $50.00. (Photo courtesy Gene Florence)

Prelude, creamer or sugar bowl, crystal, ea **12.50**

Prelude, mayonnaise, crystal, 3-pc set.............................**35.00**

Prelude, plate, crystal, 18" ...**85.00**

Prelude, plate, dinner; crystal, 10" **37.50**

Prelude, relish, crystal, 5-part, 13" **35.00**

Prelude, stem, cordial; crystal, 1-oz.....................................**40.00**

Prelude, tray, crystal, center handle, 11" **35.00**

Franciscan

When most people think of the Franciscan name, their Apple or Desert Rose patterns come to mind immediately, and without a doubt these are the most collectible of the hundreds of lines produced by

Gladding McBean. Located in Los Angeles, they produced quality dinnerware under the trade name Franciscan from the mid-1930s until 1984, when they were bought out by a company from England. Many marks were used; most included the Franciscan name. An 'F' in a square with 'Made in USA' below it dates from 1938, and a double-line script F was used later. Some of this dinnerware is still being produced in England, so be sure to look for the USA mark. For an expanded listing, see *Schroeder's Antiques Price Guide* (Collector Books).

Desert Rose, rectangular baking dish, 1½-quart, 13½x8½", $285.00; Bouillon bowl, with lid, $325.00.

Apple, ashtray, individual **22.00**
Apple, bowl, divided vegetable ..**50.00**
Apple, butter dish **50.00**
Apple, pitcher, milk **95.00**
Apple, sherbet **27.50**
Coronado, bowl, cereal; from $15 to **20.00**
Coronado, butter dish, from $35 to **45.00**
Coronado, plate, 9½", from $15 to..................................**18.00**
Desert Rose, bowl, fruit **8.00**
Desert Rose, compote, lg.......**75.00**

Desert Rose, gravy boat........**32.00**
Desert Rose, plate, chop; 14"..**125.00**
Desert Rose, tumbler, juice; 6-oz...............................**55.00**
El Patio, bowl, salad; lg, from $35 to....................................**50.00**
El Patio, butter dish, from $35 to..................................**45.00**
El Patio, teacup & saucer, from $12 to.............................**15.00**
Forget-Me-Not, plate, 6½" **6.00**
Forget-Me-Not, salt & pepper shakers, pr **35.00**
Ivy, bowl, fruit......................**10.00**
Ivy, tumbler, 10-oz................**45.00**
Meadow Rose, plate, chop; 12"..**75.00**
Meadow Rose, sherbet **25.00**
Poppy, bowl, cereal **22.50**
Poppy, plate, 8" **18.00**
Poppy, sugar bowl **48.00**
Starburst, butter dish...........**45.00**
Starburst, crescent salad......**40.00**
Starburst, mug, sm **60.00**
Starburst, plate, 8".................**8.00**
Starburst, salt & pepper shakers, sm, pr.............................**20.00**

Frankoma

Since 1933 the Frankoma Pottery Company has been producing dinnerware, novelty items, vases, etc. In 1965 they became the first American company to produce a line of collector plates. The body of the ware prior to 1954 was a honey tan that collectors refer to as 'Ada clay.' A brick red clay (called 'Sapulpa') was used from then on, and this and the colors of the glazes help determine the period of production.

For more information refer to *Frankoma and Other Oklahoma Potteries* by Phyllis and Tom Bess (Schiffer), and *Frankoma Pottery, Value Guide and More*, by Susan N. Cox. See Clubs and Newsletters for information on the Frankoma Family Collectors Association

Ashtray, Aztec design, Sapulpa clay, #471, 9".....................**9.00**
Ashtray, Gracetone, 2AT1, Pink Champagne, 7"..............**15.00**
Baker, Lazybones, Peach Glow, #4V, 2-qt.........................**23.00**
Bank, boot, Sapulpa clay, #383, 6"...............................**23.00**
Bank, owl, Sapulpa clay, #84, 7"...............................**15.00**
Bookend, puma on the rocks, Ada clay, #422 ....**185.00**
Bottle vase, Prairie Green, 1983, #V-15, from $85 to **100.00**
Bottle vase, Prairie Green & black, #V-1, from $125 to........**150.00**
Bowl, abalone shell, Ivory, #216, 1942, 11".........................**25.00**
Bowl, Oriental, low, Ada clay, #205, 10".........................**32.00**
Bowl w/pedestal, Gracetone, #101P, aqua, 6" **30.00**
Candle holder, Double Cactus, Red Bud, #306, 1949.....**50.00**
Candle holder, Wedding Day, Ada clay, #300......................**22.00**
Christmas card, Grace Lee & Milton Smith, FE, 1975..............**135.00**
Christmas card, 1950-60, from $70 to **85.00**
Christmas card, 1971-75, from $30 to **40.00**
Cigarette box, Prairie Green, #459, ca 1942, 7¼x3½"...........**125.00**

Cookie jar, Trojan horse on lid, Ada clay, #99, 3-qt **250.00**
Dealer's sign, Pacing Leopard, green............................**300.00**
Egg plate, Peach Glow, #819, 12"...............................**29.00**
Flower frog, cross, Woodland Moss, #804, 6½" **26.00**

Gravy boat and undertray, Plainsman, Prairie Green, $35.00.

Gravy boat, Westwind, Autumn Yellow, 2-spout, #6S **12.00**
Jug, Uncle Slug, Ada clay, 2¼".....**25.00**
Lazy Susan, #94FC, 1947-63, 15"..**75.00**
Mug, Bush/Quayle, Peach, 1989..**30.00**
Mug, Nixon/Agnew, Flame, 1969, from $65 to **85.00**
Mug, Woodland Moss, #C13, 1960-79 ....**10.00**
Napkin ring, rabbit, Sapulpa clay, #261 ....**3.00**
Pipe rest, #454, black, ca. 1935-40 ....**$175.00**
Pitcher, Gracetone, Pink Champagne, #2D, 3-qt.............**20.00**
Pitcher, snail, Ada clay, #558, miniature.......................**13.50**
Planter, Alamo, Sapulpa clay, #397, 1988-91, 6½".........**18.00**
Planter, Gracetone, Madonna, #231D **55.00**
Plaque, Indian w/feathers, Sapulpa clay, #6-131, miniature...**12.00**

Plate, Easter, 1972.................**12.00**
Plate, Mayan Aztec, Woodland
  Moss, #7F, 9"..................**10.00**
Plate, Wildlife, Wild Turkey,
  1978, 7"............................**75.00**
Plate, Youthful Madonna, rubbed
  bisque, 8½"......................**30.00**
Platter, Wagon Wheel, Red Bud,
  #94Q, 13"........................**26.00**
Sculpture, bull, sitting; Sapulpa clay,
  #166, miniature, 2"..........**105.00**
Sculpture, Gracetone, swan,
  white, #213, miniature..**52.00**
Sculpture, squirrel, White Sand,
  #105, 6"............................**27.00**
Sugar bowl, Wagon Wheel, Ada
  clay, #510, individual.....**10.00**
Tissue box, Sapulpa clay, #255...**8.50**
Tray, Butterfly, Sapulpa clay,
  #482, 1989-91, 4"..............**5.00**
Trivet, White Buffalo, Sapulpa
  clay, #WBTR, 1988-91 ...**10.00**
Trivet, 5 Civilized Tribes, Sapulpa
  clay, #OK3, 6" dia **8.00**

**Vase, bottle;
with base,
#V15, 1983,
3,000 made,
$65.00.**

Vase, bud; snail, Ada clay w/pot &
  leopard mark, #31, 6" **40.00**
Vase, free-form, Sapulpa clay,
  #95, 8½"...........................**10.50**
Vase, hexagonal, Sapulpa clay,
  #65, 6½".........................**10.50**

Vase, Lazybones, Ada clay, #15,
  12"....................................**45.00**
Wall pocket, Phoebe, Ada clay,
  #730, 7".........................**120.00**

Fruit Jars

Some of the earliest glass jars used for food preservation were blown, and corks were used for seals. During the nineteenth century, hundreds of manufacturers designed over 4,000 styles of fruit jars. Lids were held in place either by a wax seal, wire bail, or the later screw-on band. Jars were usually made in aqua or clear, though other colors were also used. Amber jars are popular with collectors, milk glass jars are rare, and cobalt and black glass jars often bring $3,000.00 and up, if they can be found! Condition, age, scarcity, and unusual features are also to be considered when evaluating old fruit jars.

Acme Seal (script), qt, clear, regu-
  lar mouth........................**50.00**
Atlas E-Z Seal, pt, green, w/green
  lid...................................**18.00**
Atlas E-Z Seal, 48-oz, aqua ..**30.00**
Atlas Mason's Patent Nov 30th
  1848, ½-gal, aqua.............**9.00**
Atlas Whole Fruit, qt, clear **2.00**
Ball Improved, pt, blue.........**12.00**
Ball Improved Ghost Mason, pt,
  aqua...............................**20.00**
Ball Mason's Patent 1858, pt,
  aqua................................**5.00**
Ball Perfect Mason, qt, blue,
  sq **10.00**

Ball Refrigerator & Freezer Jar, pt, clear..............................**3.00**
Ball Special, qt, blue...............**8.00**
Ball Special, qt, blue, shoulder seal...................................**50.00**
Ball Standard, ½-gal, aqua, wax sealer, tin lid..................**20.00**
Bernardin (script) Underlined Mason, pt, clear...............**10.00**
Canadian Jewel Made in Canada, qt, clear.............................**4.00**
Clyde (script), qt, clear.........**15.00**
Converse Jar, ½-pt................**80.00**
Drey Improved Ever Seal, ½-gal, clear, glass boss ears.....**12.00**

The Empire, quart, aqua, Pat Feb 13 1866 on base, correct glass lid and metal yoke, $95.00.

Excelsior, ½-gal (unlisted size), aqua.................................**65.00**
Franklin Dexter Fruit Jar, qt, aqua, regular zinc lid.....**30.00**
Gem (1 line), qt, aqua.............**8.00**
Hero, ½-gal, aqua, 2-pc lid....**80.00**
Howe Jar Scranton PA, qt, aqua............................**90.00**
Ideal, midget, aqua...............**75.00**
Ideal, qt, aqua......................**25.00**
Jewel Jar (block letters in frame), qt, clear............................**15.00**
Kerr's Self Sealing Mason, qt, amber...............................**30.00**

Lamb Mason, qt, clear, zinc lid ..**3.00**
Lustre RE Tongue & Bros Inc Phila (in circle), pt, blue ..**7.00**
Mason's Crystal Jar, ½-gal, clear...................................**35.00**
Mason's KGBCo Patent Nov 30th 1858, pt, aqua................**30.00**
Mason's Patent Nov 30th 1858, ½-gal, aqua........................**48.00**
Mason's 16 (underlined) Patent Nov 30th 1858, ½-gal, aqua...................**28.00**
Mid West Canadian Made, qt, clear...................................**14.00**
Mrs Chapin's Mayonnaise Boston Mass, pt, clear..................**6.00**
Putnam (base), qt, amber.....**45.00**
S Mason's Patent 1858, qt, med teal blue..........................**75.00**
Safe Seal (in circle), pt, blue...**5.00**
Silicon (in circle), pt, aqua....**18.00**
Standard (Mason in flag), qt, light green..............................**10.00**
TM Lightning, pt, apple green .**65.00**
Trade Mark Lightning Putman, 24-oz, aqua.....................**75.00**
Trade Mark Masons CFJ Improved, ½-gal, aqua...**12.00**
Victory (in shield) on lid, pt, clear, twin side clamps..............**4.00**

Games

The ideal collectible game is one that combines playability (i.e., good strategy, interaction, surprise, etc.) with interesting graphics and unique components. Especially desirable are the very old games from the nineteenth and early twentieth centuries as well as those relating to early or popular TV shows and movies. As always, value depends on rarity and condition of the box and playing pieces. For a greatly expanded list and more information, see *Schroeder's Collectible Toys, Antique to Modern* (Collector Books).

Addams Family Reunion, 1991, EXIB **25.00**
All in the Family, Milton Bradley, 1972, EXIB **20.00**
Annie Oakley, Game Gems/T Cohn, 1965, EXIB **50.00**
As the World Turns, Parker Bros, 1966, EXIB **45.00**
Bandersnatch, Mattel, 1969, NMIB..............................**70.00**
Bat Masterson, Lowell, 1958, EXIB **65.00**
Batman & Robin Target, Hasbro, 1966, MIB......................**200.00**
Beany & Cecil Jumping DJ, 1961, EXIB **65.00**
Ben Casey, Transogram, 1961, EXIB **30.00**
Big Town News Reporting, Lowell, 1950s, rare, NMIB ...**75.00**
Bonanza Rummy, Parker Bros, 1964, EXIB **35.00**
Brady Bunch, Whitman, 1973, NMIB..............................**85.00**
Bucket of Fun, Milton Bradley, 1968, EXIB **35.00**
Bullwinkle & Rocky, Ideal, 1963, EXIB **55.00**
Camp Runamuck, Ideal, 1965, EXIB **45.00**
Captain America, Milton Bradley, 1966, MIB......................**100.00**
CHiPs, Milton Bradley, 1977, MIB..............................**25.00**

Cinderella, Parker Bros, 1964, EXIB..............................**65.00**
Concentration, Milton Bradley, 1959, 1st edition, EXIB, from $40 to..............................**50.00**

Cootie, W.H. Schaper Mfg. Co., 1950s, MIB, $45.00. (Photo courtesy June Moon)

Davy Crockett Indian Scouting, Whitman, NMIB, from $65 to..................................**85.00**
Dennis the Menace, Standard/ Toykraft, 1960, EXIB.....**75.00**
Doc Holliday Wild West, Transogram, 1960, NMIB..........................**65.00**
Dr Dolittle, Mattel, 1967, EXIB..**45.00**
Dr Kildare, Ideal, 1962, NMIB...**65.00**
Elmer Wheeler's Fat Boys, Parker Bros, 1951, NMIB..........**50.00**
Emergency!, Milton Bradley, 1974, EXIB **20.00**
Family Affair, Remco, 1968, MIB **100.00**
Family Ties, Applestreet, 1986, EXIB **30.00**
Fantasy Island, Ideal, 1978, MIB..............................**30.00**
Fess Parker Trail Blazers, Milton Bradley, 1964, EXIB......**75.00**
Flintstones Brake Ball, 1962, EXIB **85.00**
Flying Nun, Milton Bradley, 1968, EXIB **75.00**

George of the Jungle, Parker Bros, 1968, NMIB....................50.00

Gilligan's Island, Game Gems/T Cohn, 1965, EXIB........350.00

Gong Show, 1977, NMIB......50.00

Happy Days, Parker Bros, 1976, EXIB...............................20.00

Hogan's Heroes Bluff Out, Transogram, 1966, EXIB...............100.00

Hollywood Squares, Watkins-Strathmore, 1966, EXIB .25.00

Hopalong Cassidy, Milton Bradley, 1950, EXIB....150.00

Howdy Doody TV Game, Milton Bradley, 1950s, EXIB ..100.00

Huckleberry Hound Spin-O, Bardell, 1959, EXIB.......50.00

Hungry Henry, Ideal, 1969, EXIB.............................30.00

I Dream of Jeannie, Milton Bradley, 1966, MIB, minimum value 100.00

It's a Small World, Parker Bros, 1967, EXIB......................55.00

Jetsons Out of This World, Transogram, 1962, EXIB..............125.00

John Drake Secret Agent, Milton Bradley, 1966, EXIB......60.00

King Kong, Ideal, 1976, NMIB .25.00

Knight Rider High Speed Adventure, Parker Bros, 1983, EXIB ..20.00

Last Straw, Schraper, 1966, EXIB.............................30.00

Let's Make a Deal, Ideal, 1964, EXIB 25.00

Mandrake the Magician, Transogram, 1966, NMIB.............100.00

Marlin Perkin's Zoo Parade, Cadaco, 1955, NMIB......60.00

Mighty Heroes on the Scene, Transogram, 1966, EXIB.........95.00

Mork & Mindy, Parker Bros, 1979, MIB (sealed).........30.00

Man from UNCLE, Ideal, 1965, EX (EX box), $50.00. (Photo courtesy John and Sheri Pavone)

Mystery Date, Milton Bradley, 1965, EXIB...................125.00

Nancy Drew Mystery, Parker Bros, 1957, EXIB.........100.00

New Zoo Review, Ungame, 1981, EXIB..............................30.00

Pac-Man, Milton Bradley, 1982, NMIB..............................15.00

Patty Duke, Milton Bradley, 1963, EXIB..............................50.00

Patty Playpal, Ideal, 1961, EXIB..............................35.00

Petticoat Junction, Standard Toykraft, 1964, EXIB ..100.00

Police Patrol, Hasbro, 1957, EXIB.............................100.00

Quick Draw McGraw Private Eye, Milton Bradley, 1960, NMIB 50.00

Restless Gun, Milton Bradley, 1959, NMIB....................50.00

Road Runner, Milton Bradley, 1968, NMIB....................40.00

Rocky & Bullwinkle Magic Dot, Whitman, 1962, EXIB ...75.00

Simon Says, Cardinal, 1964, EXIB 25.00

Skatterbug, Parker Bros, 1951, EXIB 45.00

Smurf Ahoy, Milton Bradley, 1982, EXIB 20.00

Supercar to the Rescue, Milton Bradley, 1962, EXIB....100.00

Superman Flying Bingo, Whitman, 1966, EXIB............**50.00**
Talking Football, Mattel, 1971, NMIB............................**100.00**
Tiger Island, Ideal, 1966, EXIB.........................**50.00**
Tom & Jerry, Milton Bradley, 1977, EXIB.....................**35.00**
Top Secret, National Games, 1956, EXIB.....................**75.00**
Twiggy, Milton Bradley, 1967, EXIB.............................**100.00**
Underdog, Milton Bradley, 1964, EXIB..............................**50.00**

Wally Gator Game, Transogram, EX (EX box), from $50.00 to $65.00. (Photo courtesy Bill Bruegman)

Waltons, Milton Bradley, 1975, MIB..................................**45.00**
White Shadow, Cadaco, 1970s, rare, EXIB.......................**85.00**
Yogi Bear Go Fly a Kite, Transogram, 1961, NMIB.............**50.00**

Garfield

America's favorite grumpy cat, Garfield has his own band of devotees who are able to find a good variety of merchandise modeled after his likeness. Garfield was created in 1976 by Jim Davis. He underwent many changes by the time he debuted in newspaper in 1978. By 1980 his first book was released, followed quickly in 1981 by a line of collectibles in by Dakin and Enesco. The stuffed plush animals and ceramic figures were a huge success. There have been thousands of items made since, with many that are hard to find being produced in Germany, the Netherlands, England, and other European countries. Banks, displays, PVCs, and figurines are the most desirable items of import from these countries.

Bank, Feed the Kitty, Enesco, 6"................................**35.00**
Bank, as bowler, Enesco, NM, from $35 to.....................**45.00**
Bookends, pushing against wall, Enesco, pr, from $150 to.**175.00**
Christmas ornament, as Santa w/sack of toys, Polonaise, 4½x4½"...........................**45.00**
Christmas ornament, Hallmark, 1992, 2½"........................**10.00**
Christmas ornament, Odie as 'Deer One,' Enesco, MIB...........**85.00**

Clock, Sunbeam #89230, Assembled in China, 6½", EX, $55.00.

Cookie jar, lying on stack of cookies, Enesco, 9"..............**270.00**

Doll, plush, sitting, w/tag, Dakin, 1981, 10x11", EX..............**6.00**

Doll, plush, window sticker, 4 suction cups, w/tag, Dakin, 1981, 8".......................................**5.00**

Doll, talker, Mattel, 1983, 10", EX, from $45 to..............**60.00**

Figurine, as fireman w/Odie, Ever Have a Day...Was Off, 5x5", NM.................................**80.00**

Figurine, as referee, It's Official I Love You on base, 3"......**20.00**

Figurine, as tennis player, 4"..**20.00**

Figurine, as Uncle Sam, I Want You on base, Enesco.......**20.00**

Figurine, as witch or Santa, vinyl, 6", ea...............................**25.00**

Figurine, I Quit (The Mad Telemarketer), Enesco, 1978, 3x4"...............................**36.00**

Figurine, in work-out suit, 4½"...........................**20.00**

Figurine, Lake-Tip-A-Canoe, Danbury Mint, M.................**50.00**

Figurine, Let the Honeymoon Begin, Enesco, 1980, MIB.............**40.00**

Figurine, To Dad From a Chip Off the Old Block.................**12.00**

Figurine, w/Odie (wearing Dunce cap), Let's Do It Until..., Enesco, 5"..........................**70.00**

Gumball machine, Superior, 1988, EX..................................**20.00**

Jack-in-the-box, Pop Goes the Odie, MIB, from $20 to..**30.00**

Kitchen timer, 60-minute, Sunbeam, 1978, MIP............**40.00**

Lamp, figural w/Party Animal shade, Prestigeline, 1980s, 14", NMIB.....................**50.00**

Music box, Baby's First Christmas, train circles & plays 'Toyland'.........................**25.00**

Music box, Oh, What a Beautiful Morning, Danbury Mint, EX..............................**55.00**

Music box, The Entertainer, plays piano w/Arlene on top, Enesco, NM....................**36.00**

Necklace, Avon, MIB.............**10.00**

Night light, head shape........**10.00**

Nodder, Wacky Wobbler, 7½", EXIB..............................**27.00**

Pin dish, 4"............................**10.00**

Plate, Christmas; A One Dog Open Sleigh, Danbury Mint, MIB..................**50.00**

Plate, Christmas; The Finishing Touches, Danbury Mint, EX....................**35.00**

Plate, Dear Diary Series, Danbury Mint, 1991, 8½"..............**35.00**

Play money, MIP....................**3.00**

Puzzle, slide-tile; MIP.............**5.00**

PVC figure w/suction cup, several variations, ea....................**5.00**

Salt & pepper shakers, Garfield & Arlene, Enesco, pr, from $75 to.....................................**85.00**

Salt & pepper shakers, Garfield Santa heads, Enesco, 1993, pr...................................**15.00**

Toothbrush holder, wall mount, United Features, copyright 1978, from $10.00 to $15.00.

Snow dome, Big Fat Hairy Deal, M **18.00**

Trinket box, ceramic, Be My Valentine, Enesco **30.00**

Trivet, cartoon w/Garfield eating at table, 9x4¾" **10.00**

Yo-yo **10.00**

Gas Station Collectibles

From the invention of the automobile came the need for gas service stations, seeking to attract customers through a wide variety of advertising methods. Gas and oil companies issued thermometers, signs, calendars, clocks, banks, and scores of other items emblazoned with their logos and catchy slogans. Though a rather specialized area, gas station collectibles encompass a wide variety of items that appeal to automobilia and advertising collectors as well. For further information we recommend *Huxford's Collectible Advertising* by Sharon and Bob Huxford, and *Value Guide to Gas Station Memorabilia* by B.J. Summers and Wayne Priddy. Both are published by Collector Books.

Air pump, Eco Tireflator, model #97, 53", NM **450.00**

Antifreeze can, Thermo, red, white & blue, full, ca 1945, 6x4", VG **60.00**

Antifreeze tester, 20", VG.....**30.00**

Ashtray, Cities Service, chrome w/plastic dome logo, 8" dia, MIB................................**50.00**

Ashtray, Unico Motor Oil, cast-iron derby hat, 2½x6" dia, EX.................................**30.00**

Badge, Esso Service, cloisonne on nickel, 1½x2", VG+ **130.00**

Badge, Rainbow Gasoline/Secret Agent K-7 Club, diecut tin, premium, NM...............**110.00**

Badge, Station Manager, cloisonne Chevron emblem, 1½x1¼", NM.................**230.00**

Bank, Save at Your Esso Dealer, clear plastic footed oval, 4x6", EX.................................**25.00**

Bank, Texaco, plastic fat attendant figure, 4⅞", EX+..**110.00**

Banner, Esso/World's First Choice, oil drip man, canvas, 83x36", VG **120.00**

Booklet, Standard Oil Personalized Tourist Information, 1955, EX..........................**5.00**

Calendar, Mobilgas, 1953, Along the Magnolia Trail, 23", complete, EX..........................**50.00**

Clock, Mobil Oil horse, reverse-painted glass, metal case, 15" dia, EX..........................**625.00**

Clock, Quaker State, battery-operated, 1970s-90s, 16x16", VG **35.00**

Clothespin bag, Mobile Station dealer advertising on canvas, 13", NM **65.00**

Coffee urn, Monroe Shock Absorbers, yellow on black, 15x12" dia, NM **150.00**

Credit card, Texaco/The Texas Co National Credit Card, paper, 1956, EX.......................**160.00**

Decal, Standard, torch & oval logo w/name, 32x40", unused, M **20.00**

Display, Buss Auto Fuses, tin litho, counter-top w/shelves, 7x9", EX+......................**180.00**

Display, Goodyear Radiator Hose/Fan Belts, sign/5 wire arm hangers, NM.........**210.00**

Display, Trico Wipers, diecut litho tin, wall mount, 14x10x3", EX...............**425.00**

Doorstop, Texaco, cast-iron lollipop sign, 9½", VG......**230.00**

Fan, Hudson Gasoline, cardboard w/wooden handle, 2-sided, 14", EX.........................**160.00**

Flag, Shell, cloth, black & orange on yellow, 47x70", NM.**350.00**

Flag, Texaco, round star logo on green, loops for rope, 48x75", EX.**500.00**

Fly swatter, Socony, oblong wire mesh w/wire handle, 17", EX...............................**50.00**

Globe, Shell, milk glass shell form w/red lettering, 1-pc, 18½", VG+..............................**325.00**

Globe, Standard Oil crown, gold & white, 1-pc w/mount & base, NM+..............................**450.00**

Hat, Mobiloil, cloth service type w/horse logo, blue & white on red, M **150.00**

Helmet, Texaco Fire Chief, red plastic with battery-operated microphone and speaker, NMIB, $220.00.

Kerosene dispenser, Keroboy, metal & cast iron, model #555, 53", EX................**115.00**

Key chain, Esso, molded metal full-figure Esso Tiger, 1966, 2", EX.............................**20.00**

Letter opener, Atlantic Refining Co, brass, shows early truck, 9", VG **30.00**

Lighter, Huskey, slimline pocket style, logo on red inlay, 2", NM **85.00**

Lighter, Texaco, silver-tone metal w/round gold star logo, 2", EX.................**160.00**

Map rack, Cities Service Motoring Aids, green painted metal, 13x19", $80.00. (Photo courtesy B.J. Summers and Wayne Priddy)

Map rack, Sohio, metal, Help Yourself/Pleasant Motoring, 12x17", EX....................**375.00**

Mechanical pencil, Gilmore Lion Head Motor Oil, w/calendar, 5½", NM **190.00**

Mug, Mobiloil, white ceramic w/red gargoyle & 2 blue stripes, NM **140.00**

Notepad & pen, Cities Services, metal case w/lid & magnetic pen, NM..........................**50.00**

Oil can, Polarine Medium, ½-gal, rectangular, labels, NM+......**135.00**

Oil can, Red Bell, 2-gal, 11½", VG+ **50.00**

Oil can, Sinclair Motor Oil, 5-gal, round easy-pour, 14x15", EX+ **200.00**

Oil can, Texaco 574 Motor Oil, 1-qt, logos on green, screw lid, EX+ **60.00**

Oil can, Valvoline Oil Co, 1-gal, vertical, 11½", VG **300.00**

Oil rack, Atlantic, wire cone shape w/3 levels, w/10 cans, 35", EX **175.00**

Oil rack, Quaker State, sign atop 2-shelf wire stand, 39x22", EX..............................**470.00**

Oil rack, Sunoco, wire, holds 8 glass bottles w/nozzles, 18", VG+ **415.00**

Paperweight/mirror, Phillips 66 Silver Anniversary, 1955, 3½", NM **120.00**

Parts cabinet, Stewart Warner, metal w/8 drawers, 33½", VG+ .**110.00**

Pen & pencil set, Sunoco DX, sterling & cloisonne, Parker, 1960s, EXIB **65.00**

Pen holder, Standard, Service Station Cleanliness Award, 2-pc, EX+ **135.00**

Pennant, Firestone, felt, orange on blue, 8x28", EX..........**45.00**

Pin, Shell, diecut w/cloisonne inlay, ½" dia, NM+.........**80.00**

Pocketknife w/scissors, Shell, Mileage Is Our Business, 2½", EX **50.00**

Pump sign, Mobilgas, porcelain 5-point emblem w/horse logo, 13x13", VG **100.00**

Radio, Champion Spark Plug form, plastic, 15", NM ..**200.00**

Sign, American Amoco Gas, porcelain, 2-sided, 1940s, 15x24", EX **110.00**

Sign, Castrol, decal on oval board, lady attendant w/oil can, 8x6", NM........................**60.00**

Sign, Exide, painted metal diecut battery, flange, 13x15", EX **180.00**

Sign, Humble/Restroom, porcelain, The Next User..., 9x7", NM+.............................**375.00**

Sign, Let Us Check Your Oil For Safety, reverse-painted, 8x15", NM+ **30.00**

Sign, Marathon/Best In The Long Run, porcelain, w/runner, 72" dia, EX....................**1,200.00**

Sign, Mobil, neon-outlined plastic Mobil horse, 53" L, newer, EX+..............................**725.00**

Sign, Phillips 66, porcelain, red and black double-sided shield, 29½x29½", EX, $450.00.

Sign, Phillips 66 diecut porcelain emblem, 2-sided, 30", VG+.**300.00**

Sign, Pro-Tex-U-Lite for Cars & Trucks, diecut cardboard, 21x17", NM.....................**25.00**

Sign, Sinclair, metal Dino figure clipped to bracket, 18x29", NM..............................**375.00**

Sign, White Rose Gasoline, porcelain, shows boy w/sign, 12" dia **325.00**

Spark plug cleaning device, Auto-Lite Cleaning Service, 20", VG **50.00**

Thermometer, Prestone Anti-Freeze, porcelain, gray, 36x9", EX **160.00**

Thermometer, Sunoco, embossed tin, logo on white, 14x4½", NM **75.00**

Tin, Rex Anti-Slip Brake Wafers, 2x1¼" dia, VG+ **70.00**

Watch fob, Golden Shell Oil, round w/embossed inlayed logo, EX **200.00**

Gay Fad

Here's another new area of collecting that's just now taking off. The company started out on a very small scale in the late 1930s, but before long, business was booming! Their first products were hand-decorated kitchenwares, but it's their frosted tumblers, trays, pitchers, and decanters that are being sought out today. In addition to souvenir items and lines with a holiday theme, they made glassware to coordinate with Royal China's popular dinnerware, Currier and Ives. They're also known for their 'bentware' — quirky cocktail glasses with stems that were actually bent. Look for an interlocking 'G' and 'F' or the name 'Gay Fad,' the latter mark indicating pieces from the late 1950s to the early 1960s.

Our advisor for this category is Donna S. McGrady; she is listed in the Directory under Indiana.

See also Anchor Hocking/Fire-King.

Ashtray, Trout Flies, clear **6.00**

Batter bowl, Fruits, milk white, marked w/F (Federal Glass), handled **70.00**

Bent tray, Stylized Cats, clear, marked Gay Fad, 11½" dia..**14.00**

Beverage set, Colonial Home-stead, 85-oz pitcher & 6 tumblers, frosted **60.00**

Canister set, Red Rose, red lids, white interior, 3-pc **55.00**

Cocktail shaker, Ballerina Shoes, frosted w/red metal screw-top, 7" **20.00**

Cocktail shaker, The Last Hurdle (fox hunt scenes), 32-oz .**35.00**

Cruet set, Oil & Vinegar, Cherry, clear **15.00**

Goblet, Bow Pete, Hoffman Beer, 16-oz **15.00**

Ice Tub, Gay '90s, frosted **16.00**

Luncheon set, Cattails, sq plate, cup & saucer, tumbler, clear, 4-pc **18.00**

Luncheon set, Fantasia Hawaiian Flower, sq plate, cup & saucer **15.00**

Mug, Notre Dame, frosted, 16-oz **15.00**

Pitcher, Currier & Ives, frosted w/blue & white, 86-oz **60.00**

Pitcher, juice; Ada Orange, frosted, 36-oz.......................... **30.00**

Plate, Fruits, lace edge, Hazel Atlas, 8½" **17.50**

Range set, Rooster, frosted w/red metal caps, 8-oz, 4-pc.....**40.00**

Stem, bent cocktail; Beau Brummel, clear, marked Gay Fad, 3½-oz **14.00**

Tea & toast, Magnolia, sq plate
w/cup indent & cup, clear..**11.00**
Tom & Jerry set, Christmas bells,
bowl & 6 cups, milk white,
marked GF **70.00**
Tumbler, Say When, frosted, 4-
oz **5.00**
Tumbler, Zombie, flamingo, frost-
ed, marked GF, 14-oz.....**18.00**
Vanity set, Butterflies in Meadow,
pink inside, 5-pc.............**60.00**
Vase, Red Poppy, clear, footed,
10" **22.00**
Wine set, Grapes, decanter & 4
2½-oz stemmed wines,
clear............................**40.00**

**Waffle set, Rosemaling, 48-ounce waf-
fle batter jug and 11½-ounce syrup
jug, from $25.00 to $35.00.** (Photo courtesy Donna McGrady)

Geisha Girl China

More than sixty-five different
patterns of tea services were
exported from Japan around the
turn of the century, each depicting
geishas going about the everyday
activities of Japanese life. Mt. Fuji
is often featured in the background. Geisha Girl Porcelain is a
generic term collectors use to
identify them all. Many of our
lines contain reference to the color
of the rim bands, which many collectors use to tentatively date the
ware.

Our advisor for this category
is Elyce Litts; she is listed in the
Directory under New Jersey.

Ashtray, Temple A, heart form,
red w/gold, M-in-Wreath
mark.............................**35.00**
Bonbon, Battledore, mum-shaped,
olive green.....................**22.00**
Bowl, Dragon Boat, 6-lobed, blue
w/gold, 7" **35.00**
Butter pat, Flower Gathering B,
cobalt w/gold, round, 3" ...**8.00**
Cocoa pot, Battledore, ewer shape,
yellow-green, 9"..............**55.00**
Condiment tray, Meeting C, plum
blossom form, red-orange,
7½" **16.00**

**Cocoa pot, Gar-
den Platform
and Parasol L
variant patterns,
light olive-green
border, ornate
backdrop for
patterns in
reserves, gold
detailing,
$125.00.** (Photo
courtesy Elyce
Litts)

Cup & saucer, tea; Bamboo Trellis, dark green **10.00**
Dresser box, Garden Bench B,
cobalt w/gold, 6" dia.......**38.00**

Dresser tray, Blind Man's Bluff, cobalt, ground **85.00**

Egg cup, Cloud A, red **12.00**

Match holder, Garden Bench A, blue-green, hanging **35.00**

Napkin ring, Flower Gathering C, semicircular, red.............**28.00**

Olive dish, Mother & Son, oval, red-orange w/gold, 7".....**25.00**

Plate, Battledore, red-orange, scalloped swirl, 6¼" **15.00**

Plate, Bird Cage, red-orange w/gold, 6".........................**10.00**

Powder jar, Pug, brick red, 4¼" **35.00**

Salt dish, Cloud A, red-orange w/flowers **8.00**

Tea strainer, Parasol/Lesson A, red, 2-pc..........................**55.00**

Tea tile, Feather Fan, Nippon, round **35.00**

Vase, Bamboo Trellis, red-orange, #14, 4½", pr **30.00**

GI Joe

Introduced by Hasbro in 1964, 12" GI Joe dolls were offered in four basic packages: Action Soldier, Action Sailor, Action Marine, and Action Pilot. A Black figure was included in the line, and there were representatives of many nations as well. Talking dolls followed a few years later, and scores of accessory items such as vehicles, guns, uniforms, etc., were made to go with them all. Even though the line was discontinued in 1976, it was evident the market was still there, and kids were clamoring for more. So in 1982, Hasbro brought out the 'lit-tle' 3¾" GI Joe dolls, each with his own descriptive name. Sales were unprecedented. The small figures are easy to find, but most of them are 'loose' and played with. Collectors prefer old store stock still in the original packaging; such examples are worth from two to four times more than those without the package.

For more information we recommend *Collectible Male Action Figures, Second Edition,* by Paris and Susan Manos; *Schroeder's Collectible Toys, Antique to Modern*; and *Dolls in Uniform* by Joseph Bourgeois. All of these books are published by Collector Books.

12" Figures and Accessories

Accessory, Action Flame Thrower, green w/helmet sticker, MOC **60.00**

Accessory, Action Rescue Raft Backpack, w/instructions, EX................................**15.00**

Accessory, Adventure Team Fire Suit, silver, EX...............**25.00**

Accessory, Adventure Team Raft, orange or black, EX **10.00**

Accessory, Air Force Cadet Jacket, w/bar & wings, VG+.......**45.00**

Accessory, Air Force Dress Jacket, MOC **235.00**

Accessory, Army Poncho, green, EX..................................**35.00**

Accessory, Battle Gear Pack #1, 1983, MIP.......................**16.00**

Accessory, Cobra Condor Z25 Plane, 1988, MIB **80.00**

Accessory, Combat Mess Kit, #7509, complete, MOC...**70.00**

Accessory, Crash Crew Extension Ladder Holder, EX.........**40.00**

Accessory, Crash Crew Jacket, EX..................**28.00**

Accessory, Dog Tag, VG........**25.00**

Accessory, Fighter Pilot Helmet, EX...................**80.00**

Accessory, Grenade Launcher Rifle, w/strap, EX...........**35.00**

Accessory, Fight for Survival, 1969, complete with Polar Explorer figure, NMIB, $450.00. (Photo courtesy Paris and Susan Manos)

Accessory, Heavy Weapons Vest, complete, EX+................**75.00**

Accessory, Jeep Search Light, EX..................**15.00**

Accessory, Motorized Battle Wagon, 1991, MIP.........**35.00**

Accessory, Phanton X-19 Stealth Fighter, 1988, MIB........**70.00**

Accessory, Q Force Battle Gear, Action Force, MIP............**5.00**

Accessory, Russian Ammo Disk, EX..................**10.00**

Accessory, Scuba Wrist Depth Gauge, decal on face, EX..**15.00**

Accessory, Ski Patrol Jacket, EX...........................**32.00**

Accessory, Sleeping Bag, EX.**25.00**

Accessory, Special Force Battle Gear, Action Force, MIP..**5.00**

Accessory, Stretcher, white, VG...................................**50.00**

Figure, Action Marine, 30th Anniversary, 1994, NRFB...............**80.00**

Figure, Action Pilot, complete, MIB.............................**450.00**

Figure, Action Sailor, complete, VG.............................**125.00**

Figure, Action Soldier, NM (EX+ box), $300.00. (Photo courtesy McMasters Auctions)

Figure, Action Soldier, complete, EX+..............................**145.00**

Figure, Adventure Team Land Adventurer, complete, NM............**150.00**

Figure, Adventure Team Man of Action, no beard, complete, EX..................................**150.00**

Figure, Adventure Team Talking Astronaut, complete, EX.**200.00**

Figure, Airborne Military Police, Kay Bee Toys, NRFB.....**55.00**

Figure, Annihilator, 1989, MOC..........................**15.00**

Figure, Battle of the Bulge, Toys-R-Us, NRFB..................**45.00**

Figure, British Commando w/ Chevrons, complete, VG....**385.00**

Figure, Captain Grid Iron, 1990, MIP..............................**12.00**

Figure, Combat Soldier (Action Man), complete, MIB...**120.00**

Figure, Crimson Guard, 1984, w/accessories, EX...........**15.00**

Figure, Deep Freeze, complete, NM..............................**285.00**

Figure, Fighter Pilot, complete, NM **550.00**

Figure, German Storm Trooper, complete, VG **395.00**

Figure, Green Beret, complete, EX **325.00**

Figure, LSO, complete, EX ..**290.00**

Figure, Marine, Toys-R-Us, NRFB **42.00**

Figure, Mountain Troops, complete, VG **165.00**

Figure, Space Ranger Patroller (Action Man), complete, MIB **95.00**

Figure, Tank Commander, complete, EX **350.00**

Figure, West Point Cadet, complete, EX **350.00**

3¾" Figures and Accessories

Accessory, Arctic Blast, 1988, EX **12.00**

Accessory, Battlefield Robot Radar Rat, 1988, NRFB **30.00**

Accessory, Cobra Emperor w/Air Chariot, 1986, NRFB **60.00**

Accessory, Earth Borer Cobra Action Pack, 1987, MOC ..**15.00**

Accessory, Hovercraft, mail-in, 1984, MIP **40.00**

Accessory, Jet Pack Jump & Platform, 1982, MIP (Canadian) **50.00**

Accessory, Mauler MBT Tank, 1985, NRFB **80.00**

Accessory, Missile Defense Unit, 1984, MIP **20.00**

Accessory, Mobile Missile System, complete, EX **45.00**

Accessory, Python Conquest, 1988, complete, EX **15.00**

Accessory, Skyhawk, complete, EX (G box) **18.00**

Accessory, Tiger Shark, 1988, complete, EX **12.00**

Figure, Airborne, 1983, complete, EX **16.00**

Figure, Barbecue, 1983-85, complete, EX **15.00**

Figure, Beachhead, 1983-85, MIP **30.00**

Figure, Buzzer, 1985, MIP ...**35.00**

Figure, Chuckles, 1987, MOC ..**26.00**

Figure, Cobra Commander, 1983, MIP **125.00**

Figure, Cutter, 1984, MOC...**15.00**

Figure, Eels, 1992, MOC **10.00**

Figure, Iceberg, 1983-85, MOC ..**32.00**

Figure, Darklon, 1989, EX, $5.00.

Accessory, GI Joe Arctic Blast, 1988, complete, MIB, $30.00.

Figure, Iron Grenadier, 1988, MOC **18.00**

Figure, Leatherneck, 1983-85, MOC **25.00**
Figure, Ozone, 1993, MOC **5.00**
Figure, Road Pig, 1988, MOC...**20.00**

Glass Animals and Birds

Nearly every glasshouse of note has at some point over the years produced these beautiful models, some of which double for vases, bookends, and flower frogs. Many were made during the 1930s through the 1950s and 1960s, and these are the most collectible. But you'll also be seeing brand new examples, and you need to study to know the difference. A good reference to help you sort them all out is *Glass Animals of the Depression Era* by Lee Garmon and Dick Spencer (Collector Books). See also Boyd; Fenton.

Alley Cat, pink carnival, Fenton, 11" **100.00**
Angelfish, amber, Viking, 7x7" ..**125.00**
Bird, candle holder, crystal, Fostoria, 1½" **20.00**
Bird, med dark blue, Viking, 9½" **40.00**
Blue Jay, flower holder, crystal, Cambridge....................**135.00**
Bunny, pale yellow, Fenton..**25.00**
Camel, cobalt, LE Smith.......**95.00**
Cardinal, Green Mist, Westmoreland................................**20.00**
Cat, black satin, raised bumps, Tiffin, #9445, 6¼" **140.00**
Cat, light blue, Fostoria, 3¾" ..**35.00**
Chick, frosted, New Martinsville, 1" **25.00**

Chick w/head down, milk glass, Imperial.........................**10.00**

Chinese Pheasant, medium blue, Paden City, 13¾" long, $175.00. (Photo courtesy Lee Garmon and Dick Spencer)

Colt rearing, crystal, Heisey...**200.00**
Colt standing, amber, Imperial..............................**125.00**
Cygnet, black, Imperial, 2½"...**55.00**
Dolphin, blue, Fostoria, 4¾" ...**35.00**
Donkey, crystal, Duncan & Miller **120.00**
Donkey, crystal, Heisey......**295.00**
Duck, ashtray, crystal, Duncan & Miller, 4"........................**20.00**
Elephant, caramel slag, Imperial, sm **85.00**
Elephant, crystal, Heisey, sm..**225.00**
Elephant, crystal, LE Smith, 1½"..............................**20.00**
Fish, bowl, crystal, Heisey, 9½"..**450.00**
Fish, red w/amberina tail & fins, Fenton, 2½" **55.00**
Frog, crystal satin, Cambridge..**25.00**
German Shepard, lamp base, pink, New Martinsville..........**125.00**
Goose w/wings up, crystal, Heisey.....................**110.00**
Heron, crystal, Duncan & Miller.....................**150.00**
Horse, bookends, crystal, Fostoria, 7¾", ea **45.00**

Horse rearing, crystal, Paden City.............................**150.00**

Mallard w/wings up, caramel slag, Imperial..........................**40.00**

Owl, dark blue, shiny eyes, Westmoreland, 5½"................**65.00**

Owl, purple slag, shiny, Imperial..................................**95.00**

Panther walking, amber, Indiana.............................**300.00**

Pony, crystal, Paden City, 12"..**100.00**

Pouter Pigeon, bookend, crystal, Paden City, 6¼".............**95.00**

Ram's head, stopper, crystal, Heisey, 3½"..................**160.00**

Rooster, amber, Imperial....**475.00**

Rooster, crystal, Heisey, 5½x5"..**350.00**

Russian wolfhound, crystal, New Martinsville, 7¼", $95.00.

Sea Horse, cocktail, crystal, Heisey...........................**160.00**

Seal (baby) w/ball, crystal, New Martinsville....................**60.00**

Sparrow w/head up, crystal, LE Smith, 3½".....................**15.00**

Squirrel on curved log, crystal, Paden City, 5½".............**65.00**

Squirrel sitting, amber, Fostoria................................**45.00**

Swan, ebony, Cambridge, 3".**65.00**

Swan, milk glass w/decor, LE Smith, 8½"....................**45.00**

Tiger w/head down, frosted, New Martinsville, 7¼".........**200.00**

Tropical Fish, ashtray, pink opal, Duncan & Miller, 3½"....**50.00**

Turtle, cigarette box, crystal, Westmoreland................**45.00**

Wren on perch, light blue on white, 2-pc, Westmoreland........**45.00**

Glass Shoes

While many glass shoes were made simply as whimseys, you'll also find thimble holders, perfumes, inkwells, salts, candy containers, and bottles made to resemble shoes of many types. Our advisor for this category is Libby Yalom; author of *Shoes of Glass;* see the Directory under Maryland for information on how to order her book. Another useful source is *Collectible Glass Shoes* by Earlene Wheatley. See also Boyd; Degenhart.

Baby shoe, embossed laced-up front, hollow sole, frosted, 1930, 3⅛"......................**50.00**

Boot, Daisy & Button, canary yellow, Fenton....................**40.00**

Boot, hobnail w/embossed front laces, milk glass, Fenton, 1970s.............................**30.00**

Boot, stylized Santa-type w/cuff & turned-up toe, amethyst, 2¾"..............................**20.00**

Boot, textured w/6 embossed side buttons, green, 4¾", 1970s, 4¾"................................**15.00**

Boot on base, smooth w/hobnail top, scalloped edge, any color, 4", ea.............................**25.00**

Bootie, Daisy & Button, French opalescent, Fenton **50.00**

Bootie, solid w/ribbed & hobnail design, Waterford, 1986, 4⅛" **85.00**

Bottle boot, lady's hightop w/embossed detail, crystal, 1900, 4¼" **50.00**

Bottle shoe, embossed flowers on vamp, crystal, 1890s, 4" L **75.00**

Button shoe, 3 buttons on side, milk glass, ca 1900, 6" ...**85.00**

Cat shoe, hobnail, Colonial Blue, Fenton, 1960s, 3x5⅛" **45.00**

Cat shoe, hobnail, topaz opalescent, Fenton, 1939-44/reissued 1962 ....**50.00**

Covered shoe, hobnail, w/dome lid, milk glass, Fenton, 1970s, 6½" **65.00**

Cowboy boot, stippled w/embossed steer, handled, green, 1950s, 10" **35.00**

Cuban heel, stippled, blue, 1930s/reissued 1960s, 4½" **50.00**

Finecut roller skate, aqua, 3x4", $75.00.

High heel, smooth crystal w/gold-trimmed bow, 1980s, 5" .**25.00**

Rose shoe, embossed roses, various colors, Tony Rosena/Fenton, 1990 ....**25.00**

Skate shoe, Daisy & Square, amber, LE Smith, 1970s, 4¼" **15.00**

Slipper, applied flowers on blue front, crystal high heel, 6" **65.00**

Slipper, floral on blue, crystal ruffle, pointed upturned toe, 5⅛" **35.00**

Tassel boot, ribbed, beaded edge, crystal, Gillinder & Sons, 4¼" **150.00**

Golden Foliage

If you can remember when this glassware came packed in boxes of laundry soap, you're telling your age. Along with 'white' margarine, Golden Foliage was a product of the 1950s. It was made by the Libbey Glass Company, and the line was rather limited; as far as we know, we've listed the entire assortment here. The glassware features a satin band with various leaves and gold trim. (It also came in silver.)

Our advisors for this category are Debbie and Randy Coe; they are listed in the Directory under Oregon.

Drink set, 8 9-oz tumblers, ice tub & brass-finished caddy ..**75.00**

Drink set, 8 9-oz tumblers & brass-finished caddy **48.00**

Goblet, cocktail; 4-oz **6.00**

Goblet, cordial; 1-oz **9.50**

Goblet, pilsner; 11-oz **9.50**

Goblet, sherbet; 6½-oz **4.50**

Goblet, water; 9-oz **6.50**

Ice tub, w/metal 3-footed frame...**22.50**

Jigger, 2-oz **7.00**

Pitcher, metal frame, 5¼", $16.50.

Salad dressing set, 3 4" bowls &
   brass-finished caddy **19.50**
Tumbler, beverage; 12½-oz.....**9.50**
Tumbler, cooler; 14-oz.............**9.50**
Tumbler, juice; 6-oz.................**5.00**
Tumbler, old-fashioned; 9-oz ..**6.00**
Tumbler, water; 10-oz.............**7.50**

Graniteware

   Graniteware is actually a
base metal with a coating of
enamel. It was first made in the
1870s, but graniteware of sorts
was made well into the 1950s. In
fact, some of what you'll find
today is brand new. But new
pieces are much lighter in weight
than the old ones. Look for
seamed construction, metal handles, and graniteware lids on such
things as tea- and coffeepots. All
these are indicators of age. Colors
are another, and swirled pieces —
cobalt blue and white, green and
white, brown and white, and red
and white — are generally older,
harder to find, and therefore more
expensive. For a comprehensive
look at this popular collectible, we
recommend *The Collector's Encyclopedia of Graniteware, Colors,
Shapes and Value, Books I* and *II*,
by Helen Greguire (Collector
Books).

Baking pan, cobalt & white lg mottle
   w/black trim, oblong, EX ..**135.00**
Bowl, vegetable; red & white lg
   swirl w/black trim, oblong,
   1950s **165.00**
Bucket, water; solid yellow
   w/black trim, white interior,
   10½", VG **55.00**
Chamber pot, blue & white lg swirl
   w/black trim, wooden bail .**250.00**
Clock, Delft-style scene, marked
   8-day Germany **395.00**
Coffeepot, white w/green veins, med
   mottle, marked Elite, G..**145.00**
Colander, solid white, 7½", VG...**60.00**
Cup, clabber; gray med mottle,
   seamed, riveted handle &
   foot, VG.........................**200.00**
Dipper, suds; gray med mottle,
   seamless, tubular open-end
   handle, NM **95.00**
Egg plate, red & white lg mottle
   w/red, white interior, handles,
   VG................................**225.00**
Fruit jar filler, gray lg mottle, riv-
   eted strap handle, EX....**35.00**
Fry pan, green & white lg swirl,
   white interior, EX........**140.00**
Funnel, dark green & white fine
   mottle, white interior, Elite,
   EX **125.00**
Gravy boat, white & light blue lg
   mottle w/cobalt trim **325.00**

Kettle, cream w/green trim, 16 embossed ribs, 7½".......**40.00**

Measure, cobalt & white swirl w/black trim, white interior, 3½"..**595.00**

Milk can (Boston), fine red-brown & white mottle, seamed, strap handle...........................**195.00**

Mold, Turk's-head turban style, solid cobalt, white interior, 9", VG...................................**95.00**

Muffin pan, 6-cup, aqua & white lg swirl w/cobalt, white interior **650.00**

Muffin pan, 8-cup, redipped brown & white lg mottle **285.00**

Pie plate, brown & blue-gray lg swirl................................**85.00**

Pitcher, molasses; gray lg mottle, thumblift on lid, VG.....**225.00**

Pitcher, water; cobalt & white lg swirl, gray interior, 10½", VG **475.00**

Platter, red & white lg swirl w/black, 1950s, 17½x13"................**175.00**

Roaster, cobalt & white lg swirl, flat top, metal vent on lid, 3-pc **245.00**

Scoop, American Gray medium mottle, 13" long, NM, $245.00.

Scoop, gray lg mottle, rolled edges, handleless style, 8½", VG..**265.00**

Soap dish, solid blue, fluted bottom, hanging, EX...........**60.00**

Spittoon, brown & white lg swirl, black trim, white interior, seamless **425.00**

Strainer, cobalt & white med mottle, 3-footed, 8-sided, eyelet...............................**95.00**

Teakettle, blue shading to white, wooden bail, Bluebelle Ware...............**295.00**

Teapot, blue & white sm mottle, Belle shape, seamless, VG...........................**425.00**

Toothbrush holder, white & light blue lg mottle, perforated lid, VG...................................**65.00**

Trivet, Delft-style windmill scene, round, handled, EX........**90.00**

Wash basin, lavender-blue & white lg swirl, lg............**45.00**

Washboard, cobalt, metal soap saver, EX.....................**165.00**

Griswold

Cast-iron cooking ware was used extensively in the nineteenth century, and even today a lot of folks think no other type of cookware can measure up. But whether they buy it to use or are strictly collectors, Griswold is the name they hold in highest regard. During the latter part of the nineteenth century, the Griswold company began to manufacture the finest cast-iron kitchenware items available at that time. Soon after they became established, they introduced a line of lightweight, cast-aluminum ware that revolutionized the industry. The company enjoyed many prosperous years until its closing in the late 1950s. You'll recognize most items by the marks, which generally will include the Griswold name; for instance, 'Seldon Griswold' and 'Griswold Mfg. Co.' But don't overlook the 'Erie' mark, which the company used as well.

Our advisor for this category is Grant Windsor; he is listed in the Directory under Virginia. See Clubs and Newsletters for information on the Griswold and Cast Iron Cookware Association.

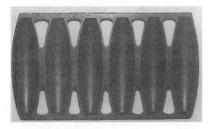

Vienna roll pan, Griswold #6, fully marked, $250.00.

Ashtray, #770, sq **20.00**
Bowl, patty; #72 ....**30.00**
Griddle, #7, handle, block trademark **35.00**
Lemon squeezer, #2 Classic.**125.00**
Muffin pan, #10, pattern #949 w/cutouts **30.00**
Popover pan, #18, wide handle, fully marked...................**65.00**
Sad iron, Griswald Erie, 5½-lb..**85.00**
Skillet, #05, heat ring, slant/EPU trademark **40.00**
Skillet, #07, heat ring, block trademark **50.00**
Skillet, #08, smooth bottom, block trademark **25.00**
Skillet, #10, slant/EPU trademark **100.00**
Skillet griddle, #109, slant/EPU trademark **125.00**

Stick pan, #954, 11-stick **25.00**
Trivet, #1740, star **35.00**
Waffle iron, #8 American (#885 & 886), w/low side handle (#975)............................**45.00**

Guardian Ware

The Guardian Service company was in business from 1935 until 1955. They produced a very successful line of hammered aluminum that's just as popular today as it ever was. Sold through the home party plan, special hostess gifts were offered as incentives. Until 1940 metal lids were used, but during the war when the government restricted the supply of available aluminum, glass lids were introduced.

The company's logo is a knight with crossed weapons and if you find a piece with the trademark that includes the words 'Patent Pending,' you'll know you have one of the earlier pieces.

In 1980 Tad and Suzie Kohara bought the rights to the Guardian Service name as well as the original molds. The new company is based in California, and is presently producing eight of the original pieces, canning racks, pressure cooker parts, serving handles, and replacement glass lids.

Be sure to judge condition when evaluating Guardian Service. Wear, baked-on grease, scratches, and obvious signs of use devaluate its worth. Our prices range from pieces in average to exceptional condition. To be graded exceptional, the interior of the pan must have no pitting, and the surface must be bright and clean. An item with a metal lid is worth 25% more than the same piece with a glass lid.

Ashtray, glass, w/knight & white stars logo, hostess gift, $25 to **30.00**
Beverage urn (coffeepot), glass lid, no screen or dripper, common **20.00**

Beverage urn (coffeepot), glass lid, complete, $50.00.

Can of cleaner, unopened **15.00**
Cookbook, Guardian Service or Pressure Cooker, $20 to..**35.00**
Cookbook, Silver Seal, 1936, 48-pg, EX **45.00**
Dome cooker, Tom Thumb; w/handles, glass lid, 3½x4⅞", $25 to **35.00**
Dome cooker, 1-qt, w/handles, glass lid, 6¾", $25 to......**45.00**
Fryer, breakfast; glass lid, 10", $45 to **60.00**
Fryer, chicken; glass lid, 12", $75 to **100.00**
Gravy boat, w/undertray, $30 to...............................**50.00**

Griddle broiler, octagon, polished center, w/handles, 16½", $20 to **35.00**
Handle, clamp-on style, $10 to..**15.00**
Ice bucket, glass lid, liner & tongs, 9", $50 to........................**90.00**
Kettle oven, bail handle, glass lid, w/rack, 8x12" dia, $135 to ...**165.00**
Omelet pan, hinged in center, black handle on each half, $75 to.**100.00**
Pot, triangular, glass lid, 7" to top of finial, 11" long, $25 to..**45.00**
Pressure cooker, $125 to.....**165.00**
Roaster, glass lid, 4x15" long, $85 to **100.00**
Roaster, turkey; glass lid, no rack, 16½" long, $100 to **135.00**
Tray, serving; hammered center, w/handles, 13" dia, $20 to..**30.00**
Tumbler & coaster set, glass, knight & shield in silver, metal rack **80.00**
Tumbler & coaster set, glass, silver knight & shield, w/rack, 9-pc **80.00**
Tureen, bottom; glass lid, $40 to **65.00**
Tureen, casserole; glass lid, $65 to **90.00**
Tureen, top; glass lid, $30 to...**45.00**

Gurley Candles

Santas, choir boys, turkeys, and angels are among the figural candles made by this company from the 1940s until as late as the 1960s, possibly even longer. They range in size from 2½" to nearly 9", and they're marked 'Gurley' on the bottom. Because they were so appealing, people were reluctant to burn them and instead stored them away and used them again and again. You can still find them today, especially at the flea market level. Tavern candles (they're marked as well) were made by a company owned by Gurley; they're also collectible.

Our advisors for this category are Debbie and Randy Coe; they are listed in the Directory under Oregon.

Halloween, witch with pumpkin and broom, 8", $18.50.

Birthday, boy, marked Tavern, 3" **6.00**
Christmas, angel, 5" **850.00**
Christmas, choir boy or girl, 2¾", ea **6.00**
Christmas, church w/choir boy inside, 6" **12.50**
Christmas, grotto w/shepherd & sheep..............................**14.50**
Christmas, grotto w/star, angel & baby, 4½" **10.00**
Christmas, reindeer, marked Tavern, 3½" **2.50**
Christmas, Rudolph w/red nose, 3" **2.50**
Christmas, Santa, 6¼"..........**12.00**
Christmas, snowman w/red pipe & green hat, 5" **5.00**
Easter, chick, pink or yellow, 3" **5.00**
Easter, pink egg w/squirrel inside, 3" **12.00**
Easter, rabbit, pink or yellow, 3" **5.00**
Halloween, Frankenstein, later issue but harder to find, 6", MIB................................**24.00**
Halloween, owl (4" orange cutout) w/7½" black candle behind it.......................**20.00**
Halloween, pumpkin w/black cat, 2½" **8.00**

Thanksgiving, acorns & leaves, 3½" **6.50**
Thanksgiving, Pilgrim girl or boy, 2½", ea **4.50**
Thanksgiving, turkey, 5¾"...**15.00**
Wedding, bride & groom, 4½", ea **12.50**

Hall

Most famous for their extensive lines of teapots and colorful dinnerwares, the Hall China Company still operates in East Liverpool, Ohio, where they were established in 1903. Refer to *The Collector's Encyclopedia of Hall China* by Margaret and Kenn Whitmyer (Collector Books) for more information. See Clubs and Newsletters for information on the Hall China Collector's Club. For listings of Hall's most popular dinnerware line, see Autumn Leaf.

Acacia, bean pot, New England, #4 ....**110.00**

Arizona, casserole, Tomorrow's Classic, 2-qt....................35.00

Arizona, vinegar bottle, Tomorrow's Classic...................27.00

Beauty, marmite, w/lid.........37.00

Blue Blossom, casserole, Sundial, * #1 ....60.00

Blue Bouquet, bowl, Thick Rim, 8½"....................................30.00

Blue Bouquet, plate, D-style, 9" 14.00

Blue Crocus, salt and pepper shakers, $60.00 for the pair. (Photo courtesy Margaret and Kenn Whitmyer)

Blue Floral, bowl, 9" 18.00

Blue Garden, jug, ball; #4.....90.00

Bouquet, ashtray, Tomorrow's Classic 10.00

Bouquet, platter, Tomorrow's Classic, 17"......................35.00

Buckingham, bowl, cereal; Tomorrow's Classic, 6" 9.00

Buckingham, casserole, Tomorrow's Classic, 1¼-qt 35.00

Cactus, bowl, Five band, 8¾"..27.00

Cameo Rose, bowl, fruit; E-style, 5¼" 6.50

Cameo Rose, butter dish, E-style, ¼-lb.................................50.00

Cameo Rose, plate, E-style, 9¼"..9.00

Caprice, candlestick, Tomorrow's Classic, 4½".....................22.00

Carrot/Golden Carrot, bowl, Radiance, 9" 32.00

Christmas Tree & Holly, cup, E-style 18.00

Clover (Pink), bowl, Thick Rim, 6" 12.00

Crocus, creamer, Medallion..16.00

Crocus, sugar bowl, Modern, w/lid..............................25.00

Crocus, tidbit, D-style, 3-tier ..60.00

Eggshell, custard, Dot.............9.00

Fantasy, bowl, fruit; Tomorrow's Classic, 5¾" 5.00

Fantasy, jug, Tomorrow's Classic, 1¼-qt................................25.00

Fern, jug, Century.................18.00

Five Band, casserole, colors other than red or cobalt, 8" 25.00

Five Band, cookie jar, red or cobalt..............................85.00

Flamingo, bowl, batter; Five band 95.00

Flareware, bowl, Radial, 8" 7.00

Flareware, cookie jar, Heather Rose 30.00

Floral Lattice, tea tile, round, 6"....................................55.00

French Flower, teapot, McCormick 110.00

Frost Flowers, egg cup, Tomorrow's Classic...................27.00

Frost Flowers, vase, Tomorrow's Classic 30.00

Game Bird, bowl, fruit; E-style, 5½".....................................8.00

Game Bird, bowl, Thick Rim, china, 8½"......................22.00

Game Bird, cup, E-style........14.00

Gold Label, bowl, salad; 9" ...18.00

Golden Glo, mug, #343.........12.00

Harlequin, plate, Tomorrow's Classic, 6".........................3.50

Harlequin, vase, Tomorrow's Classic...................................27.00

Heather Rose, bowl, Flare-shape, E-style, 8¾"...............15.00

Heather Rose, plate, E-style, 10"...............8.50

Holiday, candlestick, Tomorrow's Classic, 8"...............30.00

Holiday, plate, Tomorrow's Classic, 8"...............5.00

Homewood, bowl, fruit; D-style, 5½"...............5.50

Homewood, salt & pepper shakers, handled, pr...............36.00

Lyric/Mulberry, platter, Tomorrow's Classic, 15"...............25.00

Meadow Flower, custard, Thick Rim...............16.00

Medallion, bowl, Lettuce, #3, 6"...............9.00

Medallion, casserole, ivory...11.00

Morning Glory, bowl, straight sides, 9"...............25.00

Morning Glory, bowl, Thick Rim, 6"...............13.00

Morning Glory, teapot, Aladdin.125.00

Mums, bowl, radiance, 9"......22.00

Mums, custard, New York....16.00

Mums, pie baker...............32.00

No 488, bowl, Radiance, 6"...14.00

No 488, jug, Medallion...........70.00

Orange Poppy, bowl, fruit; C-style, 5½"...............7.00

Orange Poppy, custard...........7.00

Orange Poppy, casserole, oval, with lid, 8", $45.00.

Pastel Morning Glory, bowl, cereal; D-style, 6"...............10.00

Pastel Morning Glory, cup, St Denis...............35.00

Peach Blossom, gravy boat, Tomorrow's Classic........25.00

Peach Blossom, vase, Tomorrow's Classic...............32.00

Pert, jug, Cadet, 7½".............13.00

Pine Cone, bowl, fruit; E-style, 5¼"...............6.50

Primrose, jug, Rated, E-style.16.00

Red Poppy, cake safe, metal...35.00

Red Poppy, creamer, Daniel.15.00

Red Poppy, pie baker............35.00

Ribbed, ramekin, russet or red, 6-oz...............5.00

Rose Parade, casserole, tab handled...............35.00

Rose White, bowl, Medallion, 8½"...............22.00

Sear's Arlington, bowl, vegetable; E-style, w/lid...............28.00

Sear's Fairfax, plate, E-style, 10"...............7.00

Sear's Monticello, creamer, E-style...............9.00

Sear's Mount Vernon, bowl, oval, E-style, 9¼"...............16.00

Serenade, bowl, Radiance, 9"..16.00

Shaggy Tulip, custard, Radiance...............13.00

Silhouette, bowl, flat soup; D-style, 8½"...............20.00

Silhouette, mug, beverage....45.00

Spring, butter dish, Tomorrow's Classic...............80.00

Springtime, cake plate..........16.00

Stonewall, casserole, Radiance..32.00

Sunglow, jug, Century..........18.00

Tulip, bowl, Radiance, 9"......22.00

Wild Poppy, baker, oval........55.00

Wildfire, casserole, Thick Rim..30.00

Wildfire, salt & pepper shakers, handled, pr **36.00**
Yellow Rose, custard **11.00**

Teapots

Airflow, cobalt w/gold trim, 6-cup **65.00**
Airflow, red, 8-cup **165.00**
Albany, mahob w/gold trim, 6-cup **65.00**
Bellvue, red, 6 or 10 cup **75.00**

Automobile, cobalt, six-cup, $650.00.

Birdcage, maroon w/gold trim..**275.00**
Damascus, turquoise, 6-cup .**150.00**
French, cadet blue w/gold flowers...**55.00**
French, Gold Label (Gold decal), 6-cup **37.00**
Manhattan, colors other than red, 2-cup **55.00**
Manhattan, warm yellow, 6-cup..**85.00**
Moderne, turquoise w/gold trim, 6-cup **50.00**
New York, red, 6-cup **125.00**
Streamline, blue w/gold, 6-cup..**75.00**
Surfside, emerald or canary, 6-cup............................. **100.00**
Windshield, cobalt, 6-cup ...**125.00**
Windshield, warm yellow, 6-cup..**75.00**

Hallmark

Since 1973 the Hallmark Company has made Christmas ornaments, some of which are today worth many times their original price. Our suggested values reflect the worth of those in mint condition and in their original boxes.

Our advisors for this category are the proprietors of *The Baggage Car*, which is listed in the Directory under Iowa as well as Clubs and Newsletters.

A Savior Is Born, QX254-1, 1984 .... **35.00**
Across the Miles, QX315-7, 1991 .... **15.00**
Baby's First Christmas, QX440-2, 1981 .... **50.00**
Barbie/Dolls of the World, Chinese, QX616-2, 1997 .... **30.00**
Batman, QX585-3, 1994 .... **30.00**
Betsy Clark, QX508-5, 1985 .**30.00**
Betsy Clark, XHD100-2, 1973..**85.00**
Big Shot, QX587-3, 1994....... **20.00**
Birds of Winter, QX205-1, 1976..**85.00**
Boy Caroler, XHD83-2, 1973 .**24.00**
Caring Nurse, QX578-5, 1993..**20.00**
Cat Naps, QX620-5, 1997 .....**20.00**
Charmers, QX109-1, 1974 ....**45.00**
Charmers, QX153-5, 1977 ....**65.00**
Cheerful Santa, QX515-4, 1992..**25.00**
Cherry Jubilee, QX453-2, 1989...**20.00**
Christmas at Home, QX210-1, 1980 .... **38.00**
Christmas Morning, QLX701-3, 1987 .... **50.00**
Cool Juggler, QX487-4, 1988 .**20.00**
Cozy Goose, QX496-6, 1990..**15.00**
Currier & Ives, QX197-1, 1976..**50.00**
Dad, QX467-4, 1992 .... **25.00**
Engineering Mouse, QX521-2, 1985 .... **25.00**
Festive Angel, QX463-5, 1989..**30.00**

First Christmas Together, QX208-9, 1983 ....35.00

Flamingo, QX483-1, 1988 .....35.00

Friends Are Fun, QX528-9, 1991 ....25.00

Gold King, QBG683-6, 1998 .32.00

Golf's My Bag, QX490-3, 1990 ..30.00

Good Cheer Blimp, QLZ704-6, 1987 ....60.00

Good Luck Dice, QX681-3, 1998 ....20.00

Grandaughter, QX273-6, 1986 ....35.00

Grandmother, QX267-6, 1978 ....50.00

Hillside Express, QX613-4, 1996 ....28.00

In a Heartbeat, QX581-7, 1995 ....25.00

Keep on Glowin', QLX707-6, 1986 ....50.00

Little Drummer Boy, QX537-2, 1993 ....25.00

Lou Rankin Bear, QX406-9, 1995 ....200.00

Love, QX268-3, 1978 ....60.00

Madonna & Child, QX632-4, 1996 ....28.00

Matchless Christmas, QX132-7, 1979 ....85.00

Mountains, QX158-2, 1977 ...45.00

Muppets, QX2510-4, 1984 ....35.00

Norman Rockwell, QX166-1, 1975 ....55.00

Peanuts, QX212-7, 1983 ....40.00

Raggedy Ann, QX165-1, 1975 ..60.00

Santa & Reindeer, QX467-6, 1982 ....50.00

Snowflake Chimes, QX165-4, 1980 ....35.00

Snowgoose, QX107-1, 1974 ...75.00

Touchdown Santa, QX423-3, 1986 ....45.00

Winnie the Pooh, QX206-7, 1979 ....50.00

Yesteryears: Train, QX181-1, 1976, MIB, from $170.00 to $175.00.

Halloween

Halloween items are fast becoming the most popular holiday-related collectibles on the market today. Although originally linked to pagan rituals and superstitions, Halloween has long since evolved into a fun-filled event; and the masks, noisemakers, and jack-o'-lanterns of earlier years are great fun to look for. Within the last ten years, the ranks of Halloween collectors have grown from only a few to thousands, with many overcompensating for lost time! Prices have risen rapidly and are only now leveling off and reaching a more reasonable level. As people become aware of their values, more items are appearing on the market for sale, and warehouse finds turn up more frequently.

Our advisor for this category is Pamela E. Apkarian-Russell, the Halloween Queen, author of *Collectible Halloween, Salem Witchcraft and Souvenirs, More Halloween Collectibles, Halloween: Decorations and Games, Washday Collectibles,* and *Anthropomorphic Beings of Halloween* (all published by Schiffer). *Around Swanzey* and *The Armenians of Worcester* were published by Arcadia. Her newest book is *The Tastes and Smells of Halloween* (a Trick or Treat Trader Publication, available from the author). She is listed in the Directory under New Hampshire. See Clubs and Newsletters for information concerning *The Trick or Treat Trader.*

Bank, Snoopy & Woodstock lying atop jack-'o-lantern, Whitman Candy, EX **14.00**

Bendee, pumpkin-faced man, Burger King premium, EX **10.00**

Book, Best Witches, by Robert Heitmann, 1960, 30 pages, EX...........**40.00**

Candle holder, jack-'o-lantern, papier-mache, wire bail, 1950s, 6", EX..................**65.00**

Candy box, cardboard w/image of owl on branch, EX..........**20.00**

Candy container, ball form w/face, hat, feet, cardboard, W Germany, EX........................**75.00**

Candy container, jack-'o-lantern w/bug eyes, glass, original paint, EX **95.00**

Candy container, lemon-head girl, composition, Germany, EX **135.00**

Candy container, pumpkin-face man, composition, 3½", EX...................**175.00**

Candy holder, cat pulling pumpkin coach, cardboard, EX..................................**45.00**

Costume, Batman, Ben Cooper, 1969, complete, NMIB ...**95.00**

Costume, Charlie's Angels, any character, Collegeville, 1976, MIB, ea...........................**75.00**

Costume, Dracula, Ben Cooper, 1950s, complete, EXIB ..**100.00**

Costume, flipper, Collegeville, 1964, MIB.......................**80.00**

Costume, Great Grape Ape, Ben Cooper, 1975, complete, EXIB.............................**50.00**

Costume, Mork, Ben Cooper, 1978, complete, NM, $35.00. (Photo courtesy Greg Davis and Bill Morgan)

Decoration, bat w/movable wings, paper................................**6.00**

Decoration, Halloween a GoGo Dancers, cardboard, 1960s, 14", MIP.......................**55.00**

Decoration, scarecrow w/pleated haystack, cardboard, MIP..**30.00**

Diecut, owl & man in the moon, embossed cardboard, Germany, EX.....................**130.00**

Figure, owl, pulp, American, 1940s, 6½", NM............**150.00**

Figure, scarecrow, celluloid, EX...........................**100.00**

Finger puppets, Kooky Spookys, glow-in-the-dark, MIP, ea **10.00**

Hat, owl front w/fold-around black & orange check band, paper, EX.................................**20.00**

Horn, cardboard litho, wooden mouth bit, EX.................**65.00**

Jack-'o-lantern, pulp, American, 1940s, 5", NM...............**150.00**

Lantern, black cat, papier-mache, bail handle, 6", NM......**350.00**

Lantern, devil, cardboard with **o r i g i n a l** inserts, double-sided, American, 1950s, 7½", EX, **$125.00.** (Photo courtesy Dunbar Gallery)

Lantern, owl, cast iron, open-work forms feathers, reproduction **15.00**

Noisemaker, drum type w/hanging bells, wood & paper, EX..**95.00**

Noisemaker, tin rachet type w/witch, jack-'o-lantern & owl on moon, EX...................**15.00**

Nut cup, jack-o-lantern, papier-mache, EX **20.00**

Paddle ball, wooden w/goggle-eyed pumpkin faces, High Flyer, MIP..................................**5.00**

Paper doll sheet from magazine, Dolly Dingle's Halloween, unused, EX.....................**20.00**

Party set, Halloween Party Material Box, Whitman, complete, NMIB...........................**200.00**

Postcard, pumpkin-face children & black cat, easel back, EX...**22.00**

Push-button puppet, pumpkin man standing on pumpkin, plastic, EX......................**35.00**

Snow globe, Trick or Treat, figures & jack-'o-lanterns, Hallmark, NM......................**14.00**

Stickers, jack-'o-lanterns, 1 sheet, M.....................................**12.00**

Tambourine, laughing devil's face, tin, EX **100.00**

Yo-yo, jack-'o-lantern, tin, modern **8.00**

Handkerchiefs

Lovely to behold, handkerchiefs remain as feminine keepsakes of a time past. Largely replaced by disposable tissues of more modern times, handkerchiefs found today are often those that had special meaning, keepsakes of special occasions, or souvenirs. Many collectible handkerchiefs were never meant for everyday use, but intended to be a feminine addition to the lady's total ensemble. Made in a wide variety of styles and tucked away in grandmother's dresser, handkerchiefs are now being brought out and displayed for their dainty loveliness and fine craftsmanship. For further information we recommend *Ladies' Vintage Accessories, Identification & Value Guide,* by LaRee Johnson Bruton (Collector Books).

Gift package of three white cotton handkerchiefs with embroidered rose in corners, original tag and ribbon, unused, from $12.00 to $18.00. (Photo courtesy LaRee Johnson Bruton)

Cotton, white w/drawn work, from $5 to **12.00**

Cotton, white w/modern Battenburg lace, from $5 to **12.00**

Cotton (multicolor w/embroidery), set of 3 in gift package, from $15 to **20.00**

Cotton applique & embroidery, Made in China tag, 1950s, from $5 to **12.00**

Cotton lawn w/Madeira work, from $10 to **18.00**

Cotton w/applique hemstitching, rolled hem, from $10 to .**18.00**

Cotton w/cutwork trim or narrow tatted edge, from $7 to...**15.00**

Cotton w/embroidered florals, from $9 to **15.00**

Cotton w/embroidered monogram & trim, crochet edge, from $7 to **15.00**

Cotton w/green & black Deco design, plain rolled hem, from $10 to **18.00**

Cotton w/hand-embroidered design, 1920s, from $5 to **12.00**

Cotton w/printed floral pattern, 1940s-50s, from $5 to.....**12.00**

Irish linen w/colored crochet trim, from $5 to **15.00**

Lawn, white, hemstitched w/fine hairpin lace, from $25 to...............................**55.00**

Linen, pink, filet lace butterfly on 1 corner, from $25 to......**55.00**

Linen, white w/Battenburg-type lace & butterfly corners, 1900s, from $65 to..........**85.00**

Linen (fine) w/Madeira work, hemstitching & embroidery, from $10 to **15.00**

Machine-made lace, ivory, from $5 to **12.00**

Pongee silk, embroidered trim, from $5 to **15.00**

Princess lace, ecru, on net background, from $25 to **55.00**

Printed cotton, 1959 calendar, scalloped edges, from $10 to **30.00**

Printed cotton, 1961 calendar w/autos, from $10 to **30.00**

Silk, aqua, deep embroidered sheer silk border, 14" sq, from $15 to **25.00**

Silk, colored, embroidered floral & eyelet work, from $10 to **18.00**

Silk commemorative, printed American/British flags, 17" sq, from $20 to...............**40.00**

Silk georgette, peach, hand-painted floral, original tag, 9½" sq..........................**15.00**

Silk georgette w/delicate ecru lace, 16" sq, from $15 to **25.00**

Silk w/delicate embroidered flowers, orig '100% Silk' tag, from $10 to **20.00**

Silk w/machine lace & embroidered: Souvenir of France, WWI era, from $15 to **20.00**
Wedding, fine lawn w/wide machine-lace border, ca 1900, 17", from $25 to.............**35.00**

Harker

One of the oldest potteries in the East Liverpool, Ohio, area, the Harker company produced many lines of dinnerware from the late 1920s until it closed around 1970. Refer to *A Collector's Guide to Harker Pottery* by Neva W. Colbert (Collector Books) for more information.

Amy, plate, dinner................**10.00**
Basket of Flowers, bowl, vegetable.............................**15.00**
Cactus, pie baker...................**25.00**
Carnivale, salad fork server.**20.00**
Chesterton (Pink Cocoa), plate, 6".....................................**5.00**
Cock O'Morn, platter, Olympic..**14.00**
Crayon Apples, batter jug.....**25.00**
Dainty Flower, swirl cup......**10.00**

Deco Dahlia, Pie baker, 10", $25.00; Server, $22.00. (Photo courtesy Jo Cunningham)

Dogwood, plate, luncheon.......**8.00**

English Ivy, bowl, mixing.....**40.00**
Gladiola, bowl, mixing..........**40.00**
Holly & Berries, plate, luncheon..**8.00**
Lovelace, cake lifter..............**13.00**
Old Carriages, plate, dinner.**10.00**
Petit Point, rolling pin........**120.00**
Red & Black Lines, teapot, Cameoware shape (squashed sides)...............................**25.00**
Republic, shaving mug, pastel roses...............................**30.00**
Rosebud, shakers, Skyscraper, pr...................................**22.00**
Spanish Gold, plate, luncheon..**25.00**
Vintage, platter.....................**11.00**
Winter Asters, plate, dinner...**15.00**

Hartland

Hartland Plastics Inc. of Hartland, Wisconsin, produced a line of Western and Historic Horsemen and Standing Gunfighter figures during the 1950s, which are now very collectible. Using a material called virgin acetate, they molded such well-known characters as Annie Oakley, Bret Maverick, Matt Dillon, and many others, which they painted with highest attention to detail. In addition to these, they made a line of sports greats as well as religious statues.

Our advisor for sports figures is James Watson; he is listed in the Directory under New York.

Gunfighter, Bat Masterson, NMIB **500.00**
Gunfighter, Bret Maverick, NM........................**150.00**

Gunfighter, Chris Colt, NM ..**150.00**
Gunfighter, Clay Holister, NM ..**225.00**
Gunfighter, Dan Troop, NM...**500.00**
Gunfighter, Jim Hardy, NM..**150.00**
Gunfighter, Johnny McKay, NM **800.00**
Gunfighter, Paladin, NM....**400.00**
Gunfighter, Vint Bonner, w/tag, NMIB...........................**650.00**
Gunfighter, Wyatt Earp, NM **150.00**
Horseman, Annie Oakley, NM ..**275.00**
Horseman, Brave Eagle, NMIB..**300.00**
Horseman, Cochise, NM **150.00**
Horseman, Dale Evans, purple, NM...............................**250.00**
Horseman, Gil Favor, prancing, NM...............................**650.00**

Horseman, Lone Ranger, NM, $150.00.

Horseman, Matt Dillon, w/tag, NMIB...........................**300.00**
Horseman, Rifleman, NMIB .**350.00**
Horseman, Roy Rogers, walking, NMIB...........................**300.00**
Horseman, Tom Jeffords, NM..**175.00**
Sports figure, Babe Ruth, NM/M, $175 to **200.00**

Sports figure, Don Drysdale, NM/M, $325 to **400.00**
Sports figure, Duke Snider, M, $500 to **600.00**
Sports figure, Ernie Banks, NM/M, $250 to **350.00**
Sports figure, Henry Aaron, NM/M, $200 to **250.00**
Sports figure, Mickey Mantle, NM/M, $250 to **350.00**

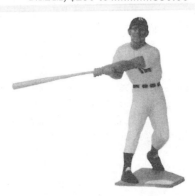

Sports figure, Roger Maris, NM/M, from $350.00 to $400.00. (Photo courtesy R. Craig Raycraft)

Sports figure, Stan Musial, NM/M, $200 to **250.00**
Sports figure, Ted Williams, NM/M, $225 to **300.00**
Sports figure, Willie Mays, NM/M, $225 to **250.00**

Head Vases

Many of them Japanese imports, head vases were made primarily for the florist trade. They were styled as children, teenagers, clowns, and famous people. There are heads of religious figures, Blacks, Orientals, and even some animals. One of the most common types are ladies wearing pearl earrings and necklaces. Refer to *Head Vases, Identification and Value Guide,* by Kathleen Cole (Collector Books) for more information. See Clubs and Newsletters for information concerning the *Head Hunter's Newsletter.*

Baby, Enesco, #2185, w/telephone, ruffled bonnet, pearl necklace, 5" **45.00**

Baby, Replo, #2013, scalloped bonnet & collar, pink & white, 6"........................**50.00**

Baby, VCAGCO (paper label), head tilted, blue bow atop head, 6"...........................**50.00**

Boy, praying, Inarco, #E978, 5"...**40.00**

Boy, unmarked, freckled face, plaid bodice w/real ribbon bow, 7" **45.00**

Boy fireman, Inarco (paper label), holding hose nozzle, 5"...**75.00**

Boy Indian, Inarco, #E3155, in chief's headdress, eyes closed, 5½"...................................**40.00**

Boy soldier, Inarco, #E3250, eyes closed, black w/red & white trim, 6" **50.00**

Clown, Napco, #IH-2243, hand w/finger pointing up, gold trim, 6¼" **50.00**

Geisha girl, unmarked, fan to mouth, head decor, gold eyelashes, 5" **40.00**

Girl, Inarco, #E2520, hat, eyes open, 6½".......................**50.00**

Girl, Inarco, #E2965, pigtails & scarf, glancing eyes, gold trim, 7" **60.00**

Girl, Inarco, #E3157, side-swept hair w/daisy, eyes open, 5½"...................**45.00**

Girl, Nancy Pew, #2262, mod hat w/bow above bill, long hair, 5½"...............................**75.00**

Girl, praying, Inarco, #E1579, 6" **45.00**

Glamour girl, unmarked, shoulder to chin, white, gold features, 6½"...................................**23.00**

Graduate girl, unmarked, #609, glancing eyes, open mouth, hair bow, 5" **40.00**

Lady, Art Deco, Japan, #KKS230A, looking up, wide hat, white, 7½"..............**30.00**

Lady, Inarco, #E1062, colonial, gloved hand w/fan to cheek, curls, 6"...........................**60.00**

Lady, Inarco, #E1066, hat, rose on bow on bodice, gold trim, 4½" **65.00**

Lady, Inarco, #E190/M, hat, hand to chin, upswept hair, gold trim, 5" **50.00**

Lady, Inarco, #E195, poinsettia on hat, gold trim, 4½".........**65.00**

Lady, Inarco, #E2966, frosted upswept hair, scalloped bodice, 11" **450.00**

Lady, Napco, #C3282A, feather hat, hand to cheek, gold trim, 6"....................................**50.00**

Lady, Napcoware, #C569, hat w/row of cut-out circles, hand to face, 5".......................**50.00**

Lady, Orion (paper label), hat, head tilted, eyes closed, 6½" **45.00**

Lady, Parma, #A219, frosted hair w/side flip, eyes open, 8½".....................................**300.00**

Lady, Relpo, #A-1229, pillbox, gloved hands to tilted face, 6½" **65.00**

Lady, Relpo, #K1175L, pillbox, chin on clasped hands, 6½" **75.00**

Lady, Relpo, #K1335, long white curls, ruffled bodice with bow and gold trim, 8", $160.00. (Photo courtesy Kathleen Cole)

Lady, Rubens, #497M, hair rose, leaf bodice, gold/pearl trim, 6½" **60.00**

Lady, Rubens, #499B, straw hat, ponytail, gold/pearl trim, 6" **70.00**

Lady, Rubens, #501, head turned, upswept hair w/braided crown, 6½" **50.00**

Lady, VCAGCO (paper label), scarf, head tilted, sq bodice, 6" **55.00**

Madonna, Royal Windsor, praying, blue & white, 8" **48.00**

Majorette, unmarked, open eyes & wide open-mouth smile, gold trim, 6" **150.00**

Nun, Napco (paper label), praying hands, black & white, 5½" ..**28.00**

Southern Belle, Acme Ware, bonnet w/lg chin bow, gold trim, 6" **50.00**

Teen girl, Inarco, #E2967, blond flip w/head band, eyes open, 5½" **65.00**

Teen girls, Inarco, #E3143, 7½", and United Import (on paper label), 7½", $250.00 each. (Photo courtesy Kathleen Cole)

Teen girl, Inarco, #E6211, eyes open, bodice w/high ruffled collar, 5" **55.00**

Teen girl, Lark, #JN-4113, eyes open, short hair w/ribbon bow, 7" **150.00**

Holly Hobbie and Friends

About 1970 a young homemaker and mother, Holly Hobbie, approached the American Greeting Company with some charming country-styled drawings of children. Since that time over four hundred items have been made with almost all being marked HH, H. Hobbie, or Holly Hobbie.

Our advisor for this category is Helen McCale; she is listed in the Directory under Missouri.

Doll, Holly Hobbie, Amy, Carrie, Heather, Knickerbocker, 6", MIB, ea **10.00**

Doll, Holly Hobbie, stuffed cloth with vinyl head and hands, Knickerbocker, 9", M, $10.00. (Photo courtesy Helen McCale)

Doll, Holly Hobbie, Amy, Carrie, Heather, Knickerbocker, 9", MIB, ea **15.00**

Doll, Holly Hobbie, Amy, Carrie, Heather, Knickerbocker, 16", MIB, ea **25.00**

Doll, Holly Hobbie, Amy, Carrie, Heather, Knickerbocker, 27", MIB, ea **35.00**

Doll, Holly Hobbie, Amy, Carrie, Heather, Knickerbocker, 33", MIB, ea **45.00**

Doll, Holly Hobbie, scented, ornament around neck, 1988, 18", NRFB **40.00**

Doll, Holly Hobbie (Bicentennial), Knickerbocker, 12", MIB **30.00**

Doll, Holly Hobbie (Country Fun), 1989, 16", NRFB **25.00**

Doll, Holly Hobbie (Day 'N Night), Knickerbocker, 14", MIB..**20.00**

Doll, Holly Hobbie (Dream Along), any, Knickerbocker, 9", MIB, ea **15.00**

Doll, Holly Hobbie (Dream Along), any, Knickerbocker, 12", MIB, ea **20.00**

Doll, Holly Hobbie (Grandma), Knickerbocker, 14", MIB..**20.00**

Doll, Holly Hobbie (Grandma), Knickerbocker, 24", MIB..**30.00**

Doll, Holly Hobbie (Little Girl), Knickerbocker, 1980, 15", MIB **30.00**

Doll, Holly Hobbie (Talker), 16", MIB **30.00**

Doll, Holly Hobbie (25th Anniversary), Meritus, 1994, 26", MIB, $45 to....................**55.00**

Doll, Robby, Knickerbocker, 9", MIB **20.00**

Doll, Robby, Knickerbocker, 16", MIB **30.00**

Doll house, M **300.00**

Sewing Machine, battery-op, Durham, 1975, 5x9", EX.**40.00**

Sing-A-Long Electric Parlor Player, Vanity Fair, 1970s, NMIB **45.00**

Holt Howard

Ceramic novelty items marked Holt Howard are hot! From the late 1950s, collectors search for the pixie kitchenware items such as cruets, condiments, etc., all with flat, disk-like pixie heads for stoppers. In the 1960s the company designed and distributed a line of roosters — egg cups, napkin holders, salt and pepper shakers, etc. Items with a Christmas theme featuring Santa or angels, for instance, were sold from the 1950s through the 1970s, and you'll also find a line of white cats collectors call Kozy Kitten. Most pieces are not only marked but dated as well.

Our advisors for this category are Pat and Ann Duncan, who are listed in the Directory under Missouri.

Bartender theme, cocktail shaker w/4 tumblers **75.00**
Bride & Groom, candle holders, 4", pr **50.00**
Bull, planter, figural, white w/ring in nose **35.00**
Christmas, butter pats, holly leaves & berries, set of 4, 2¾" **32.00**
Christmas, candelabra, Santa trio, packages hold candles, 5x8" **60.00**
Christmas, candle holders, camel figures, 4", pr..................**50.00**
Christmas, candle holders, cowboy Santa in coach w/gifts, 3x4", pr.....................................**42.00**
Christmas, candle huggers, snowman in Christmas tree hats, pr, $30 to **35.00**

Christmas, Cookie/candy jar, Santa, three-piece, hard to find, $250.00. (Photo courtesy Pat and Ann Duncan)

Christmas, dish, Santa face, 7¼x5½"...........................**42.00**
Christmas, match holder, Santa w/bongo drum, 4½" **30.00**

Christmas, place-card holders/figurines, elves, set of 4, 3" .**55.00**
Christmas, salt & pepper shakers, angel figures, 3½", pr.....**22.00**
Christmas, salt & pepper shakers, 2 stacked gifts, pr...........**15.00**
Christmas, snack set, Santa waving on plate, red cup, 8½".......**28.00**
Christmas, tray, Santa, beard forms tray, 7¾", $25 to ..**30.00**
Christmas, tree, bottle-brush style w/fruit, foil ornaments/birds, 15"...................................**40.00**
Christmas, tree, electric, 10" .**70.00**
Christmas, votive candle holder, Santa, dated 1968, 3".....**20.00**
Coin Kitty, bank, bobbing head, $100 to **135.00**
Dandy Lion, bank, bobbing head, $100 to **135.00**
Golfer, ashtray, figural, 5½"...**95.00**
Goose & Golden Egg, salt & pepper shakers, pr **40.00**
Hamburger, mustard jar, hamburger-head finial, 5½"..**85.00**
Honey Bunnies, candle climbers, w/bases, set of 4 ....**50.00**
Hot Stuff, super scooper, red & white, w/lid, 6" **50.00**
Jeeves the Butler, martini shaker, 9"...................................**200.00**
Jeeves the Butler, tray, 4¾"..**150.00**
Kozy Kitten, ashtray, cat on sq plaid base, 4 corner rests, $60 to **75.00**
Kozy Kitten, cleanser shaker, lady cat figure in apron w/broom **125.00**
Kozy Kitten, cookie jar, head form, $40 to **50.00**
Kozy Kitten, memo finder, full-bodied cat, legs cradle pad, $100 to **125.00**

Kozy Kitten, salt & pepper shakers, tall cats, pr **45.00**

Kozy Kitten, spice shaker, cat head w/loop atop for hanging, 2½x3" **35.00**

Kozy Kitten, tape measure, cat on cushion **85.00**

Kozy Kitten, wall pocket, cat's head, $60 to **75.00**

Nixon, mug, face on currency ...**60.00**

Nursery Rhymes, mug, footed, verse printed in wide graphic band................................**25.00**

Pig, votive candle holder, pastel, dated 1958, 5½" **45.00**

Pixie Ware, cocktail cherries, $175 to **200.00**

Pixie Ware, cocktail onions, onion-head finial, $160 to **175.00**

Pixie Ware, decanter, Whiskey, winking head stopper, minimum value **225.00**

Pixie Ware, dish, flat-head handle, pickle nose, minimum value............................**100.00**

Pixie Ware, instant coffee jar, blond-headed finial, minimum value **250.00**

Pixie Ware, Italian dressing bottle, from $160 to **175.00**

Pixie Ware, jam & jelly jar, flat-headed finial on lid **75.00**

Pixie Ware, mustard jar, yellow head finial on lid, from $75 to................................**100.00**

Pixie Ware, oil & vinegar cruets, Sally & Sam, pr, minimum value **250.00**

Pixie Ware, onion jar, flat onion-head finial, on lid, 1958 ....**200.00**

Pixie Ware, relish jar, green flat head on lid....................**200.00**

Pixie Ware, Russian dressing bottle, from $165 to...........**175.00**

Pixie Ware, towel hook, flat head w/sm loop hanger, minimum value **200.00**

Ponytail Princess, candle holder, figure-8 platform, $50 to..**60.00**

Ponytail Princess, lipstick holder, $50 to **65.00**

Ponytail Princess, salt & pepper shakers, pr **45.00**

Ponytail Princess, tray, girl between 2 flower cups, $50 to **65.00**

Poodle & Cat, salt & pepper shakers, 4"-4½", pr................**40.00**

Rake 'N Spade, plate, MIB ...**20.00**

Rock 'N Roll Kids, salt & pepper shakers, bobbin' heads, pr **125.00**

Rooster, ashtray/tea-bag holders, set of 4, $35 to **40.00**

Rooster, bowl, cereal; 6"........**12.00**

Rooster, bud vase, figural, $25 to **30.00**

Rooster, butter dish, embossed, ¼-lb **65.00**

Rooster, coffeepot, embossed .**65.00**

Rooster, Cigarette holder, wooden, $150.00; Recipe box, wooden, from $75.00 to $100.00; Pitcher, cylindrical, no handle, $50.00. (Photo courtesy Pat and Ann Duncan)

Rooster, egg cup, double; figural **25.00**

Rooster, mustard jar, embossed, w/lid **35.00**

Rooster, pincushion, 3¼x4", $50 to **65.00**

Rooster, pitcher, syrup; embossed, tail handle **30.00**

Rooster, pitcher, water; flaring sides, tail handle, tall, $45 to....................................**50.00**

Rooster, recipe box, wood w/painted decor, from $75 to ...**100.00**

Rooster, spoon rest, figural, $15 to **20.00**

Rooster, tray, facing left **20.00**

Rooster, trivet, tile w/rooster in iron framework **40.00**

Tiger, salt & pepper shakers, big smile, 3½", pr **25.00**

Watermelon, bowl, rind exterior, pink interior w/seeds, 2½x6" **40.00**

Whale, pencil sharpener, figural, sharpener in mouth, 3¾"..**55.00**

Homer Laughlin

The Homer Laughlin China Company has produced millions of pieces of dinnerware, toiletry items, art china, children's dishes, and hotel ware since its inception in 1874. On most pieces the backstamp includes company name, date, and plant where the piece was produced, and nearly always the shape name is included. We have listed samples from many of the decaled lines; some of the more desirable patterns will go considerably higher. Refer to *The Collector's Encyclopedia of Homer Laughlin China* by Joanne Jasper; *Homer Laughlin China Company, A Giant Among Dishes,* by Jo Cunningham; and *The Collector's Encyclopedia of Fiesta, Ninth Edition,* by Sharon and Bob Huxford.

Our advisor for this category is Darlene Nossaman; she is listed in the Directory under Texas. See Clubs and Newsletters for information concerning *The Laughlin Eagle,* a newsletter for collectors of Homer Laughlin dinnerware. See also Fiesta.

Brittany Shape
(available in Lady Alice, Emerald, Sylvan, and Hemlock)

Bowl, deep, 5" **15.00**

Creamer................................**14.00**

Pickle dish **10.00**

Plate, 6" **6.00**

Platter, 11½" **18.00**

Sauce boat **24.00**

Sugar bowl, w/lid..................**20.00**

Cavalier Shape
(available in Berkshire, Crinoline, Jade Rose, and Turquoise Melody)

Bowl, cereal/soup; Charm House ..**10.00**

Casserole, w/lid **50.00**

Plate, 10" **14.00**

Sugar bowl, w/lid..................**22.00**

Tea cup **10.00**

Tea saucer **5.00**

Teapot....................................**65.00**

Debutante Shape
(available in Blue Mist, Champagne, Gray Laurel, and Wild Grapes)

Chop plate, 15" **20.00**

Covered sugar bowl, from $12.00 to $18.00 (in Wild Grapes pattern). (Photo courtesy Joanne Jasper)

Egg cup, double	15.00
Pie server	30.00
Plate, 10"	9.00
Platter, 11"	16.00
Salt & pepper shakers, pr	15.00
Teapot	45.00

Empress Shape, early 1900s
(available in Flying Bluebirds, Pink Moss Rose, Rose & Lattice, Garland Gold Garland Border)

Baker, 7"	16.00
Bowl, fruit; 6"	8.00
Cake plate, 10"	20.00
Creamer, 5-oz	15.00
Nappy, 8"	18.00
Plate, 10"	12.00
Sugar bowl, w/lid, 4"	22.00
Tea cup	8.00

Kwaker Shape, 1920s
(available in Dream Poppy, Vestal Rose, Vandemere, and Presidental)

Bowl, deep, 6-oz	14.00
Bowl, oatmeal, 6"	8.00

Casserole, w/lid	50.00
Celery tray, 11"	24.00
Cream soup	18.00
Jug, 24s, 3⅛-pt	45.00
Plate, 7"	8.00
Platter, 17"	40.00

Liberty Shape
(available in Calirose, Dogwood, Greenbrier, and Stratford)

Baker, oval	24.00
Bowl, deep, 5"	10.00
Bowl, fruit	7.00
Casserole, w/lid	65.00
Plate, 9"	10.00
Sugar bowl	16.00
Teapot	75.00

Nautilus Regular Shape, 1930s
(available in Cardinal, Colonial, Old Curiosity Shop, and Magnolia)

Baker, oval, 9"	20.00
Bowl, fruit	6.00
Casserole, w/lid	60.00
Cup, after dinner	20.00
Mug, Baltimore	22.00
Plate, 10"	13.00
Saucer, after dinner	8.00

Newell: 1927 Design
(available in Yellow Glow, Puritan, Song of Spring, Southern Pride, and Poppy)

Baker, 10"	24.00
Bowl, deep, 1⅛-pt	15.00
Bowl, oyster; 1¼-pt	20.00
Jug, 42s, 1-pt	26.00
Nappy, 9"	22.00
Pickle dish, handled	16.00
Plate, coupe; 8"	10.00

Republic Shape
(available in Jean, Calais, Priscilla, and Wayside)

Baker, 10" **24.00**
Bone dish **12.00**
Butter dish, w/lid **75.00**
Cup, after dinner **18.00**
Plate, 6" **7.00**
Sauce boat **30.00**
Sugar bowl **24.00**

Rhythm Shape
(available in Allegro, Daybreak, Rybaiyat, and Something Blue)

Bowl, coupe soup **12.00**
Jug, 2-qt **35.00**
Plate, 8" **8.00**
Platter, 11½" **20.00**
Sauce boat **22.00**
Sauce-boat stand **8.00**
Tidbit tray **45.00**

Swing Shape
(available in Blue Flax, Chinese Three, Moss Rose, and Pate Sur Pate)

Bowl, oatmeal **10.00**
Casserole, w/lid **55.00**
Coffeepot, after dinner **55.00**
Cream soup **25.00**
Creamer **18.00**
Plate, rim soup **13.00**
Utility tray **22.00**

Virginia Rose, 1930
(available in pink Wild Rose, Rose & Daisy, Patrician, Nosegay; add 20% for JJ59 and VR128)

Bowl, coupe soup **22.00**

Bread plate, rare **40.00**
Creamer **16.00**
Nappy, 9" **25.00**
Plate, 10" **22.00**
Plate, 6" **8.00**
Platter, 11½" **26.00**

Wells, 1930
(available in Flight of the Swallows, Cosmos, Flowers of the Dell, Gold Stripe, and Hollyhock)

Bouillon **14.00**
Bowl, deep, 6" **18.00**
Egg cup, double **22.00**
Muffin cover **75.00**
Plate, chop **28.00**
Plate, 6" **7.00**
Sauce boat **25.00**

Yellowstone, 1927
(available in Moss Rose, Poppy Pastel, Golden Rose, Buttercup, and Floral Spray)

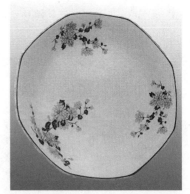

Coupe soup plate (Golden Rose pattern), 7", from $6.00 to $8.00. (Photo courtesy Joanne Jasper)

Cup, after dinner **18.00**
Grape fruit **15.00**
Relish dish **20.00**

Saucer, after dinner 8.00
Sugar bowl, individual.........16.00
Tea saucer 4.00
Teacup 8.00

Hot Wheels

An instant success in 1968, Hot Wheels are known for there racy style and custom paint jobs. Kids loved them for the fact that they were the fastest model cars on the market. Keeping up with new trends in the big car industry, Hot Wheels also included futuristic vehicles, muscle cars, trucks, hot rods, racers, and some military vehicles. A lot of these can still be found for very little, but if you want to buy the older models (collectors call them 'Red Lines' because of their red sidewall tires), its going to cost you a little more, though many can still be found under $25.00. By 1971, earlier on some models, black-wall tires had become standard.

Though recent re-releases have dampened the collector market somewhat, cars mint in the original packages are holding their values and still moving well. Near-mint examples (no package) are worth about 50% to 60% less than those mint and still in their original package, excellent condition about 65% to 75% less.

'40s Woody, 1980s, black walls, turquoise w/black fenders, MOC 10.00

'56 Flahsider Pickup, 1990s, black walls, turquoise, MOC...........................5.00
Air France Delivery Truck, 1990, black walls, white, MOC..10.00
Alive '55, 1973, red line, plum, EX+..............................120.00
Beatnik Bandit, 1968, red line, creamer pink, VG...........25.00
Blazer 4x4, 1990, black walls, blue, MOC......................12.00
Boss Hoss, 1971, red line, metallic aqua, #2 tampo, M.........20.00

Captain America Hot Bird, 1979, red, white, and blue, NM, $25.00. (Photo courtesy June Moon)

Cadillac Seville, 1983, black walls, metal-flake gold, M..........5.00
Classic '35 Caddy, 1982, black walls, tan w/brown interior, M 6.00
Classic Cobra, 1990s, black walls, red, MOC.........................5.00
Classic Nomad, 1970, red line, metallic green, NM 55.00
Classic Nomad, 1970, red line, red, MOC.......................55.00
Corvette Stingray, 1988, black walls, yellow w/multicolored tampo, MOC.....................5.00
Custom Barracuda, 1968, red line, metallic aqua, NM 70.00
Custom Cougar, 1968, red line, metallic orange, MIP ...325.00

Custom Dodge Charger, 1969, red line, red, MOC..............**100.00**

Custom Mustang, 1968, red line, ice blue, NM.................**100.00**

Custom T-Bird, 1968, red line, gold, rare color, NM.....**100.00**

Double Demon, 1990, black walls, lime green, MOC..............**5.00**

Emergency Squad, 1977, black walls, red, M (EX card)....**8.00**

Ford Mk IV, 1969, red line, metallic blue w/black interior, NM..........................**20.00**

Fuel Tanker, 1971, red line, white, EX........................**35.00**

Goodyear Blimp, MOC.............**5.00**

Heavy Chevy, 1970, red line, olive, #7 tampo, rare color, EX+.....**150.00**

Ice T, 1971, red line, yellow w/black interior, EX.......**20.00**

Jet Threat II, 1976, red line, plum w/yellow tampo, MOC....**65.00**

King Kuda, 1970, red line, blue w/#1 tampo, NM..............**50.00**

Lamborghini Countach, 1990s, black walls, red, MOC.....**5.00**

Limozeen, black walls, metalflake blue, MOC...............**6.00**

Mantis, 1970, red line, metallic green, NM.......................**35.00**

Mazed MX5, 1991, black walls, MOC.................................**4.00**

Mercedes C-11, 1972, red line, metallic blue w/cream interior, NM..........................**120.00**

Mercedes 280SL, 1973, red line, red w/gray interior, EX.................................**65.00**

Mighty Maverick, 1970, red line, metallic pink, rare, NM.**100.00**

Mongoose, 1970, red line, red w/original cage & prop, NM...........................**20.00**

Monster Vette, 1980s, black walls, purple, MOC...................**15.00**

Motorcross I, 1975, red line, red w/yellow & black tampo, NM.............................**100.00**

Mustang Stocker, 1975, red line, yellow, rare red & blue tampo, EX.....................**125.00**

Nissan Custom Z, 1990s, black walls, metallic red, MOC.**5.00**

No Fear F1 Racer, 1990s, black walls, MOC........................**5.00**

Odd Job, 1973, red line, light blue w/black interior, NM....**150.00**

Paramedic, 1975, red line, white w/red & yellow tampo, MOC...............**65.00**

Peeping Bomb, 1970, red line, metallic orange, M.........**65.00**

Porsche 930, 1991, black walls, red w/multicolored tampo, M.**4.00**

Proper Chopper, 1993, black walls, MOC......................**5.00**

Prowler, 1978, Super Chromes series, NM, $16.00. (Photo courtesy June Moon)

Range Rover, 1991, black walls, white, Getty promotion, MOC...............................**4.00**

Rigor Motor, 1992, black walls, metallic red, MOC...........**5.00**

Rock Buster, 1976, red line, yellow w/multicolored tampo, NM................................**30.00**

Seaside, 1970, red line, metallic yellow w/black interior, NM.**80.00**

Short Order, 1971, red line, blue, rare color, MOC..............**60.00**

Side Kick, 1972, red line, light metallic green, EX.........**45.00**

Snake II, 1971, red line, white, NM..................................**40.00**

Sol-Aire CX4, 1990s, black walls, blue, MOC **5.00**

Splittin' Image, 1969, red line, metallic green, M...........**60.00**

Staff Car, 1976, red line, olive w/white tampo, rare, NM .**125.00**

Street Roader Suzuki 4x4, 1990s, black walls, white, MOC..**5.00**

Street Snorter, 1973, red line, flourescent pink, EX......**50.00**

T-4-2, 1971, red line, metallic green, scarce color, M **35.00**

TNT Bird, 1970, red line, metallic blue w/#3 tampo, NM **25.00**

Tough Customer, 1975, red line, olive w/white Army tampo, MOC **60.00**

Trailbuster, 1990s, black walls, turquoise w/hot pink interior, MOC **4.00**

Troop Convoy, olive, MOC..**100.00**

Twin Mill, 1969, red line, metallic blue, EX...........................**35.00**

Vampyra, 1990s, black walls, black, MOC........................**5.00**

Winnipeg, 1974, red line, yellow w/blue & orange tampo, M.**130.00**

Zombot, 1990s, black walls, MOC **5.00**

Hull

Established in Zanesville, Ohio, in 1905, Hull manufactured stoneware, florist ware, art pottery, and tile until about 1935, when they began to produce the lines of pastel matt-glazed artware which are today very collectible. The pottery was destroyed by flood and fire in 1950. The factory was rebuilt and equipped with the most modern machinery which they soon discovered was not geared to duplicate the matt glazes. As a result, new lines — Parchment and Pine, and Ebb Tide, for example — were introduced in a glossy finish. During the '40s and into the '50s, their kitchenware and novelty lines were very successful. Refer to *Roberts' Ultimate Encyclopedia of Hull Pottery* and *The Companion Guide,* both by Brenda Roberts (Walsworth Publishing), for more information. Brenda also has authored a third book, *The Collector's Encyclopedia of Hull Pottery,* which is published by Collector Books.

Bow-Knot, bell, loop handle, 6" ..**375.00**

Calla Lily, vase, angle handles, #550/33, 7½", from $165.00 to $200.00.
(Photo courtesy Brenda Roberts)

Butterfly, ewer, #B-11, 8¾"..**175.00**

Calla Lily, console bowl, #590/33, 4x13".............**210.00**

Capri, basket, #48, 12¼".......**75.00**

Capri, swan planter, #23, 8½"......**60.00**

Continental, basket, #55, 12¾"...**175.00**

Continental, bud vase, #66, 9½"...**40.00**

Dogwood, cornucopia, #522, 3¾"..............**125.00**

Dogwood, vase, #513, 6½"...**150.00**

Early Art, jardiniere, #546, 7"...**135.00**

Early Art, vase, #39, 8".......**150.00**

Ebb Tide, candle holder, #E-13, 2¾"................**35.00**

Ebb Tide, ewer, #E-10, 14".**225.00**

Fiesta, flower pot, #40, 4½"..**30.00**

Imperial, window box, #82, 12½"...........**35.00**

Iris, basket, #408, 7"..........**325.00**

Iris, candle holder, #411, 5"..**130.00**

Iris, rose bowl, #412, 7"......**200.00**

Magnolia, gloss; basket, #H-14, 10½".............**400.00**

Magnolia, gloss; teapot, #20, 6½"...........**200.00**

Magnolia, matt; candle holder, #27, 4"...........**65.00**

Magnolia, matt; double cornu-copia, #6, 12"...............**225.00**

Mardi Gras/Granada, basket, #32, 8"......................**200.00**

Mardi Gras/Granada, ewer, #63, 10½".............**550.00**

Novelty, figurine, rooster, #951, 7".................**65.00**

Novelty, planter, giraffe, #115, 8"...................**65.00**

Novelty, planter, girl w/basket, #954, 8"...........**45.00**

Novelty, planter, kitten, #61, 7½"..........**45.00**

Novelty, planter, lamb, #965, 8".................**45.00**

Open Rose, bud vase, #129, 7"........................**185.00**

Open Rose, hanging basket, #132, 7"...................**300.00**

Orchid, console bowl, #314, 13"..........**350.00**

Orchid, jardiniere, #310, 6"..**250.00**

Parchment & Pine, ashtray, #S-14, 14"..........**165.00**

Parchment & Pine, basket, #S-8, 16½" L..........**225.00**

Poppy, planter, #602, 6½"..**250.00**

Poppy, wall pocket, #609, 9"..**375.00**

Rosella, cornucopia, #R-13, 8½"..........**150.00**

Rosella, ewer, #R-9, 6½".......**95.00**

Serenade, candy dish, w/lid, #S3, 8¼".............**175.00**

Serenade, vase, #S4, 5¼"......**80.00**

Sueno, ewer, #109-33, 13"..**500.00**

Sueno, jardiniere, #115-33, 7"...**345.00**

Sunglow, bell, 6½", from $125.00 to $150.00.

Sunglow, casserole, w/lid, #51, 7½"..............**70.00**

Sunglow, flowerpot, #97, 5½"..**40.00**

Tropicana, vase, #54, 12½"...**500.00**

Tuscany, basket, #11, 10½"..**140.00**

Tuscany, candy dish, w/lid, #9, 8½"...............**125.00**

Water Lily, basket, #L-14, 10½"........................**400.00**

Water Lily, ewer, #L-3, 5½"..**100.00**

Water Lily, jardiniere, #L-23,
5½" **150.00**

Wildflower, cornucopia, #W-10,
8½" **185.00**

Wildflower (Number Series), vase,
#78, 8½" **325.00**

Woodland, matt; cornucopia, #W2,
5½" **100.00**

Woodland, two-tone; window box,
#W14, 10" **85.00**

Dinnerware

Avocado, butter dish, 7¾", from
$20 to **25.00**

Avocado, plate, dinner; 10¼"..**8.00**

Country Belle, platter, oval..**25.00**

Country Belle, souffle dish ...**29.00**

Country Squire, bowl, spaghetti;
10¼" **17.00**

Country Squire, plate, dinner;
10¼" **9.00**

Crestone, bowl, fruit; 6" **6.00**

Crestone, casserole, w/lid, 32-
oz **25.00**

Gingerbread Man, cookie jar,
brown..............................**125.00**

Gingerbread Man, server, brown,
10x10" **30.00**

Heartland, coffeepot...............**50.00**

Heartland, pitcher, 36-oz......**40.00**

Mirror Almond, bowl, 10¼", from
$25 to **30.00**

Mirror Almond, plate, 9⅜", from
$8 to **10.00**

Mirror Almond, steak plate, 11¾",
from $20 to **25.00**

Mirror Brown, baker, open, 3-pt,
from $15 to **20.00**

Mirror Brown, butter dish, ¼-lb,
from $20 to **25.00**

Mirror Brown, chip 'n dip, 11½",
from $45 to **65.00**

Mirror Brown, baker with chicken cover, #560, 11½x13½", $225.00. (Photo courtesy Brenda Roberts)

Mirror Brown, cookie jar, 94-oz,
from $30 to **45.00**

Mirror Brown, jug, 1-qt, from $25
to **35.00**

Mirror Brown, pie plate, 9¼",
from $18 to **24.00**

Mirror Brown, server, 10", from
$12 to **16.00**

Mirror Brown, steak plate, 14",
from $20 to **25.00**

Provencial, bowl, mixing; 6¾" ..**20.00**

Provencial, plate, salad; 6½"..**11.00**

Rainbow, mug, 9-oz, from $4 to.......**6.00**

Rainbow, plate, 10¼", from $8 to ..**10.00**

Ridge, creamer, any color **10.00**

Ridge, cup & saucer, any color..**10.00**

Ring, coffeepot, brown...........**50.00**

Ring, platter, oval, brown.....**18.00**

Tangerine, plate, salad; 6½"...**5.00**

Tangerine, teapot, 5-cup.......**30.00**

Indiana Carnival Glass

Though this glass looks old, it really isn't. It's very reminiscent of old Northwood carnival glass with its grape clusters and detailed leaves and vines, but this line was actually introduced in 1972! Made by the Indiana Glass Company,

Harvest (the pattern name assigned by the company) was produced in blue, lime green, and marigold. Although they made a few other carnival patterns in addition to this one, none are as collectible or as easy to recognize

This glassware is a little difficult to evaluate as there seems to be a wide range of 'asking' prices simply because some dealers are unsure of its age and therefore its value. If you like it, now is the time to buy it!

Harvest values given below are based on items in blue. Adjust them downward a price point or two for lime green and even a little more so for marigold. For further information we recommend *Garage Sale and Flea Market Annual* (Collector Books).

Iridescent Amethyst (Heritage)

Basket, footed, 9x5x7", from $35 to **40.00**
Candle holder, 5½", ea, from $20 to **25.00**
Goblet, 8-oz, from $15 to.......**20.00**
Punch set, 10" bowl & pedestal, 8 cups, w/ladle, 11-pc......**250.00**
Swung vase, slender & footed w/irregular rim, 11x3"..**35.00**

Iridescent Blue

Butter dish, Harvest, ¼-lb, 8" L, from $25 to **40.00**
Candy box, Harvest, laced edge, w/lid, 6½", from $20 to....................................**35.00**
Canister/candy jar, Harvest, 7".**30.00**

Canister/cookie jar, Harvest, 9", from $80 to..................................**150.00**
Cooler (iced tea tumbler), Harvest, 14-oz, ea from $10 to...........**15.00**
Garland bowl (comport), paneled, 7½x8½" dia, from $15 to..**20.00**
Hen on nest, from $15 to **25.00**
Plate, Bicentennial; American Eagle, from $10 to..........**15.00**
Punch set, Princess, 26-pc, from $100 to.........................**125.00**

Iridescent Gold

Basket, Monticello, lg faceted allover diamonds, sq, 7x6", from $30 to **35.00**
Egg/relish plate, 11", from $15 to..................................**35.00**
Hen on nest, 5½", from $10 to..**20.00**

Plate, Bicentennial; American Eagle, $10.00 (made in blue iridescent as well, same value).

Relish tray, Vintage, 6 sections, 9x12¾", from $15 to.......**18.00**
Wedding bowl (sm comport), 5x5", from $9 to **12.00**

Iridescent Lime

Compote, Harvest, embossed grapes, 7 x 6", from $15 to **20.00**

Cream and sugar bowl on tray, Harvest, embossed grapes, 3-pc, from $25 to **35.00**
Egg plate, 11", from $15 to ...**25.00**
Hen on nest, from $20 to **25.00**
Plate, hostess; allover diamond points, flared & crimped sides, 10", from $15 to ...**25.00**
Punch set, Princess, 26-pc, complete **125.00**
Salad set, Vintage, embossed fruit, apple-shaped rim w/applied stem, 13", w/fork & spoon, 3-pc, from $20 to **30.00**

Iridescent Sunset (Amberina)

Basket, squared, 9½x7½", from $50 to.............................**60.00**
Basket, 9x5x7", from $30 to..**50.00**
Bowl, crimped, 3¾x10", from $40 to....................................**50.00**
Butter dish, 5x7½" dia, from $35 to....................................**40.00**
Center bowl, 4¾x8½", from $40 to....................................**45.00**
Creamer & sugar bowl..........**40.00**
Dessert set, 8½" bowl, 12" plate, 2-pc, from $40 to **50.00**
Goblet, 8-oz, from $12 to.......**18.00**
Pitcher, 7¼", from $40 to......**55.00**
Pitcher, 8¼", from $40 to......**50.00**
Punch set, 10" bowl, pedestal, 8 cups, w/ladle, 11-pc, from $150 to .**225.00**
Rose bowl, 6½x6½", from $25 to ..**35.00**
Swung vase, slender, footed, w/irregular rim, 11x3" ...**65.00**
Tumbler, 3½", from $10 to....**15.00**

Japan Ceramics

Though Japanese ceramics

marked Nippon, Noritake, and Occupied Japan have long been collected, some of the newest fun-type collectibles on today's market are the figural ashtrays, pincushions, wall pockets, toothbrush holders, etc., that are marked 'Made in Japan' or simply 'Japan.' In her books called *Collector's Guide to Made in Japan Ceramics* (there are three in the series), Carole Bess White explains the pitfalls you will encounter when you try to determine production dates. Collectors refer to anything produced before WWII as 'old' and anything made after 1952 as 'new.' You'll find all you need to know to be a wise shopper in these books.

Our advisor for this category is Carole Bess White; she is listed in the Directory under Oregon. (Please enclose an SASE if you contact her.)

See also Black Cats; Blue Willow; Cat Collectibles; Egg Timers; Enesco; Fishbowl Ornaments; Flower Frogs; Geisha Girl; Head Vases; Holt Howard; Lefton; Moss Rose; Nippon; Noritake; Occupied Japan; Rooster and Roses; Sewing Items; Toothbrush Holders; Wall Pockets.

Ashtray, clown sits in middle of tray, prewar, from $75.00 to $125.00 (Photo courtesy Carol Bess White)

Ashtray, hand form, glossy white, 2¾", $12 to......................18.00

Ashtray, 3-sided horseshoes w/horsehead & suit of cubs, 4", $18 to.........................32.00

Bank, cat form, geometric Deco style, glossy blue, 4¼", $20 to.................................35.00

Bank, money-bag shape w/dollar symbol, gray lustre w/red trim, 4½".........................22.00

Basket, embossed flowers on blue lustre, white interior, 3", $18 to.....................................28.00

Bell, bust of Asian lady w/long black hair, blue top, glossy, 4½".................................40.00

Biscuit jar, fruits on basketweave, wrapped handle, 5"........45.00

Biscuit jar, round house w/wrapped handle, pale glossy colors, 8"..............60.00

Bonbon, frog on lily pad bowl, orange/tan/blue lustre, 4¾", $30 to...........................45.00

Bonbon, majolica-style w/twisted 2-branch handle, 4½......45.00

Bookends, dog & books, glossy green, pre-WWII, 3¾", pr, $22 to.................................35.00

Bookends, sailboat on angled wave, glossy colors, 4¾", pr, $30 to............................50.00

Bowl, angled w/scalloped rim, applied flowers & butterflies, 6½"..................................45.00

Cache pot, Big Bad Wolf beside house on base, glossy colors, 5"...................................20.00

Cache pot, pixie seated on upright leaves, glossy, 5¼", $20 to..35.00

Cache pot/cigarette holder, pig form, glossy colors, 2¾" .22.00

Candlesticks, trumpet form w/flowers & berries on blue, 7½", pr.........................145.00

Celery & salt set, shell-shaped, white lustre, 5-pc, 13", $55 to.................................85.00

Cigarette box, cowboy motif on glossy white, 5¼"..........45.00

Clown dish, fan collar, derby hat, glossy colors, 10" L, $25 to .55.00

Condiment set, boat w/shakers & pot, floral on white w/blue lustre...............................45.00

Condiment set, elephant pot carrying shakers, tan lustre, 3¾"...............................50.00

Condiment set, 3 wise monkeys w/tray, tan w/blue lustre, $60 to......................................90.00

Creamer & sugar bowl, elephants w/trunks up, Oriental w/tan lustre, pr........................65.00

Figurine, calico dog, glossy, 4½".............................20.00

Figurine, colonial couple w/man seated at mirrored vanity, 7½"...............................40.00

Figurine, lady skier, matt colors, 7¾"...............................58.00

Figurine, monkey on oval base scratching head, green, 5" .30.00

Figurine, pheasant, majolica style, glossy, 6", $35 to 55.00

Figurine set, musician trio, matt, 4¾", $35 to.....................50.00

Flower frog, rose bud on tan 6-sided base, blue lustre leaves, 2½"...............................25.00

Flowerpot, bluebirds & tulips on glossy yellow, 3½", $15 to..25.00

Flowerpot, Dutch girl scene on tapered sq pot w/saucer, 3½"...............................25.00

Flowerpot, elephants banded on ribbed bowl, yellow crackle, 4" **18.00**

Flowerpot, 3-sided footed Deco style w/colored design on blue, 6" W **45.00**

Hair receiver, roses w/cobalt trim, 2¼" **60.00**

Incense burner, man seated w/pipe in mouth, glossy, 4¼", $30 to **45.00**

Kitchen shakers, Salt/Sugar/Flour & flowers on sq basketweave, 5", ea **20.00**

Lamp, colonial couple by tree trunk in glossy white w/gold trim, 8" **35.00**

Lamp, owl form on leaf branch, blue & tan lustre, 2-pc, 5½", $60 to **95.00**

Leaf dish, 2 overlapping 2-tone green leaves w/gold handle, 7¾" **8.00**

Lemon server, lemon w/leaves & blossoms on blue lustre, gold trim, 6" **42.00**

Liquor flask, Life Preserver, w/bathing beauty, bisque, 4¾", $65 to....................**125.00**

Marmalade, strawberry form, glossy red w/green leaf lid, 4½" **25.00**

Mayonnaise set, cup/saucer/spoon, bird/blossoms on blue/tan lustre, 6" **60.00**

Pincushion, elephant, glossy white, post-1960, 2¼" **8.00**

Pincushion, sailor boy, painted bisque, 3¼", $23 to **33.00**

Pitcher, embossed scene on green w/black cat handle, glossy, 6¾"....................................**38.00**

Pitcher, horse form, glossy colors, 4"...................................**25.00**

Pitcher, palm tree motif on glossy orange w/tan lustre, 8½", $55 to...................................**115.00**

Powder box, clown seated on lid, glossy colors & cream, 5½", $35 to..............................**45.00**

Powder box, colonial lady holding up flower, glossy, 7", $150 to **185.00**

Relish dish, 3-part heart form w/floral finial, green crackle, 7½"...................................**25.00**

Ring/vanity box, flower basket motif on lid, blue/tan lustre, 1¾"...................................**20.00**

Salt & pepper shakers, calico cat, yellow & green on white, 3½", pr....................................**25.00**

Salt & pepper shakers, carrot form, glossy orange w/green, 4¼", pr **15.00**

Sauce cup/saucer, w/spout, flowers on blue/tan lustre, 3", $30 to **60.00**

Sewing set, candlestick phone w/sewing items, complete, 6½", $35 to....................**45.00**

Shoe, side buttons, blue & tan lustre w/orange trim, 5¾", $18 to **28.00**

Syrup pitcher/liner bowl, flowers on white, blue lustre trim, w/lid **60.00**

Pincushion, dog sits beside radio with cushion top, lustre glazes, 3", $38.00. (Photo courtesy Carol Bess White)

Teapot, floral motif on crackle, wrapped handle, 6¾", $35 to **62.00**

Teapot/tile, geometric form & motif, colors on white w/blue lustre, 8" **50.00**

Teapot/4 cups, tomato face, red-orange w/green at top, 5¾", $68 to **85.00**

Toast rack, arched 'bamboo' dividers on base, blue/tan lustre, 5¼" **50.00**

Vase, basket shape w/side handles, floral on blue & tan lustre, 3¾" **45.00**

Vase, bulbous w/stylized flowers & vase on pink crackle, 7¼"..**45.00**

Vase, column form w/white embossed sailboats on glossy blue, 7¾" **35.00**

Vase, frog pulling flower blossom cart, glossy colors w/tan lustre, 4" **35.00**

Vase, gate type w/3 birds between 2 tree-trunk vases, glossy, 8" **45.00**

Vase, sq w/flared top, island scene on yellow lustre, tan base, 7" **70.00**

Jewelry

Anyone interested in buying gems will soon find out that antique gems are the best values. Not only are prices from one-third to one-half less than on comparable new jewelry, but the older pieces display a degree of craftsmanship and styling seldom observed in modern-day jewelry. Costume jewelry from all periods is popular, especially Art Nouveau and Art Deco examples. Signed pieces are particularly good, such as those by Miriam Haskell, Eisenberg, Trifari, Hollycraft, and Weiss, among others.

There are some excellent reference books available if you'd like more information. Marcia 'Sparkles' Brown has written *Unsigned Beauties of Costume Jewelry;* Lilian Baker has written several: *Art Nouveau and Art Deco Jewelry; Twentieth Century Fashionable Plastic Jewelry; 50 Years of Collectible Fashion Jewelry;* and *100 Years of Collectible Jewelry.* Books by other authors include *Costume Jewelry* and *Collectible Silver Jewelry* by Fred Rezazadeh; *Collector's Encyclopedia of Hairwork Jewelry* by C. Jeanenne Bell, G.G.; *Collectible Costume Jewelry* by Cherri Simonds; *Christmas Pins* by Jill Gallina; and *Collecting Antique Stickpins* by Jack and 'Pet' Kerins. All are published by Collector Books. See Clubs and Newsletters for information on the Vintage Fashion & Costume Jewelry newsletter and club.

Bracelet, Boucher, gold-tone metal w/faux coral stones, $90 to .**125.00**

Bracelet, Ciner, black Bakelite & gilded brass links, 1950s, $135 to **150.00**

Bracelet, Eisenberg, flexible rhodium links w/rhinestones, 1960s **125.00**

Bracelet, Emmons, silver-tone lacy chain w/black opaque stones **30.00**

Bracelet, Kramer, single strand of clear rhinestones, $35 to .**50.00**

Bracelet, Napier, gold-plated flexible mesh w/faux jade stone at clasp **55.00**

Bracelet, Nettie Rosenstein, gold-tone w/pavé-set rhinestones, 1950s **125.00**

Bracelet, S Coventry, metal links & enamel grape leaves, $20 to **35.00**

Bracelet, Trifari, silver-tone Trifanium-plated pear-shaped links with pear-cut white iridescent plastic stones, 1960s, from $50.00 to $75.00. (Photo courtesy Cherri Simonds)

Brooch, Boucher, enameled fish form, 1955, $65 to **90.00**

Brooch, BSK, enameled autumn-tone leaf form, $45 to **60.00**

Brooch, BSK, gold-tone bird on perch w/faux ruby accents, 1950s, sm **35.00**

Brooch, BSK, gold-tone cat form w/faux gem eyes, 1960s .**35.00**

Brooch, Coro, gold-plated peacock w/enameling & rhinestones, 1950s..............................**65.00**

Brooch, Hobe, 3-D frog on lily pad, etched gold-tone, 2", from $75 to **95.00**

Brooch, JJ, owl form, jewel middle, $30 to **45.00**

Brooch, Kramer, gold-tone w/blue aurora borealis stones, 1960s, $45 to **65.00**

Brooch, Krementz, cultured pearls on flower form, $65 to **95.00**

Brooch, Mimi, silver-tone ribbon design w/rhinestones, 1960s, $65 to **85.00**

Brooch, S Coventry, rhodium abstract cushion type w/clear rhinestones.....................**65.00**

Brooch, silver musical note form, sm, $15 to **20.00**

Brooch, Trifari, rhodium fleur-de-lis w/cultured pearls, 1950s, $55 to **75.00**

Brooch, Weiss, rhinestones of various shapes, lg, $80 to..**120.00**

Brooch & earrings, Austrian, green chatons & green cabochon flat backs **50.00**

Brooch & earrings, Sherman, floral shape w/topaz rhinestones, $65 to **95.00**

Earrings, Chanel, clustered aurora borealis stones, 1950s, pr **20.00**

Earrings, Judy Lee, button-style with pearlized center surrounded by Austrian crystal rhinestones, simulated pearls and faceted beads, silver-tone filigree backings, 1950s, 1¾", from $60.00 to $80.00 for the pair. (Photo courtesy Cherri Simonds)

Earrings, Coro, aurora borealis stones, pr, $20 to **30.00**

Earrings, Coro, cluster of plastic flowers w/rhinestones, $40 to **75.00**

Earrings, Danecraft, sterling leaf shapes, pr **22.00**

Earrings, Eisenberg Ice, blue & pink imitation zircons, 1950s **65.00**

Earrings, Laguna, cut crystal drops, pr, $25 to **30.00**

Earrings, Lisner, leaf form w/rhinestones, pr, $15 to **25.00**

Earrings, Newhouse, clip style w/3-color rhinestones, pr, $30 to **45.00**

Earrings, Ora, rhinestone flowers, sm, pr.............................**35.00**

Earrings, Regency, blue iridescent rhinestones, pr, $90 to.**125.00**

Earrings, Robert, seed pearls w/aurora borealis stones, 1960s...............................**55.00**

Earrings, S Coventry, gold-plated dangles w/clear rhinestones, pr.......................................**70.00**

Earrings, Weiss, drop style w/blue rhinestones, pr, $35 to ...**50.00**

Necklace, BSK, gold-tone floral design w/pink rhinestones **45.00**

Necklace, Coro, gold-tone w/bright aqua rhinestone dangle, $125 to **140.00**

Necklace, Hobe, cross w/antiqued gold filigree & garnets, $175 to **225.00**

Necklace, Monet, choker-length Art Moderne rhodium links, 1950s...............................**45.00**

Necklace, Pam, floral motif w/iridescent stones & enamel leaves.............................**50.00**

Necklace, Regency, glass moonstones & iridescent rhinestones, $100 to **150.00**

Necklace, Trifari, 2-strand faux turquoise beads, from $40 to **65.00**

Ring, Avon, inset faux stone, $10 to...................................**25.00**

Ring, Bakelite, ¾" wide, $25 to..............................**45.00**

Ring, Cire Perdu, 14 karat yellow gold w/lg citron **65.00**

Ring, Eisenberg Ice, teardrop-shaped topaz stone, $80 to **140.00**

Ring, Emmons, simulated pearls & turquoise, $30 to **45.00**

Ring, Judy Lee, green & citrine rhinestones, $45 to.........**65.00**

Johnson Brothers

Dinnerware marked Johnson Brothers, Staffordshire, has lately become the target of some aggressive collector activity, and for good reason. They made many lovely patterns, some scenic and some florals. Most are decorated with multicolor transfer designs, though you'll see blue or red transferware as well. Some, such as Friendly Village (one of their most popular lines), are still being produced, but the lines are much less extensive now, so the secondary market is being tapped to replace broken items that are no longer available anywhere else.

For more information refer to *Johnson Brothers Dinnerware* by

Mary J. Finegan. She is listed in the Directory under North Carolina.

Coaching Scenes

Have this fid" 1968 32 pieces $50.00

Bowl, rimmed soup	**15.00**
Bowl, vegetable; oval	**35.00**
Coaster	**9.00**
Coffee mug, minimum value	**20.00**
Creamer	**32.00**
Cup & saucer	**17.00**
Plate, dinner; 10"	**16.00**

Platter, 14", $70.00.

Friendly Village

Bowl, fruit/berry	**8.00**
Bowl, vegetable; round	**25.00**
Bowl, vegetable; w/lid	**90.00**
Butter dish	**50.00**
Coaster	**8.00**
Coffee mug	**18.00**
Coffeepot, minimum value	**80.00**
Creamer	**30.00**
Cup & saucer, demitasse	**20.00**
Egg cup	**15.00**
Plate, bread & butter	**6.00**
Plate, luncheon	**12.00**
Platter, sm (up tp 12")	**35.00**
Platter, turkey	**200.00**

Sauceboat	**40.00**
Sugar bowl, w/lid	**40.00**

Old Britain Castles

Bowl, berry; 5"	**10.00**
Bowl, cereal; 6"	**12.00**
Bowl, vegetable; oval	**35.00**
Coffeepot, minimum value	**90.00**
Gravy boat	**48.00**
Plate, bread & butter	**8.00**
Plate, dinner; minimum value	**20.00**
Plate, luncheon	**16.00**
Platter, med, 13½"	**55.00**
Teapot, minimum value	**90.00**
Tureen, minimum value	**200.00**

Rose Chintz

Bowl, cereal	**11.00**
Bowl, vegetable; round	**28.00**
Cup & saucer, demitasse	**22.00**
Gravy boat	**45.00**
Gravy boat underplate	**22.00**
Mug	**18.00**
Pitcher, 5½"	**50.00**
Plate, dinner	**16.00**
Platter, lg, 15", minimum value	**70.00**
Platter, sm, 11½"	**40.00**
Teapot	**85.00**

Kentucky Derby Glasses

Kentucky Derby glasses are the official souvenir glasses sold filled with mint juleps on Derby Day. The first glass (1938), picturing a black horse within a black and white rose garland and the Churchill Downs stadium in the background, is said to have either been given away as a souvenir or used for drinks among the elite at the Downs. This glass, the 1939, and two glasses said to have been used in 1940 are worth thousands and are nearly impossible to find at any price.

Our advisor for this category is Betty Hornback; she is listed in the Directory under Kentucky.

1961, front and back views, $110.00. (Photo courtesy Betty L. Hornback/Photographer Dean Langdon)

1938	**4,000.00**
1939	**6,500.00**
1940, aluminum	**800.00**
1940, French Lick, aluminum	**800.00**
1941-44, Beetleware, from $2,500 to	**4,000.00**
1945, jigger	**1,000.00**
1945, regular	**1,600.00**
1945, tall	**450.00**
1946, clear frosted w/frosted bottom, L in circle	**100.00**
1947, clear frosted w/frosted bottom, L in circle	**100.00**
1948, clear bottom	**225.00**
1948, frosted bottom	**250.00**
1949	**225.00**
1950	**450.00**
1951	**650.00**
1952, Gold Cup	**225.00**
1953	**175.00**
1954	**200.00**
1955	**150.00**
1956, 1 star, 2 tails	**200.00**
1956, 1 star, 3 tails	**400.00**
1956, 2 stars, 2 tails	**200.00**
1956, 2 stars, 3 tails	**250.00**
1957, gold & black on frosted	**125.00**
1958, Gold Bar	**175.00**
1958, Iron Leige	**225.00**
1959-60, ea	**100.00**
1962, Churchill Downs, red, gold & black on clear	**80.00**
1963-64	**50.00**
1965	**75.00**
1966	**60.00**
1967-68, ea	**60.00**
1969	**65.00**
1970	**70.00**
1971	**50.00**
1972	**45.00**
1973	**55.00**
1974, Federal, regular & mistake, ea	**200.00**
1974, Libbey, mistake, Canonero in 1971 listing on back	**18.00**
1974, regular, Canonero II in 1971 listing on back	**16.00**
1975	**16.00**
1976	**16.00**
1976, plastic	**16.00**
1977	**14.00**
1978-79, ea	**16.00**
1980	**22.00**
1981	**14.00**
1981	**14.00**
1982	**14.00**
1983-85, ea	**12.00**
1986	**14.00**
1986 (1985 copy)	**20.00**
1987-89, ea	**12.00**

1984, $12.00.

Apple peeler, Baldwin, cast iron **125.00**

Baby bottle warmer, Sunbeam, chrome bullet shape, 1940s, 12½" **30.00**

Batter jug, Jenkins #570, green .**150.00**

Bean slicer, Alexanderwerk Johenschneider, cast iron crank type, EX **18.00**

Bean stringer & slicer, Bean-X, 6" **25.00**

1990-92, ea **10.00**
1993-95, ea **9.00**
1996-97, ea **8.00**
1998-99, ea **6.00**
2000-2001, ea **5.00**

Beater jar, Delphite, painted green wooden handle, from $60.00 to $70.00.

Kitchen Collectibles

From the early patented apple peelers, cherry pitters, and food choppers to the gadgets of the '20s through the '40s, many collectors find special appeal in kitchen tools. Refer to *Kitchen Antiques, 1790 – 1940,* by Kathryn McNerney and *Kitchen Glassware of the Depression Years, Fifth Edition,* by Gene Florence for more information. Both are published by Collector Books.

See also Aluminum; Clothes Sprinkler Bottles; Cookie Cutters and Molds; Egg Timers; Enesco; Graniteware; Griswold.

Apple corer, White Mountain, cast iron w/wooden handle, 10x6", EX **26.00**

Beverage cooler, Porcelier, high or low barrel, ea **60.00**

Biscuit cutter, Ekco, plastic **6.00**

Biscuit cutter, Kreamer, strap handle, sm **8.00**

Blender, Kenmore #116-82421, 2-speed, 1951 ....**65.00**

Blender, Osterizer #10 Vitra Mix, chrome beehive shape, EX ..**25.00**

Blender, Waring Imperial RL-6, chrome & glass, EX **35.00**

Butter dish, Jeannette, 2-lb, pink w/B embossed on lid **185.00**

Can opener, Dazey, electric, 1960s **28.00**

Can opener, Sunbeam, electric, turquoise, 1950s, 9", EX ..**32.00**

Canister set, Century, spun aluminum w/copper-tone lids, set of 4, EX **15.00**

Canisters, Porcelier, Serv-All Line, coffee, salt, sugar or tea, ea 80.00

Cheese slicer, iron w/sharp wire blade, 1920s, 7" 18.00

Chopper, Hazel Atlas, glass jar w/wooden handle, 11" 12.00

Chopper, wooden handle w/double blades............................25.00

Chopper, wrought-iron crescent-shaped blade, wooden handle, 7½x7" 50.00

Churn, Dazey #40, 4-qt, w/patent date............................140.00

Coffee urn, Porcelier, electric ..130.00

Coffeepot, Presto, chrome Deco style w/black base, EX ..20.00

Cookie press, Wear-Ever, aluminum, 11-pc, MIB 15.00

Crimper, brass wheel, waffle design on tamper end 45.00

Decanter, Porcelier, Oriental Deco 60.00

Egg basket, collapsible wire w/wire feet, lg.................45.00

Egg beater, A&J High Speed, Bakelite handles, stainless blades, EX 20.00

Egg beater, Flint, Ekco, 1950s-60s, NM 8.50

Egg poacher, Mirro, 4 cups, aluminum w/Bakelite handle, 8" dia, NM...........................20.00

Egg poacher, Pyrex, 4 cups, glass w/rack & lid, 10" 35.00

Egg separator, JA Frost Grocer, tin 14.00

Funnel, Nesco 5 Articles in 1, tin w/red handle, 8¼"..........20.00

Funnel, Sanitary Fruit Jar Funnel, white ironstone, 4¾"......20.00

Garnishing set, Acme, 4-pc, 1935, MIB..............................35.00

Glass knife, Dur-X 3-leaf, crystal, 8½" or 9" 20.00

Glass knife, Dur-X 3-leaf, pink, 8½" or 9"..................................45.00

Glass knife, Dur-X 5-leaf, crystal, 9"..35.00

Glass knife, Dur-X 5-leaf, green, 9"..60.00

Glass knife, Dur-X 3-leaf, crystal, 8½" or 9" 20.00

Glass knife, Stonex, amber, 8½"..250.00

Glass knife, Stonex, green, 8½" 80.00

Glass knife, Vitex (Star & Diamond), blue, 8½" or 9" ...20.00

Glass knife, Vitex (Star & Diamond), pink, 8½" or 9" ...40.00

Grater, Moran's 5-in-I Kitchenaid, fits over bowl, 9½" dia ...12.00

Grinder, Griswold #3, NMIB .60.00

Grinder, Regal, cast iron clamp-on w/wooden handle, 1900s..............................35.00

Grinder, Universal #2, 3 cutters w/5 accessories, EX........20.00

Ice bucket, Paden City Party Line, amber..............................32.50

Ice cream scoop, thumb release, stainless steel w/Bakelite handle............................55.00

Ice pick, cast-iron tulip-shaped end w/sm side opener, EX......20.00

Jar wrench, adjustable loop style, marked Berthoud Patented 18.00

Jar wrench, Triumph, adjusts for 4 sizes, EX 15.00

Juicer, Acme Juicerator 5001, 17 lbs, EXIB 75.00

Juicer, Atlas, 1950s-60s, EX...65.00

Knife sharpener, metal w/Bakelite handle............................20.00

Knife holder, Nuway, red and white, box dated 1939, M, from $15.00 to $20.00.

Lemon squeezer, Sunkist, steel, 9½" L **15.00**

Measuring cup, Jeannette, 1-cup, crystal **45.00**

Measuring pitcher, McKee, 2-cup, red or black Diamond Check, $35 to **40.00**

Measuring-spoon holder, ceramic apple shape w/3 slots **10.00**

Melon baller, stainless w/Bakelite handle **18.00**

Mixer, Betty Crocker, Kenmore #303.82250, 1950s..........**40.00**

Mixer, hand; GE #10M47, 3-speed, pink, EX **35.00**

Napkin holder, Fan Fold, green, $135 to **150.00**

Paper towel/waxed paper dispenser, Kromax, aluminum/black plastic, EX **22.00**

Percolator, GE, 9-cup, chrome & Bakelite, squatty egg shape, 1950s, EX **20.00**

Percolator, Porcelier #120, electric, Golden Wheat.........**85.00**

Percolator, Westinghouse, floral & white Deco style, 12", EX.**15.00**

Popcorn set, Mirro, lg bowl w/4 servers, spun aluminum, EX **20.00**

Potato masher, Bakelite handle, 1940s, 8¾" **30.00**

Potato masher, cast iron, flat circular form w/decorative design, 10" **35.00**

Pretzel jar, Porcelier, Serv-All Line, platinum **75.00**

Reamer, Fry, straight sides, rose pink................................**60.00**

Reamer, Hazel Atlas, crystal Crisscross w/tab handle, $18 to **22.00**

Reamer, Hazel Atlas, white w/red trim................................**25.00**

Reamer, Japan, 2-pc pitcher w/floral decor, 5¼" **110.00**

Reamer, Vitrock, green 2-cup pitcher, 2-pc...................**35.00**

Refrigerator dish, Hazel Atlas, pink Crisscross, 4x4" **30.00**

Refrigerator dish, Pyrex, fired-on blue w/clear lid, 4x6¾" ..**15.00**

Rolling pin, chrome w/red plastic handles, 1940s-50s, 15".**15.00**

Rolling pin, maple, 1-pc........**20.00**

Rolling pin, Roll-Rite, Good Houskeeping Institute, 14", NM................................**40.00**

Salt & pepper shakers, Kromax, spun aluminum, EX, pr.**15.00**

Sandwich grill, Porcelier, Scalloped Wildflowers Line...........**350.00**

Server, Emerald-Glo, metal frame, $50.00. (Photo courtesy Gene Florence)

281

Sifter, Androck Hand-i-Sifter, painted tin, red wood handle, EX..................................22.50

Sifter, Gem Sifter...JL Clark...Rockford IL, tin .25.00

Sifter, Hunter's Sifter...made in USA, tin w/wooden knob, 6½", EX..................................20.00

Skillet, Pyrex, clip-on handle, 6½"...............................35.00

Spatula, heart shape w/Bakelite handle, EX......................12.50

Spatula, Red Moon Flour on handle w/bottle opener end, 11¾" 15.00

Spoon, Rumford Cake Mix & Cream Whip, Pat Oct 6-08 on handle, 12" 18.00

Steel-ite, green, 8½"..............75.00

Sugar shaker, West Sanitary Automatic Sugar, crystal..........25.00

Syrup pitcher, Heisey, green glass w/metal lid......................75.00

Syrup pitcher, Standard Glass, pink w/metal lid.............55.00

Timer, Lux, white plastic w/black ribbing, chrome-plated dial, 1950s..............................15.00

Toaster, GE #129T81, 2-slice, chrome w/Bakelite handles, EX, minimum..................15.00

Toaster, Sears Tip Out 75.00

Toaster, Sunbeam T-20B, chrome, Deco style, EX...............40.00

Tongs, Magic Hostess, gold-tone aluminum, lg....................5.00

Waffle iron, GE, cast aluminum..45.00

Waffle iron, Porcelier, Scalloped Wild Flowers Pattern, $225 to..................................300.00

Waffle iron, Torrid 40.00

Water bottle, Hocking, transparent green w/embossed ribs, EX ..35.00

Water dispenser, McKee, custard glass, EX, from $110 to .125.00

Whip/mixer, Kwik-Whip, aluminum jar style w/Bakelite top, 1950s, 8"....................8.50

Kliban

B. Kliban, artist and satirist, was extremely fond of cats and usually had more than one as companion to him in his California home. This led to his first book (published in 1975), simply titled *Cat*. The popularity of the cat character led to a series of merchandising with the Kliban cat that continues today. He can be found on calendars, mugs, note pads, Christmas cards, stuffed toys, and even golf balls along with many other items, the majority of which are of recent production.

Candy jar, Sigma, 10", $85.00.

Bank, wearing red shoes, 1979, 6½"..................................85.00

Bookends, bookcase shape w/4 cats & 1 mouse, Sigma, 8", pr.....140.00

Box, cowboy (lid) sitting in Western hat (base), Sigma, from $150 to............175.00
Box, in bathtub, Sigma......300.00
Box, in top hat, w/lid, Sigma, from $60 to...........75.00
Box, lying on back of heart-shaped box, 1970s, Sigma........130.00
Butter dish, in bathtub, sm chip on ear, Sigma, 1980s, 7x3½".95.00
Candy jar, playing guitar, Sigma..........85.00
Clock, on roller skates, Figi Giftware, 1970s, 13x13"........90.00
Cookie jar, in long pants, Sigma, from $165 to.................180.00
Cookie jar, playing guitar, Sigma, from $165 to.................180.00
Cookie jar, sitting upright w/kitten, marked Taste Setter Sigma...........475.00
Figurine, in tree, EX.............55.00
Ice bucket, in red cape flying over city skyline, vinyl, 8", NM.......................75.00
Ink stamps, Rubber Stampede, 1990-92, 4 w/different poses.........75.00
Mug, face only, Sigma #209, from $15 to...........20.00
Music box, listening to old phonograph on sq base, Sigma #540.............275.00
Picture frame, w/heart on cheek, Love a Cat, Sigma, from $100 to..................125.00
Plush doll, in Sumo outfit, w/orig tag, 14", M.............42.00
Salt & pepper shakers, hatching from egg, Sigma #224, 2-pc, minimum.................200.00
Soap dish, lying on back, Sigma #531.............150.00

Sugar bowl, head only, w/lid, Sigma, from $60 to.........75.00
Sweatshirt, 4 Christmas stockings hanging w/cats inside, NM.........................50.00
Teapot, in airplane, Sigma #246, from $325 to.............375.00
Wastebasket, 12"..............22.50

Kreiss

These novelties were imported from Japan during the 1950s. There are several lines. One is a totally off-the-wall group of caricatures called Psycho Ceramics. There's a Beatnik series, Bums, and Cave People (all of which are strange little creatures), as well as some that are very well done and tasteful. Others you find will be inset with colored 'jewels.' Many are marked either with an ink stamp or an in-mold trademark (some are dated).

For more information we recommend *Kreiss Novelty Ceramics*, written by and available from Mike King, see the Directory under Ohio.

Ashtray, Psycho, blue in bib overalls w/ashtray on head, 5".....125.00
Ashtray, Psycho, blue w/lg open mouth for ashtray, 4½"................100.00
Ashtray, Psycho, green w/belly for ashtray, 3x6".............125.00
Ashtray, Psycho, pink holding ashtray overhead, 4"....100.00
Ashtray, Psycho, pink w/wide eyes, I'm All Thumbs, 5".......125.00

Figurine, Christmas Psycho, man in black w/kisses all over face, 5"......................................**75.00**

Figurine, Elegant Heirs, bum w/cane & cigar, 7¼".......**75.00**

Figurine, Elegant Heirs, convict w/ball & chain, 6¼"........**60.00**

Figurine, Elegant Heirs, drunk holding up drink, 7".......**60.00**

Figurine, Good Time Charlie with elephant, either size, $100.00. (Photo courtesy Phil and Nyla Thurston)

Figurine, Moon Being, pink, bird-like, 4¾"..........................**175.00**

Figurine, Moon Being, tan creature w/black spots looking up, 4½"................................**175.00**

Figurine, Nudie, in plaid vest, 6½"..............................**100.00**

Figurine, Psycho, blue w/footprints allover himself, 5¼"......**125.00**

Figurine, Psycho, blue w/frown, holding hands together, 5"......**100.00**

Figurine, Psycho, brown w/white face, 4½"..........................**90.00**

Figurine, Psycho, orange w/lg smile, 4¾"......................**100.00**

Figurine, Psycho, orange w/plastic hair, mouth wide open, 5".**150.00**

Figurine, Psycho, pink elephant w/raised trunk, 5¼".....**150.00**

Figurine, Psycho, pink lady lying down w/flowers, 4¼"......**75.00**

Figurine, Psycho, pink w/light bulb antlers, 5"..............**90.00**

Figurine, Psycho, pink, man in over-sized shirt collar, 4".**90.00**

Figurine, Psycho, pink, man w/open mouth wearing white hat w/band, 5"................**75.00**

Figurine, Psycho, purple w/fingers in mouth, 5"....................**90.00**

Figurine, Psycho, screaming woman in green dress, 5½"...........**70.00**

Figurine, Psycho, smiling graduate in blue, 4¾"...............**75.00**

Figurine, Psycho, yellow w/big nose & arms crossed, 5"...........**75.00**

Figurine, Psycho, yellow w/pcs (of himself) falling out, 4½"..**100.00**

Figurines, Green-Eyed Monsters, Caveman & Family, 4-pc set...........**100.00**

Mug, Psycho, gold w/big nose, 5"..**75.00**

Mug, Psycho, smiling graduate w/hand-to-head handle, 5"..**75.00**

Lefton China

Since 1940 the Lefton China Co. has been importing and producing ceramic giftware which may be found in shops throughout the world. Because of the quality of the workmanship and the beauty of these items, they are eagerly sought by collectors of today. Lefton pieces are usually marked with a fired-on trademark or a paper label.

Our advisor for this category is Loretta De Lozier, author of *Collector's Encyclopedia of Lefton China, Books I* and *II*; she is listed in the Directory under Iowa. See

Clubs and Newsletters for information concerning the National Society of Lefton Collectors.

Ashtray, White Holly, leaf shape, #6056, 7" **20.00**

Bank, Love Nest, bluebirds in birdhouse, #7485, 7" **125.00**

Bank, Root of All Evil, devil on money bag, #4923, 8" **65.00**

Bowl, Pink Clover, #2503, 6¼"..**15.00**

Bowl, swan w/roses, #1388, 5¾"..**35.00**

Box, Green Holly, $40.00.

Cake plate, Green Heritage, #719 ....**40.00**

Canister set, Sweet Vilets, #2875, 4-pc **100.00**

Coffeepot, Floral Chintz, #8033..**150.00**

Colonial Village, Country Post Office, #07341 ....**65.00**

Colonial Village, Ryman Auditorium, #08010 ....**65.00**

Cookie jar, daisies on white, #39 ....**40.00**

Cookie jar, elf head, #3969, 8½" **300.00**

Cookie jar, yellow bird, #291, 10½" **50.00**

Cup & saucer, Four Seasons, #780 ....**40.00**

Dish, Green Holly, 3-compartment, #1351 ....**25.00**

Figurine, bay horse, #2211, 7"..**75.00**

Figurine, boy & girl w/rabbits at feet, #7453, 6½", ea **65.00**

Figurine, cat w/hat & organ grinder, #7567, 4" **18.00**

Figurine, cocker spaniel, #00412, 4½" **22.50**

Figurine, heron, naturalistic, #1541, 6½" **40.00**

Figurine, Kewpie on leaf, #2992, 3½" **30.00**

Figurine, Madonna bust, pink matt, #1720, 8" **35.00**

Figurine, man holding boy in arms, #7778, 6½" **85.00**

Figurine, nurse holding baby, #2739, 5½" **45.00**

Figurine, old man w/dog, #6885, 8" **65.00**

Figurine, rabbit, white, #880 ..**30.00**

Figurine, tabby cat, #6364, 4½"..**25.00**

Figurine, Valentine girl, #033, 4" **20.00**

Frame, Heavenly Hobos, house shape w/bride & groom, #04638, 4¾" **35.00**

Jam jar, grape cluster, #4852, 5" **30.00**

Lamp, Green Holly, #4229, 5½" **45.00**

Music box, Valentine angel, from $40.00 to $50.00. (Photo courtesy Lee Garmon)

Mug, Miss Priss, blue cat head, #1503, 4".........................**75.00**

Music box, Christmas angel on bell shape, #637, 7"........**60.00**

Perfume set, Only a Rose, #385, 3-pc **110.00**

Pitcher, Poinsettia, #4389, 6¼".**85.00**

Pitcher & bowl, green daisy, #5777, 4¼".......................**22.00**

Planter, ABC block, #2128, 4"..**12.00**

Planter, Santa on white reindeer, #1496, 6".........................**30.00**

Salt & pepper shakers, egg boy & girl, #7782, pr.................**15.00**

Salt & pepper shakers, White Christmas, #825, pr.......**25.00**

Sleigh, Green Holly, #2637, 10½" **55.00**

Snack set, Rose Chintz, #637.**35.00**

Teapot, Cardinal w/holly on white, #1655 ....**125.00**

Teapot, elf's head, #3973 ....**185.00**

Teapot, 25th Anniversary, musical, #1137 ....**45.00**

Tidbit tray, Festival, 2-tier, #2624 ....**45.00**

Vase, Brown Heritage Fruit, #3117, 8¾".......................**75.00**

Vase, Only a Rose, #420, 6"..**45.00**

Wall plaque, mermaid, #4574, 6", pr....................................**75.00**

Wall pocket, Green Heritage, rose cluster on oval, #045, 6½".**45.00**

Letter Openers

Here's a chance to get into a hobby that offers more than enough diversification to be both interesting and challenging, yet requires very little room for display. Whether you prefer the advertising letter openers or the more imaginative models with handles sculpted as a dimensional figure or incorporating a gadget such as a penknife or a cigarette lighter, you should be able to locate enough for a nice assortment. Materials are varied as well, ranging from silverplate to wood. Some are inlaid with semiprecious stones.

Our advisor for this category is Everett Grist, author of *Collector's Guide to Letter Openers* (Collector Books). Mr. Grist is listed in the Directory under Tennessee.

Brass, Revolutionary patriot on horse, England, $10.00. (Photo courtesy Everett Grist)

Advertising, celluloid & French Ivory, Henry Grady Hotel, Atlanta **30.00**

Advertising, gold-plated, Holiday Inns of America **6.00**

Advertising, plastic, yellow w/Yellow Pages lettered in black.......**3.00**

Advertising, steel, Pittsburgh Steel, also stamped on nail head **18.00**

Brass, Chinese man (smiling) w/long beard forming blade **15.00**

Brass, derringer form, Stamford CT **10.00**

Brass, elephant handle **10.00**

Brass, lion on wall, ornate blade, Belguim **10.00**

Brass, sword & stone, combination paperweight & opener **15.00**

Bronze, griffin over lion head ..**12.00**

Copper, Arts & Crafts style, Roanoke Island NC **10.00**

Enamel & brass, overall floral detail, red tassel..............**30.00**

Gold-plated, eagle form handle .**8.00**

Ivory, crocodile (carved) w/tail as blade **85.00**

Leather handle w/black braided border, wooden blade **6.00**

Lucite handle w/reverse-carved & painted fish, Gulf Shores Alabama **15.00**

Mother of Pearl, carved Victorian design **65.00**

Pewter, dancing frog handle, Metzke 1979..........................**12.00**

Pewter, sand dollar, Metzke...**6.00**

Plastic, braille alphabet, beige .**10.00**

Plastic & steel, religious motto, M-Cor, USA......................**3.00**

Porcelain, hand-painted roses, signed R Riddle **45.00**

Resin, Hawaiian totem handle .**4.00**

Rhinestone, gold-plated w/jeweled handle..............................**8.00**

Silver-plated, bamboo-style handle....................................**10.00**

Stag handle, steel blade........**10.00**

Turquoise handle, brass blade, India **15.00**

White metal, golf bag w/clubs forms handle, Metzke 1985 ....**15.00**

White metal, Old Faithful/ Yellowstone...........................**4.00**

Wood, African native head ...**10.00**

Wood & abalone, dragon form w/inlay **15.00**

Liberty Blue

'Take home a piece of American history!,' stated an ad from the 1970s for this dinnerware made in Staffordshire, England. Blue and white depictions of George Washington at Valley Forge, Paul Revere, Independence Hall — fourteen historic scenes in all — were offered on different place-setting pieces. The ad goes on to describe this 'unique...truly unusual..museum-quality...future family heirloom.'

For every five dollars spent on groceries you could purchase a basic piece (dinner plate, bread and butter plate, cup, saucer, or dessert dish) for fifty-nine cents on alternate weeks of the promotion. During the promotion, completer pieces could also be purchased. The soup tureen was the most expensive item, originally selling for $24.99. Nineteen completer pieces in all were offered along with a five-year open stock guarantee. For more information we recommend Jo Cunningham's book, *The Best of Collectible Dinnerware.*

Our advisor for this category is Gary Beegle; he is listed in the Directory under New York.

Bowl, cereal; from $10 to **12.50**
bowl, flat soup; 8¾", from $15 to **18.00**
Bowl, fruit; 5", from $4.50 to ..**5.50**
Bowl, vegetable; oval **40.00**
Bowl, vegetable; round **40.00**
Butter dish, w/lid, ¼-lb **55.00**
Casserole, w/lid, from $65 to..**75.00**
Coaster, from $8 to **10.00**
Creamer..................................**18.00**
Creamer & sugar bowl, w/lid, original box **80.00**
Cup & saucer, from $7 to........**9.00**
Gravy boat, from $30 to **35.00**
Gravy-boat liner....................**15.00**
Mug, from $10 to...................**12.00**
Pitcher, milk.........................**115.00**
Plate, bread & butter; 6".........**3.00**
Plate, dinner; 10", from $7 to .**9.00**
Plate, luncheon; scarce, 8¾".**17.00**
Plate, scarce, 7" **9.50**

Platter, 14", $80.00.

Platter, 12", from $35 to **45.00**
Salt & pepper shakers, pr.....**38.00**
Soup ladle, plain white, no decal, from $30 to **35.00**
Soup tureen, w/lid, from $250 to...............................**300.00**
Sugar bowl, no lid **15.00**
Sugar bowl, w/lid...................**35.00**
Teapot, w/lid, from $95 to...**125.00**

License Plates

Early porcelain license plates are treasured by collectors and often sell for more than $500.00 per pair when found in excellent condition. The best examples are first-year plates from each state, but some of the more modern plates with special graphics are collectible too. Prices given below are for plates in good or better condition unless noted otherwise.

Our advisor for this category is Richard Diehl, who is listed in the Directory under Colorado.

Alabama, 1984.........................**3.50**
Alaska, 1962...........................**12.50**
Arizona, 1931, fair **8.50**
California, 1933....................**20.00**
Connecticut, 1919, fair..........**10.50**
Connecticut, 1936 ....**12.50**
Georgia, 1996, Olympics.......**20.00**
Hawaii, 1976 ....**8.50**
Idaho, 1935.............................**20.00**
Idaho, 1992, Sesquicentennial .**10.50**
Indiana, 1948 ....**9.50**
Kansas, 1943, tab....................**8.50**
Kentucky, 1961 ....**10.50**
Louisiana, 1964-65.................**10.50**
Maine, 1916, poor..................**10.50**

Massachusetts, 1919.............**25.00**
Michigan, 1940......................**15.50**
Minnesota, 1949....................**25.00**
Montana, 1957 ....**12.50**
Nebraska, 1934 ....**8.50**
Nevada, 1933........................**30.00**

New Hampshire, 1926, $125.00 for the pair. (Photo courtesy Dunbar Gallery)

New Jersey, 1920 ....**20.00**
New Mexico, 1924, repainted..**30.00**
New York, 1962, pr **15.00**
North Carolina, 1975, First in Freedom.........................**10.50**
North Dakota, 1988, 'Teddy'...**9.50**
Ohio, 1958...............................**7.50**
Oklahoma, 1976, Bicentennial..**10.50**
Oregon, 1948 ....**18.50**
Oregon, 1977, Pacific Wonderland...............................**25.00**
Rhode Island, 1930 ....**17.50**
South Carolina, 1968 ....**5.50**
South Dakota, 1918 ....**18.50**
Texas, 1958, pr.....................**18.00**
Utah, 1964.............................**12.50**
Vermont, 2000.......................**10.50**
Virginia, 1953........................**10.50**
Washington DC, 1981, Inaugural **10.50**
West Virginia, 1970 ....**8.50**
Wyoming, 1958......................**8.50**

Little Red Riding Hood

This line of novelties and kitchenware has always commanded good prices on the collectibles market. In fact, it became valuable enough to make it attractive to counterfeiters, and now you'll see reproductions everywhere. They're easy to spot, though, watch for one-color eyes. Though there are other differences, you should be able to identify the imposters armed with this information alone.

Little Red Riding Hood was produced from 1943 to 1957. The Regal China Company was by far the major manufacturer of this line, though a rather insignificant number of items were made by the Hull Pottery of Crooksville, Ohio, who sent their whiteware to the Royal China and Novelty Company (a division of Regal China) of Chicago, Illinois, to be decorated. For further information we recommend *The Collector's Encyclopedia of Cookie Jars, Vol I*, by Joyce and Fred Roerig (Collector Books).

Bank, standing...................**750.00**
Bank, wall hanging..........**1,200.00**
Butter dish, from $325 to ...**350.00**

Canister, Flour, from $650.00 to $850.00.

Canister, salt **1,100.00**
Cookie jar, red spray w/gold bows,
  red shoes, from $700 to..**750.00**
Creamer, top pour, no tab handle,
  from $400 to **425.00**
Creamer, top pour, tab handle,
  from $350 to **375.00**
Mustard jar, w/spoon **350.00**
Pitcher, 8", from $325 to........**375.00**
Planter, hanging, from $375 to ..**450.00**
Salt & pepper shakers, 3¼", pr,
  from $60 to **90.00**
Sugar bowl, w/lid, from $350 to..**425.00**
Teapot, from $325 to...........**375.00**
Wolf jar, red base, from $925
  to...............................**975.00**
Wolf jar, yellow base, from $750
  to **800.00**

Lu Ray Pastels

Introduced in 1938 by Taylor,
Smith, and Taylor of East Liverpool, Ohio, Lu-Ray Pastels is
today a very sought-after line of
collectible American dinnerware.
It was first made in these solid
colors: Windsor Blue, Surf Green,
Persian Cream, and Sharon Pink.
Chatham Gray was introduced in
1948 and is today priced higher
than the other colors.

Our advisor for this category
is Shirley Moore; she is listed in
the Directory under Oklahoma.
For more information, we recommend *Collector's Guide to Lu-
Ray Pastels* by Kathy and Bill
Meehan.

Bowl, '36s oatmeal **60.00**
Bowl, cream soup **70.00**

Bowl, lug soup; tab handled .**19.00**
Bowl, mixing; 7" **125.00**
Bowl, salad; yellow...............**55.00**
Butter dish, any color except
  Chatham Gray, rare color,
  w/lid **50.00**
Chocolate cup, AD; straight
  sides.............................**80.00**
Coffee cup, AD......................**20.00**
Creamer, AD; individual **40.00**
Epergne **110.00**
Muffin cover **125.00**
Pitcher, any color other than
  yellow, bulbous w/flat bot-
  tom..........................**125.00**
Pitcher, yellow, bulbous bot-
  tom............................**95.00**
Plate, chop; 15".....................**38.00**
Plate, 6" **3.00**
Plate, 9" **10.00**

Platter, 13", $19.00.

Relish dish, 4-part.................**95.00**
Saucer, coffee; AD **8.50**
Saucer, tea..............................**3.00**
Sugar bowl, AD; w/lid, individ-
  ual.................................**40.00**
Teacup **8.00**
Teapot, flat spout, w/lid......**160.00**
Tray, pickle............................**28.00**
Tumbler, water **80.00**
Vase, bud **400.00**

Lunch Boxes

In the early years of this century, tobacco companies often packaged their products in tins that could later be used for lunch boxes. By the 1930s oval lunch boxes designed to appeal to school children were being produced. The rectangular shape that is now popular was preferred in the 1950s. Character lunch boxes decorated with the faces of TV personalities, super heroes, Disney, and cartoon characters are especially sought after by collectors today. Our values are for excellent condition lunch boxes only (without the Thermos unless one is mentioned in the line).

Our advisor for this category is Terri Ivers; she is listed in the Directory under Oklahoma. Refer to *Pictorial Price Guide to Vinyl and Plastic Lunch Boxes and Thermoses* and *Pictorial Price Guide to Metal Lunch Boxes and Thermoses* by Larry Aikens (L-W Book Sales) and *Collector's Guide ot Lunchboxes* by Carole Bess White and L.M. White (Collector Books) for more information. For an expanded listing, see *Schroeder's Collectible Toys, Antique to Modern* (Collector Books).

Addams Family, metal, 1974, w/Thermos, EX+ **125.00**
Airport Control Tower, vinyl, 1972, EX......................**150.00**
American Gladiators, plastic, 1992, red, EX.................**15.00**
Archies, metal, 1969, w/Thermos, NM..............................**125.00**

Battlestar Galactica, metal, 1978, w/Thermos, EX..............**75.00**
Betsy Clark, w/Thermos, M..**90.00**
Big Jim, plastic, 1972, dome top, w/Thermos, M **125.00**

Bionic Woman, metal, 1978, EX, $85.00. (Photo courtesy Greg Davis and Bill Morgan)

Bionic Woman, plastic, 1970s, NM..**50.00**
Black Hole, metal, 1979, EX..**70.00**
Bobby Sherman, metal, 1972, w/Thermos, EX.............**100.00**
Bugaloos, metal, 1971, EX..**100.00**
Casper the Friendly Ghost, plastic, 1996, w/Thermos, M **15.00**
Corsage, vinyl, 1970, EX.......**75.00**
Cracker Jack, metal, 1979, EX..**50.00**
Dawn, vinyl, 1970, w/Thermos, EX **175.00**
Dick Tracy, plastic, 1990, w/Thermos, M **40.00**
Disney World, metal, 1970, w/Thermos, EX..............**40.00**
Donnie & Marie, vinyl, 1976, NM...............................**75.00**
Fall Guy, metal, 1981, w/Thermos, EX **50.00**
Girl Scout, vinyl, 1960, w/Thermos, EX **175.00**
Gunsmoke, metal, 1959, EX..**150.00**
He-Man, metal, 1984, w/Thermos, EX **40.00**

Hulk Hogan, plastic, 1989, EX .20.00

Incredible Hulk, metal, 1978, w/Thermos, EX..............65.00

Jabberjaw Shark, plastic, 1977, EX....................50.00

King Kong, metal, 1977, EX.50.00

Kung Fu, metal, 1974, w/Thermos, NM 100.00

Marvel Super Heroes, metal, 1976, EX........................45.00

Mickey Mouse Club, metal, 1967, yellow, EX 85.00

Mighty Mouse, metal, 1979, EX..35.00

Mork & Mindy, plastic, 1978, w/Thermos, NM 40.00

Mr T, plastic, 1984, orange, w/Thermos, EX..............30.00

Pac-Man, metal, 1980, EX....35.00

Pee Wee Herman, plastic, 1988, EX....................35.00

Pete's Dragon, metal, 1978, EX..45.00

Pink Panther, vinyl, 1980, EX ...95.00

Raggedy Ann & Andy, plastic, 1988, w/Thermos, NM ...30.00

Rambo, metal, 1985, M.........65.00

Road Runner, metal, 1979, EX..75.00

Roy Rogers and Dale Evans Double R Bar Ranch, metal, with Thermos, EX, $165.00. (Photo courtesy June Moon)

Six Million Dollar Man, metal, 1978, w/Thermos, EX.....70.00

Smurfette, plastic, 1984, pink, EX...................15.00

Snoopy, vinyl brunch bag, 1977, w/Thermos, EX..............95.00

Swan Lake, vinyl, EX 150.00

Three Little Pigs, metal, 1982, EX................125.00

Tom & Jerry, plastic, 1992, M ..15.00

Twiggy, plastic brunch bag, zipper closure, EX, $250.00.

Welcome Back Kotter, metal, 1976, EX........................85.00

Wild Frontier, metal, 1977, EX..40.00

Wonder Woman, vinyl, 1977, yellow, w/Thermos, EX.....150.00

Woody Woodpecker, metal, 1972, EX................120.00

Ziggy, vinyl, 1979, orange, EX ..90.00

Thermos Bottles

ABC Wide World of Sports, metal, 1976, EX........................35.00

Batman & Robin, metal, 1966, EX+................100.00

Bugs Bunny, plastic, 1977, EX..15.00

Casper the Friendly Ghost, metal, 1966, NM......................75.00

CHiPs, plastic, 1977, EX 20.00

Donny & Marie, plastic, 1976, NM 10.00

Emergency, plastic, 1973, EX..25.00

Get Smart, metal, 1966, EX .65.00

Gunsmoke, plastic, 1959, EX+..**90.00**

Hopalong Cassidy, metal, 1950, EX....................................**75.00**

Krazy Daisies, metal, 1970, EX.**40.00**

Kung Fu, plastic, 1974, EX...**20.00**

Lost in Space, metal, 1963, EX...**65.00**

Mighty Mouse, plastic, 1979, EX...**25.00**

Mork & Mindy, plastic, 1978, EX..**15.00**

New Zoo Revue, plastic, 1972, EX..**35.00**

Pete's Dagon, metal, 1978, EX..**25.00**

Rainbow Brite, plastic, 1984, EX **8.00**

Rifleman, metal, 1960, EX.**125.00**

Sabrina, plastic, 1972, EX....**45.00**

Spider-Man, plastic, 1990, EX..**10.00**

Universal Monsters, plastic, 1979, EX....................................**25.00**

Wizard of Oz, plastic, 1989, EX..**15.00**

Yogi Bear, metal, 1963, EX+...**75.00**

101 Dalmatians, plastic, 1990, EX....................................**10.00**

Magazines

Some of the most collectible magazines are *Life* (because of the celebrities and important events they feature on their covers), *Saturday Evening Post, Ladies' Home Journal* (especially those featuring the work of famous illustrators such as Parrish, Rockwell, and Wyeth), and *National Geographics* (pre-WWI issues in particular). As is true with any type of ephemera, condition and value are closely related. Unless they're in fine condition (clean, no missing or clipped pages, and very little other damage), they're worth very little; and cover interest and content are far more important than age.

After Dark, 1957, December, Carroll Baker, EX **40.00**

American Heritage, 1968, April, Mickey Mouse cover, VG .**25.00**

Avante Garde, 1969, #8, Picasso, NM **35.00**

Better Homes & Gardens, 1940, January, Walt Disney, EX........**18.00**

Boy's Life, 1981, Keith Hernandez, EX............................**3.00**

Chatelaine, 1937, February, Dionne Quints, VG **10.00**

Collier's, 1935, May 18, HG Wells, EX **13.00**

Collier's, 1953, August, Brooklyn Dodgers, EX **20.00**

Cosmopolitan, 1955, October, Audrey Hepburn article, EX **11.00**

Cosmopolitan, 1959, February, VG.....................................**4.00**

Country Song Roundup, 1957, August, Elvis, VG **15.00**

Crawdaddy, 1970, #14, Jimi Hendrix, EX **78.00**

Esquire, 1951, September, Marilyn Monroe gatefold, EX...............................**125.00**

Esquire, 1952, September, Esther Williams, EX **15.00**

Esquire, 1978, August 15, Robert Kennedy, EX **3.00**

Family Circle, 1942, October 16, Judy Garland, EX..........**20.00**

Family Circle, 1946, July 26, Susan Hayward, EX **6.00**

Family Circle, 1953, May, Marilyn Monroe article (part 1), EX **20.00**

Famous Models, 1950, April-May, VG.................................**28.00**

Favorite Westerns, 1960, August, John Wayne, EX **8.00**

Good Housekeeping, 1936, October, Pearl S Buck/Petty ads, EX **20.00**

Good Housekeeping, 1969, February, Paul Newman, VG................**7.00**

Gourmet, 1960s-80s, VG to VG+, ea from $3 to **4.00**

Hollywood Stars, 1958, May, Rock Hudson/Elvis, EX...........**18.00**

Jack & Jill, 1961, May, Roy Rogers, EX.....................**10.00**

Ladies' Home Journal, November 1960, Pat Nixon and Jackie Kennedy on cover, EX, $7.00.

Ladies' Home Journal, 1960, January, Pat Boone, EX **5.00**

Ladies' Home Journal, 1973, July, Marilyn Monroe article, EX .**13.00**

Liberty, 1941, September 4, Dionne Quints, EX.........**10.00**

Life, 1938, February 7, Gary Cooper, EX **38.00**

Life, 1943, March 29, Joseph Stalin, EX..............................**12.00**

Life, 1945, April 16, Eisenhower, EX **12.00**

Life, 1950, June 12, Hopalong Cassidy, EX+.................**50.00**

Life, 1951, September 3, Gina Lollobrigida, EX **10.00**

Life, 1953, December 14, Richard Nixon, EX **12.00**

Life, 1953, July 20, Senator John Kennedy, EX **10.00**

Life, 1958, December 1, Ricky Nelson, EX......................**20.00**

Life, 1962, January 5, Lucille Ball, EX **8.00**

Life, 1964, August 28, Beatles, EX **40.00**

Life, 1969, May 23, Rowan & Martin, EX **10.00**

Life, 1971, July 23, Clint Eastwood, VG **10.00**

Life, 1971, March 19, Ali/Frazier, EX **35.00**

Life, 1972, July 14, Mick Jagger, EX **15.00**

Look, 1939, July 18, Vivian Leigh, EX **28.00**

Look, 1940, February 13, WWII ..**22.00**

Look, 1943, January 12, Jimmy Stewart, EX....................**16.00**

Look, 1946, October 15, Ted Williams, NM.................**85.00**

Look, 1954, June 1, Jackie Gleason, EX **12.00**

Look, 1956, November 13, Elvis, EX **65.00**

Look, 1963, December 3, Kennedys, EX.................**12.00**

Look, 1963, February 12, Grace Kelly, EX **25.00**

Look, 1963, January 9, Beatles article, EX **28.00**

Look, 1966, December 13, John Lennon, VG+ **28.00**

Mad Magazine, 1982, July, Greatest American Hero, NM...........**5.00**

McCall's, 1951, August, Betsy McCall paper dolls, M....**15.00**

McCall's, 1951, June, Greta Garbo, EX.................12.00

McCall's, 1958, September, Joanne Woodward, VG 8.00

McCall's, 1968, May, Raquel Welch, EX.................5.00

McCall's, 1993, November, Oprah Winfrey, VG+.................4.00

Model Life Illustrated, 1967, EX.................13.00

Modern Screen, June 1936, Christy cover, VG, $18.00.

Modern Screen, 1953, April, Doris Day, EX.................18.00

Modern Teen, 1957, August, Elvis, EX.................60.00

Movie Life, 1949, February, Alan Ladd, NM.................15.00

National Geographic, 1915-16, ea..15.00

National Geographic, 1917-24, ea....9.00

National Geographic, 1925-29, ea....8.00

National Geographic, 1930-45, ea....7.00

National Geographic, 1946-55, ea...6.00

National Geographic, 1956-57, ea..5.50

National Geographic, 1968-89, ea..4.50

National Geographic, 1990-present, ea.................2.00

Newsweek, 1941, September 8, Hitler, VG.................10.00

Newsweek, 1957, July 1, Stan Musial, EX.................25.00

Newsweek, 1964, February 24, Beatles, EX.................25.00

Parade, 1960, April, Jane Fonda..15.00

Parade, 1962, June, Liz Taylor, NM.................25.00

Photoplay, 1938, July, Clark Gable, EX.................30.00

Photoplay, 1966, April, Peyton Place cast, NM.................8.00

Photoplay, 1968, April, Lennon Sisters, EX+.................8.00

Photoplay, 1978, May, John Lennon, NM.................7.00

PIC, 1944, October 24, Lucille Ball, EX.................20.00

Picture Week, 1955, Jayne Mansfield, 4x6", EX.................40.00

Playboy, 1955, February, Jayne Mansfield, EX.................150.00

Playboy, 1958, May, Tina Louise...24.00

Playboy, 1964, January, Marilyn Monroe tribute, EX.................50.00

Playboy, 1971, December, Karen Christy, VG+.................14.00

Playboy, 1971, July, Linda Evans..15.00

Playboy, 1979, December, Raquel Welch, EX.................17.00

Playboy, 1983, February, Kim Basinger.................12.00

Playboy, 1993, January, Barbi Twins, NM.................18.00

Reader's Digest, 1940s, ea, from $3 to.................5.00

Redbook, 1934, December, Carole Lombard.................25.00

Redbook, 1953, March, Marilyn Monroe cover & article, EX.........57.00

Redbook, 1954, November, Grace Kelly cover, EX.................15.00

Redbook, 1956, March, Frank Sinatra, EX........................**7.00**

Rolling Stone, 1968, April 27, #9, Beatles, NM **100.00**

Rolling Stone, 1968, August 10, #15, Mick Jagger, NM .**130.00**

Rolling Stone, 1968, February, 24, #6, Janis Joplin, EX+...**185.00**

Rolling Stone, 1968, September 28, #18, The Who, EX....**55.00**

Rolling Stone, 1969, #37, Elvis Presley, EX....................**20.00**

Rolling Stone, 1971, November 11, #95, Beach Boys, EX......**16.00**

Rolling Stone, 1974, March 14, #156, Bob Dylan, M **20.00**

Rolling Stone, 1974, November 7, #173, Evel Knievel, NM..**18.00**

Rolling Stone, 1975, #198, Bob Dylan, EX..........................**8.00**

Rolling Stone, 1981, January 22, nude John Lennon, VG..**40.00**

Rolling Stone, 1984, #415, Beatles, EX..............................**7.00**

Saturday Evening Post, 1946, April 6, Norman Rockwell art, VG....................................**65.00**

Saturday Evening Post, 1957, April 20, Yogi Berra, EX...........**40.00**

Saturday Evening Post, 1957, Rockwell Cover, Groucho Marx article, VG.............**10.00**

Saturday Evening Post, 1966, July 30, Bob Dylan, EX .**12.00**

Screen Stars, 1946, February, Rita Hayworth, EX........**25.00**

Silver Screen, 1958, June, Mitzi Gaynor, EX....................**12.00**

Sport, 1974, Pete Rose, EX...**10.00**

Sports Illustrated, 1962, July 2, Mickey Mantle, EX......**100.00**

Sports Illustrated, 1963, March 4, Sandy Koufax, EX..........**20.00**

Sports Illustrated, 1968, January 15, swimsuit issue, EX..**38.00**

Sports Illustrated, 1974, December 23, Muhammad Ali, EX..**20.00**

Sports Illustrated, 1983, January 3, Wayne Gretzky, EX...**10.00**

Sports Illustrated, 1984, December 10, Michael Jordan, EX..**35.00**

Sports Illustrated, 1988, March 21, Larry Bird, EX.........**10.00**

Time, 1935, April 15, Dizzy Dean, EX....................................**65.00**

Time, 1941, October 10, Joe Louis, EX....................................**25.00**

Time, 1971, March 8, Ali/Frazier, EX....................................**12.00**

True Crime, May, 1955, VG ...**5.00**

True Story, 1935, April, Zoe Mozert art cover, EX.............**30.00**

True Story, 1938, July, Myrna Loy, EX..........................**12.00**

Tuff Stuff, 1990, July, Nolan Ryan cover, VG.........................**5.00**

TV Guide, 1954, May, Nelson Family........................**75.00**

TV Guide, 1970, April 4, Cast of The Brady Bunch, $125.00. (Photo courtesy Greg Davis and Bill Morgan)

TV Guide, 1956, July 7, Lassie..**84.00**

TV Guide, 1958, August 16, Wagon Train cast..........**45.00**

TV Guide, 1961, July 29, Captain Kangaroo.......................**22.00**

TV Guide, 1963, February 23, Carol Burnett.................**26.00**

TV Guide, 1967, January 28, Monkees...............................**125.00**

TV Guide, 1971, July 10, Cookie Monster...........................**6.00**

TV Guide, 1972, March 18, Sonny & Cher...........................**28.00**

TV Guide, 1977, June 11, Grizzly Adams...........................**12.00**

TV Guide, 1978, February 4, The Love Boat..........................**9.00**

TV Guide, 1984, April 14, Knight Rider cast.......................**33.00**

TV Guide, 1990, March 24, Billy Crystal...........................**10.00**

TV Guide, 1990, November 17, Muppets...........................**7.00**

TV Guide, 1993, July 3, Vanna White.................................**8.00**

TV Guide, 1993, September 25, Raymond Burr...............**20.00**

TV Guide, 1997, November 15, X-Files cast.......................**15.00**

Venture, 1964, August, Beirut/Port-Cros/etc, EX..........**12.00**

Vogue, 1940, January, swimsuit cover, EX.......................**14.00**

Walt Disney Magazine, 1958, February, Annette Funicello article, NM...........................**15.00**

Woman's Day, 1940, September, Jimmy Stewart, VG.........**6.00**

Woman's Home Companion, 1925, October, Our Gang paper dolls, EX..........................**50.00**

Yankee, 1977, May, Maxfield Parrish cover, EX.................**20.00**

Marbles

Because there are so many kinds of marbles that interest today's collectors, we suggest you study a book on that specific subject such as one by Everett Grist (see Directory, Tennessee), published by Collector Books. In addition to his earlier work, *Antique and Collectible Marbles*, he has written a book on *Machine-Made and Contemporary Marbles* as well, now in its second edition. His latest title is *Everett Grist's Big Book of Marbles*, which includes both antique and modern varieties. All are published by Collector Books.

Remember that condition is extremely important. Naturally, chips occurred; and though some may be ground down and polished, the values of badly chipped and repolished marbles are low. In our listings, values are for marbles in the standard small size and in excellent to near-mint condition unless noted otherwise. Watch for reproductions of the comic character marbles. Repros have the design printed on a large area of plain white glass with color swirled through the back and sides. While common sulfides may run as low as $100.00, those with a more unusual subject or made of colored glass are considerably higher, sometimes as much as $1,000.00 or more. See Clubs and Newsletters for information concerning the Marble Collectors' Society of America.

Artist-Made, angelfish or sea horse, David Salazar, 1⅜".........**100.00**

Aventurine, Akro Agate, 9/16"..**25.00**

Blue oxblood, ⅝"..................**120.00**

Clambroth, 2-color swirl, ⅝".**125.00**

Comic, Annie........................**100.00**

Comic, Skeezix....................**100.00**

Corkscrew, limeade (green colors), Akro Agate, ⅝"...............**40.00**

Corkscrew, Popeye, Akro Agate, ⅝"..................................**25.00**

Corkscrew, tricolor, Akro Agate, ⅝"..................................**15.00**

Divided core swirl, peewee, any color variation, ½"..........**25.00**

Master Made Marbles, in box stamped 'Clearies,' $160.00. (Photo courtesy Everett Grist)

Divided core, yellow and red with outer red, white, and blue ribbons, inner threads of alternating white and yellow, ⅝", $25.00. (Photo courtesy Everett Grist)

Goldstone, glass w/copper flakes, ¾"....................................**35.00**

Hurricane, Christensen Agate..**10.00**

Joseph swirl, ⅝"..................**150.00**

Lutz, clear swirl, ¾"..............**85.00**

Lutz, gold sparkle & white swirl on sky blue, ⅝"............**350.00**

Mica, transparent blue, green or amber w/mica flecks, ¾".**35.00**

Moonies, Akro Agate, ⅝"........**3.00**

Opaque swirl, any 3-color, Christensen, 11/16"....................**35.00**

Peppermint swirl, red, white & blue opaque, ⅝"............**100.00**

Ribbon core swirl, any color variation, ½".........................**150.00**

Slag, red, Akro Agate, ⅝".....**10.00**

Solid core swirl, ¾"...............**15.00**

Sulfide, bull, 1⅞"................**200.00**

Sulfide, chicken, 1¼".............**75.00**

Sulfide, owl, 1¾"................**175.00**

Sulfide, papoose, 1¾"..........**700.00**

Sulfide, rabbit, 1¾".............**250.00**

Tiger eye, Master Marble, 9/16" or 11/16", ea............................**20.00**

Transparent swirl, latticinio yellow core, red/white outer bands, ⅝"........................**25.00**

Transparent swirl, solid core, ¾"..............................**75.00**

Marilyn Monroe

Her life was full of tumult, her career short, and the end tragic, but in less than a decade she managed to establish herself as the ultimate Hollywood sex goddess, and though there have been many try, none has ever came close to evoking the same devotion movie goers have always felt for Marilyn Monroe. Her sexuality was innocent, almost unintentional. She was one of the last from the era when stars wore designer fashions, perfectly arranged hair styles, and flawless makeup. Her relationships with the men in her life, though all were unfortunate, only added to the legend. Fans today look for the dolls, photographs, and various other collectibles that have been produced over the years.

Book, Legend The Life & Death of Marilyn Monroe, 524 pages, EX **12.00**

Book, The Joy Of Marilyn, Sam Shaw, 1979, 160 pages, hardcover, VG+ **25.00**

Box, black high-heel pump replica, blue w/faux signature, 2½", NM **22.00**

Calender, nude photos, 1955, VG+ **55.00**

Key chain, in black teddy outfit, black & white, 1993, NM..**8.00**

Model car, 1955 Cadillac Convertible, Solido, 1/18th scale, MIB **25.00**

Ornament, in white dress (over street vent), Hallmark, 1998, MIB................................**25.00**

Pin, cloisonne; mk Andy Warhol 1964 on back, EX **15.00**

Plate, A Twinkle in Her Eye, Reflections of Marilyn Collection, EX...........................**32.00**

Plate, Graceful Beauty **25.00**

Doll, Seven Year Itch, Tristar, 1982, 11½", MIB, $100.00. (Photo courtesy Henri Yunes)

Matchbox Cars

Introduced in 1953, the Matchbox Miniatures series has always been the mainstay of the company. There were seventy-five models in all but with enough variations to make collecting them a real challenge. Larger, more detailed models were introduced in 1957. This series, called Major Pack, was replaced a few years later by a similar line called King Size. To compete with Hot Wheels, Matchbox converted most models over to a line called SuperFast that sported thinner, low-friction axles and wheels. (These are much more readily available from the original 'regular wheels,' the last of which was made in 1959.) At about the same time, the King size series became known as Speed Kings; in 1977 the line was reintroduced under the name Super Kings.

Another line that's become very popular is their Models of Yesteryear. These are slightly larger replicas of antique and vintage vehicles. Values of $20.00 to $60.00 for mint-in-box examples are average, though a few sell for even more.

Sky Busters, introduced in 1973, are small-scale aircraft measuring an average of 3½" in length. Models currently being produced sell for about $4.00 each.

To learn more we recommend *Matchbox Toys, 1948 to 1993,* and *Matchbox Toys, 1974 — 1996,* by Dana Johnson; and a series of books by Charlie Mack: *Lesney's Matchbox Toys* (there are three: Regular Wheels, SuperFast Years, and Universal years).

To determine values of examples in conditions other than given in our listings, based on MIB or MOC prices, deduct a minimum of 10% if the original container is missing, 30% if the condition is excellent, and as much as 70% for a toy graded only very good.

Key:
LW — Laser Wheels (introduced in 1987)

reg — regular wheels (Matchbox Miniatures)
SF — SuperFast

King Size, Speed Kings, and Super Kings

K-1-C, O&K Excavator, 1970, MIP, from $18 to............**20.00**

K-3-A, Caterpillar Bulldozer, 1960, MIP, from $30 to..**40.00**

K-5-B, Racing Car Tansporter, 1967, MIP, from $25 to..**35.00**

K-6-D, Motorcycle Transporter, 1975, MIP, from $12 to..**15.00**

K-10-B, Pipe Truck, 1967, M, from $20.00 to $25.00. (Photo courtesy Dana Johnson)

K-10-C, Auto Transporter, 1976, from $15 to **20.00**

K-15-B, Londoner Bus, The Royal Wedding, 1981, M..........**20.00**

K-19-B, Security Truck, 1979, MIP, from $12 to............**18.00**

K-22-A, Dodge Charger, 1969, MIP, from $15 to............**20.00**

K-29-A, Miura Seaburst Set, 1971, MIP, from $25 to............**30.00**

K-33-B, Cargo Hauler, 1978, MIP, from $16 to **24.00**

K-38-B, Dodge Ambulance, 1980, MIP, from $12 to............**15.00**

K-44-C, Bridge Transporter, 1981, MIP, from $12 to............**15.00**

K-49-A, Ambulance, 1973, red, MIP, from $30 to............**40.00**

K-90-A, Matra Rancho, 1982, MIP, from $12 to............**15.00**

Models of Yesteryears

Y-1-B, 1911 Ford Model T, 1965, silver, MIP, from $50 to..**60.00**

Y-3-B, 1910 Benz Limosine, 1966, light green w/green roof, MIP......................**75.00**

Y-8-A, 1926 Morris Crowley Bullnose, 1958, MIP, from $60 to............................**75.00**

Y-11-B, 1912 Packard Landaulet, 1964, metallic red, M, from $25.00 to $35.00. (Photo courtesy Dana Johnson)

Y-13-B, 1911 Daimler, 1966, silver or gold, MIP, ea, from $50 to............................**60.00**

Y-21-C, 1957 BMW 507, 1988, from $20 to......................**25.00**

Y-23-B, 1930 Mack Tanker, 1989, MIP, from $12 to............**15.00**

Y-45-A, 1930 Bugatti Royale, 1991, MIP, from $15 to..**20.00**

Y-61-A, 1933 Cadillac Fire Engine, 1992, MIP, from $25 to..................................**30.00**

Skybusters

SB-2-A, Corsair A7D, 1973, dark green & white, MIP, from $8 to....................................**10.00**

SB-4-A, Mirage F1 122-18, 1973, orange & brown, MIP......**6.00**

SB-9-A, Cessna 402, 1973, brown & beige, MIP, from $6 to .**8.00**

SB-17-A, Ram Rod, 1976, red, MIP..............................**10.00**

SB-19-A, Piper Commanche XP, 1977, white, MIP............**10.00**

SB-30-A, Grumman Navy F-14 Tomcat, 1989, gray & white, MIP..................................**5.00**

SB-34-A, Lockheed A130/C-130 Hercules, 1990, white with USCG decal, M, $5.00. (Photo courtesy Dana Johnson)

1–75 Series

2-F, Jeep Hot Rod, reg, 1971, pink or red, from $12 to..........**18.00**

4-E, Dodge Stake Truck, SF, 1970, MIP, from $15 to............**20.00**

5-A, London Bus, reg, 1954, red, MIP, from $60 to............**70.00**

7-D, Ford Refuse Pickup, SF, 1970, MIP, from $15 to..**20.00**

7-H, Ruff Rabbit 4x4, reg, 1983, MIP, from $3 to................**5.00**

8-G, Ford Mustang Rat Rod Dragster, reg, 1970, MIP, from $20 to....................................**25.00**

9-D, Boat & Trailer, reg, 1966, bright blue deck, MIP, from $5 to **8.00**

10-F, Mustang Piston Popper, reg, 1973, white, MIP, from $200 to..................................**250.00**

11-E, Scaffolding Truck, SF, 1970, silver, complete, M.........**24.00**

11-H, Mustang Cobra, reg, 1982, MIP, from $5 to................**8.00**

12-I, Pontiac Firebird S/E, reg, 1982, black, Firebird tampo, MIP...................................**5.00**

13-I, 4x4 Minim Pickup, reg, 1983, w/reef foil, MIP, from $2 to...............................**4.00**

17-E, Horse Bo, SF, 1970, red, no horses, M (NM+ box) **23.00**

19-F, Road Dragster, reg, 1970, metallic red, MIP, from $15 to **20.00**

21-E, Foden Concrete Truck, SF, 1970, MIP, from $20 to..**25.00**

23-F, Mustang GT350, reg, 1979, MIP, from $10 to............**12.00**

25-A, Bedford Dunlop 12CWT Van, reg, 1956, MIP, from $40 to **55.00**

26-D, GMC Tipper Truck, SF, 1970, red w/gray box, MIP, from $15 to **20.00**

28-C, Jaguar, reg, 1964, black plastic wheels, MIP, from $15 to **20.00**

29-A, Bedford Milk Delivery Van, reg, 1956, MIP, from $45 to **60.00**

29-E, Racing Mini, reg, 1970, orange, MIP, from $9 to...**12.00**

30-E, Beach Buggy, SF, 1970, lavender, EX+ **11.00**

31-D, Lincoln Continental, SF, 1970, green-gold, NM+ ..**26.00**

34-F, Vantastic, reg, 1975, orange w/white base, exposed engine, MIP...................................**12.00**

33-E, Datsun 126X, 1973, yellow with orange base, black and red flame tampo, M, from $12.00 to $18.00. (Photo courtesy Dana Johnson)

36-C, Opel Diplomat, SF, 1970, MIP, from $15 to............**20.00**

36-E, Hot Rod Draguar, reg, 1970, MIP, from $15 to............**20.00**

42-C, Iron Fairy Crane, reg, 1969, MIP, from $6 to................**9.00**

42-E, Tyre Fryer Jaffa Mobile, reg, 1972, blue, from $12 to.....................................**18.00**

44-C, GMC Refrigerator Truck, reg, 1967, MIP, from $6 to........**9.00**

47-D, DAF Tipper Truck, SF, 1970, silver & yellow, M **24.00**

47-F, Pannier Tank Locomotive, 1979, MIP, from $4 to......**6.00**

48-C, Dodge Pickup, reg, 1966, MIP, from $6 to................**9.00**

49-E, Crane Truck, reg, 1976, red, MIP, from $65 to............**75.00**

49-E, Crane Truck, reg, 1976, yellow, MIP, from $5 to **10.00**

51-D, AEC Ergomatic 8-Wheel Tippe, SF, 1970, MIP, from $15 to **20.00**

53-D, Ford Zodiac, SF, 1970, metallic green w/unpainted base, 1970, M **20.00**

54-D, Ford Capri, reg, 1971, MIP, from $9 to **15.00**

58-D, DAF Girder Truck, SF, 1970, MIP, from $20 to..**25.00**

61-C, Blue Shark, SF, 1971, dark blue w/unpainted base, #86 label, EX+ **10.00**

63-C, Dodge Crane Truck, 1968, yellow, M **25.00**

66-C, Greyhound Bus, reg, 1967, clear windows, MIP, from $60 to **75.00**

67-C, Volkswagen 1600TL, SF, 1970, red, MIP, from $30 to **40.00**

71-D, Ford Heavy Wreck Esso Truck, SF, 1970, blue, MIP, from $100 to **120.00**

71-E, Jumbo Jet Motorcycle, reg, 1973, MIP, from $15 to ..**20.00**

72-C, Standard Jeep CJ5, SF, 1970, MIP, from $15 to ..**20.00**

75-D, Alfa Carabo, 1971, M, $10.00.
(Photo courtesy Dana Johnson)

McCoy

A popular collectible with flea market goers, McCoy pottery was made in Roseville, Ohio, from 1910 until the late 1980s. They are most famous for their extensive line of figural cookie jars, more than two hundred in all. They also made amusing figural planters, etc., as well as dinnerware, and vases and pots for the florist trade. Though some pieces are unmarked, most bear one of several McCoy trademarks. Beware of reproductions made by a company in Tennessee who until recently used a very close facsimile of the old McCoy mark. They made several cookie jars once produced by McCoy as well as other now-defunct potteries. Some of these (but by no means all) were dated with the number '93' below the mark.

For more information refer to *The Collector's Encyclopedia of McCoy Pottery* by Sharon and Bob Huxford and *McCoy Pottery, Collector's Reference & Value Guide, Volumes I* and *II,* by Margaret Hanson, Craig Nissen, and Bob Hanson (all available from Collector Books). See also Cookie Jars. See Clubs and Newsletters for information concerning the newsletter *The Nelson McCoy Express.*

Astray, sq w/diagonal rest, brown, 1960s, from $15 to..........**20.00**

Bank, Lucky Penny Puppy, from $50 to **60.00**

Bank, teapot form, pink, 1940s, from $60.00 to $85.00. (Photo courtesy Margaret and Bob Hanson and Craig Nissen)

Basket, embossed flowers at base of handle, 1960s, 8x5", from $35 to **45.00**

Bookends, birds & blossoms form, pastels, 1940s, 6", pr, from $175 to..........................**225.00**

Bowl, Early American, footed, blue accents, 1960s, 7", from $30 to **40.00**

Candy boat, gondola form, gold trim, 1955, from $60 to..**75.00**

Candy dish, Golden Brocade Line, pedestal foot, 1970, 8", from $25 to..............................**35.00**

Casserole, Brown Antique Rose, w/lid, 1959, from $35 to.**45.00**

Centerpiece, leaf form, 1920s-30s, from $50 to **70.00**

Centerpiece, overlapping leaves, 1950s, 10½x7", from $40 to....................................**50.00**

Centerpiece & candle holders, Starburst, 1970s, 3-pc, from $80 to.............................**100.00**

Coffeepot & 4 mugs, steaming cup motif, 1965, 5-pc set, from $100 to...........................**120.00**

Creamer, pineapple design, Islander Kitchenware, 1970s, from $15 to **25.00**

Creamer & sugar, ivy motif on cream, gold trim, 1950s, ea from $40 to **50.00**

Cruets, oil & vinegar; drip glazes, cork stoppers, 1970s, pr, from $15 to..............................**25.00**

Flower bowl, Grecian design around incurvate rim, from $25 to..............................**35.00**

Flowerpot, orange on leaf saucer, natural green leaf, 1950s, from $40 to **60.00**

Grease jar, cabbage form, 1950s, 7", from $100 to...........**125.00**

Hanging planter, burlap sack, 1977, from $15 to **20.00**

Hanging planter, owl, Lancaster mark, 1976, from $35 to...**45.00**

Jardiniere, Harmony, 7½", from $40 to...............................**50.00**

Jardiniere, swirl design w/pedestal foot, 1962, 7", from $20 to..............................**25.00**

Lamp, berries & leaves w/tassels, 1930s, from $125 to **175.00**

Lamp, wagon wheel, w/original shade, 1950s, 8", from $75 to...............................**100.00**

Mug, strawberries & flowers on white, 1970s, from $10 to..**15.00**

Pitcher, ball form w/hobnail design, solid pastel, 1940s, 6", from $100 to **150.00**

Pitcher, strawberries & flowers on white, 1970s, 32-oz, from $35 to **50.00**

Pitcher & bowl set, sailing ship motif, 1973, 8", from $60 to...........**80.00**

Planter, baby grand piano form, gold trim, 1959, 5x6", from $150 to...........................**200.00**

Planter, baby's skirted bassinet, pink or blue, 1954, from $60 to...................................**70.00**

Planter, coal bucket, eagle decor, bail handle, 1974, 10", from $35 to..............................**75.00**

Planter, dachshund, Stretch Animal, 1940s, from $175 to **225.00**

Planter, Dutch shoe w/rose on top, late 1940s, 7½", from $25 to...........................**50.00**

Planter, frog w/separate umbrella, 1950s, from $125 to **175.00**

Planter, kittens & basket on stool, gold trim, 1950s, 7", from $60 to...................................**70.00**

Planter, lamb, gold trim, 1954, 8½", from $95 to...........**120.00**

Planter, log w/axe, gold trim, 1954, 4x8½", $80 to......**110.00**

Planter, log w/wagon wheel, gold trim, 1956, 4x12½", from $100 to............**125.00**

Planter, oblong w/pedestal, zigzag design, 1950s, 9" L, from $20 to.....................**30.00**

Planter, oblong w/scrolled footed base, 1959, 10", from $40 to...........................**60.00**

Planter, oblong w/sunburst fluting, 1940s, 3x5", from $35 to.................................**50.00**

Planter, panther, chartreuse, 1950s, from $40 to..........**60.00**

Planter, poodle prancing, pink & white, 1950s, 7½", from $100 to.....................................**150.00**

Planter, rabbits (2) & stump, pink & blue, 1950s, from $100 to...........................**125.00**

Planter, rolling pin w/Blue Boy, 1950s, 7½", from $60 to.**75.00**

Planter, squirrel form, rare metallic gold, 1950s, from $75 to...**100.00**

Planter, turtle, green, 1970s, 5x8", from $20 to......................**25.00**

Planter, watering can, pink rose on white, gold trim, 7", from $50 to...............................**60.00**

Platter, oval w/turkey motif, airbrushed, 1960s, 19", from $80 to......................................**100.00**

Salt & pepper shakers, both form cabbage head, 1950s, pr, from $75 to............................**100.00**

Spoon rest, spoon bowl shape, various decorations, 1975, ea, from $15 to......................**25.00**

Strawberry jar, red clay w/green or white gloss, 1975, 9", from $35 to.............................**40.00**

Teapot, cat figural (beware of German look-alike), 1969, from $95.00 to $150.00. (Photo courtesy Margaret and Bob Hanson and Craig Nissen)

Tray, open hands w/leaf motif, 8½", from $100 to.........**125.00**

Umbrella stand, cylindrical w/leaf columns, 1940s, 19", from $250 to...........................**350.00**

Utensil holder, wall mount, Islander Kitchenware, 1979, from $15 to.....................**25.00**

Vase, cylindrical w/scrolled foot, white, green or fawn, 14", from $75 to....................**100.00**

Vase, cylindrical w/vertical ribbing, banded rim, 1950s, 10", from $50 to.....................**60.00**

Vase, Deco style w/concentric circles, footed, 1940s, 7", from $80 to............................**100.00**

Vase, fan; fluted w/berries & leaves at base, cobalt, 6", from $40 to.............................**60.00**

Vase, hyacinth form w/leaves, standard glazes, 1950s, 8", from $100 to.................**125.00**

Vase, ivy decor w/angled twig handles, 1950s, 9", from $100 to.................................**150.00**

Vase, mug w/pedestal foot, Floraline, 6", from $15 to **25.00**

Vase, sq top w/twisted body & round bottom, Floraline, 9", from $25 to **30.00**

Vase, sq w/leaves & berries, 1940s, 10", from $80 to **110.00**

Vase, 5-finger; grapes & leaves motif, 1962, from $60 to ..**75.00**

Wall pocket, apple on 2 crossed leafy branches, 7"...........**30.00**

Wall pocket, cuckoo clock, 1950s, from $125 to **150.00**

Wall pocket, urn form, gold trim, 1950s, 6½x4½", from $50 to **74.00**

Melmac Dinnerware

Melmac was a product of the postwar era, a thermoplastic material formed by the interaction of melamine and formaldehyde. It was popular because of its attractive colors and patterns, and it was practically indestructible. But eventually it faded, became scratched or burned, and housewives tired of it. By the late 1960s and early 1970s, it fell from favor.

Collectors, however, are finding its mid-century colors and shapes appealing again, and they're beginning to reassemble melmac table services when pristine, well designed items can be found.

Our advisor for this category is Gregory R. Zimmer, who along with Alvin Daigle Jr., has written *Melmac Dinnerware*; Gregg is list-ed in the Directory under Minnesota. See also Russel Wright.

Aztec, Debonaire, Flite-Lane, Mar-Crest, Restraware, Rivieraware, Stetson, Westinghouse

Bowl, serving; from $4 to **5.00**
Butter dish, from $5 to **7.00**
Plate, bread; from $1 to **2.00**
Plate, dinner; from $2 to.........**3.00**
Salt & pepper shakers, from $4 to **5.00**
Sugar bowl, w/lid, from $3 to..**4.00**
Tumbler, 6-oz, from $6 to **7.00**

Boontoon, Branchell, Brookpark, Harmony House, Prolon, Watertown Lifetime Ware

Bowl, divided vegetable; from $8 to **10.00**
Bowl, fruit; from $3 to.............**4.00**
Bowl, soup; w/lid, from $5 to ..**6.00**
Casserole, w/lid, from $20 to .**25.00**
Creamer, from $5 to **6.00**
Cup & saucer, from $3 to........**4.00**

Brookpark, divided dinner plates, from $10.00 to $12.00 each. (Photo courtesy Gregory R. Zimmer and Alvin Daigle Jr.)

Gravy boat, from $6 to............**8.00**
Plate, bread; from $2 to..........**3.00**
Plate, salad; from $4 to...........**5.00**
Platter, from $8 to.................**10.00**
Salad tongs, from $12 to.......**15.00**
Sugar bowl, from $6 to............**8.00**
Tidbit tray, 3-tier, from $15 to ..**18.00**
Tumbler, 10-oz, from $12 to .**15.00**
Tumbler, 6-oz, from $10 to ...**12.00**

Fostoria, Lucent

Bowl, cereal; from $7 to..........**9.00**
Bowl, serving; from $15 to....**18.00**
Butter dish, from $15 to.......**18.00**
Creamer, from $8 to..............**10.00**
Plate, bread; from $3 to..........**4.00**
Plate, dinner; from $6 to........**8.00**
Platter, from $12 to...............**15.00**
Relish tray, from $15 to........**18.00**

Metlox

Since the 1940s, the Metlox company of California has been producing dinnerware lines, cookie jars, and decorative items which today have become popular collectibles. Some of their best-known patterns are California Provincial (the dark green and burgundy rooster), Red Rooster (in red, orange, and brown), Homestead Provincial (dark green and burgundy farm scenes), and Colonial Homestead (farm scenes done in red, orange, and brown). See also Cookie Jars.

Our advisor for this category is Carl Gibbs, Jr.; he is listed in the Directory under Texas. Mr. Gibbs is the author of *Collector's*

Encyclopedia of Metlox Potteries (Collector Books).

Dinnerware

Antique Grape, jam & jelly...**55.00**
Antique Grape, plate, luncheon; 9"....................................**18.00**
Antique Grape, platter, oval, 14¼"...........................**50.00**
Autumn Berry, mug, 8-oz.....**20.00**
Autumn Berry, plate, dinner; 10¾"..............................**13.00**
Blueberry Provincial, pitcher, 2¼-qt.....................................**70.00**
California Aztec, mug, cocoa ..**40.00**
California Aztec, platter, 13"..**65.00**
California Confetti, bowl, vegetable; w/lid...................**100.00**
California Confetti, plate, salad.**14.00**
California Freeform, cup, juice...**45.00**
California Freeform, flowerpot, 6"....................................**80.00**
California Geranium, gravy ladle............................**20.00**
California Geranium, plate, dinner..................................**12.00**
California Ivy, bowl, vegetable; round, w/lid, 11".............**95.00**
California Ivy, cup, jumbo **40.00**

California Ivy, bowl, divided vegetable; $50.00.

California Peach Blossom, creamer.................:.........28.00
California Peach Blossom, tumbler................................28.00
California Provincial, bread server, 9½"............................75.00
California Provincial, candle holder.......................................55.00
California Provincial, plate, dinner; 10"..........................20.00
California Tempo, chop plate, 13"................................45.00
California Tempo, tumbler, 10-oz...................................25.00
Chantilly Blue, cup...............10.00
Colonial Heritage Provincial, coffee carafe......................130.00
Colonial Heritage Provincial, egg cup....................................28.00
Colonial Heritage Provincial, platter, oval, X-lg...................80.00
Colorstax, baker, oval, 13"....45.00
Colorstax, candlestick...........28.00
Colorstax, plate, dinner; 10½"..14.00
Della Robbia, bowl, divided vegetable; 12⅛"....................55.00
Della Robbia, cup & saucer ..16.00

Homestead Provincial, creamer and sugar bowl, $70.00.

Homestead Provincial, cookie jar..............................125.00
Homestead Provincial, platter, oval, 16"..........................85.00
La Mancha, gravy boat, 12-oz ..30.00

La Mancha, teapot, 6-cup.....95.00
Lotus, bowl, cereal; 6¾"........16.00
Lotus, mug, 7-oz....................25.00
Navajo, bowl, divided vegetable; sm...................................45.00
Navajo, bowl, fruit................14.00
Navajo, pitcher, 1-pt.............40.00
Poppy Trail/#200 series, creamer.....................................20.00
Poppy Trail/#200 series, salt & pepper shakers, S&P shapes, pr....24.00
Provincial Blue, ashtray, med, 6⅜"...............................25.00
Provincial Blue, pepper mill ..55.00
Provincial Fruit, bowl, soup; 8½" .18.00
Red Rooster Provincial, egg cup ...32.00
Red Rooster Provincial, gravy boat, 1-pt........................45.00
Red Rooster Provincial, plate, dinner; 10"...........................15.00
Red Rooster Provincial, salt & pepper shakers, pr.........28.00
Sculptured Daisy, bowl, cereal; 7¼"................................14.00
Sculptured Daisy, plate, salad; 7½"................................10.00
Sculptured Grape, bowl, soup; 8⅛"................................24.00
Sculptured Grape, butter dish ..75.00
Sculptured Zinnia, plate, dinner; 10½"................................13.00
Sculptured Zinnia, teapot, 6-cup..............................100.00
Woodland Gold, mug, 8-oz 22.00
Woodland Gold, shakers, pr .24.00
Yorkshire, candle holder.......30.00
Yorkshire, celery dish...........30.00
Yorkshire, sherbet................24.00

Miscellaneous

Disney, Bambi w/butterfly .250.00
Disney, Faline....................165.00

Baby the Indian Elephant, balancing on a ball, 6½", $145.00 minimum value. (Photo courtesy Jack Chipman)

Disney, Mamma Mouse (Cinderella series) **200.00**
Disney, Three Little Pigs, 1¼", ea **200.00**
Miniatures, Burro sitting, 3"..**55.00**
Miniatures, duck w/head down, 3".................................**40.00**
Miniatures, giraffe, 5¾"......**140.00**
Nostalgia Line, Cadillac.......**85.00**
Nostalgia Line, locomotive ...**65.00**
Nostalgia Line, mail wagon..**80.00**
Nostalgia Line, Santa.........**115.00**
Poppets, Conchita, Mexican girl, 8¾"...................................**60.00**
Poppets, Eliza, flower vendor, 5⅝"...................................**55.00**
Poppets, Elliot w/4" bowl......**45.00**
Poppets, Mother Goose, 8"....**55.00**
Poppets, Penelope, nursemaid, 7¾".....................................**35.00**
Romanelli Artware, figurine, deer, 7"...................................**125.00**
Romanelli Artware, figurine, rooster, 8¼" **105.00**
Romanelli Artware, vase, mermaid & fish....................**175.00**

Miller Studio

Brightly painted chalkware plaques, bookends, thermometers, and hot pad holders modeled with subjects that range from Raggedy Ann and angels to bluebirds and sunfish were the rage during 1950s and 1960s, and even into the early 1970s you could buy them from the five-&-dime store to decorate your kitchen and bathroom walls with style and flair. Collectors who like this 'kitschy' ambience are snapping them up and using them in the vintage rooms they're re-creating with period appliances, furniture, and accessories. They're especially fond of the items marked Miller Studio, a manufacturing firm located in New Philadelphia, Pennsylvania. Most but not all of their pieces are marked and carry a copyright date. If you find an unmarked item with small holes on the back where stapled-on cardboard packaging has been torn away, chances are very good it's Miller Studio as well. Miller Studio is still in business and are today the only American firm that continues to produce hand-finished wall plaques. (Mr. Miller tells us that although they had over 300 employees back in the 1960s and 1970s, they presently have about 75.)

Angels, cherub's face, orange, 1954, pr, from $8 to........**10.00**
Angels, 2 cherubs & oval mirror, gold, 1966, 3-pc set, from $16 to.....................................**20.00**
Animals, bear toothbrush holder, M17, tan & brown, 1954, from $16 to..............................**18.00**

Animals, cat w/pencil holder, yellow & black, 1957, from $15 to.......................................**20.00**

Animals, horse head, brown, 1951, from $12 to......................**14.00**

Animals, pig, blue & white, sm, from $10 to......................**12.00**

Birds, cardinal, red, 1972, pr, from $8 to........................**10.00**

Birds, flying pheasant, M36, red, 3-pc set, from $25 to **30.00**

Birds, owl, white, 1978, 11", pr, from $8 to........................**10.00**

Birds, swan, pink, oval, 1965, pr, from $8 to........................**10.00**

Birds, swan plaques, pink, oval, 1965, pr, from $9 to........**12.00**

Birds, swan plaques, pink & white, round, 1958, pr, from $14 to..............................**16.00**

Figures, Dutch boy & girl, yellow & red, 1953, pr, from $26 to **28.00**

Figures, Raggedy Ann & Andy, blue & orange, pr, from $28 to **32.00**

Fish, family, blue, 1950s, 9", 4-pc set, from $16 to **20.00**

Fish, male & female, black, 1954, pr, from $12 to................**14.00**

Fruit, bunch, brown & yellow, round, 1968, from $6 to ...**8.00**

Fruit, carrot bunch, orange & green, 1971, from $6 to....**8.00**

Fruit, grapes on wood, gold, 1964, from $10 to......................**12.00**

Fruit, lg mushrooms, yellow & brown, 1977, pr, from $13 to **16.00**

Hot pad holder, peach w/funny face, yellow, 1972, pr, from $8 to.**12.00**

Note pad, bird, Make a Note, yellow & red, 1954, from $17 to **20.00**

Note pad, owl w/pencil holder, red & yellow, 1970, from $12 to **15.00**

Thermometer, fruit bunch, multicolor, 1981, from $10 to .**12.00**

Thermometer, fruit grouping, copyright 1966, M, from $10.00 to $14.00.

Thermometer, mermaid, aqua & white, 1976, from $14 to..**17.00**

Thermometer, Sniffy Skunk, M55, black & yellow, from $28 to..**30.00**

Model Kits

The best-known producer of model kits today is Aurora. Collectors often pay astronomical prices for some of the character kits from the 1960s. Made popular by all the monster movies of that decade, ghouls like Vampirella, Frankenstein, and the Wolfman were eagerly built up by kids everywhere. But the majority of all model kits were vehicles, ranging from 3" up to 24" long. Some of the larger model vehicle makers were AMT, MPC, and IMC. Condition is very important in assessing the value of a kit, with built-ups priced at about 50% lower than one still in the box. Other things factor into pricing as well — who is selling, who is buying, how badly they want it, locality, supply, and demand.

For information about Aurora models, we recommend *Aurora, History and Price Guide,* by Bill Bruegman (Cap'n Penny Productions, Inc); to learn more about models other than Aurora, refer to *Collectible Figure Kits of the '50s, '60s & '70s, Reference and Value Guide*, by Gordy Dutt (see Directory under Ohio for ordering information), and *Classic Plastic Model Kits*, by Rick Polizzi (Collector Books). For additional listings we recommend *Schroeder's Collectible Toys, Antique to Modern* (Collector Books). See Clubs and Newsletters for International Figure Kit Club; *Model Toy Collector Magazine.*

Addar, Evil Knievel's Wheelie, 1974, MIB....................**125.00**
Addar, Super Scenes, Spirit in a Bottle, 1975, MIB...........**50.00**
Airfix, Bristol Bloodhound, 1992, MIB...............................**15.00**
Airfix, Corythosaurus, 1970, MIB (sealed) **30.00**
AMT, Farrah's Foxy Vet, 1970s, MIB................................**35.00**
AMT, Get Smart Sunbeam Car, 1967, MIB......................**100.00**
AMT, Munster Koach, 1964, MIB............................**150.00**
AMT/Ertl, A-Team Van, 1983, MIB................................**30.00**
AMT/Ertl, Star Wars, Han Solo, 1995, MIB.......................**30.00**

Aoshima, Back to the Future, Delorian, 1989, MIB **40.00**
Arii, Orguss Flier, MIB.........**15.00**
Arii, Regult Missile Carrier, MIB..............................**25.00**
Atlantic, Mao/Chinese Revolution, 1975, MIB......................**20.00**
Aurora, Archie's Car, 1969, MIB..............................**85.00**
Aurora, Batman, 1964, MIB...**225.00**
Aurora, Captain America, 1966, MIB..............................**400.00**
Aurora, Comic Scenes, Superboy, 1974, MIB....................**100.00**
Aurora, Dick Tracy Space Coupe, 1967, MIB....................**125.00**
Aurora, Dr Dolittle & Pushmi-Pullyu, 1968, MIB..........**75.00**
Aurora, Dracula's Dragster, 1964, MIB..............................**325.00**
Aurora, Godzilla, 1972, glow-in-the-dark, MIB **150.00**

Aurora, Monster Scenes, Dr. Deadly, 1971, MIB, $65.00.

Aurora, Guys & Gals, Caballero, 1959, MIB....................**100.00**
Aurora, Monster Scenes, Dr Deadly, 1971, MIB.................**65.00**

Aurora, Monster Scenes, Vampirella, 1971, MIB..........**100.00**

Aurora, Prehistoric Scenes, Tar Pit, 1971, MIB (sealed)........**200.00**

Aurora, Tonto, 1967, MIB...**200.00**

Bachmann, Animals of the World, Lion, 1959, MIB.............**50.00**

Bachmann, Birds of the World, Scarlet Tanager, 1990, MIB.............**20.00**

Bandai, Kinggidrah, 1984, MIB..**50.00**

Bandai, Z-Ton, 1984, NMIB.**20.00**

Billiken, Mole People, 1984, vinyl, MIB.................**75.00**

Billiken, War of Colossal Beats, 1986, vinyl, MIB............**50.00**

Dark Horse, Mummy, 1995, MIB.........................**150.00**

Eldon, Moon Survey, 1966, MIB...........................**50.00**

Eldon, Pink Panther, 1970s, MIB...........................**75.00**

Hawk, Capital Airlines Viscount, 1950s, NMIB.................**50.00**

Hawk, Weird-Ohs, Francis the Foul, 1963, MIB.............**50.00**

Imai, Orguss, Thing, 1991, MIB..........................**50.00**

Kaiydo, Angurus, 1991, vinyl, NMIB............................**50.00**

Life-Like, Cro-Magnon Man, 1973, MIB................................**40.00**

Lindburg, Tyrannosaurus, 1987, MIB................................**15.00**

Lunar Models, Lost in Space, Space Pod, MIB.............**125.00**

Monogram, Snoopy on the Highwire, 1972, MIB.............**35.00**

MPC, Alien, 1979, MIB (sealed)..**75.00**

Revell, Ariane 4 Rocket, 1985, MIB................................**35.00**

Revell, CHiPs, Helicopter, 1980, MIB................................**25.00**

Revell, Robotech Commando, 1984, MIB (sealed)........**50.00**

Screamin', Bettie Page-Jungle Fever, 1994, MIB (sealed)..............**85.00**

Screamin', Star Wars, Stormtrooper, 1993, MIB....................**45.00**

Tsukuda, Frankenstein, 1985, MIB..............................**100.00**

Moon and Star

A reissue of Palace, an early pattern glass line, Moon and Star was developed for the market in the 1960s by Joseph Weishar of Island Mould and Machine Company (Wheeling, West Virginia). It was made by several companies. One of the largest producers was L.E. Smith of Mt. Pleasant, Pennsylvania, and L.G. Wright (who had their glassware made by Fostoria and Fenton, perhaps others as well) carried a wide assortment in their catalogs for many years. It is still being made on a very limited basis, but the most collectible

Lindberg, Mad Mangler, MIB, $75.00.
(Rick Polizzi)

pieces are those in red, blue, amber, and green — colors that are no longer in production. Items listed here without mention of color are red or blue. Amber, green, and crystal prices should be 30% lower.

Ashtray, moons at rim, star in base, 6-sided, 8½" **25.00**
Ashtray, moons at rim, star in base, 6-sided, 5½" **18.00**
Bell, pattern along sides, plain rim & handle, from $35 to **45.00**
Bowl, allover pattern, footed, crimped rim, 7½" **35.00**
Butter/cheese dish, patterned lid, plain base, 7" dia............**65.00**
Candle bowl, allover pattern, footed, 8", from $28 to **32.00**
Candle holder, allover pattern, flared base, 4½", pr........**25.00**
Canister, allover pattern, 1-lb or 2-lb, from $12 to.............**15.00**
Compote, allover pattern, footed, flared crimped rim, 5"....**22.00**
Compote, allover pattern, rolled edge, 12" **65.00**
Compote, allover pattern, scalloped rim, footed, 5½x8"............**35.00**
Compote, allover pattern, scalloped rim, footed, 7x10".**45.00**
Epergne, allover pattern, 2-pc, 9"...................................**65.00**
Goblet, wine; plain rim & foot, 5¾", from $15 to.............**18.00**
Jardiniere/tobacco jar, allover pattern, patterned lid & finial, 6".........................**45.00**
Lamp, miniature; amber or green, ea **145.00**
Lamp, miniature; blue........**185.00**
Lamp, miniature; milk glass..**245.00**
Lamp, miniature; red..........**235.00**

Nappy, allover pattern, crimped rim, 8"..............................**35.00**
Plate, patterned body & center, smooth rim, 8"................**35.00**
Soap dish, allover pattern, oval, 2x6"..................................**12.00**
Sugar shaker, allover pattern, metal top, 4½x3½".........**50.00**

Sugar bowl with lid and creamer, LG Wright, $75.00.

Tumbler, juice; no pattern at rim, short pedestal foot, 4¼", $18 to.....................................**22.00**

Mortens Studios

Animal models sold by Mortens Studios of Arizona during the 1940s are some of today's most interesting collectibles, especially among animal lovers. Hundreds of breeds of dogs, cats, and horses were produced from a plaster-type composition material constructed over a wire framework. They range in size from 2" up to about 7", and most are marked. Crazing and flaking are nearly always present to some degree. Our values are for animals in excellent to near-mint condition, allowing for only minor crazing.

Beagle, lying down, #554 ......**55.00**
Bloodhound, #877 ....**150.00**
Boxer, #556, miniature **65.00**
Cocker spaniel, brown, #786 .**75.00**
Collie pup, #818, miniature ..**55.00**
Dalmatian, #854....................**95.00**
Doberman, #785 ....**95.00**
German shepherd, #556 ....**75.00**
Greyhound, gray, #747, 6¾" .**100.00**

Horse, grazing on grassy base, $90.00.

Irish Setter, #856 ....**95.00**
Palomino, rearing, 9" **110.00**
Pekingese, #553, miniature ..**65.00**
Pointer pup, recumbent, #503 ..**75.00**
Poodle, gray, 4" **85.00**
Pug, #738 ....**125.00**
Springer spaniel, #745 ....**95.00**
Stag, 7½x7" **150.00**

Moss Rose

Though the Moss Rose pattern has been produced by Staffordshire and American pottery companies alike since the mid-1800s, the lines we're dealing with here are all from the twentieth century. Much was made from the late 1950s into the 1970s by Japanese manufacturers. Even today you'll occasionally see a tea set or a small candy dish for sale in some of the chain stores. (The collectors who are already picking this line up refer to it as Moss Rose, but we've seen it advertised just lately under the name Victorian Rose, and some companies called their lines Chintz Rose or French Rose, so don't be surprised if we adopt one of those names later on.)

Rosenthal made an identical pattern, and prices are generally higher for examples that carry the mark of that company. The pattern consists of a briar rose with dark green mossy leaves on stark white glaze. Occasionally an item is trimmed in gold. In addition to dinnerware, many accessories and novelties were made as well.

Our advisor for this category is Geneva Addy; she is listed in the Directory under Iowa. For further information on items made by Lefton, see *The Collector's Encyclopedia of Lefton China* by Loretta DeLozier (Collector Books). Refer to *Schroeder's Antiques Price Guide* for information on the early Moss Rose pattern.

Ashtray set, 1 tray w/4 ash-
    trays **25.00**
Bowl, serving, gold trim, square,
    2" deep, 7¼" dia **45.00**
Bowl, serving; gold trim, oval,
    5½x9¾" **40.00**
Bowl, soup; Rosenthal, Pom-
    padour shape, 1½x8½" ..**25.00**

Bowl, vegetable; sterling base,
4¼x9½"..............................**85.00**

Butter dish, Nasco, w/lid, gold
trim, rectangular, 7" L...**45.00**

Butter pat, Rosenthal, Pompadour
shape, gold trim, 4½" dia ..**20.00**

Coffeepot, Rosenthal, gold trim,
w/lid.............................**180.00**

Creamer & sugar bowl, Rosenthal,
gold trim.........................**55.00**

Cup & saucer, Rosenthal, Pompadour shape, gold trim, footed cup **30.00**

Dish, gold trim, crimped edge,
footed, oval, w/lid...........**30.00**

Dish, vanity; Japan, silver trim,
3x3" dia...........................**20.00**

Egg coddler, plastic covered metal
clip holds lid, 3¼"...........**35.00**

Egg cup, Rosenthal, beaded sterling
base, silver trim, 2¾" **30.00**

Gravy boat, Nasco, gold trim,
w/underplate **25.00**

Gravy boat, Rosenthal, gold trim,
w/underplate **55.00**

Lamp, oil; genie style, 4½x6"
(w/glass globe)................**35.00**

Plate, dinner; Royal Rose, gold
trim, 10⅛" dia **25.00**

Plate, salad; Rosenthal, Pompadour shape, gold trim,
7¾" **15.00**

Plates, bread & butter; Rosenthal,
gold trim, set of 6 ....**60.00**

Platter, Rosenthal, gold trim,
oval, 9⅝x13⅛"................**60.00**

Platter, Rosenthal, gold trim,
11x15".............................**85.00**

Set, serving for 10, 70 pcs total,
Summit Fine Chine Japan,
M **185.00**

Soup tureen, gold trim, Rosenthal,
w/lid, 6½"........................**95.00**

Teapot, $20.00; Creamer and sugar bowl, with lid, from $10.00 to $15.00.

Tea service, Royal Rose, teapot,
creamer & sugar bowl, gold
trim **65.00**

Tea set, child's; 26-pc, mk
Japan.........................**190.00**

Teapot, Rosenthal, beaded sterling base, 7½".............**165.00**

Toothpick holder, gold trim, 2" ..**16.00**

Niloak

Produced in Arkansas by
Charles Dean Hyten from the
early 1900s until the mid-1940s,
Niloak (the backward spelling of
kaolin, a type of clay) takes many
forms — figural planters, vases
in both matt and glossy glazes,
and novelty items of various
types. The company's most
famous product and the most collectible is their Swirl or Mission
Ware line. Clay in colors of
brown, blue, cream, red, and buff
are swirled within the mold, the
finished product left unglazed on
the outside to preserve the natural hues. Small vases are common;
large pieces or unusual shapes

and those with exceptional coloration are the most valuable. Refer to *The Collector's Encyclopedia of Niloak, A Reference and Value Guide,* by David Edwin Gifford (Collector Books) for more information.

Note: The terms '1st' and '2nd art mark' used in the listings refer to specific die-stamped trademarks. The earlier mark was used from 1910 to 1924, followed by the second, very similar mark used from then until the end of Mission Ware production. Letters with curving raised outlines were characteristic of both; the most obvious difference between the two was that on the first, the final upright line of the 'N' was thin with a solid club-like terminal.

Ashtray, Mission/Swirl, dog-dish shape, 2nd art mark, 4¾", $100 to **125.00**
Bowl, incurvate scalloped rim, green/tan, Hywood, 3½x8", $50 to **75.00**
Bowl, Mission/Swirl, incurvate rim, 1st art mark, 2x5", $100 to **125.00**
Candlestick, Mission/Swirl, flared bottom, early, 7¼", $250 to **300.00**
Candlestick, tulip on pancake base, pink/blue, Hywood, 3½", $25 to **50.00**
Chamberstick, Mission/Swirl, muted, 1st art mark, 4", $200 to **250.00**
Cornucopia, stepped base, Ozark Blue, Hywood, 7", $50 to ...**75.00**
Creamer, pinched spout, pink/blue, Hywood, 4¼", $25 to **50.00**

Creamer & sugar bowl, handled, w/lid, green/tan, Hywood, ea, $50 to **75.00**
Ewer, handled, footed, pink/blue, 8", $35 to **45.00**
Figurine, dog w/ears curled under snout seated, brown, 2", $75 to **100.00**
Figurine, Southern Belle in hat standing, pink/blue, 7¼", $100 to **125.00**
Flower frog, pelican, ivory, 6¾", $25 to **35.00**
Hanging basket, embossed flowers, handled, maroon, Hywood, 3", $45 to **55.00**

Humidor, predominately red, first art mark, $350.00. (Photo courtesy David Edwin Gifford)

Inkwell, Mission/Swirl, squatty, Patent Pend'g, 2½", $250 to **350.00**
Jug, ball; glossy delft blue, Hywood, 5½", $125 to **175.00**
Lamp, urn w/ribbing & scroll detail, handled, white/blue, 11", $50 to **100.00**
Mustard jar, scalloped, w/lid, unmarked, 3½", $25 to ..**50.00**
Pin tray, flower blossom shape, pink/blue, unmarked, 4", $15 to **25.00**

Pitcher, basket weave w/angled handle, upward spout, yellow, 4", $10 to.........................15.00

Pitcher, bulbous w/petal design, blue mottle, Hywood, 8¾", $100 to..........................125.00

Pitcher, bull's-eye on footed ball shape, Ozark Blue, 9¼", $75 to.....................................100.00

Planter, basket weave, no handle, Ozark blue, 2¼x4", $10 to ..15.00

Planter, cart (2-wheeled), Ozark blue, 4¼", $35 to 45.00

Planter, clown w/drum, light blue, 7½", $25 to.....................35.00

Planter, polar bear with attached basket, matt, 3½", $75.00.

Planter, swan w/upswept tail feathers, pink/blue, 6¼", $15 to.....................................25.00

Planter, teddy bear seated against basket, blue, 3¾", $50 to..75.00

Salt & pepper shakers, penguin form, Ozark Blue, 2¾", pr, $35 to.............................45.00

Strawberry jar, Ozark Blue, 5", $15 to..............................25.00

Teapot, ball shape, pink/blue, Potteries sticker, 6½", $75 to...............................100.00

Tray, straight sides w/ruffled rim, Hywood, 1¼x12¼", $25 to 50.00

Tumbler, embossed gazelle design, Ozark Blue, 5½", $35 to..45.00

Vase, bud; long ribbed neck, bulbous bottom, pinched rim, yellow, 7"............................25.00

Vase, bulbous, green/tan, Hywood, 6¼", $100 to.....................125.00

Vase, bulbous w/overlapping leaf design, green, 7", $50 to ..75.00

Vase, fan; honey, Hywood, 4", $25 to.....................................35.00

Vase, footed cylinder w/ribbed Deco design, Ozark Blue, 10", $100 to..........................150.00

Vase, Mission/Swirl, incurvate rim, 1st art mark, 7¾", $175 to.....................................225.00

Vase, ruffled rim, ribbed, pink/blue, Hywood, 6", $50 to...........75.00

Vase, 4-sided rim w/pinched corners, pink/blue, Hywood, 6", $25 to.............................50.00

Nippon

In complying with American importation regulations, from 1891 to 1921 Japanese manufacturers marked their wares 'Nippon,' meaning Japan, to indicate country of origin. The term is today used to refer to the highly decorated porcelain vases, bowls, chocolate pots, etc., that bear this term within their trademark. Many variations were used. Refer to *The Collector's Encyclopedia of Nippon Porcelain* (there are seven volumes in the series) by Joan Van Patten (Collector Books) for more information. See Clubs and Newsletters for information concerning the International Nippon Collectors Club.

Ashtray, round, rabbit in center, geometric rim, 5¼", $200 to.....................**250.00**

Basket, oblong, integral handle, bird & flower motif, 7½", $135 to.................................**175.00**

Basket/nappy, 2 pinched sides, gold trim & handle, 5" L, $60 to.......................................**90.00**

Bowl, handled, incurvate rim, acorn basket scene, 9", $160 to................................**220.00**

Bowl, octagonal w/floral & geometric border, 8½", $125 to..**160.00**

Cake plate, handled, pink stylized flowers & gold border, 10", $175 to...........................**235.00**

Candlesticks, pyramidal, footed, gold medallion decor, 8", pr, $450 to...........................**550.00**

Celery tray, Capitol building in center, rose & gold trim, 13", $85 to.............................**135.00**

Chamberstick, cup on saucer w/scroll handle, gold trim, 4" dia, $85 to.....................**135.00**

Chocolate pot, flared, palm tree, roses & gold trim, 8½", $150 to....................................**200.00**

Cigarette box, oblong, mounted knight on lid, 4½", $550 to..............**650.00**

Condiment set, pot, shakers & tray, floral swags, 6" dia, $75 to....................................**100.00**

Creamer & sugar bowl, 3-footed, w/lid, tropical scene, pr, $150 to....................................**200.00**

Dresser set, 3 round containers/tray, pink flowers/blue trim, $120 to...........................**160.00**

Mug, cylindrical, angled handle, black-outlined geese, 4½", $300 to...........................**400.00**

Mug, geese in landscape, green mark, 4½", from $300.00 to $400.00. (Photo courtesy Joan F. Van Patten)

Nappy, sq w/ruffled rim, stream w/flowers & trees, 8", $85 to **135.00**

Nut set, round, flowers w/gold-lined leaves & rim, 7-pc, $175 to...................................**225.00**

Pitcher, bulbous, outlined landscape w/moon, beaded trim, 6", $550 to....................**650.00**

Plaque, ducks in flight over marsh, 8¾", $250 to.....**325.00**

Plaque, iris, 10", $300 to.....**400.00**

Plate, black & gold geometric border, gold rim, 12" dia, $50 to **75.00**

Potpourri jar, urn w/perforated lid, bluebirds, 5½", $200 to..**275.00**

Powder box, round, flat bottom, boat by shore on lid, 3¼", $60 to **85.00**

Powder shaker, stork in flight, gold trim, 4½", $300 to..........**400.00**

Reamer, cup shape w/spout, gold trim, 4¾" wide, $150 to ..**200.00**

Stickpin holder, 1-pc holder & round scalloped tray, 1¾", $200 to **275.00**

Tankard, cylindrical, spout, stylized berries/leaves, 9¾", $275 to **350.00**

Teapot, bulbous w/short pedestal foot, floral w/gold trim, $100 to **140.00**

Toast rack, sq w/3 dividers, pink floral bands, gold trim, 5", $150 to **200.00**

Toothpick holder, hexagonal, footed, gold trim, 2⅜", from $65 to **100.00**

Tray, round w/deep sides, flowers & exotic bird on black, 12", $200 to **250.00**

Trinket box, sq pillow shape, floral decor, 2½", $80 to ...**115.00**

Vase, pinched shoulder, geese in flight over marsh, 5", $150 to **200.00**

Vase, sq w/sq shoulder handles, tropical scene, 5", $110 to **160.00**

Vase, urn w/short trumpet neck, swan scene, 9", $275 to ..**350.00**

Noritake

Since the early 1900s the Noritake China Company has been producing fine dinnerware, occasional pieces, and figural items decorated by hand in delicate florals, scenics, and wildlife studies. Azalea and Tree in the Meadow are two very popular collectible lines you will find listed here. Refer to *The Collector's Encyclopedia of Noritake, First* and *Second Series*, by Joan Van Patten; and *Early Noritake* by Aimee Neff Alden (all published by Collector Books) for more information.

Azalea

Tea tile, #169, $40.00; Toothpick holder, #192, $135.00; Egg cup, #120, $30.00.

Bowl, #12, 10" **42.50**
Bowl, deep, #310 ....**68.00**
Cake plate, #10, 9¾" **40.00**
Celery/roll tray, #99, 12"........**55.00**
Compote, #170......................**98.00**
Creamer & sugar bowl, #7....**45.00**
Egg cup, #120 ....**30.00**
Gravy boat, #40 ....**48.00**
Pickle/lemon set, #121 ....**24.50**
Plate, breakfast; #98.............**28.00**
Platter, #56, 12" **58.00**
Relish, 2-part, #171...............**58.00**
Shakers, bell form, #11, pr ...**30.00**
Teapot, #15..........................**110.00**

Tree in the Meadow

Ashtray, 5"............................**55.00**

Candy dish, #318, $400.00.

319

Bowl, oatmeal........................15.00
Cake plate 35.00
Celery dish 35.00
Creamer & sugar bowl, demi-
    tasse 40.00
Cup & saucer, breakfast.......25.00
Jam jar/dish, 4-pc..................70.00
Mayonnaise set, 3-pc.............50.00
Platter, 13¾x10¼" 60.00
Relish, divided......................35.00

Miscellaneous

Ashtray, flowers on shaded cream,
    4 rests, M in Wreath mark,
    5¾"..................................50.00
Bowl, exotic birds on white, Deco-
    style band, M in Wreath
    mark, 9¼"........................90.00
Bowl, irises on white w/blue rim,
    gold handles, M in Wreath
    mark, 10½"......................85.00
Compote, swans in river scene,
    handles, M in Wreath
    mark, 9" W................85.00
Egg cup, windmill & river scene,
    earth tones, M in Wreath
    mark, 3½"........................40.00
Lemon dish, flowering branch on
    yellow, red M in Wreath
    mark, 6½" L 40.00
Mustard set, roses in pink & yel-
    low on white, M in Wreath
    mark, 3", 4-pc.................35.00
Nappy, roses in pastels on cream,
    1 handle, M in Wreath mark,
    5"......................................40.00
Plate, windmill & river scene,
    bright colors, M in Wreath
    mark, 7½"........................65.00
Shakers, rivers scene, earth
    tones, M in Wreath mark,
    2½", pr..........................16.00

Sugar shaker, floral band on
    white, gold top, M in Wreath
    mark, 6½"........................30.00
Tile, river scene, canted corners,
    M in Wreath mark, 5"....55.00
Toast rack, bird finial, blue lustre, M
    in Wreath mark, 5½" L....125.00
Tray, river scene w/swans, blue
    Komaru mark, 12" 80.00
Vase, peacock feathers on tan,
    slim w/ruffled rim, Komaru
    mark, 8", pr 180.00
Vase, roses on long stems on
    white, handles, M in Wreath
    mark, 9½".....................165.00

Novelty Telephones

Novelty phones representing
well-known advertising or cartoon
characters are proving to be the
focus of a lot of collector activity
— the more recognizable the character the better. Telephones modeled after product containers are
collectible too, and with the
intense interest currently being
shown in anything advertising
related, competition is sometimes
stiff and values are rising. For
further information we recommend *Schroeder's Collectible Toys,
Antique to Modern* (Collector
Books).

Bart Simpson, Columbia Tel-Com,
    1990s, MIB 35.00
Batmobile (Batman Forever),
    MIB, from $35 to............50.00
Bugs Bunny, Warner Exclusive,
    MIB, from $60 to...........70.00
Crest Sparkle, MIB, from $50
    to 75.00

Darth Vader, 1983, MIB.....**195.00**

Gumball Machine, MIB **135.00**

Kermit the Frog, candlestick type, MIB.................................**80.00**

Little Orphan Annie & Sandy, Columbia Pictures, 1982, 11", EX................................**100.00**

Mickey Mouse, 1988, MIB **50.00**

New Kids on the Block, Big Step Prod, 1990, MIB, from $20 to.................................**30.00**

Raggedy Ann & Andy, Pan Phone, 1983, heart-shaped holder, EX.....................**40.00**

Snoopy & Woodstock, American Telephone Corp, 1976, touch-tone, EX........................**100.00**

Strawberry Shortcake, M **55.00**

Superman, early version with rotary dial, M, $500.00.

Winnie the Pooh, sq base, M, from $225 to..........................**250.00**

Occupied Japan

Items with the 'Occupied Japan' mark were made during the period from the end of World War II until April 1952. Porcelains, novelties, paper items, lamps, silverplate, lacquer ware, and dolls are some of the areas of exported goods that may bear this stamp. Because the Japanese were naturally resentful of the occupation, it is felt that only a small percentage of their wares were thus marked. Although you may find identical items marked simply 'Japan,' only those with the 'Occupied Japan' stamp command values such as we have suggested below. For more information we recommend *Occupied Japan Collectibles* written by Gene Florence for Collector Books. Items in our listings are ceramic unless another material is noted, and figurines are of average, small size. See Clubs and Newsletters for information concerning The Occupied Japan Club.

Ashtray, hand form, metal ...**10.00**

Ashtray holder w/4 trays, elephant form, glossy brown **20.00**

Bank, elephant trumpeting, floral design on white..............**35.00**

Box, piano form, silver-tone metal w/red velvet liner...........**25.00**

Christmas nativity figures, 2½", 7-pc set **80.00**

Clicker, chicken form, metal, 1½" **8.00**

Coasters in box, papier-mache, 8-pc set..............................**35.00**

Creamer & sugar bowl, floral sprays, blue lustre band .**14.00**

Crumb pan, embossed swan on metal................................**20.00**

Cup & saucer, crab apples on white w/gold trim............**12.50**

Cup & saucer, red hearts, black trim.................................**10.00**

Dish, fish form, tan lustre on blue, circle K mark...................**12.50**

Doll, celluloid, baby in snowsuit ..**45.00**

Figurine, Black fiddler, 5" **40.00**

Figurine, boy seated w/duck, multicolor, 4" **11.00**

Figurine, cowboy w/rope, 6½"..**20.00**

Figurine, Cupid on sled, bisque, 5"......................................**35.00**

Figurine, donkey w/prospecting gear..................................**12.50**

Figurine, frog w/accordion, bisque, 4"......................................**20.00**

Figurine, hula girl, 4½" **20.00**

Figurine, lady w/tambourine, Delft blue, 4¾" **20.00**

Figurine, ladybug baseball player w/bat, 2¼"..........................**8.00**

Figurine, Oriental flutist seated, 4½"..................................**12.00**

Figurine, villian in black w/captive lady, 7½" **55.00**

Ice bucket w/tongs, multicolored flowers on red lacquered metal, sm........................**45.00**

Lamp, courting couple, 6½", pr..**75.00**

Lamp, cowboy figure on sq base, bisque, red mark, 7½"....**40.00**

Leaf dish, white w/multicolored fruit decal in center, gold trim **17.50**

Mug, tavern scene in relief, multicolor on cobalt, 6"...........**20.00**

Planter, boot, 6½" **14.00**

Planter, boy beside cactus, 4".**8.00**

Planter, elf w/tulip pot..........**20.00**

Planter, girl w/cart, 2⅝" **8.00**

Planter, Santa figure, 6".......**35.00**

Planter, zebra, whimsical.....**12.00**

Plate, souvenir; Niagara Falls, painted scene, plain rim w/gold trim **10.00**

Platter, apple decor, 15" **25.00**

Salt & pepper shakers, chicks in a basket, pr.......................**22.50**

Shelf sitter, ballerina, net skirt, 5".....................................**30.00**

Shelf sitter, girl in dress w/bow in hair, ankles crossed **18.00**

Sugar bowl and creamer with tray, Maruhon Ware, from $25.00 to $28.00. (Photo courtesy Gene Florence)

Figurines, dancing couple, cobalt, white, and gold, signed SGK, 8¾", $175.00 for the pair. (Photo courtesy Florence Archambault)

Teapot, aluminum, 9" **35.00**

Tile, hand-painted maple leaves, 3⅜" sq **18.00**

Toby jug, Sairey Gamp, 4½x4"..**35.00**

Toby jug, winking man, 4"....**25.00**

Tray, papier-mache, rectangular, lg **18.00**
Umbrella, paper, 18" **28.00**
Vase, lg applied rose on bulbous body, 4¼" **17.00**
Vase, swan form, multicolor, 5" ..**20.00**
Vase, urn style w/scrolled handles at neck, embossed flowers, 6¼" **25.00**
Wall plaque, duck in flight, 5" ..**25.00**

Old MacDonald's Farm

Made by the Regal China Co., items from this line of novelty ware designed around characters and animals from Old MacDonald's farm can often be found at flea markets and dinnerware shows. Values of some pieces are two to three times higher than a few years ago. The milk pitcher is especially hard to find.

Our advisor for this category is Rick Spencer; he is listed in the Directory under Utah.

Creamer, rooster, $110.00; Sugar bowl, hen, $125.00.

Butter dish, cow's head.......**220.00**
Canister, flour, cereal or coffee; med, ea **220.00**

Canister, pretzels, peanuts, popcorn, chips or tidbits; lg, ea **300.00**
Canister, salt, sugar or tea; med, ea **220.00**
Canister, soup or cookies; lg, ea ..**300.00**
Cookie jar, barn...................**275.00**
Grease jar, pig....................**175.00**
Pitcher, milk........................**400.00**
Salt & pepper shakers, boy & girl, pr....................................**75.00**
Salt & pepper shakers, churn, gold trim, pr **90.00**
Salt & pepper shakers, feed sacks w/sheep, pr **195.00**
Spice jar, assorted lids, sm, ea ..**100.00**
Teapot, duck's head **250.00**

Paper Dolls

Though the history of paper dolls can be traced even farther back, by the late 1700s they were being mass produced. A century later, paper dolls were being used as an advertising medium by retail companies wishing to promote sales. But today the type most often encountered are in book form — the dolls on the cardboard covers, their wardrobe on the inside pages. These have been published since the 1920s. Celebrity and character-related dolls are the most popular with collectors, and condition is very important. If they have been cut out, even when they are still in fine condition and have all their original accessories, they're worth only about half as much as an uncut doll. In our listings, if no condition is given, values are for mint, uncut paper dolls. For more information, we recommend *Price Guide to Lowe and Whitman Paper Dolls* by Mary Young (see the Directory under Ohio). For an expanded listings of values, see *Schroeder's Collectible Toys, Antique to Modern* (Collector Books). See Clubs and Newsletters for information concerning the *Paper Doll News*.

Green Acres, Whitman #1979, 1967, $65.00. (Photo courtesy Greg Davis and Bill Morgan)

Annie Oakley, Whitman #1960, 1956, from $65 to **85.00**
Bewitched, Magic Wand, 1965, boxed set.........................**75.00**
Brady Bunch, Whitman #4784, 1972, boxed set...............**45.00**
Debbie Reynolds, Whitman #1855, 1955 ....**100.00**
Donna Reed, Artcraft #4412, 1964...............................**80.00**
Elizabeth Taylor, Whitman #968, 1949 ....**135.00**

Flying Nun, Saalfield #5121, 1968................................**65.00**
Gene Autry's Melody Ranch, Whitman #990, 1950 ...**100.00**
Gidget, Standard Toycraft (Avalon) #601, 1965..............**135.00**
Huey, Dewey & Louie Super Dooper, Whitman #1386, 1978 ....**20.00**
I Love Lucy Packaway Kit, Whitman, 1953, EX.............**125.00**
It's a Small World, Whitman #1981, 1966 ....**30.00**
Josie & the Pussycats, Whitman #1982, 1971 ....**35.00**
Karen Goes to College, Merrill #1564, 1955 ....**50.00**
Little Lulu, Whitman #1970, 1971, A...........................**35.00**
McGuire Sisters, Whitman #1983, 1959 ....**100.00**
Natalie Wood, Whitman #1962, 1957 ....**150.00**
National Velvet, Whitman #1958, 1961 ....**40.00**
Oklahoma!, Whitman #1954, 1956...............................**100.00**
Patty Duke, Whitman #1991, 1964 ....**40.00**

Tender Love'n Kisses, Whitman #1944-1, 1978, $25.00.

Princess Diana, Whitman #1530, 1985 ....**50.00**

Ricky Nelson, Whitman #2081, 1959 ....**100.00**

Rita Hayworth Dancing Star, Merrill #3478, 1942 .....**300.00**

Roy Rogers & Dale Evans, Whitman #998, 1950............**145.00**

Sandra Dee, Saalfield #4417, 1959 ....**65.00**

Tabatha, Magic Wand #115, 1966..**95.00**

Umbrella Girls, Merrill #2562, 1956 ....**65.00**

Virginia Mayo, Saalfield #4422, 1957 ....**125.00**

Ziegfield Girls, Merrill #3466, 1941 ....**400.00**

Peanuts Collectibles

First introduced in 1950, the *Peanuts* comic strip soon became the world's most widely read cartoon, ultimately appearing in about 2,200 daily newspapers. From that funny cartoon about kids (that seemed to relate to readers of any age) sprung an entertainment arsenal featuring movies, books, Broadway shows, toys theme parks, etc. At any flea market you'll always spot several *Peanuts* collectibles. United Media, the company that syndicates and licenses the *Peanuts* comic strip, estimates there are approximately 20,000 new products produced each year. If you want to collect, you should know that authenticity is important. The United Features Syndicate logo and copyright dates must appear somewhere on the item. In most cases the copyright date simply indicates the date that the character and his pose as depicted on the item first appeared in the comic strip.

For more information we recommend *Peanuts Collectibles* by Andrea Podley with Derrick Bang (Collector Books).

Alarm clock, faces & numbers, Japan, 1988, 3½" dia, MIB.**50.00**

Alarm clock, Snoopy & Charlie Brown, 2-D, Janex, 1974, MIB **135.00**

Bank, Lucy at desk, ceramic, NM..............................**30.00**

Bank, Snoopy on rainbow, composition, NM......................**25.00**

Bank, Woodstock, yellow plastic, 6", NM **35.00**

Beach bag, Beagle Beach, Colgate premium, 9x8", M **20.00**

Colorforms, Peanuts Preschool, VG (VG box) **25.00**

Dish, Snoopy lying on lid, ceramic, Determined, 1977, NM.**150.00**

Doll, Charlie Brown, stuffed printed cloth pillow type, 1963, EX........................**40.00**

Doll, Charlie Brown, vinyl, 1950s, 9", VG **75.00**

Doll, Linus, Thumb & Blanket, Determined, 1983, 8", MIB..........**25.00**

Doll, Lucy, stuffed print cloth pillow type, 1963, NM........**40.00**

Doll, Peppermint Patty, Ideal/ Determined, 13½", MIB..**50.00**

Doll, Snoopy, stuffed printed cloth pillow type, VG+ **35.00**

Doll, Snoopy, talker, Wonder World, 1986, MIB........**100.00**

Guitar, crank action, Mattel, NM..**50.00**
Jam jar, Snoopy figure on domed
  lid, ceramic, M................**55.00**
Kaleidoscope, Snoopy Disco,
  Determined, 1979, EX...**20.00**
Megaphone, Charlie Brown,
  Chein, 1970, rare, EX....**45.00**

**Mother's Day plate, Linus and
Snoopy, Schmid Bros., 1976, MIB,
from $25.00 to $30.00.**

Mug, Woodstock on tree-trunk
  mug w/heart, Teleflora, 1972,
  M................**35.00**
Pillow doll, Charlie Brown, 1963,
  EX................**40.00**
Purse, canvas w/image of Snoopy
  blowing bubbles, 9x8", M.**100.00**
Tea set, Chein, MIB.............**50.00**
Top, litho tin, Chein, 1969, MIB.**75.00**
Whistle, Woodstock, Hallmark,
  1976, MIP................**45.00**

Pennsbury

From the 1950s through the
1970s, dinnerware and novelty
ware produced by the Pennsbury
company was sold through tourist
gift shops along the Pennsylvania
turnpike. Much of their ware was
decorated in an Amish theme. A
group of barbershop singers was
another popular design, and they
made a line of bird figures that
were very similar to Stangl's,
though today much harder to find.

Ashtray, Amish, 5" dia..........**40.00**
Ashtray, Pennsbury Inn, 8"..**45.00**
Bank, Hershey Kiss, chocolate
  brown, 4"........................**20.00**
Bowl, Dutch Talk, 9" dia.......**90.00**
Bowl, pretzel; Amish, 12x8".**100.00**
Bowl, pretzel; Eagle, 12x8"...**85.00**
Butter dish, Hex, w/lid, 5x4".**45.00**
Cake stand, Two Birds Over
  Heart, 11"......................**85.00**
Candle holder, Holly, 5½".....**45.00**
Candle holder, Red Rooster, 5".**40.00**
Candle holders, rooster figurals,
  4", pr.............................**85.00**
Charger, St George Slaying Drag-
  on, 13½" dia..................**225.00**
Chip & dip, Holly, 22".........**100.00**
Coaster, Doylestown Trust Co,
  1896-1958, 5".................**25.00**

Coffeepot, Rooster, 8½", $90.00.

Compote, Holly, 5"...............**45.00**
Desk basket, Lafayette, 4"....**60.00**
Dispensers, oil & vinegar; Amish,
  7", pr.............................**150.00**
Figurine, Blue Jay, #108, 10½"..**400.00**

Figurine, Cardinal, #120, 6½".**175.00**
Figurine, March Wren, #106, 6½" **120.00**
Mug, beverage; Red Barn, 5".**60.00**
Mug, beverage; Red Rooster, 5"..**35.00**
Mug, coffee; Hex....................**22.00**
Pie pan, Mother Seving Pie, 9" dia..................................**85.00**
Pitcher, Folkart, miniature, 2½"..**30.00**
Plaque, Fisherman, 5" dia....**28.00**
Plaque, Iron Horse Ramble, Reading Railroad, 7¼x5¼" **60.00**
Plaque, Making Pie, 6" dia ...**60.00**
Plaque, Ship series, The Flying Cloud, dated 1851, 9½x7".**110.00**
Plaque, Stourbridge Lion, Delaware & Hudson Railroad, 1829, 11x8".....................**55.00**
Plaque, Walking to Homestead, 6" dia...................................**40.00**
Plate, Bible Reading, w/out primary colors, 9"......................**75.00**
Plate, Boy & Girl, w/out primary colors, 11" **45.00**
Plate, Boy & Girl, w/primary colors, 11"............................**95.00**
Plate, Christmas; from 1960-69, ea....................................**45.00**
Plate, commemorative; Turkey Hunt, 11" dia..................**85.00**
Plate, Family, 11" **110.00**
Plate, Red Rooster, 10" **35.00**
Tray, cigarette; Eagle, 7½x5"..**40.00**
Wall pocket, clown w/yo-yo, square w/canted corners, pink trim, 6½" **120.00**

Pez Dispensers

Originally a breath mint targeted for smokers, by the '50s Pez had been diverted toward the kid's candy market, and to make sure the kids found them appealing, the company designed dispensers they'd be sure to like — many of them characters the kids could easily recognize. On today's collectible market, some of those dispensers bring astonishing prices!

Though early on collectors preferred the dispensers with no feet, today they concentrate primarily on the character heads. Feet were added in 1987, so if you want your collection to be complete, you'll buy both styles. For further information and more listings, see *Schroeder's Collectible Toys, Antique to Modern* (Collector Books). Our values are for mint dispensers. Very few are worth collecting if they are damaged or have missing parts. See Clubs and Newsletters for information concerning *Pez Collector News*.

Angel, no feet.........................**60.00**
Baloo, w/feet **20.00**
Baseball Glove, no feet **225.00**
Bubble Man, w/feet, neon hat .**6.00**

B e t s y Ross, no f e e t , $185.00; Casper, no feet, $225.00.

Captain Hook, no feet **85.00**
Chick in Egg, no feet **25.00**
Cool Cat, w/feet **75.00**
Dalmatian Pup, w/feet **50.00**
Donald Duck, no feet **15.00**
Dumbo, w/feet, blue head **25.00**

Road Runner, no feet **20.00**
Rooster, w/feet, whistle head. **40.00**
Scrooge McDuck (A), no feet .. **35.00**
Skull (A), no feet, from $5 to.. **10.00**
Tweety Bird, no feet **10.00**
Yappy Dog, no feet, orange or green, ea **65.00**

Eerie Spectres, $250.00 each.

Fat-Ears Rabbit, no feet, pink head **20.00**
Fat-Ears Rabbit, no feet, yellow head **15.00**
Fireman, no feet **95.00**
Fozzie Bear, w/feet, from $1 to .. **3.00**
Goofy, no feet **10.00**
Henry Hawk, no feet **65.00**
Indian, w/feet, whistle head. **20.00**
Lamb, no feet **15.00**
Lazy Garfield, w/feet **5.00**
Mickey Mouse, w/feet, from $1 to .**3.00**
Mowgli, w/feet **15.00**
Panda, w/feet, whistle head **6.00**
Penguin, w/feet, whistle head .**6.00**
Peter Pez (A), no feet **65.00**
Pluto, no feet **50.00**
Pluto, no feet, red **10.00**
Policeman, no feet **55.00**
Practical Pig (B), no feet **30.00**
Pumpkin (A), no feet, from $10 to **15.00**

Pfaltzgraff Pottery

Since early in the seventeenth century, pottery has been produced in York County, Pennsylvania. The Pfaltzgraff Company that operates there today is the outgrowth of several of these small potteries. A changeover made in 1940 redirected their efforts toward making the dinnerware lines for which they are now best known. Their earliest line, a glossy brown with a white frothy drip glaze around the rim, was called Gourmet Royale. Today collectors find an abundance of good examples and are working toward reassembling sets of their own. Village, another very successful line, is tan with a stencilled Pennsylvania Dutch-type floral design in brown. It was discontinued little more than a year ago, and already prices are starting upwards as shoppers turn to secondary market sources to replace and replenish their services. The line is so extensive and offers such an interesting array of items, it is sure to have collector appeal as well.

Giftware consisting of ashtrays, mugs, bottle stoppers, a

cookie jar, etc., all with comic character faces were made in the 1940s. This line was called Muggsy, and it is also very collectible, with the mugs starting at $35.00 each. For more information, refer to *The Collector's Encyclopedia of American Dinnerware* by Jo Cunningham (Collector Books) and *Pfaltzgraff, America's Potter*, by David A. Walsh and Polly Stetler, published in conjunction with the Historical Society of York County, York, Pennsylvania.

Gourmet Royale, baker, #321, oval, 7½", from $18 to **20.00**

Gourmet Royale, bean pot, #11-2, 2-qt, from $28 to.............**30.00**

Gourmet Royale, bean pot, #11-4, 4-qt.................................**45.00**

Gourmet Royale, bean pot warming stand.........................**12.00**

Gourmet Royale, bowl, mixing; 6", from $8 to **10.00**

Gourmet Royale, bowl, soup; 2¼x7¼", from $6 to..........**8.00**

Gourmet Royale, bowl, vegetable; 9¾".................................**15.00**

Gourmet Royale, casserole, stick handle, 1-qt **18.00**

Gourmet Royale, casserole, stick handle, 3-qt **30.00**

Gourmet Royale, coffeepot, #303, 10-cup, from $30 to **35.00**

Gourmet Royale, creamer, #382, from $5 to **7.00**

Gourmet Royale, cup, from $2 to..**3.00**

Gourmet Royale, gravy boat, #426, 2-spout, lg, +underplate, $14 to....................**16.00**

Gourmet Royale, jug, #386, ice lip, from $40 to **48.00**

Gourmet Royale, mug, #391, 12-oz, from $6 to....................**8.00**

Gourmet Royale, pie plate, #7016, 9½", from $14 to.............**18.00**

Gourmet Royale, plate, steak; 12", from $15 to **20.00**

Gourmet Royale, platter, #337, 16", from $25 to..............**30.00**

Gourmet Royale, roaster, #326, oval, 16", from $50 to **60.00**

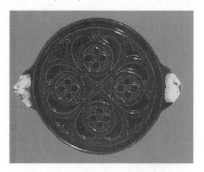

Gourmet Royale, trivet, 6½", from $8.00 to $12.00.

Muggsy, ashtray..................**125.00**

Muggsy, bottle stopper, head, ball shape **85.00**

Muggsy, canape holder, Carrie, lift-off hat pierced for toothpicks.............................**150.00**

Muggsy, cigarette server **125.00**

Muggsy, clothes sprinkler bottle, Myrtle, Black, from $225 to **260.00**

Muggsy, clothes sprinkler bottle, Myrtle, white, from $250 to **350.00**

Muggsy, cookie jar, character face, minimum value............**250.00**

Muggsy, mug, action figure (golfer, fisherman, etc), any, from $65 to **85.00**

Muggsy, mug, Black action figure **125.00**

Muggsy, mug, character face, ea, from $35 to **38.00**

Muggsy, mug, Pickled Pete, from $35 to **38.00**

Muggsy, mug, Sleepy Sam, from $35 to **38.00**

Muggsy, shot glass, character face, from $45 to **50.00**

Muggsy, tumbler **60.00**

Muggsy, utility jar, Handy Harry, from $175 to **200.00**

Village, soup tureen with lid and ladle, #160, from $40.00 to $45.00; Underplate (dinner plate), from $3.50 to $4.00.

Village, baker, #237, square, tab handles, 9", from $9 to...**12.00**

Village, baker, #240, oval, 7¾", from, $6 to **8.00**

Village, bowl, fruit; #008, 5"...**4.00**

Village, bowl, rim soup; #012, 8½"...................................**6.00**

Village, bowl, soup/cereal; #009, 6".......................................**4.50**

Village, bread tray, 12", from $15 to **18.00**

Village, canisters, #520, 4-pc set, from $50 to **60.00**

Village, coffee mug, #89F, 10-oz, from $4 to **5.50**

Village, coffeepot, lighthouse shape, 48-oz, from $30 to **35.00**

Village, creamer & sugar bowl, #020, from $9 to **12.00**

Village, flowerpot, 4½".........**15.00**

Village, pedestal mug, #90F, 10-oz **4.50**

Village, plate, dinner; #004, 10¼", from $3 to **4.50**

Village, platter, #016, 14", from $15 to **18.00**

Village, spoon rest, #515, 9" L, from $6 to **7.50**

Pie Birds

What is a pie bird? It is a functional and decorative kitchen tool most commonly found in the shape of a bird, designed to vent steam through the top crust of a pie to prevent the juices from spilling over into the oven. Other popular designs were elephants and black-faced bakers. The original vents that were used in England and Wales in the 1800s were simply shaped like funnels.

From the 1980s to the present, many novelty pie vents have been added to the market for the baker and the collector. Some of these could be obtained from Far East Imports; others have been made in England and the US (by commercial and/or local enterprises). Examples can be found in the shapes of animals (dogs, frogs, elephants, cats, goats, and dragons), people (policemen, chefs with and without pies, pilgrims, and carolers), or whimsical figurals (clowns, leprechauns, and teddy bears). New for the 1990s is an array of holiday-related pie vents.

Consequently a collector must be on guard and aware that these new pie vents are being sold by dealers (knowingly in many instances) as old or rare, often at double or triple the original cost (which is usually under $10.00). Though most of the new ones can't really be called reproductions since they never existed before, there's a black bird that is a remake, and you'll see them everywhere. Here's how you can spot them: they'll have yellow beaks and protruding white-dotted eyes. If they're on a white base and have an orange beak, they are the older ones. Another basic tip that should help you distinguish old from new: older pie vents are air-brushed versus being hand painted. Please note that incense burners, one-hole pepper shakers, dated brass toy bird whistles, and ring holders (for instance, the elephant with a clover on his tummy) should not be mistaken for pie vents.

Our advisor for this category is Linda Fields, who is listed in the Directory under Tennessee. See Clubs and Newsletters for information concerning *Pie Birds Unlimited Newsletter.*

Benny the Baker, all white, Far East Imports, 4¾".........**40.00**
Black chef, yellow, blue or green airbrushed, Japan, 1940s-60s...............................**90.00**
Blackbird, 2-pc, marked Royal Worchester, England, 1960-mid-1980s.....................**50.00**

The Arnel Mold Company (Portland, OR) has sold this three-pie-bird mold from 1977 to present. They are painted in a solid color or with good feather detail, These 4¼" pie birds are valued at $10.00 to $25.00 each. (Photo courtesy Lillian Cole)

Blackbird on log, marked Artone Pottery, England, 1950-96.......**50.00**
Bluebird, black speckles, heavy pottery, US, 1950s.........**50.00**
Canary, yellow, pink beak, Josef Originals..........................**45.00**
Canary w/puffed chest, teal or lavender, unknown maker, US, 1950s-60s.................**65.00**
Duck (or swan) head, brown w/yellow beak, from $150 to.**175.00**
Eagle, marked Sunglow, golden color, from $75 to...........**85.00**
Elephant, marked CCC, Cardinal China.............................**70.00**
Fred the Flour Grater, (original has) dots for eyes, from $65 to....................................**75.00**
Funnel, Blue Willow, unmarked, US, 1998, new.................**20.00**
Funnel, marked Rowlands Hygenic, England........**110.00**
Funnel, pagoda, Nutbrown...**95.00**
Funnel, white, unmarked, England..................................**15.00**
Golliwogs, marked England or Great Britain, 1990s......**60.00**

Rooster/hen, marked Bendigo Pottery 1858, 1998, new.......**35.00**

Songbird, cream & black body w/gold details, unmarked, US..................**65.00**

Songbird, pink, blue or cinnamon w/black details, US, 1940s-50s, ea...........................**40.00**

Welsh lady, Cymru, from $75 to..**95.00**

Witch, holding pie w/painted bird flying out, marked SB....**40.00**

Eat Fruit, Pac-Man w/cherries, 1¾".....................................**5.00**

ET, w/picture, multicolor, 2"...**3.00**

Forget Candy, Gimme Money!, Hallmark, 1986, 1½"........**7.50**

Give Me a Little Quiche, couple, 1983, 1¾"..........................**5.00**

Green Hornet Agent, 1960s, 4", EX.................................**15.00**

Happy Birthday Mickey, 1928-1978, multicolor, 1¼".....**25.00**

Pin-Back Buttons

Because most of the pin-backs prior to the 1920s were made of celluloid, collectors refer to them as 'cellos.' Many were issued in sets on related topics, Some advertising buttons had paper inserts on the back that identified the company or the product they were advertising. After the 1920s lithographed metal buttons were produced; they're now called 'lithos.'

Our advisors for miscellaneous pin-back buttons are Michael and Polly McQuillen; they are listed in the Directory under Indiana. See also The Beatles; Elvis Presley; Political.

Howdy Doody's 40th Birthday, Fries, 1988, 3½", EX, $25.00. (Photo courtesy Bill Bruegman)

Babe Ruth Baseball Club, 1970s, 1½"......................................**6.00**

Bugs Bunny, Six Flags Over Georgia, 1981, multicolor, 3".......**5.00**

Casper the Friendly Ghost, 1950s............................**20.00**

Dale Evans, black & white photo on green, 1950s, 1½"......**25.00**

Dick Tracy Secret Service Patrol, blue & gold, 1980s, 3"......**4.50**

I Love Lucy 1911-1989, 1989, 3½", EX.....................................**12.50**

I'm the Greatest, Ali, March 8, 1971, 3½"..........................**5.00**

I Yam What I Yam!, Popeye, multicolor, 1980s, 2¼"...........**4.00**

Mickey Mouse Club, 1970s, 3"..**8.00**

Mork & Mindy, multicolor portrait, 2¼"..........................**4.00**

Official Member Superman Club, Button World, 1966, 3"..**22.00**

Official Monkees Fan, Raybert, 1966, 2"...........................**8.00**

Pebbles Flintstone, 1972, 2", EX.............................**15.00**

Remington-UMC, white on red, VG.................................**15.00**

Shawn Cassidy, portrait w/signature, 3¼"..........................**5.50**

Snoopy Fan Club, litho tin, 2¼", EX **6.00**

Sundial Shoes Club, from $12.00 to $15.00.

Ted Williams, Boston Red Sox, w/portrait, 1950s, 1¼" ...**18.00**
Tom & Jerry, Sunbeam Bread premium, 1960s, 1¼" **6.00**

Pep Pins

In the late '40s and into the '50s, some cereal companies packed a pin-back button in each box of their product. Quaker Puffed Oats offered a series of movie star pin-backs, but Kellogg's Pep Pins are probably the best known of all. There were eighty-six different Pep pins, so theoretically if you wanted the whole series, as Kellogg hoped you would, you'd have to buy at the very minimum that many boxes of their cereal. Pep pins came in five sets, the first in 1945, three more in 1946, and the last in 1947. They were printed with full-color lithographs of comic characters licensed by King Features and Famous Artists — Maggie and Jiggs, the Winkles, and Dagwood and Blondie, for instance. Superman, the only D.C. Comics charac-

ter, was included in each set. Most Pep pins range in value from $10.00 to $15.00 in NM/M condition; for a complete listing we recommend *Garage Sale and Flea Market Annual (Collector Books)*.

Our advisor for Pep pins is Doug Dezso; he is listed in the Directory under New Jersey.

Bo Plenty **30.00**
Dick Tracy **30.00**
Early Bird..............................**6.00**
Goofy.....................................**10.00**
Gravel Girtie **15.00**
Harold Teen..........................**15.00**
Inspector...............................**12.50**
Judy **10.00**
Little King.............................**15.00**
Mama De Stross...................**30.00**

Orphan Annie, NM, $25.00.

Perry Winkle **15.00**
Pop Jenks **15.00**
Skeezix..................................**15.00**
Uncle Willie...........................**12.50**
Winnie Winkle **15.00**

Pinup Art

Collectors of pinup art look for blotters, calendars, prints, playing cards, etc., with illustrations of sexy girls by artists who are famous for their work in this venue: Vargas, Petty, DeVorss, Elvgren, Moran, Mozert, Ballantyne, Armstrong, and Davis among them. Though not all items will be signed, most of these artists have a distinctive style that is easy to recognize.

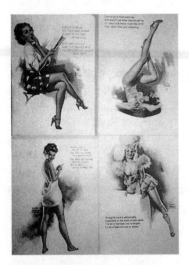

Notepads, from $8.00 to $12.00 each.
(Photo courtesy Denis Jackson)

Ashtray, metal w/painted image of nude blond by coffee table, 1950s, M **15.00**

Blotter, Elvgren, Anchors A-Wow, 1951, NM **11.00**

Blotter, Moran, Chief Attraction, Indian girl, 1944, NM **12.00**

Book, Pinup, A Modest History, Mark Garbor, 1972, hardbound, EX **35.00**

Calendar, DeVross, 1959, 32x16", complete, NM **60.00**

Calendar, Elliot, 1950, Delectable Dishes, complete, NM **50.00**

Calendar, Randall, 1961, complete, EX **55.00**

Cartoon, Petty, Talk About Gratitude, Esquire, EX..........**12.00**

Fan, Armstrong, Queen of the Ball, 1980s repro, EX..**15.00**

Letter opener, Elvgren, plastic nude, painted dress, 1950s, 8½", NM **35.00**

Matchbook cover, Petty, 1960s, unused, from $2.50 to **3.50**

Memo pad, Thompson, In Full Bloom, 1952, 3½x6½", EX.**12.00**

Mutoscope card, Elvgren, What's Cooking? EX.....................**9.00**

Playing cards, Art Studios, ea w/different nude, 1950s, complete, NMIB....................**45.00**

Playing cards, Erbit, blond in gown, 2 poses, 2 decks, complete, M...........................**60.00**

Poster, The Petty Girl, blond in maroon teddy, 22x14", VG **50.00**

Poster, Ward, The Siren, brunette, 1970s, 11x14", EX **15.00**

Print, D'Armaro, Danger!, cowgirl by fence, early 1950s, 17x12", NM.................................**35.00**

Print, DeVross, Liberty Belle, girl in patriotic attire, 16x20", EX....................**75.00**

Print, Fabian, Sheer Beauty, blond on pink blanket, 1940s, 8x10", EX.......................**18.00**

Print, Kohn, Living Art, reclining nude, 9½x7½", NM **12.50**

Print, Mozert, New Arrival, girl bottle-feeding calf, 22x29", EX................................**135.00**

Sheet music, Vargas, Adoring You, Ziegfield Follies, 1924 ....**85.00**

Shot glass, Playboy Playmate w/key printed on glass, 1960s, M..................................**40.00**

Tumbler, Petty, w/full-color illusion decal, 1940s, 4½", EX......**15.00**

Political Collectibles

Pennants, posters, badges, pamphlets — in general, anything related to a presidential campaign or politicians — are being sought by collectors who have an interest in the political history of our country. Most valued are items from a particularly eventful period or those things having to do with an especially colorful personality.

Celluloid pin-back buttons (cellos) were first widely used in the 1896 presidential campaign; before that time medals, ribbons, and badges of various kinds predominated. Prices for political pin-backs have increased considerably in the last few years, more due to speculative buying and selling rather than inherent scarcity or unusual demand. It is still possible, however, to find quality collectible items at reasonable prices. In flea markets, recent buttons tend to be overpriced; the goal, as always, is to look for less familiar items that may be priced more reasonably. Most buttons issued since the 1964 campaign, with a few notable exceptions, should be in the range of $2.00 to $10.00. Condition is critical: cracks, scratches, spots, and brown stains ('foxing') seriously reduce the value of a button.

Prices are for items in excellent condition. Reproductions are common; many are marked as such, but it takes some experience to tell the difference. The best reference book for political collectors is Edmund Sullivan's *Collecting Political Americana,* the second edition of which has been recently published.

Our advisors for this category are Michael and Polly McQuillen; they are listed in the Directory under Indiana. See Clubs and Newsletters for information concerning Political Collectors of Indiana and American Political Items Collectors.

Ashtray, I Like Ike, ceramic, sq, red, white & blue, EX....**25.00**
Ashtray, Lyndon Johnson in gold on white ceramic cowboy hat, 6½"................................**17.00**
Balloon, Vote Kennedy, blue & white, unused, EX..........**10.00**
Balloon, Wallace For President, unused, 1972....................**5.00**
Ballpoint pen, Spiro T Agnew, Vice President's seal w/name..**30.00**
Bank, FDR/Happy Days, barrel shape, 5", EX..................**15.00**
Bottle stoppers, John F Kennedy & Lyndon B Johnson, pr, MIB **150.00**
Bracelet, Nixon, pearl w/multicolor rhinestones, adult size, EX................................**15.00**
Bridge score pad, Herbert Hoover & Charles Curtis portraits, EX **10.00**
Bubble gum cigar, Goldwater in '64, El Bubble DeLuxe, 4", MIP................................**4.00**

Bumper sticker, Democrats for Nixon **2.00**

Bumper sticker, Kennedy/Johnson jugate, orange & black, NM...............................**15.00**

Button, Let the People Speak, Wallace, red, white & blue, 1968, 3½".........................**4.00**

Clicker, Click w/Dick, photo image, NM......................**10.00**

Coaster, I Like Ike in bold red letters in center, cork, EX..**15.00**

Coloring book, Amy Carter, 1977, unused, EX......................**20.00**

Coloring book, Jimmy Carter, Manor Books, 1976, unused, EX..................................**20.00**

Coloring book, John F Kennedy, Kanrom, 1962, unused, EX.........**25.00**

Dart board, Stick Dick (Nixon), 11½" sq, NM...................**25.00**

Doll, Tricky Dicky, rubber, 5", NMOC **25.00**

Doll, Lyndon Johnson, plastic, Remco, 5", MIB **35.00**

Doll, Santa w/George Bush's face, squeeze rubber, EX........**20.00**

Figure, Barry M. Goldwater, Remco, 1964, NMIB, $35.00.

Doll, Ted Kennedy, cloth caricature, 1980, 5½", EX........**15.00**

Game, Barrel of Clintons, NM .**12.00**

Game, 1964 Presidential Election, MOC **30.00**

Hand puppet, Richard Nixon, plastic head w/cloth body, 1968, NM......................**35.00**

Hat, Lyndon B Johnson, heavy paper, black & cream, folded, 3½".....................................**5.00**

Invitation, Eisenhower-Nixon inaugural ball, 1957.......**15.00**

Invitation, Ronald Reagon inaugural, 1981 ....**15.00**

Letter opener/pen, JFK, Martin Luther King & RFK memorial, EX..............................**20.00**

License plate, Herbert Hoover, enameled metal, VG **40.00**

Lighter, George Bush as Rambo, 3¼", EX...........................**10.00**

Mask, Jackie Kennedy, thin plastic, 1960, EX...................**40.00**

Medal, Ike 1953 Official Inaugural bust, bronze, M **35.00**

Money clip, John F Kennedy, 1917-1963, MIB..............**10.00**

Mug, Jimmy Carter caricature, brown ceramic................**20.00**

Nodder, I'm For Ike elephant, painted composition, 1950s, 6½", NM **100.00**

Nodders, John & Jackie Kennedy, pr **275.00**

Pamphlet, Yale Students for McGovern, 1972, 17x11", EX...............................**10.00**

Pencil, Hoover for President, 1932, red, white & blue, 7¾" **15.00**

Pin-back, Jimmy Carter for President, photo, 3" **6.00**

Pin-back button, I'm With Magic!, Clinton/Gore, M, $100.00.

Pin-back, LBJ for EX-President, blue & white, 3", EX **15.00**

Pin-back, Make Love Not War, red, white & blue, ³/₄", VG+ **15.00**

Pin-back, McGovern/Eagleton, NM **6.00**

Pin-back, McKinley & Hobart, ⁷/₈" **25.00**

Pin-back, Nixon/Agnew flasher, 2½, EX **15.00**

Pin-back, Stop the Draft, white on green, 1½", VG **15.00**

Pin-back, Vietnam — America's Hungary?, white on blue, 1½", VG...................................**25.00**

Plate, Nixon-Agnew inauguration, 1973, 8", MIB **40.00**

Plate, President & Mamie Eisenhower portraits, 12", NM...................................**25.00**

Pocket mirror, JFK portrait, black & white oval, 2¾", EX....**25.00**

Pocket mirror, RFK Destined To Become President, red, white & blue, EX **35.00**

Postcard, Nixon family portrait, black & white, Inaugural Day postmark **15.00**

Poster, Hello!, May Name Is Jimmy Carter..., cardboard, EX **16.00**

Poster, Kennedy (Robert) for President, portrait, 1968, 16x12", NM **38.00**

Poster stamp, GOP elephant, 1956, M **5.00**

Pot holder, Kennedy for President, M **32.00**

Radio, Jimmy Carter w/peanut body, vinyl strap, MIB...**30.00**

Reflector, Franklin D Roosevelt for President, M **25.00**

Ribbon, Truman Reception Committee, paper, EX...........**40.00**

Ribbon badge, Citizens for Eisenhower, white on blue, EX.**25.00**

Ribbon badge, Republican National Convention Delegate..., 1956, EX **75.00**

Ring, Jimmy Carter peanut, EX.............................**15.00**

Sheet music, Hubert Humphry March, EX **15.00**

Snowdome, Douglas McArthur, 1940s, NM **38.00**

Stickpin, Ike embossed on side of elephant, NMOC...........**15.00**

Ticket, Inaugural Gala, January 19th, 1949, $40.00.

Tie clip, PT 109, 2½" **35.00**

Tie tac, Vote Adlai, flasher, EX.**15.00**

Token, dollar; Senator Goldwater, 1964 ....**5.00**

Tray, FD Roosevelt image w/White House, 10x13", EX..........**50.00**

Wristwatch, Ross Perot, 1991, MIB................................**25.00**

Yo-yo, Jimmy Carter, plastic w/image & 39th President..., Humphery, NM................**6.00**

Poodle Collectibles

It is speculated that the return of servicemen following World War II sparked an interest in all things French. Although debatable, it was widely accepted that poodles were of French origin. Thus the poodle trend of the late '40s through the mid-'60s was born. During this era, poodles were featured in a wide variety of items that included apparel, figurines, household items, and toys. The poodle trend lost popularity and eventually faded as the flower-power movement of the late '60s and '70s brought rejection of materialism. Fortunately for collectors, poodle memorabilia survived and can be found today.

Our advisor for this category is Elaine Butler, author of *Poodle Collectibles of the '50s and '60s*; she is listed in the Directory under Tennessee.

Ashtray, ceramic, Kitchen Ashes, colored decor on white, Enesco, round.................**15.00**

Bottle opener, 3-D metal figure w/tail opener **15.00**

Compact, sq, Marhill Geniune Mother of Pearl label.....**40.00**

Cookie jar, embossed dog w/neck bow on sq form, bone finial, unmarked.......................**40.00**

Figurine, ceramic, mother bathing 2 pups, white w/gold trim, 1-pc....................................**20.00**

Figurine, ceramic, mother w/2 pups on chain, various poses, 3-pc set............................**15.00**

Figurine, ceramic, musicians in various styles & poses, ea......**15.00**

Figurine, ceramic, stylized, seated, floral decor on white, Italy, 14"..........................**60.00**

Figurine, red clay, black w/white, red & gold trim, various poses, ea...........................**8.00**

Pendant, filigreed metal frontal view w/blue rhinestone eyes, unmarked.......................**15.00**

Pin, gold-tone hammered metal figure w/smooth face & ears, unmarked.......................**12.00**

Pin, pot metal, dog w/Christmas motif on sled, rhinestone eye, Corel...............................**22.00**

Pitcher, ceramic, poodles, butterflies & flowers on white, Enesco....**25.00**

Planter, ceramic, figural w/neck bow, marked Reliable Glassware...1956......................**20.00**

Planter, ceramic, poodle cart, plaid & polka-dots on white, black trim.......................**12.00**

Plaques, ceramic, sq or round, Hand Painted by Helen DeTar..., ea pr................**50.00**

Potholder, Christmas motif on terry w/trimmed border, sq...**6.00**

Shakers, hobnail milk glass bulbous bodies, straw hats, E2167, pr........................**16.00**

Purse, labeled Princess Charming by Atlas Hollywood, Fla., from $20.00 to $25.00. (Photo courtesy Elaine Butler)

Stuffed toy, black vinyl w/white fur topknot & toes, red collar & trim **6.00**
Stuffed toy, Dream Pet **12.00**
Towel, Let's Go to Paris!, cafe & Eiffel Tower graphics on linen................................**8.00**
Trash can, metal, poodle w/umbrella & French storefronts, Ransburg **25.00**
Trivets, sq ceramic tiles w/looped wire trim, signed Yenton, Jaru, pr...........................**45.00**
Tumbler set w/rack, frosted w/black & gold, rhinestone trim, set of 6 ....**60.00**

Precious Moments

Precious Moments, little figurines with inspirational captions, were created by Samuel J. Butcher and are produced by Enesco Inc. in the Orient. They're sold through almost every gift store in the country, and the earlier, discontinued models are becoming very collectible.

Bell, May Your Christmas Be Merry, 524182, Vessel mark............................**35.00**
Box, Our Love Is Heaven-Scent, E-9266, w/lid, Dove mark ..**45.00**
Box, The Lord Bless You Keep You, E-7167, Fish mark .**50.00**
Figurine, Age 4, 136239, Ship mark **32.50**

Figurine, Bless This House, E-7164, Fish mark, $100.00.

Figurine, Eggs Over Easy, E-3118, Fish mark..............**75.00**
Figurine, God's Speed, E-3112, Fish mark.......................**35.00**
Figurine, He Cleansed My Soul, 100277, Vessel mark......**40.00**
Figurine, My Love Will Never Let You Go, 103497, Heart mark.............................**37.50**
Figurine, Thanking Him For You, E-7155, Fish mark **55.00**
Figurine, This Is Your Day To Shine, E-2822, Cross mark...........**95.00**
Figurine, Walking By Faith, E-3117, G Clef mark..........**65.00**
Figurine, You Are the Type I Love, 523542, Vessel mark......**45.00**
Frame, Jesus Loves Me, E-7171, Dove mark **65.00**

Frame, My Graduation Angel, E-7169, Hourglass mark ...**75.00**

Musical figurine, Let's Keep In Touch, 102520, Cedar Tree mark **100.00**

Musical figurine, You Have Touched So Many Hearts, 112577, Heart mark **65.00**

Nativity, Come Let Us Adore Him, 142735, Ship mark, 3-pc set **55.00**

Ornament, Angel of Mercy, 102482, Olive Branch mark..........**45.00**

Ornament, Baby's First Christmas, 15911, Dove mark...........**38.00**

Ornament, To My Forever Friend, 113956, Flower mark.....**36.00**

Ornament, Wishing You a Merry Christmas, E-5387, Cross mark **30.00**

Plate, Blessings From Me to Thee (1991), 523860, Vessel mark............**60.00**

Plate, Love Is Kind, E-2847, Fish mark **40.00**

Plate, Love One Another, E-5215, Fish mark.....................**45.00**

Thimble, Wishing You the Sweetest Christmas (1993), Butterfly mark.........................**15.00**

Purinton

Popular among collectors due to its 'country' look, Purinton Pottery's dinnerware and kitchen items are easy to learn to recognize due to their bold yet simple designs, many of them of fruit and flowers, created with basic hand-applied colors on a creamy white gloss. For more information we recommend *Purinton Pottery, An Identification and Value Guide,* by our advisor Susan Morris (Collector Books); she is listed in the Directory under Oregon.

Pitcher, beverage; Apple, two-pint, 6½", $65.00.

Baker, Intaglio, 7"................**20.00**

Bowl, cereal; Normandy Plaid, 5¼"..................**10.00**

Bowl, fruit; Cactus, 12".........**85.00**

Bowl, vegetable; Apple, 8½".**30.00**

Candle holders, Pennsylvania Dutch, 2x6", pr.............**130.00**

Coaster, Crescent Flower, 3½".**40.00**

Coffeepot, Fruit, 8-cup, 8".....**65.00**

Cookie jar, Saraband, oval, 9½".**50.00**

Creamer & sugar bowl, Chartreuse, mini, 2"..............**40.00**

Cruets, oil & vinegar; Saraband, sq, 5", pr **25.00**

Cup & saucer, Ming Tree......**20.00**

Grease jar, Normandy Plaid, w/lid, 5½".......................**60.00**

Jar, Crescent Flower, 3½" **45.00**

Lamp, TV; Red Feather, 8½".**75.00**

Mug, Apple, handled, 8-oz, 4".**35.00**

Mug, juice; Maywood, 6-oz, 2½".**15.00**

Pitcher, beverage; Ivy — Red Blossom, 2-pt, 6¼" **55.00**

Planter, Ming Tree, 5" **35.00**
Plate, dinner; Fruit, 9¾".......**20.00**
Platter, Intaglio, 12" **30.00**
Salt & pepper shakers, Seafoam,
   3", pr **55.00**
Sugar bowl, Tea Rose, w/lid, 5" .**45.00**
Teapot, Heather Plaid, 6-cup, 6"..**65.00**
Tumbler, Sunflower, 12-oz, 5" .**30.00**
Vase, Petals, 5".....................**35.00**

Puzzles

Of most interest to collectors of vintage puzzles are those made of wood or plywood, especially the early hand-cut examples. Character-related examples and those representing a well-known personality or show from the early days of television are coming on strong right now, and values are steadily climbing in these areas. For an expanded listing, see *Schroeder's Collectible Toys, Antique to Modern* (Collector Books).

Beverly Hillbillies, jigsaw, Jaymar, 1963, complete, MIB, from $25.00 to $30.00. (Photo courtesy Greg Davis and Bill Morgan)

Archies, jigsaw, Whitman, 1970,
   MIB................................**25.00**
Augie Doggie, frame-tray, Whitman,
   1960, 14x11", NM..............**20.00**
Bart Simpson, jigsaw, Milton
   Bradley, 250 pcs, MIB
   (sealed).........................**20.00**
Batman, jigsaw, Whitman, 1966,
   150 pcs, EXIB.................**40.00**
Beetle Bailey, jigsaw, Jaymar,
   1963, 60 pcs, NMIB **25.00**
Brady Bunch, frame-tray, Whitman, 1972, M **45.00**
Dark Shadows, jigsaw, Milton
   Bradley, 1969, NMIB.....**65.00**

Dr Strange, jigsaw, Third Eye,
   1971, 500 pcs, MIB **100.00**
Fonz, jigsaw, HG Toys, 1976, EX
   (EX canister).................**25.00**
Gay Purr-ee, frame-tray, Whitman, 1962, 14x11", NM ..**15.00**
Grizzly Adams, jigsaw, House of
   Games, 1978, 100 pcs, MIB .**15.00**
Impossible, frame-tray, Whitman,
   1967, 14x11", EX............**25.00**
Jetsons, frame-tray, Whitman,
   1960s, NM, from $35 to .**45.00**
Josie & the Pussycats, frame-tray,
   1971, EX **15.00**
Kristy McNichol, jigsaw, APC,
   1979, MIB......................**20.00**
Lassie, jigsaw, Whitman Big Little
   Books series, 1960s, NMIB .**50.00**
Mary Poppins, jigsaw, Jaymar,
   1964, MIB......................**40.00**
Mighty Mouse, jigsaw, Whitman,
   1967, 100 pcs, NMIB **15.00**
Nancy & Sluggo, jigsaw, Whitman, 1973, NMIB **15.00**
Pebbles Flintstone, frame-tray,
   Whitman, 1960s, NM.....**20.00**
Punky Brewster, jigsaw, 1984,
   EXIB **20.00**

Raggedy Ann and Andy, Do the Raggedy Dance, wooden board puzzle, Macmillan Inc/Playskool, 1987, MIP, $15.00.

Rookies, jigsaw, American Publishing, 1975, EX (EX container)......................................**40.00**

Silver Surfer, jigsaw, Third Eye, 1971, 500 pcs, MIB **100.00**

Sleeping Beauty, jigsaw, Jaymar, 1960s, NMIB **20.00**

Snagglepuss, jigsaw, Whitman Jr, 1962, MIB......................**25.00**

Space Kidettes, jigsaw, Whitman, 1967, 70 pcs, MIB **30.00**

Three's Company, jigsaw, APC, 1978, MIB.......................**30.00**

Thunderbirds, jigsaw, Whitman, 1968, MIB.......................**30.00**

Top Cat, frame-tray, Whitman, 1961, 14x11", NM...........**20.00**

Village People, jigsaw, APC, 1978, MIB, from $65 to.............**85.00**

Welcome Back Kotter, frame-tray, Whitman, 1977, M **10.00**

Winnie the Pooh, frame-tray, Whitman, 1979, 14x11", EX..........**10.00**

Wyatt Earp, jigsaw, Whitman, 1960s, NMIB **25.00**

Yogi Bear, frame-tray, Whitman, 1961, 14x11", M **20.00**

Zorro, frame-tray, Whitman, 1965, 14x11", NM....................**25.00**

Radios

Novelty radios are those that carry an advertising message or are shaped like a product bottle, can, or carton; others may be modeled after the likeness of a well-known cartoon character or disguised as anything but a radio — a shoe or a car, for instance. It's sometimes hard to recognize the fact that they're actually radios. To learn more, we recommend *Collector's Guide to Novelty Radios, Books I* and *II,* by Marty Bunis and Robert F. Breed (Collector Books).

Transistor radios are also popular. First introduced in 1954, many feature space-age names and futuristic designs. Prices here are for complete, undamaged examples in at least very good condition. All are battery operated and AM unless noted otherwise. For further information, we recommend *Collector's Guide to Transistor Radios, Second Edition,* by Marty and Sue Bunis (Collector Books). If you have vintage radios you need to evaluate, see *Collector's Guide to Antique Radios, Fifth Edition,* by John Slusser and the staff of *Radio Daze* (Collector Books).

Novelty Radios

Animal Crackers, Keebler, braided handle, EX.................**70.00**
Annie Sing-A-Long, LJN/Hong Kong, 8", from $35 to.....**50.00**

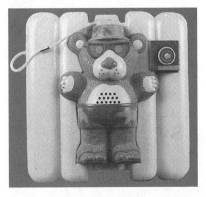

Bear on Mattress, Made in China, Fun Designs Inc., 1986, 8¼x8¼", $30.00. (Photo courtesy Marty Bunis and Robert F. Breed)

Big Bird, 2-D head image w/red & white striped bow tie, from $15 to..............**25.00**
Blabber Mouse on cheese, EX..**35.00**
Bullwinkle, figural, PAT/Hong Kong, from $200 to.....**250.00**
Cheez-It Snack Crackers, Sunshine, Isis model #39, EX..........**30.00**
Cookie Crisp, box shape, Hong Kong, from $50 to..........**75.00**
Dr Pepper, Diet can shape, from $20 to.............................**35.00**
Duracell Alkaline Battery, D cell, 5½".................................**50.00**
Flashlight w/Key Chain, round, Admiral, from $30 to.....**40.00**
French's Automash Potato Mix, EX...................................**30.00**
Gain Baby Formula, EX.......**85.00**

Hubba Bubba Soda, can shape, from $45 to.....................**60.00**
Incredible Hulk, 2-D figure, Marvel/Amico, 1978, from $50 to............................**75.00**
Little Debbie Swiss Cake Rolls, Isis model #103, EX.......**30.00**
Old El Paso Mexican Foods, can shape, from $30 to.........**45.00**
Olympia Pale Export Beer, EX..**45.00**
Orange Spot Carbonated Drink, orange can shape, from $25 to....................................**35.00**
Oscar the Grouch in Trash Can, MIB................................**35.00**
Pillsbury Doughboy, standing behind clock stove, from $40 to...................................**60.00**
Pizza Hut, pocket style w/headphones, Talbot Toys, from $25 to....................................**35.00**
Polaroid 600 Plus, China, from $20 to.............................**30.00**
Raggedy Ann & Andy, Philgee International, 1973, NM.**25.00**
Santa Bear Lunchbox, Fun Designs, 1986, from $35 to..............**50.00**
Shell Fire & Ice All Season Motor Oil 10W-40, from $25 to.....................................**35.00**
Smurf, NM...........................**10.00**
Snoopy, AM, Determined, 1970s, 7", MIB..........................**40.00**
Snoopy Flashbeagle, sq, from $15 to...................................**25.00**
Tony's Pizza, cloth cooler bag w/AM-FM radio lid, from $25 to.....................................**40.00**
Twix Cookies & Cream/Chocolate Fudge, oblong w/handle, China.............................**75.00**
V8 100% Vegetable Juice, can shape, from $35 to.........**50.00**

Wilson Tennis Balls, can shape, from $30 to **45.00**

Transistor Radios

Admiral, 4P21, horizontal, 4 transistors, AM, battery, 1957 .....**35.00**

Airline, GEN-1208A, Eldorado, horizontal, AM, shortwave/ battery, 1962 ....**30.00**

America, ST-6X, Wayfarer, vertical, 6 transistors, AM, battery, 1962 ....**40.00**

Arvin, 60R35, horizontal, 7 transistors, AM, battery, 1959 ...**30.00**

A r v i n , #86R29, 10 transistors, black plastic, Japan, $ 1 5 . 0 0. (Photo courtesy Marty and Sue Bunis)

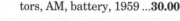

Bulova, 892, horizontal, 7 transistors, AM, battery, 1963 ..**35.00**

Continental, 160, vertical, 6 transistors, AM, battery, 1959**45.00**

Dewald, K-544, horizontal, 4 transistors, AM, battery, 1957 ...**125.00**

Eico, RA-6, horizontal, 6 transistors, AM, battery, 1961 ..**15.00**

Emerson, 977, Falcon, horizontal, 7 transistors, AM, 1961 .**35.00**

Futura, 366, vertical, 6 transistors, AM, battery, 1963 ..**30.00**

General Electric, P746A, horizontal, 5 transistors, AM, battery, 1958 ....**25.00**

General Electric, P835, Super 6, horizontal, 6 transistors, AM, 1961 ....**20.00**

Hitachi, TH-680, vertical, 6 transistors, AM, 1965 ....**25.00**

Hitachi, TH-862R, Marie, horizontal, 8 transistors, AM, 1960....**25.00**

Jewel, 10, vertical, 9 transistors, AM, battery, 1965 ....**15.00**

Kent, TR-605, vertical, 6 transistors, AM, 1965 ....**15.00**

Lloyd's, TR-6T, vertical, 6 transistors, AM, 1964 ....**10.00**

Masterwork, M2812, horizontal, 8 transistors, AM, 1965 ....**10.00**

Motorola, X36E, vertical, 6 transistors, AM, 1962 ....**20.00**

Norelco, L0X95T/62R, horizontal, 7 transistors, AM, battery, 1961 ....**30.00**

Panasonic, R-109, horizontal, 9 transistors, AM, 1964 ....**15.00**

Philco, T-68BKG, vertical, 6 transistors, AM, 1963 ....**20.00**

RCA, 1-RG-11, vertical, 6 transistors, AM, battery, 1962 .**20.00**

RCA, 1-T-4J, Hawaii, vertical, 8 transistors, AM, 1959 ....**35.00**

Silvertone, 1019, Medalist, horizontal/table, 7 transistors, AM, 1961 ....**20.00**

Sony, TR-627, horizontal/table, 6 transistors, AM, battery..**30.00**

Sony, 6R-33, horizontal, 9 transistors, AM......................**20.00**

Sylvania, 5P11R, horizontal, 5 transistors, AM, battery, 1960 ....**35.00**

Tonecrest, 2091, horizontal, 10 transistors, AM/FM, 1965 ....**15.00**

Toshiba, 8TH-428R, horizontal/ table, 8 transistors, AM/ 2SWs, 1963.................**35.00**

Valiant, AM1400, Hi Power, vertical, AM, battery **30.00**
Vista, NTR-850, horizontal, 8 transistors, AM, 1963 ....**30.00**
York, TR-103, vertical, 10 transistors, AM, battery, 1965..**15.00**

Ramp Walkers

Ramp walkers date back to at least 1873 when Ives produced a cast-iron elephant walker. Wood and composite ramp walkers were made in Czechoslovakia and the USA from the 1920s through the 1940s. The most common were made by John Wilson of Watsontown, Pennsylvania. These sold worldwide and became known as 'Wilson Walkies.' Most are two-legged and stand approximately 4½" tall.

Plastic ramp walkers were manufactured primarily by the Louis Marx Co. from the 1950s through the early 1960s. The majority were produced in Hong Kong, but some were made in the USA and sold under the Marx logo or by the Charmore Co., a subsidiary of Marx.

The three common sizes are small premiums about 1½" x 2"; the more common medium size, 2¾" x 3"; and large, approximately 4" x 5". Most of the smaller walkers were unpainted, while the medium and large sizes were hand or spray painted. Several of the walking types were sold with wooden or colorful tin lithographed ramps.

Randy Welch is our advisor for ramp walkers; he is listed in the Directory under Maryland. For more extensive listings and further information, see *Schroeder's Collectible Toys, Antique to Modern* (Collector Books).

Big Bad Wolf & Mason Pig, Marx............................**50.00**
Bison w/Native, Marx..........**40.00**
Bull, plastic **20.00**
Dairy Cow, plastic................**20.00**
Donald Duck pulling nephews in wagon, Marx..................**35.00**
Elephant, Wilson..................**30.00**
Fiddler & Fifer Pigs, Marx ...**50.00**
Goofy riding hippo, Marx......**45.00**

Hap and Hop Soldiers, Marx, $25.00.

Horse w/English Rider, plastic, lg....................................**50.00**
Mammy, Wilson **40.00**
Mickey & Donald riding alligator, Marx **40.00**
Olive Oyl, Wilson **175.00**
Pebbles on Dino, Marx..........**75.00**
Pinocchio **200.00**
Pluto, plastic w/metal legs, Marx, sm **35.00**

Popeye & Wimpy, Marx, MIB .85.00
Reindeer, plastic 45.00
Soldier, Wilson 30.00
Tin Man Robot pushing cart, plastic 150.00

Records

Records that made it to the 'Top Ten' in their day are not always the records that are prized most highly by today's collectors, though they treasure those which best represent specific types of music: jazz, rhythm and blues, country and western, rock 'n roll, etc. Many search for those cut very early in the career of artists who later became superstars, records cut on rare or interesting labels, or those aimed at ethnic groups. A fast-growing area of related interest is picture sleeves for 45s. These are often worth more than the record itself, especially if they feature superstars from the 1950s or early 1960s.

Condition is very important. Record collectors tend to be very critical, so learn to watch for loss of gloss; holes, labels, or writing on the label; warping; and scratches. Unless otherwise noted, values are for records in like-new condition — showing little sign of wear, with a playing surface that retains much of its original shine, and having only a minimal amount of surface noise. EP (extended play 45s) and LPs (long-playing 33⅓ rpm 'albums') must have their jackets (cardboard sleeves) in nice condition free of tape, stickers, tears, or obvious damage. Refer to *The American Premium Record Guide* by Les Docks, our advisor for this category, for more information. Mr. Docks is listed in the Directory under Texas. See Clubs and Newsletters for information concerning *Record Collectors Monthly*.

Children's Records

Aristocats, 33⅓ rpm, original sound track, 1970, EX (EX sleeve)............................12.00
Astro Boy, 45 rpm, theme song, Golden 1964, EX (EX sleeve) 25.00
Banana Splits Long Live Love, 45 rpm, Decca, 1969, EX (EX sleeve)............................30.00
Batman, 45 rpm, SPC, 1966, EX (EX sleeve)....................25.00
Bozo's Christmas Album, 33⅓ rpm, 1973, EX (EX sleeve).........10.00
Bozo Under the Sea, 78 rpm, Capitol, 1950, EX (EX sleeve).60.00
Bugs Bunny & the Tortoise, 78 rpm, Capitol, 1949, EX (EX sleeve)............................35.00
Bugs Bunny Meets Hiawatha, 78 rpm, Capitol, 1958, EX (EX cover) 25.00
Charlie Brown's All Star, 33⅓ rpm, 1978, EX (EX sleeve).........15.00
Chipmunks Sing w/Children, 33⅓ rpm, Liberty, 1965, EX (EX sleeve)............................12.00
Cinderella, 78 rpm, Golden, 1950s, EX (VG sleeve) ...10.00
Dr Seuss Presents Yertle & Turtle, 33⅓ rpm, RCA, EX (EX sleeve)............................15.00

Flintstones Lullaby of Pebbles, 45 rpm, Golden, 1960s, VG (VG sleeve)............................**15.00**

Flipper the King of the Sea, 45 rpm, MGM, 1960s, EX (EX sleeve)............................**20.00**

Fred and Barney Best Friends, Peter Pan, 1976, first of series, complete with booklet, EX (EX sleeve), $20.00.

He's Your Dog Charlie Brown, 33⅓ rpm, 1978, EX (EX sleeve)............................**15.00**

Heckle & Jeckle, 45 rpm, Little Golden, 1958, EX (EX sleeve)..**15.00**

Huckleberry Hound & His Friends, 45 rpm, Golden, 1959, EX (EX sleeve) **25.00**

I'm a Little Teapot, 78 rpm, Columbia Playtime, 1950, EX (EX sleeve)........................**5.00**

King Kong, 33⅓ rpm, sound track, Southern Cross, EX (EX sleeve)............................**45.00**

Mighty Mouse Theme Song, 45 rpm, Little Golden, 1958, EX (EX sleeve)......................**15.00**

Popeye, 45 rpm, 1964, EX (EX diecut sleeve)..................**15.00**

Raiders of the Lost Ark, 33⅓ rpm, Vista, 1981, EX (EX sleeve)............................**10.00**

Rocky & His Friends, 45 rpm, Little Golden, 1961, EX (EX sleeve)............................**20.00**

Roger Ramjet & the American Eagles, 33⅓ rpm, RCA, EX (EX sleeve)......................**50.00**

Roy Rogers Had a Ranch, 45 rpm, Golden, 1950s, EX (EX sleeve)............................**45.00**

Ruff & Reddy Adventures in Space, 33⅓ rpm, Colpix, EX (EX sleeve)......................**35.00**

Scuffy the Tugboat, 78 rpm, Golden, 1948, EX (EX sleeve)............................**12.00**

Sleeping Beauty, 78 rpm, Golden, 1959, VG (VG sleeve).....**15.00**

Superman, 33⅓ rpm, Power Records, 1975, EX (EX sleeve)............................**25.00**

Swamp Fox, 45 rpm, Golden, 1959, EX (EX sleeve) **12.00**

Thor, 33⅓ rpm, Golden, 1966, EX (EX sleeve)......................**25.00**

Three Little Kittens, 45 rpm, Disneyland, 1962, EX (EX sleeve) **8.00**

Voices of Marvel, 33⅓ rpm, Marvel Comics, 1964-65, EX (EX sleeve)............................**50.00**

Wagon Train, 45 rpm, Golden, 1950s, EX (EX sleeve)....**25.00**

Yankee Doodle Mickey, 78 rpm, Disneyland, 1980, EX (EX sleeve)............................**12.00**

LP Albums

Arnold, Eddy; All-Time Favorites, RCA Victor 1223, EX **20.00**

Atkins, Chet; Picks on the Beatles, RCA 3531, NM **20.00**

Belefonte, Harry; Calypso, RCA 1248, VG **30.00**

Boston, Boston, CBS/Epic, 1976, VG **6.00**

Brown, James; Please, Please, Please, EX, $50.00. (Photo courtesy Dave Torzillo)

Cadets, The; Rockin' & Rollin', Crown 5015, EX **50.00**

Carpenters, Now & Then, A&M SP-3519, 1973 ....**15.00**

Checker, Chubby; Twist With..., Parkway 7001, EX **25.00**

Clark, Petula; Color of My World, WB1673, EX **15.00**

Cline, Patsy; Patsy Cline Showcase, Coral 4202, EX........**30.00**

Croce, Jim; The JC Collection, Cashwest, 1977, EX **7.00**

Denver, John; Greatest Hits, RCA, 1973, EX+ **8.00**

Diddley, Bo; Have a Guitar Will Travel, Chess 2974, EX .**60.00**

Domino, Fats; Fats Domino Swings, Liberty, NM.....**35.00**

Flamingos, Sound of the Flamingos, End 316, EX..............**60.00**

Fleetwood Mac, Rumors, Warner Bros, 1977, EX **10.00**

Francis, Connie; More Greatest Hits, MGM E-3893, VG .**15.00**

Guess Who, Canned Wheat Packed By, RCA 4157, NM **20.00**

John, Elton; Greatest Hits, MCA, 1974, VG+.........................**6.00**

Laine, Frankie; Golden Hits, Mercury SR60587, NM.........**12.00**

Lettermen, Hurt So Bad, Capitol, 1969-70, VG.....................**8.00**

Martin, Dean; Everybody Loves Somebody, Reprise, NM **10.00**

Martin, Dean; Gentle on My Mind, Reprise RS 6330, EX......**15.00**

Nelson, Ricky; Ricky, Imperial 9048, EX **40.00**

Perkins, Carl; Whole Lotta Shakin', Columbia 1234, EX **75.00**

Presley, Elvis; GI Blues, RCA LSP-2256, NM................**20.00**

Randolph, Boots; More Yakety Sax, Monument 8037, NM **50.00**

Robbins, Marty; The Song of Robbins, Columbia 976, EX.....**20.00**

Rolling Stones, Big Hits, VG .**10.00**

Shannon, Del; Runaway, Big Top 1303, EX **50.00**

Sinatra, Frank; Greatest Hits, Capitol, 1960s, EX **8.00**

Snow, Hank; Big Country Hits — Songs I Hadn't Recorded Till Now, EX.............................**10.00**

Sons of the Pioneers, Favorites, RCA Victor 1130, EX **15.00**

Streisand, Barbra; Songbird, 1978, EX **14.00**

Supertramp, Breakfast in America, A&M, 1979, EX..........**10.00**

Valens, Richie; His Greatest Hits, Del-Fi 1225, EX.............**25.00**

Vee, Bobby; Just Today, Liberty LST-7554, EX................**20.00**

Williams, Roger; Greatest Hits, Kapp 3260, NM **40.00**

45 rpms

Abba, Dancing Queen, Atlantic 3372, 1976, NM **3.00**

Anka, Paul; Puppy Love, Paramount 10082, EX (EX sleeve) **5.00**

Anka, Paul; Put Your Head on My Shoulder, ABC-Paramount 10040, 1959 .... **35.00**

Avalon, Frankie; Venus, Chancellor 1031, M **10.00**

Avalon, Frankie; Where Are You/Tuxedo Junction, Chancellor C-1052, from $10.00 to $15.00.

Beach Boys, Fun Fun Fun, Capitol 5118, 1964, NM **30.00**

Beach Boys, Help Me Rhonda, Capitol 5372, M **15.00**

Beatles, I Want To Hold Your Hand, VG+ **45.00**

Beau Brummels, Laugh Laugh, Autumn 8, 1965, NM **10.00**

Berry, Chuck; No Particular Place To Go, Chess 1898, 1964, NM **50.00**

Big Bopper, Chantilly Lace, Mercury 71323, EX **12.00**

Boone, Pat; Friendly Persuasion, Dot 15490, maroon label, 1956, NM **25.00**

Buckinghams, Mercy Mercy Mercy, Columbia 44182, NM (EX sleeve) **10.00**

Byrds, Mr Tambourine Man, Columbia 43271, red vinyl, 1965, VG **30.00**

Cadillacs, Thrill Me So, Mercury 71738, 1960, VG **30.00**

Cannon, Freddy; Tallahassee Lassie, Swan 4031, 1959, NM **35.00**

Chad & Jeremy, Willow Weep for Me, World Artists 1034, 1964, NM **20.00**

Champs, Tequilla, Challenge 1016, 1958, NM **40.00**

Channel, Bruce; Hey! Baby, Le Cam 953, EX **20.00**

Clanton, Jimmy; Go Jimmy Go, Ace 575, 1959, NM **30.00**

Cooke, Sam; Cupid, RCA Victor 47-7883, 1961, NM **25.00**

Creedence Clearwater Revival, Proud Mary, Fantasy 619, M **5.00**

Dave Clark Five, Bits & Pieces, Epic 9671, M **10.00**

Dells, Shy Girl, Vee Jay 595, 1964, NM **30.00**

Diamonds, High Sign, Mercury 71291, 1958, NM **75.00**

Domino, Fats; I'm Walkin', Imperial 5428, 1957, NM **50.00**

Domino, Fats; Poor Poor Me, Imperial 5197, EX **30.00**

Eddy, Duane; Peter Gunn, Jamie 1168, 1960, NM **35.00**

Five Satins, I'll Be Seeing You, Ember 1061, EX **10.00**

Fleetwoods, Me Blue, Dolton 2001, EX **20.00**

Four Seasons, Sherry, Vee Jay 456, 1962, NM.................**35.00**

Francis, Connie; Second Hand Love, MGM 13074, 1967, NM.................................**10.00**

Franklin, Aretha; Respect, Atlantic 2403, 1967, NM................**12.00**

Gilley, Mickey; Susie-Q, Astro 104, EX............................**20.00**

Gore, Lesley; It's My Party, Mercury 72119, M.................**20.00**

Holly, Buddy; Slippin' & Slidin', Coral 62448, EX..............**30.00**

Hunter, Tab; Young Love, Dot 15533, M..........................**15.00**

Isley Brothers, The Drag, Gone 5048, 1958, NM............**100.00**

Jan & Dean, Surf City, Liberty 55580, 1963, NM............**30.00**

King, Ben E; Stand By Me, Atco 6194, 1961, NM...............**25.00**

Kinks, Dead End Street, Reprise #0540, 1967, NM............**20.00**

Kodaks, Teenager's Dream, Fury 1007, EX.........................**20.00**

Lee, Brenda; Sweet Nothin's, Decca 30967, 1959, NM.**75.00**

Lee, Peggy, Fever, Capitol 3998, M.....................................**10.00**

Lennon, John; Mind Games, Apple P-1868, 1973, NM..........**40.00**

Lewis, Jerry Lee; Crazy Arms, Sun 359, EX...................**15.00**

Little Richard, Tutti-Frutti, Specialty 561, EX...................**8.00**

Madonna, Like a Virgin, Sire 29210, M............................**5.00**

Manfred Man, Sha La La, Ascot, 1964, NM.......................**25.00**

Moonglos, Foolish Me, Chess 1568, EX..........................**16.00**

O'Jays, Miracles, Apollo 759, 1961, NM.......................**20.00**

Orbison, Roy; Crying/Candy Man, Monument 447, 1961, NM.**30.00**

Orbison, Roy; Only the Lonely, Monument 421, M.........**20.00**

Orioles, If You Believe, Jubilee 5161, EX.........................**15.00**

Page, Patti; Allegheny Moon, Mercury 70878, M.................**10.00**

Paul & Paula, Young Lovers, Philips 40096, 1963, NM.**20.00**

Pitney, Gene; Town Without Pity, Musicor 1009, 1961, NM.**25.00**

Platters, Great Pretender, Mercury 70753, M.................**15.00**

Presley, Elvis; Love Me Tender, RCA Victor 47-6643, 1956, VG.................................**30.00**

Quaker City Boys, Teasin', Swan 4023, 1959, NM.............**20.00**

Rivers, Johnny; Maybelline, Imperial 66056, 1964, NM................**15.00**

Robbins, Marty; Long Tall Sally, Columbia 40679, EX......**20.00**

Santo & Johnny, Sleep Walk, Canadian American 103, 1959, NM.......................**40.00**

Shannon, Del; Runaway, Big Top 3067, 1961, NM..............**35.00**

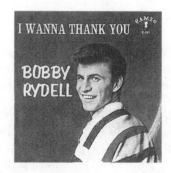

Rydell, Bobby, I Wanna Thank You/The Door to Paradise, Cameo C-201, $15.00.

Shirelles, Mama Said, Scepter 1217, M.............**15.00**

Shirelles, Will You Love Me Tomorrow, Scepter 1211, EX..........**15.00**

Teardrops, The Stars Are Out Tonight, Josie 766, EX...**75.00**

Temptations, My Girl, Gordy 7038, 1965, VG.............**20.00**

XTurtles, Happy Together, White, Whale 244, M....................**6.00**

Ventures, Walk Don't Run/The McCoy, Dolton 25X, 1960, NM................**35.00**

XVinton, Bobby; Roses Are Red, Epic 9509, M.....................**8.00**

Wells, Mary; My Guy, Motown 1056, 1964, NM.............**20.00**

X-Tremes, Facts of Life, Star Trek, 1966, NM.............**15.00**

Yardbirds, For Your Love, Epic 97-9, 1965, NM.............**40.00**

Youngbloods, Grizzly Bear, RCA Victor 47-9015, 1966, NM................**25.00**

Zombies, Tell Her No, Parrot 9723, 1965, NM.............**25.00**

Big Richard, Pig Meat Mama, Varsity 6063, EX.............**15.00**

Cash, Johnny; I Walk the Line, Sun 241, EX....................**15.00**

Crosby, Bing; Out of Nowhere, Brunswick 6090, NM.....**12.00**

Del Vikings, Come Go With Me, Dot 15538, EX................**40.00**

Dells, Time Makes You Change, Vee-Jay 258, EX.............**30.00**

Domino, Fats; Boogie Woogie Baby, Imperial 5065, EX..........**15.00**

Eddy, Duane; Rebel-'Rouser, Jaime 1104, EX..............**15.00**

Ellington, Duke; Got Everything But You, Victor 21703, NM......**30.00**

Everly Brothers, Bird Dog, Cadence 1350, EX..........**30.00**

Garland, Judy; Stompin' at the Savoy, Decca 848, NM...**10.00**

Hall's Jazz Band, West End Blues, Banner 7248, NM...........**15.00**

Holiday, Billy; Practice Makes Perfect, Okeh 5806, EX.**10.00**

Ink Spots, The Gypsy, Decca 18817, VG.....................**15.00**

78 rpms

Armstrong, Louis; Hot Jazz Classics, Columbia, 1940s, set of 4, EX...............**65.00**

Autry, Gene; Wild Cat Mama, Victor 23642, EX.................**75.00**

Avalon, Frankie; De De Dinah, Chancellor 1011, EX...................**20.00**

Baker, Buddy; Box Car Blues, Victor 21549, VG.................**15.00**

Basie, Count; Pennies From Heaven, Decca 1121, NM.........**10.00**

Basin Street Blues, Vogue, 1930s, EX................**125.00**

Lewis, Shari; Aren't You Glad You're You?, Golden, 1958, EX (EX cover), from $8.00 to $10.00. (Photo courtesy Peter Muldavin)

Little Richard, Long Tall Sally, Specialty 572, EX...........**15.00**

Nelson, Ricky; Lonesome Town, Imperial 5545, EX..........**25.00**

Page, Patti; I Went to Your Wedding, Mercury 5899, EX....**20.00**

Prairie Ramblers, Blue River, Bluebird 5302.................**25.00**

Presley, Elvis; Heartbreak Hotel, RCA 6420, EX................**20.00**

Price, Lloyd; Stagger Lee, ABC 9972, EX.........................**30.00**

Reeves, Jim; I've Never Been So Blue, Macy's 132, EX.....**50.00**

Ritter, Tex; Bill the Bar Fly, Decca 5305, EX..............**12.00**

Ritter, Tex; Nobody's Darling But Mine, Champion 45153, NM...............................**10.00**

Rodgers, Jimmy; Honeycomb, Roulette 4015, EX..........**20.00**

Williams, Hank; Message to My Mother, MGM 11875, EX .**12.00**

Red Glass

Ever popular with collectors, red glass has been used to create decorative items such as one might find in gift shops, utilitarian bottles and kitchenware, figurines and dinnerware lines such as were popular during the Depression era. For further information and study, we recommend *Ruby Glass of the 20th Century* by Naomi Over (Collector Books).

Ashtray, bowl shape w/scrolled-up end, gold decor, Venetian .**10.00**

Banana boat, English Hobnail, Westmoreland, 1980, 6¾x9½" **75.00**

Basket, bulbous w/ruffled rim, clear twisted handle, Morgantown, 12"......................**100.00**

Basket, hobnail, ruffled rim, low foot, American Glass, 1990s, 7½".................................**20.00**

Basket, Pineapple pattern, LE Smith, 1997, 14½".........**40.00**

Bell, Butterfly pattern, ruby carnival, Fenton, 1998, 7"...**30.00**

Bookends, pillow design, Blenko, ca 1982, 5½", ea **15.00**

Bowl, ruffled rim, Blenko, 1932-53, 15"............................**60.00**

Bowl, ruffled rim, Blenko, 1980, 9½"................................**25.00**

Box, treasure chest form, Sandwich pattern, Tiara Exclusives, 1980-90.................**20.00**

Candlestick, Eiffel Tower form, AA Imports, 10½" **30.00**

Candlesticks, Early American Hobnail, Fenton, 1988, 3¾", pr..**45.00**

Candy dish, Eyewinker pattern, pedestal foot, LG Wright, 1960s, 6" **35.00**

Coaster, smooth w/faint pie-wedge design, Hazel-Atlas, 3½" dia.........................**20.00**

Cornucopia, unknown maker, 5¾x5", $85.00. (Photo courtesy Naomi Over)

Cookie cutter, star shape, Taiwan, 2½".....................**6.00**

Decanter, crackle glass, Blenko, 1980s, 10".......................**20.00**

Figurine, bird, sleek, Pilgrim Glass, 1980, 5½"..............**20.00**

Figurine, teddy bear, Boyd Crystal Art Glass, ca 1980, 2¾"..**12.00**

Figurine, Victorian girl, Kemple Glass Works, miniature..**20.00**

Figurine, whale, solid, Rainbow Glass, ca 1980, 3½"........**12.00**

Open salt, wheelbarrow form, Summit Art Glass, 3½" W.........**35.00**

Pencil holder, dog figure, Boyd Crystal Art Glass, 1980, 1".........**10.00**

Pitcher, cherry blossom design, AA Imports, 1980s, 6½"................................**25.00**

Plate, American pattern, Fostoria, ca 1980, 14".....................**75.00**

Plate, plain, Venetian, 16"....**25.00**

Reamer, marked B in circle, by Edna Barnes, 1981, 4½".**15.00**

Salt & pepper shakers, metal caps, Viking Glass, 1980s, 3½", pr **20.00**

Spooner, acorn design, footed, carnival, Mosser Art Glass, 1997, 5"......................................**60.00**

Top hat, Daisy & Button pattern, LG Wright, 2¼"..............**15.00**

Tumbler, juice; Beaded Rings pattern, Hocking, 1927-32, 4-oz...............................**15.00**

Tumbler, Swirl pattern, Cambridge, 1949-53, 12-oz...................**35.00**

Vase, cup shape w/twisted crystal stem, Venetian, 1980, 10¾".............................**30.00**

Vase, footed, white decoration w/crystal handles, Venetian, 6¼"................................**125.00**

Vase, twisted stem, Blenko, 1980, 13½"...............................**20.00**

Water glass, bubble pattern, Blenko, 1982, 7-oz.........**15.00**

Red Wing

Taking their name from the location in Minnesota where they located in the late 1870s, the Red Wing Company produced a variety of wares, all of which are today considered noteworthy by pottery and dinnerware collectors. Their early stoneware lines, Cherry Band and Sponge Band (Gray Line), are especially valuable and often fetch prices of several hundred dollars per piece on today's market. Production of dinnerware began in the '30s and continued until the pottery closed in 1967. Some of their more popular lines — all of which were hand painted — were Bob White, Lexington, Tampico, Normandie, Capistrano, and Random Harvest. Commercial artware was also produced. Perhaps the ware most easily associated with Red Wing is their Brushware line, unique in its appearance and decoration. Cattails, rushes, florals, and similar nature subjects are 'carved' in relief on a stoneware-type body with a matt green wash its only finish.

For more information, we recommend *Collector's Encyclopedia of Red Wing Art Pottery* and *Red Wing Art Pottery, Book II,* by B.L. and R.L. Dollen. To learn about their stoneware production, refer to *Red Wing Stoneware, An Identification and Value Guide,* and *Red Wing Collectibles,* both by Dan and Gail de Pasquale and Larry Peterson. All are published by Collector Books.

Artware

Ash receiver, pelican, white, #880.............................**170.00**
Ashtray, angelfish form, deep green, #933....................**125.00**
Bowl, console; scalloped rim, white semimatt, #1620, 10" **42.00**
Bowl, console; Tropicana, chartreuse, #B-2014, 14".......**25.00**
Bowl, sgrafitto, #M-4001, 7".**50.00**
Candle holders, star shape, white semimatt, #B1411, 4", pr.**28.00**
Candle holders, teardrop form, glossy cinnamon, #1409, 5", pr.....................................**25.00**
Compote, med pedestal, white semimatt, #M1597, 7"....**28.00**
Ewer, Magnolia, #1012, 7"....**35.00**
Figurine, bird w/tail up perched on base, glossy forest green, 10"....................................**22.00**

Figurine, four piggyback dolphins on wave, purple with pink, 9", $70.00.

Flower frog, Fern, white, #1046 .**150.00**
Lamp, green, elephant handles, 9" **175.00**

Leaf dish, blue lustre exterior w/coral interior, #1251, 12" **25.00**
Pitcher, ball form, yellow, #547, 7½"...................................**35.00**
Pitcher, Gypsy Trail, cobalt w/wood handle................**50.00**
Planter, deer form, glossy turquoise, #1338, 5½" **38.00**
Planter, ram's head, #739, 10".**125.00**
Planter, violin form, glossy Zephyr Pink (flecked), #M1484, 13"..................**50.00**

Vase, #1162, leaves and vines, late 1930s, 9", $50.00. (Photo courtesy B.L. Dollen)

Vase, Belle 100, Dutch Blue, #792, 10"...................................**100.00**
Vase, bird; yellow, #1296, 10" .**75.00**
Vase, fan; white, #892, 7½" ..**30.00**
Vase, Magnolia, #976, 10" ..**150.00**
Vase, Seafoam, #744, 7"........**75.00**
Vase, snifter form, glossy yellow, #M1442, 8½" **38.00**
Vase, urn shape, cocoa semimatt, #M5000, 8" **28.00**
Wall pocket, guitar form, blue, #M-1484, 13½" **50.00**

Dinnerware

Blossom Time, butter dish, rectangular.........................**22.50**

Blossom Time, plate, dinner; 10½".................12.50
Bob White, bowl, rim soup....20.00
Bob White, bowl, sauce.........12.00
Bob White, cup & saucer......10.00

Bob White, dinner plate, $20.00.

Brittany, nappy, 9".............32.00
Brittany, plate, chop; 14"......60.00
Brittany, plate, dinner; 10"..22.50
Capistrano, egg plate.............68.00
Capistrano, salt & pepper shakers, pr..............................20.00
Capistrano, spoon rest.........17.50
Chevron, plate, salad; 8".........7.50
Chevron, teapot, 6-cup.........55.00
Iris, creamer......................14.00
Iris, plate, chop.....................42.50
Iris, plate, 6½"......................10.00
Lexington, bowl, cereal...........8.00
Lexington, creamer & sugar bowl, w/lid...............................30.00
Lexington, pitcher, water.....40.00
Lexington, plate, dinner; 10½".12.50
Lotus, creamer......................14.00
Lotus, plate, dinner; 10½"....20.00
Lotus, spoon rest...................18.00
Lute Song, bowl, fruit.............7.50
Lute Song, bread tray...........32.50
Lute Song, platter, sm.........22.50
Morning Glory, creamer.......15.00
Morning Glory, plate, 10½"..22.00

Normandy, bowl, vegetable..22.00
Normandy, gravy boat.........28.00
Normandy, water jug............60.00
Orleans, nappy, 9"................30.00
Orleans, plate, 6"...................8.00
Orleans, teapot....................115.00
Pepe, butter dish, rectangular.32.50
Pepe, celery tray....................17.50
Pepe, platter, 15"..................30.00
Random House, bowl, divided vegetable..............................30.00
Random House, plate, luncheon; 8½"..................................20.00
Random House, platter, 15".28.00
Reed, plate, 8½"......................7.50
Reed, teapot, 6-cup...............48.00
Round-Up, bowl, salad; 5½".42.50
Round-Up, cup & saucer.......75.00
Round-Up, salt & pepper shakers, pr.....................................95.00

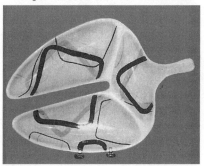

Smart Set, relish tray, three-part, from $65.00 to $75.00. (Photo courtesy Ted Haun)

Tampico, bowl, cereal............16.00
Tampico, mug.......................45.00
Tampico, plate, dinner; 10½".35.00
Town & Country, bowl, salad; 6"...................................18.00
Town & Country, syrup jug..50.00
Village Green, casserole, lg ..28.00
Village Green, mug...............25.00
Zinnia, plate, 10½"................24.00

Zinnia, salt & pepper shakers, pr.................................**22.50**

Restaurant China

Restaurant china is specifically designed for use in commercial food service. Not limited to restaurants, this dinnerware is used on planes, ships, and trains, as well as hotel, railroad, and airport dining rooms. Churches, clubs, and department and drug stores also put it to good use.

The popularity of high quality American-made heavy gauge vitrified china with traditional styling is very popular today. Some collectors look for transportation system top-marked pieces, others may prefer those with military logos, etc. It is currently considered fashionable to serve home-cooked meals on mismatched top-marked hotel ware, adding a touch of nostalgia and remembrances of elegant times past. For a more thorough study of the subject, we recommend *Restaurant China, Identification & Value Guide for Restaurant, Airline, Ship & Railroad Dinnerware, Volume 1* and *Volume 2*, by our advisor Barbara Conroy (Collector Books). She is listed in the Directory under California.

Ashtray, Ken's House of Pancakes, round, Shenango.**20.00**
Bowl, rice; Blue Willow pattern, Hall, c 1930s...................**28.00**
Creamer, El Rancho pattern, brown on tan, Wallace, 1950s ...**45.00**

Cup, Dunkin' Donuts script letter & doughboy, tan, Jackson, 1960s...............................**72.00**
Cup, Mister Donut chef w/bow tie, Buffalo, 1970s, ...**27.00**
Cup, Peking Gourmet Inn script logo, Homer Laughlin, early 1990s.................................**5.00**
Cup & saucer, AD; Roosevelt Hotel (New Orleans), Shenango, 1964 ....**35.00**
Cup & saucer, Ox Head, brown on tan, Homer Laughlin, late 1960s...............................**35.00**

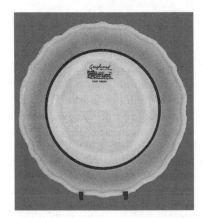

Greyhound Post House top-marked plate, Syracuse, 6¼", $22.00. (Photo courtesy Barbara Conroy)

Grapefruit, Denny's Coffee Shop, Tepco, 1950s...................**35.00**
Mug, Chicken in the Rough, Syracuse, 1950s **80.00**
Mug, Copper Penny, Shenango, 1960s...............................**25.00**
Mug, Hobo Joe logo, Hall, 1960s..**26.00**
Mug, IHOP logo, blue Fiesta, Homer Laughlin, 1990s.**100.00**
Mug, Little Tavern Shops, Shenango, 1953 date code **55.00**

Mug, Qwikee Donuts, ...get your daily dozen..., brown, Shenango, 1969 ....**110.00**

Mug, White Castle black King Size logo, Mayer, 1961 date code .**50.00**

Mug, Woolworth's script logo, Syracuse, 1924 date code **175.00**

Pitcher, 4½", Veterans Administration, Shenango, 1930s.**25.00**

Plate, compartment; Plymouth pattern on white, Buffalo, 1926-28 ....**20.00**

Plate, grill; Howard Johnson's, maroon scenic border, Mayer, 1951 ....**50.00**

Plate, grill; Red Lion, red on white, Shenango, 1960s.**33.00**

Plate, grill; Walgreen's, tan, Syracuse Econo-Rim, 1946 date code **47.00**

Plate, soup; Anderson Pea Soup logo, Jackson, 1970s **32.00**

Plate, 5½", Montgomery Ward's stylized M above W, Syracuse, 1964 ....**17.00**

Plate, 6", Disneyland, melamine, Plastic Mug Co, 1980s ...**18.00**

Plate, 6", St Francis Hotel, Syracuse, 1957 date code **21.00**

Plate, 6", Western Traveler, red on white, Tepco, 1950s...**32.00**

Plate, 6¼", Steak 'n Shake, black logo on white, Shenango, 1970 ....**18.00**

Plate, 7", Fairmont Hotel black script logo, Shenango, 1960s **12.00**

Plate, 7", Foster's brown script logo, Trenton (Scammell), 1940s **16.00**

Plate, 7¼", Clancy's, man's portrait in center, Buffalo, 1962 ....**18.00**

Plate, 8", Holiday Inn's Granny Holiday logo, Shenango, 1968 ....**30.00**

Plate, 8", MGM Grand Casino, Dudson, 1992-94 ....**30.00**

Plate, 8", 3 multicolored bands on ivory, Iroquois, 1960s.......**9.00**

Plate, 9", Hilton Hotel's H logo, Corning Pyrex, late 1960s **18.00**

Plate, 9¾", Wilson's Restrunt (sic) hillbilly logo, Jackson, 1940s **30.00**

Plate, 10", Aunt Jemima's Kitchens, Wellsville, 1950s, minimum **150.00**

Plate, 10", 20th Century Fox rust logo, Syracuse, 1993 date code, ...**35.00**

Platter, 11¼", Downyflake Waffles, ivory, oblong, Iroquois, 1940s **50.00**

Sauce boat, Amelio's, red & blue on white, Jackson, 1960 date code **22.00**

Rock 'n Roll

Concert posters, tour books, magazines, sheet music, and other items featuring rock 'n roll stars from the 1950s up to the present are today being sought out by collectors who appreciate this type of music and like having these mementos of their favorite performers around to enjoy.

Our advisor for this category is Bojo (Bob Guttuso); he is listed in the Directory under Pennsylvania. See also Beatles; Elvis Presley; Records.

Alice Cooper, concert ticket, Jackson MS, June 6, 1975, NM (unused)..........................**25.00**

Bee Gees, backpack, cloth, Image Factory, 1978, NM, $50 to.**75.00**

Bee Gees, fan club kit, 1979, complete, NM, from $75 to..**100.00**

Bob Dylan, poster, House of Blues, Atlanta, Aug 3-4, 1996, 17x11", NM.....................**50.00**

Bobby Sherman, Love Beads, 1971, M, from $40 to......**50.00**

Bobby Sherman, ring, Love & Peace, 1971, M **25.00**

Bonnie Raitt, concert poster, Smith Center, April 9, 1978, 18x12", NM.....................**75.00**

Boy George & Culture Club, puffy stickers, 1984, set of 6, M **15.00**

Cars, matchbook, Candy-O, Elektra (unused)......................**15.00**

Crosby Stills & Nash, whistle, Whistling Down the Wire, promotion, EX................**20.00**

David Cassidy, fan club kit, Laufer, 1972, complete, M **100.00**

Dick Clark, doll, Juro, 1958, 24", MIB...............................**250.00**

Donny & Marie Osmond, Poster Pen Set, Craft House, 1977, NRFB............................**40.00**

Donny & Marie Osmond, record case, Peerless Vidtronic Corp, 1977, NM **35.00**

Doors, bumper sticker, WPU NY rock station promotion, 1970s, 12", M....................**8.00**

Doors, stationery, 1960s, NM .**100.00**

Grateful Dead, postcard, BG-263, Dec 31, 1970, NM...........**30.00**

Jackson Five, banner, I Love the..., felt, 1960s-70s, 29", NM..**25.00**

Joe Cocker, concert button, Central Park Music Festival, 1980, EX.........................**10.00**

KISS, fan club kit, KISS Army, complete, M **75.00**

KISS, key chains, head images, 1977, NM, ea..................**50.00**

KISS, poster put-ons, 1976, MOC **20.00**

Led Zeppelin, blimp, inflatable vinyl, store promotion, M.........**100.00**

Led Zeppelin, program, Knebworth Park, Aug 11, 1979, VG+...............................**200.00**

Michael Jackson, key chain, 1988 concert promotion, brass, M.....**12.00**

Monkees, book, Monkees Annual, Raybert Productions, 1967, NM, $40 to......................**50.00**

Monkees, fan club kit, 1967, complete, EX (EX mailer) ..**200.00**

Monkees, tambourine, EX, $85.00.
(Photo courtesy Bob Gottuso)

Olivia Newton John, T-shirt iron-on, photo image, 1976, M **10.00**

Ozzy Osborn, scarf, Blizzard of Ozz album tour, 48", M (unused).........................**18.00**

Peter, Paul & Mary, concert ticket, April 8, 1966, unused, NM .**75.00**

Pink Floyd, postcard, Cheetah Club, color, 1980s, M **8.00**

Police, cap, 1983 Syncronicity Tour, M............................**15.00**
Rolling Stones, pennant, felt, 1960s, M.........................**75.00**
Rolling Stones, program, 1966 US Tour, EX.......................**150.00**
Rolling Stones, puffy stickers, variations, Musidor, 1983, MOC, ea...........................**10.00**
Shaun Cassidy, record case, cardboard, Vanity Fair, 1978, EX.......................**35.00**
Sonny & Cher, tour program, 1972-73, 10x13", EX.......**35.00**
Three Dog Night, banner, I Love..., felt, 1960s-70s, 29", NM.**35.00**
U2, T-shirt, Unforgetable Fire tour, 1984, M (never worn)......**18.00**
ZZ Top, mirror, 1980s, 6x6", M.**10.00**

Rooster and Roses

Here's a line of dinnerware that seemed to appear out of the blue — suddenly there it was, by the tables full at the flea markets, by the *boothfuls* at the antique malls. It's Rooster and Roses, a quaint and provincial line of dinnerware made in Japan from the 1940s and 1950s. The rooster has a yellow breast with black cross-hatching, a brown head, and a red crest and waddle. There are full-blown roses, and the borders are yellow with groups of brown diagonals. Several companies seem to have made the line, which is very extensive. In the short time we've been recording shapes, we've found more than 75. Already it's becoming harder to find!

Our advisor for this category is Jacki Elliott; she is listed in the Directory under California. For a complete listing of the line, see *Garage Sale and Flea Market Annual* (Collector Books).

Ashtray, rectagular, 3x2"........**9.50**
Basket, flared sides, 6", from $35 to....................................**45.00**
Bonbon dish, pedestal base, minimum value.....................**55.00**
Box, 4½x3½", from $25 to.....**35.00**
Candy dish, w/3 dimensional leaf handle, from $17 to........**25.00**
Carafe, no handle, w/stopper lid, 8", from $55 to................**65.00**
Chamberstick, saucer base, ring handle, from $20 to........**25.00**
Coffee grinder, rare, from $75 to...............................**85.00**
Cookie jar, ceramic handles, from $85 to...........................**100.00**
Creamer & sugar bowl, w/lid.**25.00**
Cruets, cojoined w/twisted necks, sm...................................**20.00**
Cup & saucer, from $15 to....**25.00**
Egg plate...............................**28.00**
Jam jar, attached underplate, from $25 to....................**35.00**

Lazy susan, $150.00. (Photo courtesy Jacki Elliot)

Match holder, wall hanging, from $40 to **45.00**
Mug, rounded bottom, med, from $12 to **15.00**
Pipe holder/ashtray, from $30 to **40.00**
Pitcher, 3½", from $12 to **14.00**
Plate, dinner; from $25 to **35.00**
Plate, luncheon; from $15 to .**25.00**
Recipe box, from $25 to **35.00**
Relish tray, 3 wells w/center handle **45.00**
Rolling pin, minimum value .**50.00**
Salt box, wooden lid, from $45 to **55.00**
Toast holder, minimum value .**75.00**
Wall pocket, scalloped top, bulbous bottom....................**45.00**

Roselane Sparklers

A line of small figures with a soft shaded finish and luminous jewel eyes was produced during the late 1950s by the Roselane Pottery Company who operated in Pasadena, California, from the late 1930s until possibly the 1970s. The line was a huge success. Twenty-nine different models were made, including elephants, burros, raccoons, fawns, dogs, cats, and fish. Not all pieces are marked, but some carry an incised 'Roselane Pasadena, Calif.,' or 'Calif. U.S.A'; others may have a paper label.

Angelfish, 4½", from $20 to ..**25.00**
Basset hound pup, 2", from $12 to **15.00**

Cat, Siamese, sitting, looking straight ahead, jewelled collar, 7" **28.00**
Cat, sitting, head turned right, tail out behind, from $25 to..**28.00**
Chihuahua, sitting, left paw raised, looking straight ahead, 6½"......................**25.00**

Elephant, jeweled headpiece, 6", **$25.00**. (Photo courtesy Lee Garmon)

Elephant, sitting on hind quarters, 6" **25.00**
Elephant, trunk raised, striding, jewelled headpiece, 6"....**25.00**
Fawn, legs folded under body, 4x3½"..............................**25.00**
Fawn, upturned head, 4x3½".**20.00**
Kangaroo mama w/babies **35.00**
Kitten, sitting, 1¾" **12.00**
Owl, very stylized, lg round eyes, teardrop-shaped body, lg .**25.00**
Owl, 3½" **15.00**
Owl, 5¼" **25.00**
Owl, 7" **30.00**
Owl baby, 2¼", from $12 to ..**15.00**
Pig, lg....................................**25.00**
Pouter pigeon, 3½"................**20.00**
Racoon, standing, 4½", from $20 to **25.00**

Whippet, sitting, 7½", from $25
to **28.00**

Rosemeade

Novelty items made by the Wapheton Pottery Company of North Dakota from 1941 to 1960 are beginning to attract collectors of American pottery. Though smaller items (salt and pepper shakers, figurines, trays, etc.) are readily found, the larger examples are scarce and can be very expensive. The name of the novelty ware, 'Rosemeade,' is indicated on the paper labels (many of which are still intact) or by the ink stamp.

Our advisor for this category is Bryce L. Farnsworth; he is listed in the Directory under North Dakota. For more information refer to *Collector's Encyclopedia of the Dakota Potteries* by Darlene Hurst Dommel (Collector Books).

Ashtray, flat fish form w/tall top
fin & tail wrapped under,
6½" **125.00**

Bell, peacock figural, with sticker, 5", from $250.00 to $300.00.

Bowl, fluted rim, hand-thrown,
signed F Lantz, 8¾" dia..**175.00**

Butter dish, incised rooster head, blue & red on rosy pink, ¼-lb **225.00**

Candle holders, bowl shape w/fluted rim, 2x3¾", from $75 to .**100.00**

Candy dish, shell shape w/upturned end, 2¾x4½", from $50 to **75.00**

Cheese plate, mouse embossed in center, upturned rim, 6", from $75 to **100.00**

Cotton dispenser, rabbit figure w/1 ear up & 1 sticking out, 4¾" **175.00**

Figurine, circus horse, solid, 4 x 4", from $350 to............**400.00**

Figurine, jack rabbit on base, solid, 3¼", $250 to **300.00**

Figurine, penguin family, 3-pc set, from $250 to **300.00**

Figurine, raccoon w/striped tail, 1x2½" & 1¼x1½", pr **275.00**

Incense burner, elephant seated, trumpeting, 4¼", from $150 to..................................**200.00**

Jam jar, barrel form w/various fruit finials, 5", ea, from $125 to **150.00**

Mug, 3 different Les Kouba wildlife decals, 4¾", ea, from $125 to..........................**150.00**

Planter, circus horse, 5x6½", from $75 to..............................**100.00**

Planter, Dutch shoe, 2¾x5¾", from $45 to **65.00**

Planter, sq w/grapes & leaves in relief, 4½", from $85 to..................................**100.00**

Planter, swan form, 5", from $35 to **65.00**

Plaque, fish (various kinds) on oval dish, 3½x6", ea, from $225 to **275.00**

Relish dish, oval w/2 compart-
ments, flat rim, 5½x9", from
$50 to...............................**75.00**

Salt & pepper shakers, bobwhites,
1½" & 2¼", pr, from $50 to..**75.00**

Salt & pepper shakers, fighting
cocks, 3" & 3¼", pr, from
$150 to........................**200.00**

Snack tray, w/rooster-form pick
holder, 4-compartment, 9½",
$125 to...........................**150.00**

Spoon rest, flowering prickly
pear cactus form, 5½", from
$65 to.............................**85.00**

Spoon rest, incised rooster/hen
heads, 8¾", from $100 to.**150.00**

Strawberry planter, w/chain
hanger, 6x7¼"...............**225.00**

Vase, peacock form, 7¾", from
$250 to...........................**300.00**

Wall pocket, ribbed leaf form
w/embossed smaller leaves,
4½"...................................**50.00**

Roseville

This company took its name
from the city in Ohio where they
operated for a few years before
moving to Zanesville in the late
1890s. They're recognized as one
of the giants in the industry, having produced many lines in art
pottery from the beginning to the
end of their production. Even
when machinery took over many
of the procedures once carefully
done by hand, the pottery they
produced continued the fine
artistry and standards of quality
the company had always insisted
upon.

Several marks were used
along with a paper label. The very
early art lines often carried an
applied ceramic seal with the
name of the line under a circle
containing the words Rozane
Ware. From 1910 until 1928 an
Rv mark was used. Paper labels
were common from 1914 until
1937. From 1932 until closure in
1952, the mark was Roseville in
script or R USA, Pieces marked
RRP Co Roseville, Ohio, were not
made by Roseville Pottery but by
Robinson Ransbottom of Roseville,
Ohio. Don't be confused. There are
many jardinieres and pedestals in
a brown and green blended glaze
that are being sold at flea markets
and antique malls as Roseville
that were actually made by Robinson Ransbottom as late as the
1970s and 1980s. That isn't to say
they don't have some worth of
their own, but don't buy them for
old Roseville.

If you'd like to learn more
about the subject, we recommend
*The Collector's Encyclopedia of
Roseville Pottery Revised Edition,
Vols. 1* and *2,* by Sharon and Bob
Huxford and our advisor Mike
Nickel. Mr. Nickel is listed in the
Directory under Michigan.

Note: Watch for reproductions!
They're flooding the market right
now; be especially wary at flea
markets and auctions. These
pieces are usually marked only
Roseville (no USA), though there
are exceptions. These have a 'paint
by number' style of decoration with
little if any attempt at blending.

See Clubs and Newsletters for information concerning *Rosevilles of the Past* newsletter.

Apple Blossom, vase, #390-12, green or pink, 12½", $400 to **450.00**

Apple Blossom, window box, #368-8, blue, 2½x10½", $200 to ..**225.00**

Artwood, planter, #1055-9, 7x9½", $85 to **95.00**

Baneda, candle holders, #1087, pink, 5½", pr, $600 to ..**675.00**

Baneda, vase, #610, green, 7", $725 to **800.00**

Bittersweet, cornucopia, #857-4, 4½", $100 to...................**125.00**

Bittersweet, planter, #828-10, 10½", $150 to................**175.00**

Blackberry, jardiniere, 4", $400 to.................................**450.00**

Bleeding Heart, bowl vase, #651-3, blue, 3½", $125 to **150.00**

Bleeding Heart, candlesticks, #1139-4½, blue, 5", $275 to........**325.00**

Bushberry, cornucopia, double; #155-8, blue, 6", $200 to..**225.00**

Bushberry, vase, blue, 8", from $250.00 to $275.00 (green, from $225.00 to $250.00; orange, from $200.00 to $225.00).

Cameo II, flowerpot, 5½", $350 to...............................**450.00**

Cameo II, wall pocket, 9½", $500 to...............................**600.00**

Capri, ashtray, #598-9, 9", $40 to **50.00**

Capri, shell bowl, #C-1120, 13½", $50 to..............................**60.00**

Carnelian I, console bowl, flared, 5x12½", $125 to............**150.00**

Carnelian I, fan vase, 6", $70 to..**80.00**

Carnelian II, basket, 4x10", $200 to.................................**250.00**

Carnelian II, planter, footed, 2-handled, 3x8", $100 to.**125.00**

Clemana, flower frog, #23, blue, $200 to.........................**225.00**

Clemana, vase, #750, tan, 6½", $200 to.........................**225.00**

Clematis, center bowl, #456-6, blue, 9", $150 to **175.00**

Clematis, vase, #102-6, 6½", blue, $110 to..........................**130.00**

Columbine, bookend planters, #8, blue or tan, 5", pr, $350 to **400.00**

Columbine, vase, #151-8, pink, 8", $275 to..........................**325.00**

Cosmos, hanging basket, #361, blue, 7", $400 to **425.00**

Cosmos, vase, #134-4, tan, 4", $125 to..........................**150.00**

Cosmos, vase, #956-12, blue, 12½", $650 to................**750.00**

Cremona, urn, 4", $150 to...**175.00**

Dahlrose, vase, #366, 8", $225 to **275.00**

Dahlrose, vase, #418, 6", $150 to **175.00**

Dawn, vase, #833-12, green, 12", $500 to.........................**600.00**

Dogwood I, bud vase, double; 8", $150 to..........................**175.00**

Dogwood I, tub, handled, 4x7", $125 to..........................**150.00**

Dogwood II, hanging basket, 7", $250 to.........................**300.00**

Donatello, ashtray, 3", $175 to .**225.00**

Donatello, vase, 12", $350 to ..**400.00**

Earlam, candlesticks, #1080, 4", pr, $600 to **650.00**

Falline vases in tan: Flared body looped handles, unmarked, 8¼"; Bulbous with upturned handles, foil label, 6", from $600.00 to $700.00 each.

Earlam, planter, #89, 5½x10½", $400 to **450.00**

Falline, center bowl, #244, tan, 11", $350 to **450.00**

Falline, vase, #647, tan, 7½", $600 to **700.00**

Ferella, vase, #498, tan, 4", $350 to **400.00**

Ferella, vase, #499, red, $550 to ..**650.00**

Florane, bowl, 10", $30 to **35.00**

Florane, bud vase, flared base, 7", $30 to **35.00**

Florentine, candlesticks, 10½", ea, $150 to **175.00**

Florentine, jardiniere, 5", $150 to **175.00**

Foxglove, hanging basket, #466, green/pink, 6½", $325 to .**400.00**

Foxglove, tray, #419, pink, $150 to **175.00**

Foxglove, vase, #51-10, blue, 10", $300 to **350.00**

Freesia, bowl, #465-8, tangerine, $125 to **150.00**

Freesia, flower pot/saucer, #670-5, 5½", $225 to **250.00**

Fuchsia, center bowl, #351-10, brown/tan, 4x15½", $275 to .**325.00**

Fuchsia, vase, #892-6, green, 6", $200 to **225.00**

Futura, jardiniere, #616, 6", $550 to **650.00**

Futura, pillow vase, #81, 5x6", $450 to **550.00**

Gardenia, bowl, #641-5, 5", $125 to **150.00**

Gardenia, vase, #686-10, 10½", $225 to **250.00**

Imperial I, basket, #7, 9", $200 to **250.00**

Imperial I, planter, 14" to 16", $350 to **400.00**

Imperial II, bowl, 4½", $400 to ..**450.00**

Imperial II, vase, tapered, 5½", $250 to **300.00**

Iris, basket, #355-10, blue, 9½", $475 to **550.00**

Iris, pillow vase, #922-8, pink or tan, 8½", $275 to **300.00**

Ivory II, cornucopia, #2, 5½x12", $75 to **95.00**

Ivory II, jardiniere, #574-4, 4", $40 to **40.00**

Ixia, center bowl, #330-7, 3½x10½", $200 to.........**250.00**

Ixia, vase, #856-8, 8½", $200 to **250.00**

Jonquil, candlesticks, #1082, 4", pr, $450 to **550.00**

Jonquil, vase, #524, 4", $250 to ..**275.00**

Juvenile, creamer, chicks, 3", $150 to **200.00**

Juvenile, egg cup, rabbit, 3½", $250 to **275.00**

La Rose, bowl, 3", $125 to...**150.00**

La Rose, jardiniere, 6½", $150 to **175.00**

Laurel, bowl, #252, gold, 3½", $350 to...............................**400.00**

Laurel, vase, #676, 10", russet, $650 to...............................**750.00**

Lombardy, jardiniere, 6½", $200 to...............................**250.00**

Luffa, candlesticks, #1097, brown or green, 5", pr, from $500 to...............................**600.00**

Luffa, jardiniere, #631, brown or green, 7", from $350 to.**400.00**

Lustre, basket, 10", $200 to.**250.00**

Magnolia, #388-6, 8½", from $85 to...............................**95.00**

Magnolia, ewer, #14-10, 10", $175 to...............................**200.00**

Mayfair, jardiniere, #1109-4, 4", $60 to...............................**75.00**

Mayfair, teapot, #1121, 5", $125 to...............................**150.00**

Ming Tree, conch shell, #563, 8½", $90 to...............................**110.00**

Ming Tree, hanging basket, 6", $225 to...............................**250.00**

Ming Tree, vase, #585-14, 14½", $400 to...............................**450.00**

Mock Orange, pillow vase, #930-8, 7", $150 to...............................**175.00**

Mock Orange, window box, #956-8, 8½x4½", $100 to.......**125.00**

Moderne, compote, #295, 5", $250 to...............................**275.00**

Moderne, vase, #787, 6½", $175 to...............................**225.00**

Montacello, vase, bulbous, handled, tan, 5", $350 to....**400.00**

Morning Glory, center bowl, #270, green, 4½x11½", $475 to...............................**550.00**

Morning Glory, pillow vase, #120, 7", ivory, $400 to.........**450.00**

Moss, bowl vase, #290, blue, 6", $300 to...............................**350.00**

Moss, pillow vase, #781, pink/green or orange/green, 8", $350 to.....................**400.00**

Mostique, compote, 7", $300 to .**350.00**

Mostique, hanging basket, 7", $400 to...............................**500.00**

Orian, candle holders, #1108, turquoise, 4½", $275 to..**325.00**

Orian, compote, #272, yellow, 4½x10½", $225 to.........**250.00**

Peony, bookends, #11, 5½", pr, $200 to...............................**250.00**

Peony, mug, #2-3½", 3½", $100 to...............................**125.00**

Pine Cone, #1283, brown, 9", $750 to...............................**850.00**

Pine Cone, ashtray, #499, green, 4½", $150 to.................**175.00**

Pine Cone, planter, #124, brown, 5", $200 to.....................**250.00**

Poppy, basket, #348-12, gray or green, $275 to...............**325.00**

Poppy, bowl, #336-10, 12", pink, $275 to...............................**300.00**

Primrose, vase, #760-6, tan, 7", $150 to...............................**175.00**

Raymor, gravy boat, #190, 9½", $30 to...............................**35.00**

Raymor, vegetable bowl, #160, 9", $30 to...............................**40.00**

Rosecraft, window box, brown, 6x12", $400 to...............**450.00**

Rosecraft Black & Colors, compote, 4x11", $125 to......**150.00**

Rosecraft Black & Colors, ginger jar, 8", $300 to..............**350.00**

Rosecraft Blended, bud vase, #36-6, 6", $90 to...................**110.00**

Rosecraft Hexagon, candlesticks, brown, 8", ea, $350 to...............................**400.00**

Rosecraft Panel, covered jar, brown, 10", $500 to **550.00**

Rosecraft Vintage, bowl, 3", $125 to.................................150.00

Royal Capri, leaf dish, #533-10, 2x10½", $200 to............225.00

Royal Capri, vase, #583-9, 9", $250 to.........................275.00

Rozane, vase, #5-8, 8½", $225 to 275.00

Rozane (1917), basket, blue, 11", $300 to.........................350.00

Rozane (1917), compote, 6½", $150 to.........................175.00

Savona, console bowl, 4x10", $125 to.................................150.00

Silhouette, ewer, #716-6, 6½", $100 to.........................125.00

Silhouette, vase, #781-6, 6", $90 to...............................110.00

Snowberry, basket, #IBK-12, green, 12½", $275 to 325.00

Snowberry, flowerpot/saucer, #1PS-5, blue or pink, 5½", $225 to.........................250.00

Sunflower, vase, #486, 5", $800 to 900.00

Teasal, vase, #888-12, light blue or tan, 12", $450 to.......550.00

Thorn Apple, bowl vase, #305-6, 6½", $200 to.................250.00

Thorn Apple, hanging basket, 7" dia, $300 to...................350.00

Topeo, bowl, blue, 3x11½", $200 to.................................250.00

Tourmaline, candlesticks, cup on flared base, ribbed, 5", pr, $175 to.........................200.00

Tourmaline, cornucopia, 7", $75 to.................................100.00

Tuscany, bowl vase, flared, pedestal foot, handled, pink, 4", $100 to.....................125.00

Tuscany, vase, bulbous w/handles, pink, 6", $100 to...........125.00

Volpato, covered urn, 8", from $300.00 to $350.00.

Velmoss, bowl, #266, green, 3x11", $175 to.........................225.00

Velmoss, vase, #719, blue, 9½", $350 to.........................400.00

Vista, vase, flared base, 10", $750 to.................................850.00

Water Lily, candlesticks, #1155-4½", rose w/green, 5", pr, $225 to.........................250.00

Water Lily, vase, #78-9, 9", blue, $325 to.........................350.00

White Rose, flower frog, #41, $150 to.................................200.00

White Rose, vase, #978-4, 4", $80 to.................................90.00

Wincraft, bookends, #259, 6½", pr, $175 to.........................225.00

Wincraft, wall pocket, #267-5, 5", $250 to.........................300.00

Windsor, center bowl, blue, 3x10", $400 to.........................450.00

Windsor, vase, rust, #546, $400 to.................................450.00

Zephyr Lily, bud vase, #201-7, green, 7½", $125 to 150.00

Zephyr Lily, tray, blue, 14½", $250 to.........................275.00

Royal China

Several lines of the dinnerware made by Royal China (Sebring, Ohio) are very collectible. Their Currier and Ives pattern (decorated with scenes of early American life in blue on a white background) and the Blue Willow line are well known, but many of their others are starting to take off as well. Since the same blanks were used for all patterns, shapes and sizes will all be the same from line to line. Both Currier and Ives and Willow were made in pink as well as the more familiar blue, but pink is hard to find and not especially collectible in either pattern.

Our advisors for this category are BA Wellman and John Canfield; they are listed in the Directory under Massachusetts. See Clubs and Newsletters for information on *Currier & Ives China by Royal*.

Blue Willow

Water pitcher, $65.00.

Ashtray, 5½".............................**12.00**
Bowl,soup; 8¼".....................**10.00**
Butter dish, ¼-lb..................**35.00**
Cup & saucer...........................**6.00**
Plate, bread & butter; 6¼"......**3.00**
Plate, salad; 7¼" **7.00**
Salt & pepper shakers, pr.....**18.00**
Tray, tidbit; 2-tier **65.00**

Colonial Homestead

Bowl, cereal; 6¼"...................**10.00**
Bowl, vegetable; 10".............**20.00**
Gravy boat............................**15.00**
Pie plate................................**25.00**
Plate, chop; 12"......................**18.00**
Plate, dinner; 10" **4.00**
Platter, oval, 13" **24.00**
Teapot...................................**85.00**

Currier and Ives

Ashtray 5½"...........................**15.00**
Bowl, fruit nappy; 5½" **5.00**
Bowl, soup; 8½".....................**14.00**
Bowl, vegetable; 9"................**22.00**
Butter dish, Road Winter, ¼-lb .**40.00**
Clock plate, factory, electric..**190.00**
Creamer, angle handle **8.00**
Cup & saucer...........................**6.00**
Gravy boat, tab handles, w/liner like
  7" plate), from $100 to **135.00**
Lamp, candle; w/globe **250.00**
Plate, bread & butter; 6⅜"......**2.00**
Plate, chop; Getting Ice, 11½"..**35.00**

Teapot, $150.00.

367

Plate, chop; Rocky Mountains, 11½" 65.00
Plate, luncheon; very rare, 9"..25.00
Plate, salad; rare, 7" 15.00
Platter, oval, 13" 35.00
Salt & pepper shakers, pr.....30.00
Sugar bowl, no handles, flared top 48.00
Teapot, many different styles & stampings, from $110 to .150.00
Tumbler, iced tea; glass, 12-oz, 5½" 18.00
Tumbler, old-fashioned; glass, 3¼" 7.00

Memory Lane

Ashtray, $12.00; Dinner plate, 10", $5.00; Cup & saucer, $5.00.

Bowl, cereal; 6¼" 9.00
Bowl, fruit nappy; 5½" 3.00
Bowl, vegetable; 10" 25.00
Butter dish, ¼-lb 30.00
Creamer 6.00
Gravy boat 18.00
Gravy-boat liner, from $12 to.15.00
Plate, chop; 12" 25.00
Plate, luncheon; rare, 9¼" 25.00
Platter, tab handles, 10½"....15.00
Platter, 13" 25.00
Sugar bowl, w/lid....................9.00
Tumbler, iced tea; glass........15.00

Tumbler, juice; glass...............8.00

Old Curiosity Shop

Bowl, fruit nappy; 5½" 4.00
Bowl, soup/cereal; 6½" 10.00
Bowl, vegetable; 9"...............22.00
Casserole 90.00
Creamer.................................6.00
Plate, bread & butter; 6⅜"......3.00
Plate, dinner; 10" 5.00
Salt & pepper shakers, pr.....15.00
Sugar bowl, w/lid....................9.00
Teapot.................................115.00

Royal Copley

Produced by the Spaulding China Company of Sebring, Ohio, Royal Copley is a line of novelty planters, vases, ashtrays, and wall pockets modeled after appealing puppy dogs, lovely birds, innocent-eyed children, etc. The decoration is airbrushed and underglazed; the line is of good quality and is well received by today's pottery collectors.

Our advisor for this category is Joe Devine, editor of *Royal Copley, Books I* and *II,* originally published by Leslie Wolfe; Mr. Devine is listed in the Directory under Iowa. See Clubs and Newsletters for information concerning *The Copley Currier.*

Ashtray, heart shape w/lovebirds, raised letters, 5½"..........55.00
Ashtray, various shapes w/solid or speckled colors, about 5" to 6", ea 18.00

Bank, pig w/lettering on chest, 7½" to 8", from $75 to **85.00**

Candle holder/planter, ribbed star shape, paper label, 6¾" .**25.00**

Candy/tidbit dish, various shapes w/brass handles, USA, ea, $25 to **30.00**

Creamer & sugar bowl, overlapping leaf form w/leaf handle, 3", ea **35.00**

Figurine, canary on stump, paper label, 5½" **60.00**

Figurine, cockatoo on stump, raised letters, 8¼" **45.00**

Figurines, Royal Windsor Green-Winged Teal hen and drake, from The Game Birds of North America series, designed by A.D. Priolo, 7½", 7½", from $200.00 to $250.00 for the pair. (Photo courtesy Joe Devine)

Figurine, sea gull in flight w/wings vertical, white w/gold trim, 8" **55.00**

Figurine, warbler w/head up on stump, stamp or raised letters, 5" **20.00**

Hot pad holder, rooster form, designed by AD Priolo, USA, 8¾" **55.00**

Lamp, cocker spaniel sitting upright begging, 10", from $100 to **125.00**

Lamp, Oriental boy or girl holding jug, w/original shade, 7½", ea **85.00**

Leaf dish, various shapes & speckled colors, USA, ea **25.00**

Mug, Baby, w/fish handle, 4⅛".**85.00**

Pitcher, Floral Beauty, green stamp or raised letters, 8" **50.00**

Planter, bear cub clinging to tree stump, paper label, 8¼"..**40.00**

Planter, bear playing concertina, paper label, rare, 7½" **95.00**

Planter, bear with basket, from $75.00 to $80.00.

Planter, bird on roof of birdhouse w/branch base, 8" **100.00**

Planter, bust of bare-shouldered lady, paper label, 6" **55.00**

Planter, elf on dark green shoe, paper label, 6" **40.00**

Planter, Oriental boy or girl kneeling w/basket on back, 8", ea ...**45.00**

Planter, ram's head, paper label, 6½" **30.00**

Planter, triple leaves embossed on pot, white on black or green, 4" **16.00**

Planter, wheelbarrow w/duck, paper label, 3¾" **20.00**

Planter/wall pocket, cocker spaniel head, raised letters, 5" ...**35.00**

Vase, cylindrical w/leafy branch, white on black or green, 8½" **18.00**

Vase, Floral Elegance, cobalt, 8"..**32.00**
Vase, pillow; Ivy, gold trim, footed, paper label, 6¼" **28.00**

Royal Haeger

Manufactured in Dundee, Illinois, Haeger pottery has recently become the focus of much collector interest, especially the artware line and animal figures designed by Royal Hickman. These were produced from 1938 through the 1950s and are recognized by their strong lines and distinctive glazes. For more information we recommend *Haeger Potteries Through the Years* by our advisor David Dilley (L-W Books); he is listed in the Directory under Indiana.

Ashtray, #SP-12, palette shape, 13½" L **15.00**
Astray, #128, triangular, 13¼" .**10.00**
Basket, #R-1640, metal handle & bracket, 10½" **50.00**
Bookend, #R-132 (unmarked), ram, stylized form, spotted glaze, 8", pr **150.00**
Bowl, #489, scalloped rim, footed, 4⅛x4" dia........................**40.00**
Candle holders, #R-312 (unmarked), cornucopia, foil label, 5", pr **35.00**
Candle holders, #3004, Peacock color, 1⅜x3¼x5¾", pr **30.00**
Candy dish, #R-431, lily finial, 7½" dia...........................**65.00**
Candy dish, #8004-H, Mandarin Orange, 6½x8¾"............**20.00**
Centerpiece, #R-1824, palm leaf, 26" L **35.00**

Centerpiece, #R-309, 3x8x15".**40.00**
Centerpiece, #329-H, pheasant bowl, Gold Tweed, 5½x7¼x21½"..................**50.00**
Cigarette box, #R-685, triple horse head finial, 5x4x6¾"......**70.00**
Cigarette lighter, #812-H, fish form, 10"..........................**35.00**
Compote, #3003, low oval w/4 flutes, 4½x12" L.............**20.00**
Ewer, #4103, floral relief, Peasant Yellow, 18"......................**35.00**

Figurine, #R-319, Russian Wolfhound, white, 8½", $75.00.

Figurine, #R-413 (unmarked), fawn sitting, stylized, 6½" L **40.00**
Figurine, #R-777 (unmarked), cocker spaniel lying w/legs spread, 6" L **50.00**
Figurine, #R-1224 (unmarked), gypsy girl standing w/2 baskets, 16½"....................**100.00**
Figurine, #612, rooster, 11x8½".**50.00**
Figurine, #613, hen, 10x8½".**50.00**
Flower frog, #86 (unmarked), mermaid w/child, 7" **200.00**
Lamp, #5190 (unmarked), bucking bronco w/cactus, 26".....**225.00**
Lavabo, #R-1506/#R-1507, 2-pc set, ea 6½" T..................**75.00**

Pitcher, #R-G42, 10" **35.00**
Pitcher, #R-1679-S, bulbous, 10¼".................................**65.00**
Pitcher & bowl set, #4058/4060 (pitcher w/no # mark), 10" T **60.00**
Planter, #R-271, sailfish, 9x13" .**45.00**

Planter, fish, 19x18", $450.00 minimum value.

Planter, #R-525, double tulip, 4¼x9¾" **75.00**
Planter, #R-540, turtle, 13½" L .**50.00**
Planter, #3910 (unmarked), clown jack-in-the-box, 8½x6x7" .**20.00**
Planter, #394, pilgrim hat, 4⅝" .**25.00**
Planter, #8008, bird, 7¾x4¾" .**15.00**
Shell bowl, #R-297, 2¾x7½x14" .**30.00**
Tidbit, #8010/8011, sq 2-tier w/floral relief, 10½" **30.00**
Toothbrush holder/soap dish/cup holder, blue, #920, 2x5x6½" **20.00**
Tray, #873, chicken shape w/deviled-egg holders on tail, 14¾" **75.00**
Tray, #878-H, double leaf, Mandarin Orange, 2x9x14" **20.00**
TV Lamp, #6140 (unmarked), sailfish & waves, 9x9¼".......**40.00**
Vase, #R-284, trout, Mauve Agate, 7x4½x9" **100.00**
Vase, #R-455, bow around trumpet neck, bulbous bottom, 14".**75.00**

Vase, #R-455, 14" **75.00**
Vase, #R-456, spiral form w/fluted base, Yellow Drip, 14"....**75.00**
Vase, #R-1190, pinecone, 12" .**50.00**
Vase, #RG-68, Flowerware, 7⅛" .**10.00**
Vase, #4002, hexagonal, 10¼" .**40.00**
Vase, #4181 (unmarked), tower style, Green Earth Graphic Wrap, 13".........................**75.00**
Vase, #4243 (unmarked), bottle style, 9½".........................**15.00**
Vase, #4248 (unmarked), bottle style, Earth Graphic Wrap, 4"....................................**40.00**
Vase, #483, Cobra in Mandarin Orange, 16" **50.00**
Wall pocket, #R-1135, flower form **85.00**

Russel Wright Dinnerware

Dinnerware designed by Wright, at one time one of America's top industrial engineers, is today attracting the interest of many. Some of his more popular lines are American Modern, manufactured by the Steubenville Pottery Company (1939 – 1959), and Casual by Iroquois, introduced in 1944. He also introduced several patterns of melmac dinnerware and an interesting assortment of spun aluminum serving and decorative items such as candleholders, ice buckets, vases, and bowls.

To calculate values for items in American Modern, use the high end for Cedar, Black, Chutney, and Seafoam; add 50% for Bean Brown, White, Glacier

Blue, and Cantaloupe. For patterned lines, deduct 25%. In Casual, Brick Red, Cantaloupe, and Aqua items go for about 200% more than any other color, while those in Avocado Yellow are priced at the low end of our range of suggested values. Other colors are in between, with Oyster, White, and Charcoal at the higher end of the scale. Glassware prices are given for Flair in Crystal and Pink; other colors are higher. Add 100% for Imperial Pinch in Cantaloupe. Ruby is very rare, and market value has not yet been established. For more information refer to *The Collector's Encyclopedia of Russel Wright Designs, Second Edition,* by Ann Kerr (Collector Books).

Ashtray, White Clover, clover decoration, from $40 to **45.00**

Sterling, ashtray, $75.00; relish, four-compartment, 16½", from $50.00 to $65.00. (Photo courtesy Ann Kerr)

Bowl, bouillon; Sterling, 7-oz, from $14 to.....................................**16.00**
Bowl, cereal; Iroquois Casual, 5", from $10 to **15.00**

Bowl, lug fruit; American Modern, from $15 to **20.00**
Bowl, soup; Meladur, 12-oz, from $10 to.............................**12.00**
Bowl, soup/cereal; Knowles, 6¼", from $14 to **16.00**
Bowl, vegetable; Residential, #713, w/lid, from $25 to .**30.00**
Butter dish, Iroquois Casual, ½-lb, from $85 to..............**100.00**
Casserole, Spun Aluminum, from $150 to..........................**200.00**
Celery dish, Sterling, 11¼", from $20 to.............................**30.00**
Coffeepot, AD; American Modern, from $100 to **150.00**

Creamer and sugar bowl, stacking set, Casual, from $30.00 to $36.00.

Creamer, Home Decorator, #711, from $10 to **12.00**
Creamer, Iroquois Casual (redesigned), from $15 to ..**25.00**
Cup & saucer, AD; American Modern, from $24 to **30.00**
Cup & saucer, Flair, #701/#702, from $8 to **11.00**
Flower ring, Spun Aluminum, from $125 to **150.00**
Gravy boat, American Modern, from $20 to **30.00**

Ice bucket, Spun Aluminum, from $75 to............**100.00**

Pickle dish, American Modern, from $15 to.............**18.00**

Pitcher, Knowles, 2-qt, from $150 to...............**170.00**

Pitcher, sherry; Spun Aluminum, from $250 to.............**300.00**

Plate, bread & butter; Sterling, 6", from $5 to.............**10.00**

Plate, chop; White Clover, clover decorated, 11", from $25 to...........**28.00**

Plate, dessert; Residential, 6¼", from $5 to............**6.00**

Plate, dinner; Home Decorator, #703, from $8 to............**10.00**

Plate, dinner; Iroquois Casual, 10", from $10 to.............**12.00**

Plate, dinner; Meladur, 9", from $8 to...............**10.00**

Plate, salad; American Modern, 8", from $12 to.............**15.00**

Platter, Iroquois Casual, oval, 14½", from $40 to..........**50.00**

Platter, Knowles, oval, 13", from $25 to.............**45.00**

Platter, Sterling, oval, 7½", from $15 to.............**20.00**

Salt & pepper shakers, Knowles, pr, from $30 to.............**40.00**

Salt & pepper shakers, White Clover, either size, pr, from $30 to.............**35.00**

Sauce boat, Knowles, from $25 to...............**35.00**

Sugar bowl, Flair, w/lid, #712, from $12 to............**15.00**

Teapot, American Modern, 6x10", from $100 to.............**125.00**

Teapot, Knowles, from $175 to.**250.00**

Tumbler, Flair, #715, from $15 to...............**18.00**

Wastebasket, Spun Aluminum, from $125 to.............**150.00**

Salt Shakers

You'll probably see more salt and pepper shakers during your flea market forays than T-shirts and tube socks! Since the 1920s they've been popular souvenir items, and a considerable number has been issued by companies to advertise their products. These advertising shakers are always good, and along with miniature shakers (1½" or under) are some of the more valuable. Of course, those that have a crossover interest into other categories of collecting — Black Americana, Disney, Rosemeade, Shawnee, Ceramic Arts Studios, etc. — are often expensive as well. There are many good books on the market; among them are *Salt & Pepper Shakers, Identification & Values, Books I, II, III,* and *IV,* by Helene Guarnaccia; and *The Collector's Encyclopedia of Salt & Pepper Shakers* (there are two in the series) by Melva Davern. All are published by Collector Books. See also Advertising Collectibles; Ceramic Arts Studio; Character Collectibles; Disney; Gas Station Collectibles; Shawnee; Rosemeade.

Ace of Hearts & Deuce of Clubs, ceramic, Arcadia, miniature, pr....................**30.00**

Amish couple, ceramic, black & white w/red, pr, $8 to........**15.00**

Asparagus spears, ceramic, realistic, pr **5.00**

Bahama policeman, ceramic, 1950s, 4⅜", pr **38.00**

Bananas, ceramic, realistic, pr .**7.00**

Baseball pitcher & catcher, ceramic, Japan, 4½", pr .**80.00**

Birds pecking, ceramic, blue lustre w/gold trim, yellow bases, pr **10.00**

Black boy on cotton bale, ceramic, Parkcraft, 3½x2½", pr .**250.00**

Black boys shooting dice on tray, bisque, multicolored, 3-pc .**95.00**

Black chefs w/carving knives, ceramic, Japan, 3", pr **95.00**

Blue Nun Wine, from $125.00 to $150.00 for the pair. (Photo courtesy Helene Guarnaccia)

Bowling ball & pin, ceramic, from $8 to **10.00**

Burger Chef, plastic, marked Nowhere Else, pr **15.00**

Candlesticks, ceramic, Arcadia, miniature, 1½", pr..........**30.00**

Cat & the Fiddle, ceramic, 2-pc..**40.00**

Cats stretching, ceramic, stylized, black, Dan Brechner, from $15 to **35.00**

Caveman & woman, ceramic, unmarked, vintage, 4", pr..**60.00**

Children praying, ceramic, white w/gold trim, 4¼", pr **12.00**

Cigarettes & lighter, ceramic, vintage, pr **26.00**

Circus lion rearing on tub, ceramic, 2-pc, from $15 to........**20.00**

Coffee grinder & coffeepot, ceramic, pr, from $18 to...........**22.00**

Cookies, ceramic, Oreo-type marked Cookies, glossy, pr.............**22.00**

Devils, chalkware, half-figures, red w/yellow & green, pr **25.00**

Doctor & nurse, ceramic, child-like faces, pr, from $12 to......**25.00**

Dog in doghouse, ceramic, marked Sad Sack/Beware of Dog, pr...........................**35.00**

Donald Duck & Daisy shaking hands, ceramic, Japan, 1950s, 4", pr **45.00**

Eggplant & cabbage referees, ceramic, glossy, pr..........**65.00**

Fish in top hats, ceramic, upright, pr....................................**25.00**

Glee & Glum clowns, ceramic, white & black w/gold trim, pr **45.00**

Grasshoppers on watermelon slices, ceramic, glossy, realistic, pr **15.00**

Horse heads, ceramic, Japan paper label, 3½", pr........**15.00**

Horses rearing, bone china, black & white & tan & white, pr..**15.00**

Little Orphan Annie & Sandy, chalkware, pr **45.00**

Mason jars, glass w/metal caps, pr **10.00**

Michigan's Mackinac Bridge, ceramic, ea is half of bridge, Japan, pr **45.00**

Onion people reclining, ceramic, pr, from $18 to.................**22.00**

Ostriches, ceramic, cartoon features, on grassy bases, pr............**22.00**

Peaches, ceramic, coated w/fuzz, pr.....................................**12.00**

Pebbles & Bamm-Bamm, ceramic, Harry James, 4", pr **65.00**

Penguins, painted wood, 1950s, 2½x2", pr **12.00**

Piano, plastic, upright, black & gold, 3-pc **12.00**

Pig nursing baby pig, ceramic, white w/black spots, pr..**25.00**

Pigs, interlocking, plastic, Fitz & Floyd, 1976, 3x4", pr......**40.00**

Pilgrim boy & girl, ceramic, Hallmark, 1970, pr.................**15.00**

Pineapple slices, ceramic, pr, from $10 to..............................**12.00**

✗ Pixies, ceramic, Elbee Art, 3", pr...................................**18.00**

Quaker State Motor Oil cans, heavy cardboard, 1940s-50s, 1½", pr **40.00**

Santa & Mrs Claus in rocking chairs, ceramic, pr, from $10 to....................................**20.00**

Santa & tree, ceramic, Santa standing, coiled tree, pr.**15.00**

Scarecrow couple, ceramic, 3", pr.................................**28.00**

Schlitz Beer bottles, glass w/paper labels, metal tops, 4½", pr.**28.00**

Sea horses, ceramic, Leyden Arts, California, 4¼", pr **22.00**

Sewing machine & dress form, ceramic, 2", pr **95.00**

Snakes coiled w/heads up ready to strike, ceramic, pr..........**10.00**

Snoopy as Red Baron, chalkware, pr.....................................**50.00**

Telephone, ceramic, glossy black rotary dial type, 2-pc......**35.00**

Television, plastic, turn knobs & shakers pop up, 1950s, MIB **28.00**

Washington Monument, Bakelite, 4¼", pr...........................**65.00**

Yosemite Sam, ceramic, Lego paper label, 1960s, pr..**125.00**

Ziggy & dog, ceramic, Universal Press Syndicated 1979, 3" Ziggy, pr **40.00**

Zodiac girls, ceramic, Japan, 4½", pr...................................**55.00**

Shopping couple, ceramic, 6", from $85.00 to $95.00 for the pair. (Photo courtesy Judy Posner)

Scottie Dogs

An amazing array of Scottie dog collectibles can be found in a wide range of prices. Collectors might choose to specialize in a particular area, or they may enjoy looking for everything from bridge tallies to original portraits or paintings. Most of the items are from the 1930s and 1940s. Many were used for advertising purposes; others are simply novelties.

For further information we recommend *A Treasury of Scottie Dog Collectibles, Volumes I, II,* and *III,* by Candace Sten Davis and Patricia Baugh (Collector Books).

Ashtray, etched crystal, 1940s, 4x2½", $20 to...................**35.00**
Bank, plastic, Reliable, 1950-60s, 7½", $60 to......................**80.00**
Brush holder, pressed wood w/black & white Scotties, Swank, 4x3"...................**30.00**
Figurine, flocked plastic, 1950s, 3½x3x1½", $5 to.............**10.00**

Figurines, orange with black collars, Goldscheider, 6", $50.00 for the pair.

Figurine, white milk glass, red collar, LE Smith, 2½x6x5", $35 to..............................**50.00**
Frame, ceramic, curved sides, oval center, Scottie figure, 5x4", $5 to....................................**15.00**
Ice-cream mold, metal, 2-pc, 1950s, 8x2x6", $125 to.**150.00**
Jar, clear glass w/black Scottie, red plastic lid, 1990s, 3x7", $2 to......................................**5.00**
Pin, gold-tone metal, Krementz.**40.00**
Planter, ceramic, dog at mailbox, 1950s, 6x6x4", $25 to.....**35.00**
Salt & pepper shakers, silver-tone metal, 1940s, 2x3", pr, $25 to............................**40.00**

Stuffed dog, vinyl, 1950s, 6x8x9", $20 to..............................**40.00**
Trinket box, porcelain, red plaid w/Scottie on lid, 1990s, 2", $10 to..............................**30.00**
Wall plaque, black Scottie face, ceramic, 1940-50s, 4x2½", $10 to......................................**20.00**
Wisk broom, pressed wood Scottie handle, 5", $30 to...........**40.00**

Scouting Collectibles

Founded in England in 1907 by Major General Lord Baden-Powell, scouting remains an important institution in the life of young boys and girls everywhere. Recently scouting-related memorabilia has attracted a following, and values of many items have escalated dramatically in the last few years. Early first edition handbooks often bring prices of $100.00 and more. Vintage uniforms are scarce and highly valued, and one of the rarer medals, the Life Saving Honor Medal, is worth several hundred dollars to collectors.

Our advisor for this category is Rolland J. Sayers, author of *A Complete Guide to Scouting Collectibles*; he is listed in the Directory under North Carolina.

Boy Scouts

Bank, Cub Scout bust, composition.................................**20.00**
Belt Buckle, National Jamboree 1957, double lock............**20.00**

Binoculars, plastic, 12 power, 1950 ....**12.00**

Book, National Jamboree Souvenir, 1973.....................**2.50**

Book, The Merit Badge Chronicle, Hubbard, 1986 ....**5.00**

Bookends, Official Boy Scout, composition logo, 1940-52, pr .**15.00**

Canteen, plastic, w/plastic screw top, 1970 ....**4.00**

Christmas cards, w/envelopes, 25 in red box, set................**10.00**

Compass, red plastic, 8-point side, 1930 ....**20.00**

Decal, Exploring Is the Program, black **2.00**

Figurine, Boy Scout hiker w/staff, color, hollow, Barclay.....**25.00**

Handkerchief, Cub Scout, blue w/Cub promise **4.00**

Hat, Garrison type, ca 1940-60..**15.00**

Hatchet, Tru-Temper, oak handle, 1950s..............................**22.00**

Knife, plastic handles, unused, ca 1940s, 3½", in original box, $100.00.

Pamphlet, Fun Around the Campfire, BSA, 1944 ....**4.00**

Pencil box, color scene of camp activities, 1930 ....**25.00**

Pennant, World Jamboree 1963, blue, woven w/logo **15.00**

Pocketknife, Ulster, 4-blade, black plastic handle w/Tenderfoot shield **6.00**

Postcard, World Jamboree 1959, w/logo..............................**5.00**

Ring, Sea Scout, w/anchor, sterling................................**40.00**

Signal set, Official Triple; #1092, metal, 1950....................**30.00**

Tie bar, Eagle Scout, sterling, clip-on logo **5.00**

Wallet, Cub Scout, National Issue, vinyl................................**4.00**

Woodburning kit, w/wood & cord...............................**50.00**

Wristwatch, Timex, 1950s, w/original band **15.00**

Girl Scouts

Armband, Senior Service Scout .**20.00**

Book, Girl Scout Collectibles, Degenhardt, 1989 ....**40.00**

Camera, Official GSA, Univex, 1937 ....**50.00**

Catalog, uniform; Official GSA, Univex, 1930s.................**15.00**

Cup, aluminum, collapsible, 1950 ....**5.00**

Doll, Girl Scout, Effanbee, 1965, MIB................................**30.00**

Flag, Official Brownie, sm, 1930s **25.00**

Handbook, 1955 ....**15.00**

Pin, Mariner, 1940................**15.00**

Pin, Wing Scouting, 1941 .....**35.00**

Postcards, Girls Scouts of America, color, 1951-52, set of 4 ......**5.00**

Sewing kit, Official; tin, green w/gold, Boye Needle Co, 4x2½" **35.00**

Signal flags, Official GSA, wooden handles, 1920 ....**15.00**

Uniform, Brownie dress, w/orange necktie, membership card, 1950s..............................**20.00**

Uniform, Official GSA, top & skirt, khaki, 1917-23, no badges .**75.00**

Sewing Items

Sewing notions from the 1800s and early 1900s, such as whimsical figural tape measures, beaded satin pincushions, blown glass darning eggs, and silver and gold thimbles are pleasant reminders of a bygone era — ladies' sewing circles, quilting bees, and beautifully hand-stitched finery. With the emphasis collectors of today have put on figural ceramic items, the pincushions such as we've listed below are coming on strong. Most were made in Japan; some were modeled after the likenesses of Disney characters.

Our advisor for figural sewing items is Carole Bess White (see the Directory under Oregon); she is the author of *Collector's Guide to Made in Japan Ceramics, Identification and Values* (there are three in the series). If you're interested in sewing machines, we recommend *Toy and Miniature Sewing Machines, An Identification and Value Guide,* by Glenda Thomas. All of these books are published by Collector Books.

Darner, Bakelite mushroom form w/handle, speckled gray & white, 3¾" **35.00**
Darner, celluloid egg form of blue & ivory, 2½" **15.00**
Darner, glass mushroom form w/blue swirls, 3¼" **50.00**

Darner, glass pear shape w/blue, maroon & white swirl, 7⅛"..**145.00**
Darner, plastic dome box marked Always Darn w/GLISTA Yarn, 2¾" dia **30.00**
Darner, silver, twisted w/sm & lg egg-shaped ends, 4⅛" ..**100.00**
Darner, wood door knob style w/wire spring fabric holder, 4" **20.00**
Darner, wood elongated egg shape w/multicolored swirl enamel, 3" **12.50**
Dress form, cardboard full body w/brass neck, 60" **45.00**
Dress form, cloth-covered, on cast-iron base, Wolf...1939, 61".........**190.00**
Needle book, Old Safeway, Cragmont soft drinks ad, VG **7.00**
Needle book, S&H Green Stamps, Queen Victoria...Needles, Germany...........................**7.50**
Needle box, Sewing Susan, gold-eye needles, w/threader, NM **5.00**
Oil can, Singer, red, white & blue, 5¼", EX............................**15.00**
Pattern, Advance, sheath silhouette dress, 1950s **7.00**

Pincushion, calico horse and yellow lustre cart, Japan, $32.00. (Photo courtesy Carole Bess White)

Pincushion, ceramic, elephant, calico, jointed, Made in Japan, 2x4"....................**25.00**

Pincushion, ceramic, poodle nodder w/jewel eyes, Florenza, 3½"....................................**60.00**

Pincushion, porcelain, boy in top hat, yellow lustre, Japan, 2¾".**25.00**

Pincushion, porcelain, dog, Made in Japan, 4½" **22.00**

Pincushion, porcelain, figure by basket cushion, Occupied Japan, 3".........................**40.00**

Pincushion, porcelain, Hummel-like girl figure, Japan **12.50**

Pincushion, porcelain, shoe, white w/red & blue trim, Occupied Japan..............................**25.00**

Pincushion, silk w/beadwork, Victorian, 8x11"..................**55.00**

Pincushion, velvet heart form w/beadwork, late 19th century, 2½x5" **75.00**

Pinking machine, Singer, w/box.**40.00**

Scissors, brass stork form, Italy.**10.00**

Scissors, stainless steel, stork & fox, Germany, ca 1920 ...**40.00**

Scissors, sterling, floral work, USA, 1915 ....**40.00**

Sewing machine, Artcraft Jr Miss, wood base, 1940s-50s, $50 to **75.00**

Sewing machine, Baby Brother, metallic, Japan, 1960s, $75 to **100.00**

Sewing machine, Cornet, heavy metal, white rabbit in circle, 9"...................................**170.00**

Sewing machine, KAYanEE Sew Master, hand-operated, sheet metal, $75 to **100.00**

Sewing machine, Little Mary Mix Up, sheet metal, 1930s ..**75.00**

Sewing machine, Olympia, manual or battery-operated, Japan, EX **75.00**

Sewing machine, Princess, belt drive, Japan **175.00**

Sewing machine, Sew-n-Play, plastic, manual or battery-operated.........................**25.00**

Sewing machine, Singer, Sewhandy Model 20, 1950s, $100 to **125.00**

Shuttle, Bakelite, black........**16.00**

Spool caddy, guilded cast iron, pedestal foot, pincushion top **80.00**

Tape measure, advertising, Fab Detergent **25.00**

Tape measure, celluloid pig, 2½" long, $75.00.

Tape measure, brass, turtle figure, w/motto, 2x1½".......**65.00**

Tape measure, celluloid, fish figure..................................**100.00**

Thimble, cloisonne flowers on gold-tone, China, 1980...**15.00**

Thimble, silver w/abalone & mother-of-pearl inlay, Mexico, ca 1980...........................**20.00**

Thimble, sterling, feather design, Stern Bros **25.00**

Thimble, sterling, Greek Key design, Simons, ...**25.00**

Thimble, sterling w/gold-plated band, Ketchum & McDougall **65.00**

Thimble, sterling w/spider turquoise set, Navajo, 1994..............**25.00**

Thimble holder, goat cart, cast
metal.............................**125.00**
X Tracing wheel, Bakelite, Dritz,
EX................................**12.50**

Shawnee

The novelty planters, vases,
cookie jars, salt and pepper shakers, and 'Corn' dinnerware made
by the Shawnee Pottery of Ohio
are attractive, fun to collect, and
still available at reasonable
prices. The company operated
from 1937 until 1961, marking
their wares with 'Shawnee,
U.S.A.,' and a number series, or
'Kenwood.'

Our advisor for this category
is Rick Spencer; he is listed in the
Directory under Utah. Refer to
*The Collector's Guide to Shawnee
Pottery* by Janice and Duane Van-
derbilt, and *Shawnee Pottery, An
Identification and Value Guide,* by
Jim and Bev Mangus (both by Col-
lector Books) for more informa-
tion. See also Cookie Jars. See
Clubs and Newsletters for infor-
mation concerning the Shawnee
Pottery Collectors' Club.

Bowl, mixing; Corn Line, marked
Shawnee #8, 8"..............**50.00**
Bowl, mixing; Valencia, 10"..**35.00**
Bowl, salad/spaghetti; Lobster
Ware, #922 ....**80.00**
Butter dish, Lobster Ware, marked
Kenwood USA 927 ....**65.00**
Carafe, Valencia....................**75.00**
Casserole, Corn Line, marked
Shawnee #74, lg..............**55.00**

**Coffeepot, Sunflower, marked
USA, $150.00.**

Casserole, French; Lobster Ware,
10-oz **20.00**
Cookie jar, Valencia............**140.00**
Creamer, Laurel Wreath, marked
USA **22.00**
Creamer, Wave, marked USA..**25.00**
Jug, ball; Sunflower, marked
USA, 48-oz....................**145.00**
Mug, Lobster Ware, marked Ken-
wood USA 911, 8-oz...........**85.00**
Nappie, Valencia, 9½"...........**25.00**
Pie plate, Valencia, 9¼".......**85.00**
Pitcher, Laurel Wreath, marked
USA **24.00**
Pitcher, Stars & Stripes, marked
USA **18.00**
Pitcher, Wave, marked USA.**24.00**
Planter, bird on shell, marked
USA **18.00**
Planter, Buddha, marked USA
524 ....**24.00**
Planter, dogs (2), gold, marked
USA 611 ....**24.00**
Planter, hound dog, marked
USA **8.00**
Planter, squirrel at stump,
marked USA...................**10.00**
Plate, Valencia, 9¾".............**14.00**

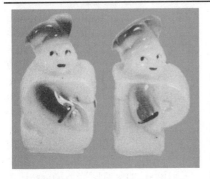

Salt and pepper shakers, chefs, from $20.00 to $25.00 for the pair.

Relish tray, Corn Line, King or Queen, marked Shawnee #79 ....**45.00**
Shakers, Cottage, sm, pr **275.00**
Shakers, Dutch boy & girl, blue & gold, lg, pr.......................**85.00**
Shakers, Dutch boy & girl, brown, lg, pr **40.00**
Shakers, Fruits, lg, pr...........**45.00**
Shakers, Jack & Jill, lg, pr ...**60.00**
Shakers, Lobster Ware, claw form, marked USA, pr..............**35.00**
Shakers, Lobster Ware, jug style, marked USA.................**110.00**
Shakers, wheelbarrows, gold, sm, pr.....................................**80.00**
Shakers, wheelbarrows, plain, sm, pr.....................................**24.00**
Shakers, White Corn, 3¼", pr.**40.00**
Sugar bowl, Corn Line, King or Queen, w/lid **45.00**
Teapot, Drape, marked USA, 4-cup **40.00**
Teapot, elephant, marked USA, 5-cup **140.00**
Teapot, Rosette, marked USA..**40.00**
Utility jar, Lobster Ware, w/lid, #907 ....**31.00**
Vase, Valencia, 8" **28.00**

Sheet Music

The most valuable examples of sheet music are those related to early transportation, ethnic themes, Disney characters, a particularly popular actor, singer, or composer, or with a cover illustration done by a well-known artist. Production of sheet music peaked during the 'Tin Pan Alley Days,' from the 1880s until the 1930s. Covers were made as attractive as possible to lure potential buyers, and today's collectors sometimes frame and hang them as they would a print. Flea markets are a good source for sheet music, and prices are usually very reasonable. Most are available for under $5.00. Some of the better examples are listed here. Refer to *The Sheet Music Reference and Price Guide, Second Edition* (Collector Books), by Anna Marie Guiheen and Marie-Reine A. Pafik and *Collector's Guide to Sheet Music* by Debbie Dillon (L-W Book Sales) for more information.

After Twelve O'Clock, Hoagy Carmichael & Johnny Mercer, 1932 ....**5.00**
Arms for the Love of America, Irving Berlin, 1941 ....**10.00**
Barnum Had the Right Idea, George M Cohan **15.00**
Basin Street Blues, Spencer Williams, Phil Harris photo cover, 1933.......................**5.00**
Bible Tells Me So, Dale Evans, R Rogers & D Evans photo cover, 1945 ....**10.00**

About a Quarter to Nine, Al Dubin and Harry Warren, from the movie *Go Into Your Dance*, Jolson and Keeler photo cover, 1935, $15.00.
(Photo courtesy Guiheen and Pafik)

Blue September, Mitchell Parish & Peter DeRose, 1940......**5.00**

Both Sides Now, Joni Mitchell, photo cover, 1967...........**10.00**

Cherries, Marois & Dartmouth, Doris Day phto cover, 1952 .**3.00**

Chicka Boom, Bob Merrill, 1953 .**5.00**

Crying in the Chapel, Darrel Glenn, photo cover, 1953.**10.00**

Cuban Pete, Jose Norman, Desi Arnaz & King Sisters, 1946.....................................**5.00**

Dime a Dozen, Cindy Walker, Sammy Kaye photo cover, 1949.................................**3.00**

Down T'Uncle Bill's, Hoagy Carmichael & Johnny Mercer, 1934.................................**5.00**

Dr No, James Bond Theme, Sean Connery & girls cover, 1962..............................**35.00**

El Dorado, Movie: El Dorado, John Wayne & Robert Mitchum cover, 1966.....**20.00**

Encore, J Fred Coots, Eddy Howard photo cover, 1947...............**5.00**

Extra, Extra, Irving Berlin, Musical: Miss Liberty, 1949...............**5.00**

Fire & Rain, James Taylor, James Taylor photo cover, 1969 .**5.00**

Fly Me to the Moon, Bart Howard photo cover, 1954.............**5.00**

Free Bird, Lynard Skynard, group photo cover, 1975.............**8.00**

Galveston, Webb, Glen Campbell photo cover, 1968.............**5.00**

Halls of Ivy, Henry Russell & Vicki Knight, 1950...........**5.00**

Hello Dolly, Jerry Herman, 1963..............................**5.00**

I Love You, Cole Porter, Movie: Mexican Hayride, 1943....**5.00**

I'm a Believer, Monkees, group photo cover, 1966...........**20.00**

I Walk Alone, Herbert W Wilson, 1943................................**5.00**

Jambalaya, Hank Williams, Hank Williams photo cover, 1952 .**3.00**

La Cucaracha, Carl Field, Don Pedro photo cover, 1935...**5.00**

Lament to Love, Mel Torme, 1941................................**3.00**

Lawrence of Arabia, Maurice Jarre, 1962......................**5.00**

Maybelline, Chuck Berry, guitar drawing on cover, 1955..**10.00**

Mutt and Jeff in the Wild and Wooley West, cartoon cover, $25.00.

Me & My Melinda, Irving Berlin, 1942 ....**10.00**

Mr Sandman, The Cordettes, group photo cover, 1953 .**15.00**

Night of My Nights, Robert Wright & Chet Forest, Musical: Kismet, 1953...............**5.00**

Oklahoma, Rodgers & Hammerstein II, Holley cover artist, 1943 ....**5.00**

On Top of Old Smokey, Pete Seeger, 1951 ....**3.00**

Pretend, Nat King Cole, photo cover, 1952 ....**12.00**

Rainbow, Russ Hamilton, 1957 .**5.00**

Rock With You, Jackson Five, Michael on cover, 1979 ..**10.00**

Sealed With a Kiss, Bobby Vinton, photo cover, 1960 ....**15.00**

Tequila, Chuck Rio & the Champs, group photo cover, 1958 .**15.00**

There'll Always Be an England!, Ross Parker & Hughie Charles, 1939 ....**10.00**

Tie a Yellow Ribbon..., Tony Orlando & Dawn, photo cover, 1972 ....**10.00**

Twist, Hank Ballard, 1959 .....**3.00**

When I Write My Song, Ted Mossman & Bill Anson, 1947...............**5.00**

When the Saints Come Marchin' In, T Elli, 1957 ....**2.00**

Woodpecker Song, Andrew Sisters, photo cover, 1940...**17.00**

Yesterday, John Lennon & Paul McCartney, 1965..............**5.00**

You've Got Something, Cole Porter, Movie: Red, Hot & Blue, 1936 ....**10.00**

You've Lost That Lovin' Feelin', Righteous Bros, Screen Gems, 1964 ....**15.00**

Shot Glasses

Shot glasses, old and new, are whetting the interest of today's collectors, and they're relatively easy to find. Basic values are given for various categories of shot glasses in mint condition. These are general prices only. Glasses that are in less-than-mint condition will obviously be worth less than the price given here. Very rare and unique items will be worth more. Sample glasses and other individual one-of-a-kind oddities are a bit harder to classify and really need to be evaluated on an individual basis.

Our advisor for this category is Mark Pickvet, author of *Shot Glasses: An American Tradition*. He is listed in the Directory under Michigan. See Clubs and Newsletters for information concerning the Shot Glass Club of America.

Barrel shape, from $6 to **8.00**

Black porcelain replica, from $3.00 to **4.00**

Carnival colors, plain or fluted, from $65 to **85.00**

Carnival colors, w/patterns, from $150 to **200.00**

Colored glass tourist, from $4 to **6.00**

Culver 22k gold, from $6 to **8.00**

Depression, colors, from $8 to **12.50**

Depression, colors w/patterns or etchings, from $15.00 to .**25.00**

Depression, tall, general designs, from $12.50 to **15.00**

Depression, tall, tourist, from $5 to **7.50**

Frosted w/gold designs, from $6 to **8.00**

General, etched designs, from $5 to **7.50**

General, porcelain, from $4 to .**6.00**

General, w/enameled design, from $3 to **4.00**

General, w/frosted designs, from $3 to **4.00**

General, w/gold designs, from $6 to **8.00**

General advertising, from $4 to .**6.00**

General tourist, from $3 to **5.00**

Inside eyes, from $5 to............**7.50**

Iridized silver, from $5 to **7.50**

Liquor store advertising, Hi-Way Liquors, Frederick MD, in fired-on red, $4.00.

Mary Gregory or Anchor Hocking Ships, from $135 to......**185.00**

Nudes, from $25 to................**35.00**

Plain, w/ or w/out flutes, from 50¢ to **75**

Pop or soda advertising, from $12.50 to.........................**15.00**

Porcelain tourist, from $3.50 to..**5.00**

Rounded European designs w/gold rims, from $4 to................**5.00**

Ruby flashed, from $35 to.....**45.00**

Sayings & toasts, 1940s-50s, from $5 to **7.50**

Sports, professional teams, from $5 to **7.50**

Square, general, from $5 to **7.50**

Square, w/2-tone bronze & pewter, from $15 to **17.50**

Square, w/etching, from $7.50 to.**10.00**

Square, w/pewter, from $12.50 to.**15.00**

Standard glass w/pewter, from $8 to **12.00**

Steuben crystal, from $150 to.**200.00**

Taiwan tourist, from $2 to......**3.00**

Tiffany, Galle or fancy art, from $500 to **750.00**

Turquoise or gold tourist, from $6 to **8.00**

Whiskey or beer advertising, modern, from $5 to..................**7.50**

Whiskey sample glasses, from $45 to **85.00**

19th-century cut patterns, from $75 to **125.00**

Silhouette Pictures

Silhouettes and reverse paintings on glass were commercially produced in the US from the 1920s through the 1950s. Some were hand painted, but most were silkscreened. Artists and companies used either flat or convex glass. Common subjects include romantic couples, children, horses, dogs, and cats. Many different styles, sizes, colors, and materials were used for frames. Backgrounds also vary from textured paper to foils, colorful lithographs, wildflowers, or butterfly wings. Sometimes the backgrounds were painted on the back of the glass in gold or cream color. These inexpensive pictures were usually sold in pairs, except for the advertising kind, which were given by merchants as gifts. Our advisor for this category is Shirley Mace, author of *The Encyclopedia of Silhouette Collectibles on Glass* and *Vintage Silhouettes on Glass and Reverse Paintings* (Shadow Enterprises); she is listed in the Directory under New Mexico.

Lady with outstretched arm looking at birdcage, Benton Glass, 6x8", $38.00. (Photo courtesy Shirley and Ray Mace)

Art Publishing Co, children blowing bubbles, plain ground, 5x3½"............................**40.00**

Art Publishing Co, hunt scene, plain ground, 8x10"........**35.00**

Benton, children watching puppets, floral & bird ground, 5x4"..**40.00**

Benton, couple at gate, golden landscape ground, 4½x3½".....**35.00**

Benton, couple courting under tree, plain ground, 5x4".**30.00**

Benton, couple dancing the minuet, plain ground, 8x6"..**40.00**

Benton, couple on a sleigh ride, plain ground, 8x6"..........**45.00**

Benton, couple waving, sailing ship ground, 5x4"...........**40.00**

Benton, gondola scene, Venice ground, 8x6"...................**45.00**

Benton, Indian maiden waving, valley w/wagon train ground, 8x6"................................**65.00**

Benton, profile bust of lady in bonnet, rose over moire ground, 8x6"...................**75.00**

Benton, sailboat on choppy sea w/clouds, plain ground, 5x4".**35.00**

Benton, shepherd trumpeting, landscape ground, 8x6"..**40.00**

Benton/Charlotte Becker art, kitten/curtain, baby & bear ground, 8x6"...................**60.00**

Buckbee-Brehm/Kaiser art, Little Jack Horner, plain ground, 4x6"...................................**40.00**

Buckbee-Brehm/Kaiser art, Saturday Night, plain ground, 6x4" **35.00**

Blossom Time, Reliance, $30.00. (Photo courtesy Shirley and Ray Mace)

C&A Richards, Tallimit art, Sunday (2 ladies & church steeple), 9x7".................**40.00**

C&A Richards/Diedenbach art, nymph on goat cart, sunset ground, 4x5"................**185.00**

C&A Richards/Diefenbach art, nymph on flower, rainbow ground, 5x4" **240.00**

C&A Richards/EV Dowd, Fishing Party (in boat), plain ground, 5x6" **50.00**

C&A Richards/Fidus art, The Four Seasons, gold ground, 36½" L, ea......................**150.00**

Erickson, advertising/Thank You, eagle descending, mountain lake, 9x3".........................**50.00**

Erickson, advertising/thermometer, elk on mountain lake ground, 8x6"...................**40.00**

Fisher Studios, couple kissing, wildflower ground, triangular, 6"............................**120.00**

Fisher Studios, lady watering flowers, wildflower ground, 5½x3½"............................**40.00**

Flowercraft, boy w/cat & dog, wildflower ground, 3½x2½" ..**40.00**

Newton, advertising/thermometer, duck in flight on marsh ground, 6x8"...................**30.00**

Ohio Art, couple escaping raindrops under parasol, 4½x3½" **40.00**

Ohio Art, fish jumping before sailing ship ground, 5x4".....**35.00**

West Coast, girl studying bird in tree, dusky ground, 12x9".**40.00**

Slag Glass

Slag glass is marbleized opaque glassware that first came in to vogue about 1870 and continued to be produced until the turn of the century. It has been revived in recent years by several American glassmakers, L.E. Smith, Westmoreland, and Imperial among them. The listings below reflect values for items with excellent color.

Fenton, basket, #8634RX, ruby, 6½"...................................**85.00**

Fenton, basket, Orange Tree & Cherry, #9136PS, purple **150.00**

Fenton, bell, Hobnail, #3667PS, purple, 5½" **50.00**

Fenton, figurine, bear cub, #515RX, ruby **65.00**

Fenton, figurine, butterfly on stand, #5171RX, ruby....**75.00**

Fenton, tobacco jar, Grape & Cable, #9188RX **195.00**

Fenton, vase, Peacock, #8257PS, purple, 8", from $95 to..**110.00**

Imperial, ashtray, shell form, #291, purple, 1961-67, 4½" **45.00**

Imperial, basket, Sawtooth, #475, ruby, 1969-70, 5½".........**65.00**

Imperial, bowl, Crimped Rose, #62C, purple, 1960.........**50.00**

Imperial, bowl, Dewdrop, #641, purple, 1961-70, 8½"......**65.00**

Imperial, box, Heart Leaf, #312, purple, 1962-67 ....**125.00**

Imperial, candle holder, Dolphin, #779, caramel, 1964-68, 5".................................**40.00**

Imperial, candy dish w/lid, #1519/59, caramel, 1964-70, 4¾x5½".........................**125.00**

Imperial, cornucopia, #123, ruby, 1969 ....**25.00**

Imperial, creamer & sugar bowl, #30, caramel, 1964-70, set **65.00**

Imperial, figurine, Hoot (Less) Owl, #18, caramel, 1969-77, 3½"...................................**35.00**

Imperial, figurine, Scolding Bird, #43931CS, caramel, 1983-83, 5".................................**75.00**

Imperial, salt dip, #61, ruby, 1971-74.........................**20.00**

Imperial, tumbler, #552, caramel, 1962-64, 11-oz................**35.00**

Kanawha, ashtray, Hobnail, #885ED, blue, green or red, 1972, 6½".......................**20.00**

Kanawha, basket, Hobnail, #296ED, blue, green or red, 1971, 7", ea.....................**45.00**

Kanawha, cruet set, Hobnail, #291ED, blue, green or red, 1973, 6", pr....................**50.00**

Kanawha red slag, Praying Hands, 5", from $65.00 to $75.00. (Photo courtesy Frank Grizel)

LE Smith, nappy, heart form, Almond Nouveau, #4630A, blended, 1980, 6"............**25.00**

LE Smith, vase, bud; Almond Nouveau, #33a, blended, 1980, 6½"........................**30.00**

LG Wright, bowl, Cherry, #7-16, caramel or purple, 10" ...**95.00**

LG Wright, goblet, #7-12, caramel, ruby or purple, ea, from $25 to.....................**35.00**

LG Wright, trough planter, #77-96, purple **45.00**

Westmoreland, basket, Pansy, #757, green, from $35 to..**45.00**

Westmoreland, candle holder, Spiral, #1933, green.............**30.00**

Westmoreland, centerpiece bowl, #300, butterscotch, from $65 to.....................................**85.00**

Snow Domes

Snow domes are water-filled paperweights. The earliest type was made in two pieces with a glass globe on a separate base. First made in the mid-nineteenth century, they were revived during the 1930s and 1940s. The most common snow domes on today's market are the plastic half-moon shapes made as souvenirs or Christmas toys, a style that originated in West Germany during the 1950s. Other shapes such as round and square bottles, tall and short rectangles, cubes and other simple shapes are found as well. Today's collectors buy them all, old or new. See Clubs and Newsletters for information concerning the newsletter *Snow Biz*.

Advertising, Santa w/Coca-Cola bottle, music box base, MIB **75.00**

Advertising, Texaco tanker truck against cityscape in round dome, ...**65.00**

Advertising, The Whole Family Stays at Days, sm oval plastic dome **10.00**

Birth announcement, babies on seesaw w/stork in middle, plastic dome **8.00**

Birthday, It's Down Hill From Here, Garfield/floating numbers, Enesco **20.00**

Character, Betty Boop, Bully, King Features/Fleischer Studios, 1986 .... **18.00**

Character, Creature From the Black Lagoon, figural, MIB **15.00**

Character, Little Mermaid, tall plastic dome on round base **20.00**

Character, Mickey Mouse in space suit w/arms stretched, Monogram **45.00**

Character, Paul Bunyan & Blue Ox, plastic dome on white footed base **15.00**

Character, Yosemite Sam, Home on the Range, glass dome, wood base **50.00**

Christmas, figural Santa on lamppost **12.00**

Christmas, figural snowman couple w/dome tummies, ea, from $15 to **20.00**

Christmas, Santa w/domed tummy, deer over shoulders **18.00**

Christmas, tree in glass dome, marked Made in USA, 4" . **45.00**

Easter, rabbit w/eggs standing next to pine tree, Austrian glass dome **10.00**

Figural, cat playing drum (drum is water compartment) .. **12.00**

Figural, coffeepot, clear plastic w/girl & snowman inside, old **10.00**

Figural, orange w/leaves **30.00**

Graduation, cap cocked atop dome w/Congratulations lettered inside **8.00**

Graduation, Garfield dressed as graduate, Congratulations on base **20.00**

Halloween, Trick or Treat!, witch atop house w/skeletons in dome **10.00**

Memphis, paddlewheeler and street scene, black base, EX, $10.00. (Photo courtesy Helene Guarnaccia)

New Arrival, stork delivering baby, pink base with blue lettering, EX, $8.00. (Photo courtesy Helene Guarnaccia)

Souvenir of Alabama, State Capitol building & missile **20.00**

Souvenir of Galveston Island, dolphin atop dome **15.00**

Souvenir of New York City, Statue of Liberty & Skyscrapers . **12.00**

Soda Pop

A specialty area of the advertising field, soft drink memorabilia is a favorite of many collectors.

Now that vintage Coca-Cola items have become rather expensive, interest is expanding to include some of the less widely known flavors — Dr. Pepper, Nehi, and Orange-Crush, for instance.

If you want more pricing information, we recommend *Huxford's Collectible Advertising* by Sharon and Bob Huxford. Our advisor for this category is Craig Stifter; he is listed in the directory under Illinois. See also Coca-Cola.

Dr. Pepper

A young pharmacist, Charles C. Alderton, was hired by W.B. Morrison, owner of Morrison's Old Corner Drug Store in Waco, Texas, around 1884. Alderton, an observant sort, noticed that the drugstore's patrons could never quite make up their minds as to which flavor of extract to order. He concocted a formula that combined many flavors, and Dr. Pepper was born. The name was chosen by Morrison in honor of a beautiful young girl with whom he had once been in love. The girl's father, a Virginia doctor by the name of Pepper, had discouraged the relationship due to their youth, but Morrison had never forgotten her. On December 1, 1885, a U.S. patent was issued to the creators of Dr. Pepper.

Apron, grocer's type w/logo on bib, NM..............................125.00
Ashtray, clear glass, red decal w/white lettering, 4" wide .9.00

Badge, metal w/celluloid name plate, Good for Life/10-2-4 logo, EX+ 325.00
Bottle carrier, cardboard 6-pack, 1940s, EX 100.00
Bottle opener, slide-type w/enameled logo, G....................85.00
Bottle topper, Cindy Garner, EX+............................165.00
Bottle topper, Edith Luce, EX+ .225.00
Calendar, 1947, complete, NM .300.00
Calendar, 1960, 75th Anniversary, EX..........................35.00
Clock, Drink A Bite To Eat, round w/glass front & metal frame, EX................................150.00
Fan pull, diecut cardboard featuring Madalon Mason, 1940s, 7", NM 100.00

Sign, aluminum with black and red enameling, 1930s, 10" diameter, NM, $375.00.

Sign, aluminum, red oval logo on textured ground, framed, 12x27", NM+ 100.00
Sign, cardboard, lady w/bottle leaning on railing, 1930s, 21x26, EX 725.00
Sign, celluloid disk, Drink a Bite to Eat w/grid logo & clock, 9", EX+............................1,050.00

Sign, neon, name in white upper & lower case lettering, 13x21", NM **130.00**

Sign, porcelain, round, Drink... & 10-2-5 on red/white/red, 10", NM..............................**700.00**

Sign, porcelain, triangle, Dr Pepper Bottling Co, 1940s, 14x22", EX+..................**300.00**

Sign, tin, bottle on white, raised border, 1950s-60s, 48x14", VG+..............................**200.00**

Sign, tin, Dr Pepper, oval logo on maroon, self-framed, 22x35", M.....................................**30.00**

Sign, tin bottle cap, 10-2-4 logo on white/red/white, 24", NM **300.00**

Thermometer, plastic, white bottle cap shape w/10-2-4 logo, 11", NM **100.00**

Tray, tin, Drink A Bite To Eat, girl w/2 bottles, 1939, EX ...**350.00**

Tumbler, Good For Life, tapered, applied label, 1940s, EX.**150.00**

Hires

Did you know that Hires Root Beer was first served to fairgoers at the Philadelphia Centennial in 1876? It was developed by Charles E. Hires, a druggist who experimented with roots and herbs to come up with the final recipe. The company originally chose the Hires boy as their logo, and if you'll study his attire, you can sometimes approximate a guess as to when an item he appears on was manufactured. Very early on he appeared in a dress, and from 1906 until 1914 it was a bathrobe.

He sported a dinner jacket from 1915 until 1926.

Ashtray, glass bottle shape w/orange & white logos, EX..............**12.00**

Banner for truck, canvas, 1940s, EX..................................**375.00**

Cup, waxed paper, 1960s, 4x3" dia, EX..............................**2.00**

Decal, Drink Hires Root Beer on bottle cap, EX..................**15.00**

Display sign, cardboard shadow box, party viewed through window, VG+................**950.00**

Door push, tin, It's High Time For Hires..., chrome frame, 4x30", G+ **35.00**

Ice-cream scoop, plastic, Only One Taste Says Hires To You, EX **10.00**

Pin-back, Hires To You...A Treat In Every Bottle, R-J logo, 2", EX **30.00**

Puzzle book, elephant pictured on front, EX.........................**35.00**

Sign, cardboard diecut, Hires Ice Cream Soda, soda w/spoon, 12", NM **40.00**

Sign, cardboard, easel back, party scene, 16x12", NM, $225.00. (Photo courtesy Autopia, Inc.)

Sign, diecut paper, R-J logo & bubbly glass, 22x12", NM+ ...**80.00**

Sign, diecut tin bottle, embossed, Since 1876 logo, 1940-50s, 58", NM **400.00**

Sign, paper, Hires Float & glass, striped ground, 7x22", NM+ **20.00**

Sign, tin, embossed, R-J logo/In Bottle-Ice Cold on blue, 19x28", NM **125.00**

Sign, tin diecut oval w/bottle, embossed, striped ground, 16x24", VG **200.00**

Sign, tin hanger on bracket, Fountain Service, 1876 logo, 15x16", VG **475.00**

Sticker, features Hires boy pointing, NM...........................**50.00**

Thermometer, dial-type w/glass front, frothy mug on woodtone, EX+ **50.00**

Thermometer, diecut tin bottle shape, Since 1876 logo, 28½", NM+ **215.00**

Nehi

Bingo Card, wood, Par-T-Pak, 8x5", EX...........................**15.00**

Blotter, Drink Nehi/Bottle Energy!, VG.............................**11.00**

Bottle, clear w/red & white label, 1967, 10-oz, EX **8.00**

Bottle carrier, cardboard, Family Package, holds 4, NM **5.00**

Bottle topper, keyhole shape w/2 bathers sipping from bottle, NM................................**115.00**

Calendar, 1938, Rolf Armstrong art, complete, 24x12", VG+...**365.00**

Cooler, metal, legs w/rollers & open shelf, VG..............**485.00**

Coupon, Drink...For Health & Happiness w/bottle at right, NM+.**65.00**

Decal, Nehi Orange...And Other Flavors, bottle over sun rays, 12x7", M **22.00**

Miniature bottle on globe marked Top of the World, glass, 4½", NM+...............................**430.00**

Pocketknife, Remington, engraved metal boot-shaped handle, EX **110.00**

Sign, painted tin, 18x45", EX, $75.00.
(Photo courtesy B.J. Summers)

Sign, tin, Curb Service/Nehi Sold Here Ice Cold, 1940s, 28x20", NM+..............................**140.00**

Sign, tin, embossed, ladies' legs & bottles flank Nehi, 14x19", G+................................**770.00**

Sign, tin, embossed, name above lg bottle, 26x7", NM.....**125.00**

Tray, bathing beauty caught up in ocean wave, 13", VG+ ..**145.00**

Nesbitt's

Door push bar, porcelain, ...Take Home A Carton, w/bottle, 32½", VG **150.00**

Sign, cardboard, 2 girls having party w/dolls at table, 25x36", NM..............................**350.00**

Sign, cardboard diecut, lady in hat & gloves w/bottle, 23x21", VG **50.00**

Sign, tin, Drink.../Take A Carton Home, 6-pack on black, 18x54", NM **550.00**

Sign, tin, graphics on black dot on yellow, curved corners, 24x24", NM **200.00**

Sign, tin bottle shape, 84x24", NM+............................**850.00**

Thermometer, 1950s, 26", EX, $125.00. (Photo courtesy Craig Stifter)

Thermometer, metal, curved corners, lg bottle on dot, 1950s, 24", NM **275.00**

Orange-Crush

Blotter, Compliments of..., king/queen, Canada, 1930s, NM+ **30.00**

Bottle opener, metal Crushy figure, NM+ **25.00**

Card hanger for phone numbers, EX+ **40.00**

Clock, light-up, sq white face w/metal frame, Discover, 15½", EX......................**150.00**

Decal, Enjoy a Fresh New Taste, peel & stick, 1967, 10x10", EX..................................**6.00**

Decal, lg amber bottle, 30x9", EX+................................**35.00**

Dispenser, ribbed glass bowl on aluminum base, porcelain top, EX+..............................**350.00**

Door push, porcelain, orange dot on green, curved ends, 1930s-40s, NM+......................**375.00**

Matchbook, Sign, flange, tin, diamond shape, Feel Fresh!..., NM+............................**400.00**

Menu board, cardboard, Today's Menu, bottle & sandwich below, 27", EX..............**180.00**

Menu board, tin chalkboard w/Crushy & Drink...Frosty Cold, 28x19", VG+........**250.00**

Sign, cardboard diecut standup, bottle shape w/Crushy, 30", NM..............................**140.00**

Sign, cardboard, tennis couple, 1940s, 20x36", EX, $180.00.

Sign, celluloid disk, Crushy mascot & name on orange, 9", VG+..............................**170.00**

Sign, flange, There's Only One...5¢, orange arrow on blue, 8x18", EX+ **725.00**

Sign, glass light-up, Enjoy...Frosty Cold 10¢/20¢, framed, 11x14", EX+..............................**400.00**

Sign, masonite, Rush-Rush for..., Crushy figure, 1940s, 18x48", EX **300.00**

Sign, paper, Serve These Favorites..., hand-held 6-pack, 14x22", EX............**20.00**

Sign, plastic, embossed, bottle/phrase w/'icy' bottom edge, 9x11", EX..............**30.00**

Sign, tin, Feel Fresh!...Drink, w/Crushy mascot, 1943, 16x12", NM..................**350.00**

Sign, tin bottle cap shape, Enjoy..., 36" dia, NM....**525.00**

Soda jerk's hat, paper, w/Crushy, NM....................................**6.00**

Thermometer, dial-type, daisies on orange ground, 12" dia, NM+.............................**125.00**

Thermometer, tin, bottle shape, 1950s, 30", EX..............**125.00**

Thermometer, wood, curved top, Crushy mascot & bottle on white, VG+...................**170.00**

Tray, Drink...Carbonated Beverage, raised rim, round, G.........**45.00**

Yo-yo, wood, Crushy Ski Top/Drink..., EX+...........**50.00**

Pepsi-Cola

Pepsi-Cola has been around about as long as Coca-Cola, but since collectors are just now beginning to discover how fascinating this line of advertising memorabilia can be, it's generally much less expensive. You'll be able to determine the approximate date your items were made by the style of logo they carry. The familiar oval was used in the early 1940s, about the time the two 'dots' (represented in our listings by '=') between the words were changed to one. But the double dots are used nowadays as well, especially on items designed to be reminiscent of the old ones - beware! The bottle cap logo was used from about 1943 until the early to mid-'60s with variations. For more information refer to *Pepsi-Cola Collectibles* by Bill Vehling and Michael Hunt and *Introduction to Pepsi Collecting* by Bob Stoddard.

Apron, canvas, vendor's type, red, white & blue, 22", NM...**42.00**

Ashtray, glass, bottle cap logo, oval, NM.......................**100.00**

Bank, plastic, 5¢ vending machine form, Marx, 1945, 7x3", EX+....................**110.00**

Baseball cards, set of 12 Mark McGuire, 1989, M.........**35.00**

Bottle, painted label, Pepsi-Cola, 8-oz, NM...........................**6.00**

Bottle, painted label, Pepsi=Cola, 8-oz, NM..........................**10.00**

Bottle, paper label, Pepsi=Cola, 12-oz, EX........................**20.00**

Bottle, swirl design w/oval Sparkling Pepsi-Cola labels, 1-qt, EX........................**130.00**

Bottle carrier, wood, triangular w/cutout handle, holds 6, EX..............................**65.00**

Bottle opener, silver-plated, The Drink of Friendship, 1950s, EX...................................**50.00**

Calendar, 1945, features famous artists, complete, EX+...**55.00**

Calendar, 1954, self-framed cardboard standup, incomplete, EX+................................**45.00**

Can, cone top, 12-oz, EX.....**200.00**

Clock, light-up, cap next to clock on yellow, 1950s, 13x17", EX+.............................**250.00**

Clock, logo at 12 w/numbers 3, 6 & 9, metal frame, 1960s, 18x14", EX+...................**65.00**

Coaster, cork, Pepsi=Cola logo in red, white & blue, 1940s, 4" dia, NM...........................**22.00**

Compact, brass finish, angled sides, 1960s, VG..............**80.00**

Cooler, picnic type, med blue w/metal handle, Drink..., 1950s, VG+...................**135.00**

Door push-plate, tin, Enjoy A Pepsi, caps top & bottom, 1950s, 13", EX..............**150.00**

Lighter, slanted bottle cap logo, Scripto, 1950s, EX+.......**75.00**

Menu board, tin chalkboard w/rope-like border, 30x20", G...............................**100.00**

Paperweight, etched glass bottle cap shape w/oval logo, NM......**55.00**

Radio, can form, 1970s, 5", NMIB...........................**35.00**

Radio, vending machine w/leather case, 1950s, 7", NM......**230.00**

Sign, cardboard, garden girl w/bottle, oval logo, 1940s, 35x28", VG **600.00**

Sign, cardboard diecut standup, Santa w/bottle in snow, 1950s, 20", EX................**60.00**

Sign, celluloid disk, Ice Cold Pepsi=Cola Sold Here, 1930s-40s, 9", VG....................**100.00**

Sign, celluloid disk, More Bounce... ribbon tag & cap on gold, 9", EX...................**220.00**

Sign, flange, bottle cap form, masonite & metal, 1940s, 13", EX+...............................**425.00**

Sign, flange, Ice Cold Pepsi=Cola Sold Here, 1940, 10x15", EX+ **350.00**

Sign, light-up cap, plastic & metal, Drink...Ice Cold, 1950s, 16", EX..............**250.00**

Sign, tin, embossed, bottle cap & ribbon, 1950s, 27x31", EX+.**160.00**

Sign, tin bottle cap form, embossed, Drink Pepsi-Cola, 1950s, 18", NM.............**275.00**

Sign, tin, More Bounce to the Ounce, 1950s, NM, $475.00. (Photo courtesy Craig Stifter)

Tip tray, black w/floral design, 1950s, 5x7", G+ **30.00**

Toy truck, plastic & tin, enclosed cargo bed, 1960s, 4", NM .**80.00**

Toy truck, tin, van w/logo on top, friction, 1950s, 4", EX+ .**200.00**

Tray, celebrating 50 years, 1987, oval, 11½x14½", NM......**25.00**

Royal Crown Cola

Ashtray, reverse-painted glass, 3x3", G............................**33.00**

Blotter, 1940s, NM................**35.00**

Bottle, clear w/red & white label, 1971, 10-oz, EX **5.00**

Calendar, 1955, complete, 25x12½", VG **30.00**

Cooler, metal, yellow w/Deco design, embossed logo, 1950s, 17x13", VG **65.00**

Decal, bottle w/sun rays, 12x7",
NM................................**22.00**
Fan, shows all-American girl,
1950s, EX **30.00**
Miniature bottle, glass w/pyramid
logo on decal label, EX+ .**25.00**
Sign, cardboard, bat boy cheering his team, 1940s, 11x28",
EX+.............................**40.00**
Sign, cardboard, Yes...Bring RC!,
girl on phone w/bottle,
11x28", EX.....................**75.00**
Sign, mirror w/painted-on
graphics, metal frame,
8x16", EX+.................**600.00**
Sign, tin, embossed, Drink...,
white diamond on red, 1950s,
10x13", NM **400.00**
Sign, tin diecut hanger, 2-sided,
name & bottle on emblem,
1940, NM......................**350.00**
Sign, tin hanger on replicated
bracket, 2-sided, 1940,
16x24", EX+.................**800.00**

**Thermometer,
tin, 1960s, 14x6",
NM, $75.00.**
(Photo courtesy
Dunbar Gallery)

Thermometer/barometer, mirrored top, Best By Taste-Test,
24x12", VG+ **250.00**

Seven-Up

Though it was originally tout-
ed to have medicinal qualities, by
1930 7-Up had been reformulated
and was simply sold as a refreshing drink. The company who first
made it was the Howdy Company,
who by 1940 had changed its
name to 7-Up to correspond with
the name of the soft drink. Collectors search for the signs, thermometers, point-of-sale items,
etc., that carry the 7-Up slogans.

Ashtray, brown glass w/white
lettering, 3 rests, 5½" dia,
NM **15.00**
Ashtray, plastic, 7-UP/Seven-
UP/The International Drink,
5½" sq **10.00**
Bill hook, celluloid button, I'd
Hang For a Chilled 7-Up,
EX+.............................**35.00**
Bottle stopper & opener, Locklite,
EXIB............................**75.00**
Bottle topper, Easter Fresh-Up,
10", EX.........................**15.00**
Bottle topper, Enjoy a 'Float!,'
green arrow & logo, EX ...**5.00**
Calendar, 1942, pinup art, com-
plete, EX+....................**140.00**
Calendar, 1953, complete, EX+ .**75.00**
Calendar, 1960, complete,
NM **25.00**
Can, flat top, white w/red 7-Up
logo w/bubbles, EX+.......**25.00**
Can, push top, Superman Sweep-
stakes, Canada, NM........**18.00**
Clip board, masonite, Diet.../Side
Track Attack, white on red,
G+ **20.00**
Clock, light-up w/sq wooden frame,
You Like It..., EX+........**100.00**
Door push, aluminum, Come In
above 7-Up oval, Likes You
below, 9", EX................**150.00**

Menu board, framed glass w/8 slots, Real 7-Up Sold Here, 17x10", VG+ **120.00**

School Zone curb sign, double-sided metal, 61½x24", EX, **$1,900.00.**

Dad's Root Beer, tin sign, 30" diameter, NM, **$300.00.**

Sign, cardboard diecut hanger, 3-D flower basket, 1940s, 20", EX+ **300.00**

Sign, cardboard standup, cartoon man w/lg bottle & dog, 1930s, 20", EX..........................**130.00**

Sign, neon, 7-Up lettered sideways on bubbly cup w/straw, 28x13", NM **200.00**

Sign, tin, colorful '60s mod design, 34", EX..........................**125.00**

Sign, tin, embossed, 7-Up Your Thirst Away, 15x33", VG.**60.00**

Sign, tin, octagonal w/raised border, Fresh Up! w/7-Up..., 14", NM+..............................**300.00**

Sign, tin, oval w/fan detail, raised edge, red w/silver, 1963, 41", VG...............................**350.00**

Sign, tin diecut bottle, 1962, 45x13", EX.....................**90.00**

Tie clip, enameled logo on bar, EX **15.00**

Miscellaneous

Bubble-Up, thermometer, tin, Kiss of Lemon/Kiss of Lime, 17", G.**40.00**

Double Cola, sign, tin flange, fancy oval, Drink..., 1947, 15x18", EX+..................**775.00**

Dr Swett's Root Beer, display, cardboard, 6 bottles, 1940s, 13x16", EX....................**140.00**

Frostie Root Beer, menu board, diecut Frosty holding board, 21x13", EX......................**80.00**

Grapette, sign, cardboard diecut, lady in raincoat w/dog, 21x13", EX+..................**160.00**

Howel's Root Beer, mechanical toy, wooden elf on trapeze, NM.................................**50.00**

Howel's Root Beer, tin diecut bottle, 1940s-50s, 58x16", EX ...**350.00**

Kayo, sign, tin, embossed, Kayo w/bottle, raised rim, 27x14", NM...............................**325.00**

King Cola, matchbox holder, celluloid, red & black on white, EX+.................................**85.00**

Kist, sign, cardboard, girl at table w/rag doll, 25x32", EX+ .**300.00**

Mason's Root Beer, bottle topper & bottle, boy in sailboat, 1940s, EX **160.00**

Mountain Dew, license plate, Yahooo!, red & green on white, EX **35.00**

Nu Icy, sign, tin, bottle & phrase, raised rim, 1940s, 18x36", EX+...............................**400.00**

NuGrape, Auto Sharp Razor, razor in tin box w/logo, VG......**40.00**

NuGrape, sign, cardboard diecut standup, lady & snowman, 13x17", EX+....................**50.00**

R-Pep, sign, tin, embossed, Drink...5¢ w/bottle & sun rays, 20x28", NM.........**250.00**

Smile, sign, vertical flange disk, Drink..., w/mascot, 1940s, 12x10", EX+..................**325.00**

Squirt, cuff links, diecut metal Squirt Boy, enameled, M, pr.........**30.00**

Squirt, doll, Squirt Boy, squeeze vinyl, 1961, 6", M.........**450.00**

Squirt, menu board, embossed chalkboard, swirl bottle, 1960s, 28", NM.............**250.00**

Sun Crest Beverages, clock, Swihart, 8x6½x2½", EX........**100.00**

Triple AAA Root Beer, sign, tin diecut bottle, 1940s-50s, 45x12", NM **120.00**

Whistle, bottle display w/bottle, cardboard, 3 elves, 1948, 11x13", EX....................**250.00**

Whistle, sign, tin, embossed, elf w/bottle on cart, 1940s, 30x26", NM **750.00**

Whistle, sign, tin bottle cap form, 1950s, 24", EX+............**350.00**

Wynola, bottle display, cardboard diecut, Sir Cola-Nut Says..., EX+...............................**110.00**

Souvenir Spoons

Originating with the Salem Witch spoons designed by Daniel Low, the souvenir spoon movement continues today as a popular hobby among collectors. Reasonably priced, easily displayed, and noted for fine artwork and craftsmanship, spoons are found with a wide range of subject matter including advertising, commemorative, historic sites, American Indians, famed personalities, and more. Souvenir spoons continue to capture the imaginations of thousands of collectors with their timeless appeal. For further information we recommend *Collectible Souvenir Spoons, The Grand Tour, Book I* and *II,* by Wayne Bednersh (Collector Books).

Abraham Lincoln, bust image on handle, plain bowl, Shiebler, $30 to **50.00**

Alligator, figural handle, customized versions, $25 to **100.00**

Apostles, figural handle, plain bowl, Gorham, reissue 1974, ea, $50 to **75.00**

Ascension, scalloped edge, Wallace, $100 to **150.00**

Betsy Ross, image on handle, heart-shaped bowl, Durgin, $30 to **50.00**

California, bear/poppies figural handle, plain bowl, Shiebler, $75 to **125.00**

Camp Grant, soldier w/rifle on cutout handle, Robbins, $10 to **20.00**

Century of Progress 1833-1933/Chinese Temple, Deco style, $25 to **50.00**

Colorado Gateway to Garden of the Gods, scene on handle & bowl, $40 to **75.00**

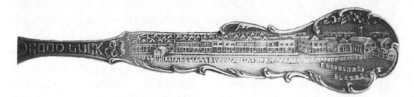

Fairbanks, Alaska, Good Luck & skyline handle, J.B. Erd, from $125.00 to $150.00. (Photo courtesy Wayne Bednersh)

Cowboy roping steer (Roundup), plain bowl, Meyer Bros, $75 to **100.00**

Cowgirl on horse, frontal figural handle, plain bowl, Watson, $90 to **150.00**

Daniel Boone, tobacco leaf handle, image on round bowl, Gorham **100.00**

Draped nude, figural (front/back), plain bowl, Mechanics, $100 to **200.00**

Egyptian mummy, enameled hinged finial, painted scene in bowl, $150 to **300.00**

Fort Sumter Charleston SC, gold-washed bowl, Towle, $25 to **50.00**

Geisha w/open parasol, Mt Fuji image engraved in bowl, $25 to **45.00**

George Washington, full-figure handle, Spokane Falls bowl, Shepard **100.00**

Gettysburg/High Water Mark, Baronial pattern, Frank Smith Co, $40 to **75.00**

Golden Gate International Exposition, sterling, demitasse, $20 to **40.00**

Graduate (female), figural handle, engraved bowl, Mechanics, $30 to **70.00**

Graduate (male), figural handle, enameled bowl, Mechanics, $40 to **80.00**

Hershey's, name enameled on handle, silver plate, $5 to........**10.00**

Indian in canoe, various bowls, Lunt, $20 to....................**45.00**

Indian scout kneeling, various bowls, Manchester/Baker, $30 to **75.00**

Indian w/hands clasped above head, plain bowl, Paye & Baker, $50 to..................**70.00**

Indian-Made, Navajo, profile head on handle, eagle in bowl, $35 to **65.00**

Indian-Made, swastika on end of handle & bowl w/detailed trim, $35 to.....................**70.00**

Indian-Made, totum pole figural handle, plain bowl, $30 to........**70.00**

Japanese painted porcelain scenes, sq finial, sterling, ea, $20 to **30.00**

Louisiana/You Kaint Fool This Chicken, engraved bowl, Shepard, $60 to............**125.00**

Mickey Mouse, enameled figural finial, round bowl, Branford, $5 to **15.00**

Miner standing w/pan of gold, Grass Valley Cal & image in bowl **150.00**

Mickey Mouse figural handle finial with multi-color enameling on stainless steel, Japan, from $15.00 to $25.00.

Miner w/pipe in mouth, Denver Colo in bowl, Hirsch & Oppenheimer, demitasse..........**40.00**

Monkeys (Speak/See/Hear No Evil), plain bowl, Paye & Baker, $40 to..................**80.00**

Monte Carlo, mechanical enameled roulette wheel finial, $40 to.....................................**85.00**

New York skyline, figural handle (7 types), Shepard, $40 to ...**65.00**

Pikes Peak, pack mule on twisted handle, embossed bowl, demitasse, $10 to **25.00**

Princess Angeline/Seattle Wash, totem handle, engraved bowl, $40 to..............................**60.00**

Rip Van Winkle, image on handle, pear-shaped bowl, Durgin, $40 to..............................**70.00**

Scrimshaw art, Eskimo scene on ivory finial w/twisted handle, $20 to............................**50.00**

Stock Exchange St Joseph Missouri, engraved image, Watson, $40 to **80.00**

Sutters Fort Sacramento Cal, engraved image in bowl, Shepard, $25 to..............**50.00**

Teddy Roosevelt, enameled bust image in bowl, Mechanic, $40 to.....................................**60.00**

Uncle Sam, full-figure profile on handle, plain bowl, Alvin, $100 to..........................**200.00**

Vicksburg/Cemetery Gate, engraved image on bowl, Shepard, $30 to..............**60.00**

Wausau Fleet/Wisconsin, painted scene in bead-trimmed bowl, $100 to..........................**150.00**

Wisconsin Dells, Chimney Rock image on cutout handle, $10 to.....................................**20.00**

Woman in bathing dress (risque), embossed bowl, Paye & Baker, $75 to................**125.00**

Woody Woodpecker, figural handle, plain bowl, IS, $5 to .**15.00**

Yellowstone Park, Great Falls image on cutout handle, Robbins, $15 to.....................**30.00**

Sporting Collectibles

When sports cards became so widely collectible several years, other types of related memorabilia started to interest sports fans. Now they search for baseball uniforms, autographed baseballs, game-used bats and gloves, and all sorts of ephemera. Although baseball is America's all-time favorite, other sports have their own groups of interested collectors.

Badge, Masters golf tournament, green & white, 1978, EX..**40.00**

Banner, Indiana University NCAA Champs, 1940/1953/1976/ 1981/1987, M **35.00**

Baseball bats, each Model 125 Louisville Sluggers, Mickey Mantle and Jackie Robinson stamps on side, NM, $100.00 each.

Baseball, Ted Williams autograph, McPhail American League ball, NM **90.00**

Basketball, Kareem Abdul-Jabbar autograph **150.00**

Bat, Stan Musial autograph .**175.00**

Book, Lou Gehrig — Boy of the Sand Lot, Riper, 1949, EX **20.00**

Book cover, Yankees team photo w/Mickey Mantle in center, 1968, NM **25.00**

Cap, Troy Aikman autograph.**45.00**

Figurine, Don Drysdale, Salvino, signed, 1989, NMIB **55.00**

Figurine, Sandy Koufax, Salvino, signed, 1989, NMIB **100.00**

Fountain pen, St Louis Cardinals 'World's Champions,' 1940s, EX **10.00**

Game, Sam Snead Tee Off, 1973, VG+ **30.00**

Golf ball, Jack Nicklaus autograph **50.00**

Golf ball, Tiger Woods autograph .**40.00**

Hockey puck, Wayne Gretzky autograph **100.00**

Magazine, Baseball Digest, Mickey Mantle cover, June 1, 1962 .... **35.00**

Media Guide, Chicago Cubs, 1966 .... **50.00**

Pen & pencil set, Philadelphia Phillies, blue jay logo, 1940s, EXIB **135.00**

Pennant, LA Dodgers, blue & white, early 1960s, 14x5", EX **20.00**

Pennant, Philadelphia Eagles, 1960s, EX+ **35.00**

Pennant, Superbowl XX, Bears.**20.00**

Photo, Davey Allison, NASCAR, 8x10" **75.00**

Photo, Jeff Gordon, NASCAR, 8x10" **35.00**

Photo, Richard Petty, NASCAR, 8x10" **40.00**

Photo, Terry Bradshaw, football, 8x10" **30.00**

Photo, Wayne Gretzky, hockey, 8x10" **30.00**

Postcard, copy of serigraph of Jordan, Leroy Neiman, 1991, 8x6", M **10.00**

Poster, Boston Celtics, 1986-87, pictures all 5 starters, 17x13", M **15.00**

Press pass, 1957 World Series, game #4 at Milwaukee, cardboard, EX........................**35.00**

Press pin, Super Bowl XXVII, NM **30.00**

Program, Harlem Globetrotters, 31st season, 1957, EX....**25.00**

Program, Tennis, Wimbledon, 1979 .... **50.00**

Program, World Series, Brooklyn, 1949, unscored, EX **135.00**

Program, Yankees/Pirates World Series, 1960, EX.............**75.00**

Ruler, lists home games for 1957 Chicago White Sox...........**6.00**

Ring, Joe DiMaggio club, silver-colored metal with signature and embossed figure of DiMaggio at bat, 1940s, VG, $330.00.

Sports card, Ernie Banks, Topps, #94, 1954, VG+..............**50.00**

Sports card, Jerry Rice, Topps, #161, 1986, NM+...........**55.00**

Sports card, Joe Namath, Topps, #96, 1966, VG+..............**55.00**

Sports card, Ken Griffey Jr, Upper Deck, #1, 1989, NM+ ...**132.00**

Sports card, Lew Alcindor, Topps, #25, 1969, VG+.............**110.00**

Sports card, Mark McGuire, Topps, 1984, NM+, from $150 to...................................**200.00**

Sports card, Roberto Clemente, Topps, #440, 1964, NM..**88.00**

Sports card, Sandy Koufax, Topps, #79, 1956, VG.................**90.00**

Sports card, Ted Williams, Topps, #1, 1957, EX.................**150.00**

Sports card, Walter Payton, Topps, #148, Rookie issue, 1976, NM.......................**88.00**

Standee, Ken Griffey Jr, Upper Deck, logo & facsimile signature, MIB......................**35.00**

Ticket, 1980 Olympics at Lake Placid (ice hockey), w/stub, EX **25.00**

Ticket stub, All-Star game at New York, 1960, EX..............**45.00**

Yearbook, Detroit Tigers, 1955, EX...................................**75.00**

Yearbook, New York Mets, 1983...........................**25.00**

Stangl

The Stangl Company of Trenton, New Jersey, produced many striking lines of dinnerware from the 1920s until they closed in the late 1970s. Though white clay was used earlier, the red-clay patterns made from 1942 on are most often encountered and are preferred by collectors. Decorated with both hand painting and sgraffito work (hand carving), Stangl's lines are very distinctive and easily recognized. Virtually all is marked, and most pieces carry the pattern name as well.

Ashtray, Apple Delight, fluted.**12.00**

Ashtray, Fruit, fluted, 5".......**15.00**

Bean pot, Town & Country, blue, 3-quart..........................**135.00**

Bowl, Apple Delight, 9".........**30.00**

Bowl, cereal; Country Garden.**20.00**

Bowl, cereal; Festival............**12.00**

Bowl, Country Garden, 8".....**35.00**

Bowl, flat soup; Cranberry ...**25.00**

Bowl, fruit; Apple Delight, 5½".**12.00**

Bowl, fruit; Country Life, rooster, 5½".....................................**35.00**

Bowl, fruit; Country Life, w/pony..**65.00**

Bowl, fruit; Yellow Tulip, 5½".**15.00**

Bowl, mixing; Fruit, 5½".......**55.00**

Bowl, mixing; Thistle, 4".......**55.00**

Bowl, salad; Blueberry, 12".**100.00**

Bowl, salad; Chicory, 12".......**95.00**

Bowl, salad; Garden Flower, Campanula, round, 10".........**55.00**

Bowl, salad; Golden Harvest, 10".................................**35.00**

Bowl, flat soup; Country Garden, $20.00.

Bowl, salad; Holly, 10".........**75.00**
Bowl, salad; Rooster, 10"......**55.00**
Bowl, soup; Lyric, lug handle, 5½"....................**20.00**
Bowl, vegetable; Fruit, oval, 2-part...............................**45.00**
Bowl, vegetable; Fruit & Flowers, 8".....................................**40.00**
Bowl, vegetable; Golden Harvest, divided............................**25.00**
Bowl, vegetable; Magnolia, divided....................................**30.00**
Butter dish, Blueberry..........**70.00**
Butter dish, Festival, ¼-lb....**50.00**
Butter dish, Thistle...............**55.00**
Cake stand, Country Garden..**30.00**
Casserole, Flora, w/lid, 8".....**65.00**
Casserole, Orchid Song, skillet shape, 8".......................**25.00**
Casserole, Wild Rose, w/handles & lid, 6"..............................**30.00**
Casserole, Yellow Tulip, 8"...**75.00**
Clock, Fruit...........................**45.00**
Clock, Town & Country, blue, skillet shape, battery powered....**75.00**
Coaster, Country Life, duckling.**45.00**
Coaster, Garden Flower........**16.00**
Coaster/ashtray, Blueberry..**25.00**

Coffee Warmer, Fruit & Flowers, $30.00 to................................**40.00**
Coffee warmer, Thistle.........**45.00**
Coffepot, Country Garden, 8-cup.............................**100.00**
Condiment tray, Carnival, #415.**25.00**
Creamer, Blueberry..............**20.00**
Creamer, Garden Flower, Calendula & Morning Glory...........**22.00**
Cruet, Fruit, w/stopper.........**45.00**
Cup, Concord.........................**11.00**
Cup, Kiddieware, Ginger Cat.**180.00**
Cup, Kiddieware, Ranger.....**95.00**
Cup & saucer, Apple Delight..**22.00**
Cup & saucer, Golden Harvest.**18.00**
Dish, Kiddieware, Ducky Dinner, 3-part, w/cup................**225.00**
Egg cup, Amber Glo..............**12.00**
Egg cup, Water Lily..............**20.00**
Gravy boat, Chicory..............**32.00**
Gravy boat, Golden Harvest.**15.00**
Gravy liner, Blueberry..........**20.00**
Mug, Apple Delight, 2-cup....**45.00**
Mug, coffee; Country Garden, low.................................**25.00**
Mug, coffee; Lyric, low..........**40.00**
Mug, Country Garden...........**45.00**

Pitchers, Festival (left) and Laurita (right), 3¾", ½-pint, $22.50 for each.

Pitcher, Fruit, ½-pt...............**30.00**
Pitcher, Golden Blossom, 2-quart.............................**45.00**
Pitcher, Magnolia, 1-qt.........**55.00**
Pitcher, Wild Rose, 1-pt........**30.00**
Plate, Apple Delight, 6"..........**7.00**

Teapot, Blueberry, from $90.00 to $110.00.

Plate, Apple Delight, 8" **12.00**
Plate, Banquet, 12" **150.00**
Plate, Bittersweet, 10" **13.00**
Plate, Blueberry, 11" **35.00**
Plate, chop; Country Garden, 12" **55.00**
Plate, chop; Country Garden, 14½" **80.00**
Plate, chop; Country Life, farmhouse, 12½" **400.00**
Plate, chop; Thistle, 12½" **50.00**
Plate, Country Garden, 10" ..**22.00**
Plate, Country Life, farmer's wife, 10" **125.00**
Plate, dinner; Jewelled Christmas Tree, 10" **50.00**
Plate, Festival, 6" **10.00**
Plate, Fruit & Flowers, 8" **18.00**
Plate, Garden Flower, Tiger Lily, 9" **18.00**
Plate, Garden Flower, 10" **22.00**
Plate, Golden Harvest, 6" **5.00**
Plate, grill; Fruit & Flowers, 9"..**50.00**
Plate, Kiddieware, Mother Hubbard **175.00**
Plate, Rooster, 8" **20.00**
Plate & cup, Kiddieware, Peter Rabbit **255.00**
Platter, Blueberry, oval, 11½", $115 to **130.00**
Platter, Blueberry, oval, 14¾" .**115.00**

Saucer, Country Life, 3 little eggs **15.00**
Saucer, Fruit, jumbo **20.00**
Server, Antique Gold, center handle, 10" **12.00**
Server, Country Garden, 2-tier .**35.00**
Shakers, Amber Glo, pr **15.00**
Skillet, Chicory, w/handle, 8".**40.00**
Tile, Apple Delight **20.00**
Tray, bread; Blueberry **55.00**
Tray, Fruit, sq, 7½" **45.00**

Star Wars

Capitalizing on the ever-popular space travel theme, the movie *Star Wars* with it's fantastic special effects was a mega box office hit of the late 1970s. A sequel called *Empire Strikes Back* (1980) and a third adventure called *Return of the Jedi* (1983) did just as well, and as a result, licensed merchandise flooded the market, much of it produced by the Kenner company. The last film was entitled *Star Wars Episode I;* it was released in 1998.

Original packaging is very important in assessing a toy's worth. As each movie was released, packaging was updated, making approximate dating relatively simple. A figure on an original *Star Wars* card is worth more than the same character on an *Empire Strikes Back* card, etc.; and the same *Star Wars* figure valued at $50.00 in mint-on-card condition might be worth as little as $5.00 'loose.' Especially prized are the original 12-back *Star Wars* cards (meaning 12 figures were shown on the back). Second issue cards showed eight more, and so on. Our advisor for this category is Brian Semling, author of *Everything You Need to Know About Collecting Star Wars Collectibles*; he is listed in the Directory under Wisconsin. For more information we recommend *Modern Toys, American Toys, 1930 to 1980*, by Linda Baker, and *Schroeder's Collectible Toys, Antique to Modern*. Both are published by Collector Books.

Figure, Boba Fett, Star Wars, 3¾", M (EX 21-back card), $1,200.00.

Bank, Yoda, SW, Sigma, M .**150.00**

Bookends, Darth Vader/Chewbacca, Sigma, ceramic..............**100.00**

Color 'N Clean Machine, Craftmaster, M......................**50.00**

Doll, Paploo, Ewok, ROTJ, plush, MIB..............................**135.00**

Figure, A-Wing Pilot, POTF, M (NM card)....................**100.00**

Figure, AT-AT Commander, ROTJ, M (VG+ card)......**40.00**

Figure, Barada, Tri-logo, M (VG+ card)..............................**75.00**

Figure, Ben Obi-Wan Kenobi, ROTJ, M (NM card).....**100.00**

Figure, Bespin Security Guard (Black), ESB, complete, NM...........................**12.00**

Figure, Boba Fett, ESB, M (NM unpunched card)..........**550.00**

Figure, Bosek, ESB, M (NM Canadian card).....................**175.00**

Figure, Boss Nass, Episode 1/Wave 3, MOC..............**12.00**

Figure, C-3PO, POTF, M (EX card)...............................**70.00**

Figure, Captain Piet, POTF, 1995-present, MOC (gr w/slide) .**20.00**

Figure, Chewbacca, ROTJ, Endor photo, M (NM card)........**90.00**

Figure, Chief Chirpa, Tri-logo, M (NM+ card).....................**65.00**

Figure, Darth Vader, ROTJ, M (NM Canadian card)....**120.00**

Figure, Darth Vader, SW, 12", MIB..............................**325.00**

Figure, Death Star Droid, ESB, M (EX+ card)....................**120.00**

Figure, Death Star Gunner, POTF, 1995-present, MOC (red)..............................**15.00**

Figure, Dengar, Tri-logo, M (EX+ card)..............................**60.00**

Figure, Emperor, ROTJ, M (NM Canadian card)..............**75.00**

Figure, FX-7, ESB, complete, NM..............................**8.00**

Figure, General Madine, ROTJ, M (EX card) **35.00**

Figure, Greedo, ESB, M (NM card) **120.00**

Figure, Han Solo, ESB, M (NM card)...........................**260.00**

Figure, Han Solo, ROTJ, M (EX card)..............................**150.00**

Figure, Han Solo, SW, 12", M (VG+ box)......................**395.00**

Figure, IG-88, Tri-logo, M (EX card)..............................**240.00**

Figure, Imperial Gunner, POTF, M (EX+ card)................**120.00**

Figure, Jann Tosh, Droids, complete, NM.........................**40.00**

Figure, Jawa, POTF, M (NM card)...........................**135.00**

Figure, Klaastu, ROTJ, M (NM card)................................**35.00**

Figure, Lando Skiff, Tri-logo, M (VG card)........................**20.00**

Figure, Logray, ROTJ, complete, NM...................................**10.00**

Figure, Luke Skywalker, POTF, X-Wing Pilot outfit, M (NM card)..............................**175.00**

Figure, Luke Skywalker, ROTJ, Jedi Knight outfit, blue saber, NM...................................**50.00**

Figure, Luke Skywalker, SW, M (NM card) (12-back).....**795.00**

Figure, Lumat, POTF, complete, NM...................................**35.00**

Figure, Nikto, ROTJ, complete, NM...................................**18.00**

Figure, Paploo, ROTJ, NM (NM card)................................**60.00**

Figure, Princess Leia Organa, ESB, Bespin outfit, M (VG card)................................**95.00**

Figure, Princess Leia Organa, ESB, M (NM+ card).....**260.00**

Figure, Princess Leia Organa, ROTJ, Hoth gear, M (NM+ card).**175.00**

Figure, Prune Face, ROTJ, NM (NM card).......................**40.00**

Figure, Rancor Keeper, ROTJ, complete, NM.................**12.00**

Figure, Rebel Commander, ROTJ, M (NM card)...................**30.00**

Figure, R2-D2, Episode I/Wave 5, MOC...............................**20.00**

Figure, R2-D2, SW, complete, EX...............................**12.00**

Figure, R2-D2, SW, M (NM card) (12-back)......................**450.00**

Figure, R5-D4, SW, complete, NM...............................**12.00**

Figure, Sio Bibble, Episode I/Wave 9, MOC...............**20.00**

Figure, Stormtrooper, ROTJ, M (NM+ card)...................**100.00**

Figure, Teebo, POTF, M (EX card)...........................**135.00**

Figure, TIE Fighter Pilot, ROTJ, M (EX card)....................**55.00**

Figure, Ugnaught, ESB, M (NM card)................................**90.00**

Figure, Walrus Man, SW, M (NM card) (20/21-back)........**350.00**

Figure, Yak Face, Tri-Logo, M (EX+ card).....................**495.00**

Figure, Zuckuss, ESB, NM (NM Canadian card).............**150.00**

Figure, 8D8, ROTJ, M (NM card)...........................**40.00**

Figures, Sy Snootles and the Rebo Band, Return of the Jedi, 1983, M (NM box), $225.00.

405

Game, Laser Battle, SW, M (EX box) 75.00

Headset radio, Luke Skywalker, SW, MIB 550.00

Mug, Biker Scout, Sigma, ceramic, MIB 30.00

Pillow, Jabba the Hutt, plush, M 50.00

Playset, Bespin Gantry, Micor Collection, MIB 75.00

Playset, Bop Bag, Darth Vader, MIB 125.00

Playset, Creature Catina, EX (EX box) 100.00

Playset, Droid Factory, MIB 100.00

Playset, Ewok Fire Cart, M (NM box) 40.00

Playset, Hoth Ice Planet, MIB (sealed) 375.00

Playset, Hoth Rescue, POTF, MIB 250.00

Playset, Patrol Dewback, MIB (sealed) 125.00

Playset, Taun Taun, ESB, M (EX box) 50.00

Sit 'N Spin, Ewoks, MIB 80.00

Talking Telephone, Ewoks, MIB 50.00

Vehicle, A-Wing Fighter, POTF, 1995-present, MIB 25.00

Vehicle, AT-AT, ESB, MIB .300.00

Vehicle, ATL Interceptor, MIB 135.00

Vehicle, Desert Sail Skiff, ROTJ, MIB 40.00

Vehicle, Jawa Sandcrawler, SW, complete, NM 350.00

Vehicle, Landspeeder, SW, MIB 145.00

Vehicle, Millenium Falcon, SW, M (EX box)......................695.00

Vehicle, Scout Walker, Tri-logo, MIB 100.00

Vehicle, Speeder Bike, Tri-logo, MIB 75.00

Vehicle, TIE Fighter, ESB, M (NM box) 500.00

Vehicle, Twin Pod Cloud Car, MIB 250.00

Vehicle, Y-Wing Fighter, ROTJ, MIB (sealed)................325.00

Strawberry Shortcake Collectibles

Strawberry Shortcake came onto the market around 1980, and immediately captured the imagination of little girls everywhere. A line of related merchandise soon hit the market, including swimsuits, bed linens, blankets, anklets, underclothing, coats, shoes, sleeping bags, dolls and accessories, games, toys, and delightful items to decorate the rooms of Strawberry Shortcake fans. It was short lived, though, lasting only until near the middle of the decade.

Our advisor for this category is Geneva Addy; she is listed in the Directory under Iowa.

Big Berry Trolley, 1982, EX .40.00

Doll, 6", any except Berry Baby Orange Blossom & Cafe Ole, MIB, ea 25.00

Doll, 6", Berry Baby Orange Blossom or Cafe Ole, MIB, ea 35.00

Doll, 12", Strawberry Shortcake, NRFB................................45.00

Doll, 15", Strawberry Shortcake, Apricot, or Baby Needs a Name, NM, ea 35.00

Dollhouse, M **150.00**

Dollhouse furniture, attic, 6-pc, rare, M.........................**140.00**

Dollhouse furniture, bathroom, 5-pc, rare, M **65.00**

Dollhouse furniture, bedroom, 7-pc, rare, M **90.00**

Dollhouse furniture, kitchen, 11-pc, rare, M **100.00**

Dollhouse furniture, living room, 6-pc, M **85.00**

Figure, Merry Berry Worm, MIB **35.00**

Figure, Purple Pieman w/Berry Bird, poseable, MIB **35.00**

Figure, Sour Grapes with Dregs, Strawberryland Miniatures, MIP, from $15.00 to $20.00. (Photo courtesy Martin and Carolyn Berens)

Figure, Strawberryland Miniatures, any, MOC, ea from $15 to .**20.00**

Figure, 1", any, PVC, MOC ..**15.00**

Ice Skates, EX **35.00**

Motorized bicycle, EX **95.00**

Roller Skates, EX.................**35.00**

Storybook Play Case, M........**35.00**

Stroller, Coleco, 1981, M.......**85.00**

Teaching Clock, 1984, M, $75.00. (Photo courtesy June Moon)

Telephone, Strawberry Shortcake, figure, battery-op, EX....**85.00**

Swanky Swigs

Swanky Swigs are little decorated glass tumblers that once contained Kraft Cheese Spread. The company has used them since the Depression years of the 1930s up to the present time, and all along, because of their small size, they've been happily recycled as drinking glasses for the kids and juice glasses for adults. Their designs range from brightly colored flowers to animals, sailboats, bands, dots, stars, checkers, etc. There is a combination of 223 verified colors and patterns. In 1933 the original Swanky Swigs came in the Band pattern, and at the present time they can still be found on the grocery shelf, now a clear plain glass with an indented waffle design around the bottom.

They vary in size and fall into one of three groups: the small size sold in Canada, ranging from 3 1/16" to 3¼"; the regular size sold in the United States, ranging from 3⅜" to 3⅞"; and the large size also sold in Canada, ranging from 4 3/16" to 5⅝".

A few of the rare patterns to look for in the three different groups are small group: Band No. 5 (two red and two black bands with the red first); Galleon (two ships on each glass in black, blue, green, red, or yellow); Checkers (in black and red, black and yellow, black and orange, or black and white, with black checkers on the top row); and Fleur-de-lis (black with a bright red filigree design).

In the regular group: Dots Forming Diamonds; Lattice and Vine (white lattice with colored flowers); Texas Centennial (cowboy and horse); Special Issues with dates (1936, 1938, and 1942); and Tulip No. 2 (black, blue, green, or red).

Rare glasses in the larger group are Circles and Dots (black, blue, green, or red); Star No. 1 (small stars scattered over the glass in black, blue, green, or red); Cornflower No. 2 (dark blue, light blue, red, or yellow); Provincial Cress (red and burgundy with maple leaves); and Antique No. 2 (assorted antiques on each glass in lime green, deep red, orange, blue, and black).

Our advisor for this category is Joyce Jackson, she is listed in the Directory under Texas.

Antique #1, any color, Canadian, 1954, 4¾", ea **20.00**

Antique #1, any color, 1954, 3¼", US **8.00**

Antique #1, any color, 1954, 3¾", ea **3.00**

Antique #2, any color, Canadian, 1974, 4⅝", ea **25.00**

Bachelor Button, red, green & white, 1955, 3¾" **3.00**

Band #1, red & black, 1933, 3⅜" **3.00**

Band #1, red & white, Canadian, 1933, 4¾" **20.00**

Band #3, white & blue, 1933, 3⅜" **3.00**

Blue Tulips, 1937, 4¼", from $3 to **6.00**

Bustlin' Betty, any color, Canadian, 1953, 3¼", ea **8.00**

Carnival, any color, 1939, 3½", ea **6.00**

Checkerboard, white w/blue, green or red, 1936, 3½", ea **20.00**

Circles & Dot, any color, Canadian, 1934, 4¾", ea **20.00**

Circles & Dot, any color, 1934, 3½", ea **4.00**

Coin, clear & plain w/indented coin decor around base, 1968, 3¾" **1.00**

Cornflower #1, light blue & green, Canadian, 3¼" **8.00**

Cornflower #2, any color, 1947, 3¼", ea **3.00**

Dots Forming Diamonds, red, 1935, 3½" **25.00**

Ethnic Series, any color, Canadian, 1974, 4⅝", ea **20.00**

Forget-Me-Not, any color, Canadian, 3¼", ea **8.00**

Galleon, any, Canadian, 1936, 3⅛", ea **30.00**

Kiddie Kup, any color, Canadian, 1956, 3¼", ea **6.00**

Jonquil (Posy Pattern), yellow and green, Canada, 4⅝", $20.00; 3½", $3.00; 3¼", $8.00.

Lattice & Vine, white w/blue, green, or red, 1936, 3½", ea.........**25.00**

Petal Star, clear w/indented star base, Canadian, 1978, 3¼".**2.00**

Plain, clear, like Tulip #3 without design, 1951, 3⅞"..............**5.00**

Provencial Crest, red & burgundy, Canadian, 1974, 4⅝"......**25.00**

Sailboat #2, any color, 1936, 3½", ea.....................................**12.00**

Special Issue, Pasadena blue sailboat, Kraft, 1936, 3½"....**50.00**

Sportsmen Series, any, Canadian, 1976, 4⅝", ea..................**25.00**

Stars #1, yellow, 1935, 3½"..**25.00**

Stars #2, clear w/orange stars, Canadian, 1971, 4⅝"......**12.00**

Tulip #1, any color, Canadian, 3¼", ea..............................**8.00**

Tulip #3, any color, Canadian, 1950, 4¾", ea..................**20.00**

Violet (Posy Pattern), blue & green, 1941, 3½"..............**4.00**

Wildlife Series, any, Canadian, 1975, 4⅝", ea..................**20.00**

Teapots

The continued popularity of teatime and tea-related items has created a tighter market for col-lectors on the lookout for teapots! Vintage and finer quality teapots have become harder to find and those from the 1890s and 1920s will reflect age with three and four digit prices. Examples from the 1700s and 1800s are most often found in museums or large auction houses. Teapots listed here represent examples still available at the flea market level.

Most collectors begin with a general collection of varied teapots until they decide upon the specific category that appeals to them. Collecting categories include miniatures, doll or toy sets, those made by a certain manufacturer, figurals, or a particular style (such as Art Deco or English floral). Some of the latest trends in collecting are Chinese Yixing (pronounced yee-shing; teapots from an unglazed earthenware in forms taken from nature), 1950s pink or black teapots, Cottageware teapots, and figural teapots (those shaped like people, animals, or other objects). While teapots made in Japan have waned in collectibility, collectors have begun to realize many detailed or delicate examples are available. Of special interest are Dragonware teapots or sets where a dragon is molded in relief. Some of these sets have the highly desired lithophane cups — where a Geisha girl is molded in transparent relief in the bottom of the cup. When the cup is held up to the light, the image becomes visible.

Our advisor for this category is Tina M. Carter, author of

Teapots, The Collector's Guide; she is listed in the Directory under California. Two quarterly publications are also available; see Clubs and Newsletters for information on *Tea Talk* and *TeaTime Gazette.*

Advertising, Tetley Tea, porcelain, white w/figure on lid, newer................................**80.00**

Aluminum, paneled w/wicker-wrapped bail handle, Bakelite knob, 1950s **32.00**

Figural, chair w/kittens & pillows, porcelain w/painted detail, Taiwan...........................**25.00**

Figural, Christmas tree w/candy cane decorations & yellow star, Taiwan...................**18.00**

Figural, clown head, black w/gold hair, yellow hat, red nose, Japan.............................**30.00**

Figural, rabbit, brown airbrushing on white, blue snout, Japan, 1950s.............................**22.00**

Figural, snail, bright yellow, Japan, 1970s **38.00**

Figural, SS Tea biplane, white w/gold trim, Fitz & Floyd, 1970s.............................**38.00**

Figural, 'TEA' butler, porcelain w/black & white detail, Japan, 1950s **30.00**

Glass, clear ball shape w/etched floral design, Pyrex, 1930s-40s **100.00**

Individual, pottery, ball-shaped w/flat lid, glossy brown, USA............................**28.00**

Lustreware, sq w/dome lid, landscape & geometric, brown & blue, 1940s **55.00**

Miniature, bone china, ribbed ball shape w/wicker handle, floral decor **28.00**

Miniature, copper kettle w/bail handle, unmarked.........**15.00**

Miniature, squat w/bamboo handle, footed, floral & gold trim, Japan.............................**30.00**

Oriental, bulbous w/painted geishas in landscape w/house, loop finial.......................**80.00**

Porcelain, circular shape w/painted Victorian scene, gold trim, France............................**60.00**

Porcelain, sq footed shape w/pastel floral decor on white, England **58.00**

Pottery, ribbed bulbous w/starburst motif, light teal, USA, 1950s..............................**32.00**

Pottery, ribbed w/peacock motif & finial, rattan handle, Japan, 1960s.............................**28.00**

Satsuma-style, shiny green with gold lustre blown-out elephants, dragon spout, elephant finial, Japan mark, 5½", $60.00.

Tiara Exclusives

Collectors are just beginning to take notice of the glassware sold through Tiara in-home parties, their Sandwich line in particular. Several companies were involved in producing the lovely items they've marketed over the years, among them Indiana Glass, Fenton, Dalzell Viking, and L.E. Smith. In the late 1960s Tiara contracted with Indiana to produce their famous line of Sandwich dinnerware (a staple at Indiana Glass since the late 1920s). Their catalogs continue to carry this pattern, and over the years, it has been offered in many colors: ruby, teal, crystal, amber, green, pink, blue, and others in limited amounts. We've listed a few pieces of Tiara's Sandwich below, and though the market is unstable, our values will serve to offer an indication of current values. Unless you're sure of what you're buying, though, don't make the mistake of paying 'old' Sandwich prices for Tiara. To learn more about the two lines, we recommend *Collectible Glassware from the 40s, 50s, and 60s, Sixth Edition,* by Gene Florence (Collector Books). Also refer to *Collecting Tiara Amber Sandwich Glass* by our advisor Mandi Birkinbine; she is listed in the Directory under Idaho.

Ashtray, amber, 1¼x7½" **15.00**

Bowl, salad; crimped, amber, 4¾x10", from $15 to.......**18.00**

Butter dish, domed lid, Chantilly Green, 6" H....................**35.00**

Candy box, w/lid, amber, 7½", from $65 to **80.00**

Candle holders, Sandwich, 3¾", from $10.00 to $15.00 for the pair.

Canister, amber, 26-oz, 5⅝", from $12 to..............................**20.00**

Celery tray/oblong relish, Midnight Blue, 10⅜x4⅜"......**18.50**

Clock, wall hanging, amber, 16" dia, from $45 to..............**55.00**

Compote, amber, 8"...............**25.00**

Creamer & sugar bowl, round, flat, Midnight Blue, pr...**15.00**

Cup, coffee; amber, 9-oz..........**4.00**

Cup (snack/punch) & saucer, crystal, 2⅝x3⅜" **2.50**

Dish, club, diamond, heart or spade shape, amber, 4", ea, from $3 to **4.00**

Egg tray, amber, 12", from $10 to...................................**15.00**

Fairy lamp, egg shape, pedestal foot, amber, 2-pc, 5¾", from $14 to..............................**18.00**

Goblet, water; amber, 8-oz, 5¼", from $6 to **8.00**

Gravy boat, 3⅛x7⅜", from $45 to **60.00**

Mug, footed, amber, 5½".........**8.00**

Napkin holder, footed fan shape, amber, 4x7½", from $22 to.**28.00**

Pitcher, amber, 8¼", from $45 to **65.00**

Plate, dinner; amber, 10", from $950 to **12.50**

Plate, salad; amber, 8"............**7.00**

Plate, salad; Chantilly Green, 8¼"...................................**9.50**

Salt & pepper shakers, amber,
4¾", pr, from $18 to **25.00**
Tray, footed, amber, 1¾x12¾".**35.00**
Tumbler, amber, 8-oz, 4", from
$12 to **14.00**

Toothbrush Holders

Children's ceramic toothbrush
holders represent one of today's
popular collecting fields, with some
of the character-related examples
bringing $150.00 and up. Many
were made in Japan before WWII.

Our advisor for this category
is Marilyn Cooper, author of *A
Pictorial Guide to Toothbrush
Holders;* she is listed in the Directory under Texas. Plate numbers
in the following listings correspond with her book.

Annie Oakley, Japan, plate #11,
5¾", $100 to.................**145.00**
Baby Bunting, Germany, plate #1,
6¾"...............................**365.00**
Baby deer, marked Brush Teeth
Daily, Japan, plate #12, 4",
$110 to..........................**140.00**
Betty Boop w/toothbrush & cup,
KFS, plate #261, 4¾", $85
to **100.00**
Big Bird, Taiwan (RCC), plate
#263, 4½", from $80 to...**90.00**
Bonzo w/sidetray, Germany, plate
#23, $135 to..................**150.00**
Boy in knickers next to mailbox,
Japan, EX, 4¼" **60.00**
Boy in top hat, Japan, plate #29,
5½", $75 to.....................**95.00**
Boy w/violin, Goldcastle/Japan,
plate #30, 5½" **80.00**

**Three Little Pigs, two with instruments, one laying bricks, two holes,
Japan, pre-war, NM, $225.00.**

Candlestick Maker, Japan (Goldcastle), plate #150, 5", $70 to.**85.00**
Cat (Calico), Japan, plate #37,
5½", $90 to....................**110.00**
Clown holding mask, Japan, plate
#62, 5½", $110 to.........**150.00**
Cowboy next to cactus, Japan,
plate #70, 5½" **95.00**
Dachshund, Japan, plate #71,
5¼", $80 to....................**120.00**
Dalmatian, Germany #202, 4",
$150 to.........................**195.00**
Doctor w/satchel, Japan, plate
#206, 5¾"......................**90.00**
Dog w/basket, Japan, plate #72,
$90 to **100.00**
Dutch boy & girl kissing, Japan,
plate #88, 6", $55 to **65.00**
Flapper, plate #230, 4¼", $110
to **130.00**
Frog w/Mandolin, Goldcastle/Japan,
plate #209, 6", $85 to **110.00**
Indian Chief, Japan, plate #115,
4½", $225 to..................**275.00**
Lion, Japan, plate #118, 6", $75
to **95.00**
Mexican boy, Japan, plate #120,
5½", from $80 to...........**110.00**

Old King Cole, Japan, plate #125, 5¼", $85 to....................**100.00**

Old Mother Hubbard, German, plate #3, 6", $350 to........**410.00**

Peter Pumpkin Eater, Japan, plate #129, 4⅞", $85 to.**115.00**

Pluto, Japan, plate #133, 4½", $300 to...........................**350.00**

Schnauzer, Germany, plate #283, 3⅛", from $90 to...........**115.00**

Skippy w/jointed arms, plate #245, 5⅝".......................**100.00**

Tom, Tom the Piper's Sun, Japan, plate #154, 5¾", $95 to .**125.00**

Toys

Toy collecting remains a very popular hobby, and though some areas of the market may have softened to some extent over the past two years, classic toys remain a good investment. Especially strong are the tin windups made by such renowned companies as Strauss, Marx, Lehmann, Chein, etc., and the battery-operated toys made from the 1940s through the 1960s in Japan. Because of their complex mechanisms, few survive.

Toys from the 1800s are rarely if ever found in mint condition but should at least be working and have all their original parts. Toys manufactured in the twentieth century are evaluated more critically. Compared to one in mint condition, original box intact, even a slightly worn toy with no box may be worth only about half as much. Character-related toys, space toys, toy trains, and toys from the '60s are very desirable.

Several good books are available, if you want more information: *Modern Toys, 1930 – 1980,* by Linda Baker; *Collector's Guide to Tootsietoys, Second Edition,* by David E. Richter; *Toys, Antique and Collectible,* by David Longest; *Matchbox Toys, 1947 – 1998, Third Edition,* by Dana Johnson; *Hake's Price Guide to Character Toys, Third Edition,* by Ted Hake; *TV Toys and Memorabilia, Second Edition,* by Greg Davis and Bill Morgan; and *Schroeder's Collectible Toys, Antique to Modern.* All are published by Collector Books. See also Action Figures; Breyer Horses; Hartland; Character Collectibles; Star Wars; Western Heroes; Club and Newsletters.

Battery-Operated

Air Control Tower, Bandai, 1960s, 11", EX..........................**400.00**

Arthur A-Go-Go Drummer, Alps, 1960s, 10", NMIB.........**600.00**

Batmobile Magic Car, Tri-Ang Minic, 1966, 5", rare, NMIB.......**500.00**

Blacksmith Bear, A1, 1950s, 10", NMIB............................**375.00**

Bongo Monkey, Alps, 1960s, 9½", MIB..............................**250.00**

Bowling Bank, MB Daniel, 1960s, 10", MIB **225.00**

Buick Patrol Car, 1966, remote control, 13", MIB..........**650.00**

Captain Blushwell, Y, 1960s, 11", MIB..............................**175.00**

Busy Secretary, Linemar, 1950s, several actions, 7½", MIB, $400.00. (Photo courtesy Don Hultzman)

Chippy the Chipmunk, Alps, 1950s, MIB **225.00**

Chirping Grasshopper, MT, 1950s, 8½", EX **175.00**

Clancy the Great, Ideal, 1960s, MIB **375.00**

Clown Circus Car, MT, 1960s, 8½", EX **275.00**

Colonel Hap Hazard, Marx, 1968, 11", EX **700.00**

Cragston One-Arm Bandit, Y, 1960s, 6", MIB **250.00**

Dancing Nicky the Clown, Marbo, 1960s, 6", EX **100.00**

Dashee the Derby Hat Dachshund, Mego, 1971, remote control, 8", EX **85.00**

Donald Duck Locomotive, MT, 1970, 9", EX **300.00**

Drinking Captain, S&E, 1960s, 12", MIB **175.00**

Drumming Polar Bears, Alps, 1960s, 12", EX **200.00**

Flintstone Yacht, Remco, 1961, 17", EX **200.00**

Ford Mustang Stunt Car, Japan, 1969, NMIB **175.00**

Funland Cup Ride, Sonsco, 1960s, NMIB **250.00**

Funland Locomotive, Daya, 1950s, 9", EX **100.00**

Happy 'N Sad Face Magic Clown, Y, 1960s, 10", NMIB **275.00**

Hasty Chimp, Y, 1960s, 9", MIB **125.00**

Highway Skill Driving, K, 1960s, 13", NMIB **150.00**

Jetspeed Racer, Y, 1960s, 17½", EX **30.00**

Kiddie Trolley, MT, 1960s, 8", EX **100.00**

Magic Action Bulldozer, TN, 1950s, 9½", EX **200.00**

Marvelous Fire Engine, Y, 1960s, 11", EX **200.00**

Marx-A-Copter, Marx, 1961, remote control, NMIB..**350.00**

Melody Camping Car, Y, 1970s, 10", EX **125.00**

Mexicalli Pete, Alps, 1960s, MIB **325.00**

Moby Dick Whaling Boat, Linemar, 1950s, remote control, NM **200.00**

Musical Clown, TN, 1960s, 9", EXIB **275.00**

Nutty Mads Car, Linemar, 1960s, MIB **675.00**

Pee Pee Puppy, TN, 1960s, 9", NMIB **200.00**

Perky Pup, Alps, 1960s, 8½", EX **100.00**

Playful Pup in Shoe, Y, 1960s, 10", M **175.00**

Royal Cub in Buggy, S&E, 1950s, 8", EX **300.00**

Santa Copter, MT, 1950s, 8½", MIB **225.00**

Skipping Monkey, TN, 1960s, 9½", MIB **100.00**

Slurpy Pup, TN, 1960s, 6½", MIB **125.00**

Shutter-Bug, TN, 1950s, several actions, lithographed tin, NMIB, $800.00. (Photo courtesy Don Hultzman)

Whirlybird Helicopter, Remco, 1960s, 25", NMIB.........**250.00**

Friction

Ambulance, KKK, 1960s, litho tin, 6", NMIB **100.00**
Armored Van Savings Bank, H, 1060s, litho tin, NM.....**100.00**
Avenue Coach Bus, Y, 1950s, litho tin, 15", NM..................**185.00**
Barney Rubble's Wreck, Marx, 1962, tin w/vinyl-headed figure, 7", VG....................**350.00**

Smoking Bunny, SAN, 1950s, 10½", MIB **325.00**
Smoking Grandpa, SAN, 1950s, eyes closed, 9", rare, MIB........**475.00**
Smoking Grandpa, SAN, 1950s, eyes open, 9", MIB **300.00**
Snowmobile, Bandai, 1960s, NMIB............................**175.00**
Speed Jack Hot Rod, Taiyo, 1960s, 11", NMIB **100.00**
Stunt Plane, TPS, 1960s, 10½" wingspan, MIB..............**275.00**
Surry Jeep, TN, 1960s, 11", EX..**100.00**
Talking Batmobile, Hong Kong, 1977, 9½", rare, MIB ...**300.00**
Talking Police Car, Y, 1960s, 14", NM................................**150.00**
Teddy Go-Kart, Alps, 1960s, 10½", EXIB **200.00**
Tom & Jerry Auto, Rico/Spain, 1960s, 13", NMIB.........**500.00**
Tricky Doghouse, Y, 1960s, MIB **225.00**
Tumbles the Bear, Yanoman, 1960s, 8½", MIB...........**165.00**
TV Broadcasting Van, Gakken, 1960s, 7½", NM............**375.00**

Cadillac Old Timer Convertible, 1933 model, Bandai, red, 8", NMIB, $200.00 at auction.

Circus Choo Choo, Daiya, 1960s, 1960s, litho tin, 6½", M .**100.00**
Circus Clown Cycle, Haiji, tin w/vinyl-headed figure, 5", EXIB **200.00**
Disneyland Jeep, Marx, litho tin, 10", EXIB......................**275.00**
Duck on Tricycle, Alps, 1950s, litho tin w/felt trim, 6½"........**100.00**
Dum Dum & Touche Turtle, Marx, 1963, plastic, 4", rare, MIB .**200.00**
Flintstone Log Car, Marx, 1977, Fred driving, plastic, 5", MIB............................**200.00**

Flying Jeep, Linemar, litho tin, 6", EXIB **225.00**
Ford 60 Dump Truck, S&E, 1960, litho tin, 15½", NMIB ..**350.00**
Greyhound Scenicruiser, Japan, 1960s, litho tin, 16", NMIB **300.00**
Harbor Patrol Boat P-110, S&E, litho tin, 9", VG **100.00**
Helicopter, S&E, litho tin, 12", NMIB **100.00**
Highway Patrol Car, Ichiko, litho tin, 8", EXIB **125.00**
Jet Boat J-105, litho tin, 11", EX **175.00**
Little Audrey, Linemar, 1959, litho tin, 5", EXIB **250.00**
Livestock Truck, TN, 1950s, litho tin, 10", NMIB **200.00**
Mickey Mouse Scooter, Marx, plastic, 4", EXIB **225.00**
Mystery Police Cycle, KO, litho tin, 6", NMIB **450.00**
Pan Am DC-8 Airport Lift Truck, Japan, 1960s, 14", NM .**250.00**
Quick Draw McGraw, Marx, 1962, tin w/vinyl figure, 4", EXIB **400.00**
Racer #18, ASC, 1960s, litho tin, 11", EX **125.00**
Sand Conveyor Truck, TPS, 1960s, litho tin, extends to 16", EXIB **100.00**
School Bus System #15, Japan, 1960s, litho tin, 11", NM.**125.00**
Sparkling Jet Plane, Marx, 1950s, plastic, 12", MIB **100.00**
Stock Car #15, Japan, 1960s, litho tin, 12½", EX **200.00**
Taxi Cab, Sanyo, 1960s, litho tin, 6", NMIB **100.00**
Thunderbird Racer #2, Japan, 1960s, Mobil/Esso/Shell/STP logo, 12", NM **140.00**

Yellow Taxi #2, MT, 1960s, litho tin, 5½", NMIB **100.00**
Yogi Bear Car, Marx, 1962, litho tin w/vinyl figure, 4", EXIB **400.00**

Wind-Ups

Airport, Ohio Art, ca 1950, litho tin, 9", NMIB **250.00**
Amphibious Boat Silver Queen, Yonezawa, litho tin, 11", EXIB **150.00**
Androcles Lion, Linemar, plush over tin, 6", EXIB **100.00**
Babes in Toyland Soldier, Linemar, 1961, litho tin, EX, $325 to **400.00**
Banjo Player Monkey, Toyland Toys, 1950s, tin & cloth, 5", NMIB **175.00**
Big Joe Chef, Yonezawa, litho tin, 7", MIB **150.00**
Blacksmith Teddy, TN, litho tin & plush, 6", EXIB **200.00**
Captain America, Marx, 1967, vinyl, 5½", EXIB **100.00**
Casper the Friendly Ghost, Linemar, litho tin, 5", VG.....**250.00**
Charlie Chaplin, Spain, 1950s, plastic, 6½", EX............**200.00**
Circus Bot Clown, Japan, 1950s, litho tin, 6", EX **185.00**
Clarabelle the Clown, Linemar, litho tin, 5", EX **300.00**
Clarabelle the Clown, Linemar, litho tin, 5", NMIB **450.00**
Donald Duck & Nephews, Japan, plastic, 11", NM **175.00**
Donald Duck Drummer, Linemar, litho tin, VG **400.00**
Flapping Lovebird, Japan, litho tin, 6", EXIB **100.00**

Duck, Kohler, 1950s, quacks and flaps wings, lithographed tin, NM, from $75.00 to $85.00. (Photo courtesy June Moon)

Monkey Cycle, Bandai, litho tin, 5", NMIB **350.00**

Music Box Carousel, Mattel, 1953, litho tin & plastic, 9", NMIB **150.00**

Musical Baby Television, West Germany, litho tin, NMIB........**200.00**

Racing Car, Irwin, 1950s, plastic, 12½", scarce, MIB **200.00**

Sea Elizabeth U-35, Japan, 1950s, litho tin, EXIB..............**125.00**

Skipping Puppy, TN, litho tin, 6", EXIB **150.00**

Flintstone Turnover Tank, Linemar, 1961, 4", MIB........**925.00**

Fred Flintstone Flivver, Marx, 1962, tin w/vinyl-headed figure, 7", NM...................**450.00**

Funny Tiger, Marx, 1960s, litho tin, 6½", NMIB..............**200.00**

Gama 520, Germany, 1950s, litho tin, 3½", NMIB..............**125.00**

Harley-Davidson Motorcycle (Auto Cycle), TN, 9", NMIB...**550.00**

Honey Bear, Alps, plush & tin w/cloth clothes, 7", MIB.**200.00**

Howdy Doody Acrobat, Arnold, litho tin w/cloth clothes, 15", VG................................**250.00**

Humphery Mobile, Wyandotte, 1950, litho tin, 8½", EX..**400.00**

Jumping Rabbit, litho tin w/plush ears, 7", EXIB **140.00**

Kitty & Butterfly, TN, plush over tin, 5", MIB...................**150.00**

Little Audrey, Linemar, 1959, litho tin, 5", EXIB **250.00**

Magic Fish, Japan, litho tin, 6½", NMIB...........................**225.00**

Mary Poppins, Marx, 1964, plastic, 8", NMIB **175.00**

Pango-Pango African Dancer, TPS, lithographed tin, NM (NM box), $350.00. (Photo courtesy June Moon)

Squirrel on Treadmill, K, 1950s, extend to 20", EXIB **250.00**

Toto Clown Acrobat, Japan, celluloid, 12", EXIB **200.00**

Tumbling Jocko, Occupied Japan, celluloid, 5", NMIB **125.00**

Typewriting Dog, Bandai, litho tin & plush, 4", EXIB **300.00**

Venus Motorcycle, TN, litho tin & plastic, 9", NMIB **475.00**

Violin Player, Linemar, litho tin, 5", NM **350.00**

Wagon Fantasyland, TPS, litho tin, 12", NMIB..............**275.00**

Xylophone Player, MT, celluloid, 6", NMIB **175.00**

101 Dalmatians Lucky Pup, Linemar, plush over tin, 6", rare, EXIB..............................**275.00**

Trolls

The first trolls to come to the United States were molded after a 1952 design by Marti and Helena Kuuskoski of Tampere, Finland. The first to be mass produced in America were molded from wood carvings made by Thomas Dam of Denmark. As the demand for these trolls increased, several US manufacturers became licensed to produce them. The most noteworthy of these were Uneeda doll company's Wishnik line and Inga Dykin's Scandia House True Trolls. Thomas Dam continued to import his Dam Things line.

The troll craze from the 1960s spawned many items other than dolls such as wall plaques, salt and pepper shakers, pins, squirt guns, rings, clay trolls, lamps, Halloween costumes, animals, lawn ornaments, coat racks, notebooks, folders, and even a car.

In the 1970s, 1980s, and 1990s, more new trolls were produced. While these trolls are collectible to some, the avid troll collector still prefers those produced in the '60s. Remember, trolls that receive top dollar must be in mint condition.

Batman, Uneeda Wishnik, original outfit, 1966, 6", NM **100.00**
Boy w/Guitar, Norwegian, Nyform, painted-on clothes, 6", NM **50.00**
Bride & Groom, Uneeda Wishnik, 1970s, 6", EX, pr **35.00**

Caveman, Dam, 1964, felt outfit, 12", NM, from $135 to .**155.00**
Cousin Claus, Dam, 1984, original outfit, 10", EX.................**25.00**
Cow, Dam, 3½", EX...............**45.00**
Girl w/Accordion, Norwegian, Nyform, painted-on clothes, 6", NM **50.00**
Graduate, Uneeda Wishnik, 1970s, original robe & hat, 6", EX **25.00**
Hula-Nik, Uneeda Wishnik, rooted skirt, 5", EX...............**30.00**
Leprechaun Man & Woman, Scandia House, 1960s, stuffed, 10", EX, pr **175.00**
Lion, Dam, 1960s, white mane & tail, 5", NM, $125 to.........**150.00**
Little Red Riding Hood, Russ Storybook series, w/basket, 4½", NM.................................**15.00**
Norfin Bride or Groom, Dam, 1977, original outfits, 9⅛", NM, ea.......**40.00**
Norfin Turtle, Dam, 1984, 4", NM **50.00**

Pirate boy and girl, felt clothes, red hair, green eyes, 7", NM, $55.00 each. (Photo courtesy Pat Peterson)

Ranch-Nik, Uneeda Wishnik, 1980s, reissue, 5", NM...**20.00**
Sock-It-To-Me, Uneeda Wishnik, original outfit, 6", NM ...**50.00**
Troll Baby, Dam, 1974, 10", NM, from $55 to **65.00**

Viking Dam, 1967, 5½", NM, from
$150 to **275.00**
Werewolf Monster, 1980, 3",
NM............................**25.00**

Largo, sugar bowl, no lid **4.00**
Rambler Rose, milk pitcher..**25.00**
Woodvine, bowl, vegetable....**15.00**
Woodvine, utility tray...........**22.00**

Universal

Located in Cambridge, Ohio,
Universal Potteries Incorporated
produced various lines of dinnerware from 1934 to the late 1950s,
several of which are very attractive, readily available, and therefore quite collectible. Refer to *The
Collector's Encyclopedia of American Dinnerware* by Jo Cunningham (Collector Books) for more
information. See also Cattail.
Ballerina (Mist), cake plate..**20.00**
Ballerina Rose, creamer **15.00**

**Mixed Fruit, refrigerator jar, 4",
$12.00.**

Blue & White, coffe server....**25.00**
Calico Fruit, bowl, 4¼" **25.00**
Calico Fruit, gravy boat........**50.00**
Cattail, cookie jar, tab handles..**85.00**
Cattail, plate, luncheon **11.00**
Harvest, cup & saucer **19.00**
Harvest, plate, dinner...........**18.00**
Highland, bowl, cereal **15.00**
Iris, platter, tab handles, 11½" .**32.00**
Largo, plate, dessert; 6" **3.00**

Van Briggle

The Van Briggle Pottery of
Colorado Springs, Colorado, was
established in 1901 by Artus Van
Briggle upon the completion of his
quest to perfect a complete flat
matt glaze. His wife, Ann, worked
with him and they, along with
George Young, were responsible
for the modeling of the wares.
Known for their flowing Art Nouveau shapes, much of the ware
was eventually made from molds
with each piece carefully trimmed
and refined before the glaze was
sprayed on. Their most popular
colors were Persian Rose, Ming
Blue, and Mustard Yellow.

Van Briggle died in 1904, but
the work was continued by his
wife. With new facilities built in
1908, tiles, gardenware, and commercial lines were added to the
earlier artware lines. Reproductions of some early designs
continue to be made, The Double
AA mark has always been in use,
but after 1920 the dates and/or
shape numbers were dropped.
Mention should be made here as
well that the Anna Van Briggle
glaze is a later line which was
made between 1956 and 1968.

Our advisor for this category
is Michele Ross; she is listed in
the Directory under Michigan.

Bowl, stylized leaves, Persian Rose, 1940s, marked, 6" diameter, from $100.00 to $150.00; Vase, stylized leaves encircle shoulder, mulberry matt with bluish-green overspray, #780, 1920s, marked, 7½", from $200.00 to $250.00; Vase, leaves, blue and light green, 1917, marked, 4½", from $200.00 to $250.00.

Ashtray, sq dish w/center handle, turquoise, 1950s-60s, $45 to..............................**60.00**

Bookends, lamb, blue/burgundy, post 1930s, 5", pr **300.00**

Bookends, owl w/wings spread on open book, turquoise, 1922-26, pr **300.00**

Bowl w/flower frog (Water Nymph), scalloped oval, turquoise, 1930s-40s....**425.00**

Candlesticks, plain w/flared base, turquoise, 1940s-50s, pr, $55 to......................................**75.00**

Candlesticks, tulip form w/leafy stem, Golden Rod, 1980s, pr, $45 to..............................**60.00**

Creamer & sugar bowl, hexagonal, turquoise, 1930s-40s, ea, $35 to..............................**40.00**

Ewer, long-neck bulbous bottle form, long handle, turquoise, 1950s-60s......................**60.00**

Figurine, bird on stump w/tail up, glossy brown, 1980s, $40 to **50.00**

Figurine, cat seated on base, stylized, turquoise, 1980s, $50 to...........................**75.00**

Figurine, Indian maiden grinding corn, Golden Rod, 1980s-91, $90 to..............................**135.00**

Flower bowl w/frog, flower petal form, turquoise, 1970 to present .**50.00**

Lamp, long-neck gourd form, turquoise, butterfly shade, 1980s, $75 to **105.00**

Lamp, woman kneeling w/pot on shoulder, mulberry, no shade, 1946-50s **375.00**

Mug, wood-look barrel shape w/handle, brown w/gray rim, 1968-70s **25.00**

Paperweight, rabbit, turquoise, early 1980s, $40 to.........**60.00**

Planter, oblong, swan design, scalloped, footed, mulberry, 1930s-40s......................**120.00**

Teapot, embossed floral band, brown, 1940s-50s, $175 to............**225.00**

Vase, crescent moon on oval foot, mulberry, 1940s-60s, $110 to..**150.00**

Vase, rose motif, ruffled rim, round foot, mulberry, 1940s-50s, $80 to **110.00**

Vase, triple cornucopia, turquoise, 1960s-70s, $30 to **50.00**

Vernon Kilns

From 1931 until 1958, Vernon Kilns produced hundreds of patterns of fine dinnerware that today's collectors enjoy reassembling. They retained the services of famous artists and designers such as Rockwell Kent and Walt Disney, who designed both dinnerware lines and novelty items. Examples of their work are at a premium. See Clubs and Newsletters for information concerning *Vernon Views* newsletter.

Anytime, bowl; chowder..........**8.00**

Brown-Eyed Susan, bowl, chowder; tab handle, 6"..........**12.00**

Brown-Eyed Susan, plate, bread & butter; 6".......................**5.00**

Calico, creamer.....................**20.00**

Calico, plate, chop; 14"..........**75.00**

Chintz, cup **8.00**

Coral Reef, cup & saucer **26.00**

Fantasia, plate, salad; Nutcracker, 7½" **165.00**

Gingham, coaster **26.00**

Harvest, plate, 12", $30.00.

Hawaiian Flowers, plate, chop; 12", from $60 to..............**85.00**

Homespun, pitcher, 2-qt.......**47.50**

Homespun, salt & pepper shakers, pr.....................................**18.00**

Lei Lani, plate, chop; 14"....**125.00**

Lei Lani, salt & pepper shakers, Ultra shape, pr...............**45.00**

May Flower, bowl, salad; 12"..**60.00**

May Flower, cup & saucer....**15.00**

Moby Dick, mug, maroon......**75.00**

Moby Dick, plate, 10½".........**55.00**

Mojave, bowl, mixing; 5".......**15.00**

Organdie, bowl, chowder; tab handle, 6"............................**10.00**

Organdie, cup & saucer **7.00**

Organdie, plate, bread & butter .**3.00**

Organdie, salt & pepper shakers, pr.....................................**12.00**

Our America, cup & saucer .**100.00**

Plate, Bits Mission, San Diego, 14"...................................**95.00**

Plate, Edward Greig, Composer, 8½"...................................**25.00**

Plate, Mount Rushmore, 10½"..**15.00**

Salamina, cup & saucer......**100.00**

Salamina, plate, chop; 12"..**285.00**

Santa Maria, bowl, serving; 9".**42.00**

Tam O'Shanter, bowls, mixing; nesting set of 5.............**125.00**

Tam O'Shanter, plate, bread & butter; 6¼" **6.00**

Tickled Pink, bowl, vegetable; 8" **12.00**

Tickled Pink, gravy boat.......**18.00**

Tickled Pink, sugar bowl, w/lid .**18.00**

Tweed, sugar bowl, w/lid **40.00**

Vernon 1860, plate, chop; 14" .**50.00**

Winchester 73, plate, 6½", $32.00. (Photo courtesy Maxine Nelson)

Winchester 73, cup & saucer .**75.00**
Winchester 73, plate, chop; 12"..**100.00**
Winchester 73, platter, 12½".**130.00**
Winchester 73, tumbler **45.00**

Wall Pockets

Here's a collectible that is easily found, relatively inexpensive, and very diversified. They were made in Japan, Czechoslovakia, and by many, many companies in the United States. Those made by companies best known for their art pottery (Weller, Roseville, etc.) are in a class of their own, but the novelty, just-for-fun wall pockets stand on their own merits. Examples with large, colorful birds or those with unusual modeling are usually the more desirable. For more information we recommend *Collector's Encyclopedia of Wall Pockets* by Betty and Bill Newbound, and *Collector's Guide to Made in Japan Ceramics* (three in series) by our advisor, Carole Bess White, who is listed in the Directory under Oregon. (They are all published by Collector Books.) See also Cleminson; McCoy; Shawnee; other specific manufacturers.

Baby seated in crook of swan's neck, ivory lustre, Bradley Exclusives......................**22.00**
Basket w/ram's head handles, flower on front, ruffled rim, Japan, 5"........................**25.00**
Bird at nest hole on bamboo shoot, Germany, 6⅞" **22.00**

Bird w/tail up on purple grape cluster, Japan, 6½" **20.00**
Cat's head w/flower basket in mouth, Lefton, 6" **20.00**
Cornucopia w/flared scalloped top, curled tail, glossy, unmarked, 8"....................................**10.00**
Cup & saucer, bright yellow, Camark, 7½" **20.00**
Daffodils & leaves form, yellow & green, glossy, Japan, 4" .**12.00**
Duck in flight on crescent vase, glossy, Japan, 6¼" **15.00**
Elf leaning on stone well, Treasure Craft, 5"..................**25.00**
Fish mounted on wood-look plaque, glossy air-brushing, Japan, 3¼".....................**22.00**
Geisha girls (2) on conical form, red & gold on green, Japan, 8¾"....................................**25.00**
Goat & palm trees form, glossy, Japan, 5½x7"..................**20.00**
Grape cluster & 2 flowers on oval basket, Japan, 6¾".........**15.00**
Iron w/floral motif, 2 openings, UCAGO China, 5½".......**15.00**
Japanese lady w/basket on back, multicolored, Japan, 8"..**25.00**

Parrot and flowers, 7½" diameter, $24.00.

Papoose sleeping, aqua & black on
ivory, unmarked, 6½"....**25.00**
Pine cone form, Cortney, 4¾".**8.00**
Ribbon bow form, Shawnee,
3¾x4¾"...........................**15.00**
Rooster, stylized, Engle Studio,
12".................................**60.00**
Skillet w/cherries & leaves (applied),
Jan's California, 7"...........**25.00**
Teapot w/strawberries & leaves,
cold-painted colors on creamy
white..............................**25.00**
Violin w/pansies, gold trim, 6½".**12.00**
Wagon wheel w/leafy branch,
unmarked (1940s American-
made)............................**25.00**
Wiskbroom, Sunglow, Hull, ca
1952, 8½".......................**50.00**

Western Heroes

Interest is very strong right
now in western memorabilia —
not only that, but the kids that lis-
tened so intently to those after-
school radio episodes featuring
one of the many cowboy stars that
sparked the air-waves in the '50s
are now some of today's more
affluent collectors, able and want-
ing to search out and buy toys
they had in their youth. Put those
two factors together, and it's easy
to see why these items are so popular. For more information, we
recommend *Character Toys and
Collectibles, First* and *Second
Series*, by David Longest; *The
Lone Ranger* by Lee Felbinger;
and *The W.F. Cody Buffalo Bill
Collector's Guide* by James W.
Wojtowicz. All are published by
Collector Books. See also Banks;
Coloring Books; Comic Books;
Games; Puzzles.

Davy Crockett

Davy Crockett had long been
a favorite in fact and folklore.
Then with the opening of Disney's
Frontierland and his continuing
adventures on 1950s television
came a surge of interest in all
sorts of items featuring the likeness of Fess Parker in a coonskin
cap. Millions were drawn to the
mystic and excitement surround-
ing the settlement of our great
country. Due to demand, there
were many types of items produced for eager fans ready to role
play their favorite adventures.

Chalk, Creston Crayon Co, 1950s,
EXIB..............................**40.00**
Color TV Set, w/viewer & 4 rolls of
film, WDP, NMOC.......**175.00**
Doll, composition w/clothes &
coonskin cap, Fortune Toy, 8",
NMIB..........................**175.00**
Doll, stuffed cloth w/vinyl face,
name on chest, 1950s, 27",
EX................................**150.00**
Guitar, fiberboard, w/pick & song
book, Peter Puppet, 25",
EXIB............................**200.00**
Hobbyhorse, wood w/springs,
23x33", EX+.................**200.00**
Pants, fringed jeans w/pocket label,
Blue Bell/WDP, NM........**75.00**
Penknife, Imperial/WDP, 1950s,
4", NM **35.00**
Pistol & knife, black plastic, Mul-
tiple, NMOC.................**65.00**

Ring, face, bronze, 1950s, NM .50.00

Shirt, flannel w/images & signatures, Blue Bell/WDP, NM............75.00

Slide-tile puzzle, Roalex, 1950s, NMOC 50.00

Soap Bubbles, w/wand, Chemical Sundries, 5", EX.............75.00

Teepee, canvas w/graphics, ...Official Fess Parker..., 70", EX...225.00

Tool kit, Liberty Steel, 1955, lithographed tin chest, complete with tools and manual, M, $450.00.

Toss-Up Balloon, Oak Rubber/ WDP, MOC...................135.00

Wagon Train, horse-drawn coach w/3 units, plastic, Marx, 1950s, NMIB 425.00

Yo-yo, blue-paint w/gold stamp, tournament shape, 1960s, NM, $5 to.......................10.00

Gene Autry

First breaking into show business as a recording star with Columbia Records, Gene went on to become one of Hollywood's most famous singing cowboys. From the late 1930s until the mid-'50s, he rode his wonder horse 'Champion' through almost ninety feature films. He did radio and TV as well, and naturally his fame spawned a wealth of memorabilia

originally aimed at his young audiences, now grabbed up just as quickly by collectors.

Cap gun, .44, diecast w/plastic grips, Leslie-Henry, 1950s, NMIB...........................250.00

Cap gun, cast iron w/red plastic grips, Kenton, 8", EXIB .250.00

Cap gun, diecast w/plastic grips, Leslie-Henry, 9", VG....125.00

Official Cowboy Spurs, MIB, $185.00.
(Photo courtesy Phil Helley)

Pin-back button w/attached gun & holster, 8", NM..............50.00

Ring, Flag, NM...................100.00

Vest & chaps, suede w/felt trim, Leslie-Henry, 1940s, NMIB, $200 to.........................300.00

Wallet, leather w/color image of Gene on Champion, ca 1950, NMIB...........................125.00

Hopalong Cassidy

One of the most popular western heroes of all time, Hoppy was the epitome of the highly moral, role-model cowboys of radio and the silver screen that many of us grew up with in the 1940s and 1950s. He was portrayed by Bill Boyd who personally endorsed more than 2,200 items targeting Hoppy's loyal followers. If you just happen to be a modern-day Hoppy aficionado, you'll want to read *Collector's Guide to Hopalong Cassidy Memorabilia* by Joseph Caro (L-W Book Sales).

Tie and scarf set, printed silk, MIB, $350.00. (Photo courtesy Phil Helley)

Belt, Switch-A-Buckle, NMOC .**225.00**
Binoculars, metal & plastic w/decals, Sports Glass Chicago, EX **165.00**
Bow tie, cloth w/western scenes, 1950, NMOC **75.00**
Cap gun, diecast w/white grips, Schmidt, 1950s, 9½", EX.**350.00**
Coloring Outfit, Transogram, 1950, NMIB..................**300.00**
Decal sheet, set of 4, 8x3" sheet, M....................................**50.00**
Film viewer, green plastic TV w/disk inside, 1950s, 1¼", EX.....**60.00**
Membership kit, Savings Rodeo Club, complete, EX (EX mailer)..................................**250.00**

Photo album, brown leather w/embossed color image, 1950s, unused, EX **150.00**
Ring, hat, NM.....................**225.00**

The Lone Ranger

Recalling 'those thrilling days of yesteryear,' we can't help but remember the adventures of our hero, The Lone Ranger. He's been admired since that first radio show in 1933, and today's collectors seek a wide variety of his memorabilia; premiums, cereal boxes, and even carnival chalkware prizes are a few examples. See Clubs and Newsletters for information on *The Silver Bullet.*

Wallet, Hidecraft, 1948, EX, $125.00.

Bank, Lone Ranger figure on rearing Silver, plastic, NM, $100 to...................................**135.00**
Bat-O-Ball, 1940, NM, $75 to .**125.00**
Bop bag, inflatable vinyl, Carlin Playthings, 1970, MIP...**45.00**
Cartoon Kit, Colorforms, 1966, MIB (sealed), $75 to.....**100.00**
Deputy kit, complete, 1956, NM, from $150 to **175.00**

Doll, talker, stuffed cloth, Mego, 1972, 24", MIB **100.00**
Flashlight gun, plastic, General Mills, 1952, 6", EX (EX mailer)................................**200.00**
Microscope, Cheerios, 1947, NM, $125 to..........................**150.00**
Party horn, litho tin, 1950, EX..**25.00**
Rifle, silver plastic w/diecast works, Marx, 1950s, 26", VG **85.00**
Scrapbook, 1940, EX.............**85.00**

Roy Rogers

Growing up during the Great Depression, Leonard Frank Sly was determined to make his mark in the entertainment industry. In 1938 after landing small roles in films featuring Gene Autry and others, Republic Studios (recognizing his talents) renamed their singing cowboy Roy Rogers and placed him in his first leading role in *Under Western Stars.* By 1943 he had become America's 'King of the Cowboys.' And his beloved wife Dale Evans and his horse Trigger were at the top with him.

Our advisor for this category is Robert W. Phillips; he is listed in the Directory under Oklahoma. Mr. Phillips is the author of *Silver Screen Cowboys, Hollywood Cowboy Heroes, Roy Rogers, Singing Cowboy Stars,* and *Western Comics;* all are highly recommended. Also recommended is *Roy Rogers and Dale Evans Toys & Memorabilia* by P. Allan Coyle. See Clubs and Newsletters for information on the Roy Rogers — Dale Evans Collectors Association.

Binoculars, MIB, $295.00.

Camera, plastic w/metal front plate, Herbert George, EXIB..........................**150.00**
Cap gun, diecast w/cross-hatched metal grips, Schmidt, 1950, 10", EX..........................**200.00**
Cowboy & Indian Kit, Colorforms, complete, NMIB...........**150.00**
Crayon set, Standard Toykraft, 1950s, complete, VG (VG box) **75.00**
Guitar, red w/white image of Roy on Trigger, Range Rythm, 1950s, EX **185.00**
Harmonica, Reed, 1955, NMOC.**95.00**
Ring, microscope, 1950s, EX..**125.00**
School bag, brown vinyl w/strap, image of Roy on Trigger, 14" L, EX............................**100.00**

Miscellaneous

Annie Oakley, blouse & fringed shirt, image on pockets, NMIB..........................**200.00**
Bat Masterson, Indian Fighter playset, Multiple, NMIB **200.00**
Cisco Kid, hobbyhorse, vinyl w/wood handle, VG **50.00**

Daniel Boone, Fess Parker Cartoon Kit, Colorforms, 1964, MIB................................**35.00**

Daniel Boone, Fess Parker Super Slate, Whitman, 1964, NM.**50.00**

Gabby Hayes, ring, cannon, 1951, EX................................**185.00**

Johnny Ringo, outfit, Yankeeboy, 1950s, complete, EXIB..**125.00**

Rin-Tin-Tin, pen, black plastic rifle, Nabisco, 1950s, EX.........**50.00**

Rin-Tin-Tin, Wonda Scoop, EX..........................**65.00**

Sky King, Secret Signal Scope, 1947, NM (NM mailer)..**250.00**

Sky King, stamp kit, complete, EX (EX mailer)...................**100.00**

Tom Mix, spinner, Good Luck, EX................................**75.00**

Tom Mix, spurs, glow-in-the-dark, MIB................................**150.00**

Tonto, ring, picture, EX........**55.00**

Wild Bill Hickok, treasure map, Sugar Pops, 1950s, NM (NM mailer)...........................**150.00**

Wild Bill Hickok & Jingles, Ranch Bunkhouse Kit, 1950s, NMIP.................**65.00**

Wyatt Earp, spurs, plastic, Selco, NMOC **50.00**

Zorro, charm bracelet, gold-painted metal, w/3 charms, WDP, 1950s, EX **50.00**

Zorro, pocketknife, Riders of the Silver Screen Collector Series, MIB, $45.00.

Zorro, domimoes, Halsam, MIB.**65.00**

Zorro, magic slate, Strathmore/ WDP, 1955, EX **50.00**

Zorro, wrist flashlight, black plastic w/red & green filters, 1958, VG......................**30.00**

Westmoreland

Originally an Ohio company, Westmoreland relocated in Grapesville, Pennsylvania, where by the 1920s they had became known as one of the country's largest manufacturers of carnival glass. They are best known today for the high quality milk glass which accounted for 90% of their production. For further information we recommend *Westmoreland Glass* by Charles West Wilson and contacting the Westmoreland Glass Society, Inc., listed in Clubs and Newsletters. See also Glass Animals and Birds.

Ashtray, Beaded Grape/#1884, Brandywine Blue, 6½ sq.**30.00**

Ashtray, English Hobnail/#555, amber or crystal, 4½" sq..**7.50**

Banana bowl, Paneled Grape/ #1881, footed, 12".........**160.00**

Basket, English Hobnail/#555, amber or crystal, 5" **20.00**

Basket, Paneled Grape/#1881, milk glass, ruffled, 8".....**65.00**

Basket, Thousand Eye, crystal, oval, 8"............................**45.00**

Bell, Cameo/#754, any color w/Beaded Bouquet trim..**35.00**

Bonbon, Daisy/#205, Brown Mist...........................**30.00**

Bonbon, Waterford/#1932, crystal or ruby, handled.............**38.00**

Bowl, English Hobnail/#555, amber or crystal, 7" **15.00**

Bowl, Lotus/#1921, milk glass, oval **30.00**

Bowl, Striped/#1814, Apricot Mist, round, footed, lg.............**35.00**

Box, chocolate; Paneled Grape/ #1991, milk glass, w/lid, 6½" dia **45.00**

Box, trinket; Crystal Mist w/Roses & Bows, sq, 4-footed **35.00**

Butter/cheese dish, Old Quilt/#500, milk glass, round, w/lid **45.00**

Cake Plate, Beaded Grape/#1884, milk glass, sq, footed, 11".**95.00**

Cake plate, Waterford/#1932, crystal or ruby, low foot, 12".........**95.00**

Candle holders, crystal or ruby, Waterford/#1932, 6", pr.**65.00**

Candle holders, Paneled Grape/ #1881, milk glass, octagonal, 4", pr **27.50**

Candle holders, Waterford/#1932, crystal or ruby, 6", pr.....**65.00**

Candy dish, Beaded Bouquet/ #1700, milk glass, Colonial pattern.............................**35.00**

Candy dish, Beaded Grape/#1884, Brandywine Blue, w/lid, 3½" .**35.00**

Candy dish, English Hobnail/#555, amber or crystal, 3-footed.**30.00**

Candy dish, Paneled Grape/#1881, Dark Blue Mist, crimped, 3-footed **35.00**

Candy dish, Paneled Grape/#1881, milk glass, w/lid, 6¼".....**25.00**

Compote, English Hobnail/#555, amber or crystal, round, footed, 6"...............................**18.00**

Creamer, Beaded Edge/#22, decorated milk glass, footed .**17.50**

Cup, Beaded Edge/#22, plain milk glass..................................**5.00**

Cup, Thousand Eye, crystal, footed, beaded handle **8.00**

Decanter, Paneled Grape, milk glass, $145.00; Matching wines, $22.00 each. (Photo courtesy Frank Grizel)

Egg cup, English Hobnail/#555, amber or crystal.............**14.00**

Egg plate, Paneled Grape/#1881, milk glass, 12"................**85.00**

Flowerpot, Paneled Grape/#1881, milk glass **47.50**

Goblet, water; Old Quilt/#500, milk glass, footed, 8-oz ..**15.00**

Goblet, wine; Paneled Grape/#1881, milk glass, footed, 2-oz.....**22.00**

Lamp, boudoir; English Hobnail/ #555, milk glass, stick w/flat base...............................**45.00**

Lamp, fairy; Waterford/#1932, cyrstal or ruby, footed....**65.00**

Mayonnaise, Paneled Grape/#1881, milk glass, footed, 4"........**27.50**

Nappy, Beaded Edge/#22, plain milk glass, 5"....................**4.50**

Oil bottle, English Hobnail/#555, amber or crstal, handled, 6-oz................................**30.00**

Pin tray, Heart/#1820, Blue Mist............................**30.00**

Pitcher, English Hobnail/#555, amber or crystal, rounded, 23-oz **50.00**

Pitcher, Paneled Grape/#1881, milk glass, 32-oz **37.50**

Place setting: Plate, American Hobnail, #77, milk glass; Matching goblet, cup and saucer, $35.00 for the set.
(Photo courtesy Frank Grizel)

Plate, Beaded Edge/#22, red-edged milk glass, 6" **7.00**

Plate, English Hobnail/#555, amber or crystal, 8" dia ...**7.50**

Plate, Forget-Me-Not/#2, black w/Mary Gregory style, 8".**55.00**

Plate, Paneled Grape/#1881, decorated milk glass, 8½" **40.00**

Plate, Thousand Eye, crystal, 10" **22.50**

Platter, Beaded Edge/#22, decorated milk glass, oval, tab handles, 12" **95.00**

Relish, Beaded Edge/#22, plain milk glass, 3-part **25.00**

Salt & pepper shakers, Beaded Edge/#22, red-edged milk glass, pr **35.00**

Saucer, Beaded Edge/#22, decorated milk glass **4.00**

Saucer, Thousand Eye, crystal .**3.00**

Sherbet, Beaded Edge/#22, red-edged milk glass, footed..**12.00**

Stem, Thousand Eye, crystal, 8-oz....................................**10.00**

Tidbit, Beaded Grape/#1884, milk glass, 2-tier.....................**95.00**

Toothpick holder, Paneled Grape/#1881, milk glass **24.00**

Tumbler, iced tea; Thousand Eye, crystal, 12-oz.................**12.50**

Tumbler, juice; Old Quilt/#500, milk glass, flat, 5-oz.......**25.00**

Vase, Paneled Grape/#1881, milk glass, 15" **22.00**

Water set, Old Quilt/#500, purple slag, 3-pt pitcher & 6 9-oz tumblers **280.00**

World's Fairs and Expositions

Souvenir items have been issued since the mid-1800s for every world's fair and exposition. Few fairgoers have left the grounds without purchasing at least one. Some of the older items were often manufactured right on the fairgrounds by glass or pottery companies who erected working kilns and furnaces just for the duration of the fair. Of course, the older items are usually more valuable, but even souvenirs from the past 50 years are worth hanging on to.

See Clubs and Newsletters for information concerning the World's Fair Collectors' Society, Inc.

1939 New York

Book, Official Guide, illustrated, 1st edition, 256-pages, 5x8", EX **24.00**

Booklet, Futurama, 20-pages,
EX **12.00**

Dish, ceramic, Trylon and Perisphere, Japan, 7½", from $35.00 to $50.00.

Folder, mailing; 18 multicolor
views of the fair **18.00**
Pin, embossed letters spelling
Heinz on green pickle shape,
1¼", EX **5.00**
Seal, Boy Scout Camp, gummed,
NM **6.00**
Swizzle stick, cobalt glass, Brass
Rail (restaurant), 6" **7.50**
Tie clip, Trylon & Perisphere
design, 2½" **24.00**

1939 San Francisco

Bookmark, butterfly form, yel-
low on acetate w/paper,
MIP **26.50**
Folder, general fair information,
dated 1939, 3½x6", NM . **6.50**
Ice pick, World's Fair mark on
wooden handle, 8", NM.. **22.50**
Medal, Petroleum Exhibit, brass,
1⅜", NM **8.50**
Ticket, Cavalcade of the Golden
West, 2x1¼" **4.00**
Token, aluminum, Road of
Streamliners & Challengers,
EX **8.50**

1962 Seattle

Bottle opener, steel w/multicolor enamel, Space Needle, MIB **16.50**
Brochure, w/map of grounds & week's
schedule of events, NM **4.50**
Dish, Space Needle & fairgrounds
on china, 11" dia **22.50**
Lapel pin, Century 21 Expo, silver
on blue **12.00**
Pennant, Space Needle, red &
black felt, 7¾" **2.50**
Tray, Space Needle & fair scenes,
multicolor enamel on tin, 11"
dia **4.50**

Tumblers, single colors with black and white matt finish on frosted glass with gold trim, 16-ounce, from $7.00 to $9.00 each.

Tumblers, buildings, scenes, etc, different colors, set of 8, M ...**45.00**

1964 New York

Badge, Ford Motors Pavilion, New
York, plastic **15.00**
Book, Official Souvenir, softcover,
M **8.00**
Booklet, Elsie (the cow) at the New
...Fair, 14-pages, 7x5", G......**35.00**
Booklet, Vatican Pavilion at the
World's Fair, M **12.50**

Charm, world globe in frame, 14k gold, eng, NM **140.00**

Cuff links, globe w/engraved NYWF, gold tone, w/matching tis clasp, EX **33.00**

Decanter, Jim Beam, 11½", NM .**60.00**

Dish, multicolored fair scenes on glass, 4x4½", NM **10.00**

Flash cards, Official Souvenir, set of 28, M in original mailing box **25.00**

Hat, Adam Burmuda, NMIB (fair logo on lid) **25.00**

License plate, blue & orange, world in center, VG+ **40.00**

Map, Visitor's Guide & Map, Squibb & Sons, M **6.50**

Paperweight, Unisphere, base metal, US Steel, 2½x5½" .**6.00**

Pin-back button, Meet Me at the Smoke Ring, EX **12.00**

Playing cards, Unisphere backs, full deck, M **20.00**

Program, Progressland, 10-pages, 8½x11" **45.00**

Spoon, demitasse; Unisphere, silver-plated, w/sleeve **12.50**

Tray, Unisphere, Peace Through Understanding, US Steel, 11¾" dia **25.00**

Viewmaster reel set, Federal & State Area, three reels, EXIB **25.00**

Viewmaster reel set, Industrial Area, 21 reels, EXIB **45.00**

Viewmaster reel set, Night Scenes & Amusement Area, 3 reels, EXIB **23.00**

1982 Knoxville

Pen, floaty; fair scene, Denmark on pocket clip, EX **15.00**

Pocket knife, white Bakelite w/red Coco-Cola logo, 2-blade, NM **10.00**

Postcard, Gondola Sky Ride ...**2.50**

Postcard, United States Pavilion **2.50**

Wrestling Collectibles

The World Wrestling Federation boasts such popular members as the Iron Shiek, Hulk Hogan, the colorful Sycho Sid, and The Undertaker. Recent tag-team wrestlers include the Legion of Doom, Cactus Jack and Chainsaw Charlie. With these colorful names and (to put it mildly) assertive personalities, one can only imagine the vast merchandising possiblities. Posters, videos, trade cards, calendars, lighters, and magazines are all popular collectibles, but the variety of items available is limitless.

Badge, 1953 World Championship in Naples, enameled, EX .**30.00**

Book, Scientific Wrestling by George Bothner, 1912, 174 pages, EX **80.00**

Book, Wrestling by Frank Gotch, Fox's Athletic Library #20, EX **110.00**

Book, Wrestling by Kenney & Law, 1952, college/amateur, 171 pgs, EX **35.00**

Figure, Atom Bomb, Hasbro, Green Card Series, MOC **50.00**

Figure, Don Muraco, LJN, 1984-89, MOC **33.00**

Figure, Jimmy Snuka, LJN, 1985, w/free poster, 8½", MIP .**35.00**

Figure, Nick Bockwinkel, Remco, 1982-86, NM.................. **32.00**

Figure, Ric Flair, Galoob, 1990, MOC **40.00**

Figure, Ultimate Warrior, WWF, LJN, 1989, EX................**70.00**

Figure set, Legion of Doom, Hawk & Animal, Hasbro, MOC .**48.00**

Flag, WCW, Goldberg, nylon, 2/hanging pole & cord, 20x36", MIP....................**35.00**

Game, WWF Wrestling Ring, Hasbro, 1991, MIB **38.00**

Guide, Official NCAA Wrestling; Spalding, 1951, 108 pages, EX **120.00**

Guide, Official NCAA Wrestling; Spalding, 1939, EX......**115.00**

Magazine, Girl Wrestling, Spring 1965, Vol 1 #2, 70 pages, EX...........**50.00**

Magazine, TV Wrestling, 1950s, Buddy Rogers on cover, EX .**40.00**

Jacket, Hulk Hogan, World Wrestling Federation, Titan Sports, polyester, 1990, NM, $25.00.

Magazine, Wrestling Revue, 1959, 1st issue, NM **140.00**

Poster, Dan Gable at Munich Olympiad, 1972, rolled, 22x33", NM....................**35.00**

Trading card, Frank Gotch, Topps Magic Photos, 1948, EX..**38.00**

DIRECTORY

The editor and staff take this opportunity to express our sincere gratitude and appreciation to each person who have in any way contributed to the preparation of this guide. We believe the credibility of out book is greatly enhanced through their participation. Check these listings for information concerning their specific areas of expertise.

If you care to correspond with anyone listed here in our Directory, you must send a SASE with your letter.

If you are among these listed, please advise us of any changes in your address, phone number or e-mail. SASE with your letter.

Alabama

Cataldo, C.E.
4726 Panorama Dr. SE
Huntsville, 35801
256-536-6893

California

Ales, Beverly L.
4046 Graham St.
Pleasanton, 94566-5619
925-846-5297
E-mail: Beverlyales@hotmail.com
Specializing in knife rests; editor of *Knife Rests of Yesterday and Today*

Carter, Tina
882 S. Mollison
El Cajon, 92020-6506
619-440-5043
Specializing in teapots, tea-related items, tea tins, children's and toy tea sets, plastic cookie cutters, etc. Book on teapots available. Send $16 (includes postage) or $17 for California residents, Canada: add $5 to above address

Conroy, Barbara J.
P.O. Box 2369
Santa Clara, CA 95055-2369
E-mail: restaurantchina@home.com
Author of *Restaurant China, Restaurant, Airline, Ship & Railroad Dinnerware, Vol I and II* (Collector Books)

Elliott, Jacki
9790 Twin Cities Rd.
Galt, 95632
209-745-3860
Specializing in Rooster and Roses

Harrison, Gwynne
P.O. Box 1
Mira Loma, 91752-0001
951-685-5434
E-mail: morgan99@pe.net
Buys and appraises Autumn Leaf; edits newsletter

Lewis, Kathy and Don
187 N Marcello Ave.
Thousand Oaks, 91360
805-499-8101
E-mail: chatty@ix.netcom.com

Authors of *Chatty Cathy Dolls, An Identification and Value Guide,* and *Talking Toys of the 20th Century*

Rosewitz, Michele A.
3165 McKinley
San Bernardino, 92404
909-862-8534
Specializing in glass knives made in USA circa 1920s through 1950s

Synchef, Richard M.
208 Summit Dr.
Corte Madera, 94925
415-927-8844
Specializing in Beatnik and Hippie collectibles; Peter Max

Utley, Bill; Editor
Flashlight Collectors of America
P.O. Box 40945
Tustin, 92781
714-730-1252 or fax 714-505-4067
Specializing in flashlights

Van Ausdall, Marci
P.O. Box 946
Quincy, 95971-0946
530-283-2770
Specializing in Betsy McCall dolls and accessories; edits newsletter

Colorado

Diehl, Richard
5965 W Colgate Pl.
Denver, 80227
Specializing in license plates

Connecticut

Sabulis, Cindy
P.O. Box 642
Shelton, 06484
203-926-0176
Specializing in dolls from the '60s-'70s (Liddle Kiddles, Barbie, Tammy, Tressy, etc.); co-author of *The Collector's Guide to Tammy, The Ideal Teen,* and author of *Collector's Guide to Dolls of the 1960s & 1970s* (Collector Books)

District of Columbia

McMichael, Nancy
P.O. Box 53262

Washington, 20009
Author of *Snowdomes,* (Abbeville Press)

Florida

Grubaugh, Joan
2332 Brookfield Greens Circle
Sun City, 33573
Author of *Gerber Baby Dolls and Advertising Collectibles* ($39.95 plus $4 postage)

Kuritzky, Lewis
4510 NW 17th Pl.
Gainesville, 32605
352-377-3193
Author of *Collector's Guide to Bookends*

Poe, Bill and Pat
220 Dominica Cir. E
Niceville, 32578-4085
850-897-4163 or fax 850-897-2606
e-mail: McPoes@aol.com
Buy, sell, trade fast-food collectibles, cartoon character glasses, PEZ, Smurfs, California Raisins, M&M items

Posner, Judy
October - May
PO Box 2194
Englewood, 34295
E-mail: judyand jef@aol.com
www.judyposner.com
Specializing in figural pottery, cookie jars, salt and pepper shakers, Black memorabilia and Disneyana; sale lists available; fee charged for appraisals

Tvorak, April and Larry
P.O. Box 493401
Leesburg, 34749-3401
Specializing in Enesco Kitchen Independence and Kitchen Prayer Ladies, Pyrex, Fire-King (guides available), and Holt Howard

Idaho

Birkinbine, Mandi
P.O. Box 121
Meridian, 83680-0121
E-mail: tiara@shop4antiques.com
www.shop4antiques.com
Author of *Collecting Tiara Amber Sandwich Glass*, available from the author for $18.45 ppd. Please allow 4 to 6 weeks for delivery

McVey, Jeff
1810 W State St. #427
Boise, 83702-3955
Author of *Tire Ashtray Collector's Guide* available from the author

Illinois

Garmon, Lee
1529 Whittier St.
Springfield, 62704

217-789-9574
Specializing in Borden's Elsie, Reddy Kilowatt, Elvis Presley, and Marilyn Monroe

Jungnickel, Eric
P.O. Box 4674
Naperville, 60567-4674
630-983-8339
Specializing in Indy 500 memorabilia

Kadet, Jeff
TV Guide Specialists
P.O. Box 20
Macomb, 61455
Buying and selling of *TV Guide* from 1948 through the 1990s

Klompus, Eugene R.
The National Cuff Link Society
P.O. Box 5700
Vernon Hills, 60061
847-816-0035
E-mail: genek@cufflink.com
Specializing in cuff links and men's accessories

Stifter, Craig
218 S. Adams St.
Hinsdale 60521
630-789-5780
E-mail: cocacola@enteract.com
Specializing in soda memorabilia such as Coca-Cola, Hires, Pepsi, 7-Up, etc.

Indiana

Dilley, David
Indianapolis
317-251-0575
E-mail: glazebears@aol.com or bearpots@aol.com
Author of book on Royal Haeger; available from the author

Hoover, Dave
1023 Skyview Dr.
New Albany, 47150
Specializing in fishing collectibles, miniature boats and motors

McGrady, Donna S.
P.O. Box 14, 301 E. Walnut St.
Waynetown, 47990
765-234-2187
Specializing in Gay Fad glassware

McQuillen, Michael and Polly
P.O. Box 50022
Indianapolis, 46250-0022
317-845-1721
e-mail: michael@politicalparade.com
www.politicalparade.com
Specializing in political memorabilia

Iowa

Addy, Geneva D.

Winterset, 50273
515-462-3027
Specializing in Imperial Porcelain, Pink
Pigs, Moss Rose, and Strawberry Shortcake
collectibles

The Baggage Car
3100 Justin Dr., Ste. B
Des Moines, 50322
515-270-9080
Specializing in Hallmark

Devine, Joe
D&D Antique Mall
1411 3rd St.
Council Bluffs, 51503
712-232-5233 or 712-328-7305
Author of *Collector's Guide to Royal Copley With
Royal Winton and Spaulding, Books I and II*

Kansas
Anthony, Dorothy J.
World of Bells Publications
2401 S Horton
Ft. Scott, 66701-2790
316-223-3404
Author of *World of Bells,* #5 ($8.95); *Bell
Tidings* ($9.95); *Lure of Bells* ($9.95); *Col-
lectible Bells* ($10.95); and *More Bell Lore*
($11.95); autographed copies available from
the author; please enclose $2.00 for postage

Kentucky
Hornback, Betty
707 Sunrise Ln.
Elizabethtown, 42701
270-765-2441
e-mail:bettysantiques@KVNET.org
Specializing in Kentucky Derby and horse
racing memorabilia; send for informative
booklet, $15 ppd.

Langford, Paris
415 Dodge Ave.
Jefferson, 70121
504-733-0676
Author of *Liddle Kiddles*; specializing in
dolls of the 1960s-70s

Smith, Don
Don Smith's National Geographic
Magazine
3930 Rankin St.
Louisville, 40214
502-366-7504
Specializing in *National Geographic* maga-
zines and related material; guide available

Maryland
Losonsky, Joyce and Terry
7506 Summer Leave Ln.
Columbia, 21046-2455
Authors of: *The Illustrated Collector's Guide to
McDonald's® Happy Meal® Boxes, Premiums,
and Promotions©,* ($11 postpaid); *McDonald's*

Happy Meal Toys in the USA in full color
($27.95 postpaid); *McDonald's® Happy Meal®
Toys Around the World,* full color, ($27.95
postpaid); and *Illustrated Collector's Guide to
McDonald's® McCAPS ®,* ($6 postpaid); auto-
graphed copies available from the authors

Welch, Randy
Raven'tiques
27965 Peach Orchard Rd.
Easton, 21601-8203
410-822-5441
Specializing in walking figures, and tin
wind-up toys

Yalom, Libby
The Shoe Lady
P.O. Box 7146
Adelphi, 20783-2758
301-442-2026
Specializing in glass and china shoes and
boots. Author of *Shoes of Glass* (with updated values) available from the author by
sending $15.95 plus $2 to above address

Massachusetts
Wellman, BA
P.O. Box 673
Westminster, 01473-0673
E-mail: ba@dishinitout.com or
www.dish.uni.cc
Specializing in all areas of American ceram-
ics; researches Royal China

White, Larry
108 Central St.
Rowley, 01969-1317
978-948-8187; e-mail: larrydw@erols.com
Specializing in Cracker Jack; author of
books; has newsletter

Michigan
Nickel, Mike; and Cindy Horvath
P.O. Box 456
Portland, 48875
517-647-7646
e-mail: mandc@voyager.net
Specializing in Ohio art pottery, Kay Finch,
Author of *Kay Finch Ceramics, Her
Enchanted World,,* available from the
authors; Co-author of *Collector's Encyclope-
dia of Roseville Pottery Revised Edition, Vol
I and Vol II* (Collector Books)

Pickvet, Mark
5071 Watson Dr.
Flint, 48506
Author of *Shot Glasses: An American Tradition,* available for $12.95 plus $2.50 postage
and handling from Antique Publications,
P.O. Box 553, Marietta, OH 45750

Ross, Michele
P.O. Box 94
Berrien Center, 49102

616-925-1604
E-mail: motherclay@cs.com
Specializing in Van Briggle and other American pottery

Minnesota

Zimmer, Gregg
4017 16th Ave. S
Minneapolis, 55407
Co-author of book; specializing in Melmac

Missouri

Allen, Col. Bob
P.O. Box 56
St. James, 65559
Author of *A Guide to Collecting Cookbooks;* specializing in cookbooks, leaflets, and Jell-O memorabilia

Bowman, Kevin R.
P.O. Box 471
Neosho, 64850-0471
417-781-6418 (6pm-9pm CST, weekends: after 10am CST)
E-mail: Ozrktrmnl@clandjop.com
Specializing in sporting goods; lists available

Duncan, Pat and Ann
Box 175
Cape Fair, 65624
417-538-2311
Specializing in Holt Howard, Lefton and Roseville

Nevada

Hunter, Tim
4301 W Hidden Valley Dr.
Reno, NV 89502
702-856-4357
E-mail: thunter885@aol.com
Author of *The Bobbing Head Collector and Price Guide*

New Hampshire

Apkarian-Russel, Pamela
Halloween Queen Antiques
P.O. Box 499
Winchester, 03470
Specializing in Halloween collectibles, postcards of all kinds, and Joe Camel

Holt, Jane
P.O. Box 115
Derry, 03038
Specializing in Annalee dolls

New Jersey

Dezso, Doug
864 Paterson Ave.
Maywood, 07607-2119
201-488-1311
Author of *Candy Containers* (Collector Books); specializing in candy containers,

nodders, Kellogg's Pep pin-back buttons, Shafford cats, and Tonka toys

Litts, Elyce
P.O. Box 394
Morris Plains, 07950
973-361-4087
happy.memories@worldnet.att.net
Specializing in Geisha Girl (author of book); also ladies' compacts

Palmieri, Jo Ann
27 Pepper Rd.
Towaco, 07082-1357
201-334-5829
Specializing in Skookum Indian dolls

Sigg, Walter
3-D Entertainment
P.O. Box 208
Swartswood, 07877
Specializing in View-Master and Tru-View reels and packets

Sparacio, George
P.O. Box 791
Malaga, 08328
609-694-4167; fax 609-694-4536
E-mail: mrvesta@aol.com
Specializing in match safes

Visakay, Stephen
P.O. Box 1517
W Caldwell, 07007-1517
SVisakay@aol.com
Specializing in vintage cocktail shakers (by mail and appointment only); author of *Vintage Bar Ware*

Yunes, Henri
971 Main St., Apt. 2
Hackensack, 07601
201-488-2236
Specializing in celebrity and character dolls

New Mexico

Mace, Shirley
Shadow Enterprises
P.O. Box 1602
Mesilla Park, 88047
505-524-6717; fax 505-523-0940
e-mail: shadow-ent@zianet.com
www.geocities.com/MadisonAvenue/Boardroom/1631
Author of *Encyclopedia of Silhouette Collectibles on Glass* (available from the author)

New York

Beegle, Gary
92 River St.
Montgomery, 12549
914-457-3623
Liberty Blue dinnerware, also most lines of collectible modern American dinnerware as well as character glasses

Dinner, Craig
Box 4399
Sunnyside, 11104
718-729-3850
Specializing in figural cast-iron items (door knockers, lawn sprinklers, doorstops, windmill weights, etc.)

Eisenstadt, Robert
P.O. Box 020767
Brooklyn, 11202-0017
718-625-3553 or fax 718-522-1087
Specializing in gambling chips and other gambling-related items

Gerson, Roselyn
P.O. Box 40
Lynbrook, 11563
516-593-8746
Collector specializing in unusual, gadgetry, figural compacts and vanity bags and purses; author of *Ladies' Compacts of the 19th and 20th Centuries* ($36.95 plus $2 postpaid), *Vintage Vanity Bags and Purses,* and *Vintage and Contemporary Purse Accessories* (Collector Books); edits newsletter

Iranpour, Sharon
24 San Rafel Dr.
Rochester, 14618-3702
716-381-9467 or fax 716-383-9248
watcher1@rochester.rr.com
Specializing in advertising and promotional wrist watches; editor of *The Premium Watch Watch*

Watson, James
25 Gilmore St.
Whitehall, 12887
Specializing in Hartland sports figures

Weitman, Stan and Arlene
101 Cypress St.
Massapequa Park, 11758
516-799-2619 or fax 516-797-3039
www.crackleglass.com
Authors of *Crackle Glass, Identification and Value Guide, Volumes I and II* (Collector Books)

North Carolina
Brooks, Ken and Barbara
4121 Gladstone Ln.
Charlotte, 28205
Specializing in Cat-Tail Dinnerware

Finegan, Mary
Marfine Antiques
P.O. Box 3618
Boone, 28607
828-262-3441
Author of book on Johnson Brothers dinnerware; available from the author

Retskin, Bill
P.O. Box 18481

Asheville, 28814
704-254-4487 or fax 704-254-1066
e-mail: bill@matchcovers.com
Author of *The Matchcover Collector's Price Guide,* and editor of *The Front Striker Bulletin,* the official publication of the American Matchcover Collecting Club (AMCC)

Sayers, Rolland J.
Southwestern Antiques and Appraisals
305 N. Main St.
Hendersonville, 28792
828-697-6064
Researches Pisgah Forest pottery; Author of *Guide to Scouting Collectibles,* available from the author for $32.95 pp.

North Dakota
Farnsworth, Bryce L.
1334 14 1/2 St.
S Fargo, 58103
701-237-3597
Specializing in Rosemeade

Ohio
Bruegman, Bill
137 Casterton Ave.
Akron, 44303
330-836-0668 or fax 330-869-8668
E-mail: toyscouts@toyscouts.com
www.toyscouts.com
Author of *Toys of the Sixties; Aurora History and Price Guide;* and *Cartoon Friends of the Baby Boom Era.* Write for information about his mail-order catalog

Budin, Nicki
679 High St.
Worthington, OH 43085
614-885-1986
Specializing in Beatrix Potter and Royal Doulton

Dutt, Gordy
Box 201
Sharon Center, 44274-0201
330-239-1657 or fax 330-239-2991
Specializing in model kits, especially figure-related

King, Michelle and Mike
P.O. Box 3519
Alliance, 44601
330-829-5946
www.quest-for-toys.com
Author of book on Kreiss; available from the author; also vintage toys, memorabilia from the 1960s - '80s, novelty and character ceramics, vintage Barbies, ad characters, Arts & Crafts

Young, Mary
P.O. Box 9244

Wright Bros. Branch
937-298-4838
Dayton, 45409
Author of books; specializing in paper dolls

Oklahoma

Ivers, Terri
Terri's Toys and Nostalgia
206 E. Grand
Ponca City, 74601
580-762-8697 or 580-762-5174
toylady@cableone.net
Specializing in character collectibles, lunch boxes, advertising items, Breyer and Hartland figures, etc.

Moore, Shirley and Art
4423 E. 13th St.
Tulsa, 74135
918-747-4164
Specializing in Lu-Ray Pastels and depression glass

Phillips, Robert W.
Phillips Archives of Western Memorabilia
1703 N Aster Pl.
Broken Arrow, 74012-1308
918-254-8205
rawhidebob@aol.com
One of the most widely published writers in the field of cowboy memorabila, biographer of the Golden Boots Awards, and author of: *Roy Rogers, Singing Cowboy Stars, Silver Screen Cowboys, Hollywood Cowboy Heroes,* and *Western Comics: A Comprehensive Reference*; research consultant for TV documentary *Roy Rogers, King of the Cowboys* (AMC-TV/Republic Pictures/Galen Films)

Oregon

Coe, Debbie and Randy
Coes Mercantile
Lafayette School House Mall #2
748 3rd (Hwy. 99W)
Lafayette, 97127
Specializing in Elegant and Depression glass, art pottery, Cape Cod by Avon, Golden Foliage by Libbey Glass Company, Gurley candles, and Liberty Blue dinnerware

Morris, Tom
Prize Publishers
P.O. Box 8307
Medford, 97504
chalkman@cdsnet.net
Author of *The Carnival Chalk Prize*

White, Carole Bess
PO Box 819
Portland, 97207
Specializing in Japan ceramics; author of books

Pennsylvania

BOJO/Bob Gottuso
P.O. Box 1403
Cranberry Twp., 16066-0403
Phone or fax 724-776-0621
e-mail: bojo@zbzoom.net
Specializing in the Beatles and rock 'n roll memorabilia

Greenfield, Jeannie
310 Parker Rd.
Stoneboro, 16153-2810
724-376-2584
Specializing in cake toppers and egg timers

Kreider, Katherine
Kingsbury Antiques
P.O. Box 7957
Lancaster, 17604-7957
717-892-3001
e-mail: Kingsbry@aol.com
Specializing in Valentines from the 1800s to 1960s; Author of *Valentines With Values* ($22.90 includes shipping and handling; PA residents please include 6% sales tax) and *One Hundred Years of Valentines* (book available from author)

Posner, Judy
June – September:
R.R. 1, Box 273 SC
Effort, 18330
e-mail: judyandjef@aol.com
Specializing in figural pottery, cookie jars, salt and pepper shakers, Black memorabilia, and Disneyana; sale lists available; fee charged for appraisal

Turner, Art and Judy
Homestead Collectibles
P.O. Box 173
Mill Hall, 17751
570-726-3597
Specializing in Jim Beam decanters and Ertl diecast metal banks

South Carolina

Cassity, Brad
2391 Hunter's Trail
Myrtle Beach, 29574
843-236-8697
Specializing in Fisher-Price pull toys and playsets up to 1986 (author of book)

Tennessee

Butler, Elaine
233 S Kingston Ave.
Rockwood, 37854
Author of *Poodle Collectibles of the '50s and '60s* ($21.95 postpaid)

Daigle, Alvin Jr.
Boomerang Antiques

Gray, 37615
423-915-0666
Co-author of book; specializing in Melmac

DeLozier, Loretta
P.O. Box 50201
Knoxville, 37950-0201
Author of *Collector's Encyclopedia of Lefton China, Identification and Values* (Collector Books)

Fields, Linda
158 Bagsby Hill Lane
Dover, 37058
931-232-5099 after 6 pm
e-mail:Fpiebird@compu.net.
Specializing in pie birds

Grist, Everett
P.O. Box 91375
Chattanooga, 37412-3955
423-510-8052
Author of books on animal dishes, aluminum, advertising playing cards, letter openers, and marbles

Texas

Cooper, Marilyn M.
8408 Lofland Dr.
Houston, 77055-4811
or summer address:
PO Box 755
Douglas, MI 49406
Author of *The Pictorial Guide to Toothbrush Holders* ($22.95 postpaid)

Docks, L.R. 'Les'
Shellac Shack; Discollector
Box 691035
San Antonio, 78269-1035
Author of *American Premium Record Guide;* Specializing in vintage records

Gibbs, Carl, Jr.
P.O. Box 131583
Houston, 77219-1584
713-521-9661
Author of *Collector's Encyclopedia of Metlox Potteries* (Collector Books); specializing in American dinnerware

Jackson, Joyce
900 Jenkins Rd.
Aledo, 76008-2410
817-441-8864
e-mail: jjpick3@earthlink.net
Specializing in Swanky Swigs

Nossaman, Darlene
5419 Lake Charles
Waco, 76710
Specializing in Homer Laughlin China information and Horton Ceramics

Pringle, Joyce
Antiques and Moore
3708 W Pioneer Pky.
Arlington, 76013
e-mail: chipdale@flash.net
www.Antiquesandmoore.com/glas
Specializing in Boyd art glass, Summit, and Moser

Woodard, Dannie
P.O. Box 1346
Weatherford, 76086
871-594-4680
Author of *Hammered Aluminum, Hand Wrought Collectibles*

Utah

Spencer, Rick
Salt Lake City
801-973-0805
Specializing in Shawnee, Roseville, Weller, Van Telligen, Regal, Bendel, Coors, Rookwood, Watt; also salt and pepper shakers, cookie jars, etc., cut glass, radios, and silver flatware

Virginia

Cranor, Rosalind
P.O. Box 859
Blacksburg, 24063
Author of *Elvis Collectibles* and *Best of Elvis Collectibles* ($21.70 pp), available from the author

Henry, Rosemary
9610 Greenview Ln.
Manassas, 20109-3320
703-361-5898; checkers@erols.com
Specializing in cookie cutters, stamps, and molds

Reynolds, Charlie
Reynolds Toys
2836 Monroe St.
Falls Church, 22042-2007
703-533-1322
e-mail: reynoldstoys@erols.com
Specializing in banks, figural bottle openers, toys, etc.

Windsor, Grant
P.O. Box 72606
Richmond, 23235-8017
Specializing in Griswold

Washington

Morris, Susan and Dave
P.O. Box 1684
Port Orchard, 98366
Authors of *Watt Pottery - An Identification and Value Guide,* and *Purinton Pottery — An Identification and Value Guide* (Collector Books) '

Wisconsin

Semling, Brian
Brian's Toys
W 730 Hwy 35

P.O. Box 95
Fountain City 54621
608-687-7572; fax 608-687-7573
www.brianstoys.com
Author of book on Star Wars; available from
the author

Helley, Phil
Old Kilbourn Antiques
629 Indiana Ave.
Wisconsin Dells, 53965
608-254-8770
Specializing in Cracker Jack items, radio
premiums, dexterity games, toys (especially
Japanese wind-up toys), banks, and old
Dells souvenir items marked Kilbourn

Wanvig, Nancy
Nancy's Collectibles
P.O. Box 12
Thiensville, WI 53092
Author of book; specializing in ashtrays

Watson, James
25 Gilmore St.
Whitehall, NY 12887
Specializing in Hartland sports figures

CLUBS AND NEWSLETTERS

Akro Agate Collectors Club
Clarksburg Crow
Roger Hardy
10 Bailey St.
Clarksburg, WV 26301-2524
304-624-4523
www.akro-agate.com
Annual membership fee: $25

American Bell Assn. International, Inc.
P.O. Box 19443
Indianapolis, IN 46219
E-mail: joanforman@earthlink.net

Antique and Collector Reproduction News
Mark Chervenka, Editor
P.O. Box 12130
Des Moines, IA 50312-9403
800-227-5531 (subscriptions only) or 515-
274-5886
Monthly newsletter showing differences
between old originals and new reproductions; subscription: $32 per year

The Antique Trader Weekly
P.O. Box 1050
Dubuque, IA 52004-1050
www.collect.com
Subscription: $37 (52 issues) per year; sample: $1

Autographs of America
Tim Anderson
P.O. Box 461
Provo, UT 84603
801-226-1787 (afternoons, please)
www.AutgraphsOfAmerica.com
Free sample catalog of hundreds of auto-
graphs for sale
Autumn Leaf
Bill Swanson, Editor
807 Roaring Springs Dr.
Allen, TX 75002-2112

972-727-5527
Avon Times
c/o Dwight or Vera Young
P.O. Box 9868, Dept. P.
Kansas City, MO 64134
Send SASE for information

The Baggage Car
3100 Justin Dr., Ste. B
Des Moines, IA 50322
515-270-9080 or fax 515-223-1398
E-mail: baggagecar@aol.com
Includes show and company information
along with current Hallmark listings

Betsy McCall's Fan Club
Marci Van Ausdell, Editor
P.O. Box 946
Quincy, CA 95971
530-283-2770
dreams707@aol.com
Subscription: $16 per year or send $3 for
sample copy

The Bobbing Head Doll Newsletter
Tim Hunter
4301 W Hidden Valley Dr.
Reno, NV 89502
thunter885@aol.com

Bookend Collector Club
Louis Kuritzky, M.D.
4510 NW 17th Place
Gainsville, FL 32650
352-377-3193
E-mail: lkuritzky@aol.com
Membership (includes newsletter): $25 per year

Boyd Crystal Art Glass
Jody & Darrell's Glass Collectibles Newsletter
P.O. Box 180833

440

Arlington, TX 76096-0833
Published 6 times a year; subscription includes an exclusive glass collectible produced by Boyd's Crystal Art Glass. LSASE for current subscription rates or send $3 for sample copy

The Candy Gram Newsletter
Joyce L. Doyle
P.O. Box 426
North Reading, MA 01864-0426

Cat Collectors Club
Cat Talk Newsletter
Karen Shank
PO Box 150784
Nashville, TN 37215-0784
615-297-7403
E-mail: musiccitykitty@yahoo.com
www.CatCollectors.com

Collectible Flea Market Finds Magazine
Magazines of America
13400 Madison Ave.
New York, NY 44107
800-528-9648
Subscription: $15.96 for 4 issues per year

Collector Glass News
P.O. Box 308
Slippery Rock, PA 16057
E-mail: cgn@glassnews.com
www.glassnews.com

Compact Collector Chronicles
Powder Puff Newsletter
P.O. Box 40
Lynbrook, NY 11563
E-mail: compactlady@aol.com
Contains information covering all aspects of compact collecting, restoration, vintage ads, patents, history, and articles by members and prominent guest writers. A 'Seekers and Sellers' column and dealer listing is offered free to members.

Cookie Jarrin' With Joyce: The Cookie Jar
Newsletter
1501 Maple Ridge
Walterboro, SC 29488

Cookies
Rosemary Henry
9610 Greenview Ln.
Manassas, VA 22110
Subscription: $12 per year (6 issues)

The Copley Courier
1639 N Catalina St.
Burbank, CA 91505

Czechoslovakian Collectors Guild International
Alan Bodia, Membership
15006 Meadowlake St.
Odessa, FL 33556-3126
www.czechartglass.com/ccgi

The DAZE
Teri Steel, Editor/Publisher
Box 57
Otisville, MI 48463
800-336-9927 for trial subscription
E-mail: dgdaze@aol.com
The nation's marketplace for glass, china, and pottery

Doll Castle News Magazine
United Federation of Doll Clubs
PO Box 247
Washington, NJ 07882
908-689-7042 or fax 908-689-6320
Subscription: $19.95 per year

Doorstop Collectors of America
Jeanie Bertoia
2413 Madison Ave.
Vineland, NJ 08630
609-692-4092
Membership: $20 per year, includes 2 newsletters and convention; send 2-stamp SASE for sample

FBOC (Figural Bottle Opener Collectors)
Linda Fitzsimmons
9697 Gwynn Park Dr.
Ellicot City, MD 21042
410-465-9296

Fenton Art Glass Collectors of America, Inc.
Butterfly Net newsletter
P.O. Box 384
702 W. 5th St.
Williamstown, WV 26187
E-mail: kkenworthy@foth.com

Fiesta Collector's Quarterly
P.O. Box 471
Valley City, OH 44280
www.chinaspecialties.com/fiesta.html
Subscription: $12 per year

Fisher-Price Collector's Club
Jeanne Kennedy
1442 N Ogden
Mesa, AZ 85205
Monthly newsletter with information and ads; send SASE for more information

Flashlight Collectors of America Newsletter
Bill Utley
P.O. Box 4095
Tustin, CA 92781
714-730-1252 or fax 714-505-4067
E-mail: flashlights@ home.com
Subscription: $12 per year; *Flashlights, Early Flashlight Makers of the First 100 years of Ever Ready*, full color, 320 pgs. now available.

Frankoma Family Collectors Assn.
c/o Nancy Littrell
P.O. Box 32591
Oklahoma City, OK 73123-0771

Membership dues: $25 (includes quarterly newsletter and annual convention)

The Front Striker Bulletin
Bill Retskin
P.O. Box 18481
Asheville, NC 28814-0481
704-254-4487 or fax 704-254-1066
E-mail: bill@matchcovers.com
www.matchcovers.com
Quarterly newsletter for matchcover collectors $17.50 per year for 1st class mailing + $2 for new member registration

Griswold & Cast Iron Cookware Assn.
Grant Windsor
P.O. Box 12606
Richmond, VA 23235
804-320-0386
Membership: $15 per individual or $20 per family (2 members per address) payable to club

Hall China Collectors' Club Newsletter
P.O. Box 360488
Cleveland, OH 44136

Head Hunters Newsletter
c/o Maddy Gordon
P.O. Box 83 H
Scarsdale, NY 10583
For collectors of head vases; subscription: $20 yearly for 4 quarterly issues; ads free to subscribers

International Nippon Collectors Club (INCC)
c/o Dave Przech
1531 Independence Ave., SE
Washington DC 20003
www.nipponcollectorsclub.com
Membership: $30 per year includes newsletter (published 6 times per year)

International Perfume and Scent Bottle Collectors Association
c/o Randall B. Monsen
P.O. Box 529
Vienna, VA 22183
fax 703-242-1357

Just for Openers
John Stanley
PO Box 64
Chapel Hill, NC 27514
919-419-1546
www.just-for-openers.org
For collectors of bottle openers

Knife Rests of Yesterday and Today
Beverly L. Ales
4046 Graham St.
Pleasanton, CA 94566-5619
Subscription: $20 per year for 6 issues

The Laughlin Eagle
c/o Richard Racheter
1270 63rd Terrace South
St. Petersburg, FL 33705
813-867-3982
Subscription: $14 per year

Marble Collectors' Society of America
P.O. Box 222
Trumbull, CT 06611
E-mail: BlockMCSA@aol.com
www.blocksite.com

McDonald's® Collector Club
www.mcdclub.com
Membership: $20 per year

National Association of Avon Collectors
Department AT
6100 Walnut
Kansas City, MO 64113
Send large SASE for information

National Blue Ridge Newsletter
Norma Lilly
144 Highland Dr.
Bloutville, TN 37617
Subscription: $15 per year (6 issues)

The National Cuff Link Society
Eugene R. Klompus, President
P.O. 5700
Vernon Hills, IL 60070
847-816-0035
E-mail: genek@cufflinks.com
www.cufflink.com
Membership: $30 per year

National Depression Glass Assn.
Anita Woods
P.O. Box 69843
Odessa, TX 79769
915-337-1297
www.glassshow.com/NDGA

National Graniteware Society
P.O. Box 9248
Cedar Rapids, IA 52409-9248
www.graniteware.org
Membership: $20 per year

National Imperial Glass Collectors' Society, Inc.
P.O. Box 534
Bellaire, OH 43906
www.imperialglass.org
Membership: $15 per year (+$1 for each associate member), quarterly newsletter

National Reamer Association
c/o Debbie Gilham
47 Midline Ct.
Gaithersburg, MD 20878
E-mail: reamers@erols.com
www.reamers.org

National Society of Lefton Collectors
The Lefton Collector Newsletter
Loretta DeLozier
PO Box 50201
Knocksville, TN 3795-0201
E-mail: leftonlady@aol.com

National Valentine Collectors Assn.
Evalene Pulati
P.O. Box 1404
Santa Ana, CA 92702
714-547-1355

NM (Nelson McCoy) Xpress
Carol Seman, Editor
8934 Brecksville Rd., Suite 406
Brecksville, OH 44141-2318
E-mail: McCjs@aol.com
www.members.aol.com/nmxpress

The Occupied Japan Club
c/o Florence Archambault
29 Freeborn St.
Newport, RI 02840-1821
E-mail: florence@aiconnect.com
Publishes *The Upside Down World of an O.J. Collector,* a bimonthly newsletter. Information requires SASE

On the LIGHTER Side
International Lighter Collectors
Judith Sanders, Editor
136 Circle Dr.
Quitman, TX 75783
903-763-2795 or fax 703-763-4953
Annual convention held in different cities in the US; send SASE when requesting information

Paper Collectors' Marketplace
PO Box 128
Scandinavia, WI 54977-0128
715-467-2379 or fax 715-467-2243 (8 am to 8 pm)
E-mail: pcmpaper@gglbbs.com
www.pcmpaper.com
Subscription: $19.95 for 12 issues per year

Paper Doll News
Emma Terry
P.O. Box 807
Vivian, LA 71082
Subscription: $12 per year, $3 for sample and illustrated list

Paper Pile Quarterly
Ada Fitzsimmons, Publisher
P.O. Box 337
San Anselmo, CA 94979-0337
415-454-5552
E-mail: apaperpile@aol.com
www.paperpilecollectibles.com
Subscription: $20 per year

Peanut Pals
Judith Walthall, Founder
P.O. Box 4465
Huntsville, AL 35815; 205-881-9198
Associated collectors of Planters Peanuts memorabilia, bimonthly newsletter *Peanut Papers;* annual directory sent to members; annual convention and regional conventions. Dues: $20 per year (+$3 for each additional household member); membership information: P.O. Box 652, St. Clairsville, OH, 43950. Sample newsletter: $2

Pez Collector News
Richard & Marianne Belyski, Editors
P.O. Box 14956
Surfside Beach, SC 29587
E-mail: peznews@juno.com
www.pezcollectorsnews.com

Pie Birds Unlimited Newsletter
Linda Fields
158 Bagsby Hill Lane
Dover, TN 37058
931-232-5099
E-mail: Fpiebird@compu.net

The Premium Watch Watch©
Sharon Iranpour, Editor
24 San Rafael Dr.
Rochester, NY 14618-3702
716-381-9467 or fax 716-383-9248
SIranpour@aol.com

Political Collectors of Indiana
Michael McQuillen
P.O. Box 50022
Indianapolis, IN 46250-0022
317-845-1721
E-mail: michael@politicalparade.com
www.politicalparade.com
Official APIC (American Political Items Collectors) Chapter comprised of over 100 collectors of presidential and local political items

The Prize Insider Newsletter for Cracker Jack Collectors
Larry White
108 Central St.
Rowley, MA 01969
978-948-8187
E-mail: larrydw@erols.com

Quint News
Dionne Quint Collectors
Jimmy Rodolfos
P.O. Box 2527
Woburn, MA 01888
781-933-2219

Record Collectors Monthly
P.O. Box 75
Mendham, NJ 07845
201-543-9520
E-mail: dgmennie@netscape.net

The Replica
Craig Percell, Editor
Hwys. 136 & 20
Dyersville, IA 52040
319-875-2000
Please include SASE when requesting info.

Rosevilles of the Past Newsletter
Nancy Bomm, Editor
P.O. Box 656
Clarcona, FL 32710-0656
407-294-3980
Send $19.95 per year for 6 newsletters

Roy Rogers - Dale Evans Collectors Assn.
Nancy Horsley, Exec. Secretary
P.O. Box 1166
Portsmouth, OH 45662-1166

Shawnee Pottery Collectors' Club
c/o Pamela Curran
P.O. Box 713
New Smyrna Beach, FL 32170-0713
Send $3 for sample copy

The Shot Glass Club of America
Mark Pickvet, Editor
P.O. Box 90404
Flint, MI 48509

The Silver Bullet
Terry and Kay Klepey
P.O. Box 553
Forks, WA 98331
For Lone Ranger enthusiasts and collectors;
send SASE for current subscription information

Snow Biz
c/o Nancy McMichael
P.O. Box 53262
Washington, D.C. 20009
Quarterly newsletter (subscription: $10 per year) and collector's club, annual meeting/swap meet

The Soup Collector Club
David Young, Editor and Founder
414 Country Lane Ct.
Wauconda, IL 60084
847-487-4917
dyoung@soupcollector.com
Membership: 6 issues per year for $22 donation per address

Tea Talk
P.O. Box 860
Sausalito, CA, 94966
415-331-1557

The TeaTime Gazette
P.O. Box 40276
St. Paul, MN 55104

Toy Scouts, Inc.
Bill Bruegman
137 Casterton Ave.
Akron, OH 44303-1552
330-836-0668 or fax 330-869-8668
E-mail: toyscouts@toyscouts.com
www.toyscouts.com

Toy Shop
700 E State St.
Iola, WI 54990
715-445-2214
www.toyshopmag.com
Subscription (3rd class) $33.98 (US) for 26 issues

The Trick or Treat Trader
C.J. Russell
and The Halloween Queen
P.O. Box 499
4 Lawrence St. & Rt. 10
Winchester, NH 03470
603-239-8875
halloweenqueen@cheshire.net; subscription:
$15 per year for 4 issues or $4 for sample copy

Vernon Views Newsletter for Vernon Kilns
collectors
P.O. Box 24234
Tempe, AZ 85285
Quarterly issue available by sending $10 for a year's subscription

View-Master Reel Collector
Roger Nazeley
4921 Castor Ave.
Philadelphia, PA 19124
215-743-8999 or fax 215-288-8030
E-mail: vmreelguy@aol.com

Vintage Fashion & Costume Jewelry
Newsletter/Club
P.O. Box 265
Glen Oaks, NY 11004
718-969-2320 or 718-939-3095
Yearly subscription: $15 (US) for 4 issues;
sample copy available by sending $5

The Wade Watch, Ltd.
8199 Pierson Ct.
Arvada, CO 80005
303-421-9655 or 303-424-4401
fax 303-421-0317
Subscription: $8 per year (4 issues)

Westmoreland Glass Society
Steve Jensen
P.O. Box 2883
Iowa City, IA 52240-2883
Membership: $15

The Willow Word
Mary Lina Berndt, Publisher
P.O. Box 13382
Arlington, TX 76094-0382

Subscription: $23 (US) for 6 20-page issues per year; includes free ads to readers and lots of photos

World's Fair Collectors' Society, Inc.
Fair News Newsletter
Michael R. Pender, Editor

P.O. Box 20806
Sarasota, FL 34276-3806
941-923-2590
Dues: $20 per year in US and Canada, $30 overseas

Index